Is Administrative Law Unlawful?

Is Administrative Law Unlawful?

PHILIP HAMBURGER

The University of Chicago Press
Chicago and London

The University of Chicago Press, Chicago 60637
The University of Chicago Press, Ltd., London
© 2014 by The University of Chicago
All rights reserved. Published 2014.
Paperback edition 2015
Printed in the United States of America

24 23 22 21 20 19 18 17 16 15   4 5 6 7 8

ISBN-13: 978-0-226-11659-4 (cloth)
ISBN-13: 978-0-226-32463-0 (paper)
ISBN-13: 978-0-226-11645-7 (e-book)
DOI: 10.7208/chicago/9780226116457.001.0001

Library of Congress Cataloging-in-Publication Data

Hamburger, Philip, 1957– author.
   Is administrative law unlawful? / Philip Hamburger.
      pages ; cm
   Includes bibliographical references and index.
   ISBN 978-0-226-11659-4 (cloth : alkaline paper) — ISBN 978-0-226-11645-7
(e-book)   1. Administrative law—History.   2. Administrative law—Philosophy.
3. Administrative law—United States.   I. Title.
   K3400.H253 2014
   342'.06—dc23

                                                    2013040559

♾ This paper meets the requirements of ANSI/NISO Z39.48-1992
(Permanence of Paper).

For C'naan

Upon my word, if I did not know I was awake, I should be apt to think I had been in a dream, and that some fairy midnight scene had carried my imagination back an hundred and thirty or forty years, in an illusory audience of some of the speeches of a James, or Charles, or their Lord Chancellors and Lord Keepers; for with no other standard of the prerogative, that I know of, will such notions square; and *these* they will fit.

A Speech Against the Suspending and Dispensing Prerogative (1767)

[D]isregarding the lessons of history there has been a disposition to revert to the methods of tyranny in order to meet the problems of democracy. Intent on some immediate exigency, and with slight consideration of larger issues, we create autocratic power. . . . [A]nd we should know by this time that arbitrariness is quite as likely to proceed from an unrestrained administrative officer of the republic reigning by the grace of an indefinite statute as by the personal government of a despotic king.

CHARLES EVANS HUGHES, "Some Observations on Legal Education and Democratic Progress" (1920)

[T]he whole genius of administrative action through commissions endangers the doctrine of the supremacy of law. Not the least task of the common-law lawyers of the future will be to impose a legal yoke on these commissions, as Coke and his fellows did upon the organs of executive justice in Tudor and Stuart England.

ROSCOE POUND, "The Law School and the Common Law" (1920)

[T]he question of whether or not the king can issue ordinances parallels our modern question as to whether or not an executive body or officer can establish regulations; and the arguments used *pro* and *con* have followed much the same lines.

JOHN DICKINSON, *Administrative Justice and the Supremacy of the Law in the United States* (1927)

CONTENTS

Is administrative law unlawful? The question is old and may seem well settled. The problem, however, has never gone away, and with the expansion of the administrative state, it has become all the more important.

The federal government traditionally bound the people only through acts of Congress and judgments of the courts. In other words, to constrain liberty, the executive ordinarily had to rely on the other branches of government—it had to persuade the representatives of the people to enact a rule, and it had to persuade independent judges and juries to apply the rule.

Nowadays, however, the executive acts against Americans through its own legislation and adjudication. This administrative action, whether legislative or judicial, is known as "administrative law," and the executive relies on it to constrain Americans in all aspects of their lives, political, economic, social, and personal.

Administrative law thereby has transformed American government and society. Although this mode of power is unrecognized by the Constitution, it has become the government's primary mode of controlling Americans, and it increasingly imposes profound restrictions on their liberty. It therefore is time to reconsider the lawfulness of administrative law.[1]

Off-Road Driving

The problem can be put in terms of off-road driving. Although the Constitution lays out lawful avenues for issuing edicts that constrain the public, the government often takes other paths.

The Constitution generally establishes three avenues of power. It authorizes the government to issue binding edicts through legislative and judicial acts and to exercise force through executive acts. Nonetheless, like so many who enjoy the strength of their vehicles, the government frequently prefers to drive off-road, pursuing binding power down paths of its own choosing.

In challenging the off-road driving, this book does not dispute the direction of substantive policy. For example, when this book objects to off-road exercises of binding power, it does not ordinarily question the policies thereby pursued by the government. Nor does it question the policies pursued by the government in its exercise of nonbinding power, such as its distribution of welfare, social security, or other benefits.

The problem examined here is thus not where the government is heading, but how it drives. To leave the roads laid out by the Constitution can be exhilarating, at least for those in the driver's seat. All the same, it is unlawful and dangerous.

What Is Administrative Law?

It already should be evident that, in questioning administrative law, this book does not question all executive acts. In fact, many executive acts are entirely lawful. It therefore is important to go into more detail about what this book criticizes as unlawful and what it does not.

The executive often issues binding directives—whether rules, interpretations, adjudications, orders, or warrants. These executive edicts purport to bind not merely executive officers, but members of the public. To be precise, they purport to bind subjects, meaning the persons subject to the United States and its law. The executive's edicts, moreover, purport to bind subjects not merely in the sense of reaching a settled decision about them, but in the deeper sense of legally obliging, constraining, or interfering with them. This executive power to issue edicts that bind, or confine, subjects has long been recognized as the central feature of "administrative law," and it is what this book questions.[2, a]

---

a. This book self-consciously speaks of subjects rather than citizens. According to some scholars, subjects are the subjects of a monarch, in contrast to the citizens of a republic. From the traditional common law perspective, however, subjects are all persons who, on account of their allegiance to a sovereign, are subject to its laws. It thus is possible to speak of the subjects of a republic. For example, whereas the English are subject to their monarch and her laws, Americans are subject to their republic and its laws.

The word "subjects," when understood in this way, is useful in this book because it includes the relevant range of persons—namely, all persons bound by the laws. In contrast, the alternative term, "citizens," is too narrow, for it excludes all those (such as immigrants and other aliens in amity) who are bound by the laws but are not citizens.

In place of the word "subjects," this book also sometimes more casually speaks of "the

Traditionally, under the U.S. Constitution, the government could bind its subjects only through its legislative and judicial powers. And because the Constitution granted these powers, respectively, to Congress and the courts, only the acts of these institutions could impose legally obligatory constraints on persons who were subject to the laws. In contrast, the executive's acts could not create this binding effect. Although the executive could implement the confining obligation of acts of Congress or the courts, it itself could not bind, but at most could impose force, whether by bringing matters to the courts or, ultimately, by physically carrying out their binding acts. Lawful executive power thus was very different from the two types of binding power authorized by the Constitution, and when the executive makes binding edicts and thereby strays into legislative and judicial power, it is exercising what, from a historical perspective, this book understands as administrative law.[b]

---

public" or "members of the public." Again, the goal is to refer to all persons subject to the laws, not merely citizens.

Of course, there is a risk that when this book speaks of "subjects" or "the public," it will be understood to mean only the governed, not government officials. The book, however, typically uses such words to refer to all persons who are subject to the laws, including government officials.* (N.B.: An asterisk at the close of a footnote means that citations can be found at the end of the book, preceding the endnotes for each chapter.)

b. The distinction in this book between binding and nonbinding government acts echoes the familiar distinction between constraints and benefits, or between rights and privileges. In particular, binding legislative and judicial acts are understood here as those that bind persons in their liberty or rights, not those that deny mere privileges. Hence the line drawn here between government acts that bind and those that deny benefits. At the same time, it should be kept in mind that binding legislative and judicial acts are not the full range of government acts that can impinge on rights, for the executive also can do this through physical force.

Of course, the distinction between constraints and benefits, or rights and privileges, has been widely criticized, especially during the past half century. In a modest version of this criticism (propounded, for example, in *Goldberg v. Kelly* and *Mathews v. Eldridge*), it is observed that a denial of benefits can, in reality, sometimes operate in the manner of a constraint—the implication being that, in such circumstances, the benefit should be treated as if it were a right. This modest point then is often used as a foundation for more ambitious critiques, in which it is suggested that any distinction between rights and privileges is meaningless or that it threatens social justice.

The value, however, of treating some benefits as if they were rights does not call into question the rights-privileges distinction. Even where there is clarity that some benefits should be handled like constraints, this does not mean that all denials of benefits should be treated in this way. Moreover, the value of treating some benefits like constraints does not alter the reality that government constraints confine liberty and therefore need to be recognized as constraints. If the effect of treating some benefits as constraints is that constraints will be treated in the manner of mere benefits, then there will have been a profound loss.

In short, notwithstanding occasional exceptions, the general distinction between constraint and benefit, or right and privilege, remains essential. It preserves, on the one hand, the liberty of subjects and, on the other, the discretionary power of government.*

What exactly were the binding acts that the executive traditionally could not adopt? The secretary of the treasury, for example, could authorize the distribution of government largess, and could make regulations that instructed treasury officers, but he could not promulgate regulations altering tax rates. Although the Post Office could refuse a request to mail a letter, it could not issue regulations requiring subjects to avoid private carriers; and although the Interior Department could deny access to confidential government information, it could not issue an order compelling a business to supply information.

Of course, the executive decisions granting or denying government money, services, information, and other benefits were very important. Yet they could be executive decisions precisely because they did not bind Americans.[c]

Nowadays, however, the executive enjoys binding legislative and judicial power. First, its agencies make legislative rules dictating what Americans can grow, manufacture, transport, smoke, eat, and drink. Second, the agencies make binding adjudications—initially demanding information about violations of the rules, and then reaching conclusions about guilt and imposing fines. Only then, third, does the executive exercise its own power—that of coercion—to enforce its legislation and adjudication.

Hence the focus of this book. As already suggested, the power of the executive to exert or withhold the government's lawful force, including its power to distribute benefits, is not doubted here. Instead, what is questioned under the rubric of "administrative" is the executive's exercise of binding legislative and judicial powers.

Incidentally, although administrative power is centrally an executive venture, it is not exclusively executive. For example, the Tax Court is a nonexecutive tribunal that binds members of the public outside the regular courts and thus exercises administrative power. In addition, some more or less independent bodies (such as the Securities Exchange Commission) bind subjects with regulations and adjudications. When these various bodies, whether nonexecutive or not entirely executive, purport to bind, their edicts are administrative.

---

c. Although the distribution of benefits usually belonged to the executive, this did not preclude a role for the other branches of government. Congress could dictate the distribution of benefits. Moreover, it could give some of the decisions about benefits to the courts—at least where it had converted the relevant privileges to legal rights. Until then, however, decisions denying benefits or privileges did not bind, in the sense of imposing legal obligation or constraint, and they therefore could remain in the executive.

One way or another, whether exercised by executive or other bodies, administrative power is understood here to include only acts that bind—only edicts that impose legally obligatory constraints on subjects of the government. There are other possible definitions of administrative law, and different approaches undoubtedly can make sense for different purposes, but because this book aims to understand administrative law historically, it focuses on binding acts.

And this points to the danger. The power to bind is a power to constrain liberty. Although only Congress and the courts have the power to bind and thereby confine liberty, this is exactly what executive and other administrative bodies claim to do through administrative law.

Historical Approach

In popular and scholarly debates, the problem of administrative law is addressed as if it were merely a flat legal question about compliance with the Constitution. Few serious constitutional questions, however, are really as two-dimensional as the pages of the Constitution. Certainly, when it comes to administrative law, the conventional surface question about constitutionality cannot be understood, let alone answered, without first digging down to more substantial questions about the underlying unlawfulness and danger of administrative power.

In particular, it is necessary to dig into the past. The justifications for administrative law repeatedly rely on its history. It is said to be a novel development, which could not have been anticipated by the Constitution and which thus was not barred by it. Administrative law further is described as a necessary response to modernity—a response that therefore cannot be avoided, even if it originally was not constitutionally authorized. Overall, the suggestion is that administrative law does not have a deep history and that it therefore must be evaluated as sui generis, standing alone merely as it has existed in recent times.

The history of administrative law, however, reaches back many centuries. Indeed, this sort of power, which is said to be uniquely modern, is really just the most recent manifestation of a recurring problem. It thus is not a coincidence that administrative law looks remarkably similar to the sort of governance that thrived long ago in medieval and early modern England under the name of the "prerogative." In fact, the executive's administrative power revives many details of king's old prerogative power. Administrative law thus turns out to be not a uniquely modern response to modern circumstances, but the most recent expression of an old and worrisome development. Although the label "administrative" is more comforting than the old term "prerogative," the danger is no less acute.

Administrative law therefore cannot be understood simply by examining it as it exists today—halfway through a single iteration. Instead, it is necessary to study it as a repeated phenomenon, in which details vary from one iteration to another, but the essentials remain disturbingly constant. This book therefore, like the god Janus, looks both backward and forward, searching the past to recognize the nature of the present, if not quite the future.

Absolutism

The problem is not merely prerogative power, but absolute power. What Anglo-American lawyers typically discussed in terms of the "prerogative" was, in the broader sweep of legal theory, a question of absolutism. It therefore should be no surprise that when administrative power harks back to the prerogative, it also, more generally, echoes some basic features of absolute power.

First, like the old absolute power, administrative power runs outside the law. Rather than work through ordinary law and adjudication, it proceeds alongside them, often mimicking their forms, but remaining different from them. In this sense, it is an extralegal mode of constraint, and it thereby evades not only the Constitution's legislative and judicial powers but also its legislative and judicial institutions and processes and even many of its rights.

Second, this power outside the law depends on judicial deference and it thus is not only extralegal but also supralegal. As in the past, a power exercised outside the law and the courts can survive only if the judges defer to it—only if they submit to it as power above their courts and the law. In this sense, administrative power is as much above the law as its predecessors.

Third, among the effects of this power outside and above the law is the consolidation of power. The administrative regime consolidates in one branch of government the powers that the Constitution allocates to different branches. Although existing scholarship recognizes aspects of this problem, it does so mostly in terms of the separation of powers. The threat to the separation of powers, however, is merely one element of a broader consolidation of power, which results from the exercise of power outside and above the law.

Administrative power thus brings back to life three basic elements of absolute power. It is extralegal, supralegal, and consolidated.

The Depth of the Unlawfulness

The absolute character of administrative law is important for understanding its unlawfulness. It will be seen that it is unconstitutional at the flat surface of constitutional doctrine. Even to understand the extent of this sort of this surface unlawfulness, however, it is necessary to consider the underlying sort of unlawfulness and the forgotten way in which constitutional law was a response.

The underlying unlawfulness initially becomes apparent when one considers that administrative law revives the first and second elements of absolute power. Administrative law constrains outside the paths of regular law and adjudication, and in securing judicial deference, it also rises above the law and the courts.

Put in terms of the threatened ideal, administrative law abandons rule through and under the law. It is commonplace to talk rather loosely about the rule *of* law. This formulation, however, is so vague as to be a distraction from the real problems with administrative law, and it therefore needs to be left aside if such problems are to be understood.[d] What is more concretely at stake here is rule *through* and *under* law (or put another way, rule *by* and *under* law). Although the English, and then Americans, long struggled to preserve this sort of legal governance, it is exactly what prerogative and then administrative power evaded by working outside and above the law. Administrative law thus is more deeply unlawful than has hitherto been understood: Not only does it violate the law, but also it departs from the ideal of government through and under the law.

As a result, administrative power threatens the liberty enjoyed under law. When the government can bind its subjects only through and under the law, their legal liberty is the freedom defined merely by law—a liberty to do all that the law and its courts do not forbid. Prerogative or admin-

---

d. Some scholars, such as Richard Epstein, question administrative law on the ground that it is inconsistent with the "rule of law." As interpreted by most scholars, however, this ideal is so vague or minimal that it cannot be relied upon to illuminate what is at stake. The way in which unconfining conceptions of this ideal tend to leave room for administrative power can be illustrated by the work of David Dyzenhaus, who understands the "rule of law" to require nothing more than "a legal warrant for what government does." Whatever this means, it is not very revealing about the central difficulties with administrative regimes.*

istrative power, however, imposes rules and adjudications in addition to those of the law, and even where these extralegal constraints have statutory authorization, they interfere with the extent of the liberty enjoyed under the law. Thus, rather than have a liberty defined by law, Americans now enjoy a liberty defined largely by administrative power.

A further aspect of the underlying unlawfulness becomes apparent from the third element of absolute power—the consolidation of power. The specialization of authority, whether in society or government, has been the foundation of modern liberty. In government, this has been accomplished by the division of specialized powers among specialized governmental bodies, whether the legislature, the courts, or the executive. In running outside and above the law, however, administrative power, like its precursor, evades this specialization and thereby subjects the people to the dangers of consolidated power.

In all of these ways, administrative law runs contrary to the very origin and nature of Anglo-American constitutional law. Constitutional law developed in the seventeenth century primarily as a means of defeating the absolute prerogative. Faced with royal claims of consolidated power outside and above the law, Englishmen increasingly responded that the constitution allocated legislative power to the legislature and judicial power to the courts, thus making clear that the government could bind its subjects only through acts of the legislature and adjudications of the courts. The English further rejected prerogative or administrative adjudication by insisting on procedural rights in all exercises of judicial power—that is, they demanded juries and the full range of due process not only in the courts but also against any extralegal adjudication. To top it off, they concluded that all government power came from a constitution adopted by the people, and in thereby subjecting all government power to the supremacy of the law, they repudiated any judicial deference to extralegal commands, interpretations, or fact-finding. Americans took these lessons to heart in their constitutions, and ever since, American constitutions have been considered models of limited government.

It thus should be evident that, in returning to consolidated extra- and supralegal power, administrative law revives a sort of power that constitutions were emphatically designed to prohibit. Absolute power was what prompted the development of constitutional law, and constitutional law therefore forcefully bars such power, including the contemporary version. Whether called "prerogative" or "administrative," it is unlawful.

Class

Although this book focuses on the questions of law, there lurks not far below a question of class. American government was founded on ideals of popular consent and representative lawmaking, and although it initially did not live up to these ideals, it eventually went far toward making them a reality. After 1870, 1920, and 1965, American legislatures increasingly were elected by the people in a meaningful sense. Strikingly, however, as Americans came to enjoy popular participation in government, advocates of administrative law pressed for a shift of a substantial part of legislative power out of the legislatures.[3]

It therefore is necessary to consider the possibility that administrative law was an instrument of a class that took a dim view of popularly elected legislatures and a high view of its own rationality and specialized knowledge. This class drew upon popular political power, but primarily to establish another sort of power, which would be exercised by members of its own class, in a manner that reflected the alleged authority that came with their specialized knowledge. Although it did not thereby become the only ruling class, it at least made itself the rulemaking class.

Class power is thus yet another way in which administrative law tends to invert the relationship between government and the people. Like the old prerogative, administrative law asserts power outside the law made in legislatures and the adjudication done in courts. Like its predecessor, administrative law relies on judicial deference, which elevates administrative power above the courts and even above the law. Like its forbear, it consolidates all of the specialized powers of government in the executive. And even more than in the era of the prerogative, it is a means of class power—a mechanism by which a class wrests power from the people and their representatives in order to secure it in the hands of persons like themselves.

Doctrine and Danger

As already should be evident, the argument of this book is of a more expansive sort than may be expected by legally trained readers. Whereas most legal arguments rest on doctrine, the argument here, although partly doctrinal, is more substantively from the underlying danger.

Of course, legal doctrines matter, and defenders of administrative power tend to rely on some general doctrinal claims. They speak, for example, about delegation, precedent, and the contemporary rejection of original intent.

These sorts of arguments, however, are largely beside the point, for rather than confront the underlying dangers, they merely apply a veneer of doctrines over them. A kitchen broom cannot sweep away a gaping hole in the floor, and similarly, conventional doctrines cannot brush aside the realities of absolute power. What therefore is needed is a recognition of the underlying perils. Once these are understood, the justificatory doctrines offer little solace.

For example, scholars often defend administrative law on grounds of delegation, saying that Congress has delegated legislative power to administrative agencies. It will be seen (in chapter 20) that what they call "delegation" is really subdelegation, but the more immediate point is the disconnect between the doctrine and the danger. The narrow excuse that Congress has delegated power does not address the risk of allowing the government to bind the people through extralegal commands.

When the delegation defense runs thin, scholars often explain administrative law in terms of the living constitution. But even if one assumes that constitutional law must evolve over time and that judges have authority to make the changes, an interpretative doctrine as open ended as the living constitution does not tell one in what direction the law should change. In this instance, the living constitution by itself says nothing about the danger of administrative law. The central legal problem thus is not really addressed by the living constitution, and it must be examined, instead, on the merits of administrative law and evidence from past experience with it.

Similarly, although some defenses of administrative law complain about original intent, this inquiry rests on something closer to original sin. Whatever one thinks about intent—especially if one fears it as a return to the constitutional past—it should be kept in mind that this inquiry focuses on something very different: the danger that the government already has returned to the preconstitutional past. Thus, rather than appeal to any interpretative doctrine, whether the living constitution or original intent, this book draws attention to one of the central dangers that prompted the development of constitutions. Much will be said about the history of the Constitution, but the argument here mainly concerns the revival of a historically dangerous sort of power.

Eventually, layers of peril will become apparent in administrative law. Philosophically, the threat is the recurring human lust for power—often accentuated by the craving for status, and the hubris of human knowledge. Legally, the danger is that of pursuing power not through and under law, but outside and above it. At a broader level, the hazard is one of concentration, including the risk that the authority of specialized knowledge is largely displacing the authority of specialized powers. Running through all of these concerns, and even more sociologically, is the danger that administrative law has been the means by which a powerful class has enthroned its own authority within the form of republican government.

Cured by Time?

Notwithstanding the danger of administrative law, it may be thought that time has settled the constitutional problem. Open constitutional questions often get settled through the practices of government or the precedents of courts, and perhaps this is the fate of administrative law.

It will be seen, however, that administrative law was never an open question. From its beginnings, it has violated the Constitution, and the problem therefore is not whether time can settle an uncertainty, but whether time can cure a continuing unlawful exercise of power.

By the end of this book, it will become apparent that administrative law is so serious a constitutional problem that it never can be solved by time. At this introductory stage, however, there is no need to worry about what time can cure, for in fact time has exacerbated the problem.

Administrative law found a place in American government when it still could be believed that administrative regulations and adjudications would merely be exceptions within the traditional constitutional structure. On this assumption, administrative regulations could be understood as simply adding details to Congress's exercise of legislative power, and administrative adjudications could be viewed as merely supplementing the courts' exercise of judicial power.

Times have changed, however, and so too has administrative law. No system of power is entirely stable, and the exception has swallowed the rule. Administrative law has by now dwarfed statutory law and has become the federal government's pervasive mode of dealing with the public. Therefore, rather than merely a means of completing the work of Congress and the courts at the margins, administrative power has become central.

The question about the constitutionality of administrative law is therefore no longer the question it once seemed to be. Administrative law nowadays offers a large-scale alternative to governance through the acts of Congress and the judgments of the courts. Accordingly, it is not reassuring that, in a prior century, it was casually accepted as a sort of exception to the rule. Having shifted from an exception to a dominant mode of governance, administrative law poses a far more serious threat than it did at its inception, and the question about its lawfulness therefore remains as novel and worrisome as ever.

The Argument

This book builds up its argument in layers: historical, conceptual, and more narrowly legal. Historically, it places administrative law within the broader ebb and flow of irregular power. Conceptually, it thereby reveals administrative law to be extralegal, supralegal, and consolidated, and thus a version of absolute power. In a more concretely legal manner, it shows administrative law to be unconstitutional.

A pair of introductory chapters lay out the intellectual foundation. One locates the book within the debate over administrative law. The other presents some basic historical concepts, which will be essential for understanding how administrative power is absolute and thus deeply unlawful.

The book's organization then follows the three most basic elements of absolute power. Parts I and II explore extralegal power. Extralegal power consisted of extralegal lawmaking and extralegal adjudication, and part I therefore begins by focusing on English prerogative lawmaking, and part II begins by focusing on English prerogative adjudication. Although the details of absolute power in England may at first seem merely historical, it gradually will become apparent that they are disturbingly like the details of contemporary American administrative power—not exactly the same, but nonetheless remarkably close. Parts I and II therefore are not narrowly historical, and each concludes by explaining how American administrative power returns to prerogative power. Put generally, the new extralegal power echoes the old extralegal power.

Along the way, it will become evident that constitutional law developed largely to defeat such power. This antiprerogative stance developed initially in the English constitution, and it was pursued most systematically in the U.S. Constitution. Parts I and II therefore conclude by explaining how the absolutist ideal of rule outside the law and the courts was defeated with the constitutional ideal of rule through the law and the courts. It thereby becomes apparent that the administrative return to extralegal power violates many specific constitutional provisions and, indeed, that it is contrary to the very nature of Anglo-American constitutional law.

Part III examines judicial deference to prerogative or administrative actions and thereby turns to supralegal power. Again, it will be seen that the administrative present returns to the prerogative past and that this is not a coincidence. Power outside the law can be sustained only if the judges can be persuaded to defer to it as if it were as a power above the law. In other words, absolute power, in the sense of extralegal power, can be defended only if it also becomes absolute in the sense of supralegal power.

Part IV then examines the problem of consolidation—the third feature of absolute power. Extralegal power has always been a path toward consolidated power, and the United States has been no exception. Whereas the U.S. Constitution established specialized powers in specialized parts of government, the development of extralegal power consolidates these powers in the executive. As a result, the executive now enjoys a thoroughly consolidated power—a power that is unspecialized, undivided, unrepresentative, subdelegated, and unfederal. In three ways, therefore, admininstrative power returns to prerogative power.

Part V wraps up the book by exploring in greater depth the ways in which administrative power is absolute and thus deeply unlawful. It questions the tendency to justify administrative law in terms of necessity—the old excuse for absolute power. It shows, moreover, that administrative power was not merely a natural recurrence to absolutist ideas, but actually was a historical continuation of them. The book completes its argument that administrative power is unlawful by considering some of the obstacles to this conclusion.

ONE

The Debate

The debate over the lawfulness of administrative law is complex, but it consists largely of constitutional critiques on one side and justifications for extralegal power on the other. Both positions are presented with much acumen. The constitutional critiques, however, do not go far enough, and the constitutional justifications concede too much.

Critiques

The scholarship questioning the constitutionality of administrative law, although not extensive, provides a valuable foundation for this book's arguments. The writing of distinguished scholars (including Larry Alexander, Bradford Clark, Ken Kersch, Theodore Lowi, Ronald Pestritto, Saikrishna Prakash, Michael Rappaport, Martin Redish, David Schoenbrod, and especially Gary Lawson) shows that administrative law departs from a wide range of constitutional principles or provisions. Their scholarship reveals, for example, that administrative law violates the separation of powers, bicameralism, due process, judicial independence, and jury rights.[1]

On the whole, however, the legal critique of administrative law focuses on the flat question of unconstitutionality, and as already suggested, this is not enough. Such an approach reduces administrative law to an issue of law divorced from the underlying historical experience and thus separated from empirical evidence about the dangers. Indeed, the flat constitutional inquiry often abbreviates the problem to a series of discrete violations of particular constitutional requirements.

When examined in this decontextualized and disjointed manner, the various constitutional violations can easily be explained away one by one, without recognition of the broader and profoundly dangerous phenomenon of which they are a part. For example, although administrative law-making violates the separation of powers, the violation can be dismissed on the ground that it departs only from the formal allocation of authority within the government—as if there were no substantive danger of consolidated governance outside the law. Similarly, the administrative denial of procedural rights can be brushed aside with the equivocation that it is all the process that is due—as if the due process of law could really be reduced to the due process of administrative power; as if there were no systematic evasion of procedural rights; as if there were no problem of extralegal judicial power.

The narrow concentration on the flat constitutional questions thus has profound costs. It fails to recognize the underlying dangers and thereby leaves the constitutional critique looking merely formalistic. To avoid this weakness, this book digs into the history.

Some hints of the history and its legal implications appear in earlier scholarship. Charles Reich (although more concerned with benefits than binding edicts) notes the danger of "special laws and special tribunals, outside the ordinary structure of government." Gary Lawson observes: "The modern administrative state is not merely unconstitutional; it is anti-constitutional. The Constitution was designed specifically to prevent the emergence of the kinds of institutions that characterize the modern administrative state."[2] These brief observations are very apt but are only laconic intimations of the constitutional problem and its underlying history.

Once the history and the depth of the constitutional problem are understood, however, it becomes difficult to miss what is at stake. It will be seen that administrative law is the contemporary expression of the old tendency toward absolute power—toward consolidated power outside and above the law. On this foundation, the familiar constitutional violations take on unexpected significance, and yet other constitutional violations, of equal import, become painfully apparent.

Justifications

Administrative law has been defended for over a hundred years by commentators whose sophistication lends much credibility to their arguments. Ultimately, however, the leading arguments for the constitutionality of administrative law are more revealing than intended, for they tend to acknowledge—sometimes glancingly, sometimes directly—that administrative law creates extralegal and even absolute power. As a result, what is said on behalf of administrative law and its lawfulness is actually a good starting point for understanding why it is unlawful.

The most common defense of administrative law is delegation—that Congress has delegated legislative power to the executive. It will be seen that this defense runs into some serious difficulties, but what matters at this introductory stage is not the weakness of the delegation defense, but rather merely what the defense concedes about the extralegal character of administrative law: It acknowledges that administrative law creates an alternative structure of legislation and adjudication—a structure outside the law and adjudication, as well as the institutions and processes, established by the Constitution.

Another justification of the constitutionality of administrative law is that it leaves in place functional equivalents of the limits established by the Constitution. For example, it is said that the Constitution does not require a fixed allocation or separation of powers among the branches of government, but rather merely a functional separation and balance of power among them. From this point of view, administrative law still leaves a balance of power, albeit not the balance established by the Constitution. Similarly, although administrative adjudication does not offer the same procedures as judicial adjudication, it is defended on the ground that due process is a functional question and that "what procedures due process may require under any given set of circumstances" will vary according to the "nature of the government function involved."[3] The very emphasis on functional equivalents, however, practically concedes that the government is exerting power outside its constitutionally authorized powers. Once again, therefore, the justification itself acknowledges the problem.

Scholars often bluntly admit that administrative law constitutes a fourth type of power—the suggestion being that it is new and that it therefore could not have been anticipated by the Constitution. The notion of a fourth type of power, however, is not so novel. It will be seen that administrative power existed in the eighteenth and nineteenth centuries on the Continent, where the people had never successfully repudiated extralegal governance. Some Continental writers accordingly recognized that, in addition to the three conventional powers of government, there might also be a fourth, "administrative power."[4] Of course, none of this recommended such a power to Americans, and it therefore is unsurprising that when the U.S. Constitution authorized legislative, executive, and judicial powers, it said nothing about administrative power. Nowadays, however, some American scholars defend administrative law as a fourth branch of government, and this is significant, for it openly recognizes administrative power as a power distinct from those granted by the Constitution.[5]

In addition, administrative law is sometimes explained as a necessary evolution in response to the sociological complexities of modern life. This defense points to the supposedly late development of administrative law—finding beginnings in the nineteenth century, growth in the early twentieth, and maturation in the New Deal. The point is not merely that administrative law could not originally have been anticipated by the Constitution, but also that it is a sociological necessity—an almost inevitable response to modern social and economic development. It is an interesting theory, to which this book will return in part V, but what matters for now is that, in focusing on the necessity of a power not anticipated by the Constitution, this justification concedes as much as it claims.[a]

Some defenses of administrative law make the necessity argument even more bluntly, and they thereby even more clearly embrace absolute power. Although most acutely felt in emergencies, necessity also can arise in quotidian circumstances. Either way, it traditionally has been understood to transcend all law, and necessity therefore has long been the intellectual foundation for absolute power—the power exercised outside and above the law. Recognizing the force of the principle, defenders of administrative law often rely on it, and they occasionally even emphasize its lawlessness. James Landis, for example, in a widely quoted passage, argues that administrative power is required by the "exigencies of governance" and that it therefore is not a matter of great concern if administrative law "does violence to the traditional tripartite theory of governmental organization."[6, b]

Most scholars, of course, prefer to leave ambiguous whether the necessity bends or breaks the Constitution. From such a point of view, it is not very pressing to inquire whether the exigency arises merely within the law,

---

a. A variant of this history (presented in most detail by Jerry Mashaw) attempts to avoid the violence to law by combining the claim about the modern necessity of administrative law with a claim that there also has been some continuity—in particular, that elements of administrative law began to develop already in the early Republic. This argument about continuity tends to rely on early nonbinding executive acts to justify contemporary binding administrative acts—as will be discussed in chapters 6 and 12.*

b. Incidentally, although necessity long was employed to justify absolute power (both in emergencies and in mundane circumstances), it also traditionally justified the more modest and respectable position that there could be a noble departure from law. In this tradition, executive officers only briefly exceeded the law to the extent necessary for the safety of the nation, and then threw themselves on the mercy of the people and their legislature, which could indemnify the officers or leave them to their fate in the courts, as it saw fit. In contrast to absolute rulers, these officials did not claim to act with a power above law and therefore accepted that they might be punished under it.

as the Constitution's measure of what is lawful, or whether it rises above the law and thus prevails regardless of what the Constitution requires. This sort of ambiguity is not coincidental, for when arguing in a system of law for a power outside the law, it is difficult to rely entirely on either the law or matters beyond the law. It therefore makes sense to hedge one's bets—to suggest that the law itself recognizes the necessity of the extralegal power and that, in any case, the necessity requires the law to do so.

Strikingly, however, not merely Landis, but many administrative law scholars have been quite candid that administrative power, of necessity, goes outside and perhaps even above the law. In England, in the early twentieth century, Cecil Carr forthrightly defended administrative law as a revival of the prerogative, including the absolute prerogative. In America, John Dickinson made the observation adopted as one of the epigraphs to this book. Yet other twentieth-century examples will be discussed in part V. Even today some scholars discuss administrative law in unabashedly absolutist terms, as when Adrian Vermeule writes about "our Schmittian administrative law," which "inevitably" contains "black holes" and "grey holes"—"law-free zones" and standards so flexible as to allow convenient shifts toward a darker type of power.[7]

In such ways, the defense of administrative law repeatedly concedes that this sort of power establishes an extralegal mode of governance—one very different from regular law and adjudication. The defense of administrative law, indeed, often turns to claims of necessity and thereby relies on the intellectual foundations of absolutism. Nor should any of this be a surprise. Administrative power runs outside the law and adjudication established by the Constitution, and ideas about extralegal or absolute power are therefore essential for understanding it.

TWO

Conceptual Framework

This chapter introduces the concepts that frame this book's arguments. The rule of law, as already suggested, is an amorphous concept, and this book therefore talks more specifically about rule through and under law. From this perspective, the book argues that administrative law is a sort of extra- and supralegal power and that it thus is a type of prerogative and even absolute power. These conclusions may initially seem overstated. Once the underlying concepts are understood, however, their application to administrative law can begin to be recognized.

Extralegal

An initial concept requiring explanation is that of extralegal power. Governments often bind their subjects not merely through the law and the orders of the courts, but through other sorts of commands and orders. In this sense, governments sometimes exercise extralegal power.

Vocabulary

This binding extralegal power has long had its own vocabulary. Medieval commentators already described it as *extralegal*, but this was not their only label for it.

For example, because extralegal lawmaking power does not run through regular or ordinary law, it is *irregular* or *extraordinary*. And because it is exercised through edicts distinct from the law, it is a power *independent* or *apart* from the law—or, as commonly put in this book, a power *outside* the law.[a]

---

a. Extralegal lawmaking power should not be confused with some nearby phenomena. First, the problem of extralegal lawmaking did not extend to custom, because custom was un-

The same vocabulary can be applied to the extralegal exercise of judicial power. In support of their extralegal legislation, governments also have attempted to bind their subjects through extralegal adjudications, and this, too, is an *irregular* or *extraordinary* exercise of power. Not being done through the judgments of the courts, but through other judgments, it is again a power *outside* the law.

Historically, these words could have layers of meaning. In some sense, for example, the law was ordinary and regular because it was the typical or normal mode of exercising power. More fundamentally, however, it was ordinary and regular because the law was understood to be the lawful mode of imposing binding duties.[1] By the same token, extralegal power was understood to be extraordinary or irregular not merely because it was unusual, but because it was not an exercise of law. Thus, the rulers who most regularly acted through their extralegal mechanisms were those who acted most irregularly.

One way or another, the terms employed here are not new. They have been used for centuries, and they remain valuable.

Extralegal

Exactly what makes a power extralegal may not be immediately obvious. Some basic distinctions, however, both medieval and modern, can clarify the problem.

Medieval kings already attempted to govern by extralegal rules and adjudications, but such modes of governance soon provoked complaint. In England, the development of Parliament sharpened the tensions between regular and irregular governance, making clear that there was a difference between government through acts of Parliament and government through other sorts of directives. Similarly, the development of the law courts clarified that there was an ordinary sort of judicial power, which was exercised

---

derstood to be inherited rather than enacted or made. The common law, for example, was said to be ancient custom, inherited and unchanged since beyond the memory of man. Of course, where custom is understood to be made or created, it can be a type of extralegal power, but this traditionally was not the common law understanding of custom.

Second, when governments attempt to rule outside the path of law, they sometimes rely not only on binding administrative orders but also on consensual devices, such as consent decrees and conditions. There thus are multiple types of extralegal power, including not only government by extralegal edict but also government by contract. The latter, however, raises its own complex legal issues, and it therefore, on the whole, is omitted from this inquiry. Put another way, this is a study of purportedly binding administrative power, not of all extralegal governance.*

by the courts and their judges, and another sort, which was done by the king's council and his other prerogative tribunals.

From this perspective, one cannot lump together all unlawful and extralegal acts. It will be seen that extralegal legislative and judicial acts are unlawful, but this does not mean that all unlawful acts are extralegal. Even regular law and adjudication can be unlawful, but only edicts that do not come through regular law and adjudication can be extralegal.

Of course, apologists for administrative law may be inclined to suggest that it is not an extralegal power, but another sort of law. Yet not everything that mimics law is really law; nor is everything that mimics a court decision the real thing. Precisely because of prior experience with prerogative power, the English constitution and especially the U.S. Constitution confined legislative and judicial powers to the constitutionally authorized paths—that is, respectively, to the acts of the legislature and of the courts. And lurking not far below was the Lockean reasoning about consent, from which it was evident that legal obligation rests on consent and that binding laws have to be made by the society's representative legislature. On these sorts of constitutional and consensual foundations, it is difficult to avoid the conclusion that administrative rule is different from rule through and under law.

Obviously, just because a power runs outside the law, rather than through it, does not mean it lacks at least a semblance of legal authorization. It will be seen that Henry VIII secured candid statutory authorization for some of his extralegal power, that the prerogative courts made strained claims of statutory authorization, and that early English kings often left it ambiguous whether they were acting under or above the law. Similarly, today, administrative law is said to have legal authorization—sometimes in clear statutory language, sometimes in strained interpretations of statutes, and sometimes in sheer ambiguity.

But quite apart from the question of legal authorization, there remains the underlying problem of extralegal power—the problem of power imposed not through the law, but through other sorts of commands. On this basis, when this book speaks of administrative law as a power outside the law—or as an extralegal, irregular, or extraordinary power—it is observing that administrative law purports to bind subjects not through the law, but through other sorts of directives.

This extralegal power, whether legislative or judicial, could be understood merely as a departure from regular institutions and processes, and certainly this is an element of the problem. As noted by some scholars, administrative power is exercised outside Congress and the courts. The more fundamental point, however, is not merely about institutions or procedures, but about the contrast between regular law and irregular commands, between ordinary adjudication and the extraordinary substitutes for it. If government must rule through the law and through the judgments of the courts, it cannot rule through acts that are not law or court judgments. The difference between the constitutional and the administrative regimes thus ultimately rests on the distinction between law and mere state power— between the regular law by which Americans govern themselves and the irregular administrative commands by which the government imposes its will on them.

Admittedly, from a historical perspective, the development of extralegal avenues of power should not be a surprise. It is familiar that new structures, processes, and modes of power often develop just outside the walls of pre-existing institutions, and something like this seems to have happened in the United States.

Yet unexpected as this may seem historically, it is worrisome as a matter of law. Law, especially constitutional law, is a means of creating obligation and of channeling and thereby limiting authority. It therefore is of little comfort to know that there were earlier instances in which government has overrun its banks and created new streams of power.

Supralegal

In defense of extralegal power, rulers traditionally claimed that it also was supralegal. A power outside the law—that is, a power exercised not through law or the courts, but through other mechanisms—could not survive legal scrutiny in a system such as the common law. Therefore, in addition to as-serting a power outside the law, rulers also had to claim that it was above the law

The power above the law was not simply a violation of the law, for it rose above the law in the sense that it was not accountable to law. Suprale-gal power thus stood in contrast to ideas about the supremacy of the law, and judges were expected to defer to it, without holding it fully account-able under the law. More profoundly, it was understood to be above the law in the sense that it was a matter of necessity, which was understood to transcend all law.

Of course, this did not mean that supralegal power was entirely beyond judicial review. Even under James I, supralegal power often came before the courts. But the courts were expected in various ways to defer to such power, and similarly today when courts defer to administrative rules or decisions, it must be considered whether they are treating them as a sort of power above the law.

As a result of the notions of extra- and supralegal power, there traditionally were three ways of understanding the unlawfulness of government acts. Such acts could be *contra ius, extra ius,* or *supra ius:* Although most basically they could be contrary to law, they also could be outside law and even above it.[2]

Absolute Power

The traditional label for the extra- or supralegal mode of governance was "absolute power." The notion of absolute power may sound rather harsh, but as will become apparent, it is inescapably relevant for understanding administrative law.[3]

The suggestion that administrative law is absolute power is not new, for the charge was commonplace during the first half of the twentieth century. The critics at that time, however, used the word "absolute" without really understanding what it meant. Roscoe Pound, for example, loosely denounced administrative discretion as absolute power, without explaining why some discretion might be lawful and some might not. Traditionally, however, "absolute power" had a series of technical and concrete meanings.

Absolute power (as already suggested) traditionally had multiple components—three of which will matter here. Most basically, it was the power exercised outside the law. In addition, it tended to be exercised above the law. And where, as usual, it combined the otherwise separate legislative, judicial, and executive powers, it was consolidated.

In contrast, a fourth version of absolute power is much less significant for understanding administrative law—this being the conception of absolute power as unlimited. Extra- and supralegal power often escaped the limits of law, and absolute power therefore could be viewed as unlimited power. Administrative law, however, is not entirely unlimited. Although it suffers from many problems, it is absolute mostly in the first three ways mentioned here, and this is serious enough.[b]

---

b. The word "absolute" could have yet other meanings. For example, it could suggest unlimited discretion up to the limits of law. After the English in the seventeenth century defeated the king's extra- and supralegal prerogatives, lawyers continued to acknowledge that the Crown enjoyed "absolute" prerogatives. What they now meant, however, was that the Crown had complete or absolute discretion within the powers it enjoyed under the law.

It may be imagined that, historically, absolute power was a sweeping sort of authority, which defied all law, and that it therefore offers little insight into administrative power. Absolute power, however, especially in England, thrived in the context of law and sometimes was even said to be authorized or at least acknowledged by law. Rather than a total negation of law, absolute power usually was understood as an alternative mechanism for exercising control, and its development alongside legal mechanisms and even partly within them suggests how much it had in common with contemporary administrative power.[4]

In fact, absolute power was the historical foundation of administrative power. Throughout the medieval and modern eras, European rulers pressed for absolute power. Although they often relied on it for the best of purposes, even the best of rulers were apt to misuse this authority. The English therefore, already in the Middle Ages, repeatedly enacted statutes attempting to restore governance through and under the law, and in the seventeenth and eighteenth centuries the English and then the Americans attempted to settle the question constitutionally. On the Continent, however, peoples were not so fortunate, and absolute power therefore was a continuing element of Continental governance. From there, indeed, as will be seen in this book, the power that once was understood to be absolute was eventually reintroduced into Anglo-American law.

Absolute power thus offers a framework for understanding the current extra- and supralegal regime and its consolidation of powers. Old absolutist notions may seem remote from modern administrative law. Ideas of absolute power, however, were the traditional conceptual framework for understanding the sort of power examined here.

Prerogative and Administrative

The relevance of absolute power for administrative law becomes more clear when one realizes that Anglo-American law has a history of an extra- and supralegal power in what was known as the "prerogative." This was the name of the power claimed by English kings, and it corresponds to the administrative power claimed by the president or under his authority.[5]

Of course, the words "prerogative" and "administrative" can be understood in different ways. Considered broadly, prerogative power can be all power exercised by the king, and administrative power can be all power exercised by the executive. From such a perspective, prerogative or administrative power sweepingly includes any royal or executive exercise of power—regardless of whether it is executive, legislative, or judicial. (For example, books on the history of government "administration" usually encompass the development of nearly all domestic governmental operations.) More narrowly, however, from the seventeenth century to the present, the king's prerogative has sometimes been understood as his extra- or supralegal exercise of binding legislative and judicial powers. Similarly, nowadays, the executive's administrative power can be understood as the executive's extra- or supralegal exercise of such powers. From this perspective, which is adopted here, "prerogative" and "administrative" are terms of opprobrium, and where they are used in looser ways, the meaning should be clear enough from the context.[c]

For centuries, Crown lawyers seem deliberately to have cultivated ambiguity about whether the king's prerogative was entirely lawful. When a king claimed a power to bind his subjects with rules he made outside Parliament, or when he claimed a power to enforce such rules in tribunals other than the courts of law, he could seem to be asserting a power outside and even above the law. Yet there were risks in openly claiming any prerogative as an exercise of absolute power, for kings depended on the legitimacy of the law and rarely could afford to declare that they were acting outside or above it. At the same time, however, it was inadvisable for the Crown to concede that all royal attempts to bind subjects had to be exercised through the law, for this would have invited limits on royal power. Being caught between these difficulties, the Crown often remained relatively silent about the theory of absolute power, hoping through politic reticence to enjoy the best of both worlds, legal and extralegal.

By the last half of the sixteenth century, however, this studied ambiguity was increasingly untenable. Henry VIII and his successors relied upon the supremacy of the law of the land to fend off foreign, papal claims. Having thus elevated the law of the land as the measure of all power within the realm, they then could defend their power to act independently of the law only by making explicit that some of their prerogatives were apart from the law and above it. It thus became commonplace, at least among men who hoped for royal patronage, to say that the king had two types of prerogatives, lawful and absolute. Whereas ordinary or regular prerogatives were acknowledged to be subject to law and thus reviewable in the courts of law,

---

c. Another understanding of "prerogative" became evident after the king's extralegal prerogative was subdued and the word was used to mean the king's lawful executive power. On this understanding, it was recognized that "the great branch of the prerogative is the *executive* power of government," and one could speak ambidextrously of the *"prerogative* or the *executive."* The prerogative, in this sense, lawfully continued to exist, even after the unlawful prerogative was prohibited. Hence, the possibility of the lawful "absolute prerogative" discussed in note b.*

extraordinary or irregular prerogatives were said to be independent of law and even above it. By the time of James I, in the early seventeenth century, the king himself publicly asserted not only his ordinary but also his "absolute prerogative."[6]

As it happens, just as Congress has authorized much administrative power, Parliament in the sixteenth century authorized or at least acquiesced in many of the absolute prerogatives claimed by English monarchs. Four hundred years later, the theory that the monarch's absolute prerogative was inherent in his sovereignty remains familiar; but less well understood is that monarchs simultaneously relied on statutory authorization for some of the central manifestations of that prerogative—as will be seen regarding proclamations, the Star Chamber, and the High Commission. Thus, even for prerogatives defended in absolutist terms, statutory authority mattered when it came down to the concrete level of legal argument. Of course, monarchs and their prerogative tribunals frequently went beyond their statutory authorization, but this makes the similarity to American administrative power all the more striking.

With or without statutory foundations, prerogative power provoked constitutional limits. The English, especially English lawyers, had long been profoundly attached to government by and under law, and in response to open claims of absolute power, common lawyers became openly skeptical as to whether a king could lawfully exercise lawmaking power outside the law or judicial power outside the judgments of the courts. They therefore increasingly condemned the lawmaking and adjudicatory prerogatives as unlawful exercises of absolute power—unlawful both because they were outside ordinary law and adjudication and because they thereby reached above the law. Indeed, it will be seen that the English adopted ideas about an English constitution precisely in order to make clear that there could be no binding or constraining government power outside or above the law.

Following in this tradition, Americans constitutions almost uniformly authorized American governments to act against their subjects only through and under law. As put by John Adams in 1776, Americans aimed to establish governments in which a governor or president had "the whole executive power, after divesting it of those badges of domination called prerogatives," by which Adams meant, of course, the absolute prerogatives.[7]

Nowadays, however, American administrative law revives the extralegal government familiar from the royal prerogative. To be precise, it restores a version of the absolute prerogative—the extra- and supralegal power that purported to bind and that flourished before the development of constitutional law. Of course, like Adams, this book usually abbreviates its allusions to the absolute prerogative, saying merely that there has been a return to prerogative power. The point, however, should be clear enough. Whether called "prerogative" or "administrative," there has been a return to power outside the law—a reversion to the sort of power that constitutional law most centrally prohibits.

Evading the Constitution

The danger of an administrative return to an extralegal regime becomes particularly concrete when one recognizes the potential for evasion. Administrative law evades not only the law but also its institutions, processes, and rights.

The central evasion is the end run around acts of Congress and the judgments of the courts by substituting executive edicts. This suggests that there can be an alternative system of law, which is not quite law, but that nonetheless can be enforced against the public.

As if this were not enough, the evasion also gets around the Constitution's institutions and processes. For example, when the executive makes regulations, it claims to escape the constitutional requirements for the election of lawmakers, for bicameralism, for deliberation, for publication of legislative journals, and for a veto. Similarly, when the executive adjudicates disputes, it claims to sidestep most of the requirements about judicial independence, due process, grand juries, petit juries, and judicial warrants and orders. The judicial evasion is particularly troubling when one realizes that it escapes almost all of the procedural rights guaranteed by the Constitution.

Recognizing at least the due process problem, courts and commentators sometimes suggest that administrative adjudication is subject to a lesser, administrative version of due process. It remains unclear, however, how a fraction of a right can substitute for the whole, or how the due process of administrative power in an administrative tribunal can substitute for the due process of law in a court. This is like a substitution of water for whisky, and the fact that both are liquid does not hide the evasion.

It was precisely to bar prerogative or administrative evasions of law that seventeenth-century Englishmen developed ideas of constitutional law. Although the constitution of a government had long been understood as the law enacted by the community or people, it was only in the early seventeenth century that Englishmen recognized its significance as a limit on the prerogative. At the beginning of that century, English monarchs attempted to rule outside the law made by Parliament and outside the adjudications of the courts. Yet if the constitution required the government to constrain its subjects only through the law, then the monarch could not exercise any binding power outside the law. And if all government power came from the people, as granted by them in their law or constitution, there could be no power above the law. On such reasoning, constitutional law developed as a means of baring prerogative evasions of the law.

Today, however, an extralegal regime has been revived, and it again escapes the law. The justification given for this evasion is that when the Constitution confines legislative and judicial power with various institutions, processes, and rights, it limits only Congress and the courts, not the executive. Yet constitutional law developed in the seventeenth century precisely to bar extralegal power. In other words, rather than restrict only what is done in the legislative and judicial branches, it was drafted to confine all exercises of legislative and judicial power, even if by the executive. It thereby bars the evasions, regardless of whether they are called "prerogative" or "administrative." The threat of evasion from an extralegal regime has not changed much over the centuries; nor has the remedy.

⊰⊱⊰⊱⊰⊱

Administrative law thus raises profound questions. Like the old absolute prerogative, it stands outside the law and even above it, and it consolidates the powers of government. The Constitution, however, was framed to bar any such extralegal, supralegal, and consolidated power. It therefore must be asked whether administrative power is unlawful—indeed, whether it is a return to absolute power.

PART I

Extralegal Legislation

Just as English monarchs once claimed a prerogative power to make law outside acts of Parliament, so too the American executive now claims an administrative power to make law outside acts of Congress. It therefore is necessary to inquire whether administrative power returns to prerogative power and its extralegal system of legislation.

The similarities between administrative and prerogative legislation are striking. Like its contemporary counterpart, prerogative legislation evaded the regular structures and processes of lawmaking. Like its contemporary cousin, prerogative lawmaking sometimes had statutory authorization. Like its contemporary doppelgänger, it was justified in terms of interpretation, judicial deference, and ultimately necessity, the old excuse for absolute power.

Of course, much scholarship (notably that by Larry Alexander, Bradford Clark, Gary Lawson, Saikrishna Prakash, Michael Rappaport, and David Schoenbrod) has recognized that administrative law is not made by Congress and thus is not made by the legislative body, let alone the legislative process, established by the Constitution.[1] This is true as far as it goes, but the danger of administrative law runs even deeper, and to understand this it is necessary to consider the history.

The history reveals that the problem is not merely the institutional location of the lawmaking power and the associated legislative process, but more fundamentally an extralegal mode of constraint—a type of rule that runs not through the law but outside it. This was absolute power, the very opposite of constitutional power.

The history thereby shows that administrative lawmaking returns to precisely the sort of extralegal governance that constitutional law was designed to prohibit. Although it is often said that administrative regulation could not have been anticipated by the Constitution and therefore was not barred by it, it will be seen that administrative lawmaking reverts back to the extralegal legislation that provoked the development of constitutional law. In other words, the Constitution's grant of legislative power to Congress developed not only to authorize and control the acts of the legislature, but also to bar any prerogative or other extralegal legislative acts. It therefore is disturbing that administrative legislation returns to this sort of legislation—the sort of power exercised not through the law, but outside it.

Part I traces the history of extralegal lawmaking power, its defeat in constitutional law, and finally its administrative revival. It begins by showing how the English Crown engaged in extralegal lawmaking—chapter 3 focusing on how it did this through proclamations, and chapter 4 on how it did this through interpretations, regulations, and taxes. Chapter 5 then examines the Crown's extralegal suspending and dispensing powers, by which it claimed to deprive law of its obligation. It will be seen, throughout these chapters, that although aspects of the extralegal lawmaking had statutory authorization, this power was understood to be absolute—thus suggesting the character of contemporary extralegal lawmaking.

Along the way, part I also explains the constitutional response. Constitutional law gathered force in the seventeenth century in opposition to absolute power, and thus rather than simply limit the power exercised through the law, it even more basically rejected all power exercised outside the law. Most centrally, it repudiated the power to bind subjects with extralegal legislation, and it thereby defeated all extralegal lawmaking, whether in proclamations, taxes, regulations, or interpretations.

Nonetheless, as shown at the end of part I, administrative law has revived much of this extralegal lawmaking. Chapter 6 examines early federal executive actions in order to differentiate lawful executive acts from extralegal administrative lawmaking. Chapter 7 concludes with contemporary administrative lawmaking, showing how there has been a return to the extralegal legislation.

Before the historical venture begins, it may be worth repeating what already was hinted in the introduction, that this history is not simply about the past. Nor, in concentrating on England, is it narrowly about that country. The goal, instead, is to look forward—to recognize a problem that cuts across legal cultures and thereby to understand the nature of American administrative law.

THREE

Proclamations

Although English kings undoubtedly could issue proclamations that did not their bind subjects, they sometimes used their proclamations to impose binding duties. Indeed, in the sixteenth and early seventeenth centuries, they candidly claimed a prerogative to legislate through their proclamations. Monarchs thereby openly asserted a power that, in the ideals of the common law, they could exercise only through acts of Parliament. At stake, therefore, in the dispute about proclamations was extralegal lawmaking— the power to legislate outside the law, outside the legislature, and outside legislative processes.

The question of proclamations thus gets to the heart of what nowadays is administrative legislation. It even reaches the question of whether the legislature can authorize such lawmaking.

Conflicting Views of Proclamations

There were conflicting views about proclamations. From a common law perspective, proclamations could not bind, but from an absolutist civilian perspective they could.

The common law understanding of proclamations was shaped by the underlying assumption that kings could make law only in Parliament. There, monarchs participated as part of the legislative body, where the entire nation was said to be present and thus capable of consenting to new laws. In contrast, when the Crown acted alone it could do much, but not in altering the laws. For example, in his proclamations, a king could issue orders to Crown and local officers; he could exhort his subjects to obey the law; he could directly order nonsubjects to the extent they were within his coercion. But to change the legal duties of any subject, he needed to act through the law, through an act of Parliament—a conclusion that left no room for extralegal modes of legislation.[1]

In taking this approach, the English self-consciously rejected civilian jurisprudence—the academic study of Roman law. Whereas the common law was studied at the Inns of Court, the civil and canon laws were taught at the universities, and the academic study of these Roman-derived systems became a vehicle for justifying absolute power. Continental scholars of this "learned law" often harked back to the view, recorded by Justinian, that "[w]hat pleases the prince has the force of law," and on this basis they elaborated theories about the imperial power of a ruler to act on his own, outside and above the law.[2]

English lawyers, however, usually took another view. Bracton already rejected the Roman or civilian vision, writing that "there is no king where will rules rather than law." More than two centuries later, around 1470, Chief Justice John Fortescue observed that the phrase from Justinian was "a favorite maxim" of the civilians and feared that it encouraged kings to "govern by absolute regal power"—in particular, to "change laws, enact new ones, inflict punishments, and impose taxes, at their mere will and pleasure." In contrast, he emphasized, the laws of England "admit of no such maxim, or anything like it." A king of England "cannot, at his pleasure, make any alterations in the laws of the land, for the nature of his government is not only regal, but political."[3]

Nonetheless, English monarchs repeatedly pressed the boundaries of their power, often issuing proclamations that imposed new legal duties, even sometimes with criminal penalties. For example, although there was no doubt that Henry VIII could proclaim the value of coins when he issued them, it was debatable whether he subsequently could simply proclaim an alteration in their value, let alone bind subjects to accept them. Similarly, although he could use a proclamation to inform his subjects that Parliament had prohibited the sale of a commodity, he was on weaker ground when he acted alone to bar them from selling it.[4]

The question was one of obligation and thus of consent. By the end of the Middle Ages, subjects of the Crown were presumed to be free. From this perspective, they could be bound only by their personal consent or the consent of all the people in Parliament. On these principles, the king alone could not bind his subjects.

Of course, where the king used proclamations merely to instruct officials, he was only issuing orders to his servants. Such orders might have practical implication for his subjects, but they did not bind them. Moreover, where the king used his proclamations to declare his will about war and peace, foreign policy, or the treatment of enemy prisoners, he was merely exercising coercive power against nonsubjects, not altering the legally binding duties of subjects.[5] But when he issued proclamations that burdened the public with duties different from those imposed by law, he wandered into legislative territory.

Recognizing the common law division between royal and legislative power, Crown lawyers often apparently did their best in the sixteenth century to ensure that any command in a proclamation was "not stated as a new limitation on the subject's liberty."[6] The common law, however, did not offer the only theory of what kings could do. The Crown's advisors well understood that the civil law justified monarchs in exercising power outside the law, and they therefore increasingly relied on the civilian ideas to excuse proclamations, decrees, and other acts that imposed binding duties. Thus, notwithstanding the common law, the civilian theory of absolute power—of power outside the law—became the foundation for an extralegal legislative regime.[a]

The Act of Proclamations

The question of legislative authorization for administrative legislation often is assumed to lack much early history. In 1539, however, Parliament notoriously authorized prerogative lawmaking in the Act of Proclamations.

Although most English kings had been prudent enough to leave unstated whether they were using proclamations to exercise legislative power outside Parliament, Henry VIII and his advisors were bold men. Hardened in religious disputes about royal authority, they did not shy away from the question of whether proclamations were an exercise of power above or at least independent of law. They therefore initially took their stand simply on Henry's absolute power. In their view, the king's will was binding, whether expressed through acts of Parliament or outside them.[b]

a. This book distinguishes between common law and civilian views, but one could just easily distinguish between two common law views—one barring extralegal power, and the other accepting some of it. Obviously, neither division is entirely satisfying, and the key is simply to recognize that each comes with gains and loses.

On the one hand, the Crown often tried to claim extralegal power on grounds of English law, and this would suggest that there were simply different common law perspectives. On the other hand, the Crown was attempting to domesticate a civilian vision of its power; it often was candid that it was doing this; and even where the Crown succeeded in court, critics complained that it was acting contrary to the "ancient" or "old" law of the land. Accordingly, for purposes of recognizing the historical development of the different views, and their constitutional significance, it has seemed best to generalize about the tensions between the civilian and the common law perspective.

b. A glimpse of the Crown's views and the opposition can be observed in a conversation

On such assumptions, Henry used proclamations to legislate on matters as diverse as religion and trade, but without fully persuading his countrymen or the judges. Earlier, when repudiating Rome, he had relied on acts of Parliament, but now, in 1538 and '39, when he felt he needed to limit the Protestant assault on traditional doctrine and ceremonies, he relied on proclamations. To his surprise, however, his proclamations provoked complaints that he lacked authority to legislate outside Parliament. When he sought to issue proclamations regulating the grain trade, moreover, the judges warned him that this might not be lawful.[7]

Henry therefore demanded parliamentary authorization for his power to make law. The result was An Act that Proclamations Made by the King Shall be Obeyed—an early version of the sort of statutes that nowadays authorize administrative rulemaking. The preamble explained that "divers and many forward, wilful and obstinate persons have wilfully condemned and broken" the king's proclamations on religion, apparently "not considering what a king by his royal power may do." Parliament therefore concluded that the king needed a statute to bind offenders "to obey the said proclamations."[8]

The Act of Proclamations bluntly relied on the civilian theory of absolute power. Civilian academics traditionally justified such power on grounds of necessity, especially the necessity of action when there was not time to wait for the regular legislative process. Echoing these arguments, the preamble of the Act of Proclamations explained that "sudden causes and occasions" often "require speedy remedies, and that by abiding for a Parliament in the meantime might happen great prejudice to ensue to the realm." The preamble, however, then appeared to relent, stating that it was

---

vividly recorded by the bishop of Winchester, Stephen Gardiner. Henry VIII's leading minister, Thomas Cromwell, had encouraged the king to believe that "his will and pleasure" should be "regarded for a law" because this was what it "was to be a very king." In other words, Cromwell urged that absolute power was inherent in sovereignty—a conclusion he drew from civilian writers in the same manner that Jean Bodin would four decades later.

Eager to secure acquiescence in such notions, Cromwell asked Gardiner to come to Hampton Court. In the presence of the king, Cromwell asked the bishop to tell the king what he thought of the civilian doctrine. When Gardiner apparently hesitated to approve, Cromwell bullied him: "Come on . . . speak plainly and directly, and shrink not, man! Is not that . . . that pleaseth the King, a law?"

Gardiner was silent. "I stood still and wondered in my mind to what conclusion this should tend." At this point Henry intervened. He "saw me musing, and with earnest gentleness said, 'Answer him whether it be so or no.'" Gardiner later recounted, "I would not answer my Lord Cromwell, but delivered my speech to the king," telling him not that his will was law, but that "the form of his reign, to make the laws his will, was more sure and quiet." Gardiner even added, "And by this form of government you are established."

Upon hearing this, the king "turned his back" on the bishop. Henry would find it more difficult to turn his back on English law.*

desirable to spare the king and his people from an exertion of his absolute power against those who refused to accept his proclamations as binding. Parliament therefore would give regular statutory authority to his absolute power to make binding proclamations.[9]

Revealingly, Parliament hinted at a double necessity, both royal and parliamentary. The legislature thought it was "more than necessary" that the king "should make and set forth proclamations for the good and politic order and governance of this his realm . . . as the cases of necessity shall require." In addition, it was "more than necessary . . . that an ordinary law should be provided by the assent of his majesty and parliament, for the due punishment, correction, and reformation of such offenses and disobediences."[10] Thus, not only the king but also Parliament was acting of necessity. It was a hint of what later would be widely recognized: that in authorizing the king to legislate outside the legislative process, Parliament had joined him in exercising absolute power.

Getting down to details, the statute enacted that the king, with the advice of his council, "may set forth . . . proclamations, under such penalties and pains" as the king and his council consider "necessary and requisite." The act added that such proclamations "shall be obeyed, observed, and kept as though they were made by act of Parliament."[11] The statute thereby lent the obligation of ordinary law to what Henry previously had claimed as an extraordinary power above and independent of the law.

Nowadays, when Congress authorizes administrative regulations, Congress can rely on the courts to accept these merely executive pronouncements as legally binding. Henry VIII, however, had reason to fear that the courts of his era were made of sterner stuff. The judges of the law courts had an office of deciding in accord with the law of the land, and in the ideals of this office, they were expected to follow the law, regardless of any contrary royal demands. Therefore, when the Crown secured statutory authorization for binding proclamations, it also arranged for the statute to authorize enforcement of the binding proclamations in the Star Chamber. Prerogative legislation was not law, and therefore, even with parliamentary authorization, it was safest when kept in a prerogative court.[12]

Although the Act of Proclamations unabashedly gave legal cover to legislative power outside and above the law, it also attempted to limit the damage. Worried about the authorization of absolute power, Parliament added a proviso limiting how the statute could be interpreted as to property, life, and law. Under no understanding of the act should "any of the king's liege people"—that is, any of his subjects—"have any of his or their inheritances, lawful possessions, offices, liberties, privileges, franchises, goods, or chattels taken from them"; nor should any of them "by virtue of the said act suffer any pains of death, other than shall be hereafter in this act declared"; nor "by any proclamation to be made by virtue of this act" were "any acts, [or] common laws standing at this present time in strength and force" to be "infringed, broken or subverted."[13] The proviso thus generally ensured that the authorized proclamations could confine liberty only as long they did not violate property, life, or laws.[c]

This proviso would soon be viewed as entirely contradicting the main body of the statute, but in fact it was more measured. Although it seriously confined what could be done through the authorized proclamations, it still allowed the proclamations to regulate where there were no conflicting property rights, where the proclamations imposed penalties short of death, and where there was a mere absence of statutory constraint rather than a law protecting liberty.[14]

Not surprisingly, the Act of Proclamations was promptly repealed in 1547—the first year of the next reign. It lived on, however, as a memorable warning against legal authorization for prerogative or administrative power.[15]

This sober lesson was discussed in 1575, when the Lords proposed the Bill of Apparel. This was a sumptuary law, which would have given the queen authority to proclaim the apparel wearable by "every degree of persons" and to specify punishments within statutory limits. The bill thereby permitted flexibility, allowing the queen to adjust the restrictions on apparel and the penalties, as might be needed "from time to time." Unsurprisingly, the bill was "much impugned" in the Commons, and the objection of one group of members is particularly revealing. Fearing a revival of the Act of Proclamations, they complained that the Bill of Apparel gave the queen a power to bind her subjects. Traditionally, "the subjects of the land have not been . . . bound to any thing but unto such as should be certainly established by authority of Parliament." If this act were to pass, however, "a proclamation from the prince" would "take the force of law, which might prove a dangerous precedent in time to come."[16] It was only a minor bill on clothing, but it was rejected, largely because it might become a precedent for legislative authorization of lawmaking proclamations.

Later generations came to view the Act of Proclamations as one of the most abject moments in English history—the point at which the legislature

---

c. There were exceptions to these limitations. The statute excepted persons who offended against proclamations on heresies, and of course it excepted "such forfeitures, pains, and penalties" as were stated in the proclamations issued under the statute's authority.

itself authorized absolute power in violation of the English constitution. David Hume, although no Whig, scathingly observed that when Parliament "gave to the king's proclamation the same force as to a statute enacted by parliament," it "made by one act a total subversion of the English constitution."[17]

Hume understood that English kings had traditionally exercised a degree of absolute power in cases of necessity, but he also recognized that, unlike Continental rulers, English kings had enjoyed this power irregularly despite the law, not regularly, with legal legitimacy:

> [T]he kings of England had always been accustomed, from their own authority, to issue proclamations, and to exact obedience to them; and this prerogative was, no doubt, a strong symptom of absolute government: But still there was a difference between a power, which was exercised on a particular emergence, and which must be justified by the present expedience or necessity; and an authority conferred by a positive statute, which could no longer admit of control or limitation.

Hume therefore asked whether there could be "any act be more opposite to the spirit of liberty than this law."[18]

Hundreds of years later, the historian Frederic Maitland concurred that the Act of Proclamations was "the most extraordinary act in the statute book."[19] The act placed lawmaking proclamations—at least, those made in "cases of necessity"—on the footing of "an ordinary law," as if ordinary law could domesticate a power outside and above the law. Yet even with all of its power, Parliament could not really legalize prerogative or administrative lawmaking. Instead, like Congress nowadays, it merely made itself complicit in absolutism.

The Persistence of Arguments from Absolute Power

The imperiousness of Henry VIII was followed by the weakness of a child king, Edward VI, and as already noted, Parliament took the opportunity to repeal the Act of Proclamations.[20] Yet even without statutory authority, the Crown continued to issue proclamations that bound subjects, and it soon again justified itself on grounds of absolute power.

These days, it is widely assumed that administrative agencies can lawfully regulate where they have statutory authorization. In contrast, in the sixteenth century, it was assumed that, even with a statutory foundation, binding proclamations involved absolute power. Already under the Act of

Proclamations, binding proclamations were understood to be exercises of absolute power, and this remained true when the Crown issued such proclamations without a statutory mandate. As a result, binding or lawmaking proclamations were not apt to fare well in court.

A hint of this became evident under Queen Mary. Faced with her ambitious proclamations, the judges opined 1555 that proclamations could not alter the law—that "the king may make a proclamation to his subjects *quoad terrorem populi*, to put them in fear of his displeasure, but not to impose any fine, forfeiture, or imprisonment; for no proclamation can make a new law, but only confirm and ratify an ancient one."[21] The underlying principle was given a symmetrical turn by Christopher Yelverton, who eventually would become a justice of King's Bench: "The prince . . . could not of herself make laws," and "neither might she by the same reason break laws."[22]

Nonetheless, ambitious Crown lawyers under Elizabeth pressed for royal legislation outside Parliament. With their eyes on the Crown's authority and their own advancement, they urged paths that went outside and above the law, and they now found a propitious climate for their absolutist claims.

It was the era in which Jean Bodin distilled the ideas of civilian commentators, arguing that the essence of sovereignty was the power above and independent of the law. From this point of view, when a sovereign worked through the law, he was not fully sovereign unless he always reserved the capacity to act outside his law. Put another way, Bodin recognized that the highest claim of authority in any society was that which was final, unreviewable, and thus above and independent of the law.

Small-scale versions of such ideas had long coexisted with English expectations of government under and through the law. The coexistence was possible because monarchs generally had enough wisdom to exercise even their most lawless prerogatives while leaving ambiguous whether they were acting above the law. In the late sixteenth and early seventeenth centuries, however, under the influence of academically trained lawyers, English monarchs increasingly cast aside such understatement.

The open pursuit of binding proclamations, and the candid defense of them in terms of absolute power, can still be observed in detail. The prime mover seems to have been Thomas Egerton. He was among the ambitious young lawyers who acquired the academic itch for absolute power, and when in the 1590s he became lord keeper, he began to expound his theories in Star Chamber.

The initial occasion seems to have been a 1597 case in which the defendants were charged with engrossing corn and buying and selling out of the open market. As they could not have been charged under existing statutes, Lord Keeper Egerton argued that "the parts of the statutes against ingrossers and forestallers" were "to no purpose." Accordingly, the queen's council and the judges aimed to get "redress for such offences and many others in the commonwealth by the queen's prerogative only"—that is, by means of extralegal power: "[T]hus their decrees and councils, proclamations and orders, shall be a firm and [en]forceable law, and of the like force as the common law or an Act of Parliament. And this is the intent of the privy counselors in our day and time, to attribute to their counsels and orders the vigor, force and power of a firm law, and of higher virtue and force, jurisdiction and preeminence, than any positive law, whether it be the common law or statute law."[23] Whatever the intent of the judges, it clearly was the intent of Egerton and leading members of the council to elevate royal proclamations and other commands to the level of law, and even above it.[d] Bodin would have been proud.

Of course, the lord keeper's sweeping claim that the monarch could, at any time, issue proclamations with greater obligation than statutes did not lend credibility to his position, and he therefore in 1603 narrowed his argument. Rather than broadly assert a general royal power to legislate outside and above the law, he now argued in Star Chamber for a prerogative power of legislation where necessity required prompt action: "The Lord keeper sermonized that 'it is his majesty's pleasure to make known in this court'" that there were "abuses" that "will not stay to be provided for by public act." And because it was his majesty's goal "to provide for these and to execute justice to all," he "hath and intendeth by his proclamations to redress them," and he therefore charged all men "to take notice" of his proclamations and "strictly to observe and perform them." Lest this admonition not be heeded, Egerton warned that "his majesty will severely punish all condemners or neglecters."[24] In short, like contemporary administrative regulations, lawmaking proclamations were defended as necessary for addressing abuses that could not wait for the legislature.

The point was stated even more bluntly in a 1607 Star Chamber case against two men who violated its building regulations. Egerton (who had since been elevated to Lord Chancellor and Baron Ellesmere) declared, "Nihil est illicitum quod est necessarium" and "Necessitas lex temporis"—

d. Shortly after Egerton's speech, the Star Chamber reenforced his point by proceeding "against the builders of cottages . . . on the proclamation and not on the statute." Recognizing the implications, a practitioner recalled the warning from Egerton and his colleagues bout how a proclamation could have the effect of law, and concluded that, indeed, "this appears to me to be their intent."*

nothing is illicit that is necessary and necessity is a temporary law. To be sure, he acknowledged that "the king cannot take my land or goods and give it to another." Ultimately, however, "where the common state or wealth of the people or kingdom require it"—in other words, where the public interest required it—"the king's proclamation binds as a law, and need not stay [for] a parliament."[25]

Not content to pursue such ideas in Star Chamber, advocates of absolute power increasingly asserted them in public. In 1607, an academic who enjoyed episcopal patronage, John Cowell, published an academic law dictionary, *The Interpreter*, in which he defined the prerogative of the king as a power "above the ordinary course of the common law." The king thus was "absolute."[26]

The last straw came from the Crown itself. Unlike statutes, which often were permanent, proclamations traditionally were admonitions aimed at current exigencies. Thus, although the king's printer republished statutes in book-length compilations, the printer usually published proclamations only once, on large sheets of paper, like official posters, to be proclaimed in public and pasted on walls. Many men therefore were astonished when the king's printer in 1609 published all of the proclamations of the current king, James I, in a book, as if they were statutes. The rumor was that "the king intended to make laws of proclamations."[27]

The House of Commons' Protest

Although the king's lawmaking proclamations flourished in Star Chamber, they soon ran into trouble in Parliament. Monarchs had long gotten away with exercising legislative power on their own, at least while they did it quietly. But now that James I was openly pursuing this power, the House of Commons finally responded. It thereby initiated what would become the constitutional rejection of binding proclamations—an assertion of constitutional principle that would, more generally, bar all prerogative, administrative, or otherwise extralegal legislation.

In a petition against "grievances," the Commons in the summer of 1610 complained that many proclamations threatened rule by law. This point came under the title "Proclamations in prejudice of your subjects' right and liberty," and the Commons elaborated: "Amongst many other points of happiness and freedom which your majesty's subjects of this kingdom have enjoyed under your royal progenitors . . . there is none which they have accounted more dear and precious than this, to be guided and governed by the certain rule of the law, which giveth both to the head and members that which of right belongeth to them and not by any uncertain or arbitrary form of government." In particular, it was an "indubitable right of the people of this kingdom not to be made subject to any punishments that shall extend to their lives, lands, bodies or goods, other than such as are ordained by the common law of this land, or the statutes made by their common consent in parliament."[28]

It therefore was disturbing that the Crown had recently sought to bind subjects by proclamations. These declarations "have been made of late years much more frequent than heretofore," and "they are extended not only to the liberty, but also to the goods, inheritances, and livelihood of men." The proclamations thereby "tend[ed] to alter some points of the law"; they even tended to "make a new, other" sort of law.[29]

This new sort of law prompted fears for liberty: "[T]here is a general fear conceived and spread among your Majesty's people, that proclamations will by degrees grow up and increase to the strength and nature of laws, whereby not only that ancient happiness and freedom will be much blemished, if not quite taken away, which their ancestors have so long enjoyed, but the same may also in process of time bring a new form of arbitrary government upon the realm." The Commons therefore petitioned that henceforth "no fine or forfeiture of goods or other pecuniary or corporal punishment may be inflicted upon your subjects . . . unless they shall offend against some law or statute of this realm in force at the time of their offense committed."[30] In effect, the Commons protested administrative power.

The only exception that the Commons acknowledged was for temporary emergency imprisonment—what today would be called administrative detention. Thus, no punishment was to be "inflicted upon your subjects other than restraint of liberty . . . upon urgent necessity."[31] This was the sort of exception that later would be acknowledged and legalized by the U.S. Constitution in its clause allowing Congress to suspend writs of habeas corpus. Beyond this, subjects and their property could be constrained only for violations of law, not mere proclamations.

Constitutionalism

In the same year that the Commons petitioned the king against his abuse of proclamations, some members of the Commons began to frame their critique of royal lawmaking in constitutional terms. The king's attempt to legislate outside acts of Parliament thus became one of the first threats to stimulate English reliance on constitutional ideas, and it is therefore an initial illustration of how constitutional law developed to defeat extralegal power, whether prerogative or administrative.

The idea of a constitution was not new. Some scholars (led by Bernard Bailyn and Gordon Wood) suggest that the constitution of a government was typically understood to be merely its arrangement, and that the idea of a constitution as an enactment of the people developed only very late. Since Roman times, however, a constitution had been understood to be an enactment, and already in Rome it was understood that constitutions could be adopted by the people. In addition, the "constitution" of a government could be its arrangement, but the sort of constitution of government that was considered a law was a Roman-style enactment of the people or community. From this Roman conception, Europeans developed the idea of a constitution or law enacted by the community to establish and limit their ruler. Hints of this sort of constitution can be discerned in the treatise written by the medieval English judge Bracton, who explained that a king was to "temper his power by law, which is the bridle of power, that he may live according to the laws." To this, Bracton suggestively added that "the law of mankind has decreed that his own laws bind the lawgiver." Certainly, by at least the fifteenth century, the enactments of men "by which some of them are raised into kings" were said to be "constitutions."[32]

In 1610, however, the notion of a constitution began to become a popular argument against absolute prerogatives, especially against an absolute power of legislation. One advantage of constitutional arguments was that they could defeat claims made outside or above the law. If government originated from an enactment or constitution of the people, then no part of government could make law or law-like edicts, except as authorized by the constitution. On such reasoning, if the constitution placed legislative power in Parliament, there could be no independent legislative power in the king. Whatever sovereign power a king enjoyed from state necessity, such a power could not exist outside or above the constitution.

To avoid the limiting implications of such arguments from the people or community, King James I claimed that he enjoyed his absolute power from God. This, however, was of little avail, for constitutional arguments also assumed that power came from God, but claimed that God placed the original power in the people. As one member of Parliament explained in 1610, "regal power" was "from God, but the actuating thereof is from the people." This seemed evident from reason, and therefore to consider the king's power "unlimited" was "contrary to reason." Focusing on the legal implications, another member observed that the king was "the most absolute king in his Parliament; but, of himself, his power is limited by law." In response, even Attorney General Henry Hobart had to concede the general point, that the king "cannot change the law, nor any other [could change it] but they that make it," and that therefore the king "cannot make laws without assent of Parliament."[33]

It later will be seen that the constitutional arguments in 1610 also focused on taxes, but whether the immediate issue on any particular day was proclamations or taxes, it was understood that both were merely aspects of the broader question of prerogative or extralegal legislation—what nowadays would be called administrative legislation.[34] James Whitelocke—a member of Parliament and soon to be a judge—rhetorically asked, "Can any man give me a reason, why the king can only in Parliament make laws?" He answered, "it is the original right of the kingdom, and the very natural [i.e., native] constitution of our state and policy, being one of the highest rights of sovereign power." Thus, "it is *jus indigena* an old homeborn right." Later in their session, the Commons as a body resolved that the "sovereign power of making laws" was allocated by the "constitution of this your majesty's kingdom" to "the kings of this realm, with assent of the parliament."[35]

The threat of prerogative legislation was stimulating the use and popularization of constitutional ideas. And although taxes and binding proclamations were the immediate concern, the constitutional principle clearly was broader, the point being that the constitution placed legislative power in the legislature. It was a principle that Americans would remember, and that still matters for administrative law.

The Opinions of the Judges

The question of proclamations soon came before the judges. When the Commons protested against the use of proclamations for lawmaking, King James I promised them he would consult the judges, probably on the hope that he could pressure them into showing deference. The result was what became known as *The Case of Proclamations*—in fact, two advisory opinions on the unlawfulness of extralegal legislation.

Chief Justice Edward Coke later recalled that in the fall of 1610 he was asked to attend the king's council. When he arrived, Lord Chancellor Ellesmere focused the discussion on two proclamations: whether "the king by his proclamation may prohibit new buildings in and about London" and similarly whether he "may prohibit the making of starch of wheat." The first proclamation was yet another example of urban planning by royal fiat; the second was an attempt to create a monopoly, from which the Crown and its supporters could profit. These, Coke was told, were among the proclamations the Commons had complained about as "grievances, and against the law and justice."

In pressing for a favorable opinion, Ellesmere impatiently demanded judicial deference. He said the judges should "maintain the power and prerogative of the king." Especially "in cases in which there is no authority and precedent," the judges should "leave it to the king to order it according to his wisdom." This was a hint, as will be seen, about royal interpretation in the interstices of statutes and about judicial deference to such interpretation. Hundreds of years later, in its notorious *Chevron* case, the U.S. Supreme Court still justifies this sort of deference on the assumption that judges should leave the executive to act on "the incumbent administration's views of wise policy."[36]

Coke, however, refused to be bullied. He protested that "I did not hear of these questions until this morning, at nine of the clock." On this ground, he asked for time to confer with his brethren so he could give "an advised answer according to law and reason." When he nonetheless was pressed, he gave a tentative advisory opinion that "the king cannot change any part of the common law, nor create any offence by his proclamation, which was not an offence before, without Parliament."[37, e]

Rather than wait for the judges to reach a considered decision, James attempted to preempt them by issuing yet another proclamation, in which he suggested that his absolute power to legislate through proclamations rested on a constitutional footing. As a concession, he said he was ordering a review of his proclamations to revise and even drop some of them. He claimed to do so, however, on the basis of his power outside and above the law—his power "to apply speedy, proper, and convenient remedies . . . in all cases of sudden and extraordinary accidents, and in matters so variable and irregular in their nature, as are not provided for by law, nor can fitly fall under the certain rule of a law." This was an absolute power to legislate in the interstices of the law. Of course, he took care to acknowledge that "by the constitution of the frame and policy of this kingdom, royal proclamations and ordinances are not of equal force, nor in the like degrees with our laws."[38] Even in thus seeming to concede, however, that his power of

e. This meeting was not Coke's first encounter with the question of proclamations, for he had been present in the Star Chamber when it brought prosecutions merely on proclamations. At that time, Coke had been unable to do much except to limit the damage by observing that there were also legal grounds for the decisions. For example, in a 1608 Star Chamber prosecution for the violation of two proclamations against tenements, he said, "ubi non est lex ibi non est transgressio"—where there is no law, there is no transgression—and he then concluded that "these buildings are against the common law and the king's prerogative."*

proclamation did not reach above the law of the land, he simultaneously, in his backhanded way, was claiming that he had constitutional authority to act outside the law in creating new offenses where statutes were silent.

Such a maneuver could only have given greater resolve to Coke and his colleagues. The next month they reported back what the king did not want to hear. They explained that "the king by his proclamation cannot create any offence which was not an offence before." In support of this, the judges observed that the law of England was "divided into three parts, common law, statute law, and [local] custom; but the king's proclamation is none of them." Of course, "the king for prevention of offenses, may by proclamation admonish his subjects that they keep the laws, and do not offend them, upon punishment to be inflicted by the law," but this was merely another way of saying that the king "by the laws of this realm cannot by his proclamation create any thing to be an offense which not an offense before against the laws of this realm."[39, f]

The broader principle, as Coke explained in his report, was not confined to proclamations or the creation of new offenses. Rather it was that "the king by his proclamation, or other ways, cannot change any part of the common law, or statute law, or the customs of the realm." On this account, Coke noted, many proclamations had been held "void."[40]

Driving home the point that a proclamation could not alter the law, Coke touched upon the question of whether the Crown could obtain legislative power from Parliament. He drew no overt conclusion about this, but he noted an apparent contradiction in Henry VIII's Act of Proclamations: this statute had given "more power to the king than he had before, and yet there it is declared, that proclamation shall not alter the law, statutes, or customs of the realm, or impeach any in his inheritance, goods, body, life, etc."[41] In seeing this as a contradiction, Coke probably was misreading the statute, but to Coke and many of his contemporaries, the apparent contradiction was significant; evidently, not even Parliament under Henry had really thought it could give the king a power to change the law. Statutory authorization was irrelevant.

---

f. The furthest Coke went toward the position of the Crown was to suggest that violations of proclamations aggravated the underlying offense. He explained that "in all cases the king out of his providence, and to prevent dangers, which it will be too late to prevent afterwards, he may prohibit them before, which will aggravate the offense if it be afterwards committed." Coke apparently meant that the king could warn the public against violating the criminal law and that subsequent violations would be considered aggravated offenses. This, however, was not entirely consistent with his broader principles, for an aggravated version of an underling offense added to the elements of the offense and increased the penalty.*

A Constitutional Prohibition

The location of legislative power in the legislature, and the consequent bar against prerogative legislation, soon became basic maxims of political theory and constitutional law. From this perspective, as will be elaborated in chapter 20, not even legislative authorization could legalize administrative lawmaking.

Roger Twysden—a mid-seventeenth-century commentator—observed, "This maxim, that the king cannot alone alter the law" is "the basis or ground of all the liberty and franchise of the subject." The alternative seemed dire: "I cannot imagine how the subject can have any thing sure and lasting in any government where that power only depends on the monarch's will." From a more specifically constitutional angle, Chief Justice Matthew Hale summarized that the king's lack of any "legislative power" outside Parliament was settled "by the constitution of this realm."[42]

This assumption came to be wisely shared. Matthew Bacon's *New Abridgment of the Law* observed that "it seems clearly agreed, that the king cannot by his proclamation change any part of the common law, statutes, or customs of the realm; nor can he by his proclamation create any offence which was not an offence before; for . . . these things cannot be done without a legislative power, of which in our constitution the king is but a part."[43] Legislative power thus lay in the legislature.

Of course, it may be supposed that the Revolution of 1688 established legislative supremacy, and that Parliament therefore could delegate its legislative power, but there were different interpretations of the Revolution. Some commentators understood it to have simply shifted power from the Crown to Parliament, thereby giving the latter absolute power, in the sense of supralegal and unlimited power. But others understood the Revolution to have restored the English constitution, including limits on Parliament. Moreover, even many of those who accepted a sort of absolute power in the legislature assumed that this high power could constitutionally reside only in Parliament. Thus, notwithstanding divergent constitutional theories, there was a substantial body of opinion that Parliament could not transfer its lawmaking power. On this basis, as has been seen, David Hume concluded that, when Parliament "gave to the king's proclamation the same force as to a statute enacted by parliament," it "made by one act a total subversion of the English constitution."[44]

Underlying the constitutional limitation on proclamations was the theoretical assumption that a government could not bind its people except through laws made with their consent—meaning the people's ancient legal customs or the acts of their legislature. The implication, as succinctly captured in 1771 in the title of a magazine essay, was that "Proclamations have not the Force of Law." This essay noted the conventional point that proclamations were "at best . . . but instruments" for "pointing out to the people the necessity of a conformity to . . . law." In contrast, statutes "receive their authority from the three estates of the realm, known by the name of parliament." They thus "proceed not from the blind, corrupt and fluctuating humor of one man, or even a single branch of the legislature; but from the mature deliberation of the three estates, grounded on the common consent of the people." Of course, because this logic arose from consent, it did not apply merely to the king or his proclamations, for the "same reasoning holds good with respect to any other branch of the legislature." The connection between consent, the obligation of law, and a representative legislature must await chapter 19, but what was said about proclamations should already suggest how consent underlay the conclusion that "every freeman is amenable to no power but the laws of his country."[45]

One result was that the constitutional objection to binding proclamations could be stated simply by contrasting executive and legislative power—the legislative power being different because it was binding or obligatory and thus capable of altering the rights and duties of subjects. The Irish professor Francis Sullivan thus distinguished between "such proclamations, or acts of the king, as are particular exertions of the executive power, which the law and constitution hath entrusted him with," and acts that, "affecting the whole people, should in any wise alter, diminish, or impair the[ir] rights." More succinctly, Sullivan's editor, Gilbert Stuart, explained that in the English constitution the "executive power remained with the crown; but . . . the united assent of the three estates . . . constituted the legislature."[46] Perhaps the tightest account came from the celebrated French writer on the English constitution, Jean Louis DeLolme, who recognized that he need only specify the location of legislative power: "The basis of the English constitution, the capital principle on which all others depend, is that the legislative power belongs to Parliament alone; that is to say, the power of establishing laws, and of abrogating, changing, or explaining them."[47]

In this intellectual context, American constitutions placed legislative and executive powers in different branches of government and by this means barred executive attempts to enact binding duties. For example, the U.S. Constitution recited: "All legislative Powers herein granted shall be vested in a Congress of the United States" and "The executive Power shall be vested in a President of the United States of America." The grant of only executive power to the president would have been enough to limit his power, and the grant of legislative power to Congress was even more decisive. Under these provisions, the president could issue proclamations, but not to bind subjects or otherwise legislate.

సించి

Lawmaking proclamations are close to contemporary life and yet distant. The reader will have to wait until chapter 7 for the contemporary side of the story, but obviously administrative legislation has returned. As in the past, it is widespread. And as in the past, it seems justified by necessity—such as the necessity of faster legislation than can be expected from the legislature.

At least in the past, however, the extralegal legislation was widely recognized as dangerous. At least in the past, it was recognized as a threat to government through and under law. At least in the past, it was understood to be the epitome of absolute power, regardless of parliamentary authorization. At least in the past, the judges resolutely declared it unlawful. At least in the past, moreover, the extralegal legislation did much to provoke the development of constitutional law, including the conclusion that executive power belongs to the Crown or executive, and that legislative power belongs to the legislature.

These days, however, neither the danger nor the unconstitutionality is well understood. The executive recognizes that, regardless of any congressional authorization, it cannot use proclamations to bind subjects. It assumes, however, that it can bind members of the public when it acts through other "rules" or "interpretations"—as if the constitutional objection merely concerned proclamations, not the extralegal exercise of legislative power. On other occasions, the executive acknowledges that the constitutional objection goes beyond proclamations but emphasizes that it does not use its rules or interpretations to impose criminal penalties—as if the constitutional objection were confined to criminal matters.

In fact, the constitutional danger arises from any attempt to rule through extralegal legislation, regardless of whether it is done through prerogative proclamations or administrative rules, and regardless of whether it is civil or criminal. The U.S. Constitution therefore does not bar proclamations, let alone merely criminal proclamations, but instead simply places all legislative powers in Congress. Consequently, whenever the executive issues rules outside the law, with or without the label of "proclamations," it is returning to the preconstitutional past—to extralegal legislation and thus absolute power.

FOUR

Interpretation, Regulation, and Taxation

The danger of extralegal legislation can take many forms. The Crown, for example, tried to make binding law not only through proclamations but also through prerogative interpretations, regulations, and taxes. Like its proclamations, however, these other modes of prerogative lawmaking provoked the development of constitutional law, which clarified that there could be no extralegal legislative power. Government could impose binding rules only through and under the law.

These days, administrative agencies have revived the imposition of extralegal interpretation, regulation, and taxing. They thereby return to familiar modes of extralegal lawmaking—modes that were long ago prohibited by constitutional law. Once again, therefore, administrative legislation leads back to the era, prior to constitutional law, when prerogative power ran outside the law.

Lawmaking Interpretation

Although it usually is assumed that administrative interpretation in the interstices of statutes has no constitutional history, nothing could be further from the truth. At the same time that James I attempted to legislate through his proclamations, he and his prerogative courts also asserted a power to interpret statutes in a manner that amounted to lawmaking. Drawing on imperial Roman ideas, they claimed a prerogative to fill the gaps in statutes and insisted that the law courts had to defer to such "interpretation." Although in retrospect, the Roman foundations of their lawmaking interpretation may seem arcane, it suggests the imperial and absolute character of such interpretation and the sobering implications of its administrative revival.

At common law, there was no difference between interpreting and expounding a statute. Whereas Parliament exercised will in making the law,
the judges had an office of judgment, in which they were expected to decide cases by exercising their judgment or understanding in accord with
the law. Their office thus required them to discern and expound the law
in cases, and although this was not all they did, it increasingly seemed the
core of their office. Consequently, as long as the judges merely discerned
and expounded the law in the course of deciding cases, their exposition of
the law had the authority of their office, and their precedents were authoritative evidence of what the law was.[1]

A competing vision of judicial authority, however, was familiar from
Roman law, which viewed interpretation as a form of legislation and thus
beyond the authority of a judge. According to Justinian's *Digest*, the emperor was the lawmaker, and thus "whenever a new contingency arises,"
it was the "the imperial function" to "correct and settle it"—or as Julian
had written, "if anything defective be found, the want should be supplied
by imperial legislation."[2] From this perspective, much of what common
lawyers would consider the exposition of law was actually lawmaking, and
although the *Codex* allowed that judges could decide cases according to
their understanding of the law, it precluded any authority for judicial exposition of the law—cautioning, in the words of Constantine, "It is part of
our duty, and is lawful for us alone to interpret questions involving equity
and law."[3]

In England, although Parliament was the lawmaking body, not even
Parliament had this imperial power to make law by interpreting in the
interstices of statutes. In its statutes, Parliament could make new law and
declare old law, but the legislature could not otherwise give authoritative interpretations of its statutes, let alone the sort of interpretations that
made law.[4]

At the beginning of the seventeenth century, however, James I claimed
for himself and his prerogative tribunals the power that not even Parliament enjoyed. He thereby explored the sort of lawmaking interpretation
that has been revived in administrative law.

James had learned about Roman imperial interpretation when studying the civil law as a teenage king in Scotland, and when he later became
king of England, some English civilians encouraged him to assert this
legislative-style interpretation. They suggested that the power to interpret
had originally rested in him, and that although he had delegated it to the
common law judges, he still could take it back and exercise it himself, either personally or through his prerogative courts. Dr. Thomas Ridley, for

example, urged that the judges exercised a delegated lawmaking authority when they expounded law and that the king "by communicating his authority to his judges to expound his laws, doth not thereby [so completely] abdicate the same from himself, but that he may assume it again . . . as often as him pleaseth." Ridley even argued, in Roman manner, that judicial interpretation was not generally authoritative, but that royal interpretation was binding as law—that "his judges' interpretation maketh right only to them between whom the cause is, but his highnesse['s] exposition is a law unto all, from which it is not lawful for any subject to recede."[5] Similarly, Archbishop Richard Bancroft informed James that in anything ecclesiastical "or in any other case in which there is not express authority in law, the king himself may decide it in his royal person." Bancroft thus relied on an exaggerated view of uncertainty in English law to open up space for imperial interpretation—interpretation that was candidly a matter of legislative will. Bancroft added that "the judges are but the delegates of the king, and that the king may take what causes he shall please . . . from . . . the judges, and may determine them himself."[6, a]

Encouraged by such arguments, James memorably complained: "If the judges interpret the laws themselves and suffer none else to interpret, then they may easily make of the laws shipmens hose." Unwilling to accept this risk, James asserted that he was "the supreme judge," that "inferior judges" were "his shadows and ministers," and even that "the king may, if he please, sit and judge in Westminster Hall in any court there," for "[t]he king being the author of the law is the interpreter of the law."[7]

Although these claims of lawmaking authority were framed in terms of the king's personal prerogative, the real question—as today—was whether prerogative or administrative bodies could legislate through interpretation. By claiming for himself the power to interpret, the king implied that the power to expound the law was really the ambitious Roman power to legislate through interpretation, and that he could withdraw this from the judges of the law courts and exercise it through his prerogative tribunals.

All of this concentrated the minds of the law judges. Coke declared on

---

a. The advice James received in England was very different from what he had been taught as a child king in Scotland. According to his learned tutor, George Buchanan: "I shall tell you . . . plainly, that you may understand it. When you grant the interpretation of laws to a king, you grant him such a licence, as the law doth not tell what the lawgiver meaneth, or what is good and equal for all persons in general, but what may make for the interpreters benefit." Royal interpretation thus would make law "useless," for if it were admitted, "it will be to no purpose to make good laws for teaching a good prince his duty; and hem in an ill king. Yea, let me tell you more plainly, it would be better to have no laws at all." James respected his tutor, but what he thought of this plain speaking can only be imagined.[*]

behalf of the barons of the Exchequer and all the justices that "the king in his own person cannot adjudge any case . . . but this ought to be determined and adjudged in some court of justice, according to the law and custom of England." James protested that "the law was founded upon reason, and that he and others had reason, as well as the judges"; and this made sense if the judges' interpretation of statutes was really a delegated exercise of a royal lawmaking power, for lawmaking required the use of natural reason to determine a just policy prior to the exercise of legislative will in enacting it.

Coke, however, famously answered that cases "are not to be decided by natural reason, but by artificial reason and judgment of law, which law is an act which requires long study and experience, before . . . a man can attain to the cognizance of it."[8] Natural reason might be adequate for the exercise of legislative will, but not for judgments in cases, in which the judges had to discern and explain the law of the land. Coke thus rejected the lawmaking sort of interpretation by distinguishing the common law vision of reasoning and judgment.

James's aspirations for imperial interpretation—what now would be considered administrative interpretation—collapsed even further in the controversy over proclamations, for although this dispute concerned direct prerogative lawmaking, it sometimes rested on the claim about imperial interpretation. For example, it will be recalled that when James attempted to legislate through his proclamations, Chancellor Ellesmere urged that the judges should "leave it to the king to order it according to his wisdom" where "there is no authority and precedent." Like some contemporary justifications of administrative power, this was a suggestion about lawmaking interpretation in the interstices of the law. As has been seen, however, Coke answered that the king outside Parliament could not create any new offense or otherwise "change the law," thus puncturing Ellesmere's inflated hopes about prerogative lawmaking, whether directly or by interpretation.[9]

The fate of claims for royal lawmaking interpretation thus ran aground on the competing claims for both judicial office and legislative power. And the logic that defeated prerogative lawmaking interpretation still applies to administrative lawmaking interpretation. Because the power to make law belonged to the king only in Parliament, he could not make law alone; and because the office of judgment belonged to the judges, the king could not interpret with judicial authority, and they could not defer to his views.

Later commentators echoed all of this, including the points about interpretation and deference. According to Roger Twysden, the king had no prerogative or administrative power of interpretation, for "he cannot alone, but in his courts of justice, by sworn judges, interpret those laws, whose office it is . . . to expound." In other words, the king had to rely on the judges of his regular courts to interpret or expound the law. Bacon's *Abridgment* similarly explained that the king "cannot execute any office relating to the administration of justice, although all such offices derive their authority from the Crown, and although he hath such offices in him to grant to others." The judges, moreover, could not defer to the king: "The judges are bound by oath to determine according to the known laws and ancient customs of the realm; and their rule herein must be the judicial decisions and resolutions of great numbers of learned, wise and upright judges, upon variety of particular facts and cases, and not their own arbitrary will and pleasure, or that of their prince's."[10] The judges by virtue of their office could defer only to the law and their precedents, not anyone's irregular will, whether their own or their monarch's.

Nowadays, administrative agencies have revived the old prerogative claim to make law by interpreting in the interstices of statutes. As in the past, they demand that the judges defer to their "interpretations." As in the past, the lawmaking interpretation intrudes on the power of the legislature and the office of the judges. Unlike in the past, however, the judges defer. They do not recognize the constitutional history, and viewing administrative interpretation as a novel question, they assist in the revival of an old constitutional problem.

Regulation

What could not be done directly through proclamations or indirectly through interpretation might nonetheless be accomplished by means of regulations—not yet administrative regulations issued by administrative agencies, but prerogative regulations issued by prerogative courts, particularly the Star Chamber. It thus turns out that administrative regulations have a history. Their history, however, is not reassuring about their constitutionality, for regulations were simply another mode of extralegal legislation that was eventually barred by law.

The primary issuer of regulations was the Court of Star Chamber. It took its name from a spacious room, decorated with gold stars on its ceiling, located in the Palace of Westminster. The king's council had long attempted to exercise extralegal judicial power, outside the regular courts, and its judicial meetings, in the Star Chamber, developed into a distinct court—not one of the courts of law, but the leading prerogative court, which implemented royal policy as well as law.[11]

The Star Chamber had once had the rough task of taming England's magnates. Their power often placed them beyond regular legal process, and against these men who brazenly went beyond the law, it was valuable to have a court that could act outside the law. The extralegal power, however, that initially made the Star Chamber so effective against local oppression eventually made the court itself seem oppressive when the Crown relied on it in more mundane circumstances—for example, to issue trade and building regulations.[12]

It was no accident that the Star Chamber issued both proclamations and regulations. Both were a sort of extralegal legislation, imposed outside the legislature and its processes, and both therefore came from the central prerogative tribunal. It thus was in the Star Chamber that the king typically issued and enforced his proclamations, and similarly it was in this court that the Crown issued and enforced its binding regulations.

The Star Chamber issued its regulations in its decrees. Although a court ordinarily issued decrees in cases, the Star Chamber, in its administrative capacity, used its decrees to give authority to rules or regulations that bound subjects in the manner of statutes. The attorney general or another government official would produce a proposed decree in court and then would recite which government officials had drafted it. The court then would consider the recommendation and, after adopting it, would order it to be recorded as a decree and published.[13]

The Star Chamber's most notorious regulations created a system of licensing the press. By requiring printers to get permission before establishing presses and before publishing, the Star Chamber controlled the dissemination of printed materials, thus protecting the English government and church from criticism. Other regulations, for example, regulated apparel, trades, prices, and the building of tenements in London.[14]

Recognizing that it did not have an uncontested power to legislate, the Star Chamber tended to issue regulations only where it could offer at least the appearance of a legal justification. For example, in explaining its power to regulate printing independently of Parliament, the Crown took the line that it itself had originally imported printing technology to England and that its press constraints therefore did not interfere with any preexisting liberty of the subject. In rationalizing its regulation of tenements, the Star Chamber recited earlier proclamations and decrees on the subject, and it obtained an advisory judicial opinion that the forbidden types of tenements were a "public nuisance."[15] Although a public nuisance would ordinarily have justified only abatement, or prosecutions against individuals at common law, in the Star Chamber (as in later administrative bodies) it came to legitimize administrative condemnations and even regulations.

Star Chamber regulations thus offered yet another avenue for extralegal legislation, and they therefore became one of the reasons for the court's demise. Of course, some of these regulations were valuable. Coming, however, from an unrepresentative body that exercised power outside the law, they seemed both heavy handed and incompatible with liberty. As Parliament explained when it abolished the Star Chamber in 1641, the "decrees of that court" had been "found to be an intolerable burden to the subjects and the means to introduce an arbitrary power and government."[16]

Although the Star Chamber's issuance of regulations came to an end with the court itself, administrative regulations have come back to life. Not merely one administrative body, but dozens now issue regulations that constrain the public. Some agencies are directly authorized by legislation; others merely have legislative acquiescence. Either way, they bind the public outside rather than through the law, and they thereby revert to the extralegal lawmaking that was rejected in the seventeenth century.

Taxation

Taxation was yet another avenue for extralegal legislation, and once again the history is revealing. Although no topic of legislation provoked greater controversy, English monarchs in the sixteenth and seventeenth centuries claimed that they had an absolute prerogative to impose some taxes. It was not a claim, however, in which they were apt to prevail. The imposition of taxes traditionally belonged to Parliament, and in response to the claims of the Crown, it came to be settled that any prerogative taxation was unconstitutional. The history of prerogative taxation thus shows that when agencies set taxes, they revive a preconstitutional sort of legislation. Administrative taxation returns to an unconstitutional exercise of power outside the law.

Taxes lay at the heart of legislative power. Parliament had begun its development as the king's court, where he met with his lords, and the Crown expanded Parliament to include members of the commons only when it wanted their money. Although this expansion of Parliament was good policy, it also made sense theoretically. Taxes were duties or burdens on the community, and it therefore might be thought that, like any other legal constraints on freedom, taxes required the consent of the community.

At the same time, kings enjoyed some taxing powers that did not ordinarily come through Parliament. Kings had claims to hereditary dues, which were understood to be part of the inheritance of the king and therefore without any need for legislative authorization. In addition, kings had grown accustomed to collecting some other taxes on the basis of their prerogative, and over time these amounts enjoyed considerable parliamentary acquiescence.

The acquiescence, however, had been possible because neither kings nor Parliaments had pressed their authority. Kings traditionally had exercised such taxation power as they could without openly insisting that they could act beyond the law. In the late sixteenth and early seventeenth centuries, however, both Crown and Parliament openly pursued conflicting understandings of their power, the one stretching its financial prerogatives, and the other responding that all taxation was legislative. As a result, prerogative taxation came into full conflict with parliamentary taxation.[17]

The Initial Constitutional Critique

Prerogative or administrative taxes first became a constitutional issue in 1610. Eager to raise money without submitting to the demands of Parliament, the king had issued a *Book of Rates* on imports and exports. The king's ministers had carefully consulted leading merchants, and had lowered some rates, but had increased others, and also had expanded the range of taxable goods.[18] In defense of this measure, the Crown claimed that it had an absolute prerogative—a sovereign power above the law—to set "impositions" or "rates" as it saw fit. Interestingly, even Crown lawyers acknowledged that it would be "against the law" for the Crown to set internal rates; instead, they claimed that the king's prerogative gave him absolute power over rates on imports and exports.[19]

Undoubtedly, during the exigencies of wartime, some past monarchs had raised money by placing duties on foreign trade without consulting Parliament. Their emergency duties, however, had been relatively proportionate to the country's real needs. In contrast, James I did not have any clear or sudden necessity for his imposition of duties. Accordingly, when he imposed high rates on an expanding array of goods, his assertion of his prerogative seemed strained, and Crown lawyers could defend it only with exaggerated conceptions of royal prerogative. They argued that because the king was the sovereign, he had the final authority to determine the necessity of impositions and that this power stood so far above the law that it could not even be discussed in Parliament or the courts.

When Parliament met in 1610, much of the House of Commons was incensed. Members of the Commons recognized that James was undermining the role of Parliament in making law, particularly in laying taxes, and they responded with vigor. Most profoundly, some of them responded in constitutional terms. Nothing offered a better response to royal claims of a prerogative or power above the law than the idea of a constitution, for this was the enactment of the people that established their government. If all government power came from such a law, then no government power, not even an extralegal lawmaking power, could rise above the law.

The lawyer James Whitelocke was particularly clear in his reliance on the constitution to question whether the king, by himself "without assent of Parliament," was "lawfully entitled to . . . alter the property of his subjects' goods." Whitelocke observed that an imposition without parliamentary consent "is against the natural [i.e., native] frame and constitution of the policy of this kingdom." As a result, the king's imposition "subverteth the fundamental law of the realm, and induceth a new form of state and government." Revealingly, Whitelocke distinguished this sort of constitutional "ground" from his other, less elevated arguments—namely, that impositions were "against the municipal law of the land," that they were "against divers statutes made to restrain our king," and that they were "against the practice and action of our commonwealth."[20]

After listening to such arguments, the House of Commons petitioned against extralegal impositions, combining this protest with its declaration against the legislative use of proclamations. The two issues were merely different aspects of the same underlying question—whether the king had a prerogative to make law. Whitelocke bluntly summarized that "the power of imposing, and power of making laws are *convertibilia & coincidentia*; and whoever can do the one, can do the other." Against the king, therefore, the Commons petitioned that both were settled by nation's policy and by its constitution: "The policy and constitution of this your majesty's kingdom appropriates unto the kings of this realm, with assent of the parliament, as well the sovereign power of making laws, as that of taxing or imposing upon the subjects' goods or merchandises, wherein they justly have such a propriety, as may not without their consent be altered or changed." Similarly, a member of the Commons explained that, "as the kings of England are generally without exception bound from making or altering laws, so by the same rule, they are as generally bound from laying new charges or impositions on their subjects."[21] Kings could not legally bind their subjects, other than through acts of Parliament.[b]

b. A nonstatutory tax thus was either an unlawful taking or an unlawful alteration of property. Whitelocke explained about the king's impositions: "[I]f he alone out of Parliament may

Thus, already from the debates of 1610, it is apparent that administrative taxation reverts to the prerogative taxation that provoked the development of constitutional law. Whereas the constitutional ideal is to bind subjects only through the law, administrative taxation returns to the practice of binding subjects outside the law.

Expanded Prerogative Taxation and the Constitutional Response

During the ensuing decades, renewed attempts at prerogative taxation only clarified the constitutional objection. The power to tax or otherwise bind subjects belonged to Parliament, not any prerogative or administrative body.

James I and his son Charles I repeatedly pressed their subjects for money under specious claims of prerogative. Although Crown lawyers always cited precedents, the precedents tended to be medieval and minimal, and they tended to be used so expansively as to change their character. Necessity always was the underlying justification, but a real necessity rarely was apparent. The judges therefore might have been justified in holding the king's demands unlawful and void. The kings, however, systematically appointed judges who embraced the royal view of the prerogative and dismissed those who dissented, thus giving the Crown a bench with a palpable sense of deference to government outside and above the law.

Nonetheless, when the judges upheld the Crown's independent power to tax or take, they had a point. If the king, as sovereign, had an absolute prerogative or power to raise money, then he was the final judge of the matter. The king might twist old precedents into a new reality of expansive extralegal power, but if he were the final arbiter of the necessity, then the judges could not presume to delineate its bounds, and the law could never really confine it. "Necessity," as the poet Edmund Waller observed, had the effect of "dissolving all law."[22] At the very least, it required judicial deference.

---

impose, he altereth the law of England in one of these two main fundamental points. He must either take his subjects goods from them, without assent of the party, which is against the law; or else he must give his own letters patents, the force of a law, to alter the property of his subjects goods, which is also against the law."

The king's letters patent were the means by which he imposed the duties specified in his *Book of Rates*, and Whitelocke's point was that the king was acting outside Parliament to take or alter property. The latter was as worrisome as the former, for "if there be a right in the king to alter the property of that which is ours without our consent, we are but tenants at his will of that which we have." One way or another, taxation outside the legislature was mere theft: "a king cannot take one penny from his subjects without their consent, but it is violence."*

The danger of prerogative taxing and taking became especially ominous when Charles I raised money in 1626 by forcing gentlemen to give him loans. The excuse was that this emergency borrowing was required by necessity and, in any case, was not permanent and so was not a taking. When five gentlemen refused to comply with this government extortion, they soon found themselves imprisoned for their recalcitrance. Undaunted, they obtained writs of habeas corpus, arguing that they had been arrested and held contrary to the law of the land. Charles caused the returns to the writs to say that the prisoners were committed at the special command of the king—a formula that, as will be seen in chapter 11, allowed him to imprison men without judicial reconsideration.[23] He thus used an absolute prerogative of imprisonment to defend an absolute power to seize property.

Two years later, when Charles assembled Parliament, it protested in the Petition of Right. Framed as a petition, this was a last attempt to limit absolute power in a tone of deference to the king. In this posture of supplication, Parliament explained that "[t]hey do . . . humbly pray your most excellent majesty, that no man hereafter be compelled to make or yield any gift, loan, benevolence, tax, or such like charge, without common consent by act of Parliament."[24] The tone would soon change.

The question of extraparliamentary taxation did not get settled until after two revolutions, the first in 1642. When a new Parliament met in 1640, King Charles resisted its attempts to hold him to account, and two years later the resulting conflict led to civil war. In the end, in 1649, Parliament had the king executed. The Civil War and the ensuing troubles did not settle many things, but they did settle at least one large thing—the location of legislative power. With Parliament's decapitation of the king, it became clear as never before that legislative power rested in Parliament and the king therefore could not successfully challenge its exclusive power to tax.

The second revolution, that of 1688, completed the rejection of any prerogative power of taxation. Although the question already was largely settled, the conduct of James II showed that a king might stretch his statutory taxing authority, and Parliament therefore provided in its Declaration of Rights "[t]hat levying money for or to the use of the Crown by pretense of prerogative, without grant of Parliament, for longer time, or in other manner than the same is or shall be granted, is illegal."[25]

This resolved the constitutional question. It had long been assumed by most English lawyers that only Parliament could levy taxes. Now this was confirmed by an act of Parliament—an act that was understood to be declaratory of the original constitution. As Chief Justice John Holt explained in a 1698 case, taxes were an exercise of legislative power, and under "the original frame and constitution of the government," they "must be by an act made by the whole legislative authority."[26]

Statutory Delegation

Nowadays, the question about extralegal taxation is not whether there is a prerogative or administrative power to tax without statutory authorization, but rather whether the executive can tax with such authorization. Even this question, however, has a past, for in placing the power to tax in the legislature, constitutional law barred it from relinquishing this power.

From one perspective, the absolute power of the Crown had been defeated by the absolute power of Parliament, thus leaving Parliament with a supralegal power above the law. From another perspective, however, Parliament had prevailed not so much on claims of absolute power as on claims of law, and being subject to law, it was limited by law.[27] In this understanding, although Parliament was the high court, and thus was beyond any appeal to the other courts, it nonetheless was bound to adhere to the law, including the constitution made by the people. In this vision of the constitution, which would become that of radical Whigs and of Americans, only the people, not Parliament, could transfer Parliament's legislative power, including its power of taxation.

Parliament's understanding that it could not leave taxes to others can be glimpsed in a statute from 1660. When kings had relied on their prerogative to impose duties on imports and exports, they had specified the duties in royal books of rates. Now that only Parliament could impose taxes, it specified such duties in its own book of rates, written and adopted by the House of Commons.

On the assumption, however, that only Parliament as a whole could impose the rates, Parliament carefully incorporated the book of rates by reference within its statute imposing the tax: "And because no rates can be imposed upon merchandise, imported or exported by subjects or aliens, but by common consent in Parliament, Be it . . . enacted and declared . . . that the rates intended by this present act, shall be the rates mentioned and expressed in one book of rates, entitled, The Rates of Merchandise." To preclude any doubt that the rates were adopted in the statute, Parliament added that it was granting "the subsid[ies] . . . as they are rated and agreed on by the Commons House of Parliament, set down and expressed in this book" and that they were to be "effectual to all intents and purposes, as if the same were included particularly in the body of this present act."[28] The very pedantry of this recital is revealing. Although Parliament enacted rates specified in a separate volume, it went out of its way to make clear that only an act of Parliament could set rates.

The theoretical and constitutional reasons why a legislature could not relinquish its taxing or other lawmaking power must wait until part IV, particularly its chapters on specialization, representation, subdelegation, and division. Already here, however, it is apparent that the Crown's extralegal demands provoked a constitutional response. Although the Crown in the early seventeenth century persistently imposed taxes outside Parliament, many English lawyers answered that not merely the law, but even the constitution placed all taxing power in the legislature. To repeat the words of Chief Justice Holt, taxes were legislative, and therefore under "the original frame and constitution of the government," they "must be by an act made by the whole legislative authority."[29]

❦❦❦

This point about taxes completes the initial argument here about extralegal legislation and the constitutional response. The Crown relied on prerogative power to legislate outside the law—whether by means of proclamations, interpretations, regulations, or taxes. Often, its extralegal legislation even had some legislative authorization or at least acquiescence. Its extralegal legislation, however, became the primary threat that prompted the development of ideas of constitutional law, and constitutional law therefore systematically placed legislative power in the legislature, thus defeating all lawmaking outside the law.

This breadth of constitutional law in barring extralegal legislation is revealing about more than the past. The reader will have to wait patiently until chapter 7 for details of the current regime of extralegal lawmaking, but the significance of the history can already be anticipated. In an era of administrative legislation, it often is assumed that when the U.S. Constitution grants legislative power to Congress, it does not bar the executive from issuing binding rules, making interpretations, or setting taxes—as long as the executive has legislative authorization or at least acquiescence. The history of constitutional law, however, reveals that constitutions developed to bar all extralegal lawmaking—the point being to confine government to ruling through the law. Thus, administrative legislation—whether by proclamation, rulemaking, interpretation, or taxation—is not a novel form of lawmaking, and it cannot, on account of its alleged novelty, escape constitutional restrictions. On the contrary, it is a return to the extralegal legislation that constitutions were established to prohibit.

FIVE

Suspending and Dispensing Powers

Associated with extralegal lawmaking power were two extralegal powers that cut against law, the suspending and dispensing powers. Just as a legislature can enact a law, so too it can repeal or otherwise contradict it, the new enactment being the means of displacing the old. This, however, was not the only way of limiting the binding effect of law, for English kings claimed a prerogative generally to suspend a statute or at least to dispense with it for particular persons. Kings exercised these two powers not through the law, but outside it, and these extralegal powers, especially the dispensing power, came to be viewed as the epitome of the absolute and unconstitutional prerogative.

Far from being merely a matter of distant history, these prerogatives, especially the dispensing power, have acquired new life in the form of administrative waivers. During the past few decades, executive officers increasingly have issued waivers to favored persons, exempting them from administrative regulations and sometimes, in effect, even from statutes. They even have offered these waivers to suspend the operation of regulations or statutes as to all persons who otherwise would be bound. The waivers often enjoy legislative authorization, but at times they do not. Either way, they reveal an administrative revival of the old dispensing and suspending powers—powers exercised outside and above the law.

Absolute Powers

The dispensing and suspending powers were understood to be absolute. Not merely powers held under law, they developed as sovereign powers outside and above the law.

The dispensing power was among the earliest of all prerogatives to be justified as absolute. It was drawn from the learned law—the academic study of the canon and civil law—in which it was suggested if a ruler, in imitation of God, was omnipotent and above his own law, then he could grant dispensations from his law. The underlying justification was necessity, which was said to be unconstrained by law. Thus, at more than one level, dispensations seemed lawless.

At least in theory, therefore, it could not be presumed that a ruler would intend to dispense with the law. The learned lawyers, however, concluded that he could overcome this presumption by expressly stating that, *notwithstanding* a specified statute, the grantee could do what it prohibited. This was, in Latin, a non obstante clause, and by using it, a ruler could remove any question about his intent. On such assumptions, popes used non obstante clauses to free men from the penalties of the canon law, and English kings soon employed such clauses to excuse men from obedience to royal laws.[1]

Recognizing the danger, the chronicler Matthew Paris in 1251 lamented the introduction of dispensing grants in England. These clauses, he complained, amounted to saying, "Notwithstanding any old liberty, the matter shall proceed." This sort of provision provoked a judge, Roger de Thurkeby, to sigh, "Alas! alas! . . . The civil court is now tainted by the example of the ecclesiastical one, and by the sulphurous spring the whole river is poisoned." Indeed, during the ensuring centuries, Englishmen repeatedly protested that a king could "not break or dispense with the positive laws," and they asked, "What certainty should there be in anything, where all depend on one's will and affection?"[2]

The dispensing power was understood to be limited to that which belonged to the king, and in this way it came to be limited in ways contemporary administrative waivers evidently are not. For example, the king could dispense with statutes, on the theory that they were his enactments in his Parliament, but he could not dispense with common law, because this was the custom of the whole people. By the same token, although he could dispense with penal statutes and any other enactments that gave a remedy to the Crown, he could not dispense with statutes to the extent they left remedies to others, lest he release what did not belong to him. On similar reasoning, he could not dispense with statutes that prohibited things considered *mala in se*. Subject to these limitations, however, the king's capacity to dispense with his laws was an "absolute power."[3]

Closely aligned with the dispensing power was the suspending power. Under this power, medieval kings could not merely dispense with a statute for some favored individuals, but could suspend the statute in its entirety.[4]

It already can be seen that the suspending and dispensing powers were absolute in different ways. The power to suspend a statute was essentially an extralegal exercise of the legislature's power to repeal its enactments, and it therefore was simply an attempt to poach on legislative power. In contrast, the power to dispense with a statute for the benefit of particular persons was more complicated. It purported to relieve persons of compliance with a statute without repealing, modifying, or suspending it. A dispensation thus did something that not even the legislature could do. It therefore traditionally was not so much an extralegal exercise of legislative power as an extralegal power that seemed inherent in the king.

Declared Illegal

In the seventeenth century, English kings increasingly exploited the suspending and dispensing powers to avoid laws that most of the nation considered essential for its safety and freedom. The English therefore systematically questioned the lawfulness of such powers and, by the end of the century, declared these powers illegal. It is an initial hint of the unlawfulness of administrative waivers.

The dispensing power ran into difficulty already in the Statute of Monopolies. In grants of monopoly, the king sometimes used non obstante clauses to authorize men to engage in trades that were barred by statute. Angered by this application of the dispensing power, Parliament in 1624 enacted that "all . . . grants . . . to give license or toleration to do, use, or exercise anything against the tenor or purport of any law or statute . . . are altogether contrary to the laws of this realm."[5]

The unlawfulness of the dispensing and suspending powers arose again decades later, when Charles II sought to relax the laws on religion. He was an easygoing monarch whose politic tolerance, religious indifference, and sexual alliances led him to seek a moderation of the statutory constraints on religious minorities, including Catholics. In 1662, he sought parliamentary authorization for him to dispense with statutory religious restrictions, but when this provoked opposition, he desisted. Moreover, when he considered acting on his own to suspend the Act of Uniformity, he was advised that this was illegal. A decade later, however, he issued a Declaration of Indulgence, declaring that "the execution of all and all manner of penal laws in matters ecclesiastical," whether against Protestants or Catholics, "be immediately suspended." This provoked fierce opposition from the House of Commons, which voted that "penal statutes in matters ecclesiastical cannot be suspended but by act of Parliament." Anxious to secure funds from Parliament, Charles gave up and rescinded his declaration.[6]

The dispensing and the suspending powers both came to an end when they were employed by one of England's most unpopular kings, Charles's brother, James II, who came to the throne in 1685. He had the misfortune to be a Catholic monarch in a Protestant country, and when he sought to relieve his coreligionists of the legal obstacles they faced on account of their religious beliefs, he settled not their fate, but his own.

It was a time of deep and not entirely unjustified anxieties about the danger of Catholic absolutism and intolerance. Catholic doctrine seemed to Protestants to excuse lying and even regicide against Protestant rulers, and now that England had a Catholic king, Protestants feared that he would use toleration of Catholics as a first step toward suppressing Protestantism and English liberty. Giving substance to these fears, Louis XIV of France, in 1685, revoked the Edict of Nantes, thereby depriving his nation's Huguenot minority of their freedom and property.

Many English Protestants therefore reacted with horror when James II dispensed with the laws barring Catholics from the army in order to appoint Catholics officers to key positions—the danger being that he might be planning to use the army to subdue the nation and its liberty. Matters became only worse when Chief Justice Herbert upheld such a dispensation, saying rather extravagantly, "There is no law whatsoever but may be dispensed with by the supreme lawgiver." In 1687, moreover, James echoed his predecessor by issuing another Declaration of Indulgence. This generally suspended the laws penalizing religious minorities and, more specifically, promised dispensations to dissenting individuals (including Catholics) who served as civil and even military officers. On the surface, James thus seemed to espouse tolerance. He did so, however, by relying on a claim of absolute prerogative, which defeated parliamentary enactments. His use of the suspending and dispensing powers therefore only confirmed the fears that Catholicism was allied with absolutism and that what James considered toleration would soon lead to something very different for Protestants.[7]

His combination of tolerance for Catholicism and intolerance for law eventually led the English to remove James II from the throne. Seven Protestant bishops refused to read James's Declaration of Indulgence from their pulpits, explaining that it was based on the "dispensing power," which had been "often declared illegal in Parliament."[8] James therefore had the seven bishops prosecuted for seditious libel, and this marked his end. His prosecution of leading clergymen who refused to cooperate in the dispensing power seemed an assault on English religion and law. Shortly afterward, leading members of the aristocracy invited William of Orange to come to England and displace James. James was deemed in law to have abdicated; in fact, he fled ignominiously in a small boat.

Among the things that were expelled with James were the dispensing and suspending powers. When William came to England, he declared that James's evil councillors "did invent . . . the king's dispensing power, by virtue of which they pretend, that according to law, he can suspend, and dispense with the execution of the laws." They thereby had rendered the laws of "no effect," not withstanding that "no laws can be made" or "repealed or suspended" other than by the king and Parliament.[9]

After making William king, Parliament in 1689 secured limitations on the Crown by adopting the Declaration of Rights, including its provision against the dispensing power. Members of Parliament had repeatedly complained that the dispensing power was incompatible with law and the legislative power. Sir Henry Capel told the Commons: "We know the king has prerogatives, but to say, 'he has a dispensing power,' is to say, "there is no law.'" Sir William Williams asked: "Is there anything more pernicious than the dispensing power? There is an end of all the legislative power, gone and lost."[10]

In the end, the Declaration of Rights prohibited the suspending and dispensing powers, unless authorized by Parliament. As to the suspending power, the Declaration simply declared: "That the pretended power of suspending of laws or the execution of laws by regal authority without consent of Parliament is illegal." As to the dispensing power, there was less clarity that it had previously been illegal, so the Declaration enacted that "no dispensation by non obstante of or to any statute or any part thereof shall be allowed but that the same shall be held void and of no effect except a dispensation be allowed of in such statute." The suspending and dispensing powers thus were not entirely abolished. These two powers were illegal if merely asserted by the Crown, but perhaps could come back to life if allowed by Parliament.[11]

The Embargo Debate

The unconstitutionality of what nowadays would be considered waivers became a prominent question again in 1766 in circumstances that almost seemed to warrant such power. Bad weather and mistaken export policies led to a wheat shortage and riots. It was genuine crisis, and Parliament was in recess. If ever peacetime events might have justified lawless power, this seemed to be it.[12]

The Embargo and the Debate

To prevent the export of what little wheat remained in the country, the Privy Council advised the king to order an embargo, prohibiting ships holding wheat from leaving English ports. Since 1670 a statute had provided that it was lawful to export grain, but the Privy Council, led by the prime minister, Lord Chatham, justified the embargo as an act of necessity, which rose above the law. The result was an order in council, published in a royal proclamation, embargoing exports of wheat. The king later explained to Parliament: "The urgency of the necessity" required him "for the preservation of the public safety" to embargo the wheat "until the advice of parliament could be taken."[13]

When Parliament met, the ministry faced much anger. Merchants already were bringing damages actions against officers who were carrying out the embargo, and the ministry worried that there might be suits even against those who had advised the measure.[14] The ministry therefore proposed an indemnity bill. Some ministers even argued that the necessity of the embargo already rendered it lawful, and this only stoked the fury.

Of course, the question was not incontrovertibly one of dispensation or suspension, for whereas these powers traditionally concerned relief from statutory prohibitions, the Crown in this instance had forbidden what a statute permitted. Nonetheless, the embargo was denounced as a matter of suspending or dispensing with the law—the "general question" being whether the Crown had "a right to suspend an act of Parliament, in any case, or on any pretense whatever?"[15]

Throughout the debates, "the necessity of the embargo was universally allowed; and the illegality of the authority was only objected to." Of course, critics blamed the ministry for responding too slowly to the threat of famine and for proroguing Parliament even though it might be needed for a legislative suspension of the export laws. As one pamphlet complained about the king (and thereby about his ministry), "the necessity was of his contriving." Once these errors had been made, however, there was little question that the embargo was necessary.[16]

Even the recess of Parliament, however, was no excuse for dispensing or suspending the laws, for "the recess of parliament, or its not being convenient to assemble it, are distinctions not known by the constitution." The "executive" or "king," it was argued, "cannot of right suspend, any more than he can make laws," for "[t]he law is above the king; and the crown, as well as the subject, is bound by it, as much during the recess, as in the session of parliament."[17] Thus, not even a genuine necessity was an excuse.

A large part of the danger was that the necessity would be judged by the Crown rather than the legislature. It had been suggested on behalf of the Crown that "the king, with the advice of the privy council, may suspend the execution and effect [of an act of Parliament], whenever his majesty, so advised, judges it necessary for the immediate safety of the people." Yet "if the crown is the judge of that necessity, the power is unlimited" and there is a danger that "discretion degenerates into despotism." The "legislative is lodged . . . in King, Lords and Commons, who together constitute the only supreme sovereign authority of this government."[18]

No one denied government might sometimes have to act from necessity in violation of law. Rather, the point was that "legality" and "expediency" were "quite separate and distinct" considerations. This distinction seemed the very foundation of lawful government. The constitution was all about "government by law," and "an act of power, founded upon whatever motives of expediency, or emergency of state however cogent, is nevertheless a violation of the constitution established by law, an illegal act of power, whether directed to good or bad purposes." Thus, "[n]ecessity of state . . . can never render that act of the crown legal which without that necessity would be clearly illegal." Undoubtedly, in emergencies, it was the "duty" of leaders "to act at their own peril, and to violate the law for commendable and meritorious purposes." In such cases, "[t]he end will sufficiently justify the means," but "the legislature alone can absolve them of the violation of the law" by adopting an indemnification act. In the meantime, "the law is certain and absolute, though the breach of it may be sometimes necessary and meritorious; but the law is one thing, expedience, emergency, or necessity is another."[19]

The point was to keep necessitous circumstances apart from questions of law, so that absolute power would never acquire legitimacy. The error of the ministry therefore was twofold: not merely the embargo, but that "instead of acknowledging the illegality," the ministry applied to Parliament for indemnity on the basis of "the high arbitrary doctrine of a dispensing power in the crown, under the specious pretenses of state necessity." This doctrine had long ago been buried but "is again propagated in open day-light."[20, a]

a. Two vignettes illustrate the ministry's arguments from necessity and the response. Out of loyalty to the prime minister, Lord Camden went so far as to argue in the House of Lords that "[t]he necessity of a measure renders it not only excusable, but legal" and that the embargo had caused "at most but a forty day's tyranny." This prompted brutal criticism, including Lord Temple's comment, "Once establish a dispensing power, and you cannot be sure of either liberty or law for forty minutes."

The Crown eventually obtained its indemnification statute, but at a cost, for the statute began by reciting that the embargo "could not be justified by law." Only on this assumption did the statute then indemnify "all persons advising, or acting under, or in obedience to" the council's order, on the ground that the embargo "was so much for the service of the public, and so necessary for the safety and preservation of his majesty's subjects, that it ought to be justified by act of Parliament."[21] The statute thus vindicated the constitutional principle against the suspending and dispensing powers—what these days are considered administrative waivers.

Statutory Authorization

The implications for administrative waivers become all the more clear when one turns to the question of statutory authorization. Although the debate over the embargo did not focus on whether a statute could give the Crown a lawful suspending or dispensing power, the embargo debate revealed hints of an underlying shift in attitude about this.

The Declaration of Rights in 1689 had expressly left room for the Crown to exercise the dispensing and suspending powers when they were authorized by statute. Recalling this, a pamphlet protested against the embargo on the ground that it was "an assumption of authority not delegated by the legislature to the crown, and consequently is in itself a nullity."[22]

In the House of Commons, the ministry's line was taken up by William Beckford. This wealthy alderman (whose son wrote the early gothic novel *Vathek*) supported his friend Lord Chatham by arguing that "[w]henever the public is in danger, the king has a dispensing power." Upon being asked by the House to explain himself, Beckford only made matters worse by saying that the king could dispense with the law "with the advice of [his] council, whenever the *salus populi* requires it." At this point he was courting censure, and he therefore finally said something closer to what the Commons needed to hear, that "where the safety of the people called for an exertion of a power contrary to the written law of these kingdoms, such exertion of power is excusable only by necessity, and justifiable by act of parliament." The Crown or executive might have to act of necessity for the sake of the people, but this could never be legal, and could at best be indemnified by statute.

This little story had an epilogue. After being bloodied in the Commons for defending the dispensing power, Beckford repeatedly sought acclaim by taking populist stances in favor of liberty. One of his efforts along these lines occurred when he presented a petition to the king on behalf of the City of London and took the occasion to make an impromptu speech in favor of the city and the constitution. Beckford died shortly afterward, and the City of London recorded its gratitude by erecting a statue of the alderman, standing on a base inscribed with his words to the king. His position on the dispensing power, however, had not been forgotten. A satirical print depicted his statue with verbal emendations. In the print, Beckford holds a scroll reciting that, "Whenever the public is in danger, the king has a dispensing power." Underneath, a pedestal is inscribed with the line about Satan in *Paradise Lost*: "And with Necessity, the Tyrant's Plea, excus'd his Dev'lish Deeds."*

Other critics of the embargo, however, were beginning to perceive a sharper boundary between executive and legislative powers, and this left little space for any delegation of the power to suspend or dispense with the laws. Radical Whigs and some Tories had come to assume that both the Crown and Parliament rested on a constitution established by the people, and although the English constitution did not place many limits on Parliament, it seemed to confine the legislative power to the legislature, and executive power to the king or executive. As explained in Parliament's 1766 Stamp Act debates, "many people carry the idea of a parliament too far, in supposing a parliament can do every thing; but that is not true. . . . There are many things a parliament cannot do"—the first example being that "[i]t cannot make itself executive."[23]

In the embargo debates of the same year, the dispensing and suspending powers were condemned in sweeping terms, which left little opportunity for executive waivers, even if authorized by Parliament. The constitution had placed legislative power in Parliament, and on this understanding, "the wisdom of the constitution has excluded every discretion in the crown over positive laws." Noting that "suspension" was "but another word for a temporary repeal," critics of the embargo said that a suspending power could only "reside where the legislature is lodged . . . that is, in King, Lords, and Commons." Similarly, although the Declaration of Rights had left open the possibility of legislative authorization, Parliament had not, in fact, "ever allow[ed] of the dispensing power, or any thing of the kind."[24]

Such arguments did not expressly foreclose statutory authorization of the dispensing and suspending powers. Nonetheless, the arguments in 1766 recognized that the constitution placed the legislative power in Parliament, and on this basis they broadly condemned any executive power to diminish the obligation of laws. It was said, for example, that "a suspending power is not, cannot be a legal prerogative, in any circumstances, or under any pretense whatsoever, because the tendency of the exercise of such a prerogative is destructive to the Constitution." In other words, "the constitution has entrusted the crown with no power to *suspend* any act of parliament, under any circumstances whatever."[25] It was an intimation of how American constitutions would treat waivers.

America

As might be expected, American constitutions generally precluded any executive acts suspending or dispensing with the law. Nowadays, administrative agencies frequently suspend or dispense with the law by means of waivers.

In response to English experience, however, American constitutions generally barred such things. The only exception was where state constitutions anticipated emergencies by expressly leaving room for legislatures to authorize executive suspensions.

Dispensing Power

The dispensing power encountered severe obstacles in America. It went outside the law and above the law, and in both ways it was unconstitutional.

An initial difficulty was that already in England, and then in America, constitutions divided the active power of government into executive and legislative powers, and it therefore was difficult to discern a place for a power to dispense with the laws. The dispensing power was not a power to make law, nor even to make a law that carved out exceptions from a prior law, but rather was a power to act outside the law to exempt persons from a law that remained in effect as to them. It thus was neither executive or legislative: On the one hand, the dispensing power was unacceptable as an executive prerogative outside the law; on the other hand, this extralegal power could not easily be understood as part of the legislative power, for the legislature acted through law. Thus, whether in the executive or the legislature, the dispensing power usually was viewed as lawless.

An additional difficulty for dispensations was that perhaps the English constitution, and certainly American constitutions, confined governmental power under law. Dispensations relieved persons of their obligation to conform to law, and they thus were in tension, even if not in direct conflict, with the principle that all persons, including the government, were subject to law.

Although some eighteenth-century English commentators had suggested that the dispensing power was legislative, and thus could be delegated, they did so on the assumption that the legislature had absolute power. The dispensing power obviously was an expression of absolute power, and it was commonly believed—for example, by William Blackstone—that under the English constitution, Parliament enjoyed an "absolute despotic power."[26] The dispensing power thus could be considered a part of the legislative power.

Already in England, however, under parliamentary absolutism, there was skepticism about a legislative dispensing power. The dispensing power had traditionally been exercised outside the law, not through it, and the dispensing power therefore was not easily understood as part of the legislative power. By many accounts, Parliament was absolute in the sense of being supralegal and unlimited, but it nonetheless was recognized as a legislature, which was confined to acting through its legislative acts. Parliament thus was not entirely absolute, and because it was restricted to legislating, it could not really dispense with the law. It could repeal or amend a law, but could not otherwise relieve anyone of its obligation.

The obstacles to viewing the dispensing power as legislative became especially forceful in America, where constitutions clearly restricted legislatures to acting through legislation and further limited legislative power by placing it under law. As a result, the dispensing power could be defended as a legislative power only by embracing absolute legislative power and rejecting constitutional limits.

The different implications of an absolute and a limited vision of legislative power can be seen in a 1788 debate in Massachusetts over a bill for "suspending the laws" for the collection of some private debts. Although this bill was not a traditional exercise of the dispensing power, it figuratively was a dispensation, and it therefore was debated in such terms. A critic noted that the legislature was established "to make laws" and that a law was understood as a rule that "must be promulgated before the conduct takes place."[27] Accordingly, when the bill offered retrospective relief from contract law, some legislators thought it was an exercise of the dispensing power.

One representative, Colonel Lyman of Northampton, relied on an absolutist vision of legislative power to justify the legislature in exercising the dispensing power. He believed that, at least in some matters, "the legislature had a dispensing power, and therefore could in that respect do anything." He "admitted that the exercise of such dispensing power is dangerous, and ought not to be exerted but when absolutely necessary to the preservation of the public." Nonetheless, he endorsed the Blackstonian vision of absolute legislative power and concluded that no government had ever existed "without some tincture of dispensing power vested in its legislature." Citing British statutes, he added that if the legislature did not have this power "when public necessity shall require," it would be "inadequate to . . . exigencies."[28]

Not surprisingly, Lyman's opponents thought he believed the legislature "could do anything, and everything." His position provoked Dr. Jarvis of Boston to protest: "Such arguments . . . might apply in Great Britain, where there was no written constitution; but in this Commonwealth, where we have a constitution . . . they would not apply." Similarly, Representative Dawes of Boston emphasized that the state's constitution had confined the legislature, generalizing that "[t]here is a great distinction between power and authority. A man may have a physical power to do a thing, but no legal or constitutional authority."[29]

This debate over the bill is revealing. Both sides assumed that a dispensing power stood in contrast to the legislature's ordinary and lawful power to make laws. Both sides, moreover, thought that if the legislature were to exercise the dispensing power, it would be pursuing Blackstonian ideas about an absolute power, based in necessity, that rose above the law. In other words, both sides apparently assumed that, if the legislature was constitutionally limited, it could not exercise the dispensing power.

As might be expected, no American constitution authorized the dispensing power in either the executive or the legislature. Even under the Blackstonian assumption, that in all nations there had to be a final or absolute power defined by state necessity, a legislature could act only through law, and it therefore could not exercise more than a figurate dispensing power. Under the American assumption, moreover, that a legislature enjoyed only limited legislative power, even a figurative dispensation could seem beyond legislative power. It therefore is unsurprising that the only mention of the dispensing power in early American constitutions came when the Massachusetts Constitution harked back to the papal origins of the power by requiring state officials to swear that "no foreign Prince, Person, Prelate, State or Potentate, hath, or ought to have, any jurisdiction, superiority, preeminence, authority, dispensing, or other power, in any matter, civil, ecclesiastical or spiritual, within this Commonwealth."[30] Otherwise, all American constitutions omitted any mention of dispensations.

This silence about the dispensing power is all the more striking because so many American constitutions specified the location of the pardoning power.[31] The two powers were identical, in that they both relied on non obstante clauses, except that whereas one dispensed with a statute before it was violated, the other dispensed with it after it was violated. This difference, however, was profound, and thus while the dispensing power perished as a dangerous exercise of absolutism, the pardoning power thrived as a mechanism for mercy.

Even in allowing a governor to pardon offenders, a state constitution could take care to prevent him from turning it into a dispensing power—as when the Massachusetts Constitution provided that "no charter of pardon, granted . . . before conviction, shall avail the party pleading the same." Although this limitation was taken for granted in most states, it reveals the anxieties provoked by the dispensing power. Some states even confined the pardoning power to their legislature or, as in Virginia, generally allowed the governor to pardon offenders except where a statute gave the power to the House of Delegates.[32] One way or another, American constitutions permitted non obstante clauses for pardoning past offenses, but not for offering future relief from the law.

American constitutions thus precluded any power to waive or dispense with legal duties. Dispensation was a power to act outside the law to relieve persons from a law that applied to them, and this was not part of either executive or legislative power. More generally, in either branch of government, the dispensing power relieved persons of their obligation to conform to law, and it thus collided with the principle that all persons were subject to law.

Suspending Power

Whereas the dispensing power was neither executive nor legislative and thus had no place in American constitutions, the suspending power seemed clearly legislative. It was a specialized, temporary type of legislative power. State constitutions therefore did not have to convey the suspending power to state legislatures; nor did they have to confine the power to them; instead, they could simply rely on their general grants of legislative power.

In an emergency, however, a legislature might have to leave the suspension of the laws to the executive. This had been why the English Declaration of Rights had left room for Parliament to delegate a suspending power to the king, and along similar lines some state constitutions provided that the power should never be exercised except by the legislature or under its authority. The Maryland Constitution, for example, provided that "no power of suspending laws, or the execution of laws, unless by or derived from the legislature, ought to be exercised or allowed." Similarly, section 20 of the Massachusetts Declaration of Rights stated that "[t]he power of suspending the laws, or the execution of the laws, ought never to be exercised but by the legislature, or by authority derived from it." Even then, it was to be exercised "in such particular cases only as the legislature shall expressly provide for." These sorts of provisions, which appeared in a half dozen state constitutions, assumed that legislatures enjoyed a suspension power as part of their legislative power but left room for them to anticipate emergencies by delegating the suspending power.[33]

Of course, some state constitutions guaranteed the writ of habeas corpus, and this required further detail about the suspending power. It was obvious from English experience that, although habeas might sometimes have to be suspended, this power was dangerous in the Crown, and the English therefore left the power to suspend habeas solely in Parliament.[34] Americans, however, learned from their experience with Parliament that even a legislative power to suspend habeas could be dangerous. The Americans constitutions that guaranteed habeas therefore took care to specify when legislative suspension of this writ was permissible. For example, the Massachusetts Constitution provided that the writ of habeas corpus "shall not be suspended by the legislature, except upon the most urgent and pressing occasions, and for a limited time not exceeding six months."[35]

Constitutions, however, could take different paths, and what matters here is that some constitutions did not authorize their legislatures to delegate their suspending power. It has been noted that six state constitutions expressly left room for executive suspension, where there was legislative delegation. Seven other state constitutions, however, did not acknowledge legislative delegation of the suspension power to the executive, and the U.S. Constitution followed this path.[36] It qualified legislative power by confining suspensions of habeas to instances "when in Cases of Rebellion or Invasion the public Safety may require it," but it did not provide for delegation of the suspending power to the executive. The federal constitution thus stood in contrast to the state constitutions that acknowledged executive suspensions under legislative authorization. Like all American constitutions, the U.S. Constitution assumed that any suspending power was part of the legislative power, and like most state constitutions, it omitted any provision for delegation. It thereby made clear that the suspending power was to remain in the legislature.

Shortly after the adoption of the U.S. Constitution, one of its leading framers, James Wilson, led the redrafting of the Pennsylvania Constitution. The resulting 1790 constitution, like some other state constitutions, ensured that "no power of suspending laws shall be exercised, unless by the legislature or its authority."[37] This sort of provision, which permitted legislative delegation of the suspension power to the executive, was precisely what Wilson and his colleagues left out of the U.S. Constitution.

The U.S. Constitution thus precluded any executive dispensing or suspending power, including any delegation of such powers to the executive. The dispensing power was neither executive nor legislative and, in any case, was inconsistent with the binding character of law. The suspending power at least was legislative, but in contrast to some state constitutions, the U.S. Constitution did not authorize its legislature to delegate it.

Nor should this constitutional repudiation be a surprise. The dispensing power and the executive use of the suspending power stood outside and above law, and constitutional law developed to confine government to ruling through and under law. What is a surprise is that these extralegal powers have come back to life in the form of administrative waivers. The result has been a return to a notoriously extralegal sort of power that constitutions were designed to prevent.

Little v. Barreme

The general point, that the executive could not relieve anyone of the law, entered the reports of the U.S. Supreme Court in 1804 in *Little v. Barreme*. Although Chief Justice John Marshall had no occasion to address the question of legislative authorization, he clearly denied that the executive, even amid the necessities of wartime, could carve out exceptions from the law.

In 1799, during the so-called quasi-war with France, Congress had barred outward-bound trade with France. In support of this prohibition, Congress authorized American ships to seize any American vessel that sailed, directly or indirectly, from the United States to France or any port under French governance. This statute, however, banned only outward-bound trade, and it therefore did not authorize the capture of vessels sailing to the United States from French ports. Dissatisfied with this, President John Adams instructed the commanders of the armed vessels of the United States to be "vigilant" against traffic in both directions, so that American vessels "bound to or from French ports do not escape you."[38]

Inevitably, two American frigates captured an American vessel, the *Flying Fish*, coming from a port under French governance. The frigates brought it back to Boston as a prize, where the captors libeled the ship—a claim apparently justified by the president's instructions. The owners, however, made a claim against the captors for seizing the vessel without statutory authorization. The district court restored the vessel to the owners without damages, but on the owners' appeal, the circuit court added damages, thus upholding the law, without regard to the contrary presidential instructions.

When the case reached the Supreme Court, Chief Justice Marshall affirmed with an opinion that was nothing less than a defense of law against claims of presidential exceptions. As he explained for the court, executive "instructions cannot change the nature of the transaction or legalize an act which[,] without those instructions[,] would have been a plain trespass." In other words, presidential instructions, even when given in wartime to military officers, could not "excuse an act not otherwise excusable."[39]

Congressional Assumptions

Congress, incidentally, appears to have recognized that it could not authorize the executive to dispense with duties that bound subjects. At least for most of the century after *Little v. Barreme*, such waivers are difficult to find in federal law.

Earlier, a 1799 federal quarantine statute appears to have authorized the secretary of the treasury to dispense with federal statutes. The statute provided that federal officers, including customs collectors, were to comply with local quarantine laws and even were to aid in their execution. There were, however, federal rules—primarily executive conditions on permission to land goods, but also at least some federal customs statutes—that required vessels to report their arrival and their cargoes more promptly than was required under some local quarantine laws. In an attempt to reconcile these discordant reporting periods, the 1799 statute authorized the secretary of the treasury to "prolong" the federal reporting period and "to vary or dispense with any other regulations applicable to such reports."[40] Thus, at least where the reporting period was statutory, the 1799 statute seems to have authorized the secretary to relax otherwise legally binding requirements.

If the 1799 statute really granted a dispensing power, it was not of long-term significance. No evidence has thus far been found that the Treasury actually dispensed with statutory reporting periods.[41] Moreover, *Little v. Barreme* in 1804 may have been a clarifying reminder that the executive could not excuse compliance with the law. One way or another, Congress thereafter, throughout the nineteenth century, does not seem to have authorized the executive to waive or dispense with duties that bound subjects.

To be sure, there were statutes that authorized the executive to waive its own rights or to dispense with its own statutorily required duties. But in fact these statutes merely changed the executive's legal duties; they did not authorize it to relieve anyone else of their legal duties.[42] Similarly, there were statutes that subjected executive officers to rules and then allowed them to depart from these rules, but these statutes merely allowed the officers to escape their own duties by following alternative binding duties in specified circumstances. Even where the statutes stated the officers' alternative duties very loosely, the statutes did not allow the officers to grant other members of the public any relief from their legal duties.[43, b]

---

b. For example, one such statute—the 1852 act regulating the inspection and licensing of steamboats—is said (by Jerry Mashaw) to have authorized executive waivers. As a formal mat-

In short, it is remarkably difficult to find instances in nineteenth-century federal law in which the executive offered relief to anyone in the rest of the public from the legal duties that directly bound them. Toward the end of the century, there were hints of changing views, but in an era in which the English dispensing power, and the constitutional rejection of it, were still understood, it is no surprise that Congress apparently did not authorize any such power.

⋘⋘⋘

The executive, in sum, has no suspending or dispensing power—no power to excuse, waive, or otherwise relieve persons of the law. Nor can Congress convey any such power, for the dispensing power was not considered part of any constitutional grant of legislative power, and unlike some state constitutions, the U.S. Constitution did not leave room for legislative delegation of the suspending power, let alone the dispensing power.

Nonetheless, the suspending power and especially the dispensing power have returned—primarily in the form of administrative "waivers." Although the particulars must be delayed until chapter 7, it will be seen that the executive nowadays issues rules that it claims have the force of law, and then it issues waivers dispensing with these rules. Where the rules, moreover, specify standards imposed by legislation, the waivers dispense not only with the regulations but also, in effect, with the underlying statutes. Not content with this, some agencies even issue waivers that directly dispense with the statutes.

It thus will become apparent that, like the prerogative power to make law, the prerogative power to unmake law has been revived. Administrative law thereby restores the full range of extralegal powers concerning legislation—powers that constitutional law was designed to defeat.

And already here the danger should be evident—that government has

---

ter, however, the statute did not authorize inspectors to waive duties that bound other persons, but instead merely authorized inspectors to depart from their statutory licensing rules in pursuit of a looser set of statutory standards. Of course, as a substantive matter, where licensing offered relief from a constraint (as in the 1852 statute), an executive officer's decision about his statutory duty in granting a license could amount to something close to a waiver. It will be seen, however, in chapter 6, that Congress traditionally employed licensing to adjust constraints only for very limited purposes—to raise taxes, to control nonsubjects such as enemy aliens, to govern localities such as the District of Columbia, and to control cross-border or off-shore persons and vessels such as the steamboats—not generally to bind subjects in domestic matters. Thus, even if the steamboat statute were understood to have authorized a waiver, it would not be a precedent for administrative waivers of a more domestic sort.*

returned to the era before constitutions, when kings or executives ruled not through law but outside it. A return to a preconstitutional era of prerogative power may not seem worrisome, for like its predecessor, administrative power often seems benign. The peril of administrative power, however, lies not in its potential for good, but in its potential for danger by unraveling government through law.

SIX

Lawful Executive Acts Adjacent to Legislation

Having examined the historical evidence that administrative legislation returns to prerogative lawmaking, this book now must pause to caution against overreading the argument. The point thus far has been that executive lawmaking creates an extralegal regime—a regime of legislation outside the law and, indeed, outside the constitutionally established lawmaking institutions and processes. The argument, however, does not go so far as to question executive action that does not impose binding constraints on subjects.

The defense of binding executive lawmaking often rests on historical precedents that did not involve binding executive action. For example, much scholarship (by Kenneth Davis, Jerry Mashaw, Eric Posner, Cass Sunstein, and Adrian Vermeule) legitimizes administrative lawmaking by citing early congressional authorization for executive regulations, without recognizing that such regulations did not bind subjects.[1] Put another way, such scholarship conflates unlawful administrative legislation with other, entirely lawful executive action. On this confused evidentiary foundation, administrative legislation acquires early precedents, and the objections to it seem to challenge lawful and valuable executive conduct.[a]

It therefore is essential to examine the evidence more carefully, to distinguish the executive action that merely comes close to legislation from that which really amounts to an extralegal mode of legislation. Much ex-

---

a. For example, Jerry Mashaw's scholarship takes note of early federal executive regulations directing officers and placing conditions on benefits or other privileges. His work also recites instances in which the executive determined and gave notice of legal duties. As will be seen, such regulations and determinations ordinarily did not legally bind subjects of the United States. Indeed, Mashaw's work does not reveal any early federal examples of binding administrative rules or adjudications, other than in the exceptional categories discussed below.

ecutive action approaches legislation without quite amounting to an unlawful exercise of lawmaking power.

Nonbinding and Thus Nonlegislative

Even the executive frequently must make rules, but this does not mean its
rules are exercises of legislative power. To understand this, one must begin by considering the traditional distinction between legislative and nonlegislative power. Recent scholarship (by Larry Alexander and Saikrishna
Prakash) recognizes the importance of this question and suggests that legislative power was the authority to make laws or rules for the governance
of society.[2] This heads in the right direction, but it is necessary to be more
concrete.

In general, the natural dividing line between legislative and nonlegislative power was between rules that bound subjects and those that did not.
Legal obligation seemed by nature to require consent. It therefore was assumed that the enactment of legally binding rules could come only from a
representative legislature and that the resulting rules could bind only subjects, not other peoples.[3] As put by John Locke, the "legislative authority" is
that by which laws "are in force over the subjects of th[e] commonwealth."
Blackstone elaborated, "Legislators and their laws are said to compel and
oblige."[4]

This constraint, obligation, or binding effect of the laws was not the
same as the ensuing physical coercion applied by the Crown or executive to
enforce the laws. On the contrary, the constraining, binding, or obligatory
character of the law was what justified the executive coercion, and thus,
even before the executive coercion, the laws themselves were binding.

These laws that obliged included those that relaxed legal duties. Recognizing this, Edward Coke explained (in the *Case of Proclamations*) that
unlawful prerogative legislation included not merely the prerogative imposition of legally binding duties, but more generally any prerogative alteration of a legally binding duty.

All of these assumptions could usually be taken for granted. It thus did
not ordinarily have to be spelled out that binding rules were legislative or
that binding legislative acts included those relaxing duties. Instead, most
commentators simply alluded to the law's binding or obligatory character,
as will this book. In the shorthand terminology of the common law, legislative acts were centrally those that bound or constrained subjects.

Of course, even when the shorthand was fully understood, constraint
was not the full measure of legislative power. Legislative power naturally

was the power to make binding rules, and the legislative powers that the U.S. Constitution granted to Congress were generally of this sort. A constitution, however, could authorize the legislature to do all sorts of things that did not bind or constrain. Indeed, it could give the legislature nonbinding power over matters that might otherwise have been considered purely executive—for example, when the U.S. Constitution gave Congress the former royal prerogatives to declare war and to grant letters of marque and reprisal. The natural core of legislative power, however, was the power to make rules that bound or constrained subjects.

As a result, the executive could not make rules or duties that bound subjects, for these were legislative. But when the executive adopted rules that did not legally bind, it usually was not trespassing on legislative territory, for most nonbinding acts were not legislative.

This book's argument about extralegal legislation therefore largely concerns the executive rules that bind subjects. When executive rules purport to bind subjects, they create a regime of legislation outside the law and the lawmaking institutions and processes established by the Constitution. In contrast, executive acts that do not alter the binding duties of subjects typically are not legislative and therefore are not usually part of the problem examined here.

This distinction matters precisely because administrative law often is confused with lawful executive actions. Defenders of administrative law tend to rely on this confusion. Once it is understood, however, that binding rules were part of the legislative power, it becomes possible to distinguish between binding legislative rules and nonbinding executive rules. It thus becomes apparent that administrative legislation does not have early federal precedents, and that the objections to this sort of legislation do not interfere with the traditional and lawful exercise of executive power.

Executive Regulations, Instructions, and Orders

The early federal executive actions that are most commonly assumed to have been early instances of administrative legislation were executive regulations, instructions, and orders. But were these executive acts really binding in the manner of legislation?

Regulation of Executive Officers

It is true that some early federal statutes authorized the president and the heads of departments to issue regulations, instructions, and orders to lesser executive officers. These statutes, however, assumed that executive officers could issue directions merely to lesser officers, not to the rest of the public. For example, when Congress in 1789 established the Department of Foreign Affairs, it provided that the department's principle officer "shall conduct the business of the said department in such manner as the President of the United States shall from time to time order or instruct." Similarly, in its 1790 act establishing pensions for wounded soldiers (not the later statute that was questioned by some Supreme Court justices), Congress provided that invalids "shall be placed on the list of the invalids of the United States, at such rate of pay, and under such regulations as shall be directed by the President of the United States."[5] These statutes simply authorized orders, instructions, or regulations directing executive officers, and although the resulting directives could affect the benefits received by members of the public, the statutes did not authorize rules that would bind them.[b]

Even this sort of statutory authorization was unnecessary, for it could be simply assumed that the president or a head of a department had authority to direct inferior officers. For example, in the early years of the Republic, Congress did not bother generally to authorize the secretary of the treasury to issue orders, instructions, or regulations. Instead, Congress merely clarified that his directions and regulations could reach the commissioners appointed to borrow money to pay off the nation's debt. The commissioner in each state was "to observe and perform such directions and regulations

b. In their eagerness to rely on these early statutes, commentators often misdescribe them, and it therefore is important to evaluate the statutes on the basis of their words, not the scholarly summaries. For example, a widely read book on administrative law (by Cornelius Kerwin and Scott Furlong) claims that in a 1799 statute, "the president was given the authority to develop regulations that set duties on foreign goods." The book adds that in an 1813 statute, "Congress granted sweeping rulemaking powers to the secretary of the Treasury to regulate the importation of goods into the United States." Indeed, the book quotes the statute as authorizing the secretary "to establish regulations . . . for carrying this law into effect; which regulations shall be binding."

All of this may seem persuasive, until one reads the statutes. The 1799 statute set exchange rates for estimates of imported goods, and it authorized "regulations for estimating the duties on goods" where "the original cost shall be exhibited in a depreciated currency." In other words, these were not regulations setting duties on goods, but rather were merely regulations directing government officers how to estimate duties. Similarly, when the 1813 statute authorized Treasury regulations, it did not simply say that the regulations "shall be binding." Instead, it said that they "shall be binding on each assessor in the performance of the duties enjoined by or under this act." Full quotations thus reveal that these enactments authorized regulations to bind executive officers, not the rest of the public; and even as to executive officers, it will be seen that regulations of this sort were binding as a condition of employment rather than in the manner of law.*

as shall be prescribed to him by the Secretary of the Treasury, touching the execution of his office."[6] Otherwise, however, the secretary's directives required no authorization.

Although the executive departments often communicated to inferior officers by means of manuscript letters of instruction, they soon turned to printed materials—both for instructions to particular officers and for regulations governing officers as a group.[7] The busier parts of the English bureaucracy, whether the army or the customs commissioners, already had issued printed instructions, and much of the U.S. government simply continued this practice. The Treasury Department, for example, almost from the start distributed its instructions to inferior officers in printed circulars, which mimicked manuscript letters of instruction even to the point of being printed in italics and being signed by the relevant official, whether the comptroller or the treasury secretary, Alexander Hamilton.[8] As the executive grew, however, individually addressed and signed instructions could become a burdensome mode of communication, and therefore, from at least 1798 onward, some departments distributed printed regulations. In that year, for example, the Office of the War Department directed all recruiting officers in their duties by printing *Rules and Regulations Respecting the Recruiting Service*, which began by admonishing that "it is particularly forbidden, to enlist any individual, while in a state of intoxication." In the same year, the Post Office printed *Regulations to be Observed by the Deputy Postmasters in the United States*—warning, among other things, "You are not to open or suffer to be opened, any mail that is not addressed to you or your office."[9]

Revealingly, these instructions and regulations were distributed to officers rather than sold to the public, for they were not binding as law. They could determine the extent of the benefits or privileges distributed by the federal government, such as pensions and land grants. They also could affect enforcement of legal constraints where, for example, they instructed officers how to enforce the law. All such executive regulations affected the public, but did not purport to bind them.[10] That would not happen for a long time.

Even as to executive officers, executive regulations or orders were not legally binding, but rather were, at most, mere conditions of employment. Thus, when an executive officer violated his instructions, whether they came from the head of his department or from the president himself, the question was not whether the disobedient officer could be prosecuted, but merely whether he could be removed. Of course, the officer could be prosecuted if he took a bribe or otherwise violated general prohibitions defined and imposed by law, but he was not accountable at law for mere disobedience.

Regulation of Nonsubjects, Such As Enemy Aliens

Alongside the executive regulations for executive officers were executive regulations aimed at very different persons—those who were not subjects of the United States. For example, Congress at an early date authorized the executive to issue regulations governing enemy aliens—meaning not enemy combatants, but subjects of the enemy present in the United States during wartime. In defense of administrative law, it is suggested that the early statutes on enemy aliens are early examples of the delegation of legislative power. These statutes, however, authorized regulations governing persons who owed allegiance to an enemy nation, and who therefore did not, in the first instance, owe allegiance to the United States. Such persons therefore were not within the obligation or protection of the law; they were not members of the society and so were not subject to its laws.[c] Thus, when Congress authorized the executive to issue orders or regulations to them, it was not delegating legislative power, but rather was simply authorizing the executive to direct or coerce persons who were not subject to law.

Of course, some enemy aliens—those who could be presumed to have submitted allegiance to the United States, and who therefore came within the obligation and protection of its laws—were bound by acts of Congress. Most centrally, when enemy aliens accepted licenses to remain in the United States during wartime, they were understood to be subjects of the United States and subject to its laws.

In other respects, however, the laws of the United States were not binding on enemy aliens, and the executive could regulate them. The executive could use regulations to adjust or withdraw the license to stay, and it could employ regulations to direct coercion against enemy aliens who refused to accept the license or who stepped outside its scope. In such circumstances, enemy aliens were not subject to the obligation of the law, but they could be subject to executive regulations as a matter of force. During the War of 1812, for example, there were elaborate executive regulations. Some required resident enemy aliens to report to federal marshals and to remove themselves inland as directed by federal marshals—these being the terms

---

c. For this book's definition of "subjects" as persons subject to the laws, see the introduction, footnote a.

of the license to stay—and some instructed the marshals about the measures they were to take against enemy aliens who failed to comply.[11]

Far from showing early acceptance of administrative lawmaking, the regulation of enemy aliens confirms the distinction between legislative and executive power. The government could confine subjects only through the obligation of law, which was legislative, and it could confine nonsubjects only through mere command or force, which was executive.

Thus, whether aimed at executive officers or enemy aliens, executive instructions, regulations, and orders were not binding. Congress could authorize these directives, and the executive could issue them, but only because it was assumed that they did not bind subjects. These early executive rules therefore were not early examples of administrative legislation, and the argument here against administrative legislation does not question the lawfulness of nonbinding executive acts.

Executive Interpretations

As with executive regulations, so too with executive interpretations, there was no pretense of any legislative power to bind members of the public. Instead, what heads of departments claimed was simply the authority to interpret the law for their departments and thereby direct their subordinates—as can be illustrated by the Treasury.

The Power to Interpret for a Department

The extent of the power to interpret became a question in 1792 when Otho Williams—the collector of customs in Baltimore—disagreed with the secretary of the treasury, Alexander Hamilton, about the duties of custom inspectors. The Treasury had directed inspectors to assist customs surveyors in overseeing the landing and marking of casks and packages. But Williams encouraged the inspectors in Baltimore to believe that they were not legally obliged to provide this assistance, and they therefore became uncooperative, with the effect of delaying imports there.[12]

Hamilton responded with a circular letter explaining his power of interpretation. Since taking office, Hamilton and the comptroller had issued circulars instructing customs officers about the proper interpretation of relevant statutes, and he now observed that, under the act establishing the Treasury Department, it was the duty of the head of the department "to superintend the collection of the revenue." According to Hamilton, this power included "the right of settling, for the government of the officers employed in the collection . . . of the revenue, the construction of the laws relating to the revenue, in all cases of doubt." This right "is fairly implied in the force of the terms, 'to superintend,' and is essential to uniformity and system in the execution of the laws."[13]

A resolution of such problems, he noted, "might be obtained from the courts of justice," but this was "very ill suited, as an ordinary expedient." In most circumstances, "It is not possible to conceive how an officer can superintend the execution of a law . . . unless he is competent to the interpretation of the law." Hamilton concluded that if the treasury secretary had this competency as the superintendent of revenue collection, then "it must follow that his judgments are directory to those, who are merely superintendents within particular spheres"—this being an allusion to "the collectors of the customs, within their respective districts."[14] His subordinates thus had to follow his interpretations, not because his interpretations were legally binding, but rather because Congress had recognized that the head of the department needed to control his subordinates.

Hamilton clarified this point when he privately reminded Williams of the consequences of disobedience. Rather than say anything about prosecution, Hamilton simply noted that a subordinate who failed to carry out government policy could be fired—a view in which later secretaries concurred.[15] In this way, although executive interpretation could not bind the public, let alone Congress or the courts, it could direct subordinate executive officers.

Mistaken Interpretations

Of course, Hamilton could be mistaken in his interpretations, and this was a serious problem for his subordinates. When he faced difficult questions of interpretation, he consulted eminent lawyers.[16] But when he and they turned out to be wrong, neither his instructions nor the underlying advice could be of much help to the treasury officers who thereby had been induced to give up their own rights or to infringe the rights of others.

For example, when Hamilton instructed customs officers not to collect fees to which they were entitled by law, they were apt to lose compensation. And when he instructed them to impose duties unjustified by law, they were apt to be held liable in court. They therefore often had good reasons, personal and legal, to disobey Hamilton's instructions.

Hamilton understood the seriousness of the problem, and having asserted his authority in the dispute with Williams, he took the opportunity in the ensuing days to acknowledge some of his mistakes. Where his interpretation was clearly mistaken, he admitted this, as when he conceded in a circular that "the construction communicated in my circular" on the Post Office Act had been "erroneous" in light of a provision that "had escaped attention."[17]

In another instance, however, concerning the fees that custom officers could collect under the Coasting Act, Hamilton adhered to his earlier interpretation but recognized that the courts might take another view. When the question had first arisen, the attorney general, Edmund Randolph, had been absent, and Hamilton therefore had consulted two other distinguished lawyers. Some customs officers, however, being convinced that Hamilton's view was wrong, had ignored his instructions and had secured "respectable law opinions" supporting their position. Recognizing this "diversity of legal opinions," Hamilton finally obtained an opinion from Randolph, but found that he concurred with the dissentient customs officers. Hamilton therefore transmitted a copy of Randolph's opinion to all customs collectors and left them to make their own decisions: "In this state of the matter, which so directly concerns the interests of the officers, I think it proper to rescind the instructions heretofore given; though my own view of the subject remains unchanged. Each officer will then pursue that course, which appears to him conformable to law, to his own interest and safety, and to the good of the service."[18] Hamilton would no longer instruct them to follow his view, but neither would he instruct them in the contrary approach, which he considered wrong.

The head of a department had the power to instruct his subordinates, even in matters of interpretation. But neither he nor they could alter the law. None of them, therefore, could afford to treat mistaken interpretations—or even sometimes only potentially mistaken interpretations—as binding.

Systematizing Treasury Interpretations

Notwithstanding Hamilton's emphatic assertion that a department head could interpret for his department, the Treasury initially did a poor job of resolving the legal questions that arose among its dispersed subordinates.[19] This gradually would become a matter of concern for the Treasury, but it more immediately worried the subordinates, as they could ill afford to make mistakes.

Customs officers, for example, not only could be sued by members of the public for failing to respect their rights, but also could be held accountable by the Treasury for anything they failed to collect. Caught between these dangers, customs officers and other federal officers therefore sought legal advice wherever they could get it. In some districts, "when they could not have recourse in time to the head of the department," they would "call on the attorney of the district for his opinion."[20] The opinion of a local district attorney, however, was no substitute for uniform interpretations from the Treasury; and as the secretary tended to be busy and the comptroller often failed to pick up the slack, local customs officers sometimes found themselves out on a limb.[d]

In the second decade of the nineteenth century, Comptroller Joseph Anderson became more systematic in anticipating ambiguities and using circular letters to share the Treasury's interpretations with collectors. As shown by Jerry Mashaw, Treasury Secretary Albert Gallatin briefly offered detailed instructions during the 1807–09 embargo, but more through his personal energy and direction than through a regular bureaucratic process.[21] Several years later, however, Comptroller Anderson offered sustained and systematic direction for customs officers, including systematic interpretation. He began in 1818 with a circular letter observing that "[m]any articles of merchandise are so indifferently expressed in the act establishing the new tariff, that doubts in relation to the rates of duty properly demandable on them have arisen in the minds of many of the officers of the customs. . . . It may, therefore, have a beneficial effect to enumerate the articles alluded to, and to state the decisions in relation to them which have been made by this department."[22] The Treasury thus offered interpretation, but merely to direct customs officers, not to bind the public.

Among the decisions made by the department were not only the inter-

---

d. The failure of the Treasury, even in the early nineteenth century, to give adequate notice of its interpretations can be illustrated by the duties on salt. A 1797 act of Congress allowed a "bounty" or drawback to the owners and crews of fishing vessels which were burdened by an additional import duty on salt. An 1800 statute, however, made this bounty conditional on the continued existence of the act imposing the additional duty on salt. When the additional duty was repealed in 1807, there arose a difference of interpretation. The collectors of customs in Massachusetts assumed that they still had to pay the bounty to fishermen for salt that was imported before the date the 1807 act took effect and that thus had been subject to the additional duty. Indeed, some apparently assumed that the 1807 statute repealed the condition imposed in 1800. Afterward, however, the comptroller of the Treasury disagreed. He admitted that the statutes were "not free from ambiguity," but in his interpretation, the collectors were mistaken—both in assuming that the date of import mattered and in believing that the 1807 statute had repealed the condition. He therefore required the collectors to remit the full additional duty to the Treasury, without subtracting the bounty or credit allowed by the collectors after the passage of 1807 act. The collectors who already had allowed the bounty were severely affected by this decision, and they petitioned Congress for relief. Although Treasury Secretary Gallatin thought the comptroller's construction "correct," he urged Congress that the "the collectors who paid the full allowances, are entitled to legislative relief."[*]

pretations given to collectors and other officials but also letter opinions issued to members of the public, and it may be thought that at least the letter opinions could bind. Merchants would write to the comptroller with questions about the Treasury's understanding of the customs laws, and the comptroller would write back with letters that often were published in commercial newspapers. Of course, collectors and other officials needed a more systematic way of learning of such decisions, and Anderson again seems to have taken the lead, using circular letters to transmit copies of the letter decisions.

The interpretations for collectors and private persons soon accumulated into a vast mass of "decisions" about the Treasury's interpretations. Together with other instructions to inferior treasury officers, they generated hundreds of loose circulars that were not always filed together, even in the Treasury itself. The Treasury therefore, at least by 1824, began to publish its decisions and instructions in a particularly useful form—as notes attached to the official tables of duties. In the 1840s the Treasury authorized the compilation of a synopsis of its circulars, and by the next decade it had begun official publication of handy alphabetical digests of its letter decisions.[23]

In such interpretations, however, the secretary and the comptroller did not purport to bind or constrain the public and did not even really bind inferior officers. Undoubtedly, secretaries could interpret for their departments and thereby could direct their scattered subordinates, especially when the secretaries backed their interpretations with the threat of dismissal. But their interpretations were no more binding as legislation than their regulations. Thus, although such interpretations might look like administrative lawmaking, they did not really have a legislative effect, for they were not legally binding. They therefore cannot be taken as precedents for contemporary administrative interpretation.

Effect on Inferior Officers: "Directory" or Legally Binding?

Hamilton had insisted that his judgments or interpretations of the revenue laws were "directory" to his subordinates, and as already seen, he thereby did not go so far as to say that they were legally bound by his interpretations. The question arose again in more complex ways in the 1830s and '40s, and although executive interpretations eventually were said to be "binding" on inferior officers, it still was understood that they were not binding like laws, let alone on the public.

When Levi Woodbury served as secretary of the treasury, he led the department in taking very aggressive interpretations of the revenue laws. In response, some importers balked, and the resulting disputes did not escape the attention of the Supreme Court.

In an 1836 case by an importer to recover excess taxes from a customs collector, the Supreme Court noted that "[t]he construction of the law is open to both parties, and each presumed to know it." On the one side, "[a]ny instructions from the Treasury Department could not change the law or affect the rights of the plaintiff. He was not bound to take and adopt that construction," but "was at liberty to judge for himself and act accordingly." Similarly, on the other side, the Treasury's instructions could not protect the collector from liability; instead, they merely could mitigate damages, being introduced as evidence that "the collector acted in good faith."[24] In other words, executive interpretations and resulting executive instructions were legally binding on neither the public nor the collectors. At the same time, it generally was desirable for collectors to obey Treasury instructions, and a collector could not disobey and expect to keep his position.[e]

Woodbury was not in a position to resist the Court while he was at the Treasury, but in 1841 he left the Treasury to become a Senator. He soon led the debate in favor of the 1842 tariff statute, and he apparently was responsible for including a provision that made it the "duty" of collectors and other customs officers "to execute and carry into effect" the treasury secretary's instructions. In case of any "difficulty" about "the true construc-

e. Two years after the Supreme Court rebuked Woodbury, Attorney General Felix Grundy also took him to task. The Treasury planned to rely on claims of commercial and administrative necessity to justify strained interpretations of statutes. Grundy, however, dismissed this as lawless.

In one instance, the comptroller relied on commercial necessity to justify a strained interpretation of the duties on silk, and in September 1838 Woodbury sought support for this from the attorney general: "Can the Comptroller, in giving a construction to the revenue laws, which, from former erroneous practice, may prove injurious to the commercial community, if immediately acted on, legally suspend their operation, as construed by him, with the view of allowing the importers of goods time to countermand their orders for goods from abroad?" Grundy responded: "My answer to this question is decidedly in the negative. The duty of the comptroller is, to execute the revenue laws. Neither he, nor any other officer of the government, has the power to suspend the operation of an act of Congress, unless specially authorized to do so, by the act itself, or some other law." Put another way, the comptroller should "avoid the dangerous practice of repealing laws by constructive implication."

Later, in December, the Treasury relied on something like administrative necessity to justify its lax interpretation of the duties of customs collectors, and Grundy again had to caution Woodbury. The attorney general recognized that the relevant statutes seemed "wholly impracticable" and that "a departure in practice" was "indispensable," but he warned that this was no excuse. For further details of Grundy's December letter, see endnote e.*

tion or meaning" of the revenue laws, the decision of the secretary "shall be conclusive and binding upon all collectors and other officers of the customs."[25]

The next year, however, in a case against the sureties of a customs collector, the Supreme Court explained its underlying constitutional assumption, that "[t]he Treasury officers are the agents of the law." The law rather than any Treasury decision ultimately bound the collectors and the persons they dealt with: "It regulates their duties, as it does the duties and rights of the collector and his sureties." Accordingly, "[t]he officers of the Treasury cannot, by any exercise of their discretion, enlarge or restrict the obligation of the collector's bond."[26, f]

Thus, even in the wake of the 1842 statute, the secretary of the treasury could interpret for his department only in the sense that he could fire inferior officers who disobeyed. And of particular interest here, the debate about executive interpretations centered on their effect for officers. What was controversial was the extent to which executive interpretations and instructions could direct inferior officers and what this meant, not whether such directives bound the public. Once again, executive interpretations were not what they may seem to have been, and they therefore cannot be taken as precedents for contemporary attempts to legislate through administrative interpretation.

Military Orders

Military orders establishing rules may seem, in retrospect, to have been similar to contemporary binding administrative rules, for they bound military personnel to obey. Such orders, however, did not legally bind the public, and they did not bind even military personnel in the civilian legal

f. The Treasury eventually added its own caveat to Woodbury's statutory solution. The statute's phrasing—that the Treasury Secretary's constructions shall be "conclusive and binding" on customs officers—was so broad that it could seem to suggest that the secretary's interpretations were to prevail even when they contradicted judicial interpretations. Ostensibly to counter this impression, Treasury Secretary Robert J. Walker explained in an 1847 circular letter that the 1842 statute required collectors to defer to his interpretations, but that any Treasury interpretation was always subject to "the judicial powers." Thus, "notwithstanding the broad language and comprehensive authority" conferred by Congress on the Treasury's interpretations, the department "feels bound to adopt the construction of the revenue laws pronounced in solemn adjudications by the Supreme Court." Although Walker thereby seemed to defer to the judiciary, he actually was suggesting to customs collectors that they were bound by statute to follow the department's interpretations until any controversy about them was resolved by the highest court.*

system. They therefore are another example of how executive action could look like administrative legislation without really going so far.

Civilian regulations or orders traditionally were only conditions of employment. As already suggested, Congress since 1842 had moved toward making some civilian decisions "binding" on civilian officers in the performance of their duties. For example, in the 1864 Internal Revenue Act, Congress provided that the Internal Revenue Commissioner's instructions, regulations, and directions "shall be binding" on revenue officers "in the performance of the duties enjoined by or under this act." But this sort of statute did not purport to make the regulations binding on the officers outside the performance of their duties, and it thus did not bind them when they resigned.[27] Even for matters within the performance of their duties, although the Treasury could fire its disobedient officers, it could not ordinarily prosecute them except for independent criminal offenses, such embezzlement or extortion. Civilian regulations or orders thus were binding only in the sense that they were conditions of holding office.

In contrast, military orders unconditionally bound military personnel to obey. Such orders thus left military personnel no option to resign, and the government usually could punish them for disobedience. At least in this sense, military orders establishing rules may seem to offer precedents for contemporary administrative rules.

Military law, however, had long been considered separate from civilian law. Rather than generally bind the public, military orders generally were directed only at soldiers and sailors and were enforceable only in the military system of justice.[28] Accordingly, even though military orders were binding in one system, this did not mean they were instances of administrative lawmaking in the other.

Of course, military orders were recognized by the civilian law. They were acknowledged already by the Constitution's provision making the president commander in chief, and by acts of Congress making it a military crime, punishable in military courts, to disobey orders. The president's orders, however, were not binding in the civilian system of law, and therefore, to allow for civilian enforcement of military orders, the Constitution gave Congress power to make rules for the government and regulation of the military. Military orders were binding on subordinates within the military system, but only the rules and regulations adopted by Congress were binding and enforceable in the civilian system.

Thus, far from being a model for administrative lawmaking, military orders are a reminder that executive commands are very different from congressional enactments. Although military officers can command military subordinates, executive officers cannot similarly command the public.

Determinations of Legal Duties

Other executive actions that came close to legislation, and that therefore are sometimes assumed to have been an exercise of legislative power, were determinations of legal duties. In these determinations, an executive officer would determine an individual's legal duty and give him notice of it, and because the imposition of legal duties was a form of lawmaking, these executive decisions about such duties could easily stray into the legislative realm. But where executive officers confined themselves to exercising understanding or judgment in discerning the law and the underlying circumstances, they could avoid any imputation of exercising legislative will.[g]

The underlying problem is sometimes said to be that legislation must apply to facts that cannot be known at the time of enactment. But this is true of almost all legislation. In fact, the problem that gave rise to most executive determinations was the need of the government to clarify the legal duties of particular subjects so as to expedite their compliance and government enforcement. This need, not surprisingly, seemed especially important in the collection of taxes and other such dues.

The understanding that determinations had to be made without any exercise of legislative will received classical expression already in seventeenth-century England. Indeed, eighteenth- and nineteenth-century Americans tended simply to echo the English doctrine. Accordingly, to understand

g. Of course, the ideal that individuals are capable of exercising mere judgment or discernment, without an exercise of will, has been much disputed. In Protestant and derivative psychological theory, it has long been urged that human beings are profoundly willful—indeed, that they are so willful that they cannot exercise mere discernment, but inevitably are precommitted or prejudiced. They therefore can at best direct their will toward what is right or just. As put by Zechariah Chafee and Alexander Bickel, "the man himself is a part of what he decides," but if "law is the will of the justices," it is "the will of the justices trying to do that which is right." On such assumptions, it is unrealistic to expect judges, executive officers, or anyone else to exercise judgment untainted by will or precommitments.

The common law, however, long retained the ideal of mere judgment or discernment. Although most common lawyers adopted Protestant and associated psychological ideas about will, they traditionally (until the twentieth century) adhered to the ideal of judgment untainted by will—their assumption being that, even if individuals could not entirely live up to this ideal, they at least could strive to approach it. Discernment or judgment thus remained the office of a judge, and by the same token it was the means by which an executive officer could make a determination without straying into legislative power.*

how American executive determinations were not really examples of administrative legislation, it is necessary to begin in England.

Commissions of Sewers

The leading precedents for determinations concerned English commissions of sewers—the commissions issued to the men who oversaw the preservation of riverbanks and the draining of fens. The primary authorizing statute, adopted in the early fifteenth century, required the commissioners to evaluate the repairs needed along each waterway and to assess adjacent landowners for the work. Although the power of the commissioners could easily have become a legislative power, Chief Justice Coke admonished them to exercise discretion in the sense of discernment, including discernment of the law and the underlying circumstances—the point being that they had to avoid discretion in the sense of legislative will. From this perspective, although the commissioners were given an authority to act "according to their discretions," they were "to be limited and bound with the rule of reason and law."[29]

The test of law and reason was the standard by which judges traditionally discerned the law where it was unclear, and Coke recited it to emphasize that commissioners were to exercise discretion in the same way as judges—as a sort of understanding or judgment about law rather than lawmaking. As Coke added, "discretion is a science or understanding to discern between falsity and truth, between right and wrong, between shadows and substance, between equity and colorable glosses and pretenses, and not to do according to their wills and private affections." Eighteenth-century judges and law books similarly recited that, although commissioners of sewers "are to act according to their discretion, yet such discretion must be governed and directed by the rules of law and reason."[30]

This assumption that the commissioners had to avoid exercising legislative will was echoed in other doctrines. For example, the commissioners could determine and give notice of duties only for the maintenance of existing walls, which local persons by prescription already had a duty to repair. The commissioners thus were confined to determining existing legal duties and could not exercise will to create new embankments.[h]

---

h. One of the great transformations of the English landscape, the draining of the fens, occurred in the seventeenth century, and the king's council under James I and Charles I sought to advance this project by suppressing the legal obstacles to new embankments. In 1609, the council sought an opinion from the judges justifying the commissioners of sewers in ordering

The commissioners of sewers enjoyed statutory authority to make ordinances for the preservation of sea walls, marshes, and adjoining areas.[31] It came to be understood, however, that even these enactments were to be made in the spirit of determinations of legal duties—or at least in aid of such determinations. As summarized in the seventeenth century, the authorizing statute "gives not the commissioners of sewers absolute power and authority to make and ordain laws . . . for these laws which they are to make, must be for the safeguard, conservation, redress, correction and reformation." In other words, "they must not be made out of self-will, and affection, but after their wisdoms and discretions." Although these ordinances strained the distinction between legislative will and the mere discernment of legal duties, they were to be made as much as possible through mere discernment.[32]

It is possible that, in reality, commissioners of sewers frequently used their determinations to exercise will and thus, in effect, to legislate. Strikingly, however, even in their ordinances, they were expected to come as close as possible to the ideal of merely discerning legal duties and giving the affected persons notice of what the law already required. Determinations thus were not understood as exertions of legislative power.

Other English Determinations of Duties

The nonlegislative character of determinations of duties is evident from a wide range of English officers. For example, road surveyors regularly determined and gave notice of legal duties.[33] Similarly, when tax assessors determined the taxes owed by individuals, they were expected merely to exercise discernment or judgment and then to notify the taxpayers of their duty under the law. A constable also could not create a legally binding rule, but simply could give a warning or notice of duties imposed by law. At most, where there was an affray or riot, he could command participants in the king's name to keep the peace and to depart.[34] All such officers had

---

a new channel for the River Ouse. Although the judges refused to comply, the council later, in 1616, issued an order (drafted by Francis Bacon) arguing that the commissioners could impose new structures. Moreover, until 1639, the council suppressed legal challenges by threatening to imprison plaintiffs who sued the commissioners.

Rather than alter the law, such high-handed conduct only cemented the rule against new structures. As summarized in the eighteenth century, the commissioners "cannot make any new inventions to charge the people; but if there were an old wall, they may build another (if that be decayed) on the inside, or some small way distant, if it be necessary, and may compel them that repaired the former to repair it if they have no damage by the remove."*

to avoid exercising legislative will, and they therefore only put subjects on notice of their already-existing duties.

Among the officers to whom this analysis applied were justices of the peace. These men exercised both judicial and what could be considered executive powers, acting sometimes "as a judge" and sometimes "as a minister only."[35] In the latter role, they sometimes did more than merely determine legal duties—most notably when inquiring about crimes. Their criminal inquiries, however, were not legislative.

Of course, many circumstances could not be anticipated in their commissions or the underlying statutes, and therefore much was left to discretion. Yet this discretion, predictably, was to be exercised as "a knowledge or understanding to discern between truth and falsehood."[36] For example, when justices of the peace licensed alehouses, they were to exercise mere discernment, thus avoiding any exercise of legislative will.[i] Once again, determinations of duties do not point toward administrative lawmaking.

The United States

By now, it should be no surprise that executive determinations in the United States were not considered legislative. Like their English predecessors, such determinations therefore cannot be relied upon as examples of early administrative lawmaking. Nor can they be taken to suggest that a critique of administrative lawmaking is a challenge to such determinations.

In the United States, federal, state, and local officers continued to determine legal duties on the familiar assumption that they could not legislate. Road surveyors, fence viewers, health officers, tax assessors, and justices of the peace all determined legal duties, and gave notice of them, on the traditional understanding that they were to act as much as possible in a spirit of discernment or judgment.

The danger that the determination of duties would cross the line into an exercise of legislative will was especially a problem in local government. Although it could be swept under England's loose constitutional rug, it became painfully apparent in America, where the lines separating governmental powers were more sharply drawn.

The potential for conflict between local determinations and constitutional principles can be illustrated by a dispute in Fairfax County, Virginia.

i. The justices also traditionally determined legal duties when setting wages or prices for grain or bread, and this sort of determination was particularly apt to drift into lawmaking. By the mid-eighteenth-century, however, on both sides of the Atlantic, these determinations had largely fallen into disuse.*

A new courthouse had long been needed in Fairfax, but in 1789, under the leadership of George Mason, many justices of the Fairfax County Court refused to impose a levy for its construction. Although Mason had underlying political concerns, he and his allies on the court argued that "the power of levying by the [county] courts was destroyed by an express article in the bill of rights of this commonwealth"—perhaps the separation-of-powers provision, but more probably the one declaring that men "cannot be taxed or deprived of their property for public uses, without their own consent."[37] Either way, the objection was that the justices had to avoid a determination that drifted into the realm of legislative power. Traditionally, however, an assessment to replace a deteriorating courthouse had been accepted as a mere determination of a legal duty, and it therefore is not surprising that a majority of the court soon overruled Mason and his fellow protesters.

Their protest nonetheless is a reminder of the tension between American constitutional principles and the local determinations that easily could wander into legislative territory. These potentially wayward determinations had been drawn from England when America was under the English constitution, and they were retained in some states when Americans adopted their own constitutions. Accordingly, when taken too far, they could seem to be local departures or at least exceptions from American constitutional principles.

It would be a mistake, however, to assume that many local determinations of legal duties were "really" legislative. At least at the local level, most officials had local knowledge and connectedness. In such circumstances, the determinations by county justices and other county officers about local legal duties were not as legislative as now may be supposed. Of course, at the federal level—where officers often had less social accountability and more centralized expertise than local knowledge—determinations about legal duties were more likely to become a mode of legislation. But in a local setting, especially in a relatively traditional society, determinations of local duties could usually rest on a discernment of local realities.[38, j]

More generally, to the extent local determinations crossed into legislation, they are historical anomalies—inherited local exceptions from American constitutional principles rather than evidence of such principles. And

---

j. Historians tend to assume that because executive officers and justices of the peace responded to local pressures, their decisions cannot be understood as exercises of judgment. The law, however, clearly required such men to exercise discretion in the sense of mere discernment, and although it cannot be assumed that they always lived up to this ideal, their local knowledge and connectedness at least enabled them to discern the local realities.

because they occurred at the local level, they never posed the threat of centralized extralegal power that has come with federal administrative law. Thus, even the most errant of local determinations cannot be considered precedents for federal administrative legislation.

Although, in retrospect, determinations of legal duties by executive officers and justices of the peace have been viewed as early instances of administrative lawmaking, the traditional understanding was very different. Executive officers and justices of the peace could come close to legislative power by making determinations of legal duties, but in making their determinations, they were expected to act with an attitude of discernment rather than will, thus avoiding any administrative legislation. As a result, early federal determinations of legal duties (let alone local determinations) offer no legitimacy for administrative lawmaking. And by the same token, this book's objections to administrative lawmaking pose no challenge to mere determinations.

Determinations of Legal Rights: Licensing

Whereas most determinations notified Americans of their legal duties, licensing focused on what might be considered the other side of the equation: It notified them of their rights. Even so, it thereby, in effect, notified them of their duties, and although it may seem to have been an opportunity for executive lawmaking, the executive (as in other determinations) was expected to exercise judgment rather than will in giving licenses.

Licensing in the Context of Constraint

The focus here on licensing requires a preliminary explanation, for it may be thought that licensing was not a constraint, but merely a grant of a privilege. From this perspective, licensing was not legislative, and there was no reason that a town officer, justice of the peace, or other person acting in an executive capacity could not exercise will in granting licenses.

Licenses, however, were granted in different contexts. Although a license, standing alone, was a mere privilege, it could be part of a legislative constraint when it was issued against the background of a prohibition. For example, a license to sell liquor in a government office building would have been a privilege, but a license generally to sell liquor was part of a prohibition. Indeed, the latter sort of licenses, which relaxed legal prohibitions, were the equivalent of grants of monopoly, which had always combined prohibitions with exceptions or licenses. Thus, even though licenses could be privileges when used to distribute access to government property, they also could be part of broader legislative constraints when used to adjust restrictions on the public.

Although the common law did not follow this distinction with much consistency, it at least expected licensers to exercise mere judgment, not will, when granting the licenses that relaxed broader legislative prohibitions. For example, it has been seen that justices of the peace were to exercise discretion in the sense of "a knowledge or understanding to discern between truth and falsehood." To make this clear when licensing alehouses, they were to sign a certificate that "we the said justices" had "good and credible report to us made, by divers credible and honest persons," that the licensed person was "a man meet to keep a common alehouse." Like other determinations of legal duties, the licensing that was part of a framework of constraint had to be done without any exercise of legislative will.[39, k]

Just how much was at stake became explicit when licenses were denied without clear statutory foundations and thereby seemed to be a matter of will. In pre-Revolutionary Virginia, religious dissenters, especially Baptists, hoped for licenses under the English Toleration Act to hold religious meetings, but it was not clear who in the colony had the power to grant such licenses, and the authorities often refused. Although Baptists and others would soon protest against mere toleration, their initial complaint was the more mundane legal point that licensing decisions should rest on judgment, not will:

> To depend on the will of man is, in truth, the very definition of slavery, and all whom it includes must be destitute of true liberty; though they have the good fortune to be blessed with kind masters. Nothing can give perpetuity and safety to the rights of the subjects but the establishment of them by law; and the more particular and clear the law is the greater security there is to those who live under it. Obscurity and uncertainty leave such a latitude of construction as exalts the judge almost into the seat of the legislator.[40]

Where licensing provided relief from legal constraint, it was a measure of liberty. It therefore had to rest on clear statutory requirements, lest it turn licensors into legislators.

k. The grant of a license, however, was not just any determination and notice, for the license itself was necessary before the recipient could exercise his right to do the licensed activity. Somewhat similarly, an assessment was not just any determination notice, for there had to be notice of the assessment before the recipient was bound to perform his duty to pay the assessed tax.

Licensing Regulations

The licensing that offered relief from constraint most clearly became a mode of executive lawmaking where executive officers issued licensing regulations. Revealingly, however, it was unusual before the twentieth century for Congress to authorize this sort of executive power. In places such as the District of Columbia, where the federal government exercised local authority, Congress (and local legislative assemblies) imposed licensing regulations. But Congress apparently did not authorize the executive to control the public in domestic matters by issuing licensing regulations.

At the federal level, Congress authorized executive officers to issue licensing regulations on enemy aliens, and the resulting regulations have been taken to be early examples of administrative legislation. Enemy aliens, however, as already noted, were not treated as subjects until they accepted the conditions of their license to remain in the country. Accordingly, when licensing regulations laid out the conditions of licenses for enemy aliens, the regulations were not legally binding on subjects and therefore cannot be viewed as precedents for administrative lawmaking.

More intriguing are the licensing regulations that controlled cross-border or offshore matters. As may already be surmised, however, these licensing regulations concerned persons and things that, in various ways, went beyond the territory or shores of the United States and that therefore were not always subject to its laws.[1]

In 1790, Congress passed an act authorizing the president to regulate trade with Indian tribes. This statute on native Americans, like that on enemy aliens, has been taken by defenders of administrative law to suggest that early statutes authorized administrative legislation. Yet it actually created a licensing scheme to govern traders who often were not clearly subject to the law of the United States. Not all of them considered themselves subjects of the United States, and even those who were subjects tended to venture into the territory of nations that often considered themselves distinct from the United States. Congress therefore had both practical and legal reasons to rely on a licensing scheme.

Its statute provided that "no person shall be permitted to carry on any trade or intercourse with the Indian tribes, without a license for that purpose under the hand and seal of the superintendent of the department." The licensed traders were to enter $1,000 bonds "conditioned for the true

---

1. As will become apparent, the word "shores" is used here broadly to refer not only to the sea shores but also to the banks of rivers that came within admiralty jurisdiction.

and faithful observance of such rules, regulations and restrictions, as . . . shall be made for the government of trade and intercourse with the Indian tribes." The superintendents and licensed persons, moreover, "shall be governed in all things touching the said trade and intercourse, by such rules and regulations as the president shall prescribe."[41] These rules and regulations stipulated the conditions of the bonds posted by the licensed traders. As a result, although unlicensed traders (at least those who were subject to U.S. law) could be prosecuted for violating the act, licensed traders who violated the rules or regulations instead risked losing their license and paying the penalty stated in their bonds.

This regulation through licensing was singularly appropriate for controlling persons, such as Indian traders, who were not entirely subject to domestic law. When executive regulations stated the conditions of licenses that gave relief from constraint, the regulations had a binding effect, and thus in domestic matters they seemed an extralegal exercise of legislative power. Here, however, such regulations were being applied to persons and a sort of trade that often went beyond the reach of the law of the United States, and in these circumstances, such regulations apparently were permissible.

Licensing thus became the standard mode of imposing controls on cross-border or offshore problems—as evident from an 1805 statute on foreign armed vessels in the ports of the United States. Such vessels were foreign sovereign territory and therefore could not be subject to American law, but they came into American ports only under an implied license from the United States, and the president had the power to impose conditions on the license. Against this background, the 1805 statute clarified the role of customs collectors. It required the commanding officer of a foreign armed vessel entering a port of the United States to "conform himself, his vessel and crew, to such regulations respecting health, repairs, supplies, stay, intercourse and departure, as shall be signified to him by the [customs] collector," who was to act "under the authority and direction of the president of the United States." At first glance, these regulations may look like binding domestic executive legislation, but in fact they stated the conditions of the licenses granted to foreign armed vessels, which were not ordinarily subject to American law. The affected vessels thus violated the regulations at the risk of expulsion rather than of prosecution. As put by the statute, any vessel "not conforming" to the regulations "shall be required to depart from the United States."[42]

This use of executive licensing regulations to govern offshore events also explains federal quarantine regulations on foreign armed vessels. Many states and municipalities imposed quarantines and other health restrictions on vessels arriving in their jurisdictions, and federal customs collectors were instructed to assist in the enforcement of these limitations—again, as conditions of licenses. For example, in his initial circular regarding the 1805 statute, Treasury Secretary Robert Gallatin instructed customs collectors, "You will continue to enforce the regulations made by the state, health or quarantine laws." He also specified that "if by the laws of the state or port regulations already in force, a certain position in the harbor has been assigned to armed vessels, you will conform therewith." But some states had not yet imposed quarantines, and President Jefferson had not taken the 1805 statute as an occasion to add any new restrictions on foreign armed vessels. Gallatin therefore explained to customs collectors that "[y]ou may also if you shall think it of urgent necessity, make temporary regulations for that object if none yet exist."[43] The point was not that executive officers could impose legally binding rules regarding quarantines or foreign armed vessels, but rather that custom collectors could impose conditions on the licenses granted to such vessels. Once again, Congress used executive licensing regulation at the borders, but not to govern domestically.

Similarly, Congress licensed steamboats. Beginning in 1789, it authorized the executive to license coastal and fishing vessels, and in 1852, in response to the danger from steam power and exploding boilers, it further authorized the executive to license steamboats and their key personnel. In this scheme, moreover, Congress authorized the executive to issue regulations and impose them as conditions of the licenses. It has therefore been suggested (by Jerry Mashaw) that the steamboat regulations reveal an early example of administrative legislation.[44]

As might be expected, however, the regulations were not understood to be narrowly domestic. Instead, they applied to vessels of a sort that increasingly were traveling on the high seas and even to foreign countries.[45] These regulations therefore had to reach places where the law of the United States did not ordinarily have obligation, and it therefore is no surprise that Congress imposed them as conditions on licenses.

Of course, the steamboat licensing often applied to vessels that remained on internal waters, and it thus apparently went further than earlier federal licensing. Even in this, however, it largely followed admiralty jurisdiction, which was a traditional boundary of domestic law. The 1789 Judiciary Act already established admiralty jurisdiction over substantial vessels on waters "navigable from the sea," and an 1845 act gave district courts admiralty jurisdiction over the Great Lakes and the connecting navigable waterways. Revealingly, the latter statute applied only to steamboats and other large vessels that already were licensed as coastal vessels. In other words, the coastal vessels, particularly steamboats, that went in and among the Great Lakes were blurring the distinction between inland and coastal shipping, and Congress recognized this by expanding admiralty jurisdiction inward toward Canada. Congress thereby treated the banks of the relevant navigable waterways like the shoreline. Accordingly, when Congress, seven years later, subjected steamboats to executive regulation through licensing, it did so with good reason for thinking that even inland steamboats were, in a sense, beyond the nation's territory or shores.[46]

Only apparently at the beginning of the twentieth century did Congress go much further in authorizing executive licensing regulations.[47] Before then conditions on licensing were not yet generally mechanisms for the executive to exercise binding domestic legislative power or will. Instead, when executive officers decided upon licenses that provided freedom from constraint, the officers had to exercise mere judgment. Not only when directly determining duties, but also when granting licenses that offered relief from constraint, executive officers had to avoid exercising legislative will.

Determinations of Facts

Just as executive officers could determine legal duties, so too they could determine legally significant facts. In particular, the legislature could condition a statutory duty on an executive determination of fact. The executive then had a duty to make the determination, but only by exercising discernment, not legislative will.

The most prominent examples were presidential determinations about the acts of foreign nations. Congress sometimes passed statutes asking the president to make determinations about "acts of state" under the law of nations—such as whether foreign countries were at peace or war with the United States. Congress in its statutes also sometimes asked the president to make more mundane factual determinations—such as whether foreign countries had dropped their discriminatory duties against American goods.

During the 1790s and the first decade of the next century, particularly during times of conflict, Congress in several statutes authorized the president to impose embargoes or, more typically, to suspend them, based on presidential decisions that unabashedly went beyond mere factual determinations. For example, in late 1807, when Britain and France were at war with each other and were interfering with American shipping, Congress had barred imports from either combatant, but in 1808 it allowed the president to suspend the embargo where he determined this was safe. To be precise, Congress enacted:

> That in the event of such peace or suspension of hostilities between the belligerent powers of Europe, or of such changes in their measures affecting neutral commerce, as may render the United States sufficiently safe, in the judgment of the President of the United States, he is hereby authorized, during the recess of Congress, to suspend, in whole or in part, the act laying an embargo on all ships and vessels in the ports and harbors of the United States, . . . under such exceptions and restrictions, and on such bond and security being given as the public interest and circumstances of the case may appear to require.[48]

This gave the president much more than a merely factual determination, and it assumed that the suspension came from the president rather than Congress.

Although earlier suspension acts had provoked little attention, the 1808 statute led to lengthy protests in the House of Representatives and in the press. Interestingly, the most vocal concerns came from men who "anxiously" wanted the "immediate repeal" of the embargo, but insisted on a constitutional version of the bill. Representative Philip Key objected that "we cannot transfer the power of legislating from ourselves to the president," and asked how a statute could "give the president of the United States power to repeal an existing law now in force"? Recognizing that this was a "dangerous prerogative" once "claimed by the Crown," Key observed that "[i]n England it might be done, because the legislature is omnipotent; but we are limited within the sphere of our Constitution."[49]

The crux of the matter was the departure from a mere determination of fact. Of course, Congress could "give the president upon certain predicted events a power by which the embargo may be taken off," but the "repeal or suspension must be the act of the Congress . . . operating upon events or facts to which the president by his proclamation may give publicity." Similarly, Congress could not leave the president a power to set "exceptions and restrictions" as he thought in accord with the "public interest." In such ways, he would be "exercis[ing] a legislative, not an executive power." Key and his handful of fellow protesters therefore hammered away at the difference between "a case in which we ourselves by law suspend an act upon the happening of an event yet in the womb of time," and "a case in which we give the executive a power to suspend the law *ad libitum* [at pleasure] when that event does occur." One might think this merely a difference of "phraseology," but if Congress could authorize the president to do more than "notify" Americans of the fact upon which a statute was conditioned, the prerogative to suspend laws would come back to life.[50, m]

Although Key and his few allies lost in 1808, their logic prevailed for much of the rest the century. The very next year, when Congress adopted a similar statute, it made clear that Congress rather than the president was suspending the embargo, and that the president was to make only a factual determination: "That the president of the United States . . . is authorized, in case either France or Great Britain shall so revoke or modify her edicts, as that they shall cease to violate the neutral commerce of the United States, to declare the same by proclamation; after which the trade of the United States, suspended by this act, and by the act laying an embargo . . . may be renewed with the nation so doing." Adding even further clarity, a subsequent version of the statute specified that the president was merely to declare the "fact" that either Britain or France "shall cease to violate the neutral commerce of the United States."[51]

It thus is dubious whether the pre-1808 determinations should be viewed as precedents for executive officers to make law. After Congress recognized the constitutional problem, it took care to avoid any suggestion that the president was suspending the law or otherwise exercise lawmaking will. Instead, when relying on the president to determine conditions—whether war, peace, or discriminatory duties—Congress asked him merely to exercise judgment.

Eventually, executive determinations of facts would be stretched into opportunities for administrative lawmaking. At first there were only a few lapses in this direction, most clearly in 1822.[52] In the late nineteenth century, however, and especially the twentieth, Congress systematically authorized the executive to determine indeterminate facts and to suspend statutes on such determinations—most notoriously (as soon will be seen) in the 1890 tariff. Congress in such ways invited the executive to exercise lawmaking will, and determinations thereby became an avenue for administrative lawmaking.[n]

m. Outside Congress, a commentator protested that "this delegation of power from Congress to the president" was "objectionable, on constitutional grounds" and thus was a "nullity." He added: "We here behold Congress transferring their powers to the president. And this . . . is the first time I have ever heard of a constitutional delegation of power from one branch of the government to another. Nay, I had always thought that it was the true spirit of our constitution, to keep the great departments of our state distinct."*

n. Among the developments that helped to legitimize the use of determinations for administrative lawmaking were nineteenth-century plebiscites. When authorizing these popular votes, state legislatures understood that because their constitutions had given them legislative

Traditionally, however, when an executive officer made a determination of fact, he was expected to confine himself to exercising judgment or discernment. By this means, he could avoid exercising legislative will.

✧✧✧

Executive power thus could be exercised adjacent to legislation without actually trespassing on legislative power. The executive, for example, could make regulations and interpretations that merely directed executive officers and nonsubjects and could make determinations that merely discerned facts or the duties of subjects. Although these executive acts came close to legislation, they generally did not bind members of the public, and they therefore were not legislative.

As a result, early executive regulations, interpretations, and determinations are not precedents for binding administrative legislation. On the contrary, they show the difference between lawful executive action and unlawful administrative lawmaking, and they thereby reveal that the one is not threatened by the argument against the other.

---

power, they could not simply authorize the people to legislate. They therefore engaged in a subterfuge. They would enact a proposed reform, on the condition that the returns on a plebiscite showed a majority of popular votes in favor of it. When such plebiscites were challenged as unconstitutional, the courts still recited the principle that only the legislature could exercise lawmaking power, but they upheld the authorizing statutes on the ground that the statutes merely depended on determinations of fact. From this perspective, the election officers simply ascertained the majority vote, and "the majority vote is but an ascertainment of the public sentiment." As put by the Pennsylvania Supreme Court in 1873, although "the legislature cannot delegate its power to make the law, . . . it can make a law to delegate a power to determine some fact or state of things upon which the law makes, or intends to make, its own action depend."

On the face of the matter, such cases followed the traditional distinction between an exercise of will in legislation and an exercise of discernment in a determination of fact. Yet the fact thus determined was one willed by the people of the state. Accordingly, to say that the election officials (or the majority of the people) were merely determining a fact was to obscure the underlying reality of legislative will. By such reasoning any extralegal legislation could be considered a determination of fact merely by placing the wilful reality behind the fig leaf of an executive or majority determination of what was willed.*

SEVEN

Return to Extralegal Legislation

It now is time to complete part I of this book by examining how contemporary administrative legislation returns to an extralegal regime of lawmaking. Like the old prerogative bodies, administrative agencies act outside the law, the legislature, and the legislative process to impose binding rules and interpretations. The agencies thereby return to extralegal governance, which is precisely what constitutional law developed in the seventeenth century to prevent.

Multiple Modes of Legislation

As in the past, the extralegal legislation comes in different forms. Much of it developed already in the first half of the twentieth century, but it currently enjoys its authority under—or at least in the context of—the 1946 Administrative Procedure Act. Rather than establish a single model of administrative lawmaking, this statute opens up opportunities for a series of approaches, and after more than a half century of evolving practices, there now are multiple modes of administrative legislation.

Cascade of Evasions

Administrative lawmaking comes in many types of rulemaking and interpretation, and each type functions as an evasion of the others. When Congress and other institutions have tightened up one mode, agencies have simply turned to other modes. As a result, administrative legislation has developed as a cascade of evasions—initially an evasion of law, but then a series of evasions within administrative lawmaking.

The most formal mode of administrative lawmaking is "formal rulemaking," which is made on the basis of a record developed at an administrative hearing similar to a trial. On account of the adjudicatory model, interested parties can attend and even can present evidence and cross-examine opposing witnesses.[1] Of course, an adjudicatory model for extralegal lawmaking may not seem intuitive, but it is not unique, for (as will be recalled from chapter 4) the Star Chamber often issued regulations in the form of decrees.

Although this formal, adjudicatory-style rulemaking never was the predominant mode of administrative rulemaking, it remained central until mid-1960s, when agencies sought modes that allowed them to churn out regulations more rapidly. Formal rulemaking still is conventional only for setting rates for utilities and common carriers.

Similar to this formal rulemaking is formal adjudication. On its face, it merely concludes with adjudicatory decisions. The resulting decisions, however, are considered binding in the manner of precedent, and they thereby serve to make policy that functions like legislation. The National Labor Relations Board relies entirely on this mode of legislation, probably to avoid committing itself to general rules, and to escape effective judicial review. More typically, agencies rely on formal adjudication in specialized circumstances, often when granting licenses.[2]

In their search for a bureaucratically simpler approach, many agencies in the late sixties and the seventies increasingly relied on "informal rulemaking." In this mode, an agency must give notice of its plan to adopt a rule by publishing the details and supporting data in the *Federal Register*. The agency also must give an opportunity for public comment, even if merely by allowing written submissions. This therefore is often called "notice and comment" rulemaking, and the rules that are adopted in this manner are considered binding on the public.[3]

Beyond informal rulemaking are the variations on it. More onerous than the standard version is hybrid rulemaking, which is informal rulemaking with the addition of extra procedures, usually added by acts of Congress. Less onerous, and especially significant, are approaches that allow agencies to escape some rulemaking procedures (such as notice and comment) as long as the agency acts with "good cause." This could be called "very informal rulemaking."[a] Of course, these modes of rulemaking—formal, in-

a. For example, the Administrative Procedure Act allows an agency to make a rule immediately effective, without complying with the notice-and-comment requirements, where the agency "for good cause" finds that these procedures "are impracticable, unnecessary, or contrary to the public interest." Sometimes, when an agency finds "good cause" to make a rule immediately effective, it will call it an "interim final rule" and then will adjust it with more

formal, hybrid, and very informal—are only general categories, for within each there are many different versions, which vary from agency to agency.

Not content with government-proposed rules, agencies sometimes simply arrange "negotiated rulemaking," in which an agency meets with carefully selected members of the affected industries, and sometimes also a few public interest groups, to draft a regulation by consensus before the agency adopts it. One way or another, agencies use the devolution of lawmaking to co-opt potential opposition before a rule is even issued, thus securing a unified front for regulation that might otherwise have been opposed by the interests not included at the table.[4] The overall effect is to attract support for regulation by giving cooperative institutions the power to impose their will on others, including weaker competitors. Rather than government though law, or even simply government outside law, this is a return to the medieval practice of establishing a lawmaking concordat or cartel with influential private or international institutions.[b]

Indeed, agencies often leave lawmaking to bodies altogether outside the government. For example, agencies give this power to trade associations, professional associations, producers cooperatives, and international bodies (such as the World Trade Organization). The result is the privatizing and even the internationalizing of legislative power.

Apart from rulemaking, agencies also increasingly regulate through their interpretations. In the 1980s, after the courts strengthened the procedural protections in informal rulemaking, agencies avoided the procedures required for informal and even very informal rulemaking by expanding their use of lawmaking interpretation. To qualify as interpretation, and thus avoid rulemaking procedures, a putative interpretation must be derivable from the statute it implements and must avoid making too substantial a change in policy. Worried about the extent of the evasion, the Supreme Court has indicated that courts will defer to an agency's interpretation only when the agency follows its authorized procedures for making binding

---

formal modifications when it has time for notice and comment. To avoid even the good cause requirement for making rules rapidly, agencies also have developed "direct final rulemaking." In this approach, an agency can publish a rule in the *Federal Register*, with the explanation that it will become effective as a final rule in 30 days unless an adverse comment is received within that time—in which case the rule will be withdrawn. At that point, the agency can republish the rule under normal notice-and-comment procedures.*

b. On account of the "private participation in the administrative process," Walter Gellhorn claims that "administrative bodies can and very frequently do democratize our governmental processes." Government selected participants, however, are not substitutes for publicly elected representatives. For more on the supposedly democratic character of notice-and-comment regulation, see chapter 19, footnote b.*

rules—most commonly, by adopting its interpretation in the manner of informal rulemaking, with notice and comment.[5] Yet the Court's requirement has merely accelerated the shift to other forms of interpretation.

To escape even the notice-and-comment requirement for lawmaking interpretation, agencies increasingly make law simply by declaring their views about what the public should do. Agencies, for example, offer "guidance," propose "best practices," declare "policy," give "advice," take positions in briefs, or make naked demands—all of which is done with the unmistakable hint that it is advisable to comply. These statements officially are not binding on the public, and they usually evade even the notice and comment required for lawmaking interpretation.[c] Nonetheless, the Supreme Court has not rejected these statements, but rather has said that they deserve "respect" as interpretations of statutes. Of course, most statements of guidance, policy, etc. are not really interpretations of any statute. On the theory that they are interpretations, however, they tend to be backed up by the courts, thus enabling agencies (as put by John Manning) "to make an end run" around their other modes of lawmaking.[6]

As a practical matter, it is not always predictable whether guidance, etc. will get judicial "respect." Agencies therefore often enforce such demands with "arm-twisting"—something that (as will be seen in chapter 13) often amounts to extortion.[7] But with or without arm-twisting, guidance and other such modes of "interpretation" are a mode of evasion, which is difficult to reconcile with the Supreme Court's view that they are entitled to respect.

Last but not least, agencies often engage in lawmaking by granting waivers. Although waivers will be considered separately, later in this chapter, it already should be recognized that agencies often use them not simply to excuse compliance with their rules, but more ambitiously to formulate policy and thereby make law.[8] Through waivers, the exceptions become the rule.

This cascade of evasions creates many modes of administrative lawmak-

---

c. The Office of Management and Budget has published its own guidance, establishing "best practices" for the guidance given by other agencies. In particular, the OMB guidance requires agencies to comply with notice-and-comment requirements for their guidance. There are ample loopholes, however, and in any case, the requirements apply only to "economically significant" guidance—that which can reasonably be anticipated to lead to "an annual effect on the economy of $100 million or more." As a result, agencies still can issue guidance without notice and comment on a vast range of matters that, although not "significant" to OMB, are of profound significance to many Americans.*

ing, all of which revert to the extralegal lawmaking of the prerogative era. The initial administrative evasion was the shift from acts of Congress to agency rules, but it obviously has not ended there. Each administrative lawmaking procedure has spawned further evasions—the irony being that once one allows one extralegal mode, others develop alongside, thus creating a series of extralegal modes, each undermining the others. The result is not only legislative power outside the law but also outside administrative rulemaking, and then outside administrative interpretation, and so forth, hopefully not ad infinitum.

Determinations

Some specialized types of administrative legislation require further attention—for example, determinations that make law. These determinations echo the old determinations of facts, in which an executive officer determined a factual question that was a condition of a statute's application. Rather than being exercises of mere discernment or judgment, however, the newer style determinations often include overt exercises of lawmaking will.

Such determinations arise under statutes that leave plenty of room for lawmaking. For example, the administrator of the Environmental Protection Agency is required to specify the application of the EPA's ambient air quality standards by publishing a list of air pollutants that "in his judgment, cause or contribute to air pollution which may reasonably be anticipated to endanger public health or welfare."[9] Although statutes of this sort speak in terms of determinations and judgments, they provide for determinations of questions so abstract or loosely stated that the agencies inevitably must engage in policy choices—in legislative will rather than mere judgment.

As put by Justice Thurgood Marshall in a 1970 dissent, "the factual issues with which the Secretary [of Labor] must deal are frequently not subject to any definitive resolution," for "[c]ausal connections and theoretical extrapolations may be uncertain," and "when the question involves determination of the acceptable level of risk, the ultimate decision must necessarily be based on considerations of policy, as well as empirically verifiable facts." Thus, "[t]he decision to take action in conditions of uncertainty bears little resemblance to . . . empirically verifiable factual conclusions."[10] In such instances, factual determinations become exercises of lawmaking will.

Penalties and Taxes

Other specialized types of administrative legislation concern penalties and taxes. As in the era of the prerogative, administrative bodies set penalties and taxes outside rather than through the law.

Administrative rules often set the penalties for regulatory violations. The enactment of penalties traditionally was a legislative task, for the imposition of the constraint was legislative, and a penalty was simply the final measure of a constraint. Thus, when James I legislated through proclamations, the House of Commons protested against "[p]roclamations penned with penalties, in form of penal statutes."[11] Nonetheless, administrative rules return to imposing penalties outside rather than through the law.

In addition to these penalties are extralegal taxes. After 1808, when the constitutional problem was pointed out, early tariff statutes (with only an occasional deviation) authorized the president merely to exercise his judgment in determining either acts of state or relatively concrete factual conditions—such as whether a foreign nation's tariffs no longer discriminated against American goods. Such provisions, however, eventually became open ended and authorized the president himself to suspend the law. The 1890 tariff act moved far in this direction by authorizing the president, by proclamation, "to suspend" the statute's allowance of duty-free imports "whenever and so often" as he deemed the duties imposed by exporting countries to be "reciprocally unequal and unreasonable." After the Supreme Court upheld this, Congress in the early twentieth century went even further in authorizing the president to determine tariffs. Nowadays, Congress allows these questions to be decided by the Commerce Department and even the World Trade Organization.[12]

Administrative taxation also can be discerned in administrative fees. Agencies use their regulations to impose a wide range of fees, many of which are taxes in all but name. Of course, some user fees are simply sales of government property, which are comparable to private fees for the use of similar private property, and some service fees are simply sales of services, which also are comparable to private fees. Many administrative fees, however, particularly many licensing fees, are not for government property or services, but instead are for covering the expenses of government and thus are really taxes. They are taxes imposed by agency fiat rather than act of Congress.[d]

---

d. Some agencies excuse such fees on the theory that regulation is a "service" for which an agency can charge its clients. For example, when the Department of Labor proposed in 1993

Nuisances

Administrative agencies sometimes exercise legislative and judicial power through their appropriation of the law of nuisance. Although this version of extralegal power is less common in the federal government than in state and municipal governments, it reveals yet another way in which administrative power returns to the prerogative.

The Star Chamber, it will be recalled, had legislated by declaring various types of tenements to be a "public nuisance" and then had proceeded against them in its judicial proceedings. After the abolition of the Star Chamber, however, the Crown could neither legislate public nuisances nor adjudicate them. Similarly, in America, although executives or private persons could initiate the prosecution of public nuisances, legislation on the subject belonged to state or municipal legislatures, and adjudication belonged to the courts. As a result, state and municipal executive officers on their own, even when organized into boards of health, typically had no more than a power of abatement, which they could exercise only at the risk of being sued if they removed or destroyed what was not in fact a nuisance, or if they destroyed more property than was necessary.[13]

State statutes and town ordinances, however, increasingly authorized boards of health to ordain or declare what constituted a public nuisance. Continental boards of health, especially as developed in Germany, enjoyed vigorous administrative powers; and after Parliament in 1848 created Anglicized versions of these boards, American states followed suit.[14] In order to put the administrative power of the German boards in common law terms, the English and especially the American statutes gave their boards a power to legislate and adjudicate on nuisances—thereby giving a common law appearance to what was really extralegal power. Boards of health thus became the bodies that first accustomed numerous Americans to administrative power.

State statutes usually distinguished the legislative and judicial powers of boards of health. The statutes established legislative power by authorizing boards to make ordinances for the preservation of public health and against public nuisances. The states also established extralegal judicial

---

that the Mine Safety and Health Administrative should charge for approving mine operation plans, evaluating dust samples, and certifying miners, it admitted that this is "likely to result in costs being passed along to consumers." It theorized, however, that it was providing "services" to the mine industry, and on this fiction justified the "service fees," arguing that "this would mean that the cost of these materials will more accurately reflect the full cost of their production."*

power by authorizing the boards to declare any particular building, condition, business, or other activity a public nuisance, and to order it abated, and where these declarations enjoyed any deference in subsequent litigation, they were a sort of judicial power. Recognizing the trespass on the judicial role, the statutes typically required boards of health to give notice and hold hearings. State legislatures, such as that of New York, thus gave legislative and judicial nuisance powers to local boards, most notably in 1866 to the Metropolitan Board of Health.[15]

The New York Court of Appeals soon upheld the legislative power of the boards. In an 1868 case, it justified the Metropolitan Board's regulations against driving cattle through the streets, and against slaughtering cattle in southern Manhattan.[16]

The judicial power of the health boards, however, was another matter. The court in 1868 left this question for another day—although with dicta that the power to declare and abate nuisances was really "not judicial in its character" and was better understood as "an administrative duty." But when this power came before the court again in 1893, it asked, "how can these provisions conferring powers upon boards of health to interfere with and destroy property, and to impose penalties and create crimes, stand with the constitution, securing to every person due process of law before his property or personal rights or liberty can be interfered with?" Rather than a matter of substantive due process, this was, as in so many cases, a question as to how administrative process could displace a court's due process.[17, e]

Over the long term, however, such objections did not prevail, and boards of health thus acquired a combination of legislative and judicial power over nuisances. The boards were said by courts to have the power to destroy per se nuisances and "inherently harmful" property, without due

---

e. The court, in other words, rejected the proposition that "the determinations of the board of health as to the existence of nuisances" were "final and conclusive upon the owners of the premise where they are alleged to exist." On the contrary, "whoever abates an alleged nuisance, and thus destroys or injures private property, or interferes with private rights, whether he be a public officer or a private person, unless he acts under the judgment or order of a court having jurisdiction, does it at his peril." Thus, "when his act is challenged in the regular judicial tribunals it must appear that thing abated was in fact a nuisance."

The court added: "It may be said that if the determination of a board of health as to a nuisance be not final and conclusive, then the members of the board, and all persons acting under their authority in abating the alleged nuisance, act at their peril; and so they do, and no other view of the law would give adequate protection to private rights. They should not destroy property as a nuisance unless they know it to be such, and, if there be doubt as to whether it be a nuisance or not, the board should proceed by action to restrain or abate the nuisance, and thus have the protection of a judgment for what it may do."*

process. More profoundly, executive due process, consisting of notice and a hearing, increasingly seemed to avoid the need for judicial due process. Boards of health and other such bodies thus came to enjoy not only the legislative power over nuisances but also in the associated judicial power— both of which traditionally had been asserted in the worst of the prerogative courts.[18]

Licensing

Another specialized legislative path taken by administrative agencies is licensing. Although this is an increasingly common mode of administrative lawmaking, it is not well understood.[f]

A license (as seen in chapter 6) generally is a grant of a mere privilege, and the executive therefore does not, on the whole, exercise legislative power when it issues regulations stipulating the conditions on which it will grant licenses. This book consequently makes no objection to the licensing of access to government services, property, money, or information. But in many instances (as also seen in chapter 6), the executive grants licenses that offer relief from constraints on the public, and in these circumstances the licenses are part of a system of constraint.

This distinction between different licensing schemes is familiar from some free speech cases. Whereas a license to use a government resource (such as a government building) is treated in the manner of a mere privilege, a license to use public or common property (such as the sidewalk) is understood to be a means of demarcating the constraint on its use. Thus, in the speech cases, although the license to use a government resource does not ordinarily provoke free speech concerns, the license to use public or common property can directly collide with the First Amendment's speech guarantee.[g] The distinction, however, is not always so clearly recognized.

---

f. Incidentally, licensing is assumed here to include accreditation, certification, and zoning. Although these mechanisms often are distinguished from licensing, they similarly require one to get permission to escape a general constraint, and they therefore are recognized here as versions of licensing.

g. The distinction also is connected to equal protection cases such as *Rosenberger v. University of Virginia*. Although tax funds can be distributed unequally, assessment moneys cannot. The reason is that, unlike the distribution of tax funds, the allocation of moneys collected by assessment is so closely tied to the underlying constraint—the collection of the money—that the allocation is considered part of a constraining scheme, thus making it subject to the same legal limits. As a result, the discriminatory allocation of student fees creates a core equal protection problem.

Administrative agencies therefore have often been able to enjoy the legitimacy of one sort of licensing while actually exercising the other.

The result has been an easy path to extralegal legislative power. When issuing licenses in a system of constraint, officers traditionally had to confine themselves to making determinations or judgments, lest they stray into the legislative realm, and even when they merely made determinations, there was a profound risk in placing so much power in a largely unaccountable individual. Now, however, even in the context of constraints, officers often make policy decisions when issuing licenses. Indeed, they often promulgate regulations stating the availability of the licenses, and thereby the reach of the constraints, thus openly engaging in extralegal legislation.

Traditionally, however, licensing was expected to be a matter of discernment rather than will, and Congress did not authorize executive licensing regulations domestically in the context of constraints. To be precise, it has been seen (in chapter 6) that, although Congress in the nineteenth century allowed local licensing regulations, it authorized the executive to issue licensing regulations in the context of constraint only for enemy aliens, and for cross-border or offshore matters in which federal law often was not binding.

Since then, however, domestic legislation through licensing regulations has become commonplace. For example, although the airwaves are shared or common property rather than government property, Congress since 1934 has barred broadcasting without a license from the Federal Communications Commission, and the FCC grants licenses only where the licensees comply with FCC conditions (including conditions limiting speech).[19] The licenses, in other words, are part of a system of constraint, and the regulations imposing the conditions therefore are legislative in character.

Administrative legislation thus comes in many forms, including administrative rules, interpretations, penalties, taxes, declarations of public nuisances, and licensing regulations. Whatever the form, it all returns to extralegal legislation. Although this time it is administrative rather than prerogative, it reverts to lawmaking outside the law and thus to a danger that constitutions carefully barred.

Administrative Waivers

After administrators adopt a burdensome rule, they sometimes write letters to favored persons telling them that, notwithstanding the rule, they need not comply. In other words, the return of extralegal legislation has been accompanied by the return of the dispensing power, this time under the rubric of "waivers."[h]

Indeed, agencies sometimes grant the waivers to all persons subject to the waived requirements, thus using the waivers to suspend the requirements altogether. The revived dispensing power is thereby also used to revive the suspending power.

The very form of waivers harks back to dispensations. As when kings granted such things, they still come with non obstante clauses. In other words, they do not give permission to engage in specified conduct, but instead carefully inform recipients that they need not comply with a specified rule.

It is the substance of waivers, however, that is so disturbing. Like dispensations, waivers go far beyond the usual administrative usurpation of legislative or judicial power, for they do not involve lawmaking or adjudication, let alone executive force. On the contrary, they are a fourth power—one carefully not recognized by the Constitution.

Different from Special Legislation, Pardons, and Prosecutorial Discretion

Waivers often are justified by analogy to special legislation, pardons, or prosecutorial discretion. As in the prerogative past, however, waivers are very different.

When Congress uses special legislation to exempt persons from statutory duties, it at least works through other legislation. In contrast, when agencies release persons from regulatory duties, they do not act through

---

h. Although both licenses and waivers provide relief from otherwise binding law, they are different. As explained by Ernst Freund, "the licensing power sets or assumes a standard, while the dispensing power sanctions a deviation from a standard. There are borderline cases in which the two classes of power shade into each other, but on the whole they perform different functions."

Even when waivers are used to suspend statutory requirements, they are not the same as the power exercised by some agencies, under their authorizing statutes, to issue regulations modifying statutory requirements. When the latter power, astonishing even by administrative standards, first developed in England, the authorizing provisions were known as "Henry VIII clauses." An American example can be observed in the Communications Act.

Note also that this book's arguments reach only the waivers that offer relief from binding administrative or statutory rules, and there consequently are mixed implications for the waivers that adjust conditions on benefits. Some statutory conditions on benefits may be binding on the recipients, and in all such instances the waivers that adjust the conditions revive the dispensing power. Where conditions are not binding, however, waivers of the conditions do not revive that power.*

additional regulations, but through mere waiver letters. Rather than publicly alter the rules through additional rules, they privately excuse compliance by mere fiat. They thus offer private relief from public duties.[i]

Waivers or dispensations also are different from pardons. Royal dispensations and pardons were almost identical; they were drafted in the same form, and they did almost the same thing. Yet dispensations were widely viewed with horror, for whereas a pardon excused a person after he violated the law, a dispensation excused him beforehand, thus relieving him not merely of the law's penalty, but of its obligation.[20] Similarly, nowadays, waivers are much more dangerous than pardons, for they offer prior dispensation from the very obligation of the law, not merely after-the-fact abatement of its penalty.

Along the same lines, a waiver works very differently from a prosecutor's discretion to refrain from bringing charges against an individual. Whereas prosecutorial discretion spares criminals from punishment after they violate the law, a dispensation—what nowadays is called a "waiver"—purports to relieve persons from the obligation of the law itself, and it does this even before the law is violated.

Although it may be thought that a prosecutor comes close when he systematically underenforces a law, he cannot guarantee relief from the obligation of the law itself, and this is profoundly important. Consider, for example, the position of a large corporation that seeks to depart from environmental standards under federal law. If the corporation can secure a waiver, it has a guarantee, but if it must rely on a prosecutor's discretion, it has no guarantee from him, let alone other federal prosecutors in other

---

i. An early advocate of administrative law, Ernst Freund, candidly admitted that one advantage of a waiver was that "it permits relaxation without disclosing its object." He explained that where "a general policy of prohibition may have to be relaxed under exceptional circumstances," the law "may vest an appropriate dispensing power in administrative authorities." As exercised by the Crown, this power "was finally declared illegal in the seventeenth century," and it "is not claimed in America as an executive power." Nonetheless, "a similar power" is "conferred by legislation upon administrative officials."

Freund recognized that even in the most exigent circumstances, "[e]mergency dispensations" were thought to "to break down the law" and "are consequently avoided." At the same time, he defended administrative dispensations in less pressing circumstances, explaining that "[m]ost newly formulated restrictive policies bring temporary hardships to legitimate interests." Personally, he thought "[w]e should be adverse to granting such power to an administrative official, but prefer to specify the exemptions in the law." Nonetheless, he recognized the drift of administrative power. When Congress authorized administrative rules, it usually was setting out on a venture of unpredictable success and scope, and Congress therefore almost inevitably authorized "the dispensing power," for this "reflects the legislative sense of uncertainty of the wisdom or practical enforceability of the law."*

districts. Moreover, if it can get a waiver, it need not worry about departing from the law, but if it relies on a prosecutor's discretion, its departure from the environmental standards still are violations, and even where the corporation escapes prosecution, it still may be subject to civil actions. In short, waivers go much further than prosecutorial discretion, for they return to an assurance that one need not follow the law.

Waivers thus are not analogous to special legislation, pardons, or prosecutorial discretion. Such things may be worrisome, but waivers are much worse.

Different from Equity

Another analogy that is sometimes used to justify waivers is equity. Equity can be understood to carve out exceptions from law, and undoubtedly waivers also create exceptions. This is not to say, however, that waivers should be respected as instruments of equity.

Whereas equity comes in cases, waivers come prior to any case or controversy. They thus amount to a direct power over legislation rather than a power of equity. Equity, moreover, was decided by judges in an exercise of discernment or judgment, and the U.S. Constitution gives the judicial power in law and equity to the courts. Administrative waivers, on the other hand, come from executive officers and usually are exercises of will. Indeed, they sometimes are candidly a method of making policy.

When judges find equitable exceptions from rules of law, they are carving out exceptions from rules that they do not make. To be precise, judges discern equitable exceptions to rules laid down by statute or inherited in common law, not rules that they make or directly control. When administrators, however, issue waivers, they both make the rules and carve out the exceptions. Rather than exercise equity to avoid the injustice of a rule they do not control, they use waivers to adjust rules they themselves enacted. The waivers thus look less like equitable exceptions than like a power to dispense with legislation.

Ultimately, the view that waivers are equitable exceptions from rules rests on a gross misunderstanding of Anglo-American equity. According to a tradition that dates back to Aristotle, equity avoids the injustice of rules by offering exceptions in individual instances. Since the seventeenth century, however, as will be seen in chapter 8, equity has more typically consisted of a subsidiary system of rules within the law's broader system of rules. From this perspective, the justice done in equity involves subsidiary rules or principles rather than the sort of justice that cannot be reduced to generalities.

Thus, instead of carving out exceptions in individual instances, it ordinarily offers alternative generalizations in standardized circumstances.

Equity thus fails both as a constitutional justification and as an analogy. Obviously, when the Constitution grants the judicial power in equity to the courts, it does not justify any power in executive officers. And the Constitution's grant of the judicial power in equity offers a particularly feeble support for waivers, because these are not even claimed to be an exercise of the judicial power, let alone of mere judgment. What remains is merely the use of equity as an analogy—an analogy that provides an ill-defined excuse for departing from rules. This is not equity as an element of judicial power and the jurisdiction of a court; nor is it even the equitable reasoning that actually was employed in equity. Instead, it is merely an attempt to claim the legitimacy of equity for something very different—namely, the old dispensing power. If one is going to rely on legal tradition to understand a contemporary practice, one should acknowledge the relevant tradition.

Only Rules, Not Law

In justification of waivers, it often is said agencies use them to excuse compliance with administrative rules rather than law—as if this cured the problem. This excuse, however, collides with both the reality of the waivers and the theory of administrative law.

Although the waivers of administrative rules ostensibly excuse compliance with the rules, they often actually excuse compliance with the underlying statutes. Sometimes waivers directly offer relief from a statutory requirement, but more typically they do this through their effect on regulations.[21] Statues frequently require the public to comply with a standard or principle, which administrative agencies then elaborate in their rules. Accordingly, when agencies tell persons that they need not adhere to the rules, they often also end up excusing them from following the statute. For example, although the Affordable Care Act required so-called mini-med insurers to provide guaranteed levels of insurance, the Department of Health and Human Services gave waivers to favored corporations, relieving them of the duty to meet the regulatory and thus also the statutory levels.[22]

Even when waivers dispense merely with administrative rules, they nonetheless dispense with what, in administrative theory, is a type of legislation. The entire theory of administrative law is based on the assumption that agencies exercise a delegated legislative power. If administrative rules are a form of binding legislation, then it is difficult to understand how waivers are not an attempt to dispense with the law.

Only Three Types of Federal Power

It may be thought that waivers are a sort of delegated legislative power. The U.S. Constitution, however, authorizes only three types of power, none of which includes a power to excuse persons from the obligation of law.

When administrative agencies grant waivers from their regulations, they sometime act with congressional authority, and sometimes without it. It will be recalled (from chapter 5) that although the 1689 English Declaration of Rights condemned dispensations, it left open the possibility that Parliament could authorize them. Parliament, however, did not grant such authorization, for the dispensing power came to be recognized as a power incompatible with the constitutional allocation of powers.

Once the legislature had made a law, much rested with the Crown. The Crown could perhaps show restraint in enforcing the law; certainly in many instances it could pardon offenders after they had violated the law. But no part of government—not the legislature, the courts, or the Crown—could simply relieve a subject of the obligation of an enactment while it remained in effect and thus a law.

Even more clearly than the English constitution, the U.S. Constitution establishes only three powers: A legislative power to make law, a judicial power to adjudicate cases in accord with law, and an executive power to execute the lawful force of the government. None of these powers includes any authority to excuse persons from law. The power to excuse from law was the old dispensing power, and it simply does not exist in the Constitution.

Of course, as in England, executive power includes a power to grant pardons and perhaps to show restraint in prosecutions, but this does not mean it includes a power to relieve persons from the law itself. The judicial power extends to cases in equity, but waivers do not arise in cases, let alone cases in equity. All that is left is the legislative power, and to excuse someone from a law that is left in place, and that still applies to him, is a far cry from a making law. Nonetheless, agencies issue waivers.

The difficulty of understanding waivers as legislative power—let alone a delegated legislative power—is compounded by their form. Rather than declare new administrative rules, which modify or repeal prior administrative rules, waivers offer relief from rules that concededly remain in effect. Rather than apply to a group identified in general terms, each waiver excuses a specified person, usually a corporation or other such entity. Last but not least, whereas administrative rules mimic the legislative process and are published, waivers appear in letters, sent merely to the privileged recipients, and thus usually are unpublished. Waivers clearly do not even pretend to be a mode of legislation, and they therefore cannot be justified as a type of delegated legislative power.

Recognizing the weakness of the delegation explanation, commentators sometimes restate it in weaker form, saying simply that waivers have congressional authorization. This often is true, but it amounts to a concession that waivers are not a type of legislative power.

The power to waive compliance with law is evidently a fourth sort of power—one not granted by the Constitution to any part of government. Of course, Congress can authorize the executive to exercise a wide range of executive powers that are not inherent in the executive. According to administrative theory, Congress even can rearrange the constitutionally granted powers, primarily by authorizing the executive to exercise legislative and judicial powers. But Congress cannot authorize the executive to exercise a fourth sort of power that the Constitution carefully does not grant to any part of the government.

The Constitution, in other words, authorizes only limited types of power—this being an instance of what has been called the *numerus clausus* principle.[23] The Constitution thereby requires the government to work through the constitutionally authorized powers, not through others.

The resulting exclusion of waivers makes sense. In a government of laws there is no room for a power to excuse compliance with the law. And especially in a government limited to legislative, judicial, and executive powers, no amount of congressional authorization can constitutionalize this fourth, lawless power.

Dangers

Waivers or dispensations are profoundly dangerous. They were widely recognized as a threat already in the Middle Ages, and nowadays the danger is even greater.

Administrative waivers are more dangerous than the old dispensing power, for even that power could not relieve persons of duties or penalties they owed to third parties or that were *mala in se*. In contrast, administrative waivers are without any such limitations. They thus return not merely to dispensations, but to the barbaric early version of dispensations, before late medieval doctrine limited them to situations in which they would not interfere with the rights of others.

Waivers also are more lawless than most other prerogative or administrative power. When the government grants a waiver or dispensation, it does not act through law or even a delegated lawmaking power, and yet it purports to liberate the recipient from the law. In other words, when the government grants a waiver, it acts outside law to permit others to act above the law, thus making waivers doubly lawless.

Among the more concrete dangers is favoritism. One may assume that when the executive waives compliance with a law, it will grant waivers only to the most deserving applicants. Inevitably, however, it will find deserving applicants among those who have close contact with the administration, including many who are politically aligned with it.

Making matters worse, the executive tends to use waivers to co-opt political support for politically insupportable laws. When Americans are subject to severe legislation, they can unite to seek its repeal. All persons subject to a harsh law ordinarily must comply with it and will therefore cooperate to fight it. Waivers, however, allow the executive to preserve such legislation by offering relief to the most powerful of those who might demand repeal, thereby purchasing their nonresistance at the cost of other Americans.[24] Waivers thus shift the cost of objectionable laws from the powerful to others, with the overall effect of entrenching oppressive laws.

Most generally, waivers endanger equal freedom under law. The ideal that the law is the measure of freedom and equality under government has sometimes seemed elusive, but it remains one of the blessings of American society. And it has implications for waivers. Although the government can, to a degree, adopt laws that limit freedom and equality, it cannot act outside the law to excuse selected Americans from a law that applies to them. In terms of equality, the government cannot act outside the law to give some Americans a freedom from law, for this would deprive others of equality under law.

Waivers thus revert to a particularly lawless mode of prerogative power. Not merely an extralegal lawmaking power, they are an extralegal power to undo the law without even adopting extralegal legislation. They thus restore the dispensing power (and even sometimes the suspending power). Chapter 20 will show in more detail how waivers have been defended as a delegated exercise of legislative power. Already here, however, it should be apparent that they are not even an extralegal exercise of legislative power. Thus, even if Congress could delegate its legislative power, it cannot delegate a power it does not have.[j]

---

j. Much more could be said about waivers. Although waivers often are justified on the ground that they offer relief from excessive regulatory burdens, waivers also invite such burdens, for they permit congressional and administrative lawmakers to escape the political consequences of drafting onerous laws. Lawmakers ordinarily have reason to worry about imposing severe rules. Waivers, however, remove the incentives for moderation. Indeed, because of waiv-

⋘⋘⋘

In sum, part I has shown that administrative law revives prerogative legislation, together with the prerogative of suspending and dispensing with law—thus restoring an extralegal regime of making and unmaking law. And lest it be thought that this is improbable, it should be recalled that some leading advocates of administrative law candidly admitted that their project was to return to prerogative power. John Dickinson, for example, observed that "the question of whether or not the king can issue ordinances parallels our modern question as to whether or not an executive body or officer can establish regulations; and the arguments used *pro* and *con* have followed much the same lines."[25]

Put more theoretically, administrative lawmaking is not a power exercised through law, but a power outside it. Indeed, as will become more fully apparent in part III, it is a power above the law. But even when considered simply as a power outside the law, this extralegal regime revives what once was considered absolute power.

Administrative law thus returns to the very sort of power that constitutions developed in order to prohibit. The prerogative to issue law-like commands was the primary point of contention in the English constitutional struggles of the seventeenth century. In response, the English developed a constitution and Americans enacted a constitution that placed all legislative power in the legislature. It therefore is mistaken to assume that American administrative law is a novel mode of governance, which could not have been anticipated or barred by the U.S. Constitution. On the contrary, administrative power revives extralegal rulemaking, interpretation, dispensing, and suspending, and thus almost the entire regime of extralegal lawmaking once associated with absolute prerogative power. It thereby restores what constitutions barred when they located legislative power in their legislatures.

---

ers, the executive can find advantages in harsh regulations, for it thereby acquires the opportunity to issue waivers, with which it can reward its allies and create a sense of dependency in all who need relief.

Waivers also are sometimes justified with hints that the problems could be cured with transparency and consequent opportunities for accountability. It is not obvious, however, how transparency would really avoid the dangers of power above the law, favoritism, inequality, entrenching bad laws, perverse legislative incentives, and the inability of Congress to delegate what it itself cannot do. Nor is it clear how transparency would make unlawful executive acts lawful. Even if transparency could do all of this, it thus far has been largely absent. Little is known about the political realities of getting waivers.*

PART II

Extralegal Adjudication

Having examined extralegal lawmaking in part I, this book in part II must turn to extralegal adjudication—the exercise of judicial power not through the judgments of the courts, but outside them. As with lawmaking, so with adjudication, there has been an administrative reversion to extralegal power.[a]

The immediate constitutional difficulties are institutional and procedural—that administrative adjudication collides with the Constitution's grant of the judicial power to the courts, and with its due process and jury requirements—points that have been aptly observed in the scholarly literature (for example, by Gary Lawson and Caleb Nelson).[1] There is more to be said, however, for the threat comes not merely from the evasion of the courts and their proceedings, but more profoundly from the extralegal exercise of judicial power, and even simply to understand the extent of the

---

a. Legislative and judicial edicts traditionally bound in different ways, and although the differences are intuitive, they may be worth spelling out. Laws sometimes were said to be rules in the sense that they were general, but they also were understood to be rules in the sense that, prototypically, they were generally binding on the society. In contrast, judicial edicts were prototypically binding as orders in particular cases, usually directed to particular persons. For example, whereas a legislature could generally bind the society by prohibiting specified conduct, a court could order an individual in a case to pay for engaging in the conduct, and even sometimes could enjoin him not to do it. As put by St. George Tucker in the early 1790s, "the legislative power may be defined to be the power of making laws, or general rules in all cases not prohibited by the Constitution: the application of these rules to particular cases being the province of the judiciary."

The differences were evident in court. Being the command of a court in a particular instance, a judicial order could be enforced by holding a disobedient person in contempt of court. Being directed to the public as a whole, a statute (even if mere private legislation) was enforceable only by the commencement of a prosecution or cause of action.*

constitutional problems, one must first understand this underlying danger, the revival of absolute power.

To enforce a system of extralegal power in a system of law, rulers must work through extralegal adjudication. The prerogative regime therefore relied on its prerogative courts, and these days the administrative regime relies on its administrative tribunals.

The historical depth of the danger from administrative tribunals was recognized a century ago by Roscoe Pound. Looking back at the seventeenth century, he observed: "It seemed that judicial justice, administered in courts, was to be superseded by executive justice, administered in administrative tribunals or by administrative officers. In other words, there was a reaction from justice according to law to justice without law, in this respect entirely parallel to the present movement away from the common-law courts in the United States."[2]

Adding to the general danger of extralegal adjudication are myriad associated threats to judicial processes and rights—threats that once were safely buried in the past but now have resurfaced. For example, administrative courts, like their prerogative predecessors, have neither juries nor real judges; they employ inquisitorial process rather than due process; they trespass on criminal jurisdiction and the rights of criminal defendants; they create problems similar to those of general warrants; they employ systematically biased discovery and burdens of persuasion and proof. These problems may seem surprising to advocates of administrative law, but they are exactly what one would expect from an extralegal system of adjudication.

The English barred both extralegal adjudication and the associated threat to process and rights. Throughout the Middle Ages, they repeatedly insisted on the due process of law and other procedural rights and eventually, in the seventeenth century, gave them a constitutional foundation. In the same century, they further impeded extralegal adjudication by concluding that their constitution placed the judicial power in the courts. Recognizing the power of these solutions, Americans in the next century adopted them. Thus, just as the U.S. Constitution cut off one sort of extralegal power by giving legislative power to Congress and defining legislative process, it precluded the other sort by giving judicial power to the courts and guaranteeing rights of judicial process—preeminently, the due process of law. As a result, the government could issue directives legally binding or constraining its subjects only through the acts of the legislature and the acts (including the due process) of the courts.

In partial defense of administrative adjudication, it is suggested that the Constitution's procedural processes and rights apply principally to adjudications in the courts. From this perspective, these constitutional limits extend to administrative adjudications only in a secondary and weakened way. Constitutional law on judicial power, however, developed mostly in response to extralegal adjudication, whether called "prerogative" or "administrative," and constitutional law therefore limited all exercises of judicial power, whether in the courts or elsewhere. Accordingly, when the U.S. Constitution gave judicial power to the courts and stipulated judicial processes and rights, it was not merely empowering and limiting the regular adjudications of the courts; it also, no less centrally, was barring any irregular adjudications outside the courts. The history thus reveals the danger of extralegal adjudication and how the Constitution barred this peril.

Nonetheless, extralegal adjudication has come back to life—as will become apparent here in part II. This part begins with the prerogative version of this power. Chapter 8 examines the extralegal prerogative tribunals; chapter 9 observes the lack of judges and juries in such tribunals; chapter 10 traces their use of inquisitorial process rather than the due process of law; chapter 11 explores prerogative orders and warrants. All along, it will be seen that the extralegal adjudication often had at least an appearance of statutory authorization, but that it nonetheless was considered an exercise of absolute power. These chapters ultimately show that extralegal adjudication (including the abandonment of judges and juries, the departure from the due process of law, and the issuance of extralegal orders and warrants) was repudiated as unconstitutional.

Part II closes by turning to American administrative adjudication. Chapter 12 distinguishes lawful judicial acts from extralegal adjudication, and chapter 13 shows that administrative agencies have revived extralegal adjudication. Finally, chapter 14 wraps up parts I and II by showing how the prerogative path of rule outside the law and the courts was defeated with the constitutional ideal of rule through the law and the courts. On this dual principle, constitutions could preclude all extralegal governance, both legislative and judicial—at least until the principle was forgotten.

EIGHT

Prerogative Courts

The Crown enforced its prerogative legislation through prerogative adjudication. Whether in temporary commissions or the central prerogative courts, the Crown applied its extralegal power through extralegal judicial proceedings.

The English, however, had long been attached to the ideal that the government could issue binding directives in particular instances only through the judgments of the courts. On this principle, they increasingly resisted the Crown's prerogative adjudication, and in the seventeenth century they eventually barred this extralegal power by concluding that their constitution placed judicial power in the courts. Eighteenth-century Americans in their constitutions even more clearly located judicial power in the courts, and they thereby emphatically reiterated the constitutional bar to any extralegal adjudication.

The history thus once again reveals that constitutional law developed to bar the danger of extralegal governance, including, as seen here, extralegal adjudication. It therefore is worrisome that administrative law has revived such adjudication, thus restoring one of the most basic threats that constitutional law prohibited.

The Courts

The Crown needed prerogative courts because the judges of the law courts were bound to decide in accord with the law—to be precise, the law of the land. Although this law authorized and limited the king's regular prerogative power—the royal equivalent of lawful executive power—it did not so clearly authorize his absolute prerogative, and in any case this power was not carried out through law. Accordingly, when the Crown increasingly made open claims for absolute prerogatives, it increasingly sought enforcement in its prerogative tribunals.

The Crown thereby developed a version of what can be recognized as administrative adjudication. In retrospect, it is disconcerting to see how the prerogative tribunals anticipated what would later be done in administrative tribunals, for the leading prerogative bodies were nothing less than the Star Chamber and the High Commission—bodies that have become bywords for cruelty and political oppression. These courts, however, exercised most of their oppression not through political barbarism, but through mundane administrative proceedings, and once this is recognized, it can begin to be understood that adjudication outside the courts remains as dangerous as in the past.

Notwithstanding that judicial power had come to reside in the king's law courts, medieval monarchs repeatedly attempted to use the king's council to exercise some judicial power outside the course of the law and its courts. In this sense, the king's council was the most basic prerogative court. The most prominent prerogative court, however, was the Star Chamber, which (as already noted) developed as a judicial offshoot of the king's council.

The Star Chamber's role in enforcing extralegal constraints is apparent from its jurisdiction over *crimina extraordinaria*. The civil law distinguished between what it called *crimina ordinaria* (or *crimina legitima*) and what it called *crimina extraordinaria*. The former were crimes defined and punished by the ordinary law, and the latter were crimes not recognized by such law—indeed, that "have no peculiar and proper name in law, or else no certain punishment determinately appointed by law."[1] As might be expected, the prosecution of such crimes was one of the Star Chamber's specialities. In the words of a practitioner, the court punished "such things as are necessary in the commonwealth, yea although no positive law or continued custom of common law giveth warrant to it." For example, the court imposed "all punishments of breach of proclamations"—what today would be called breaches of administrative regulations.[2]

Although some of the regulatory violations or *crimina extraordinaria* were obviously political, most were not. All of the extralegal crimes, however, were matters that neither the common law nor Parliament had prohibited, and at least in this sense, they were politically sensitive. Urban planning, monopolies, the standards for clothing, the prices for food and labor, and other economic regulations were bitterly contested questions, which Parliament often hesitated to address. Therefore, when the Star Chamber enforced proclamations or its own regulations on such issues, it was no accident that the legislation occurred outside Parliament or that the enforcement took place outside the adjudications of the law courts.

Like American administrative courts, the Star Chamber seemed to have had some statutory authorization. Parliament often repudiated royal attempts at prerogative justice, but it also recognized that the Star Chamber's summary proceedings might be necessary against local strongmen, whose money corrupted juries and whose armed retainers overwhelmed sheriffs. Most prominently, Parliament in 1487 enacted that the Star Chamber could proceed on its own against such offenders without juries or other common law niceties and could punish them in the same way as if they had been "convicte[d] after the due order of the law."[3] In other words, the statute legitimized irregular proceedings to cure the weakness of regular proceedings. Although the Star Chamber probably had already been recognized as a court, and although the 1487 statute merely authorized it to address a narrow range of offenders, many lawyers came to assume that the statute was the initial foundation of the court and that it authorized the court to conduct wide-ranging proceedings outside the ordinary course of the law.[4]

The other leading prerogative court, the Court of High Commission, was an ecclesiastical tribunal, established largely to enforce conformity to the doctrines of the Church of England. Led by clerics, it applied a range of statutes and administrative religious rules, including royal proclamations and episcopal articles or injunctions. Of course, many of the royal proclamations and episcopal articles went further than what was allowed by Parliament.[5]

The High Commission's ecclesiastical jurisdiction had a statutory foundation in Queen Elizabeth's Act of Uniformity, adopted by Parliament in 1559. This statute authorized the court to impose otherworldly punishments on the public and even to deprive wayward ministers of their livings, but the court was not content with this. Taking a strained interpretation of the Act of Uniformity, it claimed a power to impose temporal punishments (including fines and imprisonment) on temporal persons, thus going beyond its narrowly ecclesiastical jurisdiction.[6] Although some members of Parliament complained, Parliament itself largely acquiesced in this extension of prerogative authority—not unlike Congress's acquiescence in contemporary extensions of administrative authority.

The awkwardness for both the Star Chamber and the High Commission was the growing recognition that the Crown was using these courts to adjudicate outside the judicial power of the regular courts. Once this was widely understood, the claim of legislative authorization or acquiescence would not save the prerogative courts from eventually being condemned as extralegal instruments of extralegal power.

The Unlawfulness of Prerogative Adjudication

The unlawfulness of prerogative adjudication had long been recognized—as can be illustrated by occasional decisions from the Middle Ages onward. These decisions concerned relatively sporadic exercises of extralegal adjudication, and by themselves they could not have determined the fate of bodies such as the Star Chamber or the High Commission, which had at least partial parliamentary authorization. Nonetheless, they reveal that prerogative or administrative adjudication already was in tension with the regular judicial power of the courts of law.

A notable medieval case arose from a 1368 royal commission to two men to seize and imprison another and take his goods. The judges held the commission void, saying it was "against the law" because it authorized the commissioners "to take a man and his goods without indictment, suit of a party, or due process." The decision became a standard citation in arguments against irregular judicial power, including that of the High Commission.[7]

Similar concerns prompted a similar result in *Scroggs' Case*. The dispute concerned the office of the exigenter of London, a clerk of the Court of Common Pleas who prepared writs called "exigents." In 1558, the exigenter of London, Thomas Hemming, died. Shortly afterward, Chief Justice Richard Brooke of Common Pleas also died, without having yet appointed a new exigenter. Queen Mary could not resist the opportunity to fill both offices, and on the same day that she made Anthony Browne the new chief justice, she also granted the place of exigenter to Robert Coleshill, who had previously been "a man of war and a soldier."[8] Shortly afterward, Justice Browne appointed his nephew, Alexander Scroggs.

Queen Mary evidently assumed that her appointment and any judgment about it was a matter of prerogative, which could be decided in a prerogative manner. She therefore appointed a commission, consisting of some judges and others, to hear the dispute between the two claimants. When Scroggs had the temerity to challenge this mode of proceeding, the commission demanded his submission, and upon his refusal, it imprisoned him. Scroggs, however, obtained his freedom on a writ of habeas corpus, and the judges who discharged him explained that the commission was unlawful. (They also held Mary's appointment of Coleshill void and awarded Scroggs the office of exigenter.) Thus, even when the monarch's own interests were at stake, she lacked the power to make "a commission to determine a question of right, depending between two parties."[9]

The danger of adjudications outside the courts arose again in the early seventeenth century, when the Crown authorized local administrative officers to punish offenses against proclamations. Unable to rely on the law courts to enforce its lawmaking proclamations, the Crown tried to use justices of the peace and other local officers. The House of Commons responded by declaring the unlawfulness of issuing "[p]roclamations referring punishment to be done by justices of [the] peace, mayors, bailiffs, constables and other officers." These administrative officers were not judges of courts, and they therefore could not inflict punishments "before lawful trial and punishment."[10] The Crown, in short, could not give judicial power to commissioners or local administrators, for the law gave this to the judges.

Unlawfulness of the Prerogative Courts

The main threat of extralegal judicial power came from the Star Chamber and High Commission. These were the central prerogative tribunals. They therefore are the primary examples of the extralegal judicial power that, although declared unlawful in the seventeenth century, has been revived in the twentieth.

Already at the close of the late sixteenth century, these tribunals encountered resistance. Religious dissenters repeatedly resisted the orders and warrants of the High Commission and complained about its "unjust and unlawful manner of proceeding." Similarly, in the last year of Elizabeth's reign, the Star Chamber worried that it was "a common thing to resist the process of this court, and with disgrace to condemn it, and to beat him who executes it." The common law critique of these courts sometimes even found expression in a sort of parody: When the Star Chamber issued a subpoena against a prisoner in the Marshalsea, the prisoners promptly hauled the serving officer before their lord chief justice—the oldest prisoner—who "adjudged" the officer's cloak "to be forfeited and to be pawned for drink" and further sentenced him to "eat the subpoena."[11]

Although the men and women who refused to comply typically began by protesting the substantive policies of the prerogative courts, they usually also soon objected to the prerogative proceedings. Nor should this be unexpected. Just as the Crown used prerogative courts to impose its prerogative policies, so those who resented the extralegal policies fought back by protesting the extralegal mechanisms used to impose them.[12]

By the early seventeenth century, the unpopular policies enforced by the prerogative courts, and their use of non-common-law proceedings, provoked protests in widely disseminated writings. For example, in a 1607 pamphlet, the bold lawyer Nicholas Fuller challenged the High Commission for imposing ex officio oaths. Although his specific complaints must be left until the next chapter, his general point was that the High Commission bound subjects outside the due course of the law: "That the laws of England are the high inheritance of the realm, by which both the king and the subjects are directed; And that such grants, charters, and commissions, as tend to charge the body, lands, or goods of the subjects, otherwise than according to the due course of the laws of the realm, are not lawful, or of force, unless the same charters and commissions, do receive life and strength, from some act of Parliament."[13] It was enough for Fuller's immediate purposes to conclude that the High Commission's temporal jurisdiction was not authorized by Parliament, but the underlying principle was that the Crown could act against subjects only through the law and its courts.

The complaint that prerogative adjudication bound subjects outside the course of the law eventually took a toll. Apologists for the prerogative courts were accustomed to defending extralegal adjudication on the ground that it was necessary, but because of the growing discontent, they increasingly felt they had to justify it as ordinary or lawful. Attempting to reconcile these conflicting arguments, a treatise on the Star Chamber simultaneously justified it as an "extraordinary and expeditious court" and yet repeatedly strained to show that it was an "ordinary court of judicature."[14] This attempt to assimilate irregular adjudication to regular judicial power was not really plausible, but it suggests how much was changing.

On the eve of the English Civil War, in 1641, Parliament voted to abolish the prerogative courts, beginning with the Star Chamber. Against this tribunal, Parliament recited the provision of Magna Charta that no one was to be deprived of his liberty or property, other than by the judgment of his peers or the law of the land. Parliament then observed that "all matters" that had been decided in Star Chamber could "have their proper remedy and redress . . . by the common law of the land and in the ordinary course of justice." Indeed, when sitting in Star Chamber, the council had "adventured to determine of the estates and liberties of the subject contrary to the law of the land and the rights and privileges of the subject." Parliament therefore enacted that the Star Chamber and "all jurisdiction, power, and authority belonging unto or exercised in the same court" was thenceforth "absolutely dissolved, taken away, and determined."[15]

The High Commission met the same fate. Although, "by color of some words" in the Act of Uniformity, the ecclesiastical commissioners had fined and imprisoned the king's subjects, to their "great and insufferable wrong and oppression," this was an "authority not belonging to ecclesiastical jurisdiction." Parliament therefore repealed the misinterpreted clause in the Act of Uniformity and added that "no . . . persons . . . exercising spiritual or ecclesiastical power, authority, or jurisdiction . . . shall . . . impose or inflict any pain, penalty, fine, amercement, imprisonment, or other corporal punishment upon any of the king's subjects for any . . . thing whatsoever belonging to spiritual or ecclesiastical cognizance or jurisdiction."[16]

In these statutes, Parliament abolished not merely the Star Chamber and the High Commission, but all prerogative adjudication—what has been revived as administrative adjudication. For example, Parliament in its statute against the Star Chamber broadly declared that the property of the subject "ought to be tried and determined in the ordinary courts of justice and by the ordinary course of the law." Thereafter, it was understood (in the words of Roger Twysden) that the king "cannot proceed against any subject, civilly or criminally, but in his ordinary courts of justice, according to the known laws of the land."[17]

Remaining "Prerogative" Courts

Of course, there remained some "prerogative" courts in England. But they were spared the fate of the Star Chamber—for reasons that confirm the unlawfulness of extralegal power in England after 1641.

The king's privy council, from which the Star Chamber had evolved, would long continue to exercise a sort of judicial power. Most notably, it heard appeals in admiralty and from the colonies. It generally, however, avoided domestic jurisdiction and thereby avoided exercising extralegal power.

Taking a different route to safety, the Court of Chancery realigned itself to clarify that it was a court of law. Although the Chancery was well established as a court, it claimed a power that cut against the law, and because it was not, in a sense, a court of law, it sometimes seemed to be a prerogative tribunal. Its power therefore often seemed inconsistent with the principle that subjects could be bound only in the ordinary courts, in accord with the law of the land.

One justification was that the Chancery enforced a law that was higher than the law of the land. Another justification was that it carved out exceptions where the law otherwise would be unjust. Either way, advocates of the Chancery sometimes suggested that the court enjoyed a sort of absolute power—a prerogative power outside and above the law. Such positions, however, increasingly raised questions about the authority of the court, for if it exercised power outside the law, its decisions might lack the force of law.

Beginning around 1618, therefore, chancellors began to trim their sails, fearing that, in pursuing absolutist theories, they might run aground on the law itself. They emphasized that equity was a part of the law of the land rather than a power above it. They also suggested that it consisted of rules and that it deferred to the law. By such means, the Chancery clarified its place within the law and so avoided any question of its being an extralegal court.[18]

Of course, the tendency of equity to depart from rules, especially those of the law, would continue to provoke complaints. Thomas Jefferson, for example, protested that equity should "not interpose in any case which does not come within a general description and admit of redress by a general and practicable rule." Equity, however, was defended, in both England and America, on the ground that "precedents and rules govern as much in chancery as they govern in courts of law."[19] On this foundation, equity and its courts could be viewed as part of the law rather than as an extralegal threat to law.

DeLolme

Although extralegal judicial power has come back to life in administrative adjudication, the danger and the constitutional barriers to it were well understood in the eighteenth century. They were expressed with particular prominence for Americans by the Swiss intellectual Jean Louis DeLolme, whose 1771 analysis of the English constitution became an instant classic on both sides of the Atlantic.

DeLolme observed that, in the 39th article of Magna Charta, "the sovereign bound itself neither to go, nor send, upon the subject, otherwise than by the trial of peers, and the law of the land." This prompted DeLolme to reflect on the prerogative power asserted through proclamations and the Star Chamber: "This article [in Magna Charta] was . . . afterwards disregarded in practice, in consequence of the lawful efficiency which the king claimed for his proclamations, and especially by the institution of the Court of Star Chamber, which grounded its proceedings not only upon these proclamations, but also upon the particular rules[, that is, the regulations] it chose to frame within itself." DeLolme explained, however, that the article of Magna Charta was restored by the abolition of the Star Chamber: "By the abolition of this court (and also of the Court of High Commission) in the reign of Charles the First, the above provision of the Great Charter was put in actual force."[20] Thenceforth, the government could act against subjects only as stipulated by Magna Charta, through the law and its courts.

Responding to the old suggestion that extralegal adjudication was necessary, DeLolme pointed out that reliance on the law and the law courts was practicable. The Crown had believed that it could not govern without recourse to the Star Chamber and its other adminstrative tribunals, but DeLolme observed that this had proved to be mistaken. DeLolme recalled how the abolition of the Star Chamber had revived the requirement that the government could "neither . . . go, nor send, upon the subject, otherwise than by the trial of peers, and the law of the land." He then added that "it has appeared by the event, that the very extraordinary restriction upon the governing authority we are alluding to, and its execution, are no more than what the intrinsic situation of things, and the strength of the constitution, can bear."[21]

The constitutional conclusion was that the executive enjoyed merely executive power and could not exercise the judicial power: "The judicial authority . . . which the executive power had imperceptibly assumed to itself, both with respect to the person and property of the individual, was abrogated by the act which abolished the Court of Star Chamber; and the Crown was thus brought back to its true constitutional office, viz. the countenancing, and supporting with its strength, the execution of the laws."[22] Historically, DeLolme was mistaken in suggesting that the Crown had originally enjoyed merely executive power. But he elegantly expressed the whig understanding that, after the abolition of the Star Chamber, the Crown was confined to its "true constitutional office," which included executing the law, but not adjudicating it. It was a history lesson with conceptual implications that Americans would remember when they placed executive and judicial powers in different branches.

✧✧✧

The lesson that DeLolme recited for his contemporaries needs to be recalled, for executive tribunals have been revived. The details of the contemporary administrative adjudication must await chapter 13, but already here the reader can anticipate that what once was done in prerogative courts is now done in administrative courts. It thus will become apparent that administrative tribunals regress to the prerogative era—the period prior to constitutional law. They support the extralegal lawmaking regime with an extralegal judicial regime, and it will be seen that, as in the past, this is unconstitutional.

NINE

Without Judges and Juries

Common law adjudication was conducted by judges and juries—judges who exercised independent judgment in accord with the law, and juries who brought charges and gave verdicts. In contrast, prerogative adjudication was done by Crown officers, who sometimes were called judges, but who did not have the office of a common law judge and did not act with juries.

Prerogative adjudication thus was profoundly different from common law adjudication in ways that added to the constitutional problems. Nonetheless, administrative law returns to the prerogative practice of exercising judicial power without juries or even real judges.

Judicial Office

The judges of the law courts had an office or duty of independent judgment in accord with the law of the land. Although they did not always live up to this ideal, they were deeply attached to it, and it profoundly affected what they did. They therefore were very different from the personnel of the prerogative tribunals, whose offices were not so closely focused on independent judgment and the law.

Independent Judgment

An initial element of judicial office was independent judgment. The independence of the judges was thus not only external but also internal.

In defense of at least a narrow category of administrative judges, the "administrative law judges," it is said that they enjoy some partial statutory protection for their independence—as if judicial independence consists

merely of formal guarantees against external impositions of will. The independent judgment of common law judges, however, has traditionally been
both internal and external. To be sure, it required constitutional protection
from external threats to tenure and salary. More fundamentally, however,
independent judgment was the office or duty of a judge, and thus, regardless of the external fortification from external threats, the deeper question
about independence has always been internal—the duty of judges to exercise independent judgment untainted even by their own will or passion.[1]

It traditionally was theorized that the faculties of the soul consisted
of intellect and will—the former being the foundation for the exercise of
judgment or understanding. In this vision of the human mind, the will
could prompt the exercise of judgment, and will was to be informed by
judgment. But judgment and will, by definition, stood in contrast, judgment being an exercise of intellect that, once begun, had to be exercised
independently of will. This had consequences for judges, for what were distinct faculties in the soul were also distinct offices in government—the legislature having the exercise of lawmaking will, and the judges the exercise
of judgment. Judges thus inherited ideals of their office that required them
to exercise judgment independent of will.[2]

The most obvious intrusion of will was external—from kings who
sought to impose their will. Although all judges were servants of the
Crown, and kings therefore could threaten to dismiss them or to lower
their salaries, kings rarely did this before the seventeenth century. Instead,
they employed other pressures.

Already in the Middle Ages, however, the judges understood they had
to follow their own judgment. When Edward II asked them to put a hold
on their proceedings against a baron for robbery, the judges resisted. As
recorded in the year books, "though letters were brought from the king
bidding the justices stay their hands, they would not for such reason give
way."[3] Letters of this sort eventually led Parliament to require judges to
swear that they would "not delay any person of common right, for the letters of the king, or of any other person, nor for any other cause; and in case
that any letters come to you contrary to the law . . . you shall proceed to do
the law, the same letters notwithstanding."[4]

Thus, even against external impositions of will, the response initially
was not to limit the external pressures, but to bolster the internal commitment of the judges to their office. In the words of Chief Justice Fortescue, in
the late fifteenth century, "the judges . . . are all bound by their oaths not
to render judgment against the laws of the land, although they should have
the commands of the sovereign to the contrary."[5]

The core of judicial office was thus the duty of independent judgment. This internal commitment distinguished the law judges from prerogative judges and (as will be seen in chapter 13) it still distinguishes them from administrative judges.

Prerogative Pressures and Constitutional Protection

In the seventeenth century, in defense of the prerogative, kings placed more pressure on the judges than they could withstand. By the end of the century, therefore, Parliament established some basic constitutional protections from external threats to judicial independence. Even with these guarantees, however, what defined the independence and very identity of a judge was his office or duty of independent judgment. And as already hinted, this matters because, like the constitutional protections for judicial independence, the office of independent judgment is something that administrative adjudicators still do not have.

James I initiated the pressure by asking the judges for informal advisory opinions, hoping to trap them into positions that would bind them on the bench. After Chief Justice Edward Coke resisted the most extreme claims for the prerogative, James went so far as to dismiss him. This was understood as an attack on the law itself, for in defense of the absolute prerogative—the power apart from law—James had fired the most eminent judge who had refused to defer.

James's heirs continued throughout the century to pressure judges to support the prerogative and to dismiss those who refused to conform. The monarchs thereby sometimes got their way, but they ultimately persuaded the nation that the judges needed formal protection against external impositions of will. Parliament in 1701 therefore gave the judges security in tenure and salary—provisions soon echoed in American constitutions. Thus, in defense against prerogative power, Parliament not only abolished prerogative courts but also protected the judges of the law courts.

Of course, neither the 1701 English statute nor American constitutions guaranteed tenure and fixed salaries for prerogative or administrative judges. But this was unnecessary, as after 1641 it could be assumed that the use of prerogative courts to bind subjects was unlawful and even unconstitutional. If the government could take action against subjects only through the law and its courts, there was no need to provide formal protection for the independence of judges who sat on other sorts of tribunals.

Although it conventionally is assumed that the constitutional protection against external intrusions of will was what ensured judicial independence, it is striking that the judges maintained so much independence even before they received this protection. Already before 1641, when law judges and prerogative judges coexisted, neither sort had guarantees of independence, but the law judges already had an office of independent judgment. Their sense of their office often secured them against both their own passions and the pressures from others, for if they could hold off their internal fears and desires—whether fears of harm or hopes for reward—they could resist the external demands.

Even after judges acquired protection against dismissal and diminished salaries, they continued to need the internal commitment to their office, for governments had many ways of influencing them. Although no longer able to punish judges who were refractory, the Crown still could offer political rewards for compliance. Some American states were even more brazen. For example, the legislature of Massachusetts satisfied constitutional guarantees with low annual salaries while keeping the judges dependent on annual bonuses.[6]

It therefore is a mistake to assume that judicial independence is simply a matter of institutional guarantees against external impositions of executive or legislative will. Ultimately, independence has always more centrally been a matter of the judges' office of independent judgment—a duty under which they were obliged to hold off their own, internal will, predispositions, or passions. In this context, the constitutional innovation was merely to bolster this internal ideal with external constitutional guarantees.

Thus, what distinguishes law judges, and still is missing in administrative judges, is the combination of two layers of independence—externally the full constitutional protection of tenure and salary, and internally the office or duty of judgment independent of will.

In Accord with the Law of the Land

Judicial office required judges not only to exercise independent judgment but also to follow the law of the land. This element of judicial office can easily be taken for granted, and it therefore often is forgotten, but it was foundational for the Anglo-American legal system.

Judges had long been expected to decide in accord with law or, at least, in accord with right. This sort of generic requirement, however, soon came to seem inadequate—probably because it left room for civil or other "foreign" law. Therefore, already early in the development of the common law, the king's commissions to his judges specified that they were "to do that which pertains to justice according to the law and custom of England."

As summarized by a popular eighteenth-century commentator, "all the commissions of judges are bounded with this limitation." The judges thus "have not power to judge according to that which they think fit; but that which by law they know to be right."[7]

As a result, there were two elements of the office of a judge. His office required him not only to exercise independent judgment but also to follow the law of the land. These two elements of judicial office defined the duty of a common law judge. Indeed, they determined his very identity. What defined a common law judge therefore stood in sharp contrast to the traits of a prerogative or administrative judge.

Prerogative Judges

The personnel of the prerogative courts did not have to exercise independent judgment or follow the law of the land. On the contrary, they held offices that often required them to exercise policy judgment and to follow prerogative regulations. Their offices thus were very similar to those held nowadays by administrative adjudicators.

Prerogative judges were servants of the Crown in a more immediate sense than the law judges, for their offices required them to carry out prerogative power or policy. For example, whereas the judges had an office that required them to exercise independent judgment in accord with the law of the land, the privy councillors who sat on the Star Chamber were sworn to support the king—to be "true and faithful" to him. Not content with this, James I even required his privy councillors to swear that they would "defend all jurisdictions, preeminences, and authorities granted to his majesty, and annexed to his Crown . . . by act of Parliament or otherwise."[8] Star Chamber judges thus had an office that drew them away from independent judgment and the law.

Although prerogative judges were appointed for their dedication to the Crown's prerogative rather than to the common law, it should not be assumed that their predispositions were mere prejudice. Just as individuals today join administrative agencies because of their commitment to administrative policy making, the men who sat on the prerogative courts tended to have sympathies with the Crown's prerogative power.

Today, the prerogative departure from the common law office of a judge has been revived in administrative agencies. The U.S. Constitution expressly vests "[t]he judicial Power of the United States" in the courts. It assumes, moreover, that the courts will consist of judges with the traditional judicial office or duty to exercise independent judgment in accord with the law of the land. On this foundation, the Constitution secures the judges in this office with guarantees of tenure and salary.[9]

Administrative agencies, however, now exercise the judicial power that the Constitution vested in the courts. The details must wait, but it already can be anticipated that whereas the judges of the courts have judicial office (the duty to exercise independent judgment and to follow the law of the land) and whereas the judges are constitutionally protected in this office, administrative adjudicators have merely adminstrative offices (in which they must exercise policy judgment and must follow administrative regulations), and in which they lack constitutional protection. Even if not personally attached to the particular administrative regulations they enforce, they are expected to be committed to the overall project of administrative power, and it will be seen that they are subject to penalty if they fail to follow administrative regulations. Administrators with administrative commitments thus exercise the power once vested exclusively in the courts and their judges, and this is yet another way in which the present seems to return to the past.

Juries

The prerogative courts not only lacked real judges but also acted without juries. They used neither a grand jury to charge defendants nor a petit jury to give verdicts. The prerogative courts thereby deprived defendants of the full range of jury rights—a constitutional problem that has been revived in administrative adjudication.

Grand Juries and Petit Juries

Jury requirements were ancient and fundamental. Since the thirteenth century, charges for felonies in English courts had to be initiated by a grand jury—an accusatory jury of twenty-four men. Only if they signed the indictment, saying it was "a true bill," could it proceed. Since the thirteenth century, moreover, a verdict had to come from a petit jury—a panel of twelve men. Upon considering the evidence and the judge's instructions, the jury could find the defendant "guilty" or "not guilty," and its decision was final. The two sorts of juries thus provided a pair of communal obstacles—one against unjustified criminal proceedings and another against unjustified convictions—with some of the disadvantages of communal procedures but at least some of their advantages.

In effect, grand and petit juries assured a specialization of labor. The importance of specialized governmental authority and the threat to it from prerogative or administrative regimes must be delayed until chapter 17, but even at this stage the advantages of specialization can be observed in the courts of law. The judicial power of the courts to try and punish was divided among the judges and the two types of juries. The judges were pre-committed to specialized public interests and were trained to pursue them with great skill. The juries, on the other hand, offered safety by segregating the powers of commencing and concluding trials and placing them in bod-ies that, unlike the judges, were selected from the general public. In this sense, their specialized role was to offer unspecialized decisionmakers— decisionmakers who were specialized in the sense that they were members of the local community who could share its understandings and could act on its behalf.

In prerogative courts, however, there were no juries—the initial prob-lem being that the courts charged defendants without using grand juries. Of course, the High Commission punished mostly ecclesiastical offences, and the Star Chamber punished mostly what it considered misdemeanors, and it therefore may be thought that these courts were under no duty to rely on grand juries. The High Commission, however, imprisoned men for refusing to answer its interrogations. Moreover, the Star Chamber some-times imposed enormous penalties for mere misdemeanors, as if they were as serious as felonies, and it sometimes punished under the rubric of "mis-demeanors" what actually were felonies at common law.[10]

Even worse than this abandonment of grand juries was that the preroga-tive courts tried defendants without petit juries. These juries were required in both civil and criminal proceedings but were unavailable in either the Star Chamber or the High Commission, thus leaving defendants subject to all of the preconceptions of the prerogative judges. As put by DeLolme, because the Star Chamber "decided matters by its own single authority, without the intervention of a jury, it was always ready to find those persons guilty, whom the court was pleased to look upon as such."[11]

The abolition of the prerogative courts solved this problem, and there-after the right to a jury became one of the most widely celebrated of con-stitutional ideals. In the late seventeenth century, John Hawles described it as one of the "fundamental points of the common law," saying even that it was "derive[d] from the fundamental constitution and laws of our coun-try."[12] This point about the right to a jury was echoed by almost all writers on law, ranging from Blackstone to anonymous scribblers, and it precluded any prerogative or administrative adjudication.

America

Far from merely inheriting jury rights as ideals, Americans had their own experiences under prerogative or administrative tribunals without juries—most notoriously when Parliament in 1765 passed the Stamp Act. The act required Americans to pay a stamp duty on the paper used for legal documents, and it gave the enforcement to admiralty courts.[13] These courts followed simplified civilian procedures, without juries, and were conducted by a single judge, who lacked tenure, thus making them convenient institutions for imposing an unpopular revenue measure that juries might find distasteful. The substitution of civilian process for the due process of law was not ordinarily a problem in admiralty courts, as they were established by English and colonial law for matters of admiralty, which lay outside the realm. Indeed, admiralty jurisdiction traditionally depended on the libelant's recitation that the cause of action arose "super altum mare"—on the high seas.[14] It therefore was ominous that Parliament now was using such courts to collect domestic taxes.

Americans vehemently objected to the use of admiralty courts and the consequent denial of jury rights. Locally, towns such as Braintree passed resolutions complaining that "[i]n these courts one judge presides alone, no juries have any concern there, the law and fact are to be decided by the same single judge whose commission is only during pleasure." Being under the influence of the Crown, "a judge of such a court" could "render us the most sordid and forlorn of slaves. We mean the slaves of the servant of a minster of state." At the continental level, the colonies formed a Congress to protest "the tyrannical acts of the British Parliament." In its Declaration of Rights and Grievances, the Congress declared that "trial by jury is the inherent and invaluable right of every British subject in these colonies" and that "by extending the jurisdiction of the courts of admiralty beyond its ancient limits," the Stamp Act had "a manifest tendency to subvert the rights and liberties of the colonists."[15]

Parliament responded in 1765 with the Declaratory Act, declaring Parliament's power "to bind the colonies and people of America . . . in all cases whatsoever." It added that "all resolutions, votes, orders, and proceedings, in any of the said colonies or plantations," that questioned the authority of Parliament to enact laws binding Americans are "utterly null and void."[16] Although this sweeping assertion of parliamentary power gratified the British, it only exacerbated the fears of Americans, who resented the denial of jury rights in circumstances that would be considered unconstitutional in England.

Recognizing the larger implications, newspaper essayists complained that the admiralty courts revived prerogative power. "If we are Englishmen. . . . [h]ow are our new laws to be adjudged and executed? Is not our property . . . to be thrown into a prerogative court? a court of admiralty? and there to be adjudged, forfeited, and condemned without a jury?" In other words, the "powers of the courts of admiralty" were being "extended to cases belonging to the courts of common pleas," with the result that "the privilege of juries" was "denied in jury actions." Although this was done by Parliament, it was no less dangerous "than if effected by royal prerogative only."[17]

Having thus been invigorated in their attachment to trial by jury, Americans carefully protected this right in their state constitutions. The New Jersey Constitution, for example, provided that "the inestimable right of trial by jury shall remain confirmed as a part of the law of this colony, without repeal, forever."[18] Of course, there remained a wide range of complexities about the different roles of judges and juries. But there was no doubt that the right to a jury was a right to a body of twelve persons and that the government could not evade the right by shifting hearings outside the regular court system. There thus was no room for administrative evasions of the right to a jury.

Military and Economic Emergencies

This sort of constitutional requirement, however, tested the patience of some state legislatures. Notwithstanding that most states in 1776 proclaimed their devotion to the right of trial by jury, they faced invasion from without and soon also financial collapse within. Across the continent, therefore, state legislatures in the late 1770s and '80s turned to legal shortcuts, including summary administrative proceedings before justices of the peace.

Like the English government two decades earlier, the states that took this path felt themselves compelled by necessity. Recognizing that their experiments skirted the law, they attempted to cure the constitutional problem by allowing appeals or other modes of review in common law courts. Nonetheless, the evasion of jury rights in the initial hearings was painfully apparent to Americans not swept up by the claims of necessity.

The state legislatures that authorized these summary proceedings placed them under the supervision of justices of the peace, who were partly judicial and partly executive officers. When sitting in groups (in monthly and quarter sessions in England and in monthly county courts in some southern states), justices of the peace exercised some general judicial powers. When they sat alone, however, they had only a very limited judicial role. In criminal matters, they could not by themselves hold trials, but could only carry out only preliminary judicial functions, such as issuing warrants for search and seizure. Even in civil cases, they could not hold trials for amounts that came within the jurisdiction of the common law (traditionally, disputes for more than forty shillings).[19] In other respects, they acted executively—as county managers at their monthly sessions and as police investigators when conducting preliminary examinations of suspected criminals.

The adoption of administrative proceedings without juries in response to a military crisis can be observed in New Jersey. In 1779, parts of the state were under British occupation, and the areas near British lines were wracked by a sort of civil war. In this dire situation, trade with the enemy was undermining the morale and loyalty of Americans and was giving the British the means to reconnoiter American territory. The legislature therefore authorized Americans to seize goods transported across enemy lines. To ensure enforcement, it authorized justices of the peace, with juries of only six men, to hear claims for forfeitures of the goods. A justice of the peace was not a regular judge, and a jury was understood to consist of twelve jurors; but the legislature thought summary proceedings were essential and therefore tried to get away with hearings in front of justices of the peace and truncated juries.

The constitutional question came before the New Jersey Supreme Court in 1780 in *Holmes & Ketcham v. Walton*. Major Elisha Walton had seized £29,000 worth of goods belonging to John Holmes and Samuel Ketcham. Alleging that these had come across the lines, Walton obtained a forfeiture judgment from a friendly justice of the peace, John Anderson, sitting with a jury of six.

The circumstances were as necessitous as any in American history—so necessitous that Walton, Anderson, and many others in New Jersey were forming themselves into an association of Retaliators. These vigilantes acted against Tories with methods far worse than administrative proceedings and justified themselves with the old maxim "Necessity has no law."[20]

Holmes and Ketcham, however, relied on the law against the administrative proceedings. They obtained a writ of certiorari from the state's supreme court on the ground that the legislature's authorization of six person juries violated the state's constitutional guarantee of "the inestimable right of trial by jury."[21] The court agreed. A jury of six was not a jury, and the legislature's emergency establishment of administrative summary proceedings had to give way to the constitution.[22]

Five years later the New Hampshire legislature responded to a financial crisis with a similar expedient and met a similar result. In the mid-1780s, a combination of bad harvests and a shortage of specie created a debt crisis so severe that many farmers could not pay their mortgages or their taxes. This was the national emergency in which Americans formed and adopted the U.S. Constitution. More immediately, the crisis led distraught farmers to demand the issuance of paper money and even the stopping of the courts, desperately hoping that these measures would save them and their farms. Eager to increase the flow of money, the legislature hoped to provide an efficient mode of justice by authorizing mere justices of the peace to hear claims of up to £10 without a jury. This "Ten Pound Act" pleased some creditors, but the debtors who were forced to defend themselves without a jury were less amused.

Many defendants who lost before the justices of the peace appealed to the Inferior Courts of Rockingham and Strafford Counties. Although they could obtain a new trial with a jury in the Inferior Courts, the defendants preferred to argue that the statute was unconstitutional. On such arguments, the courts held in one case after another that "the act of the legislature empowering a justice to hear and determine civil actions of more than forty shillings is manifestly contrary to the constitution of this state."[23] The denial of a jury in the regular courts would have been unconstitutional, and it was no less unconstitutional when defendants were deprived of this right in proceedings before semi-administrative officers.

Of course, the Ten Pound Act was defended as essential for providing an "expeditious" way of recovering small debts at a time of financial crisis, but the need was no excuse. As observed by a newspaper essay, "the law may answer the purposes of the legislative" in providing justice in an expeditious manner, but "[t]he question before us is that of *right* not utility."[24]

The *Ten Pound Cases* are particularly revealing about the right to a jury even "in the first stage of the action." The statute allowed appeals to the Inferior Courts, where either party could demand a new trial with a jury. The constitutional question was therefore whether proceedings before a semi-administrative officer acting without a jury could be rendered constitutional by the later availability of regular judicial proceedings with a jury. For example, when a defendant's lawyer in one of the cases argued that the state's bill of rights had "guaranteed a continuance of trial by jury," the plaintiff's lawyer protested that the state constitution did not guarantee "a right to trial by jury in the first instance." He added: "Nor does the law restrain the party aggrieved from appealing to the Inferior Court where he may have the same cause tried by a jury in as full and ample a manner as if it had originated at an Inferior Court." Upon hearing these arguments, the justice of the peace hearing the case overruled the defendant's constitutional objection; but on appeal to the Inferior Court, the defendant won a reversal and costs—this being one of the occasions on which the Rockingham Inferior Court held the statute "manifestly contrary to the constitution of this state."[25] Thus, even with the opportunity for an entirely de novo trial, including a jury, the denial of a jury in the first instance was unconstitutional. Nowadays, however, even on appeal, litigants in the administrative regime do not get a jury.

The U.S. Constitution carefully vests "[t]he judicial Power of the United States" in its courts and then guarantees juries. It secures grand juries whenever a person is "held to answer for a capital, or otherwise infamous crime"; it guarantees trial by jury in "[s]uits at common law" above twenty dollars; it also guarantees trial by jury in "all criminal prosecutions" and in "[t]he Trial of all Crimes." The Constitution thereby protects jury rights not merely in the courts, but in almost all exercises of judicial power, whether civil or criminal. The Constitution thus leaves no room for the government to evade jury rights by shifting proceedings from the courts to administrative hearings.

Nonetheless, administrative tribunals use neither grand juries nor petit juries, and when their determinations come up on appeal, the judges generally defer to agency determinations of the facts. The judges thereby legitimize the denial of jury rights in the administrative proceedings, and the judges themselves deny jury rights when the cases come before the courts.

The return to the prerogative denial of jury rights is all the more striking because state courts in the 1780s had no difficulty repudiating such a move. The states at that time denied jury rights in response to profound military and economic emergencies—indeed, the emergencies that gave rise to the nation. The state courts, however, recognized that it was their duty to follow the law, and they therefore repeatedly held the summary administrative proceedings unconstitutional for violating jury rights. It therefore is all the more astonishing that today, even in the absence of any sharp emergency, administrative tribunals continually deny jury rights, and that the regular courts persistently uphold these irregular proceedings.

෨෨෨

The absence of juries and real judges in administrative adjudication is yet another example of the return to the preconstitutional past. The prerogative judges did not have an office that required them to exercise independent judgment or to follow the law of the land, and they acted without either grand juries or petit juries. All of this was soon recognized as unconstitutional. What was unconstitutional in prerogative adjudication, however, has been revived and upheld as lawful in administrative adjudication—as if the change from "prerogative" to "administrative" were significant.

The current evasion of judges and juries will be examined only in chapter 13. For now, it is enough simply to recognize that administrative proceedings revert back to the old prerogative proceedings. Constitutional law carefully requires the government to act through judges and juries— not merely in its courts, but generally in its exercise of the judicial power. Nonetheless, as in the past, government purports to escape this requirement simply by exercising its judicial power administratively, outside the courts.

TEN

Inquisitorial Process

The common law had its own ideals about the personnel, structure, and mode of proceeding of its courts—ideals that could be summed up as the due process of law. The prerogative courts, however, were staffed, structured, and run largely in imitation of the civil law and its inquisitorial process. The contrast between the legal and the prerogative systems therefore echoed the broader contrast between the due process of the common law and the inquisitorial process of the civil law.

The inquisitorial procedures of the prerogative tribunals shaped much constitutional law. The threat from inquisitorial procedures already had sharpened medieval thinking about common law procedures. In the seventeenth century, the common law reaction went a step further, for in response to the growth of the inquisitorial model in the prerogative courts, the English elevated some of their old practices and principles to constitutional law. Most notably, they developed their old practices against self-incrimination, and their old ideal of due process, into constitutional principles.

This history still matters because it shows the breadth of the principles of self-incrimination and due process. In justification of administrative adjudication, it is said that these principles centrally concerned the law courts. Yet having developed to bar prerogative adjudication, these principles clearly applied, in their fullest extent, not only to regular adjudication in the courts but also against irregular adjudication outside the courts. The latter was the greatest danger, and rather than ignore this, the principles on self-incrimination and due process reached all exercises of judicial power.

It therefore is disturbing that many elements of the old inquisitorial process have reappeared in administrative tribunals. What once was dangerous and unconstitutional in such bodies now is accepted as utterly mundane.

Self-Incrimination

To understand the administrative revival of inquisitorial procedures, one can begin with self-incrimination. Whereas common law procedures tended to preclude self-incriminating testimony, the prerogative courts systematically pressured persons to incriminate themselves—as do administrative courts today.

Antiprerogative Origins

Today, self-incrimination often is assumed to be prototypically a problem arising in the law courts—indeed, merely in their demands for testimony under oath in their criminal proceedings. The constitutional right against self-incrimination, however, began to develop earlier in response to the danger in the prerogative or adminstrative courts.

The principle against self-incrimination originally came from the learned law, which flourished on the Continent. In the civil and canon law courts, judges systematically relied on forced self-incrimination under oath and even made this a guiding principle of their proceedings. To prevent the worst abuses of this approach, some canonists and civilians developed the principle that no one is is bound to testify against himself—in other words, *Nemo tenetur prodere seipsum*. Thus, the learned law was the source of both the danger and the abstract principle that might be applied against it.[1] Yet the practical development of the principle as a real obstacle to the danger had to await developments in England.

In the common law courts, there was no overt principle against self-incrimination, but also much less overt danger. At least in felony prosecutions, individuals were accountable not on the mere demand of a judge, but only upon indictment by a grand jury. In such cases, during both grand jury and petit jury proceedings, the suspect or defendant could not take an oath to testify in his defense. He could be questioned during pretrial investigations, and informally later in court, but he could not testify under oath. This disability could handicap the defendant, but it also limited the Crown, preventing it from forcing him to testify against himself under oath. Recognizing that this was more of a practice precluding self-incrimination than a principle against it, late-sixteenth-century lawyers, such as James Morice, observed, "In criminal causes and suits, whereby either the loss of life, liberty, member of the body, or good name, may ensue . . . the common laws of this land have wholly forborne . . . to urge or impose an oath upon the accused."[2]

Of course, in misdemeanor and civil proceedings, English law was more ambiguous. Individuals in such cases often had little choice but to answer incriminating questions on oath, and at the border of the common law, in equity, they similarly could be obliged to do this. In all such proceedings, however, self-incrimination was not ordinarily required unless there was an accuser who formally and publicly brought suit or made charges. On the whole, moreover, to the extent self-incrimination occurred in English law, it was more a by-product than a central principle of the proceedings.

In contrast, the prerogative courts—most prominently, the High Commission—systematically required defendants to testify against themselves. Learned lawyers theorized about when self-incrimination was justified, and following the civilian model, the Act of Uniformity apparently authorized the High Commission to impose its inquiries on the clergy. Taking a broad view of this authorization, the commission also forced laymen to answer incriminating questions—even in cases in which it claimed a jurisdiction to impose temporal penalties. Its method was to have its judges ex officio require suspects to swear that they would answer questions before they had seen the charges against them, thereby forcing a defendant to be "both . . . accuser and accused."[3] In this manner, the judges made self-incrimination the court's preeminent mode of proceeding.

The Star Chamber also relied on self-incrimination. Even before a person was called before this court, the attorney general could ask him to answer questions, thereby eliciting incriminating answers without any formal accusation or even any information about the charges against him. The attorney general, moreover, could introduce the answers in evidence in Star Chamber—at least until the court in 1606 rejected such evidence on the ground that the questions were solicited "in a mass" rather than in response to a particular charge in a particular case.[4] After charges had been brought, however, self-incrimination remained permissible—both in proceedings brought by private persons and in those commenced by the Attorney General. The coercion occurred when the defendant was asked to answer interrogatories. An evasive answer was punishable, and a refusal to answer was taken to be a confession.[5]

The government, moreover, could rely on self-incrimination when it proceeded against a suspect in the Star Chamber by the summary mode called *ore tenus*. This was the government's usual method, and it was an "extraordinary kind of proceeding," even "more short and expeditious" than other Star Chamber hearings. Under this approach, an officer of the court apprehended the suspect without any probable cause, warrant, or charges against him. The suspect then was "privately examined, without oath," by one of the judges, before any charges were brought, to see if any crime had been committed; and if the suspect confessed "without constraint," he was promptly taken before the court. Once the suspect was in court, he was shown the confession, after which, "if he acknowledge it," he was summarily convicted and sentenced.[6] The justification was that "where the queen is a party . . . then on confession the queen may proceed *viva voce*." Making the most of this, the court assumed that where a suspect refused to answer, his reluctance should be taken as a confession.[7]

The constitutional problem of self-incrimination thus arose primarily from prerogative or administrative proceedings. Most existing histories of self-incrimination (for example, by John Wigmore, Leonard Levy, and John Langbein) attempt to determine when the privilege came to be applied in the common law courts—as if this were when it became a common law right.[8] Similarly, contemporary administrative law accepts a substantial degree of administrative self-incrimination on the assumption that the privilege centrally concerns proceedings in the courts. The question of self-incrimination, however, most prominently arose in prerogative tribunals, and as will be seen shortly, it developed as a right mainly in opposition to this administrative adjudication.

Excuses

The defenders of prerogative adjudication offered many excuses for its self-incrimination—excuses of a sort that are nowadays made for administrative self-incrimination. The excuses, however, were no more persuasive about prerogative self-incrimination than they are today about the administrative version.

One excuse that has resurfaced was that prerogative or administrative proceedings were not really criminal in nature. For example, a prominent civilian apologist for the High Commission, Richard Cosin, argued that at least its privately initiated hearings were distinct from criminal inquiries. His explanation was that the "penances" enjoined by the judges in privately commenced proceedings were not really punitive, but rather were for "the reformation of the delinquent," for the "example of others," and for "the satisfaction of the Church." And because the proceedings were "not taken in law to be *poena*, but *medicinae*," the suspected persons were "not to make scruple to discover themselves"—at least not after the judges had determined that they were suspect. Along somewhat similar lines, Cosin suggested that self-incrimination should be tolerated in High Commission proceedings in the same way as in civil suits in equity, in which a defendant could be forced to make answers on oath, after the initial showing by the plaintiff.[9]

It was widely recognized, however, that the High Commission generally imposed corrective orders and temporal penalties on behalf of the government or its church, and that such proceedings, even if privately commenced, were criminal. Even Cosin acknowledged that many High Commission proceedings were "moved criminally, to the intent of public punishment," and the records of the court itself stated that most of its proceedings were for "criminal" offenses "punishable by ecclesiastical authority." As put by the court's leading historian, the various commissions that formed the High Commission were "criminal courts." Similarly, Chief Justice Edward Coke observed that "[a]ll suits in the Star Chamber, though exhibited by the party, are informations for the king." Evidently, the threat of self-incrimination arose primarily from extralegal prerogative proceedings that were criminal in nature, regardless of who began them. The victims of such proceedings therefore had good reason to protest (as did John Penry in 1589) that "in a criminal cause," the laws of the land "enforce no man to be his own accuser."[10]

Another justification for self-incrimination that has been revived was to shift the burden of proof to the defendant. Cosin and the other civilian apologists for the High Commission were willing to admit the maxim *nemo tenetur prodere seipsum*, but they equivocated by interpreting this to mean that "no man may be urged to betray himself in hidden and secret crimes." In other words, he could be forced to betray himself where there was notoriety or a widespread rumor about his crimes—what was called *fama* or fame and nowadays would be called public suspicion. As a procedural matter, this rendered the crime "public" and thereby shifted the burden of proof. And whereas *fama* traditionally had to be proved, by the sixteenth century it was simply taken for granted, thus almost always placing the burden of proof on the defendant. Accordingly, if he denied "the crime objected, then he is by law enjoined his purgation"—that is, he "must directly answer, clearing, or convicting himself."[11] The shift in the burden of proof, merely on account of prerogative suspicion, thus had the effect of forcing a defendant to vindicate or condemn himself. This was part of what English criminal procedure since the Middle Ages had substantially rejected and what American constitutional law would later prohibit. Nonetheless, as will be seen in chapter 13, administrative charges, based on administrative suspicion, nowadays again often shift the burden of proof to defendants, thus forcing them to vindicate or condemn themselves.

A further justification that has been resuscitated was to suggest that self-incrimination was a problem only when a court directly solicited confessions of guilt. In ex officio prosecutions, civilians candidly justified direct questioning about guilt, explaining that the judge may "require the oath of the supposed delinquent touching both the circumstances and the crime." In private prosecutions in ecclesiastical courts, however, English civilians recognized that direct questioning about guilt could be problematic. They therefore again admitted the maxim, *nemo tenetur prodere seipsum*, and this time equivocated that no one may be urged "simply" to betray himself in hidden and secret crimes. In other words, self-incrimination was permissible in private prosecutions as long as the defendant "is not bound to answer upon oath any articles of the very crime itself." He "may be examined by oath upon other matter of circumstance, yet he may not so be examined touching the very fact and crime, or anything nearly or presumptively tending thereunto; until by sufficient presumptions, the judge be induced, to account him greatly to be holden suspected"—at which point the court could impose more direct questions. Circumstantial questioning was thus merely the first step toward direct questioning, and once again, suspicion turned the tables. Of course, common lawyers were not satisfied with assurances that, in private prosecutions, the High Commission worked by cornering the suspect before directly demanding a confession. As a common law critic noted, the ecclesiastical judges thereby "extort[ed] by oath . . . from the party" the very "ground and foundation of the inquisition."[12]

Yet another excuse, at least for the Star Chamber, was that when it sought self-incrimination in its *ore tenus* proceedings, it did not seek sworn testimony in court—a distinction nowadays made on behalf of some administrative demands for information. Nice distinctions, however, did not reassure common lawyers, who recognized the realities and therefore tended to oppose not only sworn self-incrimination in court but also the Star Chamber's *ore tenus* questioning.

Recognizing that the excuses were weak, common lawyers and even some prerogative lawyers concluded that the English had a version of the Spanish Inquisition. For decades there had been complaints that when the High Commission forced persons "to accuse themselves," it acted as "a Court of Inquisition more than Spanish." And there soon were similar worries about the Star Chamber—even merely about its indirect questioning. Advocates of this tribunal acknowledged that such inquiries could be used "like a Spanish Inquisition, to rack men's consciences, nay to perplex them by intricate questions, thereby to make contrarieties, which may easily happen to simple men.'"[13]

The problem of self-incrimination thus was not easily excused. It could not be made to disappear by transferring criminal proceedings to prerogative or administrative tribunals, by shifting the burden of proof, or by initially confining the questioning to circumstantial evidence of guilt. Even with these excuses, the substance of the self-incrimination in prerogative or adminstrative courts was dangerous and contrary to common law traditions.

Unlawful

Common lawyers in the seventeenth century increasingly concluded that the prerogative imposition of self-incrimination was unlawful and even unconstitutional. Although centuries have passed since then, their arguments against self-incrimination are revealing, for they were framed in opposition to the prerogative courts. It thus becomes clear that the privilege against self-incrimination reached not merely criminal cases in the common law courts, but also those in other, prerogative or administrative courts.

Critics of self-incrimination had multiple complaints. The narrowest charge against the High Commission was that its questioning went beyond the commission's statutory jurisdiction, which was merely ecclesiastical. Most broadly, there were religious concerns that it tempted individuals to risk their souls and philosophical concerns that its inquiries delved into "secret deeds, words, and thoughts no way offensive to the public peace."[14]

At a middle level, however, there were two broad but concretely legal conclusions. One, as already noted, was that compulsory self-incrimination in criminal cases was contrary to the practices of the common law, at least as understood from the paradigm of felony prosecutions. The second conclusion was that a tribunal could not bind subjects to accuse themselves unless there was an accuser and a formal accusation in court—this being an argument that focused on ex officio inquiries. In the words of a prominent critic of the High Commission, it lacked "the power to imprison subjects, to fine them, or to force them to accuse themselves upon their own enforced oaths, there being no accuser known," and it thereby it "tend[ed] to charge the body, lands, or goods of the subjects, otherwise than according to the due course of the laws of the realm."[15] In the eighteenth century, the first such point, generally against self-incrimination in criminal cases, would become the basis of a guarantee along these lines in the U.S. Constitution. In contrast, the second point, against self-incrimination in ex officio inquiries, would be left to other guarantees in the Constitution—namely, those on the specification of accusations, confrontation by witnesses, and most centrally the due process of law.

Already in the seventeenth century, these legal arguments were becoming constitutional principles. One of the earliest glimpses of this constitutionalization of the debate comes from the 1590s, when some critics of the High Commission apparently argued that its self-incriminating questions were contrary to England's fundamental or constitutional law. This constitutional complaint focused on the commission's departure from the common law's traditional requirements for criminal proceedings. In response, Cosin—a leading defender of the High Commission—felt obliged to respond that "albeit the matter in some degree, happen to be criminal," this did not mean that ex officio oaths were "contrary to the fundamental laws."[16] It was early hint of where the controversy would end.

In 1641 Parliament finally ended prerogative self-incrimination. It terminated temporal authority for such questioning by abolishing the Star Chamber and similar prerogative jurisdictions. It similarly cut off ecclesiastical authority for such inquiries by abolishing the High Commission. Other ecclesiastical courts remained, however, and Parliament therefore specifically barred any such courts from requiring any self-accusation resulting in any penalty:

> [N]o . . . persons . . . exercising spiritual or ecclesiastical power, authority, or
> jurisdiction . . . shall ex officio, or at the instance or promotion of any other
> person whatsoever . . . minister unto any . . . person whatsoever any corporal
> oath whereby he or she shall or may be charged or obliged . . . to confess or
> to accuse him or herself of any crime, offence, delinquency, or misdemeanor,
> or any neglect . . . or thing [else] whereby, or by reason whereof, he or she
> shall or may be liable or exposed to any censure, pain, penalty, or punish-
> ment whatsoever . . .[17]

This provision confirms that the self-incrimination problem centrally concerned not the law courts but the prerogative courts, not only ex officio proceedings but also those initiated by private parties, and not only what were formally criminal proceedings but also any other proceedings imposing any censure or penalty for any neglect.

Tellingly, it was only after 1641 that the English developed a privilege of self-incrimination against the courts of law. Most of the existing histories dispute whether the privilege was secured in 1649 or only much later, but either way (as already noted) they assume that the key question is when and how far the privilege was recognized in the law courts.[18] This, however, misses the point. Of greater significance for understanding the breadth of the right is that it initially developed where it seemed most relevant, in the struggle against the prerogative courts—in other words, against administrative tribunals—and that in this context, it was a complete bar against any coerced self-incrimination.[a]

America

All of the American states that adopted bills of rights provided guarantees of one sort or another against self-incrimination. The Virginia Constitution, for example, stated that no man could be "compelled to give evidence against himself."[19] The U.S. Constitution assured that no person "shall be compelled in any criminal case to be a witness against himself."

As might be expected from the history, the Constitution stated its guarantee generally, not merely as to courts of law. The problem had notoriously centered in the prerogative courts, and it had concerned any self-incrimination in any proceedings of a criminal nature, not merely what were technically criminal proceedings at common law. The Constitution therefore stated the right in the passive voice, thus making clear that it barred self-incrimination generally in criminal cases, even if outside the courts. Similarly, because the problem had included privately initiated proceedings and those in which the testimony was not under oath, the Constitution did not restrict its guarantee to government-initiated proceedings or to sworn testimony.

All of this remains important, for the danger of self-incrimination is no longer a matter of the past. Administrative courts have returned to prerogative demands for self-incrimination and have gone back to the theory that their extralegal situation, outside the courts of law, and outside common law criminal cases, leaves them unbound by the constitutional right. They thereby, however, return to precisely the sort of extralegal demands that gave rise to the rule against self-incrimination. Far from escaping the constitutional barrier, they fall squarely within it.

Inquisitorial Process and Due Process

The prerogative courts not merely sought self-incrimination, but more generally employed inquisitorial process. In response, the English developed the notion of due process into a constitutional ideal and barred the gov-

a. Of course, when the bar against self-incrimination developed in the regular courts after 1641, the judges had to develop refined distinctions about when a defendant could avoid testifying against himself. At least in opposition to prerogative proceedings, however, the bar against self-incrimination tended to be understood more sweepingly to preclude any coerced self-incrimination.

ernment from judicially binding subjects, except with the due process of law. Although the constitutional due process of law thus repudiated the extralegal adjudication and its inquisitorial tendencies, administrative courts have revived such adjudication, including its inquisitorial approach.

Too often, scholars miss the breadth of what was at issue in inquisitorial process, for they focus on its dramatic use of torture and self-incrimination rather than on its administrative efficiency. The inquisitorial mode of proceeding had developed in the learned law of the Continent—a sort of law in which judges actively made inquiries or inquisitions, these being what gave the Spanish Inquisition its name. Of course, few English prerogative inquisitions were bloody, and when one considers the quotidian character of most prerogative inquisitorial proceedings, one can begin to appreciate how they were forerunners of administrative proceedings. An extralegal system of adjudication will naturally turn to inquisitorial proceedings because they allow so much administrative control. Hence the danger. Even without the worst elements of the Spanish Inquisition, extralegal adjudication not merely evades due process, but systematically substitutes inquisitorial proceedings.

Ex Officio Proceedings

There is no point in cataloguing all aspects of inquisitorial process. But it is worth noting a few of its characteristics that have recurred in administrative law—one being the ex officio proceeding.

At common law, judicial proceedings were begun and shaped by open accusations. There had to be "[a]n accuser, and accused, and a judge," and defendants therefore were counseled that "you be not bound to answer till your accusers come before you."[20] In prerogative courts, however, especially the High Commission, the judges themselves could initiate proceedings merely by virtue of their office (*ex officio mero*). Acting on the basis of a secret informant, a prerogative judge could commence inquiries on mere rumor or suspicion, and acting on his own, the judge could initiate proceedings simply because he served as "the curious eye of the state and king's council prying into the inconveniencies and mischiefs which abound in the commonwealth." As put less charitably by a critic, the "inquisition" was commenced by the judges "[e]ither upon complaint made of some crime or offense, by secret and for the most part malicious informers, or upon bare suspicion conceived of their own phantasies."[21]

Thus, without getting a formal and public accusation by an accuser, and without sharing details of any charges against a defendant, High Commission judges could force answers to questions and thereby engage in fishing expeditions to learn about compliance with prerogative regulations. Their "cases" therefore could serve as the occasion for open-ended inquiries as to whether an offense had been committed in the first place—thereby making the judges not merely judge and jury, but also the grand jury. At common law, subjects could not be forced to supply information unless it was relevant to a grand jury or to court proceedings about particular offenses, as openly charged by known persons, and supported by known evidence. As put by a critic of the High Commission, "No man is to be condemned without an accuser." Even Francis Bacon acknowledged that "to examine a man upon oath, out of the insinuation of fame, or out of accusations secret and undeclared, though it have some countenance from the civil law, yet, it is so opposite *ex diametro* to the sense and course of the common law, as it may well receive some limitation." In the High Commission, however, suspects had to answer general questions about compliance or be punished— all on the mere say-so of administrators. Thus, if the inquisition were successful, the suspect would be tried by his "own forced oath, against his will, without any witness or accuser."[22]

Even where ex officio proceedings were initiated or promoted by an accuser (*ex officio promoto*) and thus were not merely ex officio, they allowed judges at the inquiry stage to impose inquisitorial questioning, in which judges could seek information not only about the alleged offense but also about other offenses. Once again, therefore, the High Commission judges could exercise the power of a grand jury. The Star Chamber also exercised this sort of power, for it used proceedings against individuals for narrow offenses to justify interrogating them under oath about other offenses, whether by them or others. Faced with such questioning in 1638, John Lilburne refused, explaining that he could not take an unlawful "oath of inquiry."[23]

Worst of all, judges in both courts could act in a prosecutorial role. This was particularly clear in High Commission proceeding *ex officio mero*, in which there was no public accuser in court and the prerogative body itself commenced the proceedings. As put by one critic, "the judge, who imposeth the oath, is . . . the party accuser, and so both judge and promoter, which all good laws forbid." On such grounds, critics concluded that "the proceeding of the commissioners, upon the oath ex officio, without an accuser," was "not warranted by law, but erroneous and void."[24]

Forced Disclosure Concerning Others

A further trait of inquisitorial proceedings that has reappeared in administrative form was the practice of forcing information from members of the public outside judicial proceedings in court, even without any charges against anyone in such proceedings. As already hinted, although this could lead to self-incrimination, it also was a more general problem.

The unlawfulness of administratively required disclosure—even regarding other persons—became especially clear in response to the king's demands for forced loans. In 1626, Charles I attempted to raise money outside the law by claiming a prerogative to collect loans. Although the forced loans themselves will be considered in the next chapter, they already matter because Charles established commissions to interrogate and otherwise pressure gentlemen who would not pay. He hesitated to authorize the commissioners to demand self-incriminating information; so he instead had the commissioners ask the recalcitrant gentlemen for information about those who had encouraged them in their obstinacy.[25] Two years later, when Parliament adopted the Petition of Right, it complained that many men "have had an oath administered unto them not warrantable by the laws or statutes of this realm," and it prayed that "none be called to make answer, or take such oath" and that none be "molested or disquieted . . . for refusal thereof."[26]

The inquiries about forced loans were merely prerogative or administrative hearings, not common law proceedings. They were not even the sort of prerogative proceedings that were understood to be criminal. And unlike so much prerogative questioning without charges, these inquiries carefully avoided any self-incrimination. Nonetheless, it was clear to Parliament that any such questioning and punishment for refusing to provide information was unlawful.

Such questioning to incriminate others was also common in the High Commission, and it therefore was again condemned in 1641. When abolishing the High Commission, Parliament more generally prohibited any ecclesiastical attempt to exercise extralegal judicial power, and in so doing, Parliament not only forbade ecclesiastical courts from seeking self-incrimination but also barred them from requiring persons on oath to "to make any presentment of any crime or offense."[27] Extralegal tribunals could not force persons to incriminate either themselves or others.

Nonpublic Proceedings

Another characteristic of inquisitorial process that has been revived in administrative proceedings was that it often was hidden from public view. This resulted in part from the absence of juries and a corresponding reliance on written evidence, but more generally inquisitorial process was secretive at all stages—as much of it is again nowadays.

At common law, "intelligence of faults . . . by uncertain author, or suppressed name, is wholly . . . rejected." In the High Commission, however, the complaints that could trigger an ex officio inquiry could be anonymous. Even when informants were known to the commission, their identity could be suppressed. When the prerogative judges proceeded to their inquiries, moreover, they interrogated suspects not only in "public courts . . . but privately also into secret corners and privy chambers"—most notoriously, the Inner Star Chamber.[28] Even when proceedings occurred in the regular chambers of the irregular courts, there was little publicity, for the courts themselves were mostly closed to public.

This was private rather than public justice, and it led Edward Coke to remind his contemporaries that the law required "all causes to be heard, ordered, and determined before the judges of the king's courts." Indeed, it had to be heard "openly in the kings courts, whither all persons may resort," not in "chambers, or other private places: for the judges are not judges of chambers, but of courts."[29]

Due Process

Today it is widely assumed that the due process of law centrally concerns the courts, and from this perspective it is said that administrative tribunals owe only such process as is due. The process that allegedly is due, however, is a version of inquisitorial process, thus revealing how completely administrative adjudication reverts to its prerogative predecessor. This chapter therefore closes by showing how due process developed into a constitutional principle in response to the prerogative courts—particularly in response to their inquisitorial mode of proceeding.

The notion of the due process of law first came to prominence in earlier disputes over the inquisitorial power of a prerogative court, the king's council. Magna Charta's most famous provision, chapter 39, guaranteed that "[n]o freeman shall be taken or imprisoned or disseised . . . nor will [the king] go upon nor send upon him, except by the lawful judgment of his peers and by the law of the land."[30] This already was a rejection of extra-legal adjudications. In the fourteenth century, however, rather than govern through the courts of law, the king's council summarily called subjects before it for questioning and punishment. Apparently for such reasons, Parliament enacted in 1354 that "[n]o man of what estate or condition that he be, shall be put out of land or tenement, nor taken, nor imprisoned, nor disinherited, nor put to death, without being brought in answer by due process of the law." In the next decade Parliament spelled out the nature of the underlying dispute. It declared that the attempts to hold subjects accountable "before the king's council" were "against the law," and it enacted that "no man be put to answer without presentment before justices, or matter of record, or by due process and writ original, according to the ancient law of the land." Lest the implications be unclear, it concluded that "if anything henceforth be done to the contrary, it shall be void in law, and held for error." The overall principle, as stated in the traditional title of the statute, was that "[n]one shall be put to answer without due process of law."[31] Prerogative or administrative adjudications in the king's council thus provoked Parliament to assert the due process of law.

On the foundation of the medieval statutes, persons who opposed the High Commission complained that its proceedings were extralegal and unlawful—that it engaged in a "form of inquisition" in "derogation and subversion of the law and public justice of this land." Its judges "cast aside" such arguments, saying that Magna Charta and the due process statutes were "antiquated . . . and worn out of use"—this being the civilian doctrine of desuetude or what nowadays would be called the "living constitution." The critics, however, persisted in asking: "Where is now . . . the great Charter of England . . wherein is contained that no freeman shall be apprehended, imprisoned, distrained, impeached, disseised, or put from his freehold or franchise, but by the law of the land . . . ? Where is now the statute . . . whereby it is provided that no man be put to answer without presentment before justices, matter of record, due process [and] writ original, after the ancient law of the land?"[32] Although prerogative judges dismissed the old law, common lawyers stood on the law of the land and the due process of law.

James Morice, for example, complained in 1590 that the High Commission's "examinations and inquiries upon oath" stood in opposition to those of the law—that they "impugn our government and form of justice"—from which he concluded that the "king's grant or commission" establishing the court "is of no force in law."[33] Similarly, in 1607, Nicholas Fuller condemned the court's inquisitorial proceedings by reciting Magna

Charta and the 1368 statute on "due process . . . according to the old law of the land."[34]

Although it was rare before 1610 for English lawyers to argue expressly from England's constitution, Fuller came close. For example, when complaining about the High Commission's administrative power to force disclosure of information, he protested that this was "a course of arbitrary government at the discretion of the commissioners, directly contrary to the happy long continued government and course of the common laws of the realm, and directly contrary to Magna Charta." Of course, the High Commission had at least some statutory authority, and Fuller did not go so far as to say that the underlying statute was void, but he suggestively argued that "all construction of statutes contrary to Magna Charta" was "void."[35] It was a hint of what would soon be the fate of all extralegal adjudication, including inquisitorial proceedings.

The protests against the extralegal process of the prerogative courts were embraced by the House of Commons. When the Commons petitioned against proclamations in 1610, it recognized that this sort of extralegal legislation was accompanied by extralegal adjudication. Most centrally, the Commons complained about the "[p]unishment of offenders in court[s] of arbitrary discretion, [such] as Star Chamber." More generally, the Commons added that prerogative proceedings were extralegal—that they had the effect of "[d]ebarring the subjects from trying their right to and by the law."[36]

The complaints against such proceedings increasingly came from very ordinary men and women. For example, after Sara Jones and other members of a private conventicle or religious service were imprisoned in 1632, they were hauled before the High Commission. Once in court, the king's advocate demanded that they "take their oaths to answer the articles . . . against them," but all of them, beginning with Jones, refused. Their objections were partly religious, partly that they had not been shown the articles against them, and further that they did not know their accuser. More generally, some questioned the lawfulness of the court. Sara Jones archly told the High Commission, "I will answer upon my oath to end a controversy before a lawful magistrate." Later, Elizabeth Sergeant similarly explained that "she must not swear but when she is before a magistrate." This earned her the bishop of London's sarcastic question, "Why now, . . . you are called before the magistrate, are you not?" But Robert Reynolds clarified the point: "If I have done anything against the law, let me be accused by the course of law."[37]

Eventually, in 1641, Parliament abolished the prerogative courts, partly on account of their lack of due process. The downfall of the prerogative courts is often said to be have been their severity and excessive jurisdiction. Undoubtedly, their harsh punishments for religious and political dissent provoked much anger. At the same time, the men who abolished the courts made clear that they were particularly concerned about extralegal adjudication, including the substitution of inquisitorial process for due process and the resulting tendency to impose arbitrary rule in place of lawful government.

The key moment in the abolition of the Star Chamber came when a member of the House of Commons expressed disgust with a mild bill that would have merely regulated the court, apparently confining its jurisdiction more than its inquisitorial process. The complaining member protested that "the usurpations of that court" were at least as much "in the forms of their proceeding" as in their jurisdiction. The court's inquisitorial proceedings, however, were "very difficult, if not impossible, to regulate" by law, because they stood outside and sometimes even above the law. Recognizing this, the complaining member proposed "utterly to abolish" the court—a suggestion that the House promptly followed.[38]

The resulting statute began by reciting how the Star Chamber threatened the due process of law. The act recited chapter 39 of Magna Charta and various statutory confirmations, including the principle stated in 1368, that "no man be put to answer without presentment . . . by due process and writ original, according to the ancient law of the land." It also noted that the matters that came before the Star Chamber could be remedied "by the common law of the land and in the ordinary course of justice." Of course, there were many reasons to object to the Star Chamber, but one central reason was that it did justice outside the law courts and their due process of law.[39, b]

Thereafter, the English constitution and then American constitutions were understood to require that the government not issue binding or constraining edicts in particular instances—in other words, that it not issue judicial edicts—except with the due process of law in the courts of law. As put by the Fifth Amendment to the U.S. Constitution, "No person shall . . . be deprived of life, liberty, or property, without due process of law."

This right is understood these days to be centrally applicable only to

---

b. Even the 1487 statute on the Star Chamber, which was widely assumed to have established this court, seemed to be evidence that the court did not offer the due process of law. As one critic aptly observed in 1641, the statute provided for prerogative proceedings against a defendant as "if he were convict[ed] of the same crime by due process of law." The court thus "sends us to the law, and calls us back from it again."[*]

courts of law, thus allowing administrative bodies to revert to inquisitorial process. The history, however, shows that due process became a constitutional ideal precisely in response to extralegal adjudicatory bodies—what then were prerogative courts and now are administrative courts. As might therefore be expected, it was understood to guarantee the law's judicial process in the courts of law. The constitutional principle thus cannot be understood to allow administrative evasions. On the contrary, the principle requires that all judicial power be exercised with the "due process of law," which was that done through the law and its courts.

More specifically, the history shows that due process became a constitutional right in opposition to the inquisitorial processes of the prerogative courts. Due process thus included a right against inquisitorial proceedings—those in which administrative officers, outside the formal accusatory processes of the courts of law, could demand testimony or other information merely on the basis of suspicion, or otherwise could proceed against persons for not supplying information.

At stake in the due process of law, therefore, was much more than is usually understood. Rather than being merely a loose notion of procedural "fairness," the due process of law was a requirement that government could bind subjects in particular instances only through the traditional processes of the law, consisting of regular criminal or civil proceedings.[c] Even more fundamentally, it meant that government could bind members of the public in particular cases only through the regular courts, not through administrative tribunals. That is, it had to act through juries, and through judges whose office required them to exercise independent judgment in accord with the law—not through politic administrators who followed regulations or other irregular expressions of policy.

Nonetheless, as will be shown in chapter 13, administrative agencies have returned to the inquisitorial process of the prerogative courts. Although the guarantee of due process does not bar Congress from enacting disclosure or courts from ordering it, administrative bodies have gone further: they have gone back to imposing their own demands for disclosure through inquisitorial proceedings. For example, like the prerogative courts, administrative agencies often begin their proceedings not with indictments, but on the accusations of anonymous or secret informers, or merely on the suspicions or policy decisions of executive officers. Indeed, agencies

c. Criminal proceedings were commenced by indictment or presentment, and civil proceedings, by original writs. Accordingly, when Chief Justice Coke defined the due process of law, he said it is "by indictment or presentment of good and lawful men . . . or by writ original of the common law."*

impose ex officio demands for information about compliance, thus coercively fishing for violations before formal charges are brought. The agencies thereby combine functions that the due process of law separates. For example, the agencies serve as initial investigators and interrogators, then as prosecutors, then as grand juries, and then as judges and juries; in other words, they coercively collect information, formulate charges, determine their sufficiency, and finally try them. Last but not least, the agencies impose self-incriminating questions and even require persons to self-report their departures from regulations before they are questioned—thus reviving the confessional character of inquisitorial process. In all of these ways, administrative agencies return to the inquisitorial process that the due process of law repudiated.

〰〰〰

By means of its extralegal or irregular exercise of judicial power, government once again proceeds against members of the public not merely without juries and regular judges, but more generally without the due process of law. Indeed, it relies on self-incrimination and other inquisitional proceedings.

This time the inquisitorial proceedings are called "administrative" rather than "prerogative." Yet as will become apparent in chapter 13, they have much in common with the extralegal proceedings of the past.

In justification of the due process violations and the other constitutional problems examined thus far, it sometimes is hinted that the U.S. Constitution's grant of judicial power, and the limits on it, centrally concern the courts, not the executive. The history, however, shows that constitutional law developed most basically to bar extralegal power, including extralegal adjudication. Giving force to this repudiation of extralegal adjudication, the U.S. Constitution places judicial power in the courts. In addition, the Constitution applies most of its judicial processes and rights generally, not merely to the courts—thus reaching all exercises of judicial power, even those that are extralegal. The Constitution, in short, systematically bars extralegal judicial power.

Already here, therefore, before this book focuses on contemporary law, it should be evident that, when administrative agencies exercise judicial power outside the courts, without the due process of law, and without satisfying the other processes and rights that limit judicial power, they act unconstitutionally. They revert to the extralegal power that constitutional law emphatically prohibited.

ELEVEN

Prerogative Orders and Warrants

The binding effect of judicial power comes in orders and warrants. In the ordinary course of law, the courts and their judges issue orders and warrants that bind members of the public. In the prerogative past, however, extralegal judges bound members of the public with extralegal orders and warrants, and now in the administrative present, extralegal judges have revived this mode of constraint.

When the Crown's prerogative courts issued orders and warrants outside judicial channels, the English responded by developing constitutional limits. The English clarified that the constitutional power to issue binding orders and warrants was judicial and that it thus belonged exclusively to the courts and their judges. The English also made clear that all judicial power, including binding orders and warrants, was limited by due process and, more specifically, by the common law requirements for warrants. Not only in England but eventually also in America, this array of constitutional principles barred extralegal judicial orders and warrants. As a result, administrative orders and warrants can no more escape such principles than their prerogative predecessors.

At the outset, it must be recognized that the Crown or executive could lawfully issue some orders and warrants. For example (as will be explained in chapter 12), it could issue orders and warrants directing the conduct of its officers. At stake here, however, are orders and warrants that legally bind subjects, including subpoenas for the appearance of persons and the production of their papers, final orders imposing penalties, and warrants authorizing search and seizure. In issuing versions of such orders and warrants, the Crown extralegally exercised part of the judicial power. It used prerogative power to sidestep the judges and the due process of law, and nowadays the executive in its administrative power engages in a similar evasion.

Orders and Warrants from Prerogative Tribunals

Although, at law, only judges had a power to issue orders or warrants that constrained subjects, the Star Chamber and the High Commission also issued such instruments. These tribunals thereby collided with the increasingly sharp assumption that the Crown could bind subjects in particular cases only by acting through the courts and their judges.

An order, usually in the form of a subpoena, directly commanded a subject—for example, requiring him to appear, testify, or produce his papers. There was nothing remarkable about such an order when it came from a law court, but when prerogative courts issued subpoenas, it was another matter, for they were extralegal institutions, which enforced extralegal enactments.[a] Moreover, they issued their subpoenas and other orders in the course of their inquisitorial proceedings, and thus in pursuit of proceedings inimical to the due process of law.

In contrast to a subpoena, a warrant was not an order to a subject, but to an officer to constrain a subject. It was called a "warrant" because the officer later could rely upon it to warrant his conduct if he were charged with false imprisonment or some other unlawful act. At law, warrants were issued by judges or, in localities, by justices of the peace. The judges of the prerogative courts, however, also issued warrants authorizing constraints on the public, and they maintained their own officers to search for and seize wayward persons and their papers.[1]

Overall, the prerogative courts thus claimed an extralegal power to bind subjects—either by order or by way of a warrant. As observed by one of the High Commission's victims in the reign of Queen Elizabeth, the commissioners sought to "withdraw some of the most high and chief causes from her royal courts and judgment seats into their own courts," and they therefore exercised "absolute authority" on their own to "cite, summon," and "confiscate, at their pleasure whom and wherefore they list . . . not by the prince's royal writs and courts to which every soul ought to be subject."[2]

Rather than accept the resulting prerogative orders and warrants, the English increasingly questioned them. The popular opposition to Star Chamber subpoenas has already been noted, it being "a common thing" as early as 1602 "to resist the process of this Court, and with disgrace to condemn it, and to beat him who executes it."[3] Even more dramatically, re-

---

a. The term "law court" is understood broadly here to include not only courts of law but also the Chancery, for by the mid-seventeenth century (as noted in chapter 8), the Chancery had abandoned its prerogative pretensions. Although it remained a court of equity, it accepted its role within and under the law.

ligious dissenters resisted the High Commission's warrants for search and seizure.

The most notorious critic of the commission was "Martin Marprelate"—a fictional opponent of the bishops. His audacious creators avoided detection by having his antiprelatical pamphlets printed in the country houses of sympathetic gentry. The printers stayed one step ahead of the High Commission by trundling a printing press in a wagon from house to house, thereby leading the High Commission on a wild goose chase across southern England.[4]

The threat from prerogative orders and warrants ended only when Parliament abolished the Star Chamber and High Commission. In 1640 and 1641, a committee of the House of Commons spent months hearing complaints from those who had suffered under these courts. The complaints concerned extralegal orders, and warrants both for arrest and for the search and seizure of papers, and the committee carefully reported the details. After hearing the report on each case, the House of Commons repeatedly resolved that the orders or warrants were "illegal" or "against law and the liberty of the subject."[5] On such foundations, Parliament abolished the prerogative tribunals and their jurisdiction, and it thereby ended not only these courts but also the orders and warrants by which they burdened subjects outside the mechanisms of the law. At least for a while, therefore, these prerogative edicts became a matter of history.

The Judicial Character of Orders and Warrants Binding Subjects

After 1641, orders and warrants that bound subjects had to be issued by regular judicial officers. To be precise, orders had to come from the courts, and warrants (as Akhil Amar has observed) had to come from judges or at least justices of the peace.[6] There thus was no room for administrative orders or warrants.

The Exceptions and the Rule

Of course, there remained exceptions to the judicial character of binding orders and warrants, but they were exceptions that defined the rule. Parliamentary committees still issued orders for appearance and testimony on the basis of Parliament's status as a court. Military officers still gave orders to their subordinates, for they enjoyed a distinct realm of power, along lines that differed from those of the civilian world. The Crown still issued detention warrants—for a while above law, but eventually (as will be seen) under lawful suspensions of habeas corpus. Perhaps most interestingly, bankruptcy commissioners issued orders to preserve the bankrupt's estate. Beyond such instances, however, orders and warrants binding members of the public were aspects of the judicial power, and the government therefore could lawfully issue such orders or warrants only by working through judicial officers.[b]

On this principle, Chief Justice Matthew Hale explained that arrest warrants were judicial acts. "[A]ll courts and persons, that have judicial power by the common law, or by act of parliament for the conservation of the peace, have power to grant warrants for arresting of felons." In contrast, others could not issue arrest warrants. For example, officers who "are simply ministerial and have no jurisdiction, [such] as constables, cannot issue warrants for that purpose, but must do their office either alone, or with others called to their assistance." Lest it be thought that this bar against warrants from nonjudicial officers excluded only low-level or ministerial officers, he added that even royal "proclamations against persons not indicted are against law."[7]

The result was a revealing contrast between the royal or executive power of the king and the judicial power of lowly justices of the peace. Whereas "the power of justices of the peace to convene and commit felons before indictment is allowed," the Crown had no such power. And what was true of warrants against the bodies of subjects was also true of warrants for search and seizure of their goods, for these warrants were also "judicial acts."[8]

The larger point was that the government ordinarily could direct subjects in particular cases only though judicial acts. Put another way, the application of legal obligation to subjects in particular instances was understood, by its nature, to be a judicial power. Among the implications was that orders or warrants could be issued only when a party formally initiated judicial proceedings. As explained about warrants in the 1760s, "[n]othing . . . can be forcibly taken from any man, or his house entered, without some specific charge upon oath."[9]

In this context, when the U.S. Constitution gave judicial power to the courts, it gave only the courts the power to issue binding orders and warrants. Of course, there were the exceptions: orders could also come from legislative committees and military officers, and warrants could come under suspensions of habeas. In general, however, orders or warrants binding members of the public were judicial and had to come from the judges.

---

b. Another possible exception was the power of secretaries of state to issue search and seizure warrants for unlicensed printing, and for seditious libels, but this increasingly was done on the assumption that the secretaries of state had taken oaths as justices of the peace.

The Central Danger

The principle that the government could bind its subjects only through judicial orders and warrants, was profoundly important for confining the exercise of power within the channels of the law. An irregular system of government, whether prerogative or administrative, can succeed only if it has the power to impose its irregular will on its subjects. An extralegal regime therefore needs not only administrative regulations but also administrative means of applying the regulations to subjects. It thus was essential for the development of government through and under law that the English and American constitutions were understood generally to bar governments from issuing binding orders and warrants, other than through the courts and their judicial officers.

Of course, alongside this requirement that the government could bind subjects only through judicial orders and warrants was the authority of executive officers directly to coerce subjects—most commonly when constables acted on their own knowledge or suspicion to search and seize persons and their property. These officers could lawfully act without an order or warrant, and it therefore may be thought that they were inadequately restrained by the requirement that orders and warrants had to come from judges. Executive officers, however, were vulnerable to civil actions for damages if they acted unreasonably—most basically, if they acted without probable cause. The resulting space for warrantless searches and seizures was thus very narrow. It was confined to officers who had authority to enforce the law, who acted on their own knowledge or suspicion, and who did so on sufficient evidentiary grounds, for otherwise their acts would be unreasonable.

Although this lawful freedom of executive officers to act without warrants may seem dangerous, the goal of the Constitution's warrant requirement was not to prevent every unreasonable search, but to limit the danger from an extralegal regime. Local arresting officers often needed the freedom to act on their own initiative, subject to the risk of liability, and although there was some cost in allowing them in the first instance to judge the reasonableness of their conduct, the more profound danger was the administrative power to issue binding orders or warrants.

Binding extralegal orders and warrants were what allowed an extralegal regime to rule independently of the law and its courts. The U.S. Constitution's warrant requirement therefore reinforced the understanding that orders and warrants were part of the judicial power and that they thus had to come from the courts and their judges. Exactly how it did this will become apparent later in this chapter. For now it is enough to note that the Constitution's warrant requirement aimed not merely to prevent unreasonable searches and seizures, but more centrally to hold off the threat of binding orders and warrants from administrative or otherwise nonjudicial officers.

Warrants in Cases of State Necessity

Notwithstanding that the orders and warrants that bound subjects had to come from judicial officers, there remained an open question as to whether the king and his council nonetheless had to be able to issue arrest warrants in cases of extreme necessity. Although the necessity for most administrative warrants did not rise above considerations of administrative efficiency, some necessities, emergencies, were more urgent. In these circumstances, the Crown might need a power of administrative detention, and the warrants it used for these detentions were the crucial test of whether the law could really tame prerogative or administrative warrants. In no other instance was it so clear that an administrative power outside the law might sometimes be necessary, but in no other instance was the potential for abuse of power so keenly felt.

In 1591, Lord Chancellor Christopher Hatton and Lord Treasurer William Cecil asked the judges for an advisory opinion about the Crown's power of detention—in particular, whether the Crown could issue warrants to detain individuals without being required to specify the cause in later judicial proceedings on writs of habeas corpus. The Crown apparently wanted clarity about when it could successfully use administrative detention against traitors and others who seemed to threaten the state.

The judges responded with what became the leading judicial opinion on extrajudicial warrants. In general, they did not recognize any prerogative or administrative power of detention. But in deference to government necessity, they acknowledged a narrow range of three circumstances in which the Crown could hold persons without specifying the cause.

First, the Crown could issue warrants "by her majesty's special commandment," meaning an order "from her person." Second, it could issue warrants "by order of the council-board," meaning an order of the council as a body. Finally, any one or two members of the board could issue warrants for treason—or, as more narrowly stated in another version of the opinion, "for treason touching her majesty's person." On any one of these three foundations, imprisonment on a nonjudicial warrant could be impervious to a writ of habeas. Rather than have to specify the reason for the imprisonment on his return of the writ, the jailer could generally recite who had signed the warrant—merely saying, for example, that the prisoner was being held at her majesty's special command. This would suffice because the judges in such a case would let the monarch be the final judge of the governmental necessity. Outside the three exceptional circumstances identified by the judges, however, a return had to be sufficiently specific to show that the detention was done lawfully.[10]

The 1591 opinion thus left only a limited window for prerogative warrants, but it was more than enough to open up opportunities for abuse—as became clear in *Darnel's Case*. When Charles I in 1626 demanded forced loans, he was resisted by Sir Thomas Darnel and four other gentlemen. After Charles issued warrants committing them to the Fleet Prison, they obtained writs of habeas corpus, but the warden of the Fleet returned simply that they were being held at the king's special command. The judges acknowledged that this was the primary exception recognized by the 1591 opinion, and they therefore left the men in prison. The shallowness of this reasoning, however, was manifest. As Serjeant John Bramston argued for the prisoners, "our case will not stand upon precedents, but upon the fundamental laws and statutes of this realm; and though the precedents look the one way or the other, they are to be brought back unto the laws by which the kingdom is governed."[11]

These events left many Englishmen wondering whether any ruler could be entrusted with prerogative or administrative discretion to issue warrants for the detention of subjects. Undoubtedly, there might be genuine cases of necessity, in which the government might need to detain persons without explaining why. It was disturbing, however, that the king was using prerogative warrants to imprison men for reasons that seemed to have little basis in pressing national necessities. Even more worrisome, the king was relying on prerogative warrants to enforce a sort of prerogative taxation. The monarch's evasion of judicial process thus threatened to become the means of sustaining his evasion of legislative process.

Parliament responded by insisting that the Crown or executive had no power of arrest or detention outside the law. The Petition of Right in 1628 recited Magna Charta to the effect that "no freeman may be taken or imprisoned . . . but by the lawful judgment of his peers or by the law of the land." The Petition of Rights also quoted the 1368 statute that echoed Magna Charta with the provision that "no man" should be "taken, nor imprisoned . . . without being brought to answer by due process of law." On this basis, the petition observed that nevertheless "divers of your subjects have of late been imprisoned without any cause showed" and that when these subjects obtained writs of habeas, "no cause was certified, but . . .

they were detained by your majesty's special command." As a result, they "were returned back to several prisons, without being charged with anything to which they might make answer according to the law." The petition therefore protested that "no freeman, in any such manner" should "be imprisoned or detained."[12]

Although Parliament resisted the Crown's power to make emergency administrative arrests, it soon claimed this absolute power for itself. Recent kings seemed to have demonstrated that the power could not be entrusted to them, and advocates of the legislature therefore argued that if there had to be a power above law, it could "no where rest more safely than in Parliament."[13] Lawlessness, however, even parliamentary lawlessness, has never been a lasting justification for authority in Anglo-American society. Ultimately, therefore, the question could not be which part of government had the authority to engage in adventures outside the law, but rather how administrative detentions in genuine emergencies could be accommodated within the law.

Parliament achieved a lawful solution of this sort in the 1679 Habeas Corpus Act. There have recently been suggestions that the statute accomplished little.[14] In fact, it not only offered a remedy for emergency administrative arrests but also clarified how such arrests could be made lawfully. In the 1670s, discontented members of Parliament, who would soon acquire the name "Whigs," feared that their politics might eventually prompt the king to imprison them at his special command and thus without access to habeas. They therefore secured a statute requiring the judges to grant the writ and requiring jailers to specify the cause of the imprisonment in their return of the writ. Because these were statutory requirements, only Parliament thereafter could spare the Crown from writs of habeas, and thus only Parliament could allow the Crown to detain persons without showing cause.

The statute thereby placed emergency detentions on a lawful footing. From 1679 onward, administrative detentions occurred not by virtue of a state necessity above the law, but under acts of Parliament that suspended habeas and authorized the detentions.[15] There thus remained an emergency exception to the principle that warrants binding subjects had to be issued by judicial officers, but the Habeas Corpus Act reduced it to an exception within the law, as determined by the legislature. In this way, the absolute power to detain in emergencies was tamed and rendered lawful.

This approach prevailed in the next century in the United States. It will be recalled that when the U.S. Constitution enumerated limits on legislative power, it required that "the Writ of Habeas Corpus shall not be suspended, unless when in Cases of Rebellion or Invasion the public Safety may require it."[16] The Constitution thereby followed the model of the Habeas Corpus Act, authorizing administrative warrants for emergency detention, but only under law, and only with legislative authorization. The Constitution thus preserved the judicial character of warrants by incorporating a limited version of the most pressing exception.

General Warrants

Although an administrative officer generally could not issue a warrant authorizing constraint of a subject, he could try to obtain a general warrant. This was a judicial warrant that did not specify the person to be seized or place to be searched—sometimes not even the suspected offense. The unconstitutionality of such warrants is well known, but what is less well understood is the reason.

General warrants facially satisfied the principle that warrants constraining subjects had to come from judicial officers, for these warrants were signed by such men. Nonetheless, by omitting details—whether about the persons, places, or offenses—these warrants ran into difficulty. One risk was that the omissions turned the warrants into judicial authorizations to search or seize merely on suspicion that offenses would be committed in the future. As observed in the seventeenth century, "General warrants are not legal to apprehend any man upon suspicion of a fact that may, or is like to be committed."[17] Even worse, such warrants shifted the exercise of judgment, making "the party to be in effect the judge." In other words, they shifted the decision about probable cause from judicial officers to the constables and others who enforced the warrants, thus giving merely administrative officers a freedom to search and seize according to their discretion.[18]

General warrants therefore are profoundly revealing about the extent of the bar against administrative warrants. They show that even judicial warrants were unlawful if in reality they functioned as administrative warrants.

The attitudes toward general warrants can be illustrated by the reaction against Chief Justice William Scroggs. He notoriously was more dedicated to the Crown than the law, and in his brutish zeal for the royal prerogative, he "granted divers general warrants for attaching the persons, and seizing the goods of his majesty's subjects, not named or described particularly in the said warrants." In 1681 this became one of the reasons for his impeachment. As the Commons explained, his general warrants were the "means whereof many of his majesty's subjects have been vexed, their houses entered into, and they themselves grievously oppressed contrary to law."[19] Although a prorogation of Parliament cut short the impeachment, the disapproval of general warrants was obvious.[c]

The underlying legal logic was nearly inescapable. The traditional method of evading the judicial character of warrants had been for a justice of the peace to sign a warrant that left blanks where he ordinarily would insert the suspect's name and offense. Such a warrant clearly was invalid, and as noted by an early-eighteenth-century treatise writer, William Hawkins, this had implications for general warrants: "[I]f a justice cannot legally grant a blank warrant for the arrest of a single person, leaving it to the party to fill it up, surely he cannot grant such a general warrant, which might have the effect of an hundred blank warrants." It therefore seemed "very questionable, whether a constable can justify the execution of a general warrant to search for felons or stolen goods." A constable could rely on a facially valid warrant, but a general warrant "seems to be illegal in the very face of it"—the danger being that the warrant would "leave it to the discretion of a common officer to arrest what persons, and search what houses he thinks fit."[20]

On account of this administrative danger, general warrants were held in 1763 to be not merely unlawful, but unconstitutional. John Wilkes—the brilliant demagogue—had excoriated the government in his newspaper, the *North Briton*. When the government sought to prosecute him for the notorious issue number 45, Secretary of State Halifax issued a warrant "in his majesty's name" to apprehend and seize "the authors printers and publishers" of issue 45, together with their private papers. It had long been the practice of secretaries of state to sign warrants for seizing the producers of alleged seditious libels and their papers without specifying such persons by name, and the practice of issuing these general warrants could be considered an administrative precedent. On such grounds—that it was "the course of office" and that this sort of precedent had been "approved of by the crown-lawyers"—Lord Halifax signed the warrant.[21] Wilkes, however,

---

c. It is commonly assumed that objections to general warrants date back only to the Wilkes controversy, but they actually run across much of the history of English law. The antiquity of the objections is suggested by a 1338 case in which Justice William de Shareshull emphasized the need for a "special warrant." Complaints about general warrants became increasingly common, and by the late seventeenth century were prominent.

What changed after the mid-seventeenth century was that the English came to assume there were constitutional barriers to prerogative warrants. The Crown therefore increasingly relied on general warrants where it previously would have used prerogative warrants, and general warrants thereby came to seem not merely unlawful acts, but evasions of the constitution.*

was unimpressed by the course of administrative practice, and in an action for damages against the arresting officer, Robert Wood, Wilkes challenged the constitutionality of the warrant.

The initial question was whether a secretary of state was a judicial officer. In the United States, where executive and judicial powers would be more sharply drawn, a secretary of state would not be able to serve as a justice of the peace, and he therefore would not be able to issue even a special warrant for search and seizure. In England, however, because secretaries of state tended to be sworn as justices of the peace, they usually had judicial authority—albeit, as Blackstone said, only "in extraordinary cases."[22] In the case against Wood, however, it was not yet clear whether Secretary of State Halifax could be considered a justice of the peace.[23]

The case therefore turned on the other question, that of general warrants. A general warrant was facially inadequate, and thus Wood—the arresting officer—could not defend himself by relying on the warrant signed by Secretary of State Halifax. As Chief Justice Charles Pratt instructed the jury: "This warrant is unconstitutional, illegal, and absolutely void." The reason was that a general warrant delegated judicial power to Crown and its minions: "If it be good, a secretary of state can delegate and depute any one of the messengers, or any even from the lowest of the people, to take examinations, to commit or release, and, in fine, to do every act which the highest judicial officers the law knows can do or order."[24] Whether regarding a person or his papers, the decision to search and seize had to remain in a judicial officer.[d]

General warrants, moreover, could not be justified even though they were a long-standing administrative practice. Crown officers had become accustomed to issuing general warrants, but their administrative precedents and the advice of Crown lawyers could be relevant only "in mitigation of damages," not to excuse the violation of law. As put by Pratt, "the office precedents, which had been produced . . . are no justification of a practice itself illegal, and contrary to the fundamental principles of the constitution."[25]

---

d. The danger that a general warrant would become, in effect, an administrative warrant was widely recognized. For example, in a series of essays published in 1776, Francis Maseres observed: "This omission of Mr. Wilkes's name made the warrant utterly illegal, because it required the king's messenger (who was a mere ministerial officer, or rather who acted as such) to do that which was the business of a judicial officer, or magistrate, that is, to exercise an act of judgment of so high a nature by determining who were, and who were not concerned in the commission of the offense in question. . . . And much less can a magistrate delegate such a power of determining who is the person that has committed a particular offense, to a mere ministerial officer of justice . . . which is done whenever a general warrant is issued."*

The controversy over general warrants thus reveals how completely constitutional law barred administrative warrants. General warrants shifted
power to administrative officers and therefore were recognized as evasions
of the principle that warrants had to be judicial. The judicial signature
could not paper over the administrative reality.

Writs of Assistance

At the same time that the Chief Justice rejected the use of a general warrant
against Wilkes, the English Crown continued to rely on general warrants in
the more bureaucratic context of the customs office. Although these general warrants—the "writs of assistance"—were signed by judges, they left
senior customs officers to make administrative determinations of probable
cause, and they thus, in effect, functioned as administrative warrants. From
a bureaucratic perspective, they were the very model of an efficient administrative departure from law. When Parliament, however, authorized the
use of such writs against Americans, a rejection of administrative warrants
became one of the foundations of the American Revolution.

Customs officers regularly needed the protection of a warrant. Much of
their work consisted of searching warehouses and other private premises,
and although, like constables, they could act on their own suspicion or
knowledge, they typically needed to act on the knowledge of others. They
therefore usually could not conduct their searches without facially lawful
warrants. For example, when a customs officer learned from an informant
about illicit or untaxed goods, he had to go before a justice of the peace
for a warrant before he could insist on entry into the suspected warehouse,
let alone before he could break open its doors. Even if he were zealous
enough to risk a suit for damages, the legal risk was such that he would
have difficulty persuading other officers to assist him, and there were physical dangers in acting alone.

It was tedious, however, to seek a warrant from a justice of the peace.
The difficulty was not simply that the justice might be unavailable or slow.
He also might ask for details about the probable cause. At the very least,
the justice would expect a sworn statement of probable cause, and in the
shady world of customs enforcement, this sometimes might be awkward.
The requirement of a judicial warrant thus could be an impediment to efficient enforcement.

The English customs office therefore relied on the familiar evasion offered by a general warrant—the specialized version used by the customs
office being known variously as a "writ of assistance" or a "writ of assis-

tants."[26] This was a warrant, issued periodically by the Court of Exchequer, authorizing the principle customs officers, with the assistance of their servants, to search for untaxed goods.

The evasion was in the details. Although this was a judicial warrant, it was a general standing warrant, to be used at the discretion of the administrative officers. Since the first half of the eighteenth century, the commissioners of customs would apply to Exchequer for such a warrant, which did not specify the place or objects of the search. The principle customs officers then would hold it "for use by them or their subordinates as the occasion demanded." The principle officers apparently avoided abuses of this instrument by mimicking the judicial function—by requiring "the same showing of information and probable cause that a justice would have required for the issue of a special search warrant."[27] Nonetheless, writs of assistance were evasions, for they allowed administrative officers to substitute their judgment for that of judicial officers. Although a writ of assistance was signed by a judge, in reality an administrative officer decided upon the places and goods to which it applied.

One colonial American governor was slow to understand even the underlying assumption, that writs had to come from judicial officers. William Shirley became governor of Massachusetts in 1741, and some time afterward he began to issue general standing warrants—writs of assistance—to the colony's customs officers, thus sparing them from having to apply to the judges.[28] The gross unlawfulness of the practice, however, was noticed by Thomas Hutchinson, who also eventually would become governor.

Hutchinson became involved when customs officers acted on "information of iron imported from Spain being concealed" in a warehouse belonging to Hutchinson's brother. With this information (although it was mistaken) the customs officers probably could have obtained a special warrant from a judge, but instead they proceeded on their general warrant. When they were about to break open the building, Hutchinson, who was friendly with the officers, asked one of them "what authority he had to enter," at which point the officer "showed the governor's warrant." Hutchinson knew that his brother was not harboring any untaxed goods, and he therefore "sent for the keys, and caused the warehouse to be opened." At the same time, he told the officer that "if he had forced an entry, an action would have been brought against him, his warrant being of no value."

Governor Shirley responded by "examining the legality of his warrants." Recognizing that the officers had to meet the same standards as the English customs office, he "direct[ed] the officers to apply for warrants from the superior court; and, from that time, writs issued, not exactly in the form, but of the nature of writs of assistance issued from the Court of Exchequer in England."[29]

Looking back on these events late in his life, Hutchinson noted that the warrants issued by Governor Shirley did not even pretend, like writs of assistance, to be judicial warrants. Shirley had issued the warrants "as the civil magistrate," while he "was in administration"—meaning that they were candidly administrative rather than judicial. Hutchinson expostulated: "This appears [all the] more extraordinary, as Mr. Shirley was a lawyer by education, and was allowed to be a man of good sense."[30] Hutchinson's astonishment at Shirley is revealing. There was little question that warrants had to be judicial rather than administrative, and the only real dispute was whether they could be evasively general.

Americans eventually refused to submit to the evasion, for they were even more anxious than the English to enjoy the rights of Englishmen. Although customs officials in Massachusetts had become careful to rely on writs of assistance from the colony's Superior Court, they eventually needed replacement writs, issued in the name of the new king, George III, when he came to the throne in 1760. They therefore asked the court for new writs. It must have seemed like an ordinary bureaucratic request.

Americans, however, were becoming restive, and it was bad news for the customs officers that James Otis was among the lawyers who opposed the issuance of the writs. Eager to preserve his men's administrative discretion, the surveyor general of the customs, Thomas Lechmere, responded by insisting "that writs of assistance may be granted to himself and his officers as usual."[31]

When the question was debated before the Superior Court in 1761, the lawyer for the customs office, Jeremiah Gridley, apparently conceded that writs of assistance, being general warrants, would ordinarily be unlawful, but he justified them on grounds of administrative necessity: "It is true that the common privileges of Englishmen are taken away in this case, but . . . 'tis the necessity of the case and the benefit of the revenue that justifies this writ." Otis answered that the law allowed only "special writs," which could be granted only "on oath and probable suspicion." Otis recognized that the writs of assistance, in effect, restored prerogative warrants and that this was being justified on the old absolutist theory of a necessity above the law, and he therefore concluded: "It is the business of this court to demolish this monster of oppression, and tear into rags this remnant of Star Chamber tyranny."[32] Not understanding how writs of assistance harked back to prerogative warrants, modern scholars view Otis's allusion to Star Chamber tyranny as mere oratory, but his outcry accurately identified the extralegal effect of the writs and the heritage of the government's argument from administrative need.

What the English permitted, Americans thus called into question. The Massachusetts Superior Court felt bound to issue the new writs of assistance, for the barons of the English Exchequer had issued such warrants, and although the judges of the other central English courts had not upheld the practice, neither had they condemned it. Otis's arguments, however, circulated among lawyers and reached the public through the newspapers.[33]

After the Wilkes episode, moreover, even English law seemed to vindicate the American objections. Although the English government continued to use writs of assistance in England, Americans felt they had good reason to reject them as general warrants.[34]

To solve the problem, the English government (in the 1767 Townshend Revenue Act) authorized colonial courts to grant writs of assistance, but with little success.[35] Aroused by the earlier events in Boston, the courts in many colonies refrained from issuing the writs. The chief justice of Pennsylvania bluntly said that "such a general writ" was "not agreeable to law"—a point in which the colony's attorney general concurred. Similarly, the chief justice of East Florida wrote that he was not "justified by law to issue general writs . . . to be lodged in the hands, and to be executed discretionally (perhaps without proper foundation) at the will of subordinate officers, to the injury of the rights of his Majesty's other loyal subjects."[36]

After this experience with writs of assistance, Americans in their constitutions forbade all general warrants. Whereas the English generally viewed general warrants to be unconstitutional but left room for writs of assistance, Americans sweepingly barred general warrants, even the convenient administrative exception that the English retained. The Maryland Constitution, for example, prohibited "all general warrants—to search suspected places, or to apprehend suspected persons, without naming or describing the place, or the person in special," declaring that they "are illegal and ought not to be granted."[37] Taking the other drafting option, the U.S. Constitution, required that "no Warrants shall issue, but upon probable cause, supported by Oath or affirmation, and particularly describing the place to be searched, and the persons or things to be seized." Either way, these sorts of American provisions assumed that warrants had to be judicial, and they clarified that all warrants had to be particular rather than general.

The response of Americans to the writs of assistance thus reveals how systematically the U.S. Constitution barred any return to administrative orders and warrants. Most generally, the Constitution placed judicial power in the courts and thus required all binding orders and warrants to come from judges. In addition, it guaranteed the due process of law and thereby allowed the government to bind members of the public in particular instances only through the courts and their processes. Last but not least, it barred general warrants, which had been used as a subterfuge to shift search and seizure decisions to administrative officers.

Nonetheless, administrative decisions about orders and warrants have once again been revived under cover of judicial formalities. The difference is that this time the judicial fig leaf comes after rather than before the administrative decisions. Instead of getting a judicial but general order or warrant, which leaves the actual decision to administrators, administrators now issue their own orders and warrants and then get the courts deferentially to uphold them. Although the current administrative evasion is different from that employed by customs officers in the eighteenth century, the response to that earlier evasion is a reminder of the underlying principle—that binding orders and warrants must be judicial in reality, not merely in form.

⬥⬥⬥

Just as the power to impose binding rules was legislative, so the power to impose binding orders or warrants was judicial. There were, of course, the exceptions for congressional committees, military orders, and suspensions of habeas. But otherwise any orders or warrants that bound members of the public were judicial and therefore had to come from the judges.

Although the principle that binding orders and warrants had to come from the courts or their judges was ancient, for a long time it was much evaded. It was evaded directly and systematically by prerogative orders and warrants, and indirectly and sporadically by general warrants. English and especially American constitutional law therefore eventually clarified that such evasions were prohibited.

Administrative agencies, however—as will become apparent in chapter 13—have returned to the extralegal issuance of binding orders and warrants. The agencies thereby ignore how constitutional law developed in opposition to such administrative instruments. Specifically, they ignore the U.S. Constitution's grant of judicial power to the courts, its guarantee of the due process of law, and its provision against general warrants. By these means the Constitution generally barred all binding administrative orders and warrants, even if they were judicial in form. Nonetheless, administrative orders and warrants have come back to life.

TWELVE

Lawful Executive Acts Adjacent to Adjudication

Before part II concludes by examining the contemporary administrative re-turn to prerogative adjudication, this part must acknowledge that the early federal executive could do much that came close to judicial power. For example, the executive could hold judicial-like hearings and could issue orders directing its own officers. But it could do these things that might seem like judicial power only as long as it did not thereby bind subjects in the manner of actual judicial power.

Although the distinction between binding and nonbinding adjudication nowadays tends to be forgotten, some scholars (including Gary Lawson and especially Caleb Nelson) recognize it as the basis of judicial power.[1] To be precise, the core of judicial power, which belonged exclusively to the courts, was the power to make binding adjudications, not merely in the sense that they were determinative, but more basically in the sense that they bound subjects, whether by obliging them to appear, to testify, to produce documents, to pay damages, or otherwise to relinquish their liberty or rights. And already here it should be evident that these binding adjudications did not include decisions about government benefits or privileges, unless they had "vested" and become rights.

Most administrative law scholarship, however, confuses the distinction between binding and nonbinding adjudication. It thereby fails to sort out the difference between unlawful administrative adjudication and lawful executive action.

This confusion affects perceptions of precedents. It often is argued (for example, by Jerry Mashaw) that there was administrative adjudication in the 1790s—as if the decisions then were really precedents for contemporary administrative adjudication.[2] The effect is to normalize contemporary administrative adjudication and even to lend it the authority of the founders or at least the early Republic. The supposed administrative precedents, however, concerned executive actions that did not bind subjects. In contrast, the contemporary administrative adjudications that are challenged in this book do bind subjects and thereby amount to an exercise of judicial power outside the adjudications of the courts. The claim about early federal precedents for administrative adjudication thus dissipates as soon as one recognizes the distinction between adjudications that bind and those that do not. The one sort finds no support in the other.

A related misunderstanding is that the objections to administrative adjudication prove too much—that they challenge even nonbinding executive adjudications. In arguing against prerogative or administrative adjudication, however, this book takes aim only at the administrative adjudications that purport to bind subjects. Other executive proceedings, orders, and warrants, which make no attempt to bind subjects, do not amount to extralegal exercises of judicial power, and the argument here therefore does not question them. Indeed, far from challenging nonbinding executive power, the argument here clarifies its lawfulness.

Thus, whether regarding the claim of precedents or the fears of overreaching objections, the distinction between binding and nonbinding adjudications can clear up much of the difficulty. Binding administrative adjudication (like binding administrative legislation) amounts to extralegal power.

Executive Adjudication Concerning Nonsubjects

When the U.S. Constitution located judicial power in the courts, it left the executive free to use judicial-like proceedings as long as these did not impose any legal obligation. The executive therefore could rely on its own adjudications as internal mechanisms for dealing with persons not subject to American law.

Persons who were not subject to the law of the United States were neither bound nor protected by it. These persons included a host of aliens, ranging from enemy aliens to aliens in amity seeking to immigrate, and because systematic federal regulation of immigration developed only relatively late, the focus here will be on enemy aliens.

It will be recalled from chapter 6 that resident enemy aliens who were not licensed to remain in the United States (or who did not accept a license) were not subjects. And because they thus were not bound or protected by the law, the executive could issue regulations or orders that directly commanded them or stipulated the terms of their license to remain, without intruding on legislative power. Of course, because these rules and instructions were not applicable to subjects, they were without legal obligation, but they still could be effective as a matter of mere coercion.

Along similar lines, the executive could use hearings to determine whether enemy aliens failed to come within any license granted by the government, for such hearings did not purport to bind subjects. Where enemy aliens were not within the conditions of the government's license, they lacked the obligation and protection enjoyed by subjects, and they could not have judicial proceedings, let alone a judicial remedy.[3, a] The executive therefore was free to deal with such persons as it thought appropriate, subject to any legal limitations imposed by Congress. Sometimes the executive simply commanded enemy aliens to leave—as was authorized by a 1785 Virginia statute and the 1798 federal statute on enemy aliens (each of which came out of a committee headed by James Madison).[4] Sometimes, however, the executive had reason to make clear to other nations that it was dealing with unlicensed enemy aliens in accord with the laws of war or other rules, and in such instances, it could put the aliens through executive proceedings, such as those of a military tribunal. Similarly, even when enemy combatants forfeited the protection of the laws of war, the executive could demonstrate its fairness by convening a military tribunal to try and punish them—this being how General George Washington dealt with the British spy Major John André.

Such a person was not subject to American law. Consequently, although he could not be bound by judicial proceedings in the courts, he could be punished in executive proceedings. Such proceedings often adopted judicial forms, but they were not binding in the sense of imposing any domestic legal obligation, and they therefore cannot be understood as examples of executive exercises of judicial power.

Executive Adjudication Concerning Benefits or Other Privileges

Among the executive adjudications that were not binding, and that thus did not stray into judicial power, were those regarding benefits or other privileges. These adjudications could mimic judicial proceedings. Yet they

---

a. Nonetheless, when prisoners of war claimed that they had been misclassified, their friends at least could use a motion for a writ of habeas to get a prehabeas hearing on their status. If the prisoners, acting through their friends, could show at the hearing that they were within the government's license and thus within the protection of the law, the prisoners could then get a writ of habeas.[*]

did not legally oblige subjects, and they therefore cannot be viewed as early instances of binding administrative adjudication.

Claims against the Government

An initial example of these executive decisions on privileges was the sort in which the government settled its accounts with claimants. Such adjudications did not confine the public, but rather were merely a means of deciding how the government should distribute its funds.

Judicial-style decisions about government debts had the advantage of showing the justice of the government's actions. On account of the government's sovereignty, claimants could not sue the United States without its permission, and Congress had power over federal taxes and expenditures. It therefore seemed especially important for the government to make clear that it was following the law when it refused claims for payment.

The initial solution lay in the auditors and the comptroller. Already under the Articles of Confederation, the federal government began to require the Treasury to follow judicial-style procedures in paying accounts. Claimants had to present their claims to the auditors. After the adoption of a 1781 enactment of the Continental Congress, however, they could appeal an auditor's decision to the comptroller, who was required "openly and publicly" to "hear the parties," and whose decision was to be "conclusive." When Congress in 1789 authorized the formation of the Treasury under the U.S. Constitution, it took the same approach—although this time it specified merely that the comptroller should "examine all accounts settled by the auditor, and certify the balances," thus leaving the Treasury to decide the details of how the comptroller was to proceed.[5]

In recognition that the comptroller mimicked judicial decisionmaking, James Madison noted that the comptroller had duties that were "not purely of an executive nature," but rather were of a sort that "partakes strongly of the judicial character." According to Madison, this was a reason "why an officer of this kind should not hold his office at the pleasure of the executive branch."[6] Madison, however, did not persuade his colleagues of this, for it was well understood that the comptroller was an officer of the executive, whose decisions often caused regret but did not constrain. Thus, although the executive had reason to require the comptroller to adopt judicial-style decisionmaking, there was no need for Congress to require this, let alone to require decisions by a court.

The only recourse for disappointed claimants was political. Already in the states in the 1780s, when claimants failed to persuade state auditors, they had no recourse in the state courts.[7] Similarly, at the federal level, persons who failed to persuade executive officials had no legal recourse and therefore had to petition Congress.

The growing number of claims eventually required more streamlined decisionmaking. As things stood, the law left "every subordinate officer" who adjusted claims against the federal government "to erect himself into a tribunal for expounding the law," and this was awkward when so many such officers were notoriously incompetent for such purposes and, in any case, could not avoid conflicting decisions.[8] The system therefore provoked much complaint, and even when Congress made departmental decisions final, it could not prevent unhappy claimants from importuning the president and Congress.

Congress finally addressed the problem in 1855 by establishing the Court of Claims. This initially was an executive branch tribunal for hearing monetary claims against the United States, and it thus was "hardly more than a bureau for investigating claims." As a result, although it enjoyed a binding power to issue subpoenas, "its findings, drawn up in form of a bill, had no legal validity until approved by Congress."[9, b]

Eventually, in 1863, Congress authorized the Court of Claims to issue binding judgments and gave its judges tenure and security in their compensation. On this basis (after a brief hiccup that will be examined later) the Supreme Court soon accepted it as a regular court within the judicial branch.[10] The Court of Claims, however, began its life not as a court, but merely as an executive tribunal by which the executive regularized its recommendations to Congress about the disbursement of federal funds. Decisions about claims against the government, in other words, did not impose

---

b. Incidentally, the Court of Claims itself explained that the executive could exercise neither legislative nor judicial power. On legislative power, the court took the view that "[i]t is the duty of the departments to administer the law, and not to make it." Thus, "Decisions in the public offices of the government are facts, not rules of law."

Similarly, as to judicial power, "No part of the judicial power, under the Constitution of the United States, can be conferred upon an executive officer." Underlying this conclusion was the assumption that when an executive department made judgments about rights merely for purposes of deciding upon its own course of action, it was not exercising judicial power. As the court explained when parsing a statute, "the power of the secretary of the Treasury . . . is purely administrative, and in no sense judicial. This is sufficiently obvious from the very terms of the act. It did not vest the secretary of the Treasury with the power of deciding upon the rights of the claimant, except to the extent that he might be required to act upon them."

Of course, this still left the executive with unreviewable discretion within its sphere of executive power. "If the act which a ministerial officer is required to do be *executive*, and not merely *ministerial* in its character, his decision is final as regards executive action, and no appeal lies from it to the courts, nor can they revise his judgment."*

legal obligation and so could be left to executive adjudication. The executive's resolution of such claims, even in a so-called court, therefore is not a precedent for administrative adjudication.

Federal Lands

Yet other examples of executive adjudication can be observed in the distribution of federal benefits—most notably, lands. The government stimulated the settling of the West by handing out federal property, and to resolve disputes, it established a system of executive decisions and appeals.

Of course, if Congress had allowed claimants to acquire title to federal land prior to any executive decision, they would have had vested rights. Although the claimants would not have been able to sue the government, on account of its sovereign immunity, they would have been able to assert their ownership by bringing civil suits against individuals, including government officers. Congress, however, generally did not vest any right in claimants until there had been a final executive decision and a grant of a land patent.[11] Claims to federal lands thus ordinarily remained claims for benefits, and decisions resolving the claims remained executive. For example, when two claimants sought the same government land, the executive's decision between them merely granted a benefit to one and denied a benefit to the other; it did not impose any binding constraint on the disappointed party. In contrast, when there was a conflicting third-party claim, which not merely demanded a grant of the land but asserted a prior right to it, the executive's grant of a patent was not dispositive, for the claim of prior right had to be left to the courts.[c]

In the early nineteenth century, claims to acquire federal lands were decided under the supervision of the General Land Office. It was established in 1812 in the Treasury and was moved in 1849 to the Department of the Interior.

Settlers initially made their claims to the federal land office in their locality, and as the system eventually developed by the late 1850s, there were two levels of appeal. If the register and receiver at the local office refused to

---

c. This sort of question was especially common when the federal government established tribunals to settle claims against the federal government for lands relinquished by, or taken from, other governments. For example, there were many claims to land in the District of East Florida, which had been relinquished by Spain in 1819. Congress therefore appointed existing land officers in the district to serve as commissioners to decide the claims. Such decisions took effect only when confirmed by Congress, and as might be expected, they were to "operate as a release of any claim had by the United States, and not to affect the interest of third persons."*

accept a claim, the claimant could make an appeal to the commissioner of the General Land Office, and his decision was final, unless it then was appealed to the secretary of the interior.

The secretary's decision was "necessarily final, so far as respects the action of the executive." Although disappointed claimants sometimes sought relief from the president, it was "settled both by judicial decisions and by the practice of the government" that "an appeal does not lie to the president from the decisions of the heads of the different executive departments," lest the task interfere with his public duties.[12] The finality of the Interior Department decisions, however, did not extend beyond the executive, thus leaving claimants free to turn to the courts, if their vested rights were affected. As one interior secretary explained to a claimant who had complained to the president, the secretary would not reopen the case unless there was new material testimony that "could not have been obtained, or was not known at the time of the former hearing." Accordingly, the decision "will otherwise be final, so far as the executive departments are concerned, and you must resort to the courts for such relief as you may be entitled to."[13, d]

Although the decisions of the local land offices, and ultimately the General Land Office and the Department of the Interior, were not authoritative interpretations of the law, they were valuable guidance as to what these executive tribunals would do. Their decisions therefore were widely disseminated in periodicals such as *Copp's Land Owner*, thus allowing federal land officers to avoid discordant decisions, and settlers and investors to make informed investments.

The imitation of judicial proceedings and appeals, however, should not obscure the merely executive character of the decisions. Although the

---

d. Similarly, in some questions that came before the Treasury, the decision of the comptroller was final. When Robert H. Piatt sought "pecuniary compensation" from the government "for services alleged to have been rendered by him in the War of 1812," his claim was rejected, initially by the auditor, and then by the comptroller. Undeterred, the rejected claimant contacted President Millard Fillmore for help. Attorney General John J. Crittenden, however, cautioned the president:

> My clear conviction is that the decision of the comptroller on this claim is final and conclusive upon all the branches of the executive government; that the law allows of no appeal to you, and gives you no power to revise or interfere with that decision for any purposes of controlling, correcting, or altering it. Congress has properly and wisely forborne to impose on the president the impracticable duty of exercising an appellate jurisdiction in the settlement of the almost innumerable claims that are brought against the government. His . . . duties are of a higher and more general character, and the settlement and adjustment of accounts has been left to accountants.[*]

executive relied on judicial-like practices to regularize the conduct of its officers, its adjudicatory decisions of this sort did not impose binding constraints on members of the public—this being why these decisions could remain within the executive and why they were not early instances of administrative adjudication.

Patents for Inventions

The executive's proceedings when granting patents for inventions were much less like those of courts than those that it used when distributing land. Nonetheless, its patent decisions could be considered adjudicatory, and it therefore is necessary to observe that when the executive granted patents, as when it granted land, it was not understood to be imposing constraints on subjects. Its patent decisions therefore cannot be taken as precedents for binding executive adjudications.

The word "patent" originated as the shorthand name for letters patent. The Crown used these letters (which were not folded shut and thus were open or patent) to issue grants of privileges; and in the postmedieval era, a patent became simply a grant from the Crown or, in America, from the executive. A patent could grant an office, a piece of land, or the exclusive right to engage in specified activities—the last being the sort of patent at stake here.

Both in England and America, there was a sharp distinction between the grant of a patent and the recission or repeal of a patent. Once a patent of land or for an activity had been granted, it was a property right, and the government therefore could not simply rescind the patent. Instead, to bind a patent holder, it needed a judicial decision holding the patent unlawful and void. The initial grant of a patent, however, was another matter. A patent was a grant of a benefit or privilege, and because this, by itself, did not seem to bind subjects, the executive could issue patents on its own without turning to the judges.

Of course, when a patent granted what was within the rights of others, it strayed into imposing constraints on subjects, and patents therefore had to be drafted carefully to avoid this danger. To begin with a simple example, after the Crown had granted a patent of office or land, it could not grant the same office or land to another. In such instances, the courts on both sides of the Atlantic would regularly hold the second patent void.[e]

e. In 1519, for example, King's Bench held that "where the king, by his letters patent . . . grants me an office," and "then by other letters patent" he "grants the same thing to a stranger,

When the Crown or the federal executive granted patents for trades or manufactures, it similarly had to worry about imposing a constraint, for like office and land patents, patents for activities could easily end up granting what was within the rights of others. It already has been noted how an overly broad second patent for office or land could infringe on particular property rights, and this also was true of overly broad patents for trades or manufactures, where a prior patent had granted the same activity. Even more fundamentally, patents for trades or manufactures could stray into granting what all persons had been free to do, thus violating the general liberty or common right of the subject.[14] For example, if subjects already practiced a lawful trade or manufactured a lawful product, a patent for this conduct would constrain them, thus depriving them of their liberty without an act of Parliament or a court decision. In this way, patents for activities that were not novel had much in common with lawmaking proclamations, and there thus was good reason to consider them unlawful.[f]

If patents were to sidestep this danger, they had to be drafted to avoid constraining the preexisting liberty of subjects, and this is why the Crown often took care to grant patents for trades and manufactures only as to invented or newly imported matters. In retrospect, it has been assumed that patents for inventions developed as a means of encouraging national prosperity, and there is some truth to this; but the framing of patents in terms of new inventions and imports arose from the legal problem that the Crown by itself could not bind its subjects. Although the Crown's immediate purpose in granting patents for trades and manufactures was to elicit payments from the grantees, it traditionally had to draft its patents in a way that did not impinge on the liberties of the subject, and it therefore, in

---

these second letters patent are absolutely void." American decisions reached the same conclusion. A 1792 South Carolina case, for example, resolved a dispute between grantees by holding for the first. The colonial legislature eighty years earlier had sustained the second grantee, but the South Carolina Court of Common Pleas held that under the English law then applicable, "the plaintiffs could claim no title under the act in question, as it was against common right, as well as against *magna charta*, to take away the freehold of one man and vest it in another," and "the act was, therefore, *ipso facto*, void."*

f. Such was the main issue, for example, in a 1561 decision concerning the sweet Greek wine known as Malmsey. King Philip and Queen Mary had granted letters patent to the town of Southampton that no Malmsey was to be imported, except at Southampton, and that anyone who imported such wine elsewhere was to pay treble the ordinary customs to the Crown. Nonetheless, some Venetian merchants imported Malmsey to Kent and then transported it by water to London. The attorney general brought an information against them on behalf of Queen Elizabeth for the treble customs, and the case eventually came before all the judges in the Exchequer Chamber, where they held that "the letters patent were against the laws, customs and statutes of this realm" both "in respect of the principal matter, concerning the restraint in the landing of Malmseys . . . and also in the assessment of the penalty of the treble custom."*

theory, had to confine its trade and manufacturing patents to matters that were new to the kingdom, whether inventions or imports.[15, g]

In their desperation to raise money, however, Elizabeth I and James I frequently granted patents that infringed the preexisting liberties of subjects. They thereby provoked widespread public anger and elevated the question to a constitutional level.

Parliament responded in 1624 with the Statute of Monopolies, which established patents, and the Crown's authority to grant them, on the constitutional foundation that they could not constrain subjects. The statute's general point was that monopolies constrained the liberty of subjects outside Parliament and the courts. Harking back to "the ancient and fundamental laws," the statute declared that "all grants of monopolies . . . are contrary to your majesty's laws." The statute then specified that "all monopolies . . . and letters patents . . . for the sole buying, selling, making, working, or using of anything within this realm . . . or of any other monopolies . . . are altogether contrary to the laws of this realm, and so are and shall be utterly void." To ensure that this fundamental prohibition would not be evaded in prerogative or administrative proceedings, the statute added that all such monopolies and letters patents were "forever hereafter" to be "examined, heard, tried, and determined by and according to the common laws of this realm and not otherwise."[16] In other words, patents that bound were unlawful and could not be decided in administrative proceedings.

The statute recognized, however, that monopolies for inventions could encourage industry without constraining the liberty of subjects. It therefore excluded these letters patent, reciting that the statute's general prohibition "shall not extend to any letters patents and grants of privilege for the term of fourteen years or under, hereafter to be made of the sole working or making of any manner of new manufactures within this realm, to the true and first inventor and inventors of such manufactures, which others at the time of making such letters patents and grants shall not use."[17] The underlying point was that a limit on what "others at the time of making such letters patents and grants shall not use" did not diminish their liberty. This acknowledgment of a lawful realm for patents where they did not intrude

---

g. One implication of the traditional assumptions about inventions and imports was that, at the end of the period of a patent, the government could not grant a second patent or term, lest it interfere with the remainder interest or residual liberty of the people. Placing this on consequentialist foundations, a prominent legal abridgment concluded that "if a patent be granted in case of a new invention, the king cannot grant a second patent; for the charter is granted as an encouragement to invention and industry, and to secure the patentee in the profits for a reasonable time; but when that is expired, the public is to have the benefit of the discovery."*

on any preexisting liberty was part of the very definition of a monopoly. As Edward Coke explained, a monopoly was a grant of an exclusive right whereby any person would be "restrained of any freedom or liberty, that they had before, or hindered in their lawful trade."[18, h]

The American patent statute echoed the English Statute of Monopolies and its underlying constitutional assumption. The U.S. Constitution authorized Congress to "promote the Progress of Science and useful Arts, by securing for limited Times to . . . Inventors the exclusive Right to their . . . Discoveries." Under this provision, Congress in 1790 enacted that the executive could grant patents for "any useful art, manufacture, engine, machine, or device, or any improvement therein not before known or used." By granting patents only for things "not before known or used," the executive could grant exclusive rights without imposing constraints on the public.[19]

As a result, patents could be granted without resort to judicial decisions. The 1790 patent act authorized a committee (consisting of the secretary of state, the secretary of the War Department, and the attorney general, or any two of them) to receive petitions from inventors and to cause letters patent to issue "if they shall deem the invention or discovery sufficiently useful and important." In 1793, Congress authorized the secretary of state alone to cause letters patent to issue and eliminated any decision about usefulness and importance. Either way, as in England, it was necessary to minimize the risk of confining subjects. Both statutes therefore permitted letters patent to be sealed only after the attorney general certified that they were "conformable to this act," which meant (at the very least) that the letters patent did not purport to protect something previously known or used.[20]

These early patent statutes came closest to establishing an adjudicatory body when the 1793 enactment provided that "in case of interfering applications, the same shall be submitted to the arbitration of three persons, one of whom shall be chosen by each of the applicants, and the third . . . by the Secretary of State." The arbitrators' decision about the granting of the patent was to be "final," meaning that the secretary was to follow it.[21] Even their adjudication, however, did not make the patent binding on the public, for members of the public remained free to do what they had previously done and were limited only as to what the patentee had invented.

In 1836, Congress imposed more elaborate procedures and standards

h. In the debates that led up to the adoption of the statute, Coke was reminded of this distinction by another member of Parliament. Coke had observed: "The sole buying and selling of anything and sole importation and exportation is a monopoly." A colleague then added the qualification: "New manufacture the king may make monopoly, but not an old trade."*

for granting patents, and it established a patent office, with a patent commissioner, and a board of examiners under him.[22] Again, however, the somewhat adjudicatory style of the executive proceedings did not mean that they bound the public, for under traditional constitutional assumptions, inherited from the English, a grant of a patent for an invention did not prevent any subject from doing what he had done beforehand.

Obviously, the assumption that a patent for something new does not bind members of the public is somewhat artificial, and one might therefore hesitate to apply it to other areas of law. This assumption, however, was the foundation for the constitutionality of patents. And because grants of patents were thus understood to avoid imposing legal obligation on members of the public, they are not a foundation for contemporary administrative adjudication.

Post Office

Unlike the other examples recited here, the decisions of post offices to accept or deny mail, or to charge one postal rate or another, did not mimic judicial procedures. All the same, they have been proposed as examples of executive adjudication, for they reached decisions that affected members of the public.[23] From this perspective, any decision by a post office clerk about accepting or charging for mail is a precedent for contemporary administrative adjudication.

The carriage of mail, however, was merely a government service, and the decisions of postmasters about what mail they would accept thus did not bind or constrain members of the public. Of course, when there were few alternative modes of communication, such decisions could be profoundly important, and when they were biased, they even could be dangerous. They were not, however, binding adjudications, for although they could deny an essential government service, they did not bind members of the public.

Concerns about the power of postmasters became apparent already during the debates over ratification of the Constitution. The post office in the eighteenth century had often transported newspapers for free and, of particular importance, had at least allowed printers to send each other single copies of their papers without charge. In 1787, however, Postmaster General Ebenezer Hazard broke with these traditions, and Anti-Federalists feared that they were the target of his policies. Anti-Federalists complained that the new postal policy on printer's copies was a threat to the press and the new nation's liberty, but even many of the Anti-Federalists acknowledged that the free carriage of newspapers was not so much a legal right as a printer's privilege or an ancient usage, which was important for the freedom of the press in a republic. As George Washington sympathetically observed, even "[i]f the privilege was not from convention an original right, it had from prescription strong pretensions for continuance; especially at so interesting a period." In other words, only a public service had been denied, not the natural freedom of speech, let alone such a freedom as was protected by law. And when understood in this way, the decisions of post offices about the mail were not binding.[24, i]

These various executive decisions—about enemy aliens, claims against the government, the distribution of lands, the award of patents, and the transportation of mail—did not bind subjects. Even where the executive used judicial-like mechanisms to regularize its decisions, it systematically avoided imposing binding constraints on the liberty or vested rights of subjects. The resulting decisions therefore (as suggested by Caleb Nelson) did not require the exercise of judicial power.[25] Early federal executive decisions thus offer no precedents for the binding administrative adjudication that flourishes nowadays, and it shows that a rejection of such adjudication does not threaten the use of executive tribunals where subjects are not bound.

Executive Adjudication As a Means of Determining and Giving Notice of Duties

Another use of executive hearings or adjudications was to determine and give notice of legal duties. As was observed in chapter 6, and as will further be seen here, it was the law rather than any executive determination that was binding. For example, when administrators assessed taxes, it was the law that bound taxpayers to pay. Accordingly, the executive traditionally could make such determinations on its own, without any hearing or other adjudication, let alone any executive version of due process.

Nonetheless, as seen in chapter 6, determinations of legal duties could easily trespass into legislative territory, and to ensure that they did not, executive officers needed to make the determinations in a spirit of discernment or judgment. One way the executive could ensure that its officers acted in such a spirit was by having them make their determinations of legal duties in executive hearings, which mimicked aspects of judicial hear-

---

i. The misconduct of postmasters in refusing to deliver newspapers was finally addressed when, in 1794, Congress enacted that "every printer of newspapers may send one paper to each and every other printer of newspapers within the United States, free of postage, under such regulations as the Postmaster General shall provide."*

ings but concluded with the administrators issuing notices of legal duties rather than binding judgments.

Of course, these decisions could easily drift from mere determinations into extralegal adjudications, but the law went far in trying to prevent this. On the whole, therefore, these determinations are further examples of executive adjudications that could look like the exercise of judicial power but were not binding, and they thus are not precedents for administrative adjudications. They illustrate, moreover, that this book's critique of binding administrative adjudications does not reach mere determinations, even those that are adjudicatory in form.[j]

Police Warnings

A simple example of an executive determination can be found in the warnings given by constables or police officers. When policing a town, a constable could warn a person not to do a specified act—for example, not to fight. In retrospect, these warnings may seem to have been legally binding administrative adjudications or adjudicatory orders.

In fact, however, these warnings were not legally binding. To be sure, a constable or police officer could warn individuals not to do unlawful acts, but in making such statements, the officer merely informed the individuals of their legal duties. What bound the individual was the underlying law, and the officer was merely making a determination, and giving notice, of the law's implications. Of course, when an officer made a determination of probable cause to arrest a person or seize his property, it was unlawful to resist. Again, however, it was the law that bound. Thus, when an officer

j. There always was a danger that determinations of duties would slide into becoming binding adjudications. This was especially a problem where the law did not clearly dictate the outcomes, but left room for officers to exercise some will or subjective discretion. In such instances, not only the law but also the determinations bound the affected persons, thus making the determinations, in reality, binding executive ventures into legislative and judicial power. (For concerns about this danger, see the discussion below about valuations by federal tax assessors.)

There also could be subsequent due process problems—at least where determinations had the effect of shifting the burden of persuasion or proof in subsequent court proceedings. After some types of determinations, an affected person was liable or otherwise bound, unless he brought a suit to challenge the determination. This always was a difficulty where the determination itself was binding, but it also could be a problem where the determination merely gave notice of the binding effect of an underlying law. In either situation, if the affected person could avoid liability or other binding consequences only by undertaking the burden of persuasion and proof, he was in the position of a defendant, sometimes even a criminal defendant, without the corresponding procedural advantages. (For details, see the discussion of burdens of persuasion and proof in chapter 13.)

warned persons not to fight and they continued, and even when he sought to arrest them and they resisted, the subsequent prosecution was for violating the underlying law against fighting and resisting arrest.[26]

It therefore is a mistake to assume that police warnings were precedents for police officers or other executive officers to make binding adjudications or commands. The warnings given by constables and police officers were merely notices of their determinations about the duties of members of the public, not examples of binding executive adjudications.

Commissions of Sewers

The early adjudications that were merely determinations included many of those made by commissions of sewers. Persons owning land running alongside seawalls, waterways, and drainage ditches had a duty to maintain these embankments, and when they failed in this, the commissioners relied on adjudications to determine the work that was owed or the financial equivalent.[27]

Although commissions of sewers existed mostly in England, they have been taken as precedents for American administrative law on the ground that "to modern eyes the commissions look much like a true administrative agency."[28] Certainly, the commissioners had statutory authority to inspect the relevant land and to order testimony under oath. Otherwise, however, they had little if any power to bind persons. For example, they could not issue judgments. Instead, they assessed the work or money necessary to repair embankments, and like tax assessors, their most direct mode of collection was merely by distress, not a binding judgment or order.[29]

When the commissioners came closest to binding subjects, they relied on juries of at least twelve men, who served simultaneously as little grand juries and as petit juries. These juries were particularly important when the commissions pursued accusations and amercements for harm. Without a charge from the jury, no one could be forced answer an accusation, for "no other accusation is of sufficient strength in law to put a man to his answer." The commissioners also relied on the juries to make determinations about the duties of particular persons. In the words of a historian, "It was always for the jury to determine who was liable to make a particular repair—like bridge repairs, a matter of immemorial custom—though the commissioners might decide on their view what work ought to be done."[30]

To be sure, the commissioners could impose "amercements"—for harm or for work not done—but these amercements were distinguishable from binding judgments. Like the initial assessments, the amercements were enforceable by distress and evidently were understood merely as determinations of amounts owed. In contrast, if the commissioners for sewers needed to impose a fine, they could not act alone, but had to turn to a justice of the peace.[31]

Thus, although the commissioners of sewers could inspect land and bind individuals to testify, and although their amercements for harm sometimes looked like fines, their work was carefully structured in terms of determinations rather than binding adjudications. In reality, they probably exercised considerable judicial power, but it is telling that the law went so far in trying to treat their judicial power as a matter of mere determination. The commissioners of sewers therefore do not offer much legitimacy for the contemporary administrative exercise of judicial power.

English Excise Adjudications

The most important and ambitious English nonjudicial adjudications were those concerning internal excise taxes. In retrospect, they have seemed to show that the executive could hold judicial proceedings and that the objections to executive exercises of judicial power collide with essential and long-standing administrative power.[32] English excise adjudications, however, were mostly determinations of legal duties, in which royal officers merely discerned the duties and gave notice about them. Although in other respects excise officers bound members of the public outside the courts, they were widely condemned for this, and their binding orders therefore cannot be taken as a measure of what was considered lawful under American constitutions.

In eighteenth-century England, Parliament imposed internal excise taxes on a wide range of things, including beer, houses, windows, and servants. Excise assessors determined the applicability of the taxes, and the amounts owed, whereupon the taxpayer could pay or have excise officers distrain his property for the unpaid amount.[33]

Individuals who did not consider themselves subject to the taxes then could appeal to the commissioners for appeals. Afterwards, taxpayers or surveyors could ask the commissioners to state the case to the judges of the three central common law courts. In the late seventeenth century, a single judge usually would give at least a briefly reasoned opinion; by the mid-eighteenth century, all the judges available would meet and summarily, without explanation, give an "opinion" as to whether the determination of the commissioners was right or wrong.[34] At this point, the commissioners would conform to the opinion of the judges.

The decisions of the judges, however, appear to have been merely advisory opinions, and the judges therefore saw no need for full courtroom hearings, binding judgments, or even explanations. Instead, in each instance, they merely discussed the question and gave a conclusory opinion. The summary nature of the decision and opinion left the judges relatively uncommitted, and so presumably left open the theoretical possibility that an aggrieved taxpayer or surveyor could pursue a remedy in court.

To the extent discussed thus far, the excise officers merely assessed taxes and thus did not do more in their adjudications than merely determine and give notice of legal duties. The excise laws, however, went further. In the field, for example, they required businesses to allow excise officers to inspect private business records without warrants.[k]

Still worse, the excise laws allowed excise commissioners to act as judges who could bind subjects, even to the point of imposing forfeitures and penalties. By statute, excise officers could come before a justice of the peace or three excise commissioners to charge a taxpayer by information for a violation of the excise laws. After a hearing, the justices or commissioners then could levy the resulting forfeiture or penalty and could issue a distress warrant. In form, such hearings remained mere determinations, for they concluded with distress warrants rather than binding judgments. Distress, however, traditionally was a remedy for unpaid taxes, not for infractions of law. Thus, where the commissioners enforced forfeitures or penalties as if they were merely additional taxes, they were using distress to evade the ideal that only courts of law could give binding judgments. Adding to this reality of binding administrative power, commissioners holding such hearings could require testimony, even from the accused taxpayer, and could impose penalties on anyone who did not cooperate.[35, l]

The commissioners thus exercised judicial power outside the courts of law and without juries or other due process of law. An otherwise unemo-

---

k. Already during the Revolution of 1688, Parliament abolished the tax known as "hearth-money" on the ground that it was "not only a great oppression to the poorer sort but a badge of slavery upon the whole people[,] exposing every man's house to be entered into and searched at pleasure, by persons unknown to him." It thus was an unlawful invasion of the people's "rights and liberties."*

l. Incidentally, the excise commissioners were not alone in encroaching upon judicial power, for during wartime treasury commissioners could impress unemployed men for military service.*

tional treatise on taxation explained that those who paid excise taxes were "in many cases deprived of that which is the glory of Englishmen, to be tried by God and their country." As put by Blackstone, excise proceedings "are so summary and sudden, that a man may be convicted in two days time in the penalty of many thousands of pounds by two commissioners or justices of the peace; to the total exclusion of trial by jury, and disregard for the common law."[36]

This departure from common law ideals was notorious. The excise was despised, and its very name, as Blackstone observed, was "odious to the people of England." Indeed, Samuel Johnson's *Dictionary* famously defined the excise as a "hateful tax . . . adjudged not by the common judges of property, but wretches hired by those to whom excise is paid." Many Americans would soon echo such views. Thus, although English excise adjudication departed from the ideals described in this book, it cannot be considered a reliable precedent for contemporary administrative adjudication.[37]

Federal Excise and Customs Adjudications

For an understanding of what was possible in federal executive adjudication, one must to turn to the early federal taxes. Although both excises and customs offer good illustrations, the severity of the excise tax on distilled spirits makes it the best example. Adopted in a 1791 statute and subsequent amendments, this excise carefully avoided the excesses of the English excise tax. Indeed, it adopted a reporting system and thereby systematically left binding adjudications to the courts.

The 1791 federal excise statute required "entry" or filing of taxes, and it thus offers an early illustration of the reporting system that would become the model for later American taxes, including the income tax. The statute required distillers to enter or file details about their distilleries and their casks, and to pay duties on the spirits before they were removed from the distilleries. Under this approach, treasury officials did not need to engage in any binding adjudication. Instead, the officials would collect the taxes from the distillers, and when the distillers failed to make accurate reports or otherwise violated the excise law, either private persons or U.S. district attorneys could bring prosecutions to recover penalties and forfeitures in federal, territorial, or state courts. Thus, although Congress imposed a severe excise law—one that provoked a rebellion in western Pennsylvania—it did not authorize administrators to engage in the English-style excise adjudication that bound subjects.[38]

The excise system adopted in England had left revenue officers to exercise administrative powers that were difficult to square with the location of judicial power in the courts, jury rights, or other due process. It therefore is no surprise that when Congress established federal taxes, whether the internal excise or customs duties, it avoided these dangers and, instead, relied on reporting systems.

Valuations by Assessors

The clearest instance of how early federal tax determinations could stray into binding adjudications can be found in the determinations by tax assessors about the value of taxed property. Both in England and America, this was particularly a problem under a land tax, which was imposed on the value of land. Of course, in figuring out the value of the taxed property and the tax payable on it, the assessors merely engaged in the usual combination of determination and notice, and in this respect their decisions were unremarkable. Yet to the extent their perception of value rather than the law constrained taxpayers, their assessments in effect were binding adjudications. Therefore, more than most officers who made determinations, assessors seemed to exercise a sort of judicial power.

Ordinarily, a tax assessor only had to determine what was taxable, and then had to determine the tax, none of which necessarily was complicated. Where the tax rested on the value of the taxable object, however, an assessor could not determine the tax without first determining the value of the property.

In England and in America, assessors acted at their own risk when they deciding whether a particular piece of land or personal property was taxable under a statute. In other words, if they made a mistake about what was to be taxed, they were subject to later legal action by the taxpayer.

Absent some clear abuse, however, assessments generally could not easily be challenged in the courts for overstating the value of taxable property. Taxpayers could appeal a valuation to the tax commissioners in England, or to equivalent officers in the American states, but only in some states could they appeal to the courts. Following the general pattern, a 1798 federal statute on valuations allowed taxpayers to take appeals to the principal assessor on the question of whether the protested valuation was proportional to others. Again, however, this was merely part of the government's power to adjust its assessments, not a judicial remedy.[39]

Congress recognized at least part of the danger. Worried that open-ended factual determinations about value would become the basis for binding executive adjudications, Congress initially (as explained by Leonard White) set up "a revenue system which for some years avoided the necessity of discretionary valuation of property." Congress avoided such evaluations by relying on mechanistic tax calculations. For example, when Congress in 1789 placed ad valorem duties on imports, it set the duties simply at a percentage of the actual costs of imports. "Discretion thus was replaced by the bill of sale." Similarly, in the duty on domestically distilled spirits, "The operation of the act was almost automatic. The rate of duty upon spirits was fixed in the law; no valuation was required of revenue officers." Valuation, however, was a tempting instrument of taxation, and in its 1798 tax on land, dwellings, and slaves, Congress authorized valuations of the land and dwellings.[40]

Executive assessments based on evaluations may thus seem a precedent, at least in tax matters, for a type of binding administrative adjudication. Theoretically, the decisions of assessors were mere determinations, but to the extent loose evaluations rather than the law bound taxpayers, the assessments were really binding adjudications. It therefore is revealing that the federal government initially tried as best it could to avoid evaluations by relying on mechanistic tax calculations.

Licensing

Of particular importance, it is necessary to consider whether the early federal government used licensing determinations as substitutes for court adjudications. When tied to a background constraint, licensing becomes a mode of adjudication, which resolves, at least in the first instance, whether a person is bound or released from the constraint. Early federal licensing may therefore seem to be a precedent for administrative adjudication though licensing. The early licensing, however, did not go so far.

To be sure, Congress authorized licensing as mechanism for raising taxes, and at least in this way, licensing served as a mode of imposing a limited range of constraints. Moreover, Congress authorized licensing to adjust constraints in the District of Columbia and similar territories, in which Congress exercised local power. More generally, however, at least until the beginning of the twentieth century, Congress does not appear to have relied on licensing to apply domestic constraints. As seen in chapter 6, it used licensing to control enemy aliens, and to control various cross-border or offshore matters, such Indian traders, coastal vessels, and steamboats. Yet in more domestic matters, beyond the collection of taxes and the exercise of local power in territories, Congress does not seem have used licensing as a substitute for binding adjudication. Early federal licensing thus does not generally justify the federal government in domestic licensing or other administrative exercises of judicial power.

At least at the federal level, executive determinations of legal duties or rights generally were not avenues for binding administrative adjudication. Instead, the determinations confirm the distinction between binding court adjudications and nonbinding executive decisions. The court adjudications bound subjects to appear, testify, produce records, and ultimately to pay penalties or forfeitures; the executive determinations on the whole did not. The executive use of adjudicatory methods to make determinations of legal duties is thus part of a larger pattern of nonbinding executive action, and it offers little comfort for binding adjudications in contemporary administrative law.

The Executive Role of Judges

Incidentally, the varied instances of nonbinding executive adjudication included a much-misunderstood type of executive adjudication, that done by the judges. This executive decisionmaking by judges is usually associated with *Hayburn's Case*, and in the conventional misreading of this decision, the courts and their judges get lumped together under the labels of "judiciary" and "judicial branch." The Constitution, however, granted the judicial power to the *courts*, and this points to a distinction that matters for understanding the executive role of the *judges*. Courts could bind, but judges acting as executive officers could not.

In a range of statutes in the 1790s, Congress authorized and sometimes even required federal judges to carry out executive functions. For example, Congress directed district judges to lay census returns before grand juries; it authorized judges to administer oaths of office; it directed judges to inquire into petitions seeking relief from penalties or forfeitures, and to transmit the facts to executive officers; it appointed judges to boards or commissions; it authorized judges to notify the president when federal law was opposed by combinations of persons too powerful to be suppressed through ordinary judicial proceedings; it authorized judges to certify whether refugees were entitled to lands under resolutions of the Continental Congress.[41]

These statutes authorizing or requiring judicial exercises of executive power are sometimes said to reveal an early acceptance of administrative law. In particular, they are said to show that Congress could shift executive power to the courts, and on the assumption that the logic works both ways, they are said to justify the transfer of judicial power to the executive. As put by Jerry Mashaw, "The use of courts as administrative tribunals to make initial or recommended decisions seems analogous to the modern role of the administrative law judge."[42] But just because courts allegedly could exercise executive power does not mean that the executive or its officers can exercise judicial power.

In fact, the key to understanding the statutes from the 1790s is to recognize that they concerned the judges rather than the courts. The Constitution barred persons from being legislators if they held executive or judicial power—stating that "no Person holding any Office under the United States, shall be a Member of either House during his Continuance in Office." Yet the Constitution did not prevent judges from exercising executive power. Hence the distinction drawn by the statutes, which gave executive tasks to the judges, not the courts. As put by Maeva Marcus, Congress tended to "impose the duties on individuals rather than on the courts themselves."[43]

The judges in these instances served in executive roles, such as making determinations, and they did not do anything more than what executive officers could have done. In the exigent circumstances of the early federal government, the executive lacked sufficient officers to carry out all of its duties, and it therefore is no surprise that Congress turned to the judges, as individuals, to assist the executive, as was permitted by the Constitution. But this does not show that the courts were accepting a delegation of executive power or that the executive was engaged in the sort of adjudication done by the courts.

The care with which the judges understood these distinctions is evident from their response to the best known of the congressional attempts to rely on the judges for executive acts—an attempt that went astray by relying on the courts. In 1792, in the Invalid Pension Act, Congress authorized injured Revolutionary War veterans to apply for federal pensions. Rather than leave them to petition Congress for relief, the act required them to petition the federal circuit courts. Not simply the judges, but the circuit courts were to examine the proofs, determine who should receive a pension and in what amount, and transmit the conclusions to the secretary of war. The secretary at that point was to report the information to Congress, but where he had cause to suspect "imposition or mistake," he was given the power to "withhold the name of such applicant from the pension list, and make report of the same to Congress." Upon receipt of the lists and the secretary's adjustments, Congress was free to grant the pensions as it saw fit.[44]

This statute merely sought recommendations about grants of pensions, but unlike most other federal statutes that allocated executive duties to the judges, this one gave such duties to the courts. The judges therefore faced two possible problems. On the one hand, the duties were executive, and therefore, although they could be given to the judges as individuals, they could not be given to the courts as institutions, for under the Constitution, the courts could exercise only judicial power. On the other hand, if the Constitution granted the courts only judicial power, then their pension decisions would be binding final judgments, and this meant that they could not be submitted to the secretary of war and ultimately Congress for reconsideration, lest the judicial power be subordinated to the executive and legislative powers.

The circuit courts therefore hesitated to undertake the executive role given to them by statute. The judges of the circuit court for the district of New York explained that "neither the legislative nor the executive branches, can constitutionally assign to the judicial any duties but such as are properly judicial and to be performed in a judicial manner." The Invalid Pension Act, however, assigned duties to the courts that "are not of that description." Moreover, the act "subjects the decision of these courts made pursuant to those duties, first to the consideration and suspension of the Secretary at War, and then to the revision of the legislature," neither of which, under the Constitution, could "sit as a court of errors on the judicial acts or opinions of this court."

On such grounds, the circuit court in New York did not hear pension applications. The best that could be said of the statute was that it could be "considered as appointing commissioners for the purposes mentioned in it by official, instead of personal descriptions." In this charitable reading, the statute meant for the judges to act as individuals, even though it referred to them in their joint capacity as a court. This interpretation left the judges free in their personal capacity "to accept or decline that office," and the judges sitting in New York accepted it.

The judges sitting in other districts, however, did not twist the statute to make it constitutional. It clearly gave executive duties to the courts, not to the judges in their individual capacity. The circuit courts in the districts of Pennsylvania and North Carolina therefore refused to comply. For example, the judges sitting in Pennsylvania, in what is known as *Hayburn's Case*, observed that "the business directed by this act is not of a judicial nature: it forms no part of the power vested, by the Constitution, in the courts of the United States," and if the court had proceeded, its opinions or judgments could "have been revised and controlled by the legislature and an officer of the executive department," which was "radically inconsistent with the independence of that judicial power, which is vested in the courts."[45]

The objections of the circuit courts confirm, by way of contrast, that when the judges participated in executive acts under other statutes, they were acting as individuals within the executive branch. Some of the other statutes required the judges to make their decisions reviewable by the executive or by Congress, but asked the judges to act merely as individuals, and thus presumably as members of the executive. The Invalid Pension Act, however, requisitioned the services of the courts rather than merely the judges, and it thereby asked the courts to exercise more than judicial power and to subordinate judicial power to the executive and Congress.

The statutes that authorized *judges* must therefore be distinguished from the Invalid Pension Act, which authorized *courts*. Although the judges *as individuals* could serve as executive officers, the courts *as institutions* could not undertake executive power or be subject to it.

The larger principle was twofold: executive power could not be shifted to the courts, and judicial power could not be shifted to the executive. All of this remained familiar until at least the late nineteenth century. In 1863, as already noted, Congress authorized the Court of Claims to give final judgments and thereby seemed to make the court a part of the judicial branch. But Congress also required the court to submit its judgments to the Treasury Department, so that the Treasury could include these amounts within its requests for congressional appropriations. Congress thereby repeated the mistake it had made in the Invalid Pension Act. The Supreme Court in 1864 therefore held that it lacked jurisdiction to hear appeals from the Court of Claims—its point apparently being the same as in 1792, that a court could not exercise executive power and that its judicial power could not be subject to executive or legislative review.[46]

Both aspects of this conclusion are worth remembering, for (as will be seen in chapter 16) both are now largely ignored. Although the courts nowadays do not overtly exercise executive power, it will be seen that, in administrative cases, they have reduced much of their appellate process to an extension of the administrative process. Even more clearly, they submit their judgment to the executive—first, by deferring to administrative decisions and, second, by remanding their decisions against agency actions, so the agencies can take corrective action to avoid having their actions held void. In reality, therefore, even if not in form, what was recognized in *Hayburn's Case* as unconstitutional is now commonplace.[m]

m. Indeed, judicial decisions are these days formally subject to executive review, if one considers administrative adjudication to be an exercise of judicial power. The decisions of administrative law judges, for example, are often not final until adopted by agency heads, and even when they are final, they often are subject to administrative review by agency heads or review boards. Thus, what are said to be judicial decisions are subject to executive review, frequently by the most political of administrators.

More immediately, *Hayburn's Case* and the related decisions matter because, when correctly understood, they offer no support for contemporary administrative adjudication. Judges could be allocated to the executive, but the judicial and executive powers had to stay put. Thus, far from showing that executive power could be shifted to the courts—let alone that judicial power could be shifted to the executive—the pension decisions reveal that there was no room for any such reallocation of power.

Coercive and Other Physical Acts by Executive Officers

In limited circumstances, the law allowed executive officers to act against subjects without a judicial warrant or order. These executive acts, being at most merely instances of coercion, are improbable precedents for any sort of adjudication. Nonetheless, they sometimes are taken to be early examples of the administrative exercise of judicial power, and it therefore is necessary to observe that, in fact, they were not adjudications, let alone of the sort that imposed legal obligation. On the contrary, they were merely instances in which the law allowed the executive to act, and required subjects to cooperate or submit, without a prior exercise of judicial power.

Customs Officers

Prominent examples of such coercive and other executive action can be found in the powers of customs officers. As observed by Jerry Mashaw, "[c]ustoms officers seized property, held goods in shoreside warehouses, refused to return or release bonds, and held ships in port." According to Mashaw, these actions were early instances of the power—apparently, the adjudicatory power—of the "modern administrative state."[47]

Yet rather than exercises of binding judicial power, these were the statutory powers and, indeed, duties of customs officers. Just as the law itself required merchants to declare their goods and to pay duties or give bonds before removing their goods, so too the law required customs officers to collect the duties and bonds, to hold goods on which duties or bonds were still owing, and to hold bonds until ships had met legal requirements for setting sail. Of course, in all of this, the customs officers engaged in physical and sometimes even coercive acts. But the officers were merely carrying out their statutory duties, and there was no pretense that they were issuing binding edicts, as if they were administrative versions of a court.

As a result, they were vulnerable to suits for damages and other remedies when they went beyond their statutory powers. They could act physically and even coercively under the customs statutes, but they could not resolve the lawfulness of their acts, for legally binding adjudications remained the power of the courts.

That customs officers could not resolve judicial questions is further apparent from the officers' dependence on the courts for forfeitures. Although customs officers had long been able to seize goods where they had probable cause, the government did not thereby acquire a right to the property, until it or an assisting private party brought a forfeiture proceeding in a court of law. When a dispute arose in 1750 as to whether an Irish case fell within admiralty or customs jurisdiction, the English attorney general and solicitor general together opined that "clearly all forfeitures by the law relating to the customs are of common law cognizance only[,] and if goods are claimed upon that foot, the only remedy is in the courts of common law and especially the Exchequer as a court of revenue." Similarly, in America, when goods were seized by treasury officers, they could be taken as "penalties or forfeitures" only after the government or assisting private parties had gone to court. Either a private person who discovered the goods had to bring an action of debt in a district court, or the local district attorney had to bring an information in the name of the United States. Of course, seized goods sometimes remained unclaimed, but even though customs officers, with probable cause, had a power to seize them, the goods were not forfeited until there were proceedings in court.[48, n]

The coercion and other physical acts done by customs officers thus did not amount to a court-like power to make binding adjudications. Although custom officers frequently acted on their own, as authorized by statute, only the courts could issue binding judicial edicts.

Distress

Another salient instance of executive coercion was the power of distress or distraint. This often is assumed to have been an early example of binding administrative adjudication, but it actually was something much more mundane. It was simply a remedy by which creditors could seize personal property as a pledge for a delinquent debt.[49]

---

n. Other executive actions that may seem in retrospect to have involved binding adjudication involved the executive's control over prisoners, orphans, and lunatics entrusted to its care. In exercising physical control over these persons, however, the executive prototypically was not engaging in binding adjudication, but rather was carrying out the law and the binding judgments of the courts. What legally bound the confined individuals in such instances was ordinarily the law itself, and the judgments of the courts, not executive adjudication.

Landlords could use distress to obtain back rent from their tenants, and similarly the government could rely on it to collect past-due taxes. In altering possession, it had the advantage of shifting the burden of litigation onto the debtor, whether a renter or taxpayer. It also had the advantage of allowing the creditor, whether the landlord or the government, to obtain a secured interest in the property against the debtor's general creditors. Either way, it was a self-help remedy allowed by law to landlords and the government alike.[50] Thus, although the Supreme Court, in 1856, in *Murray's Lessee v. Hoboken Land & Improvement Co.*, alluded to distress as one of the government's "public rights," this was not so much a distinctively governmental power as a right available for favored private and governmental claims.[51]

It therefore is a mistake to view distress as an administrative power to make binding adjudications. Far from an executive exercise of the judicial power, it was merely an ancient self-help right of some creditors, including the government. As put by the Supreme Court in *Murray's Lessee*, the distress was not a "judicial controversy," but one of the "summary extrajudicial remedies" authorized by law.[o]

The broader point is that coercive or other physical executive action should not be confused with judicial edicts, which bound persons in particular cases. The former belonged to the executive, and the latter to the courts.

Nonbinding Orders and Warrants

Among the early executive acts that may seem to have been judicial were not merely adjudications, but executive orders and warrants. If they in-

---

o. The Court noted some familiar types of summary extrajudicial remedies: "An instance of extrajudicial redress of a private wrong is the recapture of goods by their lawful owner; of a public wrong, by a private person, is the abatement of a public nuisance; and the recovery of public dues by a summary process of distress, issued by some public officer authorized by law, is an instance of redress of a particular kind of public wrong, by the act of the public through its authorized agents."

The power of the executive, in at least some instances, to exercise coercion against subjects without first getting a judicial order or warrant is sobering, and it raises an interesting question about the limits on such coercion. One answer, evident in *Murray's Lessee*, was to assume that government generally cannot exercise coercion against subjects without the authority of a judicial act, but that there are a small number of traditional exceptions, such as distress.

Thus, although the case is often said to have held that administrative process generally can satisfy due process, the Court's opinion reached the rather different conclusion that distress was merely a traditional exception from the due process of the courts. The Court explained that "though 'due process of law' generally implies and includes *actor, reus, judex*, regular allegations, opportunity to answer, and a trial according to some settled course of judicial proceedings . . . yet this is not universally true"—most notably in cases "in which process, in its nature final, issues against the body, lands, and goods of certain public debtors without any such trial."[*]

volved an executive exercise of judicial power—that is, if they bound sub-jects in particular instances—then they could be considered precedents for contemporary administrative orders and warrants and, more generally, for extralegal judicial power.[52] There was a difference, however, between the orders and warrants that bound subjects and those that did not.

Orders and Warrants Directing Executive Officers

When executive officers requested action by their subordinates, they often issued what were called "orders" and "warrants." Of course, courts issued orders and warrants that bound subjects, and it may therefore be assumed that the executive orders and warrants had a similar effect.

The similarity of names, however, should not distract attention from the dissimilar effects. Whereas judicial orders and warrants were bind-ing on members of the public, executive orders and warrants were merely formal directives to subordinate executive officers, by which the executive ordered or authorized them to take actions within the power of the ex-ecutive. English government officials, for example, signed "warrants" in the king's name to authorize other officials to make payments on behalf of the Crown, whether salaries for Crown officers, provisions for soldiers, or pensions for favored members of the public.[53] Similarly, the Treasury of the United States traditionally issued "warrants" for payments to be made by the federal government, thereby authorizing officials to make disburse-ments of public monies. Rather than constrain or bind subjects, these ex-ecutive warrants merely gave directions to executive officers.

Distress Warrants

Among the warrants available to the executive were distress warrants, which the government used to collect delinquent taxes. Although distress warrants may seem a slim justification for something as broad as administrative ad-judication, the role of a distress warrant in *Murray's Lessee v. Hoboken Land & Improvement Co.* has been taken to show that there is an administrative power of adjudication to bind subjects in particular instances.[54]

The law on distress, however, rather than the warrant gave the govern-ment the power to distrain the property of a taxpayer. It has been seen that distress or distraint was a simply a remedy by which certain creditors could secure personal property as a pledge for a delinquent debt. It therefore should be no surprise that, when the federal executive sought distress for taxes, it worked through low-level officers, and it issued warrants authorizing them to act on behalf of the government. It has been seen that under state law, tax assessors would ascertain taxes in accord with a formula determined by statute—their assessments being attempts to discern the duty imposed by the legislature and to notify the taxpayers. The assessors then issued executive warrants authorizing and ordering tax collectors to collect specified amounts from specified persons and, if they would not pay, to collect such amounts by distress. Similarly, under acts of Congress, federal tax officials assessed taxes and signed warrants for lesser executive officers to collect unpaid amounts by distress.

These warrants merely directed lesser executive officers to do what the executive was allowed to do by law, and although the distress warrants may seem to have been administrative orders binding subjects, what actually bound the derelict taxpayers was the law on taxation and distraint. The distress warrants thus were merely the internal mechanism within the executive by which it initiated lawful executive acts. The taxpayers could pay under protest and then go to court to recover any amounts they did not owe, but the distress itself was not a judicial act, and the warrants authorizing officers to distrain for taxes did not bind taxpayers any more than they already were bound.

Among the distress warrants available to a government was the sort it could use to recover the taxes that a tax collector had failed pay the government. Again, this was an executive warrant, which did not itself bind the public but simply authorized a low-level executive officer to act for the government. As the Supreme Court explained in *Murray's Lessee*, "what was generally termed a warrant of distress, running against the body, goods, and chattels of defaulting receivers of public money, was issued to some public officer, to whom was committed the power to ascertain the amount of the default, and, by such warrant, proceed to collect it."[55] Rather than bind anyone to a new duty, distress warrants merely were instruments for authorizing lesser executive officers to pursue a remedy already available at law.

Thus, not all "orders" and "warrants" were of the sort that legally bound subjects. Although judicial orders and warrants had this effect, executive orders and warrants merely directed executive officers in their lawful powers and duties.[56, p]

p. Other examples of nonbinding executive orders and warrants were those confining persons who were outside the obligation and protection of the law, such as enemy aliens who lacked a license or who were in violation of the conditions of their license. As already noted, the executive in such cases was exercising power over persons who were not subject to the United States and its laws, and its orders and warrants concerning them therefore were not

Executive Orders to Appear, Testify, or Produce Records

Only the courts could impose binding constraints on persons in particular instances; federal executive bodies could not. The latter therefore could not issue binding orders and warrants to subjects—not even orders merely to appear, to testify, or to produce records, let alone to do so under oath. Early executive bodies thus do not justify contemporary administrative demands for appearance, testimony, or production of records. Although nowadays administrative agencies frequently issue such orders—both in open-ended investigations and in proceedings against particular persons—it is unclear how such orders can find support in the early history of the federal government.

Constitutionally, the problem has several layers. At the very least, there is the problem of self-incrimination in investigations and proceedings that could lead to penalties, or other correction on behalf of the government, and that thus are criminal in their nature. In addition, there is the broader problem that the due process of administrative power is not the due process of law. Even more generally, the difficulty is that binding orders and warrants are part of the judicial power and that the Constitution commits this to the courts rather than the executive.

In England, some administrative bodies had a limited power to demand appearance, testimony, and records. Commissioners of sewers, of bankruptcy, and of the excise followed the civilian inquisitorial process rather than the regular due process of law. As Matthew Hale explained when discussing the due process required in courts of law, these commissions proceeded by "other rule or trial than the common law." These commissions therefore could bind persons to appear, to testify, and to share their records. Bankruptcy commissioners had particularly extensive powers, for they could seize and sell assets and could break open the bankrupt's house, and they even could imprison those who did not comply.[57] Their deviations from the due process of law were justified by acts of Parliament, which claimed a power not limited by constitutional rights or allocations of powers. But would these departures be allowed under a constitution that clearly limited the legislature and guaranteed the due process of law?

As might be expected, the federal government abandoned the prerogative or administrative interrogation employed by English commissions.

---

legally binding, but merely coercive. By the same token, the executive could issue orders and warrants enforcing martial law, for martial law was a power outside the law, which amounted merely to an exercise of force, without purporting to bind.

Under federal statutes, even excise officials could not demand appearance, testimony, or records; instead, they relied on general reporting, record-keeping, and inspection requirements imposed by acts of Congress. The executive officers who distributed federal benefits, such as land officers, could receive submissions of written evidence, and could hear proof, but could not compel anything. The most substantive exception was the first Court of Claims, which beginning in 1855 could compel testimony.[58] If one goes back to the early Republic, however, it is difficult to find any federal executive body that could bind subjects to appear, testify, or produce records.

The most prominent exception occurred under the first federal bankruptcy statute. Adopted in 1800, it followed the English model of involuntary bankruptcy for merchants, at the behest of creditors, who could get a court to appoint commissioners with binding adjudicatory powers. Under the 1800 act, the commissioners appointed by district courts could apprehend the bankrupt, could take possession of his property, could summon persons to testify about his property and debts, and could commit them to prison if they failed to answer truthfully.[59] These constraining powers are suggestive. The Constitution had authorized Congress to establish a uniform system of bankruptcy, and Congress in 1800 seems to have assumed that the Constitution thereby opened up room for an English civilian-style system that did not rely on the courts and did not accord the due process of law. The Constitution, however, had placed judicial power in the courts, and the Fifth Amendment's due process guarantee limited all grants of power. It therefore is not suprising that, by 1803, Congress recognized the constitutional problem and partly on this account repealed its bankruptcy statute.[60]

When Congress finally returned to the question, in 1841, it kept the bankruptcy system within the courts and their due process. It gave jurisdiction over bankruptcy proceedings to the federal district courts, which could order a bankrupt to testify before either the court or a court-appointed commissioner. Although it relied on the commissioners for the ministerial task of collecting testimony, this departure from common law principles (like the use of masters in chancery) was acceptable for proceedings that followed the civilian model in relying mostly on paper evidence. Even then, however, Congress did not allow the commissioners to order testimony, and "all . . . proofs of debts and other claims" made before the commissioners "shall be open to contestation in the proper court having jurisdiction over the proceedings." Although the statute generally authorized voluntary bankruptcy, it also allowed some involuntary bankruptcy, and it therefore added protection for anyone declared bankrupt at the instance of a creditor, providing that such a bankrupt could petition the court to hold a trial by jury to ascertain the fact of his bankruptcy.[61] In this vision of bankruptcy, the power to bind, even if only to order testimony, had to be exercised by the courts.

It remained thus for the rest of the century, with only a little slippage in the 1867 bankruptcy act. This statute left jurisdiction in district courts, and although it appointed registers in place of commissioners to take evidence, it echoed the past statute in authorizing any party, "during the proceedings before a register," to "take the opinion of the district judge upon any point or matter arising in the course of such proceedings, or upon the result of such proceedings." The statute, however, moved toward binding administrative power, for it gave the registers the authority to summon persons to testify. To be sure, it allowed only the judges to enforce such summons, and it thereby preserved the formality that judicial power remained in the courts.[62] But this was a fig leaf for binding administrative orders—a type of fig leaf that would flourish in the next century.

Even so, the power of the bankruptcy registers was a relatively late instance of administratively compelled testimony. It therefore does not alter the overall conclusion that orders to appear, testify, and produce documents traditionally had to be issued by the courts. These demands for information bound or constrained subjects, and they therefore had to come from the courts with their due process of law.

Of course, at the state level, there were some historical anomalies, which survived from England. For example, commissioners of sewers persisted in some states and still enjoyed a judicial power to demand testimony.[63] Along similar lines, as seen in chapter 6, local justices of the peace continued in places to exercise something close to local legislative power in levying assessments for public works. It would be a mistake, however, to conclude too much from minor surviving instances of how local administrators could issue orders binding subjects in an exercise of judicial power. Like the anomalous persistence of minor legislative power in justices of the peace, the local administrative exercises of judicial power were inherited exceptions from prevailing constitutional principles rather than measures of these principles. They therefore are not revealing about federal constitutional law.

Reporting, Record Keeping, and Inspection

Although executive bodies could not bind members of the public, it may seem that something functionally similar was accomplished under statutory reporting, record-keeping, and inspection requirements. From this perspective, the old statutory requirements are precedents for contemporary administrative orders and warrants for testimony, for the production of private records, and for the inspection of businesses.[64] The statutory requirements for such things, however, were distinct from binding executive orders and warrants.

In 1791, Congress adopted reporting, record-keeping, and inspection measures in its statute placing excise taxes on distilled spirits. Congress also did this in other excise statutes, such as that on snuff, and in its statutes concerning the customs, but its excise statute on spirits was particularly prominent and invasive, and it therefore is taken as the illustration here.[q]

What applied the federal reporting, record-keeping, and inspection requirements to distillers was the general requirement of the statute, not any executive order or warrant in any particular instance. The 1791 federal excise statute required distillers to report the places where they distilled spirits and the spirits contained there; it required them to keep record books specifying what they distilled and to make them available to treasury officers; and it required them to allow treasury officers (upon request during the daytime) to inspect, inventory, and sample the spirits in the reported distilleries, and to place marks and certificates on casks. (Although Congress also authorized treasury regulations, these concerned only the forms of the marks and certificates treasury officers were to place on the casks and barrels.) In other words, Congress could make binding laws, including laws requiring reporting, record-keeping, and inspection, but this was not to say that treasury officers could trespass on the judicial power of issuing binding orders or warrants.[65]

Even the inspection requirement was very limited, for it applied only to places that the distillers reported to the government. If administrators could decide which places were to be inspected and could order subordinate officers to carry out the inspections, the inspection requirement would become, in reality, an excuse for administrative search warrants. The excise statutes therefore allowed inspection only of places that had been reported as distilleries. Distillers had a statutory duty to report their distilleries, but if they did not do so, they were under no duty to allow inspection, and treasury officers then had no power to inspect. Instead, in such instances,

---

q. Of course, there also were local inspection laws. In Massachusetts, for example, "The tythingmen shall carefully inspect all licensed houses, and give information of all disorders and misdemeanors committed in them, to a justice of the peace or to the court of sessions." Moreover, "They are authorized to enter into any part of an inn or public house on the Lord's day, and the evening preceding and succeeding; and if such entrance shall be refused, the landlord or licensed person shall forfeit the sum of forty shillings for each offense."*

a treasury officer had to prosecute the distillers and had to get a warrant from a judicial officer before entering, searching, or seizing. Indeed, when treasury officers overstepped their authority, they were liable in court actions, which had to be decided by jury. And when these actions were for any seizure, it was necessary for the defending officer "to justify himself by making it appear that there was probable cause for making the said seizure; upon which, and not otherwise, a verdict shall pass in his favor."[66]

The record-keeping and inspection requirements, moreover, did not apply to privately owned records or papers. Rather than require production or inspection of private records, the 1791 statute carefully stated that treasury officers were to supply distillers with books for recording their production of spirits, and that distillers were to enter their production of spirits in these books. The books thus were government property, and on this assumption, the statute required that distillers return the books at the end of the year and, in the meantime, keep them open for inspection.[67] Thus, although Congress dragooned private parties into maintaining government records in government books, Congress did not impose a general legislative requirement for the production and inspection of private records. Nor, of course, did it authorize legally binding executive orders or warrants for persons to produce or open up their own books.[68]

Conceptually these are important distinctions. They confirm that, as seen in chapter 6, only Congress, not administrators, could impose rules or regulations binding on subjects. They also show that to be lawful, a reporting, record-keeping, or inspection requirement had to be imposed by legislation, not by executive discretion. It also is apparent that privately owned papers were peculiarly protected: They were not subject even to general disclosure requirements, it being only government-owned records that were open to inspection.[69]

These distinctions confirm that binding orders and warrants must come from judges. Although Congress can require reporting, record-keeping, and inspection requirements, the executive cannot issue binding orders or warrants—whether for reports, records, or inspections, let alone for searches and seizures. The unlawfulness of binding executive orders or warrants may confine government, but as evident from the early excise laws, it actually leaves the government much freedom to collect information, as long as it works through general requirements of law.

⊗⊗⊗

The distinction between binding and nonbinding adjudications avoids much confusion. At the very least, it sorts out the precedents. There were, of course, some narrow exceptions (mostly for tax evaluations and cross-border or offshore licensing), in which executive determinations had the effect of binding subjects in the manner of adjudications. But early federal executive acts (including determinations, hearings, orders, and warrants) generally did not bind subjects, and they therefore cannot be viewed as precedents for the contemporary administrative regime and its usurpation of judicial power.

In addition, the distinction between the binding and the nonbinding shows that the argument here does not call into question nonbinding executive adjudications. On the contrary, a recognition of why the binding adjudications are unlawful has the advantage of clarifying the lawfulness of the nonbinding executive decisions.

THIRTEEN

Return to Extralegal Adjudication

Part II of this book has thus far examined extralegal adjudication in its prerogative form and how constitutional law defeated it; it also has distinguished extralegal adjudication from nonbinding executive action. This part therefore can now examine the administrative revival of extralegal adjudication.

Scholars generally recognize that administrative adjudication is in tension with the Constitution's grant of judicial power to the courts and its guarantee of due process and other procedural rights.[1] To this, however, it must be added that administrative adjudication dangerously restores an extralegal judicial regime. The common law has faced recurring challenges to governance through and under law, and never since the time of James I has the extralegal challenge been so profound.

In defense of administrative adjudication, many scholars and judges hint that the Constitution's grant of judicial power, and its judicial processes and rights, centrally limit the courts, and thus not so much the executive. These constitutional principles, however, developed over the centuries most basically to bar extralegal exercises of judicial power. The return to an extralegal judicial regime therefore cannot really escape these constitutional limits.

The extralegal character of administrative adjudication thus reveals the extent and seriousness of the constitutional violations. To bar extralegal adjudication, the constitutional law of England and the United States placed judicial power in the courts and limited this power with processes and rights. Accordingly, when government once again relies on extrajudicial adjudications to bind subjects, it clearly violates these constitutional provisions. Indeed, it systematically returns to the extralegal adjudication that constitutional law developed largely in order to prevent. The result is a massive evasion of fundamental constitutional limitations.

Administrative Adjudication Binding on Subjects

The executive branch (like the Crown in the early seventeenth century) enforces its administrative rules and interpretations against members of the public by resorting to its own tribunals. And the essential feature of this extralegal adjudication is that it binds or constrains subjects outside the judgments of the courts.

Already in the early twentieth century, the result was "a noticeable tendency to supplement or supersede judicial action in administrative matters." As summarized by Ernst Freund—a leading academic apologist for administrative law—administrative adjudications carved out an "exception to the general rule that final compulsion cannot be exercised except upon the mandate of a court of justice."[2]

Nowadays, administrative agencies repeatedly exercise judicial compulsion. The agencies impose themselves in proceedings against private parties and even between them. They order parties to appear and testify; to produce documents; to make their homes, places of business, and records open for inspection; and to report their compliance with regulations and even their violations of them. The agencies issue orders requiring business to turn over records, including those that the businesses have a legal duty to keep confidential. They order payment of fines, forfeitures, damages, and restitution. They issue "cease and desist" orders and even order corrective action. The only things they do not impose are imprisonment and death.

Administrative agencies thus revive the prerogative exercise of judicial power—the imposition of binding adjudication outside the courts. More detailed problems with the administrative adjudication will be examined below, but most centrally, it returns to the extralegal exercise of judicial power that existed before Anglo-American constitutions clarified that judicial power belongs to the courts.[3]

Criminal in Nature

Many administrative hearings bind subjects not merely civilly, but in proceedings that are criminal in nature. When adjudication moves out of the courts, it is apt to escape many of the limitations on the judicial power, including the distinction between civil and criminal proceedings. This was true already in the prerogative courts, and it is evident again in administrative tribunals.

Defenders of administrative adjudication take a witheringly narrow view of what constitutes a criminal case. From their vantage point, criminal cases are merely those culminating in imprisonment or capital punishment, or those brought in criminal form in the common law courts, thus conveniently excluding administrative proceedings, including even those imposing fines. Criminal proceedings, however, have long included all government proceedings culminating in fines, and the mere fact that agencies impose their fines in their own tribunals does not mean that these proceedings are not criminal in nature.

Indeed, all government proceedings brought on behalf of the government for penalties or correction have long been considered criminal in nature. In the prerogative courts, most of the government's extralegal proceedings were candidly recognized as criminal. Regardless of whether they were initiated by the attorney general, a prerogative judge, or a private person, they were understood to be criminal when they were brought on behalf of the government for orders correcting or penalizing the defendants.

Along the same lines, after the abolition of the prerogative courts, many civil proceedings were recognized as criminal in nature. To be sure, numerous late-seventeenth- and eighteenth-century statutes authorized private individuals to bring civil actions in the law courts to recover damages, and whether a plaintiff kept the recovered amount or had to share it with the government, such actions were civil in form and in nature. But when the government initiated proceedings to correct or penalize, the proceedings were recognized as criminal, and any failure to recognize this would have been an evasion. Similarly, where a statute allowed a private person to bring an information, on behalf of the government, to correct or penalize the defendant, the proceedings were recognized as criminal, notwithstanding that the private person could collect much of the penalty. Last but not least, there were many civil actions, brought by private parties in the government's name or merely in their own, that were recognized as criminal in nature because the claim was not for damages, but for a share of a statutory fine, forfeiture, or other penalty.[4, a]

The lesson from both the prerogative and the common law courts is that neither administrative nor civil forms can disguise the reality of criminal proceedings. As in the old prerogative tribunals, so too in contemporary courts and administrative agencies, proceedings to correct or penalize, whether brought by the government or in its name, are criminal, and even many private civil actions to impose penalties, forfeitures, or corrective ac-

a. Already in the Star Chamber, there were informations in which the initiating party could secure both a fine for the government and damages for himself. But the only dispute about such proceedings was not whether they were criminal, but whether the damages could be differentiated from any punishment and thus protected from the reach of a pardon.[*]

tions are criminal in nature. Although there is disagreement about which private civil actions are criminal in nature, there is little dispute about the underlying principle, that the reality of criminal proceedings cannot be evaded by noncriminal forms.[b]

The Administrative Procedure Act actually admits that agencies prosecute criminal cases in their administrative proceedings. Although the statute generally manages to avoid any hint that it concerns criminal proceedings, it distinguishes between the executive and judicial functions of administrators by referring to administrators "engaged in the performance of investigative or prosecuting functions for an agency." In fact, this phrase appears twice, thus revealing that it is not a Freudian slip, but a careful recognition of the prosecutorial realities.[5]

Of course, the point here about the criminal character of most administrative proceedings is not necessary for this chapter's main arguments about the revival of extralegal judicial power or about its danger. The criminal nature of the extralegal adjudication, however, points to the extent of

b. Such reasoning suggests when administrative and judicial proceedings for forfeitures should be considered criminal. Traditionally, forfeitures were scarcely distinguished from criminal penalties, and government actions for forfeitures were therefore criminal or at least criminal in nature. As a result, the government (or those acting on its behalf) could secure a forfeiture only in a criminal prosecution, or in a forfeiture proceeding after a criminal conviction, against the property of the persons convicted. For example, as already noted, even when a treasury officer lawfully seized goods on probable cause, he could not confiscate them for the United States as "penalties or forfeitures" until he had a district attorney successfully bring an information in a district court.

Nowadays, however, the government obtains forfeitures in non-criminal proceedings, both administrative and judicial, and sometimes even without any proceedings. The government thereby secures criminal penalties or forfeitures without criminal proceedings and convictions in court—frequently even against the property of persons who are not even accused of committing a criminal act.

Recognizing that non-common-law forfeiture proceedings failed to meet the requirements for criminal proceedings, early Americans (as noted in chapter 9) repeatedly complained about the violation of the right to a jury. This concern about forfeitures was one of their key complaints in 1765 against the Stamp Act, and they echoed it in the Declaration of Independence when they protested against George III "[f]or depriving us in many cases, of the benefits of trial by jury." The right to a jury for forfeitures thus became a foundation of the new republic. Along similar lines, the New Jersey Supreme Court in 1780 rejected the administrative forfeiture proceedings in *Holmes & Ketcham v. Walton* on the ground that even the six man jury in that case violated the constitutional right to a jury.

Indeed, because administrative forfeitures are criminal penalties imposed in extralegal proceedings, they are unconstitutional on many grounds. They fail to provide criminal proceedings, courts, real judges, juries, or the due process of law. Moreover, being imposed without judicial proceedings, and without compensation, they are unlawful takings. And as if this were not bad enough, the agencies often keep the forfeited property for themselves and therefore tend to act with all the rapaciousness of those who are judges in their own case.*

the danger. As soon will become apparent, where agencies adjudicate cases of a criminal nature, they tend to deny the associated constitutional rights, most clearly those on grand juries and self-incrimination.

The Adjudicators

Administrative adjudicators come with many of the dangers of prerogative judges, and this further suggests how their exercise of binding judicial power is unconstitutional. As noted in chapter 12, the executive can lawfully rely on judge-like officers in judicial-like hearings to regularize its exercise of its lawful power, such as the distribution of government benefits. But when it relies on executive officers to issue edicts constraining subjects, it reverts to the perils of placing judicial power in persons who are not really judges.

Delegated

The key to understanding administrative judging is that the executive authority comes from above rather than below. Administrative adjudication therefore tends to be delegated—if not literally, then at least in the sense that it is part of the hierarchy of executive power. Of course, there is also the question of congressional delegation (which will be discussed in chapter 20), but the more immediate delegation is within the executive branch.

Executive power belongs to the president, and under him it is delegated to the heads of departments, commissions, and other agencies. The heads of agencies therefore usually have the final judgment for their agencies, even in adjudicatory decisions, unless they delegate such judgment to their subordinates. But the heads of agencies are very busy, and they often find the task of hearing cases to be a burden. They therefore ordinarily do not bother much with adjudication. Instead, simply sit atop a pyramid of delegated judicial power.

At the bottom of the pyramid, decisions begin with administrative officers, some of whom are administrative law judges, but even they often delegate many of their judicial tasks to agency staff. The administrative law judges can delegate to their own staff, and other decisionmakers delegate to more general staff. Some decisions by administrative law judges are only interim decisions or recommendations, until these are adopted by the agency; some are considered final decisions, subject to appeal within the agency. The head of the agency then finalizes the interim decisions and can review the others, but either way he typically leaves much work to staff, and he often simply leaves his decisions to an appointed review board. The contrast to federal judges thus could not be more stark. As put by one commentator, "judicial action is personal, while administrative determination is normally, as a matter of fact, delegated."[6]

It is no coincidence that this delegation echoes the practices of the prerogative courts, for whether prerogative or administrative, an executive exercise of judicial power must be delegated from above. It will be recalled that James I thought he was the source of judicial power and that he therefore could delegate it to his prerogative judges. Similarly, nowadays, executive agencies and their heads are invested with judicial power but usually leave it to subordinate administrative judges. Although the administrative version of judicial power comes from above, it must be delegated below.

Unity of Duty and Power

One problem with this delegated approach to judicial power is that it alters the character of a judge. Common law judges have a profoundly personal office or duty of judgment; it is their exercise of their own intellect or judgment that gives authority to their decisions; and on this basis they enjoy the great power of their courts. They therefore tend to feel an unusually tight combination of duty and power—a personal duty to exercise judgment in accord with the law, and an institutional power to carry it out.[c]

Because of the personal character of his office of judgment, a common law judge cannot ask anyone else to share in either his duty or the resulting power. Nor can he take comfort in thinking that he is merely acting for someone else, who has the ultimate burden of judgment or power. Instead, he must judge for himself, bearing the full weight of the decision, and then must stand alone with only a few fellow judges in issuing a court order.

This tight combination of duty and power, which concentrates the minds of common law judges on their responsibility, gets lost when administrative agencies delegate judicial power. For example, because of this delegation, many of the administrative opinions given by heads of departments are "the product of a bureaucratic staff, which the ostensibly responsible

---

c. Note the underlying distinction between the power of the courts and the duty of the judges. The Constitution vests the judicial power in the courts—this being the power to bind or constrain subjects in particular cases or controversies. Judges who sit on the courts, however, have an office or duty of exercising judgment in accord with the law of the land. The contrast is significant for many reasons. For example, whereas orders to parties enjoy their binding force from the power of the courts, the authority of the judges' exposition of the law arises from their office or duty.*

but busy agency heads may have little time to consider."[7] Thus, whereas a judge sometimes will not *write* all of his opinion, an agency head often will not even *read* all of his opinion, and he therefore cannot be considered to be exercising his own judgment. To avoid this sort of difficulty, much adjudication is delegated to administrative law judges or other officers, but precisely because they have only a delegated power, they often lack the power to issue the final order, and they therefore (quite reasonably) are apt to feel that the ultimate responsibility for their decisions lies elsewhere. Thus, although the duty of judgment tends to get delegated below, the power to decide tends to remain at the top of agencies, and the resulting disjuncture of judgment and power tends to weaken responsibility at both ends.[d]

Even when an administrative officer makes a final decision, he tends to act merely on behalf of his agency—usually a massive executive branch institution—thus leaving the officer with anything but a sense of power over the organization. This is very different from the situation of real judges, who sit in small groups on their courts and thus have a keen sense of both their duty and their power. On this ground alone, it is apparent that administrative decisionmakers are not apt to feel the unity of duty and power, and the resulting sense of responsibility, that tends to be felt by judges on the bench.

To compensate for this shift away from individual responsibility, the Administrative Procedure Act requires an administrative decisionmaker to become "personally familiar with the issues." So weak a requirement, however, is less than reassuring, for it does not mean that the decisionmaker must personally hear the evidence. On the contrary, he can do this through others—for example, "by reading portions of the transcript and briefs" or by "reading a report of lower level decisionmakers, reading summaries prepared by staff members, or receiving a briefing by staff members."[8] As a result, the decisionmaker may ultimately be someone who never even attended the hearing and never even looked at the administrative record.[e]

If a common law judge were to reach a final judgment in a case that

---

d. This division between the power to decide and the duty to conduct the adjudication can have curious consequences—for example, when an administrative law judge can merely make a recommendation in a case, and the head of their agency makes the final decision. When such a decision gets appealed, the Administrative Procedure Act requires the reviewing court to review the administrative record, and the court thus ends up reviewing a record that was not produced by, or even necessarily read by, the administrative decisionmaker.*

e. At least when the English in 1552 contemplated an early statutory attempt to tame their ecclesiastical courts, they proposed the common law standard, that "[t]rial must be held in the presence of the judge and in court, and not out of court, and not [merely] in the presence of a notary or a notarial official." Nowadays, however, like the old ecclesiastical and other preroga-

came before his "agency" or court without attending the hearing or even reading the transcript, but merely on the basis of a staff summary or briefing, he would be inviting impeachment. In the administrative system, however, this low standard of judgment is offered as a guarantee of the agency's due process. And the courts shy away from upholding even this appallingly weak standard.

The delegation of judicial power within the executive branch thus has consequences that are not cured by the Administrative Procedure Act. The delegation disaggregates judicial duty and power, and it thereby undermines personal responsibility in the exercise of both.

Judicial Office

Quite apart from how administrative judges carry out their duties, they do not even have the office of judges. Later, in chapter 17, it will be seen that administrative judges tend to have personal precommitments favoring the government. For now, however, it should suffice merely to examine their formal commitments and thereby observe that their office or duty is profoundly different from that of a judge.

In defense of administrative adjudication, its apologists protest that administrative law judges are just like real judges. Undoubtedly, most are devoted to acting sincerely in accord with their duties. Yet this is not to say that they are real judges or even that they come close to having the office or duty of real judges; nor is it to say that administrative adjudication as a whole meets such a standard.

The office of a judge has traditionally been a duty of independent judgment in accord with the law of the land. A judge, in other words, has a duty to exercise his judgment independently of will and to follow the law, not other commands.

In contrast, administrative decisionmakers hold offices that require both more and less of them. Administrative decisionmakers must do more than follow the law, because they must follow administrative rules and interpretations—indeed, they often must exercise judgment about the implementation of administrative policy. They also must do less than exercise independent judgment, for they are precommitted to carrying out the government's policy in its regulations, and they must submit to having their decisions reconsidered by executive officers—neither of which is compat-

---

tive judges, administrative decisionmakers can leave hearings to subordinate officials, and the Administrative Procedure Act simply acquiesces.*

ible with judicial independence. Therefore, notwithstanding their good intentions, they do not really have the office or duty of judges.[f]

In fact, the delegation of judicial office creates a range of deviations from judicial independence in different types of administrative adjudicators. At the bottom of the heap, for "informal adjudication," there are a host of ordinary executive officers, who do not enjoy even the appearance of independence. Of higher status, there are "administrative law judges," who are not appointed with Senate confirmation, but who are largely protected in tenure and salary. Even they, however, are not really independent. Fifteen percent of administrative law judges surveyed in 1992 complained of threats to their independence, and eight percent said this was a frequent problem. Nor should this be a surprise, as they can be removed or can be demoted to a lower pay scale for failing to follow administrative regulations. Thus, even if they were secure in most matters, they lack the independence of judges on the essential question, the lawfulness of their own administrative proceedings and of administrative regulations.[9]

Standing above all such initial adjudicators, moreover, are the members of administrative review boards, and ultimately the heads of agencies. These high administrative adjudicators are typically political appointees and thus not at all independent. Nonetheless, they often adjudicate. Sometimes they hold initial hearings; more typically, they review or finalize the decisions of administrative or administrative law judges. One way or another, political appointees adjudicate.

Recognizing that the location of judges within the executive branch threatens their independence, the Administrative Procedure Act carefully establishes a separation of functions. It bars a decisionmaker from deciding a case if he has "engaged in the performance of investigative or prosecuting functions" in it. The statute, however, does less than is apparent. In taking a case-by-case approach, the statute ignores the systemic interests of administrators across cases. Moreover, in excluding only adjudicators who have "engaged in the performance" of the investigation or prosecution of a case, the statute leaves room for adjudicators who ordered or even are still overseeing the investigation or prosecution of the case. The result is comic. It is as if a statute fastidiously barred federal judges from serving

---

f. The incomplete office of administrative judges became painfully apparent in a 2012 case before the Court of Veteran's Appeals. This administrative tribunal worried that its authorizing statute did "not explicitly empower the Court to 'hold unlawful' statutes enacted by Congress," and it therefore requested additional briefs on the question of "Whether the Court has the jurisdiction and, if so, the power, to strike down a statute because it's unconstitutional?" Real judges would have had no doubt of their duty to follow the law, including the Constitution.*

as FBI agents and district attorneys in their cases, but simultaneously allowed them to oversee such persons. As a result, review boards and other high-level administrators can hear appeals, notwithstanding that they initiated or otherwise oversaw the investigation or prosecution. Even this weak protection, however, does not always apply. It does not reach decisions on initial licenses or on the rates and practices of public utilities or carriers. Nor does it apply to agency heads, even when they make the final decision.[10]

The absence of even the semblance of judicial office is especially bad at the top and the bottom. At the top, the heads of agencies have most power and are least expected to act like judges. They do not even work within the weak version of the judicial role that is established for administrative law judges. Instead, they usually are political appointees, who do not enjoy protection in tenure or salary, who can be fully engaged in investigating and prosecuting the cases they decide, and who usually can receive all sorts of internal off-the-record suggestions and advice on a case. Nonetheless, almost all decisions by administrative law judges are subject to appeal or other review by the heads of agencies or by persons appointed by them. As a result, they are the final judges, even if the least informed and the most biased. The persons least like judges thus enjoy the greatest judicial power.[11]

At the bottom, the dangers are even worse, for much adjudication is merely "informal adjudication" which can be done by ordinary agency staff. Such decisionmakers have even less of judicial office, and less protection in it, than the administrative law judges. This would not be worrisome if their proceedings were confined to claims concerning government benefits, government contracts, and other matters that Congress can lawfully leave within the power of the executive. Much informal adjudication, however, concerns equality in employment and other violations of statutes or rules, and in these decisions, administrators can issue constraining adjudications without even a semblance of being judges in the constitutional sense. Administrative adjudicators, from the top to the bottom of their agencies, thus revert to the posture of prerogative judges.

Like their predecessors in the prerogative courts, most administrative decisionmakers surely aim to act in a principled manner. But that does not make them judges. To sum up, they lack the duties of independent judgment and of following the law of the land and thus do not hold judicial office. In addition, they are not selected like judges, with the Senate's confirmation; they act without the essential combination of judicial duty and power; they often can consult and take advice about cases off the record;

they can initiate and oversee investigatory and prosecutorial decisions in their own cases; they are subject to docked salaries or removal for not following regulations. Moreover, those with the final decisions, or at least the final say on administrative appeals, are often politicians, and agency adjudications therefore are often subject in a very real sense to executive review, which is incompatible with judicial power, as explained in *Hayburn's Case*. All in all, even the least biased administrative adjudicators act in ways and under pressures that would not be tolerated in real judges. And this list does not even reach the question, to be discussed in chapter 17, as to how the judgment of administrators is apt to be tainted by their administrative precommitments.

Administrative agencies thus act through "judges" who have little in common with the judges of the courts. In the words that Frederick Maitland applied to the Star Chamber, an agency tribunal is "a court of politicians enforcing a policy, not a court of judges administering the law."[12]

Administrative Process and Due Process

The process in contemporary administrative adjudication is strikingly similar to the old inquisitorial process of the prerogative courts. Of course, it is not the same in all respects. But in pursuing judicial power outside the structures, processes, and rights established by the Constitution, administrative adjudication takes a path very close to that of the prerogative courts, and it thereby violates a wide range of procedural rights, all of which are part of the due process of law.[13]

Open-Ended Investigation outside a Grand Jury

Perhaps the least understood return to the prerogative regime has been the administrative revival of inquisitorial or general investigative inquiries. The common law traditionally confined binding open-ended inquiries to grand juries, and when the Crown pursued such inquiries in its prerogative courts, constitutional law developed to bar such courts. Nonetheless, binding open-ended investigations outside grand juries have returned.

As in the prerogative courts, the contemporary versions of these investigations do not have defined boundaries, and they thus can range from questioning about known violations to more general inquiries that search for violations or that explore the need for new legislation. As in the prerogative courts, moreover, the investigations can range from the formal to the utterly informal. An agency can require testimony at a court-like hearing, or it can simply ask for information without a formal request. Although the hearings are no longer common, the power of agencies to hold formal inquiries or to take other aggressive action generally induces cooperation with their less formal demands for information.

The constitutional problem is substantial, for the power to bind subjects in particular instances, including the authority to demand information from particular persons, is part of the judicial power. Congress can demand cooperation with its committee inquiries, but beyond the end of a session, it must rely on the courts to back it up.[14] Although individual police officers can question persons, they have no power to force answers. Even when the police and other executive officers need warrants to search places, or to seize things or persons, they must get the warrants from the judges based on probable cause about the commission of a crime. Otherwise the power to force answers to questions belongs to the courts—either in cases or controversies begun by accusation or in general investigations by grand juries.

The power to impose open-ended inquires thus resides in grand juries, which operate under a court. In contrast, the executive has no power to demand responses to general inquiries.

Nonetheless, administrative agencies enjoy "powers of original inquiry"—powers to impose open-ended investigations, either by holding hearings or by issuing orders for the production of records and other materials.[15] The agencies thereby can inform themselves about the need for new regulations and even about violations of existing regulations. Thus, quite apart from the question of self-incrimination (which will be discussed shortly), agencies can bind persons to respond to their questioning, without any showing of a violation of law, this being a power that ordinarily belongs only to grand juries.[g]

The Supreme Court even defends this investigatory power as "a power of inquisition." In *United States v. Morton Salt*, the Federal Trade Commission had "made no charge of violation," and the Court therefore recognized that the agency was "engaged in a mere 'fishing expedition' to see if it can turn up evidence of guilt." The justices acknowledged, moreover, that

---

g. With a strange sense of delicacy, agencies sometimes hesitate to make openly inquisitorial demands for confessions about violations and therefore, instead, reach administrative judgments in which they decree that, as part of the remedy, the delinquent must file compliance reports. An agency thereby can investigate violations under the guise of seeking information about compliance with the prior adjudication—as if the agency were a court of equity merely ensuring compliance with a decree in a private dispute.

courts "have often disapproved the employment of the judicial process in such an enterprise."[16, h]

Yet the Supreme Court assumed that "[b]ecause judicial power is reluctant, if not unable, to summon evidence until it is shown to be relevant to issues in litigation, it does not follow that an administrative agency charged with seeing that the laws are enforced may not have and exercise powers of original inquiry."[17] The Constitution allows coercive questioning without charges only in grand juries. Astonishingly, however, the Court assumed that because the Federal Trade Commission was working outside the courts, it was not subject to the usual constitutional limitations.

Ironically, in justifying grand jury powers outside the judicial power, the Court relied on the analogy of a grand jury. From this perspective, the agency had a nonjudicial power of inquisition: "It has a power of inquisition . . . which is not derived from the judicial function. It is more analogous to the Grand Jury, which does not depend on a case or controversy for power to get evidence, but can investigate merely on suspicion that the law is being violated, or even just because it wants assurance that it is not."[18] If the executive were exercising a "judicial function," its forced inquiry without charges would clearly be unlawful, so the Court relied on the analogy of a grand jury. But to call and oversee a grand jury is part of the judicial power—indeed, part of the judicial power of courts only in criminal matters.

To be sure, the High Commission proceeded against persons ex officio, without any formal accusations of the sort required at common law, and it thereby imposed open-ended inquisitorial inquiries without a grand jury. At law, however, the government can forcibly make open-ended inquiries only by having a court convene a grand jury, and although the grand jury can require the testimony of witnesses, it does so not as an administrative body, but as a part of the court. Thus, rather than support an open-ended power of investigation in administrative agencies, the grand jury analogy is a reminder that this power belongs to the courts.

---

h. The Court's earlier decisions had recognized "limitations upon the administrative process." The Court, however, mocked the reasoning in these earlier cases, suggesting that the constitutional limitations restricted only the courts, not the judicial power: "The courts could not go fishing, and so it followed neither could anyone else. Administrative investigations fell before the colorful and nostalgic slogan 'no fishing expeditions.'" In fact, the Constitution confined the judicial power to the courts. And when it guaranteed procedural rights, it generally established them not merely as limits on the courts, but as limits on any exercise of the judicial power.*

The Supreme Court understood that it was legitimizing a dangerous administrative power, and it therefore cautioned against investigations "of such a sweeping nature and so unrelated to the matter properly under inquiry as to exceed the investigatory power." Yet rather than acknowledge the profound danger of administrative inquisitions, or the need to confine open-ended demands for information to the courts and their grand juries, the Court offered the meaningless palliative that there was sufficient protection "in the requirement . . . that the disclosure sought shall not be unreasonable."[19, i]

Concededly, the executive has a power to investigate, but the executive does not have a power to investigate with the force of law. Orders or warrants binding subjects (whether individuals or corporations) are part of the judicial power. Therefore when the executive seeks to bind persons to give information, it traditionally must act through the courts and their judges, and when it seeks to bind subjects to give information in the absence of an accusation in court, it must act through a court's grand jury.[j]

The administrative power to force disclosure thus evades the requirement of a grand jury. It returns to what the Supreme Court itself calls a "power of inquisition"—the power by which prerogative or administrative bodies act outside the courts to force subjects to disclose information. The executive thereby revives inquisitorial process in place of due process, and more generally exercises a power of ordering persons that the Constitution gives to the courts.

Serious Criminal Charges without a Grand Jury

When an agency brings or allows charges against a defendant, there is a further grand jury problem. The Fifth Amendment requires that "[n]o person shall be held to answer for a capital, or otherwise infamous crime, unless on a presentment or indictment of a Grand Jury." The meaning of an "infamous crime" is not always clear in contemporary circumstances, but it is clear enough to raise doubts about some administrative proceedings.

i. Recognizing the weakness of its argument, the Court felt obliged to back up its position by suggesting that "corporations can claim no equality with individuals in the enjoyment of a right to privacy." At stake, however, is not privacy, but more concretely the judicial power and the due process of law—all of which the Constitution locates in the courts, without confining the benefits to individuals.*

j. Of course, a grand jury is necessary to charge a person only where he is accused of a capital or infamous crime. But this does not mean that the government can impose questioning without charges where lesser crimes or no crimes are at stake.

Administrative agencies do not use grand juries to charge regulatory offenders. On the contrary, many agencies file complaints on their own based merely on their own belief that there has been a violation of their regulations. As a result, the agencies can bring charges on the basis of nothing more than their own determinations.

Of course, the agencies do not hold common law criminal proceedings; nor do their practices even look like criminal proceedings. As has been seen, however, many administrative hearings are really criminal—most clearly where, like prerogative criminal proceedings, they are brought by the government or in its name to correct or penalize the defendants. The Administrative Procedure Act, moreover, recognizes that it authorizes what are really prosecutions. Nonetheless, the criminal nature of these proceedings is denied when it comes to the rights of the defendants.

The Constitution's grand jury requirement applies only when a person is being held to answer for "a capital, or otherwise infamous crime," and the Supreme Court has interpreted an "infamous crime" to mean a felony, which it in turn has understood to mean imprisonment for more than a year. In contrast, administrative proceedings usually seek only fines. Such proceedings, even if criminal, therefore have not seemed to be of the seriousness that would require grand jury charges.

In the last two centuries, however, penalties for many crimes have shifted from capital punishment to incarceration, and from this physical punishment to financial penalties. And when the government comes to rest on fines, it often seeks huge amounts, which go far beyond ordinary fines. It uses the amounts of the fines, moreover, to indicate the reprehensible or infamous character of the crimes. In these circumstances, the interpretation of infamous crimes to exclude financial penalties no longer is plausible. Many administrative defendants, moreover, are corporations, unions, and other artificial bodies, which cannot face capital charges or imprisonment. In this context, the Court's definition of infamous crimes systematically excludes these administrative defendants from the Constitution's right to a grand jury. Contemporary circumstances thus call into question the assumption that administrative agencies do not deal with infamous crimes and thus do not need to work through grand juries.

Unspecific Notice and Unspecified Accusers

Following civilian inquisitorial procedures, the prerogative courts often refused to let criminal defendants see the charges against them or to face their accusers. Constitutional law therefore carefully rejected these inquisitorial practices—not only in the courts but also in extralegal exercises of judicial power. Administrative proceedings, however, again prevent criminal defendants from learning details about their charges and accusers.

Administrative agencies often charge defendants in a manner much less specific than is required in criminal charges, and the agencies have no duty to provide bills of particulars. The Administrative Procedure Act requires agencies, when they charge defendants, to give them notice about "the matters of fact and law asserted"—a standard that satisfies due process in civil actions before the courts.[20] Yet at least when administrative proceedings are brought by or on behalf of agencies to penalize or correct defendants, the proceedings are really criminal, and they therefore ought to comply with the standard of notice for criminal trials.

Agencies also often suppress information about the underlying accusers. Of course, anonymity can be valuable for a whistle-blower, and prosecutors in the courts do not have to share information about a witness if the evidence is not exculpatory. Yet where the prosecuting agency is also the judge, the decisionmaker (or those he relies upon) may well know of the secret informant and his evidence, even where it is not part of the record and is not known to the defendant. This is particularly likely when cases come before heads of agencies.

Recognizing the danger in all criminal proceedings, the Sixth Amendment guarantees that, in "all criminal prosecutions, the accused shall enjoy the right . . . to be informed of the nature and cause of the accusation" and "to be confronted with the witnesses against him." The Amendment does not say that criminal defendants shall enjoy these rights only when prosecuted in courts; rather, it more generally provides protection in *all* criminal prosecutions, regardless of whether the proceedings occur in the courts or in administrative tribunals. And this is exactly what might be expected from principles that developed as constitutional rights in response to the inquisitorial practices of the prerogative courts.

In short, precisely because prerogative tribunals left defendants uninformed and unable to confront their accusers, the Constitution generally rejects these inquisitorial practices, without distinguishing between regular or irregular tribunals. Nonetheless, both as to charges and as to accusers, administrative agencies return to the inquisitorial tendency to hide the ball.

No Petit Jury

Notwithstanding the Constitution, agency adjudications go back to the prerogative practice of reaching decisions without petit juries. The Constitution calls for juries in both criminal and civil trials. For criminal trials, it requires that "The Trial of all Crimes, except in Cases of Impeachment, shall be by Jury; and such Trial shall be held in the State where the said Crimes shall have been committed." The Sixth Amendment adds that, "In all criminal prosecutions, the accused shall enjoy the right to a speedy and public trial, by an impartial jury of the State and district wherein the crime shall have been committed . . . ." As for civil trials, the Seventh Amendment provides that, "In Suits at common law, where the value in controversy shall exceed twenty dollars, the right of trial by jury shall be preserved . . . ."

The right to a jury developed into a constitutional right in response to the Crown's reliance on inquisitorial proceedings in prerogative courts. When the Crown, moreover, in the 1760s, relied on admiralty proceedings without juries to enforce the Stamp Act, Americans insisted on their jury rights. Both English history and recent colonial experience thus led Americans to understand their jury guarantees as barriers to jury-less adjudication, regardless of whether the proceedings occurred in administrative tribunals or in courts.

The significance of such guarantees for administrative hearings is all the more clear from some jury cases from the 1780s—*Holmes & Ketcham v. Walton* in New Jersey and the *Ten Pound Cases* in New Hampshire—which were discussed in chapter 9. A New Jersey statute authorized justices of the peace to impose forfeitures with only six-person juries, and a New Hampshire statute authorized justices of the peace to hear civil proceedings without juries. In other words, the statutes allowed what were, in effect, administrative trials. The defendants who were tried in this manner protested, and the regular courts held the trials and the statutes unconstitutional for failing to provide juries. Even under the New Hampshire statute, which allowed a jury on appeal, the courts held the proceedings and statute unconstitutional.[21] The constitutional guarantees of a jury trial thus protected the defendants from administrative hearings without juries, regardless of any right to an appeal—indeed, regardless of any right to a jury on appeal.

Nowadays, however, the executive blithely adjudicates both civil and criminal cases without juries.[22] Of course, where the executive hears suits in equity or admiralty, its constitutional violations do not include the denial of a jury. Otherwise, however, administrative adjudications, being without juries, collide with the Constitution's jury guarantees.

Indeed, there are two layers of violation—at trial and on appeal. One violation occurs whenever an administrative body requires a defendant to submit to an adjudication and verdict without a jury. And as seen from the foundational decisions on the subject, the *Ten Pound Cases*, this difficulty cannot be cured by the opportunity for a jury on appeal. At least in those cases, however, the defendant could get a jury trial on appeal to a court. Nowadays, however, even on appeal, he cannot get a jury. This leads to a second violation, for when the courts review administrative cases on appeal, without insisting on a jury trial in a district court, the courts themselves deny the right to jury.

One justification is that trials for petty offenses did not require juries and that administrative proceedings are trials of this sort. To be sure, the common law and Magna Charta had long seemed to require juries in all trials at law, including all criminal trials. A series of seventeenth- and eighteenth-century statutes, however, both in England and the colonies, allowed justices of the peace to hold criminal hearings for minor offenses, without a jury.[23] There thus were divergent traditions about the extent of the right to a jury in criminal cases: There was the traditional right to a jury in all cases, as guaranteed by Magna Charta and the common law, but there also was the modified version of the right, as adjusted by the recent statutes on petty offenses.

Notwithstanding the dual versions of the right to a jury, the Supreme Court casually assumes that there was a uniform understanding of the matter. Relying on nothing more than the statutes concerning petty offenses, the Court simply takes for granted that the modified right had displaced the previously unrestricted common law right. It thereby concludes that the Constitution's guarantees of jury trial do not extend to petty offenses—a position that conveniently helps to justify administrative proceedings.[24]

American constitutions, however, clearly distinguished between the two versions of the right to a jury. Some states clearly followed the statutory vision, as when the New York Constitution guaranteed "trial by jury, in all cases in which it hath heretofore been used in the colony." In contrast, other constitutions expressly protected the old common law right—the right to a jury even for petty offenses—as when the Maryland Constitution required a jury in "all criminal prosecutions." This was the approach taken by the U.S. Constitution, not once, but twice. The concept of petty offenses therefore cannot justify any federal denial of a jury in any criminal proceedings, let alone in administrative proceedings.[k]

k. The position of the Supreme Court—that early Americans had a uniform understanding of the right to a jury, and that the right did not extend to petty offenses—is plausible only if one systematically ignores the different words of different constitutions. It therefore is worth examining the words in detail.

Several states clearly guaranteed the right to a jury as adjusted by their colonial statutes,

Another justification, which harks back to the prerogative vision of justice, suggests that trials outside the courts are not fully restricted by the law's procedural rights. Thus, although the Constitution requires juries in

---

thus allowing criminal proceedings without juries for petty offenses. The Pennsylvania Constitution of 1776 succinctly stated, "Trial shall by jury as heretofore." More grandiloquently, as already noted, the New York Constitution of 1777 provided that "trial by jury, in all cases in which it hath heretofore been used in the colony of New York, shall be established and remain inviolate forever." Adopting a somewhat similar approach but a different drafting strategy, the Massachusetts Constitution stated that "the legislature shall not make any law that shall subject any person to a capital or infamous punishment, excepting for the government of the army and navy, without trial by jury." New Hampshire adopted a similar provision.

Other states, however, guaranteed juries in all criminal cases. The North Carolina Constitution provided that "no freeman shall be convicted of any crime, but by the unanimous verdict of a jury of good and lawful men, in open court, as heretofore used." Putting this in the positive form, the Virginia Bill of Rights guaranteed that "in all capital or criminal prosecutions a man hath a right . . . to a speedy trial by an impartial jury of twelve men of his vicinage, without whose unanimous consent he cannot be found guilty." Making clear that its vision of jury rights echoed Magna Charta, the state's Bill of Rights added that "no man be deprived of his liberty, except by the law of the land or the judgment of his peers." The Maryland Constitution adopted a more carefully drafted version of this guarantee, focusing on "all criminal prosecutions" and similarly echoing Magna Charta.

Two states did not specify the extent of the right. The New Jersey Constitution of 1776 stated that "the inestimable right of trial by jury shall remain confirmed as a part of the law of this Colony, without repeal, forever." The Georgia Constitution, adopted the next year, declared that "trial by jury" was "to remain inviolate forever."

The U.S. Constitution took the path laid out in North Carolina, Virginia, and Maryland. The United States did not have a prior history of adjusting jury rights, and its powers were of a sort that would not typically require it to be responsible for regulating and prosecuting petty offenses. Moreover, the power of the new government was sufficiently feared that the Constitution probably would not have been ratified if it had left any doubt about the traditional common law right to a jury in criminal cases. It therefore is unsurprising that it guaranteed a jury in *trials of all crimes* and soon emphasized that the right reached *all criminal prosecutions.*

There have been suggestions that the Constitution's requirement of juries in all criminal cases cannot be understood to mean what it says, because the federal government needs an exception to govern the District of Columbia. In providing juries for "[t]he trial of all Crimes," however, Article III excepted impeachments, and it thereby revealed that it anticipated exceptions. Indeed, Article III anticipated the District of Columbia question. It continued: "[S]uch Trial shall be held in the State where the said Crimes shall have been committed; but when not committed within any State, the Trial shall be at such Place or Places as the Congress may by law have directed." In other words, Article III recognized that crimes would occur in the District and other places outside the states, but it did not therefore limit the right to a jury trial, other than to allow Congress to specify the trial location. Even this departure from the traditional common law right troubled many Americans, and the Sixth Amendment therefore added that in all criminal prosecutions, the accused had a right to trial "by an impartial jury of the State and district wherein the crime shall have been committed."

It thus is evident that the federal constitutional right to a jury in criminal cases extends to all criminal cases. Decisions about petty offenses or about administrative equivalents cannot be excluded.*

all criminal prosecutions and almost all suits at common law, administrative proceedings are said to be outside the system of law and thus exempt.

The extralegal character of the proceedings, however, is a strange sort of justification. The constitutional right to a jury developed largely in answer to extralegal proceedings, and the Constitution therefore does not confine its jury requirements to the courts.[1] More generally, also to bar extralegal proceedings, the Constitution places the judicial power in the courts. Thus even if administrative proceedings were merely civil in nature, and even if the Seventh Amendment were understood to require civil juries only in the law courts, there still would be no excuse for relocating the judicial power out of the hands of the courts and their juries.

A third justification for the administrative denial of petit juries is the idea of "public rights"—to be precise, the notion that the sovereign's statutory claims of "public rights" escape the protection of the Seventh Amendment. In this sort of argument—made by the Supreme Court in *Atlas Roofing v. Occupational Safety and Health Review Commission*—"public rights" are contrasted to private rights and thus are distinctively governmental claims, which are said to carve out an exception from the right to a jury. As put by the Court, "At least in cases in which 'public rights' are being litigated— *e.g.,* cases in which the government sues in its sovereign capacity to enforce public rights created by statutes . . . —the Seventh Amendment does not prohibit Congress from assigning the factfinding function and initial adjudication to an administrative forum with which the jury would be incompatible."[25]

This argument, however, is odd—most immediately because it assumes that administrative adjudications are merely civil proceedings and thus are subject simply to the Seventh Amendment's jury requirement. In fact, most administrative proceedings are criminal in nature, and the Court practically concedes this when it speaks of how the government in its administrative proceedings "sues in its sovereign capacity to enforce public rights." Being criminal in nature, these proceedings must come with a jury.

It does not make sense, moreover, for the Court to argue that the statutory basis of a claim excuses the government from complying with the Seventh Amendment. Even if administrative proceedings were all civil in nature, what led to the adoption of the Seventh Amendment were demands

1. To be sure, the Seventh Amendment guarantees a jury "in Suits at common law," and nowadays this sometimes is interpreted to include only cases in the courts, not those in administrative proceedings. As will be explained below, however, this phrase was employed in the amendment to exclude cases in equity and admiralty, and the phrase therefore does not imply that the government can evade the civil jury requirement simply by acting outside the courts.

for jury rights generally in civil actions, and the amendment therefore guarantees juries in *suits at common law*—that is, in all civil cases outside of equity and admiralty—not merely in *common law actions*. It therefore is strange for the Court to assume that the statutory foundation of a claim is significant—as if an amendment that excludes criminal, equitable, and admiralty proceedings should be read to exclude a range of statutory claims.

Worst of all, the Supreme Court excludes administrative proceedings from the Seventh Amendment where (on top of the statutory foundation) the government in its sovereign capacity asserts a public right. The Court thereby elevates sovereign rights over constitutional rights. The notion of public law, and the public claims or rights of the sovereign, are Continental imports, which are not evident in the Seventh Amendment. On the Continent, prerogative or administrative decisions on behalf of the government's public power were often said to be sovereign and thus above the rights of private persons. But the whole point of the U.S. Constitution, including the Seventh Amendment, is to establish and limit the sovereign, not least by means of constitutional rights. It therefore is entirely alien to the United States and its constitution to conclude that the constitutional right to a jury melts away before the sovereign's "public rights."[m]

m. When the Supreme Court initially used the phrase "public rights" in 1856 in *Murray's Lessee v. Hoboken Land & Improvement Co.*, it was referring merely to the executive's traditional power under law and thus not to any executive power of issuing binding legislative or judicial edicts. The phrase, however, has subsequently become a springboard for claims of administrative power, and it therefore is worth examining it, to understand where it came from and why it was so open to misunderstanding.

When first encountered, the notion of the executive's "public rights" is disconcerting, for it is conventional to speak of personal rights and governmental powers. To be sure, there is no necessary difference between rights and powers, and it is not uncommon speak of the government's rights in relation to other governments. Nonetheless, in relation to domestic persons, one ordinarily says that the government exercises powers rather than rights.

How, then, did the Supreme Court come to speak of the executive's domestic "public rights"? Roman law had distinguished between *ius publicum* and *ius privatum*, and this could be translated as a distinction between public and private law. The former concerned the interests of the state, and the latter, merely private interests. This public-private distinction carried risks, for it suggested that public and private matters were not subject to the same law of the land, and it thereby could lend legitimacy to governmental claims of extra- and supralegal powers. In opposition to this dual vision of law, the common law placed the monarch under the law of the land, the same law as governed his subjects. Similarly, Anglo-American constitutions limited government on the theory that the constitution was part of the law of the land. Rather than another sort of law, the constitution was simply the highest part of the same law.

Although it was not easy at common law to accept a civilian distinction between public and private law, there was another possibility, for *ius publicum* and *ius privatum* could be understood as two types of rights: the public rights of government and the private rights that ordinarily were enjoyed by private persons. The word *ius* was notoriously capable of meaning either law or right, and it therefore is unsurprising that *ius publicum* came to be understood by

The justifications for administrative adjudications without juries are thus less than reassuring. Some even hark back to preconstitutional claims about a sovereign prerogative not subject to law. In such ways, administrative adjudications recall the prerogative proceedings that flourished before constitutions guaranteed jury trial.

Nonpublic Proceedings

Further echoing the practice of prerogative tribunals, many aspects of administrative proceedings are closed to the public. The prerogative tribunals were opaque in part for the simple reason that they did not use juries. Instead, they followed the civil law in relying heavily on written arguments, evidence, and other submissions. For similar reasons, many aspects of administrative proceedings are not apt to be publicly visible.

Making the problem worse is the tendency of agencies to close proceedings or keep matters secret to protect information. Although they sometimes reserve information for reasons of national security, they also do this to protect the anonymity of their informants or the interests of private

---

civilian-influenced commentators (such as William Blackstone) to be the government's public rights. Similarly, some American lawyers found it an appealing way to express the government's claims of power.

An initial problem was the sheer extent of the power that could be subsumed under the rubric of "public rights." Like the Continental notion that lingered in the background, the phrase "public rights" suggested the general power of government in public matters, not merely enumerated powers, let alone merely executive power.

An even greater problem was the suggestion that the government did not merely have powers derived from the people, but rather, qua government, had rights against the people. Ideas about the *ius publicum* and derivative notions of the government's public rights seemed to suggest that the government had a range of inherent power, which could not be limited by the law or rights established by the people. Recognizing this difficulty, one American commentator attempted to flip the phrase around by speaking, instead, about "the public rights of the people." Typically, however, the implications cut the other way.

Far from being merely historical, these dangers have come back to life. As in the past, the notion of *ius publicum*, or "public rights," lends itself to the idea that the executive enjoys general governmental rights that trump the legal claims of the public. The U.S. Constitution structures rights as exceptions to the powers of government; but when the executive's power is understood as a right, it becomes plausible to invert this structural relationship—to conclude that the government's public rights override merely private claims to constitutional rights.

Such is the conclusion of the Supreme Court in *Atlas Roofing*. Faced with a Seventh Amendment objection to administrative fact-finding, the Court in that case states that the executive in its administrative proceedings is asserting the government's "public rights." It then concludes that a statutory claim of public rights carves out an exception from the constitutional right to a jury. Public rights thereby override constitutional rights.*

companies. As a result, much that would be public in courts tends to be kept away from the public eye in administrative proceedings.[26]

Long ago, Coke warned of the danger of doing justice in "chambers, or other private places." The due process of the law was that which occurred "openly in the kings courts, whither all persons may resort," and it therefore could not be hidden away in prerogative or administrative offices. In contrast, in private administrative chambers, the public cannot monitor what agencies do and cannot come to the defense of defendants who are denied their rights. Defendants cannot even observe how similarly situated defendants are treated. As a result, in administrative hearings, "a man may lose his cause or receive great prejudice . . . for want of defense."[27]

Evidence, Discovery, and Burdens of Persuasion and Proof

The treatment of evidence in administrative proceedings differs from that in courts. Whereas constitutional law has long given defendants evidentiary protections, the administrative tribunals return to their prerogative roots in flipping these around to give the government special advantages.

This tendency is apparent already in the administrative rules of evidence, which allow hearsay and otherwise relax the standards for admission of evidence. Although the Constitution does not require any specific set of evidentiary rules, the evidentiary rules adopted in courts of general jurisdiction have equal effect across the full range of their cases. Administrative tribunals, however, hear a very specific slice of cases. When one considers the administrative adjudications that purport to bind, and that thus trespass on judicial power, it becomes apparent that they consist almost entirely of cases charging defendants with regulatory violations. This slanted jurisdiction gives the open approach to evidence a distinctly biased effect, which cuts against those who are charged with violating administrative regulations. The evidentiary rules are equal on the surface, but the entire game is tilted.

The administrative treatment of discovery is even more candidly unequal. Agencies typically have discretion in deciding whether or not to allow discovery to parties that appear before them, and courts will force agencies to permit discovery only in "the most extraordinary circumstances."[28] Although a private party can ask an agency to issue a subpoena for purposes of discovery, such a subpoena need not be answered until the hearing. In contrast to the limited discovery for private parties, the government enjoys the broadest possible discovery, and an agency can demand testimony and documents long before any hearing—even before the agency brings charges.

The government even enjoys discovery in cases of a criminal nature. Although the government cannot constitutionally get discovery against criminal defendants, it asserts sweeping discovery powers against such defendants when it proceeds against them in administrative tribunals—as if the use of extralegal proceedings allowed the government to escape constitutional rights.

Exacerbating these evidentiary and discovery problems, administrative adjudications rely on a diminished burden of proof. In formal administrative adjudications, the proponent of an order usually must make his case by a "preponderance of evidence." The government, however, thereby adopts the standard for civil actions, even though in many instances the proceedings are essentially criminal. This standard is even lower than the "clear and convincing" standard that courts apply in civil fraud cases. Thus, even where an agency such as the Securities Exchange Commission would not prevail in court, it still can hope to prevail in administrative proceedings.[29] Of course, in informal administrative adjudications, including those that impose constraints, the burden of proof often is even lower—usually being nothing more than whatever complies with the Administrative Procedure Act's "arbitrary and capricious" standard.[30]

Administrative law often even reverses the burdens of persuasion and proof. In the High Commission, "the presumption was always against the defendant, and the initial burden of proof lay upon him."[31] But at least since the abolition of the prerogative courts, the due process of law has been understood to include a presumption of innocence—the presumption that a defendant in a criminal proceeding is innocent until proved guilty beyond a reasonable doubt. Even in civil cases, due process traditionally includes a presumption that the defendant is not guilty, until the plaintiff has made at least a prima facie case. As in the High Commission, however, agencies often place such burdens on defendants.

The shift in burdens comes in several ways. First, in administrative adjudication, when an agency decisionmaker takes "official notice" of "legislative" or "adjudicative" facts, including disputed technical questions, the defendant acquires the burden to prove the contrary.[32] Second, this reversed burden of proof and, more generally, a reversed burden of persuasion persists in the courts. When an agency brings administrative proceedings against a defendant, he can challenge it in the courts, but he then must persuade the judges, and they defer to the underlying administrative adjudication, and in both ways the burdens of persuasion and proof come to rest on the person who was the defendant in the underlying proceeding. Third, when an executive agency refuses a license, it usually bears no burden of persuasion or proof; on the contrary, the person seeking the license has these burdens, and he again bears both of them if the license is refused and he attempts to overturn this decision.[33] Thus, at least at the agency level, and then in the courts, a person who is denied a license is in the position of a defendant but without a defendant's evidentiary advantage. Simlarly, where the executive makes determinations of facts or legal duties (including assessments and determinations of liability) it shifts the burden of persuasion and proof, and statutes sometimes make this explicit. CERCLA—the Comprehensive Environmental Response, Compensation, and Liability Act—allows the executive to impose "liability" on parties and then gives them burden of showing that they are not liable.[34] The very parties who in reality are the defendants must prove that they are not guilty.

The problem, as already suggested, is all the more serious because so many administrative proceedings are criminal in nature. Often, therefore, even when an affected party gets to court, a presumption of guilt replaces the presumption of innocence, obliterating the ideal of proof beyond a reasonable doubt. Whatever burden of persuasion or proof is compatible with the due process of law, a presumption of guilt is not it, for this assumes, in the manner of *Alice in Wonderland*, that everyone is guilty as charged, until proven innocent.

Even where the proceedings are merely civil, the reversal of the burden of proof in ways that systematically favor the government violates due process. In some civil actions, courts flip around the burden of proof to illuminate difficult factual questions. The courts in such instances require the plaintiff to offer prima facie evidence of the disputed matter, and then shift the burden of proof to the defendant. This conventional burden shifting, however, is available to all plaintiffs who happen to bring the relevant causes of action. In contrast, the administrative burden shifting applies only for the benefit of a single party, the government. Although the due process of law permits burden shifting for a judicially determined class of parties, it surely does not permit the government to flip around the burden of proof merely in favor of itself.

Lest one imagine (however improbably) that the administrative manipulation of the burden of proof comes from substantive concerns about justice, one should note that this was not the justification for it. On the contrary, as Ernst Freund observed, the shift in the burden of proof was introduced as a "method of strengthening the administrative order."[35] In other words, the government rigged the burden of proof to ensure its success in its own proceedings.

Of course, in slanting the rules—whether on evidence, discovery, or the burden of persuasion or proof—administrative tribunals do not always go as far as the old prerogative tribunals. Nonetheless, administrative proceedings go far beyond what is constitutional. By escaping court adjudications, they revert back to the old prerogative abuses.

Self-Incrimination

Among the dangers of inquisitorial proceedings has always been the risk of coerced self-incrimination. Attempting to cut off this risk, the U.S. Constitution provides that no person shall be "compelled in any criminal case to be a witness against himself."

All the same, administrative proceedings regularly require subjects to testify against themselves in proceedings of a criminal nature. In such proceedings, whether brought by the government or by private parties, defendants usually find that the privilege is of no avail. As candidly suggested by one commentator, the judges recognize that the privilege might "frustrate much regulatory activity."[36] Defendants therefore often must reveal information about their regulatory violations.

Even Congress, in its investigations, cannot force a person to answer a question where he would be obliged to supply self-incriminatory information.[37] Nonetheless, administrative agencies, allegedly acting under congressional authority, brazenly force self-incriminatory responses.

Going even further, some agencies require institutions and individuals to take the initiative to report their own regulatory violations or (what amounts to the same thing) their regulatory compliance. In other words, rather than require the reporting of facts, the agencies require the reporting of guilt. Again, Congress cannot do this, as it is a legislative demand that cuts short the due process of law in court. Nonetheless, both formally and informally, agencies make abundantly clear that safety lies in confessing one's sins and seeking mercy before one is discovered and punished. Although this sort of requirement thrived in the Inquisition, it was avoided even by the English High Commission, for it puts subjects in a confessional relationship to government.

On behalf of these various revivals of self-incrimination, it is said that administrative proceedings are not criminal—that criminal cases are merely those in the courts, not those in administrative tribunals. From this perspective, neither the mode of inquiry nor the revealed information is criminal, and the constitutional privilege against self-incrimination therefore does not interfere.

Yet a government action to correct or penalize a defendant (even when initiated by a private person, and even when brought outside the regular courts) was traditionally recognized to be criminal in nature. On this basis, as has been seen in chapter 10, the privilege against self-incrimination developed in response to the danger of self-incrimination in prerogative proceedings. The privilege thus was not merely a limit on criminal proceedings in the courts of law; nor was it a privilege merely as to information that would support prosecutions in courts of law. On the contrary, the evolution of the privilege shows that, at least as centrally, it concerns self-incrimination and the risk of conviction in extralegal proceedings.[n]

Indeed, the threat of demands for self-incrimination is most pervasive, as in the past, not simply in administrative prosecutions, but in administrative demands for information that ordinarily are possible only in a grand jury. Even before the filing of a complaint against an administrative defendant, agencies often require information in open-ended investigations and demands for information. Agencies, as already noted, even request compliance reports—what might just as well be called incrimination reports. All of this, as has been seen, is justified as part of the government's "power of inquisition."[38]

Inquisitorial administrative fishing expeditions, however, when conducted in the prerogative courts, were what first provoked the development of a right against self-incrimination. The prerogative inquisitorial practices, moreover, remain the most notorious examples of unlawful self-incrimination. It therefore is clear that demands for information in administrative proceedings, including open-ended inquisitions, are not outside the scope of the constitutional privilege against self-incrimination. In fact, they are precisely the sort of extralegal proceedings that most centrally inspired the privilege.

---

n. On similar reasoning, the privilege also applies to forfeiture proceedings. Most such proceedings (as noted above in footnote b) were and still are criminal in nature.

By the same token, ex post facto administrative legislation cannot be justified on the ground that the right against ex post facto laws applies only to statutes creating criminal offenses. For example, when an early North Carolina statute authorized sheriffs to hold manumitted slaves, and authorized county courts to auction them off, the state's Superior Court in 1778 quashed such proceedings as to the slaves manumitted prior to the adoption of the statute, on the ground that the proceedings violated the state's constitutional guarantee against ex post facto laws. In other words, this right was not confined to criminal prosecutions in the courts, but also reached administrative actions that were criminal in nature.*

Due Process of Law

More generally, the administrative return to prerogative tribunals collides with the due process of law. For more than a century, the notion of due process of law has been adopted for a range of purposes beyond traditional due process, including the protection of substantive economic rights, the protection of substantive personal rights, and the incorporation of the Bill of Rights against the states. At the same time, sadly, it has been deprived of its essential traditional role of limiting the administrative exercise of judicial power.[o]

In defense of such adjudication, it is said that the Constitution guarantees only "such process as is due."[39] This equivocation allows the government to get away with only an administrative hearing—as if the government's evasion of the courts also justified an evasion of regular process. The constitutional principle, however, is not simply due process, let alone the due process of administrative rules, but the due process of law—meaning judicial decisions following the law, in the courts of law, in accord with their essential traditional procedures.[p]

To avoid this conclusion, scholars of administrative law frequently sug-

o. There is a close connection between the denial of traditional "procedural" due process in administrative cases and the development of "substantive" due process. At least some of the late-nineteenth-century cases that, in retrospect, are said to have involved substantive due process actually arose from binding administrative adjudication, which denied the traditional procedural due process of law. Indeed, the doctrine on substantive due process became prominent only after courts in administrative cases failed to protect the traditional due process. The development of the substantive due process doctrine therefore needs to be reconsidered.*

p. Further study is needed to understand how administrative hearings came to be accepted in place of the due process of law in the courts, but there is reason to think that it was justified, in part, by a gross misreading of tax valuation cases. As noted in chapter 12, valuations by tax assessors typically were appealed only to tax commissioners or equivalent officers, and could not easily be challenged in the courts. This was the most serious exception to the general principle the government had to work through the courts to bind subjects in particular instances, and it therefore was a constitutional anomaly.

Rather than accept the anomaly, late-nineteenth-century judges did their best to assimilate it to the constitutional standard by stating that tax officers at least had to provide a hearing in an administrative appeal. Of course, such hearings usually were already available by statute, and in any case were of little value. It therefore is difficult to avoid the conclusion that the judicial requirement of a hearing provided more solace to the judges than to taxpayers.

The self-indulgence of the judges, however, was not without cost. The danger lay in the initial mistake of trying to justify a narrow exception by accepting a reduction of the general principle. The due process of law traditionally meant the procedures of the courts, not the procedures of prerogative or administrative tribunals, and therefore, when judges accepted the constitutionality of tax adjudication on the ground that there was (or eventually could be) an administrative hearing, they opened up the possibility that all sorts of binding administrative adjudications were acceptable, as long as they offered this minimal procedure. The negligible

gest that due process and other procedural rights centrally applied to the courts, not administrative tribunals. Peter Strauss, for example, writes about due process: "As originally understood, this instruction chiefly concerned the ordinary processes of law. . . . There was no reason to think that it applied to procedures followed within the government bureaucracy."[40, q]

Nothing, however, could be further from the truth. As seen in chapter 10, the principle of due process of law developed primarily in opposition to extralegal proceedings. This is apparent already in Magna Charta. More concretely, the 1354 and 1368 statutes relied on due process to bar prerogative or administrative proceedings, even those that merely forced men to appear and answer questions. After the Crown reinvigorated such proceedings, seventeenth-century lawyers restored the principle and gave it constitutional status. The main point of the principle thus has long been to prevent the Crown or executive from employing the judicial power—to prevent it from binding subjects in particular instances, even to prevent it from calling particular subjects to answer it—except through the due process of law in the courts.

Giving effect to this principle, the Fifth Amendment to the U.S. Constitution guarantees that "[n]o person shall . . . be deprived of life, liberty, or property, without due process of law." Although generations of legal scholars have parsed these words to discern which substantive rights are included in "life, liberty, or property," the provision most basically alluded to a general freedom from government acts binding subjects in particular instances, except through the courts and their criminal and civil processes. Revealingly, the Constitution recites its due process and other procedural rights at its conclusion rather than merely in Article III, and it states them in the

---

expansion of a constitutional liberty in exceptional cases thereby justified a massive contraction of the liberty in all instances.*

q. On the assumption that due process traditionally limited only the courts, many scholars believe that the requirement of a hearing (a mere part of due process) in administrative decisions is an expansion of liberty. This make some sense when one examines administrative decisions about government benefits. For example, in *Goldberg v. Kelly*, the Supreme Court held that due process requires the government to offer a hearing before denying some types of welfare benefits, and this has seemed to be an enlargement of due process.

The story, however, is more complicated. Although *Goldberg* offers a smidgeon of process for denials of some benefits, it is part of a broader jurisprudence that accepts a profound denial of process for government constraints. There once was a right to the full due process of law in the courts of law for binding adjudications. This essential right, however, has been reduced to a mere administrative hearing. The sort of doctrine evident in *Goldberg* therefore strains at a gnat and swallows the proverbial camel: It secures negligible administrative process in a few sorts of benefit cases while accepting serious denials of the due process of law in constraint cases. The overall effect is not so much to expand due process at the edges as to legitimize administrative violations of due process at the core.*

passive voice. It thereby makes clear that these rights limit all parts of government, including the executive as much as the courts.[41] St. George Tucker recognized the implications in his lectures in the early 1790s at William and Mary. After quoting the Due Process Clause, he concluded: "Due process of law must then be had before a judicial court, or a judicial magistrate."[42]

The guarantee of due process thus bars the government from holding subjects to account outside courts and their processes. This was the history of the principle from its very beginnings, and this was how the Fifth Amendment was drafted in 1791.

Since the late nineteenth century, however, government has returned to an extralegal system of judicial power. It thereby imposes trials without courts, judges, and juries and denies almost every constitutionally guaranteed judicial procedure, process, and right. Most generally, it denies the due process of law and substitutes the due process of administrative power.

Informal Adjudication

Most of the constitutional failings observed thus far occur in formal administrative adjudication. The situation, however, is even worse in informal adjudication.

Formal administrative adjudications already are summary proceedings, which violate the Constitution's grant of judicial power, its judicial processes, and its guarantees of procedural rights. But informal administrative adjudications are even worse, for they are utterly summary, without even the pretense of dispassionate adjudicators and proceedings. Such adjudications are not even within the Administrative Procedure Act's efforts to separate functions, to allow counsel, to allow confrontation of witnesses, to require a record of hearings, or to require a preponderance of the evidence.

Of course, the summary procedure in informal adjudication is not necessarily unconstitutional in decisions allocating benefits and other matters within the executive's discretion. All too often, however, agencies use this summary method to issue orders that restrict subjects.

Although the informal proceedings are grossly unconstitutional, they are more deeply a reminder that, like extralegal legislation, extralegal adjudication creates a cascade of evasions—from the legal to the extralegal, from the formal to the informal. The prerogative courts were not content with their formal proceedings and therefore increased their reliance on ex officio and *ore tenus* proceedings. Similarly, nowadays, administrative agencies work through formal proceedings where they must, but always seek loopholes, and find informal adjudication easier.

The current extralegal procedure thus returns to that of an earlier era. Not all details are the same, but administrative procedure engages in many of the same evasions as the old prerogative procedure, and this is justified on the ground that the courts are the real targets of constitutional guarantees of due process and other procedural rights.

It is not plausible, however, to suggest that administrative tribunals are less confined by procedural guarantees than the courts, or that administrative process satisfies the due process of law. Procedural rights developed in the Middle Ages, and were given constitutional status in the seventeenth century, precisely to bar extralegal adjudication. And the growth of administrative adjudication only confirms the importance of procedural rights as limits on extralegal power. Rather than satisfy the due process of law, administrative process is exactly what the guarantee of due process forbids.

Indirect Adjudicatory Force

The ways that the extralegal judicial power comes to bear on the public include licensing and administrative extortion. These are only indirect exercises of binding power, and they usually do not even mimic the adjudication of the courts, but they are powerful mechanisms by which the executive imposes its extralegal adjudication.

Licensing

Administrative adjudication often weighs on members of the public through licensing. Although only indirectly binding, it is a central mode of administrative adjudication.

The nature of the problem requires careful attention. As first noted in chapter 6, although some licensing merely allocates government property, other licensing exists against a background of constraint, and it thereby serves as the measure of that constraint. At the local level this sort of licensing has always been commonplace, but at the federal level it traditionally was very limited lest it become a path either for extralegal legislation (as seen in chapter 6) or for extralegal adjudication (as seen in chapter 12). Where it goes beyond a mere determination, it becomes a mode of extralegal legislation, but even where it is confined to mere determination, it becomes a mode of extralegal adjudication. It is this danger of extralegal adjudication that must be considered here, for where licensing gives relief from background constraints, the licensing allows executive officers to judge the application of the constraints to members of the public.

Even more emphatically than other administrative power, licensing concentrates all three of the powers of government. Administrative agencies already combine legislative, executive, and judicial powers. But when agencies act through licensing to offer relief from constraints, a single individual or office within an agency can combine all three powers. Thus, by means of licensing, a single body can impose legislative policy, can enforce it, and can adjudicate its application to members of the public, and as will be seen shortly, this combination of powers accentuates the danger of administrative extortion.

Just by itself, however, the extralegal exercise of judicial power is enough to be worrisome, for the power of an administrator to deny, withdraw, or simply delay a license can cripple a business. In making such a threat, the administrator usually can be confident that the business will suffer irreparable harm long before the question gets to court. Administrators therefore can use their power to threaten licensed institutions (even powerful banks and universities) without fear of legal consequences. For example, by relying on their background power to withdraw a license, administrators can demand acquiescence in fines and other adjudicatory measures far exceeding what is justified by regulations, let alone the laws.

Even when licensing in the context of constraint is not abused, it deprives affected persons of due process. It already has been seen that administrative process deprives persons of juries, real judges, and other due process of law in a court of law, and the licensing that offers relief from constraint shares in these general failings. Licensing proceedings, however, are particularly worrisome, for they reverse the ordinary presumption about how the government can impose constraints. Instead of requiring an agency to bring judicial or even administrative proceedings against members of the public, licensing requires members of the public to supplicate the agency for permission.[43] Thus, rather than have to prove anything against a prospective licensee, the agency can simply remain unpersuaded. Licnesing thereby (as seen earlier) reverses the ordinary burdens of persuasion and proof. Indeed, it reverses the ordinary presumption of freedom. Whereas Americans ordinarily are free to do what is not prohibited, licensing leaves them unfree until they get permission.

Licensing thereby offers an opportunity for wholesale control. The government ordinarily must enforce its laws in retail proceedings that it brings against each offender. That is, when enforcing its laws, it must act against each violator, one by one, in a court of law; even when enforcing its administrative regulations, it theoretically must initiate an action against each violator in an administrative proceeding and must make an effort to prove its case. When licensing, however, the government can simply refuse the license until persuaded otherwise. Licensing thus allows the government to impose constraints wholesale, without initiating retail proceedings, and it consequently is an unusually dangerous sort of extralegal adjudication.

For all of these reasons—the extralegal adjudication, the consolidation of powers, the potential for abuse, the denial of due process, the reversal of burdens, and danger of wholesale control—it should be no surprise that, although Congress authorized licensing to raise taxes, and to control enemy aliens and cross-border or offshore matters, it traditionally did not otherwise employ licensing as a mode of governing the nation. Even in using licensing for tax purposes, Congress relied on it only for collecting money and reports and did not add regulatory conditions. Otherwise, until the beginning of the twentieth century, Congress appears to governed the country without authorizing the domestic use of the sort of licensing that amounted to binding adjudication.[44]

Of course, Congress understood the efficacy of licensing as a mode of regulation and adjudication, and it used licensing to govern the District of Columbia and similar localities under federal control. But it therefore is all the more striking that, when governing the nation as a whole, it did not rely on licensing to determine the application of constraints. In domestic matters, such licensing could easily become a mode of extralegal lawmaking, and it almost always was a mode of extralegal adjudication. It therefore is revealing that, although Congress used licensing to collect taxes and to govern cross-border and offshore matters, and although it used licensing for local governance, Congress generally avoided the domestic use of licensing as a mode of imposing constraints or adjudicating them, lest such licensing become a substitute for acts of Congress or the adjudications of the courts.

Similarly, today, it should be recognized that the licensing that provides relief from constraints is usually a mode of extralegal legislative and judicial power. Just as this sort of licensing revives extralegal lawmaking, so too it restores extralegal adjudication.

The exceptions, to be sure, remain important. Licensing is still used for collecting taxes. Moreover, licensing is still applied to cross-border or off-shore persons and vessels. Thus, just as executive officers in the nineteenth century licensed steamboats and their essential personnel, the Federal Aviation Administration nowadays licenses planes and pilots. More generally, however, when domestic licensing offers relief from constraint, it revives a mode of extralegal adjudication—an indirect mode, but one that was sufficiently direct that Congress traditionally avoided it.

Administrative Extortion

The other indirect way that agencies impose extralegal judicial power (as well as extralegal lawmaking) is through a sort of extortion. Although it may be thought that administrative extortion is exceptional, and that it merely offers efficient enforcement of lawful restrictions, it actually is commonplace and dangerous.

The extortion sometimes is used in support of extralegal legislative power. When agencies want to impose restrictions they cannot openly adopt as administrative rules, and that they cannot plausibly call "interpretation," they typically place the restrictions in guidance, advice, or other informal directives. Of course, they cannot enforce this under-the-table administrative legislation as easily as more aboveboard administrative legislation, and they therefore often turn to under-the-table threats of an executive or judicial nature.[45] The Occupational Safety and Health Administration, for example, uses the threat of "wall-to-wall inspections" to get employers to "cooperate" in safety programs not required by its regulations.[46]

This sort of extortion—the enforcement of under-the-table legislation by resort to under-the-table executive or adjudicatory threats—usually occurs out of view. But it sometimes becomes visible, most commonly in licensing, when an agency threatens to withhold or withdraw a license unless the licensee conforms to the agency's guidance or other informal requirements. As shown by Lars Noah, many agencies rely on such threats to secure compliance with policies that they cannot put in their regulations.[47] The extortion also becomes visible in settlements and consent decrees. In many of these arrangements, agencies employ the threat of litigation under a statute—for example, CERCLA—to secure substantive constraints not authorized by the statute. Agencies thereby use their enforcement or adjudicatory powers to exercise extralegal lawmaking power of a sort that is not possible even in regulations.[48]

The extortion is most frequently used in pursuit of extralegal judicial power. Agencies almost every day quietly ask for information or other concessions ordinarily within the realm of adjudication, and they thereby evade not only the courts but also the agencies' own adjudicatory processes. They can be confident about getting cooperation because it is understood that they can punish noncomplying persons with harsh executive action in investigations and inspections, and even with harsh extralegal lawmaking in licensing and regulations. Thus, even after the Supreme Court held that OSHA inspectors must get warrants before entering places of employment, they needed warrants against less than three percent of employers, for the employers knew that if they were not cooperative, they would face measures of another sort.[49]

In private—whether at the agencies or in site visits—agencies sometimes candidly threaten such retaliation. In public, they prefer to speak in more positive terms, unctuously reciting that regulation is a cooperative effort and that the cooperation of private parties avoids the need for administrative severity.

Of course, there is nothing necessarily wrong with bargaining, as evident when prosecutors ask defendants to plead to lesser charges. A prosecutor, however, can threaten only additional executive action—such as bringing higher charges—and he has no authority to demand or threaten more than is required by law. An agency, in contrast, enjoys all three powers of government and can use them to impose more than is required by law—indeed, more than is required by regulation. An agency thereby has so many opportunities for unrestrained demands and retaliation that its offers usually cannot be refused. Rather than have to engage in express bargaining, an agency typically need only leave a hint about the potential cost of noncooperation.[50]

The combination of powers in administrative agencies thus gives them a power of extortion. As suggested by James Lindgren, extortion (like bribery) can be understood to involve the exercise of a right or power belonging to another.[51] In a somewhat similar way, when an agency secures information, an admission, a consent decree, or other judicial action by threatening executive or legislative action, it is pursuing one power by threatening the use of another. So too, when it secures compliance with guidance, interpretation, or other lawmaking policy by threatening executive or judicial action, it is pursuing one power by threatening the use of another. All of this is administrative extortion, and it gives agencies an under-the-table power that extends far beyond their open extralegal power.

Licensing and administrative extortion thus give agencies much indirect adjudicatory (and lawmaking) power. Even more central, however, as now will be seen, are the direct mechanisms of extralegal adjudication

Binding Administrative Orders and Warrants

Extralegal judicial power comes to bear most directly on members of the public mostly through administrative orders and warrants, which superficially look like judicial orders and warrants. This chapter on the return to prerogative adjudication therefore closes by examining administrative orders and warrants and whether they really are lawful.

Orders and Warrants

Binding prerogative or administrative commands were familiar from the past, and constitutional law was designed to keep them there. But it has not been very successful.

Under English and American constitutional law, as seen in chapter 11, the power to issue binding orders or warrants was judicial. The government therefore could ordinarily bind subjects in particular instances only through the courts and judges. The only exceptions, of course, were for subpoenas issued by congressional committees, warrants issued under a suspension of habeas corpus, and military orders (although they were not binding in the civilian legal system).

Even when the government acted through judicial orders and warrants, it could not rely on them when they shifted discretion to executive officers—this being why general warrants were unconstitutional. Although in form such warrants were signed by judges and thus were judicial, in reality they left discretion in administrators. This was particularly unacceptable to Americans, as evident from the controversy over writs of assistance. Recognizing that these facially judicial warrants functioned as administrative warrants, American courts generally refused to issue them and condemned them as unconstitutional.

Nonetheless, the executive has returned to the preconstitutional practice of binding persons through prerogative or administrative orders and warrants. As now will be seen, agencies issue their own binding orders; they also issue what amount to administrative warrants in their inspections; and they secure what formally are judicial warrants but actually are administrative warrants, in that the judges defer to the underlying administrative decision.

Administrative Orders

Administrative agencies act most directly through administrative orders. The agencies do this not only in final adjudicatory orders but also in orders (or "summons" or "subpoenas") for appearance, depositions, testimony, and records. Whether in open-ended investigations or in administrative cases, agencies typically can issue these orders largely at their discretion, and the courts defer to the agencies as long as the requested materials are "not plainly incompetent or irrelevant to any lawful purpose" of the agency.[52]

Administrative Warrants in Inspections

Agencies also issue what, in effect, are warrants for search and seizure, usually under inspection statutes. Although inspection statutes can be lawful, binding administrative warrants are not.

The distinction between inspections and warrants traditionally was clear. As seen in chapter 12, a statute could require private persons to allow entry to federal officers—at least where the private persons had reported that they were subject to the law, and at least for inspections of physical objects and government-owned records. In contrast, an administrative warrant could not justify entry into private property, whether a home or an industrial site. Thus, an administrator could lawfully instruct a subordinate officer to carry out an inspection imposed by statute, where the statute determined the duties of the affected persons. An administrative warrant, however, was not binding, and it therefore could have no effect in specifying or altering the owner's duties. Nor could it determine any other matter that a judicial officer ordinarily would determine in issuing a warrant. Of course, these limits could be complicated at the edges, but the point was that executive officers could not exercise binding judgment or will about the duties of the persons inspected.[r]

The Supreme Court, however, has confused the inspection and warrant questions. Although it generally has balked at allowing intrusions into homes, it has allowed agencies, when acting under open-ended inspection statutes, to exercise their own discretion in invading private property—at least when an agency sanitizes its discretion by specifying it in an inspection plan. In particular, the Court has allowed agencies such discretion in inspecting heavily regulated industries, such as alcohol and firearms—as if heavy regulation could justify unlawful entry.[53] Agencies thus often make their own decisions to send their officers onto private premises, and because these decisions are treated as legally binding, they amount to administrative warrants. In other words, it is not the inspection statutes, but the administrative decisions that dictate the duties of the private persons. Ordinarily, such duties, if not specified in an inspection statute, would have to be spelled out in a judicial warrant for search and seizure, and the problem is that the executive substitutes its decision for that of a judge.

---

r. The distinction between inspections and warrants thus lays the foundation for resolving some potentially difficult problems, such as how inspections at airports can be distinguished from situations requiring judicial warrants or not-unreasonable searches.

Recognizing the constitutional awkwardness of so candidly displacing judicial warrants, agencies and courts emphasize that agencies are merely carrying out inspections, as if the warrant problem could be avoided by simply not talking about it. Nonetheless, under the guise of authorizing inspections, administrators issue warrants that bind private persons, and they thereby usurp the warrant power that traditionally belonged to the judges.[54]

Making matters worse, the administrative decisions or warrants that determine the inspection requirements reach private business records and other private papers. Judicial warrants ordinarily cannot be used to go on fishing expeditions for information, for they must be based on probable cause, relating to a particular crime, as shown to a judge or justice of the peace. To get around this, overzealous rulers once turned to prerogative warrants, and then to general warrants—thus allowing royal or executive officials to look around for information in private papers. Although these warrants now are unconstitutional, it is no coincidence that administrative agencies have found another means of fishing through private papers—this time by making inspection decisions, which in effect are administrative warrants. The threat to private papers is one of the standard dangers of administrative warrants, and it has come back under the guise of inspections.

Judicial Warrants That Really Are Administrative

Outside the inspection of heavily regulated industries, agencies rely on the judges to issue warrants, but the judges usually accept the underlying decisions of the agencies. Therefore, notwithstanding that such warrants are signed by the judges, it is apt that they usually are called "administrative warrants."

The degree to which these warrants rest on administrative rather than judicial decisionmaking is painfully clear from the Supreme Court's decision in *Marshall v. Barlow's, Inc.*—a case involving warrantless inspections by OSHA. The Court there generally recognizes that, outside heavily regulated industries, OSHA needs warrants for its inspections, and that judges can issue the warrants only on a showing of probable cause. The Court, however, assumes that "[p]robable cause in the criminal law sense is not required." Indeed, probable cause does not even have to rest on "specific evidence of an existing violation," but instead can consist of a showing that the agency seeks the inspection under "reasonable legislative or administrative standards," such as an administrative enforcement plan.[55] In other words, judges now grant warrants to agencies not on probable cause of an actual crime, but on the agencies' own abstract standards about what it wishes to learn.

Under this approach, judges grant warrants to different agencies under slightly different tests, depending on the applicable authorizing statute. For example, the Department of Transportation can get a warrant merely by showing that it has a "valid public interest in the effective enforcement" of relevant laws and regulations "sufficient to justify the inspection or impoundment."[56] Whatever this means, it is but another illustration of how judges grant warrants to agencies not on the judges' own determination of probable cause that any crime has been committed, but in deference to the agencies' judgment of their administrative need. Thus, like general warrants, these administrative warrants are judicial only in their form, not in the reality of administrative discretion.

All of these orders and warrants—whether administrative orders, administrative warrants within inspections, or judicial warrants that defer to underlying administrative decisions—enable administrative agencies to displace the role of judges in issuing binding commands to members of the public. The agencies thus go back to the era, before the advent of constitutional law in the seventeenth century, when the Crown claimed a prerogative power outside the courts to issue binding orders and warrants. The agencies thereby violate the Constitution's grant of judicial power to the courts and its guarantees on due process and warrants.

Only Criminal Proceedings?

In defense of administrative orders and warrants, it occasionally is suggested that the constitutional restrictions on warrants apply only to criminal proceedings, which occur only in the courts. It already has been seen how this sort of argument is used to justify the privilege against self-incrimination, and it also is used, more generally, to excuse administrative orders and especially warrants.[57]

By now, however, it should be evident that binding administrative orders and warrants often arise in cases that are criminal in nature. It also should be evident that prerogative orders and warrants, both criminal and civil, were among the dangers that led to the development of constitutional limits. Such orders and warrants were extralegal exercises of judicial power, and in response, already in England, the law placed judicial power in the courts, thus requiring that all orders and warrants come from judicial officers. The law also guaranteed the due process of law, thus requiring all orders and warrants to be made through the process of the courts, and it barred general warrants, thus cutting off the evasion by which judicial warrants left room for administrative discretion about matters that had to be specified in warrants. The U.S. Constitution, moreover, adopted all of these constitutional limits, without confining them to criminal proceedings, let alone criminal proceedings in the courts.

The failure to understand the breadth of the Constitution's rejection of binding administrative orders and warrants is painfully apparent in the leading cases on the subject—for instance, *In re Meador*. This was a late-nineteenth-century challenge to an administrative summons. A federal revenue officer in Atlanta issued a summons to a tobacco company, requiring that the members of the firm appear at his office to testify under oath and to produce their business papers and records for the current tax year. The company should have prevailed simply by observing that binding orders are part of the judicial power, and that an administrator therefore could not have discretion to bind anyone. Administrators, however, were beginning to claim such a power, and the company therefore took another tack. It protested that the summons revived a sort of general warrant and even a version of a writ of assistance and that it thus violated the Fourth Amendment. In response, the district court held that the Constitution's warrant requirement applied only to criminal proceedings in the courts, not mere civil matters.[58, s]

---

s. In support of this conclusion, the court in *Meador* noted that, according to Blackstone, eighteenth-century English revenue officers could enter businesses at will to inspect their premises and records to ensure compliance with the excise laws. But (as seen in chapter 12) early American excise statutes carefully limited inspection to comply with the Constitution. The statutes generally required distillers to report their distilleries and production and to allow inspection by excise officers, but these were general congressional requirements, not binding executive orders or warrants.

Indeed, the distilled spirits statutes specified the extent of their reporting and inspection requirements, and in their attempt to avoid leaving any discretion to administrative officers, the statutes applied their inspection requirements only to those persons who made an entry or filing with the government that they fell within the restricted class. Even as to such persons, the government's access to papers or records was confined to government owned and supplied records, which the distillers had to maintain, not privately owned records. Not even in these instances, moreover, could the executive issue binding orders or warrants. Early statutes on inspection and reporting thus confirm that the Constitution barred binding administrative orders and warrants, without regard to whether the proceedings were civil or criminal.

Another nineteenth-century case was *In re Mark Strouse*. The taxpayer refused to allow the assessor to examine his books—one of his objections being that the requirement to produce his books was an unreasonable search under the Fourth Amendment. The district court, however, held that the guarantee against unreasonable searches "is applicable to criminal cases only." The taxpayer also objected that the assessor's request would incriminate him or lead to his incrimination, but the district court, as on the search and seizure question, held that assessor was conducting a civil rather than a criminal proceeding. (Incidentally, the court added

Such a conclusion was possible only on the basis of utter indifference to constitutional history. The summons in *Meador* was not really a warrant, but even a modest knowledge of history would have revealed that constitutional law on judicial power developed mostly in response to adjudication in prerogative courts. It therefore was strange to suggest that the Constitution's warrant requirement applied only to criminal proceedings in the regular courts.

Of course, it is true that warrants and some kinds of orders are lawful only in common law criminal proceedings before judges. But just because binding warrants are meant to come from judges in criminal matters does not mean that the government can evade the warrant requirement by acting outside the courts.

Judicial Power without the Limits on Such Power

The peculiar excuse for administrative power that has just been examined deserves further attention. It is structured as a strange two-step, in which agencies claim judicial power in criminal questions but disclaim the limits on such power. Of course, it is only part of a broader tendency of administrative agencies to assert judicial powers without the corresponding constitutional limits, but is particularly egregious as to criminal matters.

On the one hand, the agencies claim the powers of the judges in criminal matters. They issue orders for appearance, testimony, and records that ordinarily can be issued only by judges in criminal proceedings, whether before grand juries or petit juries. On the other hand, the agencies demur that their proceedings are not judicial and so are not fully subject to the Constitution's limits on the judicial power. They thereby get away with exercising the judicial power in criminal inquiries while simultaneously excusing themselves from the Constitution's provisions on criminal process, including its provisions on grand juries, warrants, petit juries, proof beyond a reasonable doubt, and self-incrimination. This is the power of another branch, but without its limits.[t]

---

that the self-incrimination objection "was no longer of any force" since the passage of an 1868 act of Congress providing that disclosures obtained through judicial proceedings "shall not be used against" such a taxpayer "in any manner before any court of the United States." The privilege against self-incrimination had developed precisely against the use of self-incriminating questions to convict defendants in prerogative or administrative proceedings, but the court now upheld such questions for such purposes.)*

t. Of course, this exercise of borrowed power without the associated limits is evident not only in administrative adjudication but also in administrative lawmaking. The evasion of limits, however, is particularly serious for administrative adjudication, for this adjudication es-

The constitutional response is obvious: administrative agencies cannot have it both ways. Their orders and warrants either are part of the judicial power—indeed, typically part of the judicial power in criminal matters—or they are not. Consider, for example, the orders that ordinarily are issuable only in grand juries and the warrants that ordinarily are issuable only in criminal investigations. If the administrative versions of such proceedings are not criminal, then the agencies cannot exercise the power that judges enjoy only in criminal matters. By the same token, if the proceedings are criminal, then they surely are subject to the constitutional limits on criminal proceedings.

The agencies cannot have their cake and eat it too. Even if the executive could exercise the power that the Constitution gives to the courts and their judges, the executive cannot simultaneously enjoy judicial power in criminal matters and escape the constitutional limits on such power.

Discovery Analogy

Another justification of administrative orders and warrants is that they are analogous to orders for discovery in civil litigation. The analogy, however, is poor.

Discovery occurs in private suits in court, as overseen by the courts, and it thus offers no foundation for executive demands for testimony and documents. In other words, discovery is a judicial mechanism for settling differences between private parties; in contrast, administrative subpoenas and warrants are executive mechanisms against private parties in proceedings that usually are criminal in nature.

Discovery could develop in civil suits between private parties precisely because there was no danger that the government could impose it independently of the courts to squeeze information out of private persons—let alone in extralegal criminal trials or in inquisitorial proceedings to search for offenses. Now, however, discovery is said to justify administrative subpoenas and warrants by which the agencies do exactly what they could not do through discovery. And they do this not in civil proceedings in courts, in the same way as private parties, but in their own tribunals, in proceedings that are criminal in nature, in which they themselves are the judges.

In fact, administrative subpoenas do not even come close to discovery, whether civil or criminal. In civil proceedings in courts, both sides have

capes not only the Constitution's institutions and processes for judicial power but also the associated constitutional rights.

equal access to discovery. In administrative proceedings brought by agencies, however, the private parties have no assurance of discovery, while the agencies have far-reaching powers to extract information through subpoenas. As for criminal discovery in courts, it is only prosecutors that must share information with defendants. In contrast, in administrative proceedings of a criminal nature, the reverse often is true. Where the proceedings are brought by the agencies, they have sweeping power to extract information, and the defendants have practically no such power.

Theory That Corporations or Businesses Are Not Protected

It often is said that whatever the constitutional guarantees against administrative orders and warrants, these protections do not fully apply to corporations or other commercial ventures. It has been seen that this argument is made in support of open-ended inquiries without grand juries, and it also is made, more generally, in favor of administrative orders and warrants.[59]

As suggested earlier, however, most constitutional rights are not merely individual rights, but more broadly are limits on government. They therefore generally do not exclude corporations or other artificial persons, except where (as with arrests) only natural persons could be affected.[u]

It may be supposed that the Fourth Amendment right of "the people" to be secure in their "houses" does not protect commercial or industrial buildings. The underlying principle, however, was that the power to bind belonged to judicial rather than administrative officers. On this basis, "the people" meant more than merely individuals, and "houses" meant more than simply living quarters. Religious societies, for example, were protected in their churches as much as individuals were in their homes. By the same token, businesses were protected in their buildings.

Nowadays, a factory or corporate headquarters is not apt to be considered a house. In the eighteenth century, however, most business, including most of the manufacturing and commercial activity in the United States, was conducted in people's houses. When business was not done in the main house, it often was done in a connected building, whether a back-

---

u. Although it sometimes is said (most recently in response to *Citizens United v. Federal Election Commission*) that corporations are not persons, it is abundantly clear that corporate charters establish incorporated enterprises as persons at law—the point being to ensure that they can be sued for their duties and can sue for their rights as legal persons. And if incorporated entities (which are established by charter as legal persons) are not persons for purposes of constitutional rights, what can be said for the constitutional rights of all the other entities, whether churches or political associations, that are not even incorporated?

house, shed, or barn, all of which (if connected) were part of the house. Even separate work buildings were houses, being distinguished as "bake-houses," "warehouses," or simply "outhouses."[60] Even when merchants lived in townhouses, if business was not done in the living quarters, it was done below in the shop, and goods were stored further below in the cel-lar—all of which, again, were part of the house.

Thus, already in the dispute over writs of assistance, the legal question centered on searches of "houses." These general warrants authorized searches for commercial goods and applied mostly to commercial locations. They therefore elaborated that customs officers could search "any house, shop, cellar, warehouse, or room or other place," and some Americans were nearly as specific in their complaints about the writs.[61] Other Americans, however, protested more generally about searches of "houses." The common law treatises that discussed the doctrine against general warrants tended to re-cite that special warrants were necessary for searching "houses," and when James Otis argued against the writs of assistance, he told the judges that, in "modern" law books, "you will find only special warrants to search such and such houses." In short, although the customs officers used the writs of assistance for commercial searches of all sorts of places, including shops, cellars, and warehouses, Otis followed the standard common law locution, and he therefore concluded that "one of the most essential branches of English liberty, is the freedom of one's house. A man's house is his castle."[62]

All of these considerations—the underlying principle, common law doctrine, American architecture, and the debate over writs of assistance—show that the framing of the Fourth Amendment in terms of "houses" did not exclude economic searches of economic facilities. Instead, what seems to have mattered was entry into enclosed space.[63]

Accordingly, even when the early federal government dealt with large industrial enterprises, in independent industrial buildings, it carefully sat-isfied the constitutional guarantees concerning searches and seizures as well as due process. For example, although distilleries and other businesses subject to the excise often were located in industrial buildings, the early excise statutes carefully respected the rights of due process and search and seizure.

The same logic applies today. The FBI cannot demand corporate records or break into corporate offices without a court order or a judicial warrant. Is it therefore a surprise that administrative agencies cannot lawfully do such things? The exercise of power through one agency rather than another does not relieve the executive of its constitutional limits.

Justification Based in Determinations of Legal Duties

Another defense of administrative warrants is that they merely notify subjects of the executive's determination of a subject's legal duties. Although this explanation of administrative warrants may sound esoteric, it is the most plausible in theory, at least until the realities of such warrants are examined.

Executive officers, it will be recalled, could determine the legal duties of subjects and notify them of these duties, as long as the officers exercised discretion only in the sense of discernment, understanding, or judgment. Not being an exercise of will, such determinations were not legislative, and not being binding in the manner of orders and warrants, they were not judicial. Such, for example, were the determinations made by tax assessors.

The suggestion that an executive order or warrant is similarly a mere determination of a subject's legal duty was put forward in the *Meador Case*. This was the 1869 Georgia decision in which a revenue officer issued a summons for the appearance of members of the Meador firm and for their testimony and production of business records. It will be recalled that the Meadors protested that the summons violated their Fourth Amendment right to a warrant because the summons was, in effect, a general warrant or a writ of assistance, which left discretion to the executive officer. The U.S. District Court for Georgia, however, upheld the summons, one reason being that it was "simply a notice, and similar in its nature to a summons issued by an overseer of roads requiring persons to attend with the necessary implements and to work on the public highway."[64]

Yet rather than specify any details of who had to appear, testify, or produce records, the revenue statute left all of this to the discretion of the revenue officer.[65] Therefore, unlike an assessment of taxes based on statutory tax rates, or an assessment of labor based on a statute, the summons could not have been a mere determination of duties imposed by law.

Similarly, most contemporary administrative summons and warrants cannot be justified as determinations and notices of legal duties. Statutes authorizing assessments make relatively clear who is to be assessed, and tax assessors therefore can hope to discern rather than invent the duties of taxpayers. In contrast, the statutes authorizing administrative orders to pay penalties, or to testify and produce records, tend to leave administrative officers free to choose who will receive such orders. Such a statute provides an inadequate foundation for discretion in the sense of discernment. Executive officers therefore end up exercising discretion in the sense of will—an exercise of legislative power outside the constitutionally established path for lawmaking.[v]

Judicial Rubber-Stamp Theory

A further justification for administrative orders and warrants is that they become binding only when rubber-stamped or endorsed by the courts. On this theory, when an agency issues an order for appearance, testimony, inspection, or the production of records, or when it makes an inspection

---

v. Although most administrative orders nowadays make no pretense of being anything else, there are some exceptions, in which agencies attempt to keep up the appearance of merely determining and giving notice of legal duties. Perhaps the most interesting example can be found in the Comprehensive Environmental Response, Compensation, and Liability Act, usually known as "CERCLA." This statute attributes "liability" and a cleanup duty to various parties associated with contamination—mostly the owners of contaminated sites and those who generated the contamination. It then authorizes the executive, including the Environmental Protection Agency, to determine and give notice of such liability. The statute thereby projects at least the appearance of following the determination model.

CERCLA, however, clearly goes far beyond authorizing mere determinations and notice. It authorizes the executive to seek abatement when the president determines that "there may be an imminent and substantial endangerment to the public health or welfare or the environment because of an actual or threatened release of a hazardous substance from a facility." Beginning already with the word "may," this standard is highly indeterminate, and in recognition of this, CERLA requires the EPA to issue guidelines for the executive in making the determinations. Once there is a determination about the release of a hazardous substance, and about the existence of an imminent and substantial endangerment, the EPA can order private parties to clean up contaminated property at their own cost (with an uncertain possibility of later government reimbursement or private compensation). Parties that fail to comply must pay the government's costs in cleaning up the site, and if they fail without "sufficient cause," they are subject to "punitive" triple damages.

In issuing its orders, the executive is not merely giving notice of determinations, for its "determinations" and the guidelines about them usually involve policy choices or lawmaking will. Recognizing that the EPA is issuing orders rather than mere notices of determinations, CERCLA calls the EPA's directives "unilateral administrative orders." Indeed, CERCLA acknowledges that the EPA is not really determining liability, but merely identifying "potentially responsible parties," who then must litigate to show that they do not have liability. Far from judgments or determinations of legal liability, the EPA's orders are extralegal commands, involving will as well as judgment, and forcing private parties to pay amounts that they may not really owe.

Courts have upheld the statute as consistent with the due process of law because the affected private parties can attempt to avoid the penalties in court. The initial EPA orders, however, already are extralegal adjudications and thus are violations of the due process of law. Even when the defendants obtain judicial reconsideration, the courts defer to the EPA's findings, thus preventing defendants from getting the independent judgments of judges and juries and again denying the due process of law. As if this were not enough, the defendants can prevail in court only by proving their innocence—only if they undertake the burden of showing that they are not liable under CERCLA or that an order was arbitrary and capricious or otherwise not in accord with law.*

or seeks an administrative warrant for search and seizure, the person constrained remains free to disobey until a court orders obedience or issues
a judicial version of the underlying administrative dictate. This theory—
oddly enough propounded by the courts—at least formally acknowledges
the location of judicial power in the courts, but it does not recognize the
reality of binding administrative power.

Already at the agency level, when agencies make orders during adjudication, they can enforce their orders by imposing evidentiary burdens on
parties who refuse to comply. For example, when a party refuses to comply
with a subpoena for records, an agency adjudicator can assume that the
records are unfavorable to the refusing party.[66]

More generally, the theory that binding power comes only later, in
court, cannot be reconciled with the tendency of courts to defer to agency
orders as long as they meet the minimal criterion of being "not plainly
incompetent or irrelevant."[67] Indeed, some courts candidly say that, in enforcement actions, they may only "rubber-stamp" subpoenas, and that any
such review must be conducted "summarily."[68, w]

The overall effect is administrative power to bind. Thus, for example,
when a party refuses to comply with an order to appear and testify, the
agency adjudicator can proceed to hold a hearing and issue an order that,
for all substantive purposes, is binding. As the Supreme Court has observed, once the agency issues its order, and once enforcement proceedings are commenced in a federal district court, "the sanctioned party is
not permitted to litigate the merits of its position in that court." Moreover,
"[s]hould a party choose to ignore an order" issued by the agency, the
agency "may impose monetary penalties for each day of noncompliance,"
and after it "issues an order assessing a civil penalty, a sanctioned party
may not later contest the merits of that order in an enforcement action

w. Not far from the rubber-stamp theory is the idea that the courts can treat a violation of
an administrative order as a contempt of court. On this basis, it sometimes is accepted (as in
Interstate Commerce Commission v. Brimson) that Congress can authorize administrative bodies
to "invoke the aid" of federal courts to punish the "contumacy" of anyone who disobeys an
administrative subpoena—on the theory that the disobedience is a "contempt" of court.

Mere disobedience to a court's orders, however, when done outside the court, was not traditionally, in either England or America, a contempt of court. Nor is disobedience to one court
or administrative body punishable by another court as a contempt to its dignity.

More generally, if only courts and judges can constitutionally bind persons in particular
instances, how is a refusal to obey an executive officer a contempt of court? The theory that administrative bodies invoke the aid of the courts concedes that the executive lacks the power to
issue binding orders or warrants; it even concedes that the executive lacks the power to punish
disobedience as a contempt. How then can a court can punish for contempt a mere refusal to
obey an executive demand?*

brought by the Attorney General in federal district court." In other words, "the role of the modern federal hearing examiner or administrative law judge . . . is functionally comparable to that of a judge," and to conclude that the examiner's power to issue orders "does not coerce . . . would be to blind ourselves to reality."[69]

The rubber-stamping, moreover, results in two layers of constitutional problems. Already at the administrative level, binding administrative orders and warrants are an extralegal exercise of judicial power, which violate the Constitution's grant of judicial power to the courts and its guarantees regarding due process, juries, and warrants. At the appellate level, moreover, although the rubber-stamping is designed to cure the underlying constitutional problems, it denies the parties their rights in court, including juries, due process, and the independent judgment of the judges. The difficulty with administrative orders and warrants is thus not really avoided by the subsequent court proceedings. On the contrary, in attempting to solve one problem, the subsequent proceedings merely add another.

By rubber-stamping administrative orders and warrants, the judges essentially give administrators the power to make decisions that belong to the judges. In the eighteenth century, this was the problem with general warrants, and nowadays it is a problem with all judicial ratifications of binding administrative orders and warrants. Only the judges can issue such instruments, and in issuing them they have a duty to exercise their own independent judgment. To do otherwise is to deprive Americans of the Constitution's protection, including its allocation of judicial power and its guarantees on warrants, juries, and the due process of law.

Necessity Justification

The last resort in justifying administrative orders and warrants is the claim of necessity. This argument, however, is empirically too weak and conceptually too strong.

When Crown lawyers argued in defense of general warrants and writs of assistance—the eighteenth-century versions of administrative warrants—they said that such warrants were necessary. In the *Writs of Assistance Case* (as seen in chapter 11), the government's lawyer, Gridley, acknowledged that writs of assistance ordinarily would be considered unlawful general warrants—saying that "[i]t is true that the common privileges of Englishmen are taken away in this case"—and he therefore fell back on a claim of administrative "necessity." This was the old justification for absolute power, and Otis therefore responded that Gridley was reviving "Star Chamber tyranny." Nowadays, however, necessity again is said to justify extralegal orders and warrants.

Even if taken on its own terms, the necessity argument is weak, for the empirical necessity of administrative orders and warrants has never been shown. For example, although the English government and its lawyers claimed that writs of assistance were necessary for the collection of taxes, Congress in the early Republic accepted the constitutional barrier against such warrants without evident concern about prejudice to the revenue. On the water, where customs officers were searching ships that could not be understood as houses, they did not need a warrant, and Congress authorized them to act on their own suspicion to enter the ships and search for concealed goods, subject to later proceedings. On land, however, Congress required customs officers to get judicial warrants to enter any place. As a result, if officers suspected the concealment of goods in any place on land, they had to "make proper application on oath" to a justice of the peace for "a warrant to enter such house, store, or other place (in the daytime only) and there to search for such goods."[70] Congress clearly assumed that the customs office could manage without unconstitutional writs of assistance or other general warrants.

These days it is claimed that American society and government regulation is so complex that the executive needs to use administrative rather than judicial orders and warrants, but exactly why it is so burdensome to work through judicial officers and the courts is not made clear. Nor is any evidence supplied to show the need. Apparently, the claim is merely that it is convenient to evade the constitutional requirement of judicial orders and warrants, and even in this, the convenience is unexplained and unproved. Instead, it is assumed that an unsupported claim of necessity should simply slice through the Constitution.

The justifications for binding administrative orders and warrants thus are more worrisome than reassuring. In fact, these administrative directives return to the exercise of judicial power outside the adjudications of the courts, thus reviving precisely the extralegal judicial power that was barred by constitutional law.

❧❧❧

In sum, the administrative adjudication that binds or constrains subjects rehabilitates an extralegal regime of judicial power. It thereby violates the Constitution's grant of judicial power to the courts and its provisions for the due process of law and other procedural rights.

By way of apology for the administrative adjudication, it is said, for example, that the Constitution's grant of judicial power merely authorizes the courts and that its limits on this power merely confine the courts. Indeed, it is said that some limits, such as those on self-incrimination and warrants, only restrict criminal proceedings in the courts. But the constitutional provisions on judicial power, including those limiting the judicial power in criminal matters, developed largely in response to the prerogative tribunals. These provisions were designed to limit any exercise of judicial power and to bar any exercise of that power outside the courts.

The administrative exercise of judicial power thus restores the very sort of adjudication that constitutional law emphatically forbids. Like extralegal legislation, extralegal adjudication has no place in the constitutional system.

FOURTEEN

Rule through the Law and the Courts of Law

This book has thus far traced the administrative return to prerogative rule—in part I the return to prerogative legislation, and in part II the return to prerogative adjudication. The conceptual point is that there has been a revival of an extralegal regime, in which the government rules outside the law and the adjudications of the courts. This chapter rounds out the conceptual observation by elaborating the most basic of the underlying principles. It is well known that government must govern under law, but even more fundamentally, it must govern through the law. To be precise, it can bind only through the law and its courts.

England

The English had long tended to assume that their government could rule them only through the law, and in the seventeenth century they clarified and sharpened this principle. Their kings had openly sought to govern through prerogative or administrative power, and in rejecting this extralegal regime, the English established with new clarity that the Crown could not govern outside the paths of the law. This was not the amorphous concept of the rule of law, but more concretely the dual principle that the government could rule only through the law and the courts.

Edward Coke summarized the two elements of the principle in his gnarled, old prose. First, "[t]he king being a body politic cannot command but by matter of record, for *Rex præcipit, & Lex præcipit*"—meaning, the *king orders* and the *law orders*—"are all one, for the king must command by matter of record according to the law." In saying that the king must command by matter of record, Coke meant the king could rule only through the acts of courts of record, including both Parliament and the more narrowly judicial courts. Second, even when the king merely commanded a person to be arrested, "the king cannot do it by any commandment, but by writ, or by order, or rule of some of his courts of justice, where the cause dependeth, according to law."[1] Coke stated this second element more generally in 1628 in the debates over the Petition of Right. Rejecting claims that the king could rule through his prerogative or administrative courts, Coke answered that king's commands had to come through his regular courts, for "[t]he king distributes his power by the judges."[2]

The question came to be settled in the 1640s not by lawyers, nor even by Parliament, but by Parliament's armies. After the Civil War, lawyers could be confident that the Crown could exercise power over its subjects only through the law of the land and its courts.

The most profound of common law judges, Matthew Hale, summarized this dual point: "*Potestas imperii* or *regalis* in England hath two qualifications: (1) That it is not absolute or unlimited, but bounded by rule and law. (2) It is not simple but mixed with jurisdiction, for the contempt or disobedience to his command ought to receive his punishment by that jurisdiction which the king is intrusted with, *viz.* in his courts of justice."[3] Pursing the first point, about governance under law, Hale added that in England it required governance through the law, for "by the constitution of this realm the supreme power of the king is limited and qualified that it cannot make a law or impose a charge but by the consent both of lords and commons assembled in parliament."[4] What got resolved in the mid-seventeenth century was thus not merely that government had to be under law, but more specifically that its power had to be channeled through the law and its institutions.

Roger Twysden pursued similar conclusions. The primary point was that the king had to govern through the law, not through any administrative power. Twysden explained that the king was to govern by and under the law—that he was "to govern his subjects by and according to those laws which at his coronation he is sworn to observe." This meant that "he cannot alone in any particular alter any laws already established, either common [law] or statute" and that "he cannot alone make new laws." Secondarily, the king could confine his subjects only through the law courts: "[H]e cannot proceed against any subject, civilly or criminally, but in his ordinary courts of justice, and according to the known laws of the land."[5]

Whether as expressed by Coke, Hale, or Twysden, the constitutional assumption was that there was no room for prerogative or administrative power constraining subjects outside the law and the adjudications of the courts. Instead, binding power could be exercised only through these mechanisms.

Perhaps the most eloquent declaration of this ideal—at least of its primary element—came in a pamphlet from the 1766 embargo controversy:

> It is the glory of this constitution, says one our ablest lawyers, that its true and simple definition may be comprised in three words, *government by law*. Indeed what is the difference between a free state and arbitrary power, but that in the one the law promulgated stands the certain and unerring guide of our conduct, [and] in the other the uncertain and erroneous will of one man, or a few men, in whom the executive power resides, is substituted instead of law.[6]

Government by law ensured a freedom measured by law.

It often is assumed that the cardinal achievement of the English in their constitutional struggles was to subdue the Crown under the law, particularly under the English constitution. The principle of government under law, however, was only the most general expression of what was at stake. The threat came specifically from royal efforts to rule outside the law—to exercise prerogative or administrative power outside the regular channels for lawmaking and adjudication. The seventeenth-century vindication of law therefore rested not only on the principle of rule *under* law but also on the more detailed principle of rule *through* the law and the courts.

America

The principles of government through and under law were the foundations of constitutional governance, and they were most completely expressed in American constitutions, particularly the U.S. Constitution. Being a constitution made by the people, it was the source of all of the government's power, and it thus left no room for a power above the law. Moreover, it gave legislative power to Congress and judicial power to the courts, thus leaving only executive power to the president. It thereby allowed the new government to bind subjects only through the law and its courts.[7]

The implications for administrative law were not lost on those who were willing to recognize them. Francis Lieber—who had suffered under Prussian administrators—summarized in 1853 that citizens should not be subject to "mere 'proclamations' of the crown or executive." Nor should they be subject to "a dispensing power in the executive (so much insisted on by the Stuarts, and, indeed, by all rulers who claim to rule by a higher law than the law of the land)." As for the judicial power, "The citizen . . . ought not to be subject . . . to a 'government by commissions,' nor to extraordinary courts of justice." He added that "the citizen is not free, where aught else than the administration of justice belongs to the court, and where anything that belongs to the administration of justice is decided by anyone but the courts"—for example, where "interpretation or application belongs to anyone else than to the judiciary." Thus, "[t]here must not be what are called in France *jugements administatifs*, . . . nor any decisions by the executive about the application of the law."[8, a]

During the last half of the nineteenth century, however, government by commission was again beginning to threaten the dual principle of government through the law and its courts. And, astonishingly, this principle was most severely weakened by its most prominent defender.

On both sides of the Atlantic, Alfred Dicey was the leading expositor of government through the law and its courts, but he crudely summarized it as "the rule of law." Working from this slogan rather than the underlying concerns, Dicey explained, "We mean, in the first place, that no man is punishable or can be lawfully made to suffer in body or goods except for a distinct breach of law established before the ordinary courts of the land." He then supplemented this with a caution against excusing administrative officers from accountability in the courts: "We mean in the second place, when we speak of the 'rule of law' . . . not only that . . . no man is above the law, but . . . that every man, whatever be his rank or condition, is subject to the ordinary law of the realm and amenable to the jurisdiction of the ordinary tribunals."[9] Dicey thereby focused on the significance of the courts at the cost of understating the more basic point that the government could constrain subjects only through the law. Indeed, when he wrote that "no man is punishable or can be lawfully made to suffer in body or goods except for a distinct breach of law," he did not clearly foreclose the pos-

a. Lieber explained that "[b]y extraordinary courts of justice are meant, in this connection, courts of an extraordinary composition, not those that are simply directed to sit at an unusual time." In later editions, he added:

The difference between justice, that is, right distributed among men by lawful and regularly appointed judges on the one hand, and the trials by commissioners on the other hand, is well pointed out by an anecdote, such as Plutarch would not have disdained to give in his writings. Montaign, grandmaster of the household of Charles VI., was tried, tortured, and executed by commissioners. He was buried in the church of the Celestines, and when Francis I. came to see his tomb, the king said, "This Montaign has been condemned by justice." "No, sire," answered the simple monk who guided the king, "he was condemned by commissioners."[*]

sibility that the breach might consist of violating a statute giving effect to administrative regulations.

John Dickinson—an American apologist for administrative law—further eroded the principle by simply dropping the word "law." Summarizing Dicey, Dickinson concluded merely that "every citizen is entitled, first, to have his rights adjudicated in a regular common-law court, and, secondly, to call into question in such a court the legality of any act done by an administrative official."[10] He left out the word law because he was speaking of rights under administrative regulations, and he thereby completed the process, begun by Dicey, of collapsing the dual principle, of government through the law and its courts, into its second half.

Having done this, Dickinson then admitted that the remaining element—of having rights adjudicated in a regular common court—had been "overridden" by administrative law. Nonetheless, with the optimism of a Candide, he argued that this loss was cured by subsequent judicial review—as if the judges were really apt to do much more than defer.[11] Like other advocates of administrative law, Dickinson had no real use for the old principle that government could bind persons only through the law and its courts.

This foundational ideal was thus thrown to the winds. Today, rather than impose general duties on the public through the law, government exercises power once again through extralegal legislation, whether by rulemaking, interpretation, or guidance. Similarly, rather than rely on the courts to bind members of the public in particular intances, government once again acts through extralegal adjudication. Administrative legislation and adjudication thereby restore a prerogative regime—a system of governance outside the lawful channels of legislative and judicial power. This regime is not merely contrary to law, but outside and above the law.

⋘⋘⋘

Thus, although prerogative lawmaking and adjudication are long gone, administrative versions have taken their place. The ghost of the prerogative has come back to life with little change other than in its name.

Both the danger of extralegal power, and the solution, have come full circle. Although constitutional law developed to bar extralegal power, government has reasserted a power outside the law—outside the acts, institutions, processes, and rights established by the Constitution. The administrative state thereby harks back to the situation that prevailed before the development of constitutional law. Indeed, it returns to the preeminent danger that constitutional law was understood to have defeated.

PART III

Supralegal Power and Judicial Deference

Whereas parts I and II focused on extralegal power, part III now must turn to supralegal power. An extralegal regime can survive only if it can avoid being held to account under the law in the same way as regular government. In other words, power outside the law depends on judicial deference to it as a power above the law.

This was the point of much of the early-seventeenth-century dispute over absolute power and the supremacy of the law. To protect his power outside the law, James I insisted that it also was above the law and thus above judicial reconsideration. Put another way, he argued that his administrative lawmaking and adjudication were owed deference.

Of course, the royal demand for deference did not mean that questions of prerogative or administrative power could escape coming before the courts. On the contrary, the judges frequently reviewed such questions. But where the Crown said that its power was absolute—that it was above the law—the judges felt profound pressures to defer.

What ensued was a struggle for the supremacy of the law that would define the law and the role of the judges for centuries. The demand for deference was an assertion of power above the law, and it was met with principles about judicial office, the supremacy of the law, and the constitution.

The current deference of the courts to administrative power therefore cannot be understood merely as a modern phenomenon. On the contrary—as is explained in the ensuing chapters on deference and its revival—contemporary deference returns to the old claims for absolute power.

FIFTEEN

Deference

In defense of its extralegal power, the Crown demanded judicial deference. To be precise, it sought to secure its power outside the law by seeking deference to it as a power above the law.

Judicial deference almost inevitably had to be presented as deference to a power above the law, for otherwise the judges would have had to have held the Crown's extralegal prerogative acts unlawful. The Crown therefore asserted this mode of governance as a power not only outside the law but also above it.

The demand for deference to absolute prerogatives thus collided with the supremacy of the law and the independent judgment of the judges. Eventually, after a century of struggle, the English put such questions to rest. All that then was settled, however, has been reopened by contemporary demands for deference to administrative power.

Deference to Prerogative Legislation

The royal claim for deference to prerogative legislation rested on the king's claim of absolute power. If the king's prerogative was not merely outside but above the law, the king could not be questioned for it under law. Put another way, if the king was the final judge, the judges of the law courts had to defer to his judgment rather than exercise their own. As James I told the assembled judges in 1616, "the absolute prerogative of the Crown" was "no subject for the tongue of a lawyer, nor is [it] lawful to be disputed."[1] Nowadays, the executive does not speak in such terms to the judges, but although the words have changed, the insistence on deference has not.

Of course, the king's absolute prerogative coexisted with his ordinary prerogative, the result being that he had "a double prerogative." Although "the one was ordinary and had relation to his private interest, which might be and was every day, disputed in Westminster Hall; the other was of an higher nature, referring to his supreme and imperial power and sovereignty, which ought not to be disputed or handled in vulgar argument."[2] The ordinary prerogative was that exercised under law and thus subject to judicial determinations; the other was so sovereign and absolute that the king expected it to be altogether above the law and its courts.

The implications were especially sobering when James and his advocates took an expansive view of what was within his absolute prerogative. Many matters, ranging from pardons to war and peace, did not bind subjects and thus could be exclusively in the hands of the king. Acts creating taxes, criminal offenses, and other binding constraints, however, traditionally had to be done through the law, which could be changed only by Parliament and adjudicated only in the law courts.

The difficulty was that there were always men ready to suggest that some taxes and criminal offenses belonged to the king in his absolute prerogative—as when Henry Yelverton, in 1610, defended the king's prerogative in taxes by arguing that "[w]e are where the common law cannot judge." He explained that impositions were a matter of "reason of government" and therefore, "[t]hough the imposition be excessive, yet none can judge it but the king."[3] Even the judges however, who upheld the king's taxes or impositions did not go so far, and Yelverton's arguments therefore earned him the contempt of much of the House of Commons. Indeed, such arguments increasingly spurred common lawyers and judges to recognize that all royal authority had to be exercised under law. This was particularly clear from the notion of a constitution. If the government had been established by a constitution or enactment made by the people, then there could be no prerogative above the law.

From this perspective, even where the king retained areas of absolute discretion, it was not absolute power in the sense of a power above law, but merely a discretion or power defined by law and under it. Already in responding to Yelverton in the House of Commons, Richard Martyn observed that "[t]he king of England is the most absolute king in his Parliament; but, of himself, his power is limited by law." He was part of the legislative power, which in England was unreviewable and absolute; by himself, however, he had no such authority. As Edward Coke explained in the debates over the Petition of Right, "the king's prerogative is part of the law of this kingdom, and a supreme part . . . yet it hath bounds set unto it by the laws of England."[4] The question thus came down to which was supreme, the king or the law of the land.

Although this question about deference to extralegal legislation was put to rest in the seventeenth century, it will be seen in the next chapter that it has been revived. In the meantime, a related question must be examined—the question of deference to extralegal adjudication. Here, too, the history is revealing about more than merely the past.

Deference to Prerogative Adjudication

The prerogative courts, backed by King James, sought to limit review of their proceedings by the law courts, but without much success. The judges of the law courts had a duty to exercise independent judgment in accord with the law of the land, and it therefore became apparent that they could not defer to the judgments of others, including the judgments of prerogative or administrative officers.

Already when the High Commission interrogated individuals in the 1590s, they complained of the judicial deference it had secured for its proceedings. Magna Charta assured the queen's "free born subjects" that they would enjoy "the benefit and use of her highness' laws even in any cases or causes betwixt her highness and them." Nonetheless, the "lawless and insolent dealings, oppressions, injuries, violence" of the commissioners "may not be called in question or examined by any civil magistrates or courts."[5]

The demand of the prerogative tribunals for deference from the law courts became especially bitter in the dispute over writs of prohibition. The law courts issued these writs to prevent the prerogative bodies from acting outside their jurisdiction or otherwise contrary to the law of the land. In response, the prerogative courts insisted that the law courts should defer to their judgments, including their interpretations of statutes.

The opposition to deference was vigorous, as can be observed in the argument of Nicholas Fuller for a writ of prohibition against the High Commission. On behalf of his clients, who had been prosecuted by the commission, Fuller protested that "whatsoever the commissioners do, it is examinable in every court where it shall come in question, at any time thereafter," for "their decrees and sentences are not pleadable in law, as judgments in courts of record are." Thus, whatever "allowance, or toleration" was given to commissions, if their conduct was "contrary to law," it "bindeth neither the right of the king, nor subjects, but that the judges of the law may judge thereof according to law."[6]

The underlying common law point was that the judges had an office of judgment, in which they had a duty to follow the law of the land. Having taken an oath to serve in this office, they were "sworn to execute justice according to [the] law and custom of England."[7] They therefore could not defer to the judgment of the prerogative courts about the law. Instead, where the law barred the prerogative proceedings, the common law courts (at least under Chief Justice Coke) typically did their duty and issued prohibitions.

Fact Deference

The dispute then, as today, was partly about who determined facts. In the prerogative courts, facts were decided by the prerogative judges rather than by juries. All the same, when the common law courts took cases from the prerogative courts, they did not defer to any prior administrative determinations of fact, but proceeded to decide factual questions in their regular manner, usually by leaving them to a jury.

Of course, there were some determinations of fact that belonged to the king, but far from being low-level administrative determinations, these were matters (such as certain questions of war and peace) that belonged to the king as the sovereign. As Matthew Hale explained, "Touching questions purely of fact, there be some cases wherein the conusance of the fact lies purely in the king's conusance. In which case his certificate or affirmation under his great seal is final and not examinable. . . . But on the other side, if the king will certify a matter triable otherwise and in presumption lying in the knowledge of the country, this is not conclusive."[8] Other than the few matters determinable by the sovereign, factual questions belonged to the jury, which meant there was no room for judicial deference to administrative determinations.

Interpretation Deference

The question that, as nowadays, was more openly debated was whether judges could defer to prerogative or administrative interpretations of statutes. It already has been seen, in chapter 4, that James I and his prerogative courts claimed an imperial power to legislate through interpretation. Although the judges of the law courts understood themselves to have a duty to expound the law, including statutes, James and his advisors argued that when statutes left questions open, the king had a power to interpret in the sense of exerting a gap-filling legislative will. They also hinted that he had delegated this intersticial power of interpretation to the judges of his prerogative courts. On this theory, James and his advisors argued that the prerogative courts could establish their own interpretations of statutes—interpretations to which the law courts had to defer.

The law courts, however, could not defer to prerogative or administrative interpretations of statutes any more than they could defer to parliamentary interpretations. Parliament could use a statute to amend an existing statute; and it could use the same mechanism to declare the law with the effect of amending an existing statute; but as noted by Chancellor Hatton, its mere interpretations of its statutes had no legal significance.[9] The judges therefore could not defer to such interpretations, and if they could not defer to Parliament's interpretations, they surely could not defer to those of the prerogative courts.

An underlying reason was that the law rather than the interpretative choices of judges had legal obligation. When it was said that prerogative judges could exercise delegated lawmaking will in interpreting statutes, the law judges responded that the exposition of law was not an exercise of will, but of judgment. In other words, the law itself rather than any delegated exercise of will was determinative, and the judges therefore could not defer to the interpretations of prerogative judges. This was Coke's point when, in *Bonham's Case*, he wrote that "the common law will control acts of Parliament."[10]

Moreover, the exposition of law was a matter of judgment about law, and the law gave the office of judgment, at least in cases, to the judges. It thus became apparent that the judges—indeed, only the judges in their cases—had the power to give authoritative expositions of the law.[11] Lawyers recited this in constitutional terms—for example, when a lawyer argued in King's Bench that "a power is implicitly given to this court by the fundamental constitution, which makes the judges expositors of acts of Parliament."[12] The judges therefore could not defer to interpretations by persons who were not the constitutional expositors, let alone interpretations that were administrative exercises of legislative will.

Ultimately, the question came to rest, as already noted, on the very office of the judges. They had an office or duty of judgment independent of will, including the king's will, and they therefore had to judge for themselves. They had a duty to exercise this judgment, moreover, in accord with the law of the land. Their very office thus left them no room for deference to the interpretations or other adjudications of prerogative or administrative bodies. Instead, they could defer only to the law and their own judgment of it.

The Supremacy of the Law of the Land

The struggle over judicial deference to the king's absolute prerogative came to rest not only on the office of the judges but also, as already hinted, on the supremacy of the law. The supremacy of the law of the land was one of the preeminent achievements in the development of law, for it cut off royal claims for a power above the law to which the judges had to defer. Already in discussing the history, therefore, the implications for administrative law should be obvious.

During the Reformation, the Crown resisted the legal authority of the pope by asserting the legal authority of the king, especially his supreme authority to make law in his Parliament and to provide justice in his courts of law. The underlying principle was that the law of each temporal ruler was supreme in his land. The Crown thus defeated a foreign priestly power by clarifying the supremacy of domestic temporal law.

This sixteenth-century royal emphasis on the supremacy of the law of the land and its courts framed much the conflict between the Crown and common lawyers. Although English monarchs asserted that the law of the land was supreme against Rome, they insisted at home that at least some of their prerogative, the absolute prerogative, rose above the law.

This was James I's point when he told the judges that "the absolute prerogative of the Crown" was "no subject for the tongue of a lawyer, nor is [it] lawful to be disputed."[13] His absolute prerogative—his administrative power—was above the law of the land, and the judges therefore had to defer to it.

The common law judges, however, were dedicated to the supremacy of the law of the land, and they insisted on the law's supremacy over the prerogative, including the supremacy of the law courts over the prerogative courts. For example, as already noted, the judges repudiated the royal demands for deference to prerogative interpretations of statutes, and they regularly issued writs of prohibition against the proceedings of the prerogative courts. In the words of Roscoe Pound, "A valiant fight against . . . administrative absolutism was waged by the common-law courts, and in the end the older law prevailed. . . . The chief weapon which the common law employed in this contest and the one about which the contest raged, was the doctrine of the supremacy of law. That doctrine, therefore, became established among the fundamental[s] of our legal tradition as a result of the victory."[14]

This rejection of judicial deference to prerogative or administrative power did not become complete until the late seventeenth century. Until then, the Crown carefully appointed judges who shared its ambitions or who at least would succumb to its pressures. Nonetheless, the judges generally were dedicated to their office of independent judgment in accord with the law of the land, and on account of this office some of them exhibited much courage in maintaining the supremacy of the law against the absolute prerogative.

In the struggle over deference to absolute power, constitutional law was essential, for it was the most definitive assertion of the supremacy of law. When answering royal assertions of prerogative outside and above the law, many lawyers argued that all government power was enjoyed under the law enacted by the people. Constitutional law thereby became a conclusive way of showing that there was no government power above the law, to which the judges might have to defer.

The supremacy of the law of the land, especially the constitution, thus cut off claims of prerogative power above the law. In other words, the supremacy of the law precluded any deference. Rather than defer to prerogative or adminstrative power, judges had to defer to the law.

America

In America, too, deference was barred. Because of the office of the judges and the supremacy of the law, the judges could not defer to any executive exercise of legislative or judicial power.

The Constitution

The Constitution laid the foundations for both judicial office and the supremacy of the law. In both ways, it precluded deference.

The Constitution granted judicial power to the courts and authorized the appointment of individuals as judges. As a result, although the courts had the judicial power, the judges had judicial office, and this was the office or duty to exercise judgment in accord with the law of the land. As James Iredell explained about judges under his state's constitution, "The duty of the power . . . in all cases, is to decide according to the laws of the state."[15]

Recognizing the implications for judicial power, Chief Justice Marshall wrote:

> Judicial power, as contradistinguished from the power of the laws, has no existence. Courts are the mere instruments of the law, and can will nothing. When they are said to exercise a discretion, it is a mere legal discretion, a discretion to be exercised in discerning the course prescribed by law; and, when that is discerned, it is the duty of the court to follow it. Judicial power is never exercised for the purpose of giving effect to the will of the judge, al-

ways for the purpose of giving effect to the will of the legislature; or, in other words, to the will of the law.[16]

The judicial power of the courts thus turned on the duty of the judges to follow the law, and this would mean that judicial power could not be exercised to defer to anything else.

Confirming this conclusion, the Constitution also defined the supreme law of the land: "This Constitution, and the Laws of the United States which shall be made in Pursuance thereof; and all Treaties made, or which shall be made, under the Authority of the United States, shall be the supreme Law of the Land." Recognizing that some state judges might doubt whether they had a duty to follow federal law, the Constitution added that "the judges in every state shall be bound thereby, anything in the Constitution or laws of any State to the contrary notwithstanding."[17]

The supremacy clause and its supremacy of the law of the land is often understood merely in terms of the supremacy of federal law over state law. But this is myopic, for it misses the traditional supremacy of the law of the land—a supremacy that had been assumed at common law for centuries and that the supremacy clause made explicit. It has been seen that the law of the land was supreme over both foreign papal power and domestic prerogative power. Against this background, it becomes clear that the Constitution made federal law supreme over all competing assertions of temporal power within the nation—state law being merely the most recent threat.

Thus, even within the federal government, the law of the land was supreme, and like its seventeenth-century precursor, it thereby precluded any claim for a power above the law, to which judges might defer. In England the supremacy of the law had left no room for deference to prerogative power, and in America it similarly foreclosed any deference to administrative power.

No Deference Even within Spheres of Executive Power

It may be thought that the judges were to defer to the executive at least where, by law, it had a realm of discretion or authority. Even there, however, it was the duty of the judges to defer to the law's allocation of power, not to the executive.

The degree to which judges were simply to follow the law was suggested by the Supreme Court's nineteenth-century doctrine of "public rights."[18] This was very different from the contemporary doctrine of public rights, and although often thought to be opaque, this phrase at least was clear in acknowledging that when the Court upheld executive power, it was not deferring to the executive, but was recognizing the right or power of the government under the law.

Indeed, the Court used the phrase to refer to the sphere of power that the English had come to think of as the prerogative enjoyed under law. Whereas in the early seventeenth century, Crown lawyers had distinguished between the ordinary prerogatives under law and the absolute prerogatives above the law, by the end of the century, all royal prerogatives were conceded to be "absolute," but merely in the sense that they were realms of absolute discretion granted and defined by law. The monarch thus could exercise his will as he pleased but only under law and as limited by law. Not surprisingly, his remaining prerogatives generally did not include the power to make binding rules or other decisions that constrained subjects.

Similarly, in America, the sphere of lawful executive power—of public rights—was absolute only in the sense of being discretionary, not in the sense of being above the law. It was merely the power allowed to the executive by the law, which the judges had to follow. As in England, moreover, this sphere of authority did not include any power to make binding decisions that constrained subjects, but consisted merely of executive power—such as the power to issue orders to executive officers, to seek distress, to distribute benefits, or to constrain nonsubjects.[19] Of course, the Constitution left room for military orders and warrants issued under suspensions of habeas. But generally executive power—the executive's "public rights" as understood through much of the nineteenth century—was not a power to bind subjects, this being why it could be a realm of discretion defined and allowed by law.

Thus, even when the judges acknowledged public rights or spheres of executive authority, it was a stretch to say that they were deferring to the executive. Instead, they were following the law.

The Supreme Court explained this in an 1840 case resting on a pair of pension statutes, under which the widow of Stephen Decatur claimed two pensions. One statute granted her a pension by name; the other generally granted pensions to widows of naval officers. The secretary of the navy interpreted the statutes to allow her only one pension, and when the succeeding secretary refused to reconsider this decision, she sought a mandamus against him to get both amounts. But even though the statutes were written in language that seemed to mandate payment, the Supreme Court recognized that the statutes were allocating benefits, and this left it room to conclude that they left discretion in the secretary:

If a suit should come before this court, which involved the construction of any of these laws, the court would not be bound to adopt the construction given by the head to a department. And if they supposed his decision to be wrong, they would, of course, so pronounce their judgment. But. . . . [t]he court could not entertain an appeal from the decision of one of the secretaries, nor revise his judgment in any case where the law authorized him to exercise discretion, or judgment.[20]

It is debatable whether the Court was correct in assuming that the statutes gave the secretary discretion in distributing the pensions, but the significant point for this book was the Court's lack of deference. The judges had to defer to the law, not the executive's interpretation.

Litigation

At a practical level, the implications of judicial office and the supremacy of the law became evident in the repeated decisions of the courts that reconsidered administrative decisions. There was no question of the judges' deferring to administrative interpretations, not even to the administrative interpretations that purported merely to bind executive officers. Instead, the judges repeatedly exercised their own judgment in accord with the law of the land.

Executive decisions were reexamined by the courts almost exclusively in suits brought by members of the public after they were harmed by executive officers—either when they were constrained or when they were denied government benefits to which they had a vested right. As shown by several scholars (particularly Thomas Merrill, Caleb Nelson, and Ann Woolhandler), the law traditionally left such persons to their fate but then allowed them to seek damages or other remedies against wayward executive officers.[21] For example, an assessor would assess taxes, and if necessary, a collector would distrain for the taxes, and only at this point could the taxpayer get a remedy. Yet rather than appeal from the executive decision, he would initiate an action against the collector. In other words, the taxpayer had to suffer an injury, such as distraint or payment under protest, and he then could bring an action for trespass—or, if he was imprisoned for lack of distrainable property, for false imprisonment.[22]

In retrospect, the inability to appeal from an executive adjudication until after payment or distress may seem harsh, for it required a taxpayer to wait for an injury, even if only a mild one, and then required him to commence an action. This approach, however, had the virtue of keeping the executive and the judicial proceedings apart. The actions against executive officers were ordinary actions—for trespass, for false imprisonment, or for other torts—in which the judicial proceedings were not extensions of the executive proceedings. Therefore, as put by Thomas Merrill, "the nature of the review was uniformly what we now would call de novo" and "courts generally gave no deference to agency determinations."[23] Judges decided the law, and juries gave their verdicts on the facts, without deference and, indeed, entirely independently of executive determinations and interpretations.

It was so far from the assumptions of the judges that they should or even could defer to executive interpretations that they ordinarily did not address the issue. Occasionally, however, they revealed at least one of their underlying premises, that executive interpretations and instructions were not law and thus were not binding. For example, in an 1836 case against a customs collector, the Supreme Court concluded: "The construction of the law is open to both parties, and each presumed to know it. Any instructions from the Treasury Department could not change the law or affect the rights of the plaintiff."[24, a]

The utterly nondeferential approach of the courts, even at a time of aggressive Treasury interpretations under Treasury Secretary Levi Woodbury, is further evident from a series of instructions on gunny cloth. In 1839, the Treasury was informed that this cloth was being imported in large quantities for the same purposes as cotton bagging. Eager to collect revenue, the comptroller made the most of an 1832 statute that imposed a duty on "cotton bagging." Taking an expansive interpretation of this, he issued a circular to customs collectors instructing them to levy the cotton-bagging duty "on all articles suitable for and used in making cotton bagging." The

---

a. A contrary position has sometimes been attributed to the Supreme Court, but based on a strange misreading. In 1809, in *United States v. Vowell*, the Supreme Court held that the defendant, an importer, did not owe duties under an act of Congress. Writing for the Court, Chief Justice Marshall explained that, "If the question had been doubtful, the Court would have respected the uniform construction which it is understood has been given by the Treasury Department of the United States upon similar questions." When taken out of context, this quotation has seemed to reveal a historical foundation for judicial deference. Such a conclusion, however, misunderstands the case.

The defendant had relied on prior treasury interpretations, and the Treasury now was asking the Court to reach a decision contrary to the Treasury's prior interpretations. In these circumstances, Marshall was simply observing that, even if the statute had not so clearly justified the defendant, the Court still would have held for him. That is, it would have respected the Treasury's prior interpretations for the defendant's sake, not the Treasury's. Rather than judicial deference to administrative interpretation, this was a recognition of something like reliance, estoppel, or waiver. *

importers of gunny cloth therefore had to pay the duties, but they did so only under protest, and one of them in 1841 challenged the government's position by suing the collector for the port of Boston in the circuit court. Justice Joseph Story, sitting on circuit, instructed the jury that "gunny cloth was not subject to a duty as cotton bagging within the meaning of the law," and the jury gave a verdict for the importer.[25]

The Treasury initially conceded the point by issuing a circular to collectors instructing them that gunny cloth was to be admitted free of duty. A few months later, however, the comptroller reissued his 1839 instructions. Once again, therefore, "the collector of the port of Boston . . . compelled the importers to give bonds for duties on gunny cloth as cotton bagging, which they have done under protest, and paid under protest." The merchants sued to recover these payments, and again Justice Story heard the case. He took the conventional view that, "in the construction of commercial laws and commercial contracts," it was necessary to examine "[t]he language of merchants." On this basis, he concluded that the government "must show, that gunny cloth was known as 'cotton bagging' in 1832." Rather than defer to the Treasury's persistent interpretation and instructions, he reminded the jury of the evidence that in 1832 gunny cloth was not known as "cotton bagging" and was not used for this purpose. "If this evidence be true, and be believed by the jury, then the case is made out for the plaintiff"—a conclusion the jury shared.[26]

The Treasury pressed for its interpretations, and as will be seen in the next chapter, it eventually sidestepped the question by persuading Congress and the Supreme Court to bar suits against customs collectors. But because its interpretations were not binding, the public did not have to defer, and the courts could not defer.

Executive Records

As might be expected by now, the courts could not defer to the transcripts or records developed by the executive in its proceedings. Executive records were not records in the judicial sense, and they therefore were considered merely the records of a party, which could be introduced as evidence in subsequent judicial proceedings, but which were not binding on other parties, and which could not be relied upon by the courts.

Traditionally, there was a distinction between courts of record and courts not of record. The central judicial courts at Westminister were courts of record, this being why their acts, memorialized in their records, enjoyed a presumption of validity, unless overturned by a higher court of record:

"Records are of so high a nature, that for their sublimity they import verac-ity in themselves; and none shall be received to aver anything against the record itself." Of course, Parliament was the highest court of record, and this was why its acts enjoyed an irrebuttable presumption of validity. In contrast, although courts that were not of record kept what colloquially are known as "records," these were not records at law, and their acts could not, even presumptively, be relied upon in other courts, except as evidence. Ac-cordingly, from the courts that were not of record, there could not be writs of error. Instead, there could be only de novo proceedings, in which the moving party "denied" the underlying proceedings and had the question "tried by a jury."[27]

Federal executive agencies clearly were not courts of record, and their transcripts and other records therefore enjoyed no presumption of truth or validity. Where executive decisions were examined by the courts, Congress could limit the courts to hearing evidence on issues that had been raised in the executive proceedings.[28] But even at the behest of Congress, the judges could not defer to the executive record or the facts supposedly established by it, lest they abandon their office of independent judgment and the office of juries to decide the facts.[b]

This question came before the Supreme Court in an 1843 case concern-ing Samuel Swartwout—the customs collector for the port of New York who in 1838 departed from his office with huge embezzled sums and then "Swartwouted out" to England. This left the United States to recover its back duties from his sureties. When presenting its evidence, the govern-ment did not rely on the Treasury's general accounts, but on a Treasury restatement or transcript of Swartwout's account. In response, the sureties sought to exclude this evidence on the ground that the Treasury's general accounts were a conclusive judicial record—"that the duties of the Treasury officers charged with the settlement of these accounts are in their nature ju-dicial; and that when an account is once settled it is conclusive on the gov-ernment, and can only be opened for correction by a suit in court." Both the general accounts and the restatements or transcripts, however, were merely the records of one of the parties in the case, and they did not have the conclusive effect of a court record. As the Supreme Court said about the restatement, "the transcript or restatement of the account, as explained by

---

b. Of course, where Congress authorized land officers to decide on grants of land patents, or on the release of federal claims against landowners, it could bar reviewing courts from hear-ing any evidence about the underlying merits. These were discretionary grants by the govern-ment, and the underlying merits therefore were irrelevant.

the depositions, was competent evidence to the jury," but was "only *prima facie* evidence," and "[t]he jury will determine what effect it shall have."[29]

Evidently, an executive record, even one kept by officers who were expected to exercise judgment rather than will, had no presumptive verity or validity. Administrative judgment might mimic the judgment of a court, but this did not give an executive record the presumptive effect of a court record.

🙟🙟🙟

In the early seventeenth century, the Crown asserted that its absolute prerogatives were above the law and that the judges therefore had to defer. But these demands for deference did not get very far.

For most of the history of the common law, it has been the office or duty of judges to exercise their independent judgment in accord with the law of the land, and the duty of juries then to evaluate the facts and give their verdicts—all without deference. Since the mid-seventeenth century, moreover, the law of the land has been recognized as supreme over any other claims of temporal power, foreign or domestic. It therefore came to be recognized that the judges could not defer to any power outside the law as if it were a power above the law. Rather than defer to prerogative or administrative power, the judges had to follow the law.

Times, however, have changed. Although deference was buried under constitutional barriers, it will be seen that it has crawled back to the surface and returned to life.

SIXTEEN

Return to Deference

The question of deference has not gone away. The return to extralegal power has led to revived demands for deference to such power, and in compliance, judges largely defer to administrative decisions. Of course, the new deference is different from the past deference, but the reality of deference has returned.[1]

Cutting Off Actions and Substituting Appeals

The foundation for judicial deference was laid by a pair of other developments: restrictions on legal actions against administrators and a corresponding substitution of appeals. As a result, rather than independently judge administrative proceedings, the judges have come to participate in the administrative regime, and they thereby have been drawn into circumstances that invite deference.

Although the doctrine of sovereign immunity traditionally prevented Americans from suing their governments, it has been seen that it did not bar them from bringing actions against individual executive officers, including actions for damages. Executive officers generally lacked insurance, and the actions against them therefore offered a powerful mechanism for inducing their compliance with the law. More generally, such actions gave vigor to the salutary old principle that every official had "personal liability to the ordinary law and the ordinary courts . . . for any acts without legal justification, whether or not performed in his official capacity."[2]

Court decisions against executive officers, however, increasingly provoked complaints from such officers and their friends. In the 1840s, for example, a writer associated with the Treasury protested against the injustice and inequality of a system that allowed suits against customs and excise collectors, but not against those who allocated land, pensions, and other government benefits. Of course, the tax collectors constrained Americans in a way that the distributors of government largesse did not. To officers who felt the hard edge of judicial remedies, however, this distinction seemed insignificant.[3]

A hint of the future became evident as early as 1839, when a statute seemed to protect customs collectors from lawsuits. The suits by merchants against customs collectors had long annoyed the Treasury, for the threat of liability altered the collectors' behavior. In particular, when merchants protested payments, or when duties remained unascertained, the collectors held back the payments from the Treasury, thus delaying the receipt of taxes. The collectors' control over these disputed amounts had given the New York collector, Samuel Swartwout, the opportunity for his dramatic embezzlement, and Congress responded by enacting that all money paid to customs collectors under protest, or for unascertained duties, should no longer be held personally by the collectors, but should be "placed to the credit of the Treasurer of the United States." The statute added that "whenever it shall be shown to the satisfaction of the Secretary of the Treasury, that . . . more money has been paid to the collector . . . than the law requires . . . it shall be his duty to draw his warrant upon the Treasurer in favor of the person or persons entitled to the over-payment."[4]

When this new system finally came before the Supreme Court in 1845, a majority of the judges understood it to bar suits against customs collectors. On its face, the statute merely barred collectors from holding onto disputed payments and allowed merchants to choose between suing collectors and applying to the secretary of the treasury for the return of their money. The Court concluded, however, in *Cary v. Curtis*, that the statute did not impose the risk of a double payment on the collectors. (In the Court's strained reasoning, once collectors had placed protested or unascertained amounts to the credit of the United States, the collectors could no longer be personally liable to return such money to the merchants who paid it—as if money were not fungible.) Thus, although the statute could not have withdrawn jurisdiction against collectors from state courts, it was interpreted to have the effect of barring any recovery from collectors. In place of such suits, according to the Court, the statute left merchants to apply to the secretary, thus making him the sole "tribunal for the examination of claims for duties said to have been improperly paid."[5]

Justices Joseph Story and John McLean vociferously dissented. At the very least, the Court had misinterpreted the statute. More generally, it had allowed Congress to bar causes of actions against executive officers for money they held unlawfully, and had allowed an executive officer to exercise judicial power. When "stripped of all formalities," Story wrote, the question was "[w]hether Congress have a right to take from the citizens all right of action in any court to recover back money claimed illegally, and extorted by compulsion, by its officers under color of law, but without any legal authority, and thus to deny them all remedy for an admitted wrong, and to clothe the Secretary of the Treasury with the sole and exclusive authority to withhold or restore that money according to his own notions of justice or right?" If Congress could do this, Americans no longer had "a government where the three great departments, legislative, executive, and judicial, had independent duties to perform each in its own sphere; but the judicial power, designed by the Constitution to be the final and appellate jurisdiction to interpret our laws, is superseded in its most vital and important functions." This left "no security whatsoever for the rights of the citizens." Moreover, "if Congress possess a constitutional authority to vest such summary and final power of interpretation in an executive functionary," there was "no other subject within the reach of legislation which may not be exclusively confided in the same way to an executive functionary." With this prescient observation, Story sharply concluded: "I deny the constitutional authority of Congress to delegate such functions to any executive officer, or to take away all right of action for an admitted wrong and illegal exercise of power in the levy of money from the injured citizens."[6, a]

Congress itself largely repudiated the danger feared by Story and McLean. Immediately after the Court's decision, Congress passed a statute

---

a. In answering Story and McLean, the Court excused its opinion by suggesting the merchant was not entirely "without other modes of redress, had he chosen to adopt them." What the Court meant was not that the merchant could bring an action to recover duties held unlawfully, but rather that if he had initially refused to pay duties, and had tendered only what he thought he owed, he might have been able to bring an action to recover his goods from the customs officer. As put by the Court, the merchant might have "asserted his right to the possession of the goods, or his exemption from the duties demanded, either by replevin, or in an action of detinue, or perhaps by an action of trover, upon his tendering the amount of duties admitted by him to be legally due." On this basis, the Court suggested that the "legitimate inquiry" before the Court was "not whether all right of action has been taken away from the party," and the Court therefore said that it "responds to no such inquiry."

This, however, was a weak response. For one thing, the Court's approach was financially impracticable for most merchants, as it would require them to leave their goods with the government for the duration of the litigation. More seriously, the Court's analysis was not really on point, for the case before the Court concerned the unlawful holding of money rather than the unlawful detention of goods. Put another way, it was irrelevant that Congress had not deprived merchants of all means of disputing customs duties, for the question in the particular case more narrowly concerned whether Congress could take away all right of action in court to recover money illegally held by officers under color of law.[*]

preserving the right of importers to sue customs collectors for money paid under protest and emphasizing that importers had a right to trial by jury. In addition, Congress barred the secretary of the treasury from making refunds of amounts paid under protest.[7] In other words, it almost entirely restored the adjudication of overpayment to the courts. It was a sweeping vindication of Story's position.

Later, however, courts and legislatures would gradually whittle away suits against executive officers. By the last decades of the century, at least some judges and legislators probably understood that there could be no room for suits against executive officers under an administrative regime. They seem to have recognized that, if the courts were to accept the lawfulness of binding administrative orders or warrants, they would have to avoid holding executive officers accountable for such constraints. More generally, there was much judicial and legislative solicitousness for executive officers. One way or the other, such officers increasingly were above judicial recourse, thus eventually making their will a binding power.[b]

Certainly, one result of the limitations on suits against executive officers was to free such men from any personal anxiety about the binding constraints they imposed on the public. While suits were still possible against executive officers, they tended to lean toward the safety of lawful conduct—indeed, they tended to confine themselves to what clearly was within the law. As the risk of legal responsibility decreased, however, they came to lose their fear of the law. Of course, they remained subject to disciplinary actions within their agencies, but these internal measures were mild compared to paying damages in court and were unlikely when officers were carrying out administrative policies dictated by their superiors. Thus, whereas eighteenth and early-nineteenth-century executive officers had to be fastidious about adhering to the law, twentieth-century officers could afford to be nearly indifferent.[8]

At the same time that the courts bowed out of the business of suits against executive officers, the courts increasingly were given another, more

---

b. Ernst Freund identifies four stages in the decline of damages suits against executive officers. First, the realm of protected discretion, in which liability was barred, was expanded to include licensing of otherwise prohibited activities, and then even directly binding acts, and the scope of protected ministerial acts was similarly expanded. Second, liability was limited by expanding the actions in which plaintiffs had to show fault. Third, liability was rendered of no practical consequence by government compensation for officers found guilty in the courts—a notable instance being when Congress in 1863 barred recovery from customs collectors and substituted payments from the Treasury. Fourth, actions for liability were superseded by administrative remedies. Yet another consideration, as noted by David Engdahl, was the growing tendency of the courts, in suits against officers, to view the state as the real defendant.*

appellate mode of overseeing executive action. At least something like an appeal to the federal courts can be discerned already in the late eighteenth century for federal tax assessments on carriages.[9] Appeals to the courts, however, were mostly a late-nineteenth- and twentieth-century development, which accompanied the development of binding administrative power. As already hinted, the timing probably was not an accident, for it was what might be expected when executive officers no longer simply distributed benefits and made determinations but also imposed constraints. This new sort of regime could not survive suits against officers, and it therefore required a shift to mere appeals.[c]

More to the point here, the appeals largely reduced judicial process to an extension of the administrative process. When courts frequently considered executive actions in independent lawsuits against individual executive officers, the judges tended to exercise independent judgment. They recognized that they served in an institution distinct from the executive and that they had no responsibility for the success or failure of an administrative state. Further diminishing the stakes, they were deciding cases against mere individuals, not the government. They therefore, as in any other lawsuit, considered the factual and legal questions on their merits.

Since at least the beginning of the twentieth century, however, the courts increasingly have heard challenges to administrative decisions on appeals from the administrative agencies. Whereas an affected person once would have brought a cause of action for damages in a trial court, he now typically petitions an appellate court for "judicial review." This appeals process may look efficient, for it integrates administrative and judicial efforts, allowing the judicial participation to follow immediately on administrative decisions. But it often has reduced the courts to extensions of the administrative state, nearly making the court proceedings yet another layer of administrative hearings.

Rather than feel responsibility merely to the law and the individual parties, many judges therefore feel responsibility to the government—a responsibility to make the administrative system function effectively. As a result, there is "a sort of partnership . . . between agency and court," and even the Supreme Court intones that these institutions "are to be deemed collaborative instrumentalities of justice."[10]

---

c. Note the underlying distinction here between a new cause of action and an appeal or other reconsideration in a higher tribunal. In an appeal, the question conventionally is whether the judgment below must be reversed on account of error. In a new cause of action, the question is whether the defendant must correct, or pay damages for, an injury or other violation of right.

Thus, even before one gets to the question of judicial deference, one must recognize that the role of the courts has shifted, with profound consequences both for administrators and for judges. Whereas judges once heard independent actions against executive officers, they now are the final participants in an appeals process that oversees administrative agencies. The result is that administrators feel liberated from the constraints of law, and judges feel bound to make the administrative system work.[d]

A Class above the Law

Before turning to the implications for deference, this chapter must linger on the implications for government officers. One of the basic features of Anglo-American law has been that no person is above the law. From this perspective, although government has sovereign immunity, government officers are subject to the same laws as other members of the society. All of this, however, has been transformed by the protection of officers from damages actions, for the result is to distinguish them as a specially protected class and elevate them above the law.

d. One of the ways that the judges have attempted to integrate the judicial and the administrative systems is through the doctrine of exhaustion. The doctrine ordinarily applies as a matter of comity among the different legal systems of different sovereigns—for example, a federal court will expect a plaintiff to exhaust his remedies in state court, or tribal court, before he can seek redress in federal court. As applied to administrative law, however, the doctrine does not concern the exhaustion of remedies under another sovereign. Instead, it protects the federal executive—as if it were a separate sovereign, with its own court system—by requiring parties to exhaust their administrative remedies before they can enter federal court.

The nineteenth-century approach to such questions was simply to inquire whether the action of an executive officer was final—that is, whether it was a decision of his department and thus of the executive. For example, where a subordinate officer reached a tentative decision (really a recommendation), which was not effective until a decision by the secretary of his department, the subordinate officer's decision was not final, and only when the secretary made his decision could there be a cause of action. The executive thereby could enjoy layers of reconsideration, it could place the onus of final decisions on relatively high-level officers, and it could protect their subordinates from litigation.

Contemporary doctrine, however, goes beyond inquiries about finality. In addition, it requires persons to exhaust their administrative remedies before suing an agency and sometimes also before bringing an appeal from an agency decision. Thus, even where an administrative law judge reaches a final decision for his department, the courts often will not allow a remedy in the courts if an administrative appeal (to the secretary or some review board) is available. This doctrine is said to rest on considerations of both judicial and administrative efficiency, but especially where an independent cause of action exists under state or federal law, how can the judges deny access to the courts on grounds that it would inconvenience themselves or the defendant? At least in such cases, where a cause of action already has arisen, the exhaustion of remedies amounts to little more than the exhaustion of plaintiffs by denying them access to the courts and the equal protection of the law.

Contrasting Traditions

There once was a sharp contrast between the common law and the civilian treatment of officers. Anglo-American law dealt with officials like other persons, and officials therefore were accountable for their unlawful acts, even where they acted under an official warrant. The civilian-derived law that developed on the Continent, however, elevated officials as a nearly distinct class; they therefore were not legally accountable for their acts, as long as they were following orders—an excuse the Nazis made infamous.

Of course, even at common law, officers enjoyed some protection, but only while they rested on the law. They could rely on facially valid warrants to justify ministerial acts, but where their authorization was facially unlawful, or where they went beyond it, they no longer were clothed with lawful authority, but stood alone, personally liable. At that point, rather than enjoy the protection of the law, they were acting unlawfully and were subject to the law in the same way as anyone else. For example, when a warrant or other order evidently went beyond the issuing officer's lawful authority, the acting officer could find no safety in it.

Similarly, officers traditionally were protected in their discretionary acts while they remained within their lawful discretion or jurisdiction. This doctrine protected judges in their exercise of judgment, and it also protected executive officers when they acted with discernment to determine legal duties—this being why they sometimes were called "quasi-judicial" officers. It even protected them in their wilful discretion when they were distributing benefits or doing other things that were within executive control. But executive officers were not protected when they exercised judgment to make binding adjudications or when they exercised will to make binding rules, as such things were beyond their lawful discretion or jurisdiction.

Put succinctly, officers needed facially lawful warrants for ministerial acts and actual legal authority for discretionary acts. On the whole, therefore, officers could rely only on the law, not on sovereignty or official status.[e]

---

e. Already in English law, the liability of officers was foundational—as was commonly illustrated by two judicial opinions. The judges in the fifteenth century informed Henry VI that if the king commanded a man to arrest another, the second man would have an action of false imprisonment against the first, even if the arrest were done in the king's presence—the point being that a facially unlawful order, even if directly from the king, was no justification for a ministerial act. In the same century, Chief Justice John Markham "told King Edward IV that he could not arrest a man on suspicion of treason or felony, as any of his liege subjects may, because if he does wrong the party cannot have an action"—the principle being that there had to be potential liability for the discretionary act of making an arrest without a warrant. These opinions (usually paired to cover both ministerial and discretionary acts) reached lawyers on

Because the law applied equally to officers and the public, officers tended to think twice before exercising extralegal power. Indeed, to have spared them from damages actions would have placed them above the law and would have denied their victims both the due process and the equal protection of the law. The common law therefore subjected all officers, high and low, to damages actions in the courts, and it will be recalled that Joseph Story thought this conclusion was to some extent secured by the U.S. Constitution.[11]

On the Continent, in contrast, whatever was done officially was considered a sovereign act. Reflecting absolutist civilian traditions, royal officers there and, later, administrative officers were understood to be unaccountable in the ordinary courts for their official acts. At best, they were accountable to the sovereign in prerogative or administrative courts. Thus, like the policies they carried out, they were in a sense outside and above the law.[f]

Immunity for an Official Class

The development of immunity for American government officers has shifted their status toward the Continental model. Although the immunity is not complete, it establishes them as a class largely above the ordinary law—including the ordinary tort law—that applies to other Americans.

Already in the mid-nineteenth century, when American officers sought protection from litigation, judges and legislatures gradually placed executive officers beyond legal remedies. For example, although the judges ulti-

---

both sides of the Atlantic through the writings of Coke and other commentators, and for centuries they framed common law assumptions about officer liability.[*]

f. Looking across the Channel, Albert Dicey wrote that the "most despotic" feature of the *droit administratif* was its tendency "to protect from the supervision or control of the ordinary law courts any servant of the state . . . whilst acting in *bone fide* obedience to the orders of his superiors and, as far as intention goes, in the mere discharge of his official duties." An early-twentieth-century American scholar, James Randall, explained:

It is a well-known principle of our law that government officers . . . are liable in damages for official conduct which results in private injuries, and are subject to prosecution in case such conduct bears a criminal character. In this respect the principles of American and English law differ radically from the administrative law of Europe. The essence of the continental system is to give personal immunity to officers acting under authority, and to accord distinct and separate treatment to official cases in special "administrative courts." Under American and other Anglo-Saxon jurisdictions, however, any governmental officer who injures private rights, either by omission or commission, is, but with few qualifications, subject to civil or criminal action precisely as an ordinary citizen would be. This liability of governmental agents is but one phase of the Anglo-Saxon principle that governments are not above law, and that an officer of the government is not a given a privileged character superior to that of the common law.[*]

mately refused to extend sovereign immunity to executive officers, they increasingly granted them what came to be known as "qualified immunity." This initially was a requirement that plaintiffs show that officers acted with malice or other fault, and in the twentieth century it more generally became a defense for acts that did not violate clearly established law.

One way or the other, the result was to protect government officers as a class against personal liability for most of their administrative decisions. In the words of Frank Goodnow, whereas the law traditionally had "regarded officers as subject to the law of the land in the same way as ordinary individuals," it now follows the civilian-derived Continental assumption that they are "a privileged class."[12]

The degree to which this immunity places executive officers above the law becomes evident when one contrasts it to pardons and indemnification. After an officer violates the law, and before he is punished, a pardon can protect him as an individual from criminal penalty. Similarly, after his violation of law, and before he is forced to pay damages, an indemnification statute can protect him and other officers from civil remedies. Now, however, officers as a class are largely protected from personal responsibility under law long before they have done anything wrong. The result is to remove their incentives to conform to law—indeed, to liberate them as a class from the tort and property laws that apply to other Americans.

The immunity of officers is thus a profound change in the relationship of individuals to government and in expectations of equal protection. It once could be taken for granted that officials and members of the public were equally under the law and thus were equally protected by the law. Now, however, like Continental officials, American officials are a privileged class, whose official acts are not equally subject to law, thus leaving other Americans unprotected by it.

Limits on Suits and the Extent of Power

The immediate basis for judicial deference apparently was the introduction of standards of fault and other limits on suits against officers. These suits were merely a means of redress, but when they were subjected to restrictive limits, they came to define a sphere of administrative conduct that, although not justified by law, was not remediable at law. In other words, there was a widening gap between the law that demarcated the liberty of subjects and the remedies that delineated the liability of officers.

Up through the late nineteenth century, Americans enjoyed a hodgepodge of remedies against wayward executive officers. They could bring actions against them for damages; they could seek injunctions; they could turn to writs of certiorari or mandamus. These remedies left gaps in the recourse against government, but they also offered sharp constraints. Gradually, however, the most forceful remedies, those for damages, were whittled away, until the remaining claims seemed to demarcate a policy of judicial deference.

For example, although executive officers traditionally could rely on facially lawful warrants, they otherwise could not defend themselves from actions for damages by claiming that they were following official orders or usage. Instead, if their authorization was not facially lawful—for example, if they had only an executive warrant to justify a constraint on the public— they could offer their official orders only in mitigation of damages. Officers under this old approach thus remained vulnerable in the courts, and they therefore always had to consider for themselves the lawfulness of what they did.

Increasingly, however, plaintiffs were required to show fault, with the result that officers usually could avoid liability by showing that they had merely followed official orders or usage. Individual officers thereby began to become mere instruments of official power, who rested secure under the mantle of official rules, instructions, decisions, interpretations, or practices.

Although this was judicial deference to administrative policies merely for purposes of officer liability, it did not stop with liability. Already at this point, it was only a hop and a skip to a broader deference and even an outright power of administrative rulemaking, interpretation, and adjudication. One observer in 1910 noted that the courts exhibited "an unfortunate timidity" in actions against officers and that the judges tended to treat the decisions of executive officers as "conclusive" on "the scope and application of the laws which they are to carry out." Less troubled about this development, Frank Goodnow relied on cases that limited remedies against executive officers to assert the "conclusiveness of administrative determinations."[13]

The point was that when complainants could no longer easily bring actions for damages against officers, they had to rely on other remedies, such as writs of mandamus, which directly interfered with executive acts, and which therefore were available only in very limited circumstances. The narrow standard for issuing these writs thus became the basis for broader language about judicial deference. In mandamus cases, for example, the courts generalized that they would not interfere in executive actions where the executive officers acted within their jurisdiction or official duties. Of course, as John Dickinson pointed out, "[t]he fact that the courts will not issue a writ of mandamus in a given situation" should not be taken to mean that they "would not review the executive action . . . in some other way," but the standard for writs of mandamus led the courts to adopt "broader language than they would otherwise have used"—the result being to accord administrative officers "a final power of interpreting the law."[14]

This judicial deference to administrative interpretation received prominent recognition in 1984, in the *Chevron* case (which will be discussed shortly). But already more than a half century earlier such deference was recognized to be well established as a delayed or "retarded development in the law of mandamus." As put then, mandamus seemed to leave an executive officer with a power of "interpreting ambiguous statutes relating to his department."[15]

Deference and damages have thus been intimately connected. When executive officers secured protection from damages actions, the remaining standards for relief became foundations for judicial deference. The safety of administrators thereby established safety for administrative power.

Yet a protective standard (let alone an overly protective standard) for proceedings against executive officers cannot establish the lawfulness of their power. Put another way, the attempt of legal realism to define rights by their remedies comes at a cost. Restrictions on remedies become evidence of a poverty of rights, as if limitations on remedies could legalize power that the Constitution barred.

Contemporary Judicial Deference

By now, the deference is pervasive. Early-seventeenth-century judges faced continual threats to their independence, and they often bowed to the pressure. But they simultaneously felt obliged to uphold the law and their independent judgment about it, and they therefore generally refused to accept prerogative interpretations of statutes, let alone prerogative determinations of facts. These days, in contrast, judges have ample constitutional protection for their independence, but they systematically defer to administrative agencies.

Statutory Foundations

Over the course of the twentieth century, the deference has acquired statutory foundations. It is not clear, however, how a statute can dictate the standard by which judges determine the unconstitutionality of executive acts. Indeed, it is unclear how a statute can justify the judges in deferring to anything other than the law and their own independent judgment about it.

In evaluating the unconstitutionality of a government act, judges must ask whether there is a conflict between the act and an act of greater obligation. Far from being statutory, this question about contradiction arises from assumptions about the nature of law, which were taken for granted in the Constitution. As Hamilton summarized in the *Federalist*, "If there should happen to be an irreconcileable variance" between two enactments, "that which has the superior obligation and validity ought of course to be preferred."[16] On these foundations, an executive act contrary to law must be held void.

Nonetheless, the Administrative Procedure Act sets forth a different standard of review for administrative acts. It is not usual for statutes to dictate the standard by which judges review the constitutionality or other lawfulness of government acts, but the Administrative Procedure Act recites a series of such standards.

Its standards of review include not only the Constitution and statutes, but also other measures. Most generally, as to both administrative legislation and adjudication, the Administrative Procedure Act states: "The reviewing court shall . . . hold unlawful and set aside agency action, findings, and conclusions found to be . . . arbitrary, capricious, an abuse of discretion, or otherwise not in accordance with law."[17] On this basis, the courts generally tend to uphold administrative action as lawful, unless it is so unreasonable as to be "arbitrary and capricious" or an "abuse of discretion." The result is to protect administrative action unless it goes to these extremes.[g]

The Administrative Procedure Act adds that the reviewing court shall

---

g. In defense of the arbitrary-and-capricious standard, it sometimes is said that the Administrative Procedure Act requires a higher standard for administrative acts than for acts of Congress. For example, the statute requires courts to set aside agency actions that are arbitrary or capricious—a limitation that courts cannot apply to statutes.

It should be no surprise, however, that the courts enforce acts of Congress, as long as they are constitutional, for Congress is the institution to which the Constitution grants lawmaking authority. The executive, on the other hand, lacks such authority, and its efforts at binding legislation therefore do not deserve to be enforced at all.

In this context, the effect of the arbitrary and capricious standard is to legitimize unlawful extralegal power. The judges interpret the Administrative Procedure Act to mean that, although they can set aside an agency action for being arbitrary and capricious, they otherwise generally should defer to reasonable agency rules, adjudications, and interpretations. As a result, what looks like an additional statutory limitation becomes a cover for ignoring the constitutional limitations that bar extralegal power and associated violations of constitutional rights.

"hold unlawful and set aside agency action, findings, and conclusions" found to be "unsupported by substantial evidence."[18] At first glance, this standard makes sense—until one realizes that (if taken seriously) it preserves government decisions as long as they rest on at least some evidence, regardless of the weight of contrary evidence. As it happens, the courts nowadays tend to understand the "substantial evidence" standard very much like the "arbitrary and capricious" standard, but at least when reviewing formal adjudications, courts maintain a distinct "substantial evidence" standard, and it therefore has the potential to provide another statutory avenue for deferential review.[h]

A mere statute thus invites the courts to defer in ways they otherwise would avoid, and the courts accept the invitation and run with it. When Congress acts unlawfully, the courts hold its acts void without deference. Similarly, when the executive acts in its nonadministrative capacity—that is, when it does not claim legislative or judicial power—the courts generally hold its unlawful acts void without deference. But when the executive acts in its administrative regime, the courts shy away, refusing to reject administrative acts unless they are so appalling as to be "arbitrary and capricious" or without "substantial evidence." Although the judges do not say as much, they thereby treat administrative power as if it rose above the law and the courts.

Even when an administrative action conflicts with the deferential standards of the Administrative Procedure Act, the judges do not usually hold

---

h. Whatever the "substantial evidence" standard means nowadays, it originated as the measure for overturning jury verdicts. The jury is the constitutionally guaranteed mode of deciding civil and criminal cases, and therefore, ordinarily, a jury verdict can be overturned only if there is no substantial evidence in the record to support it. Of course, an administrative agency is not a jury; indeed, it usually is one of the parties. Nonetheless, the advocates of administrative law argued that judges should review administrative fact-finding as if they were examining the verdict of a jury, and it thus came to be assumed that judges should uphold administrative fact-finding unless it was "unsupported by substantial evidence."

The 1941 Attorney General's Report on Administrative Procedure already complained about the one-sided character of this standard. Under this approach, "if what is called 'substantial evidence' is found anywhere in the record to support conclusions of fact, the courts are said to be obliged to sustain the decision without reference to how heavily the countervailing evidence may preponderate—unless indeed the stage of arbitrary decision is reached." Thus, "the courts need to read only one side of the case and, if they find any evidence there, the administrative action is to be sustained and the record to the contrary is to be ignored." On this account, the report protested that "important litigated issues of fact are in effect conclusively determined in administrative decisions based upon palpable error."

At the same time, the report simply conceded on the larger question. It emphasized that judicial review "should not be too broad and searching or it will hamper administrative efficiency."*

the administrative action void. Courts ordinarily hold an executive action void when it violates the law. According to the Administrative Procedure Act, however, a reviewing court shall "hold unlawful and set aside" any arbitrary or capricious administrative action, and courts understand this to mean that they can "set aside" such an action without going so far as to hold it void. Courts therefore usually remand such an action back to the agency for corrective proceedings—an approach that adds a deferential remedy to an already deferential standard of review.

On behalf of the deference under the Administrative Procedure Act, it is said that Congress is not constitutionally barred from authorizing deference—as if Congress can detract from the office of the judges. The office of the judges, however, was an element of the Constitution's grant of judicial power, and it required the judges to exercise independent judgment in accord with the law of the land. Put another way, when the Constitution authorized judicial power, it took for granted that judges, by their nature, had such a duty.[19]

This judicial duty was recognized very early, because it was the foundation of what nowadays is called "judicial review." When writing about the judicial power of North Carolina in 1786, James Iredell explained: "The duty of the power I conceive, in all cases, is to decide according to the laws of the state," and as "the constitution is a law of the state," a statute "inconsistent with the constitution is void." Or as put by John Marshall in *Marbury v. Madison*, where "both the law and the constitution apply to a particular case" the court "must determine which of these conflicting rules governs the case," this being "of the very essence of judicial duty."[20] Judicial review, in other words, is entailed by judicial duty—a duty that accompanies judicial power and that requires judges to exercise their own independent judgment in following the law. And another result of this duty is that a mere statute cannot justify the judges in abandoning their independent judgment or in following extralegal rules or interpretations.

As if this were not enough, the U.S. Constitution adds that no person shall be "deprived of life, liberty, or property, without due process of law." If this means anything, it surely requires a judge not to defer to one of the parties, let alone to defer systematically to the government. Nonetheless, on the basis of a mere statute, the judges generally defer.

The next step is to examine the varieties of deference, for the judges give different sorts of deference to different kinds of administrative decisions. The deference to administrative orders and warrants has already been noted in chapter 13. In addition, as now will be seen, there is rule deference, interpretation deference, and fact deference.

Rule Deference

The most basic judicial deference is the deference to binding administrative rules. When James I attempted to impose legal duties through his proclamations, the judges held this void without showing any deference, and after the prerogative tribunals tried to govern through their rules, decrees, and regulations, Parliament abolished the tribunals themselves. The English thereby rejected extralegal lawmaking, and in the next century the American people echoed the English constitutional response by placing all legislative power in Congress. Nonetheless, the courts nowadays defer to the executive's extralegal lawmaking.

The deference to administrative rules comes in at least two gradations. Rules that seem relatively minor to the judges get nearly complete deference. In contrast, the rules that seem important to them tend to get "hard look" review, which sounds tough. Certainly, it is tougher than abject deference, but it merely requires the courts to "consider whether the decision was based on consideration of the relevant factors and whether there has been a clear error of judgment." Indeed, the agency need only "examine the relevant data and articulate a satisfactory explanation of its action, including a rational connection between the facts found and the choice made." Of course, there are many reasons for adopting a rule, and thus if a rule "reasonably advances at least one of those objectives," and if the agency's "decisionmaking process was regular," the courts will uphold the rule.[21] Thus, even "hard look" review is utterly deferential and very different from simply deciding whether the executive has acted unlawfully.

Of course, the courts generally uphold acts of Congress as along as they are constitutional, without any inquiry into Congress's reasoning, but this makes sense, because Congress enjoys the Constitution's lawmaking authority. In contrast, the executive does not have any such authority, and its binding legislation therefore deserves no deference.

When the executive acts in its ordinary, constitutional spheres of action —for example, when distributing benefits—the courts show no deference to its unconstitutional acts. When, however, the executive acts administratively in imposing rules, the courts systematically defer—as if the administrative character of these executive acts placed them above regular judicial treatment. Of course, there are some ordinary spheres of executive action in which the courts say they defer to the executive, as in many questions of foreign policy, but the courts in these cases are really deferring to the law—in particular, to the Constitution's allocation of such questions to the executive. Administrative law thus stands out as a form of government action in which the courts are deferring not to the Constitution's allocation of power, but to the executive.

This deference to the executive is incompatible with the judicial duty to follow the law. Deference to the ruler—in particular, deference to the ruler's extralegal power—has long been recognized as incompatible with the duty to follow the law, and judges therefore have traditionally been bound to evaluate royal or executive conduct as they would the conduct of any other party to a proceeding. Now, however, when the executive acts administratively, the courts act with deference—following the administrative rules rather than the law.

Judges tend to excuse themselves on the ground that they lack expertise, protesting that "[w]e are not engineers, computer modelers, economists or statisticians, although many of the documents in this record require such expertise—and more."[22] But even among experts, technical data does not resolve difficult policy questions. On the contrary, in technically based matters, ranging from health care to the environment, disputes are as intense as in other areas, and this is why all legislation inevitably is a political act, which the Constitution leaves to Congress, not to administrators.

It therefore is not the difficulty of technical knowledge, but the extralegal character of administrative legislation that creates the problem. Rather than have to decide matters requiring scientific expertise, the judges need only confront the question of law: They need only decide whether the legislation has been adopted in an act of Congress.

Unwilling to confront this question about the institutional procedures for lawmaking, the judges instead ask whether the executive has met procedures for rational thinking. Judges ordinarily must accept the obligation of statutes that are made through the regular lawmaking process, which involves a series of fixed institutional steps. There is, however, no fixed institutional process for an irregular mode of governance, and the Administrative Procedure Act therefore substitutes its inquiry about arbitrary and capricious lawmaking and abuses of discretion. Taking up this hint, the judges defer to administrative rules where they have been made in a manner that seems more or less rational—the mental process thus filling the gap in the institutional process.

The substitution of mental process at least offers the judges a sense of having done their duty. Rather than admit that they are prostrating themselves before administrative lawmaking, they can stand on principle and engage in at least the formality of judicial review. Their principles, however, are not those of the Constitution, and the review is candidly a matter of deference to power—a power that could not survive ordinary, nondeferential review under law. Thus, although the judges do not say they are deferring to a power above the law, it is difficult to understand what they are doing, if they are not deferring to this sort of absolute power.

Interpretation Deference

The courts further develop their deference by deferring to administrative interpretation. The prerogative courts claimed to be able to make law by interpreting in the interstices of statutes, and in defense of this interpretation, they demanded deference from the courts of law. As has been seen, however, the judges of these courts responded that only they had the authority to expound the law, and they were confirmed in this by Parliament's abolition of the prerogative courts. Today, however, the courts systematically defer to administrative interpretation.

The Supreme Court notoriously explained "the principle of deference to administrative interpretations" in *Chevron U.S.A. Inc. v. Natural Resources Defense Council*. According to this case, where a relevant statute is "silent or ambiguous" as to whether the agency can act on a particular matter, a court must accept the agency's interpretation if it is at least a "permissible construction." In other words, the question is not whether the agency's interpretation of its statutory authority is the correct interpretation of the statute, but merely whether the agency's action is "a reasonable choice within a gap left by Congress." Predictably, in justifying this highly deferential approach, the Supreme Court added that judges "are not experts in the field" and that agencies can "rely upon the incumbent administration's views of wise policy."[23]

Obviously, agency interpretations are an opportunity for administrative legislation, and the judges therefore worry that *Chevron* deference allows lawmaking interpretations to evade the notice-and-comment process required for informal lawmaking. Concerned about this evasion—though not the larger evasion of the Constitution's lawmaking process—the judges conclude that, where agencies in effect are altering their rules by means of interpretation, they can get *Chevron* deference only by adopting their interpretations with notice-and-comment procedures.

Administrative agencies, however, can adopt lawmaking interpretations by other means, including proffers of guidance, office manuals, letter rulings, and even briefs. Does the *Chevron* deference to notice-and-comment interpretation mean that these other interpretations do not get deference?

The answer comes in so-called *Skidmore* deference—a doctrine named after an older case, *Skidmore v. Swift & Co*. In a series of cases, the Supreme Court makes clear that, even where agency interpretations are not adopted with notice and comment, they are "entitled to respect." In this lessor sort of deference, the Court does not treat an administrative interpretation as controlling, but nonetheless, to some degree, defers to it. Revealingly, the Court defers to executive interpretations even in mere opinion letters and in Customs Service ruling letters—the sort of executive interpretations that (as seen in chapters 6 and 15) are as old as the nation and that traditionally were not binding or given any special respect by the courts.[24]

Beyond the deference shown to administrative interpretations of statutes is that shown to administrative interpretations of regulations. As by now should be expected, the Supreme Court defers, saying bluntly, "We must give substantial deference to an agency's interpretation of its own regulations." The Court explains that if a requirement "is a creature of the Secretary's own regulations, his interpretation of it is, under our jurisprudence, controlling unless plainly erroneous or inconsistent with the regulation." Of course, the Court would not defer to an act of Congress interpreting a prior act, and (as observed by John Manning) it therefore should not defer to an agency's interpretations of its own regulations. Nonetheless, the Court concludes that because administrative interpretation is a "creature" of administrative power, it must get deference.[25]

Like the deference to rulemaking, the deference to interpretation is an abandonment of judicial office. The Constitution grants judicial power to the courts, consisting of judges, who were assumed to have an office or duty of independent judgment. The Constitution thereby establishes a structure for providing parties with the independent judgment of the judges, and this means their own, personal judgment, not deference to the judgment of the executive, let alone the executive when it is one of the parties. Nonetheless, the judges defer to judgments of the executive, and they thereby deliberately deny the benefit of judicial power to private parties and abandon the central feature of their office as judges.

This abandonment of office is particularly striking as to interpretation, because the judges have a distinctive authority to expound the law. Legislation belongs to Congress, but the exposition of law belongs to the judges. And (as Chief Justice Coke made clear already in the *Case of Proclamations* and in *Bonham's Case*), the judges cannot give up this power in deference to prerogative or administrative interpretation.[26] Instead, they must personally expound the law, according to their own conscience.[i] What, then, are they doing when they defer to administrative interpretation?

---

i. This argument was made already by Samuel Rutherford—the seventeenth-century political theorist. Like Chief Justice Coke, he faced royalist arguments that the king could be "an

Of course, when Congress demands deference to its interpretation of its statutes, the courts brush aside the claim as presumptuous. Similarly, when a president issues a "signing statement," the courts do not defer to it as an interpretation of the law. But when administrators interpret, and even candidly make law in their "interpretations," the judges speak of deference and respect, and this is puzzling, unless the administrators enjoy a power above the law.[27, j]

Fact Deference

A final sort of judicial deference concerns administrative determinations of facts. Rather than rely on juries, or even themselves, to decide questions of fact, the judges largely defer to administrative findings, as long as there is some evidence to support them. In other words, the judges follow the Administrative Procedure Act and therefore do not ask whether the record as a

---

interpreter of the law according to that super-dominion of absolute power, that he hath above the law." Rutherford responded by observing that the "expounding of the law judicially is an act of judging, and so a personal and incommunicable act, so as I can no more judge and expound the law according to another man's conscience, than I can believe with another man's soul, or understand with another man's understanding, see with another man's eye: The king's pleasure therefore cannot be the rule of the inferior judge's conscience."*

j. Some scholars defend judicial deference to administrative power on grounds of departmentalism. From this perspective, each department or branch has authority, within its sphere, to interpret the Constitution as to the department's own constitutional powers in relation to the other departments. This view was embraced by James Madison and some other Virginians in the 1780s, and although they did not suggest that it might justify administrative power, contemporary scholars have deployed it to this effect.

As it happens, departmentalism was not widely accepted in the late eighteenth century outside Virginia. Instead, in the more conventional approach to interpretation, only the judges had an office of independent judgment in accord with the law of the land. Accordingly, only the judges had an office of expounding the law, and this gave authority to their expositions. This understanding of judicial authority was centuries old, and even Madison did not question it outside structural constitutional questions.

More to the point, the departmentalist view of interpretation offers little comfort on judicial deference. Although it can justify the executive in interpreting its own constitutional powers in relation to the other departments, it cannot justify the executive in relying on its constitutional interpretations in relation to the public—for example, when denying their constitutional rights to have their cases decided by courts, with real judges, with juries, and with other due process of law.

Nor can the departmentalist argument justify the judges in giving up their own independent judgment in expounding the law, whether the Constitution or statutes. The whole point of the departmentalist view is that the different departments have equal interpretative authority to expound their constitutional power within their spheres of power. Thus, whatever departmentalism shows about the executive's power to interpret, it does not thereby displace the power and, indeed, the duty of the judges to exercise their own judgment in expounding the law in their cases.*

whole supports an administrative decision, but merely whether it contains evidence that could support it. This sort of deference, unsurprisingly, tends to reach the entire question of whether there has been a violation—what used to be a jury's guilty verdict. The fact deference therefore usually becomes a broader deference to administrative adjudications.

When administrative agencies adopt rules, and even more frequently when they adjudicate, they rely on evidence, which they often preserve in a written administrative record. The Administrative Procedure Act gives significance to this sort of record by specifying that when a court reviews an administrative decision, "the court shall review the whole record or those parts of it cited by a party." Courts thus are to review the agency's record rather than rehear evidence before a jury.[28]

Accentuating this focus on the administrative record, the Administrative Procedure Act provides for preenforcement judicial review in courts of appeals. It thereby channels most judicial reconsiderations directly to the appellate courts, which are accustomed to reviewing written records and do not hold jury trials.

The overall effect is to put courts in a position in which they defer to the facts as developed on the administrative record and even as determined by the agency. Indeed, it long ago was theorized that agencies serve as juries for the courts, and although the theory did not flourish (as it drew too much attention to the absence of juries), it accurately describes the reality.[29]

The courts justify themselves by saying that they are deferring to the expertise of administrators, but one of the great advantages of having jurors is to take decisions out of the hands of government officials, lest they be biased in favor of government. It would be bad enough for the courts to defer to juries of randomly chosen experts, but the courts are at best deferring to government-chosen government experts. Although such persons have been extolled as unbiased, they nonetheless are apt to have the precommitments of government employees. Worse, they are apt to have the precommitments of those who are employed in exercising extralegal power. The expertise of administrators therefore offers no reassurance about the transfer of power from juries to agencies.

Instead of being candid about the displacement of juries, the courts engage in a sort of doublespeak. They speak of an *appeal* from the *decision* of an administrative *judge*, based on the *record* arising from his *hearing*. Such words dignify the administrative proceedings, but they cannot hide the reality that there is no underlying trial court, nor any court hearing, nor any final judgment, nor any court record, nor any judge or jury. Instead, there usually is mere deference—deference to the facts as declared by one party, the prosecuting agency.

This fact deference violates several constitutional principles. It violates the Constitution's grant of judicial power to the courts, and its guarantee of due process of law. Perhaps most specifically, it denies Americans their right to trial by jury. At the very least, when a court tolerates the administrative evasion of this right, the court is in error. More seriously, when a court defers to administrative findings of facts, it allows a mere party to supplant a jury as the court's fact finder, and the court itself thereby violates the Constitution. It is one thing for a court to be in error about a constitutional violation, but quite another for it to engage in its own violation.

A Jurisprudence of Deference

The overall result is an entire jurisprudence of deference. This book has argued that administrative lawmaking and adjudication return to a version of the prerogative power claimed by James I. This argument, however, does not go far enough with respect to the current deference to administrative power, for not even James I got such consistent deference to his proclamations, regulations, interpretations, and adjudications.

In some ways the old deference to prerogative power was worse than the current deference to administrative power. Certainly, the atmospherics were worse. The old deference did not enjoy the appearance of regularity under the Administrative Procedure Act, and rather than arise from rationalistic acknowledgments of administrative expertise, it came in response to imperious royal demands for obsequiousness.

In other respects, however, the current deference is more serious. At least in the past, when courts reviewed prerogative cases, they did not abandon their regular practices to accommodate the Crown. In particular, courts did not deny a jury or otherwise defer to prerogative fact-finding; they did not usually adopt a special, permissive standard of review; they did not defer to prerogative interpretations of statutes; they did not usually recognize prerogative rules as legally binding. Indeed, the judges often stood up to the Crown, and although some bowed to the prerogative, they later were impeached or otherwise condemned for this. In such ways, the past deference was not entirely deferential, and the current deference is much more systematic.

James I expected his judges literally to bow before him. But even when Chief Justice Coke had to get down on his knees before his king, he refused to defer. He kept on speaking his mind, exercising his independent judgment. In this spirit, he and his colleagues repudiated the king's fantasies that the judges should defer to the rules and interpretations put forward by prerogative tribunals. Eventually Coke was dismissed for his temerity, but his common law understanding of judicial office survived to become a foundation of the constitutional vision of government through the law and the courts. In this vision, judges have an office of independent judgment in accord with the law of the land, and they therefore cannot defer to anyone else's judgment, let alone anyone else's will.

Nowadays, however, the judges speak not of duty, but of deference. Whereas in the past, at least some judges, in defiance of threats, struggled to preserve their independence and the supremacy of the law, all of the judges now submit to the contemporary version of the absolute prerogative—the power beyond and above the law. In the abstract, they still maintain the ideal of the supremacy of the law, as enforced by the courts, but in particular doctrines they create all sorts of escape hatches down which they pursue judicial deference. As put by Thurman Arnold, the entire structure of administrative law was "equipped with noiseless elevators and secret stairways, by means of which the choice was always open either to take a bold judicial stand or make a dignified escape."[30]

At best, judges rely on deference to avert their eyes from administrative power, as if anxious not to recognize it for what it is. More soberingly, although personally protected in tenure and salary, they seem to fear for their institution, questioning whether it really can stand up to the administrative state.[31] Either way, they abandon the supremacy of the law of the land and their office of independent judgment in accord with this law.

They undoubtedly face a more profound predicament than did Coke, for he could hope for popular or at least professional vindication against prerogative power. In contrast, the judges today must worry that, in a democratized republic, popular power will be aligned with the administrative state. They therefore seem to think they should bow to their fears and defer to extralegal power. But why bother saving the court at the cost of giving up on the law?

James I could not have imagined that his vision of absolute power would finally enjoy deference from republican rather than royal judges. Such, however, is the strange truth. Federal judges adamantly insist on their independence, and they would take umbrage at any hint that they have corrupted themselves by deferring to anyone else's judgment or will—whether that of Congress or even of other judges. Nonetheless, when confronted by administrative power, they speak in terms of deference—a sweeping deference that goes far beyond anything heard from the most subservient judges in the history of the common law.

෧෧෧

The judges thus have played a key role in reviving extralegal power. As Roscoe Pound recognized a century ago, "Nor is the legislature alone in bringing back this extralegal—if not anti-legal element to our public law." Since 1880, "the judiciary has begun to fall into line, and . . . powers which fifty years ago would have been held purely judicial and jealously guarded from executive exercise are now decided to be administrative only and are cheerfully conceded to boards and commissions."[32]

In deferring to administrative power, the judges avoid holding it unlawful, but they do not really give it the legitimacy of law. An extralegal regime can survive only by securing judicial deference—by standing to some degree above the law and thus escaping judgment in accord with the law. The deference, however, does not really alter the character of such a regime. Regardless of the deference, administrative power remains outside the law, and because of the deference, it evidently stands above the law. In both ways, it reverts to a preconstitutional vision of power.

PART IV

Consolidated Power

In creating an extralegal system of governance, administrative law also consolidates power. This point often is discussed as a matter of the separation of powers, but it actually is broader and more dangerous: It is a reversion to the third element of absolute power. Parts I and II showed how administrative law revives extralegal power, and part III showed how it resuscitates supralegal power. Part IV now shows how administrative law also restores absolutism by consolidating power.

In other words, administrative law harks back not merely to the time before the adoption of the United States Constitution, but all the way to the early Middle Ages. It then was commonplace to imagine that government power belonged to a single person or group that would be sufficiently wise, forceful, and judicious that it could be entrusted with all government power.

Since the late Middle Ages, however, the development of law, at least in Anglo-American lands, has run in another direction, largely in response to the increasingly fragmented nature of society—that is, in response to the specialization associated with sociological modernization. In societies that developed in this direction, the divided character of authority left much freedom—freedom for individuals, for estates or classes, and thereby also for different institutions. Rather than resist this, some western nations preserved their freedom by recognizing specialized and otherwise divided powers in government. They thereby adapted their governments to the nature of their societies, and no nation pursued this approach more systematically than the United States.

Administrative law therefore is a profound counter-development. It consolidates the different powers back into one branch of government, and

it thus deprives Americans of some of the most basic structural foundations of their freedom.

Put sociologically, administrative law and constitutional law take very
different approaches to the fractured character of modernity. The U.S. Constitution responds to specialization and other divisions in society with a
carefully specialized and divided government, thus allowing the society to
preserve its freedom through institutions adapted to its character. In contrast, administrative law responds to the complexity of modernized society
with administrative commands—as if the only way to deal with a complex
society were to confront it with consolidated state power.

This consolidating tendency is traced below in chapters devoted to the
unspecialized, undivided, unrepresentative, subdelegated, and unfederal
character of administrative power. In each chapter, it will become apparent how the Constitution's specialized and fragmented structure of government has given way to something very different.

SEVENTEEN

Unspecialized

Defenders of administrative law candidly acknowledge that its consolidation of powers conflicts with the separation of powers. But they offer reassurances that the Constitution requires only a separation of branches and that any stricter separation is undesirable.

The separation of powers, however, was a specialization of powers. It therefore was not so much a separation of the branches of government as, more basically, a matter of distinguishing the three specialized powers of government and vesting each in its own specialized part of government.

It thus becomes clear why the administrative consolidation of power is so dangerous. By cutting through the specialization, administrative law creates an unspecialized irregular regime alongside the specialized regular government. It thereby threatens the structural foundations of American government and freedom.

Separation of Powers or Separation of Branches?

There are several scholarly debates over separation. There is a historical controversy as to when the separation of powers developed; there also is a legal controversy about whether the separation of powers is satisfied by a functional balance of powers. Before reaching these questions, however, this chapter must take note of the dispute as to whether one should focus on a separation of powers or merely a separation of branches.

If the Constitution's separation means keeping apart only the branches of government, not the powers they exercise, then its conflict with the administrative consolidation of powers is minimal and does not require much attention. If, however, separation requires a separation of powers, then the conflict is apt to be more substantial.

Although each vision of separation has had its adherents, aspects of both visions are evident in American constitutions. There is ample evidence that the separation of powers was the pervasive underlying theory. Yet even when not recast in terms of a separation of branches, the separation of powers implied at least some separation of the branches. Accordingly, most American constitutions, including the U.S. Constitution, carried out the separation of powers by granting the separate powers to separate branches of government, subject to a host of minor exceptions.[1]

This matters, as already hinted, because it has become commonplace to defend the administrative consolidation of powers on the ground that the branches of government remain separate. The Constitution's separation of branches, however, was merely derivative of its underlying separation of powers. It therefore is not possible to escape the problem by speaking about the remaining separation of branches. Instead, it is necessary to focus on the separation of powers.

Separation As Specialization

The separation of powers assumes a specialization of powers. To be precise, it is a separation of specialized powers into specialized institutions. Specialization is not a familiar way of thinking about the separation of powers, but it reveals how much the administrative consolidation departs from the Constitution. It will also (in the next section) suggest one of the dangers of the consolidation and the corresponding advantage of the separation of powers.

From Individuals to Government

The specialization of powers was long thought to be discernible in human nature. The specialization seemed the ideal of individual self-government, and it thereby became the model for political government. Although this derivation from individuals may initially seem little more than a historical curiosity, it offers a preliminary hint of the importance of specialized powers for all rational decisionmaking, individual or institutional.

In governing their own lives, individuals traditionally were thought to exercise their faculties or powers: intellect, will, and force. In other words, they had to understand or discern, they had to chose or decide, and they had to act. Such powers came to be idealized as natural, not so much because individuals predictably exercised each in a distinct manner as because it seemed that each individual could reach his potential by doing so. By idealizing distinct exercises of judgment, will, and force, individuals could become more self-conscious about each power, and so could do better in discerning, choosing, and acting.

Of course, not all commentators were confident that the will naturally followed the judgment of the understanding. On the contrary, many writers concluded that the will naturally rebelled against judgment—a conclusion that later found expression in psychological ideas about the id and the super-ego. One way or another, the faculties of the soul—what nowadays would be called the mind—seemed to include both will and understanding, and the exercise of will seemed to dictate the physical acts or power of the body.

This vision of the specialized powers of individuals was soon extended to the powers of government. As early as the fourteenth century, some commentators speculated about what would become the familiar tripartite division of powers: lawmaking will, executive force, and judicial understanding or judgment.[2] In this analysis, the two mental faculties each belonged to a distinct branch of government—lawmaking will to the legislative body, and understanding or judgment to the courts. To these were added the physical faculty of force, by which the executive carried out the will of the body politic. The English were among those who sometimes recognized this division, as when a fourteenth-century treatise on Parliament discussed legislation "against defect of laws original, judicial, and executive."[3]

For a long time, this tripartite specialization had little visible application in England. Formally, Parliament was the king's high court, and the judges were his servants, and thus, if there were tripartite powers, they were not clearly aligned with distinct institutions. Indeed, it was conventional to say that the king in Parliament had the legislative power and that the judges were part of the king's executive power.

When thinking about individuals, however, the English were well aware of the elements of the tripartite scheme, and they increasingly held it out as an ideal for their institutions. They had, since the Middle Ages, emphasized the distinctive office of the judges in exercising judgment rather than lawmaking will, and they had upheld the ideal that the judges should not be influenced by the Crown in their cases.[4] In developing the power of Parliament, moreover, the English had long made clear that the king alone did not have legislative power. Accordingly, when Parliament in the seventeenth century finally defeated the king's judicial and lawmaking ambitions, English commentators could regularly generalize about the three powers—that executive power lay in the king, legislative power in Parliament, and judicial power in the courts. Of course, some Englishmen were slow to recognize that the judicial power lay not in House of Lords, but more realistically in independent judges; and some still thought that the king's executive power was ministerial rather than more generally a matter of force.[a] Nonetheless, there remained no serious obstacles to concluding that there were three powers of government, located in the king, the legislature, and the judges.[5]

Thus, by the beginning of the next century, Chief Justice Holt could simply assume in passing that the English government was divided into the familiar powers, saying that "the people" had elected their representatives in the House of Commons with "power and authority to act legislatively, not ministerially or judicially."[6] Evidently, the specialized powers of individuals were also becoming the specialized powers of government.[b]

A Foundation of Liberty

The specialization of government powers was not merely historical. On the contrary, it came to be viewed as a foundation of liberty.

This point was made as to prerogative or administrative power by the early-eighteenth-century essayist James Pitt. Looking back on Charles I's prerogative exercise of both legislative and judicial powers, Pitt recognized that the combination of powers threatened liberty. Under Charles, the Privy Council exercised both "a legislative, and an executive power; for they first met in the council chamber, and sent forth proclamations as law; and then the same men went into the Star Chamber, and High Commission Courts, and executed those laws, which before, as privy counselors, they

a. The nature of executive power long remained ambiguous. Legislative will and judicial office were understood as institutional manifestations of faculties of the soul, and therefore, already very early, they enjoyed conventional definitions. The definition of executive power, however, remained open to dispute even as late as the founding of the United States.

Some commentators understood it to be at least the power of executing the law, and from this perspective they said it was ministerial. St. George Tucker, for example, said that the executive power, in its "abstract definition," was "the duty of carrying the laws into effect." Others recognized that, if this power was not legislative or judicial, it was everything other than the faculties of the soul or mind, and this meant it was the entire power of exercising the physical force of the government. As put by Hamilton, the powers of government were those of will, judgment, and force.*

b. There remain historians (such as Gordon Wood) who largely deny the early development of ideals about the separation of powers. Their arguments, however, rest mainly on evidence from the slow and incomplete development of separation of powers in state constitutions rather than on evidence about ideals. Of course, inherited institutions were not instantly or systematically adjusted to the ideals, but this does not mean the ideals did not enjoy wide appeal. As suggested above, even the English had long been exploring aspects of the separation of powers.*

had made." By this means "was the constitution absolutely destroyed, and the foundation of all our liberties undermined."[7]

The preservation of liberty through the specialization of powers was most influentially expounded by the French *philosophe* Montesquieu. "When the legislative and executive powers are united in the same person, or in the same body of the magistracy, there can be then no liberty; because apprehensions may arise, lest the same monarch or senate should enact tyrannical laws, to execute them in a tyrannical manner." Similarly, "there is no liberty, if the power of judging be not separated from the legislative and executive powers," lest the judge "be then the legislator" or lest he "behave with all the violence of an oppressor."[8]

Worst of all, however, was the combination of all three powers, when "the same body" could "exercise those three powers . . . of enacting laws, . . . executing the public resolutions, and . . . of judging the crimes or differences of individuals." This was the situation in Turkey, "where the three powers are united in the Sultan's person," and "the subjects groan under the . . . oppression."[9]

Significantly, the problem of unified powers also was apparent in republics, such as those of Italy. To illustrate the danger, Montesquieu pointed to the "state inquisitors" of Venice, who could initiate prosecutions at the instance of anonymous informers. "What a situation must the poor subject be in, under those republics?" Such governments were worse than most European monarchies, for the "same body of the magistracy are possessed, as executors of the laws, of the whole power they have given themselves in quality of legislators," and they therefore could "plunder the state by their general determinations." Likewise, they have the "judiciary power in their hands," and thus "every private citizen may be ruined by their particular decisions."[10]

Nowadays, defenders of administrative law suggest that its consolidation of powers is no danger because the administrative state remains accountable to the people through Congress or the president. Like Montesquieu, however, Americans traditionally recognized the need for separate or specialized powers even in a republic. Jefferson, for example, wrote against a system in which "[a]ll the powers of government, legislative, executive, and judiciary, result to the legislative body." Although such a system was more responsive to the people than administrative law, he concluded that "[t]he concentrating [of] these in the same hands is precisely the definition of despotic government. It will be no alleviation that these powers will be exercised by a plurality of hands, and not by a single one. 173 despots would surely be as oppressive as one. . . . As little will it avail us that they are chosen by ourselves. An elective despotism was not the government we fought for." More generally, Madison wrote in the *Federalist*: "The accumulation of all powers, legislative, executive, and judiciary, in the same hands, whether of one, a few, or many, and whether hereditary, self-appointed, or elective, may justly be pronounced the very definition of tyranny."[11] Even in a republic, the separation of specialized powers was essential.

The Delegation of the Specialized Powers

The separation of powers was established in government by the people when they delegated their powers to the different parts of government. The separation of specialized powers was therefore binding not merely as a background constitutional principle, but more specifically as a result of the people's delegation of the powers.

In the state of nature—the hypothetical condition of individuals prior to the formation of civil government—individuals were bound only by the law of nature, not by civil law, but already then, at least according to John Locke, they had two of the specialized powers. Most basically, individuals in the state of nature were "judges in their own cases." Moreover, "everyone has the executive power of the law of nature"—meaning that, in the state of nature, "every man hath a right to punish the offender, and be executioner of the law of nature."[12] Thus, even in the absence of civil government, every individual had both the judicial and the executive power.

These became tripartite powers when individuals in the state of nature formed themselves into a people or society. At that point, according to Locke, the people acquired legislative power. The people thus seemed to enjoy all three powers, which they then could convey to government.[13]

On this basis, Americans assumed that the people delegated the three specialized powers to government. Edmund Randolph—the attorney general of Virginia—argued in 1782 about his state's constitution that a people "who have either never yet entered into a formal social compact, or having abolished an old one are about to conclude another . . . possess every power, legislative, executive and judiciary." The people in their constitution thus "delineat[ed] the degree, to which they have parted with legislative, executive and judiciary power." As was more succinctly said of the Pennsylvania Constitution, "The legislative, executive, and judicial powers of the people" had been "severally, delegated to different bodies."[14] The specialized powers arose in individuals, and more completely in the people, who then delegated them to the different parts of government.

Caveats

Of course, the definition of the different powers was not always clear. As put by James Madison, "Experience has instructed us that no skill in the science of government has yet been able to discriminate and define, with sufficient certainty, its three great provinces, the Legislative, Executive, and Judiciary."[15] Yet whatever the uncertainty at the edges of each power, there also was much clarity about the natural differences among the specialized powers.

Although the separation of powers was understood to be based in nature, there were many reasons for a constitution to deviate in minor ways from the separation of powers. James Madison explained that "[n]o political truth is certainly of greater intrinsic value," but the branches of government could not be "totally separate and distinct from each other," for each branch needed some "control" over the others.[16]

Accordingly, when state constitutions declared separation as a general principle, there was a danger that separation would become a rigid overgeneralization. Recognizing the difficulty, the New Hampshire Constitution announced the separation of powers with the caveat that the powers of government were to be "kept as separate and independent . . . as is consistent with that chain of connection that binds the whole fabric of the constitution in one dissoluble bond of union and amity."[17] The statement of separation as a general principle seemed to require this open-ended qualification.

Such a limit, however, usually was unnecessary, because most constitutions, including the U.S. Constitution, did not generalize about the ideal of separation. Instead, most constitutions simply granted each specialized power to its own specialized part of government, and then carved out exceptions. The result was very concrete. Rather than idealize the abstract separation of powers, and then recognize an abstract qualification, a typical American constitution carefully established its own separation of powers and then recited specified exceptions.

In this approach, a constitution's grant of specialized powers to different branches of government was the default allocation. For example, after noting how the Pennsylvania Constitution had distributed the three powers, a committee of the state's Council of Censors explained, "All power therefore, not placed out of its proper hands, belongs to the legislative, or the executive, according to its nature." St. George Tucker observed that "one of the fundamental principles of the American government" was "to keep these powers separate and distinct, except in the cases positively enumerated." Along these lines, the U.S. Constitution granted each power to the appropriate branch of the federal government, subject to specified qualifications, such as that the president can veto legislation, and that he can make binding treaties with Senate ratification. Other than as allowed by such exceptions, each specialized power belonged to its own specialized part of government.[18]

Thus, far from challenging the separation of powers, the caveats to it confirm that it was a specialization of powers, subject to the specified exceptions. This specialization already suggests the depth of the principle and its incompatibility with any administrative consolidation of powers. It also (as now will be seen) points to one of the great benefits of the principle and the corresponding cost of administrative departures from it.

Specialized Decisionmaking

A fundamental advantage of the separation of powers is that it institutionalizes specialized decisionmaking and thereby allows Americans to enjoy all of the advantages of distinct exercises of judgment, will, and force. A breakdown in the distinctions among the three powers was a fundamental part of what traditionally was understood as arbitrary or irrational decisionmaking. From this point of view, specialized decisionmaking is valuable for avoiding a type of arbitrary governance—a type encouraged by the administrative consolidation of powers.

Individuals

The fragmentation of decisions into specialized components or stages, and the way it minimizes arbitrary decisionmaking, is widely recognized as essential even for mere individuals. Unlike institutions, individuals cannot place their understanding and will in different bodies—this being why Aquinas and other philosophers observed that although these faculties were different, they were connected in any individual. Yet even in individuals, it can be important to be self-conscious about the separate, specialized character of each part of a decision.

This point has been pursued most systematically where the stakes are highest, in air combat, particularly dogfights. Fighter pilots learn to think in terms of the "OODA Loop," the series of decisions in which pilots must observe, orient, decide, and act. This is as much as to say that they must understand or judge their circumstances, must exercise will, and then must execute their decision. By internalizing this model, pilots make it second nature, doing it so fast that they can "get inside" the enemy pilot's OODA Loop. The goal is make and execute informed decisions before enemy pilots can execute theirs, thus allowing American pilots to survive and prevail.

More sedately, when simply crossing a street, children are taught to exercise the specialized powers. Children will insist that they do not need to be so methodical in separating out their observation, decision, and conduct. But parents know the risk of blurring these capacities into a single swift movement, and they therefore teach their children to be systematic: to look and listen, to decide, and only then to act.

Judgment, will, and execution thus are not merely antiquated formalities based on illusory ideas of what is natural. Among fighter pilots and children, scientists and doctors, and lawyers and corporate managers, this self-conscious specialization remains essential for adapting human nature to hard realities.

Even the mere conception of specialized powers shapes how individuals act in the world. It may not be possible for an individual to exercise entirely unprejudiced judgment, but with the ideal of judgment unaffected by will or passion, an individual can at least attempt to act with an accurate understanding of the world and of his moral and legal duties. Similarly, with self-consciousness about his will, he can have a sense of his freedom to make choices and can feel responsibility for them. And with self-consciousness about his capacity for forceful action, he can carry out his decisions with a clear sense of both the opportunities and the risks.

It thus is no coincidence that women long accepted their incapacity to govern themselves, let alone to participate in government. They had been taught to believe that they were too passionate or wilful to exercise good judgment, too fickle to pursue a consistent will, and too frail to execute their will in the world. Therefore, to attain responsibility and freedom, they had to overcome the debilitating effect of having internalized the personal failings attributed to them. They did this by recognizing their own capacities—by becoming confident in their ability to exercise judgment, will, and force.

Government

These specialized powers are not confined to individuals. Of course, individuals and institutions face many different difficulties, and it would be misleading to anthropomorphize government. At the same time, because government is a human endeavor, the specialization that is so valuable for avoiding arbitrary personal governance is also advantageous in political governance.

The means, however, are somewhat different for individuals and governments. Whereas individuals can maintain the specialized character of their powers by idealizing and practicing the separate exercise of each, government additionally needs to institutionalize the separation. This is especially important because, although individuals often can act intuitively, without self-consciously distinguishing their exercise of judgment, will, and force, governments are mere institutions, which lack the advantages of seamless, intuitive thought. Governments therefore need to formalize their separation of powers.

Montesquieu already justified the specialization of powers as a means of staving off arbitrary decisionmaking, but he focused on a crude sort of conflict of interest. For example, he feared that the executive would "plunder the state" if it were to share in the legislative power.[19] From this perspective, the concentration of powers corrupts the exercise of the specialized powers, thus making the separation of powers necessary to avoid a deprivation of liberty. The dangers of concentration, and the advantages of specialization, however, tend to be more complex.

As might be expected from the discussion of specialization in individuals, another way that governmental specialization limits arbitrary decisionmaking is by forcing the government to work through specialized institutions with specialized powers—indeed, by forcing it to work in a sequence of legislative, executive, and judicial power. For example, the government cannot restrain members of the public unless Congress first enacts a law, unless the executive then brings legal actions to enforce the law, and unless the courts then sustain the government's claims. In contrast, although in theory any one administrative agency could separately make rules, seek enforcement, and adjudicate such matters, it does not have to take these distinct steps. Rather than follow the Constitution's orderly stages of decisionmaking, an agency can blend these specialized elements together—as when it legislates through formal adjudication, or secures compliance with its adjudicatory demands by threatening severe inspections or regulation. In such ways, it can avoid separately deliberating about its legislative will, its executive force, and its adjudicatory judgment.

In precluding this consolidated sort of decisionmaking, the specialization also limits another sort of arbitrary power—one aptly summarized by Christopher Hitchens. He observes that the "true essence of a dictatorship is . . . not its regularity but the unpredictability and caprice; those who live under it must never be able to relax, must never be quite sure they have followed the rules correctly or not. Thus, the ruled can always be found to be in the wrong."[20]

Such is the danger when government can act against its populace not merely through three bodies with specialized legislative, executive, and judicial powers, but through multifarious agencies with all three powers. These agencies can almost always get to subjects by substituting one power for the others—for example, by threatening punitive regulations to secure the payment of excessive fines, or by threatening prosecutions to get compliance with the irregular legislation done through mere guidance. This use of one governmental power to exercise another is what (in chapter 13) was recognized as administrative extortion. It allows agencies to exercise a profound under-the-table power, far greater than the above-board government powers, even greater than the above-board administrative powers, and agencies thuggishly use it to secure what they euphemistically call "cooperation."

Whatever its name, the combination of powers often leaves Americans at the mercy of administrative agencies. When those who exercise the government's force also can make its laws and adjudicate violations, they come to enjoy a nearly freestanding coercive power, only distantly limited by the external formalities of authorizing statutes and deferential judicial decisions. The agencies thereby become rulers of a sort unfamiliar in a republic, and the people must jump at their commands.

In contrast, the specialization of powers protects Americans against some basic types of arbitrary governance, even if not always against arbitrary results. There are many ways in which government acts can be substantively arbitrary, and constitutional law does not bar most of them. Nor should it, for in a free society there is apt to be disagreement about what substantive policies are reasonable. At the very least, however, governmental decisions that bind subjects should be made with a nonarbitrary process, and without arbitrary power, and this means through the Constitution's specialized powers rather than through the consolidated power of the administrative state.

The extent of the current danger becomes apparent when one realizes that the Constitution's specialized powers define a sort of liberty.[21] Not being labeled as a right, the specialization of powers may initially seem a far cry from any kind of freedom; certainly, it is not a substantive liberty in the same way as the free exercise of religion or the freedom of the press. Most of the rights guaranteed by the Bill of Rights, however, merely limit judicial procedure. And similarly, the specialization of government powers confines the government to procedures—mainly by restricting legislative power to Congress and its processes and by restricting judicial power to the courts and their processes. The specialization of powers thus, at the very least, protects liberty in the same way as much of the Bill of Rights: It limits not so much the substance of what the government can do as how it can do it.

And this freedom from unspecialized power is of fundamental importance for the protection of other liberty. For example, when agencies enjoy a combination of legislative, executive, and judicial powers, they can bind Americans without giving them a rule to guide them and secure their liberty, and without giving them juries and independent judges. But when the powers of government are specialized in the three branches, the government can bind Americans only through laws, and only through courts with juries and with judges, thus preserving the most basic conditions of freedom.

Balance of Powers

A more conventional ground for worrying about the consolidating effect of administrative law is the balance of powers. But what is not sufficiently understood is the link between this balance and the specialization.

Scholars defend administrative law on the ground that it leaves in place at least a functional balance of power among the parts of government. And they give credence to this view by placing its "functionalism" in opposition to the mere "formalism" of adhering to the Constitution's separation of powers. So pervasive is this characterization of the question that even the most distinguished critics of administrative law tend to embrace the formalist label.[22]

The question, however, is not an abstract choice between functionalism and formalism. Instead, it is between two very different balances of power. On the one hand, there is any balance of power that is accepted as "functional"—whatever that means. On the other hand, there is the specific balance of power established by the Constitution, which has profound functional significance for the specialization of powers.

Put another way, the Constitution does not establish just any balance of power. On the contrary, it sets up a particular balance of specialized powers among specialized institutions. This is functionally important because it aligns the institutional balance with the specialized powers, thus bringing institutional power to bear in reenforcing the specialization.

When administrative law, however, consolidates all three powers in one part of government, it disassociates the institutional balance and the specialized powers of the branches of government. This is dangerous, for it opens up incentives for the parts of government to expand the extralegal system of consolidated power. For example, Congress increasingly relieves itself of the responsibility to legislate by leaving this to the executive, the courts happily spare themselves the burdens of adjudication by turning a blind eye to administrative adjudication, and the executive ever more brazenly avoids the need to work through the other branches and, instead, simply acts on its own to exercise their powers.

The danger is not stationary, for every expansion of administrative power further sidelines the specialized powers. Far from a balance of power, let alone of powers, this is an imbalance, which inch by inch increasingly tilts the field, shifting the weight of power in favor of consolidation and against the specialization of powers.

Judge in One's Own Case

One of the advantages of the specialization of powers has been that it places judicial power in the courts and thereby avoids the danger leaving the government to be judge in its own case. The administrative concentration of powers, however, leaves the executive and its officers precisely in this position.

At an individual level, the persons who engage in administrative adjudication tend to be judges in their own case. As noted long ago by Alfred Dicey, the decisions of administrative adjudicators are "apt to be influenced by political considerations." Of course, administrative law judges have some personal protection, but as in Dicey's day, such persons tend to be very sensitive to policy considerations. "An administrative court," therefore, "is never a completely independent tribunal."[23]

No less serious are the conflicts of interest arising simply from individual precommitments. Many administrative law judges and other administrative adjudicators originally joined the government because of their personal commitments to its policies. At the very least they tend to have commitments to administrative power.

Indeed, there tends to be a relationship between employment and dedication to a type of power. Montesquieu already worried about locating too much power, especially a combination of different powers, in any one class or profession. At stake here, however, is the link between administrative employment and an elevated sense of administrative power. Like employees of the old prerogative bodies, employees of administrative bodies become psychologically attached to the sort power of in which they play a role, and they therefore are in no position to judge the lawfulness of any exercise of that power.[24]

Even when individual administrative adjudicators rise above their personal precommitments, their institutional situation renders the executive a judge in its own case. Administrative adjudicators are administrative appointees and are subject to administrative penalties for failing to enforce agency regulations and policies. Their very office or duty requires them to follow agency regulations. They thus are really agents of the executive, whom the executive hires to enforce its rules, not simply the law. In fact, according to John Dickinson, "administrative adjudication, unlike adjudication by a court, is not usually a separate and distinct process," but rather "is a mere moment, an integral part, in a larger process, which is nothing less than the carrying on of the business of government."[25]

As a result of these various administrative commitments and circumstances, administrative adjudicators and their agencies cannot be considered indifferent judges. Instead, they are, in a sense, parties in their own proceedings. And when the executive also prosecutes, it is even more literally both judge and party. Thus, as noted already by Bruce Wyman in 1903, "the jurisdiction of the administration to determine its own controversies has been established to a degree not often appreciated."[26]

It might be countered that even regular judges have their share of biases. The bias of administrative adjudicators, however, is distinctive. For starters, when one considers the full range of administrative adjudicators, from heads of agencies down to ordinary administrative officers, most lack external protection for their independence. Moreover, most have an office that requires them to follow agency regulations, not simply the law. Indeed, most are psychologically attached to their agencies or at least administrative power. Thus, both institutionally and personally, most administrative judges are systematically and narrowly aligned with the prosecuting party. They thus are judges in their own case. In the anodyne phrasing of a defender of administrative adjudication, "there often is a closer connection between overt policy authority and case decision in administrative adjudication than in courtroom adjudication."[27]

The problem is profound, for the notion of judge in one's own case became prominent as the classical definition of the state of nature. Although it had long been considered unreasonable for a person to be both a party and a judge, John Locke took this point further. He explained that the state of nature was a condition in which individuals could not rely on government to provide the three essential advantages or specialized powers of civil government: known laws, an indifferent judge, and a power of enforcement. An individual in the state of nature lacked these things, and he therefore had to be his own accuser, judge, and executioner, thus making him judge in his own case. The condition of being judge in one's own case thus seemed to be a defining characteristic of the state of nature.[28]

It therefore is sobering that the executive makes binding adjudications, for it thereby places itself in the state of nature in relation to those whom it constrains. Even when merely adjudicating cases between private parties, it is in a sense a party by virtue of being the maker of the relevant regulations. As already noted, it even more concretely puts itself in the dual role of judge and party when it adjudicates cases in which it is the prosecutor. Either way, the executive deprives the public of an indifferent judge and makes itself judge in its own case—this being the condition that Locke associated with the absence of government.[29]

In Locke's theory, revolution and judicial redress were alternatives. From this perspective, an appeal to God could become necessary when it was not possible to find an indifferent judge on earth. An independent judiciary thus came to seem essential, and when the government acted as judge in its own case, it seemed that the people could legitimately turn to revolution.[30]

The specialization of powers thus avoids serious dangers. In placing judicial power in courts with independent judges, and in separating the judicial power from the legislative and executive powers, the specialization spares the public from being held to account by persons or institutions who are judges in their own case. And it thereby spares them from having to contemplate an appeal to the ultimate judge.[31, c]

A Single Lawmaker and a Single Court System

A further benefit of the specialization of powers is that it establishes a single, constitutionally authorized lawmaker and a single constitutionally authorized court system. Medieval life was burdened by a fragmentation of lawmaking and judicial authority. Modern life, however, depends on there

---

c. Even Blackstone reluctantly acknowledged the potential for revolution: "[I]f ever it should happen that the independence of any one of the three [powers] should be lost, or that it should become subservient to the views of either of the other two, there would soon be an end of our constitution. The legislature would be changed from that, which was originally set up by the general consent and fundamental act of the society; and such a change, however effected, is according to Mr. Locke (who perhaps carries his theory too far) at once an entire dissolution of the bands of government; and the people would be reduced to a state of anarchy, with liberty to constitute to themselves a new legislative power."*

being only one lawmaker and one court system for each nation or state. This is, in effect, another *numerus clausus* argument.[d]

The modernity of having a single lawmaker and single court system is well known. Medieval society was subject to competing authorities. Whether for lawmaking, adjudicating, or executing the law, there were competing papal and temporal systems, and within each of these, there were a host of lesser systems. In contrast, a key step in the development of the modern state, especially at common law, was to reduce the competing authorities to single specialized bodies. The result was the specialization of powers in specialized parts of government, consisting of a single legislative body, a single executive body, and a single judicial system under a high judicial court.

The existence of a single lawmaking body is essential. For one thing, it forces all lawmaking to run through the same political process. It thereby requires all interested political groups to work together in one institution and allows the public to monitor or stop lawmaking at one location or choke point. In addition, the single mode of lawmaking—an act of Congress—gives domestic federal law a stamp of authority that all persons can easily recognize. This enables both the courts and the people to discern with ease which rules are law and which are not. Although there always will remain substantive constitutional questions, the clarity about the procedural requirements for law has obvious benefits, whether calculated in terms of certainty, efficiency, reliance, democracy, or liberty.

The administrative consolidation of powers, however, subjects Americans to many lawmaking bodies with many forms of lawmaking. Rather than have to comply only with acts of Congress, Americans must comply with the acts of myriad agency heads, who engage in all sorts of lawmaking. These include formal rulemaking, informal rulemaking, various types of hybrid rulemaking, exceptional types of rulemaking, lawmaking through notice-and-comment interpretation, and the indefinite range of other sorts of lawmaking interpretation, such as that done through guidance, manuals, letter opinions, and briefs. The obligation of these alternative forms of law predictably is disputed, thus often leaving Americans uncertain about when they must comply.

Even the content of such rules and interpretations can be difficult to locate. Although the *Federal Register* gives notice of informal rulemaking,

---

d. For the notion of a *numerus clausus* argument, see chapter 7's discussion of the limited types of powers authorized by the Constitution and the implications for waivers.

there is little if any notice to the public about the lawmaking done through most interpretation, especially the vast amount done by means of guidance, etc. In fact, much of the casual administrative lawmaking is known only within the different agencies. Such lawmaking gets the "respect" of the courts but cannot be known by the public.

Overall, the uncertainty about the obligation and content of administrative lawmaking creates incalculable burdens for the courts and, more seriously, for the people. Administrative law thus painfully demonstrates the need for confining government to the single, constitutionally established legislature and its single mode of making domestic law.

The same is true of administrative adjudication. Whereas the Constitution's specialization of powers leaves Americans under a single court system, there now are myriad administrative jurisdictions, each with its own administrative process. The variation exists not merely from agency to agency, but even among different offices within a single agency. The courts accept this on the assumption that the Constitution guarantees not any fixed due process of law, but only the process that is due—the fiction being that there remains one due process, even if many applications. In reality, however, agencies constrain the public through many judicial systems, with many processes, all of which radically depart from the due process of law enjoyed in the courts.

The public thus faces a dizzying maze of administrative jurisdictions, far more complex and confusing than the scattered prerogative jurisdictions of early England. The diversity of adjudication is so great that most scholars know the details only as to one or two agencies. Thus, whereas the Constitution subjected the people to a single judicial system that is difficult enough to understand, extralegal power subjects the people to more legal systems than any one specialist in administrative law understands.[32]

The existence of multiple avenues for lawmaking and adjudication points to the most serious *numerous clausus* argument—that the multiple options allow the government to evade constitutional structures, processes, and rights. If the government cannot restrict liberty through an act of Congress, it can act through an agency rule, and if this is difficult, it can work through an agency interpretation. The government thereby can choose whether to rule through representative or unrepresentative lawmaking. Similarly, if the government cannot successfully prosecute in the courts, it can act through administrative tribunals, and it thus can decide whether to offer the due process of law or mere administrative process, whether to offer grand juries or not, whether to offer petit juries or not, and so forth.

The administrative multiplication of modes of lawmaking and adjudication thus inevitably deprives Americans of their liberty.

Indeed, the multiplicity leads to an accelerating loss of liberty. As already seen in chapters 7 and 13, once administrative agencies broke away from the constitutionally established legislative and judicial avenues, they could also break away from their own paths. The initial departures from the regular channels of lawmaking and adjudication thus almost inevitably opened up cascades of irregular conduits, each new one escaping the limits that confine the others. The goal of the agencies was candidly to avoid the burdens of the lawmaking process, and the effect has been to increase the burdens on the public with ever fewer constitutional or even substitute protections. The abandonment of the Constitution's single modes of exercising legislative and judicial powers has thus allowed the government increasingly to leave behind many of the constitutional limits on such powers, and to leave the public subject to mere administrative command.

In short, the consolidation of powers in administrative agencies returns Americans to the medieval risks of multiple paths for lawmaking and adjudication, thus enabling agencies to proceed against the public either through the law or outside it, at the agencies' discretion. In contrast, the specialization of powers avoids such dangers, for it establishes a single lawmaker and a single court system.

The Sociological Foundations of Specialization

The specialization of powers ultimately is not merely legal but sociological, for it is part of the social specialization that lies at the heart of modernity. By recognizing specialized spheres of power, and of freedom, the Constitution protects individuals and the interests of government in a manner well suited to modernized circumstances. By cutting back on the specialization of powers, therefore, administrative law puts much at risk.

That modernization has consisted largely of specialization is nothing new. Recognizing this, Adam Smith generally welcomed the division of labor as a path toward productivity, and Karl Marx regretted it, hoping to restore an undivided way of life.

The mixed blessings of specialization include both freedom and alienation, as evident from the most modernized of societies, the United States. By pursuing their lives in specialized, compartmentalized ways, Americans often find themselves so individuated as to be alone in a crowd. This specialization, however, is also their freedom, in which individuals can pursue their choices in specialized spheres of life, whether their work or their family arrangements, without feeling much constrained by demands for conformity to communal expectations.

In these circumstances, it is valuable that the Constitution establishes a government of specialized powers. It thereby avoids the consolidated government power that traditionally prevailed in consolidated societies and that seemed essential for the grim twentieth-century attempts to reimpose such societies. Indeed, the Constitution accepts the modern, specialized character of American society and ensures that it is matched by the specialized character of its government. The diverse forces in the society thus can pursue government power only through specialized institutions, none of which can exercise more than one of the government's powers. Accordingly, to capture the full range of government powers, a majority or other faction must capture all three branches. The specialization thus stands in the way of the sort of power necessary to impose a consolidated society.

Consolidated administrative law therefore is not as clearly the wave of the future as imagined by its advocates. On the contrary, if specialization is characteristic of modernized society, its institutions, and its freedom, then administrative law may be a great leap backward. Undoubtedly, for a while, administrative power could make valuable use of the energy, knowledge, and productivity of America's modernized society, but the larger danger remains that consolidated administrative power is incompatible with the specialization, diversity, and freedom of modernity. It ultimately may stifle the energy of the society it claims to serve.

Epistemological Arrogance

Perhaps the most profound implication of the consolidation of powers is epistemological, for the administrative state offers opportunities for a heady combination of concentrated power and specialized knowledge. As dryly put by Ernst Freund, the administrative state "presupposes the organization of a staff of experts acting under responsibility to an official chief."[33] It assumes, in other words, the possibility of relatively authoritative evaluations of knowledge, determined by government experts, and marshaled for purposes of administrative action. This ambitious union of expertise and power displaces the specialized authority of legislators, judges, and juries with the specialized knowledge of administrators.

Already here, hints about the intellectual foundations of this vision can be anticipated. Lorenz von Stein—the nineteenth-century German scholar of administrative law—urged in Heglian fashion that administration "brings together all knowledge available to improving society by means of the state." Commenting on this tendency, the German sociologist Max Weber concluded, "Bureaucratic administration means fundamentally domination through knowledge."[34]

Modernity and its scientific knowledge, however, are based on epistemological modesty. Whereas traditional knowledge consisted of supposedly demonstrable truths, modern science consists of testing for errors. Rather than a stable body of knowledge, science thus is more of a continuing inquiry. Scientists therefore put forward not truths, but mere hypotheses and theories, which always are open to empirical testing—the result being that none can be considered proved and that all are open to disproof.[35]

Considered sociologically, modern scientific knowledge is decentralized and never authoritative. It is based on diverse sources of authority and challenges to centralized claims of truth. Scientists internalize this spirit by separating their formulations of hypotheses or laws from their judgments about them. Tying some of these strands together, Robert Merton observes that "skepticism is a methodological and institutional mandate for scientists," who rely on "[t]he temporary suspension of judgment and the detached scrutiny of beliefs."[36]

In this context, the epistemology of the administrative state looks distinctly premodern. It assumes that the diversity of opinion, the skepticism, and the specialized faculties that inform scientific exploration can be reduced to authoritative technocratic conclusions, imposed through consolidated power. On this justification, the administrative power substitutes the specialized knowledge of administrators for the specialized authority of the branches of government. In a strange way, therefore, the administrative combination of expert knowledge and consolidated power really does hark back to the medieval monarchical vision of a wise ruler, who knows what is best for his people, and who therefore must have the full range of unspecialized power to impose justice.[37]

The result is a government ill equipped to handle modern life. Rather than take advantage of the diversity, freedom, and epistemological openness of modern science and society, administrative law responds to these conditions with epistemological arrogance and consolidated power.

જાજાજા

The administrative consolidation of power thus collides with the specialized nature of modern society and law. In the postmedieval era, almost all fields of human endeavor—ranging from science and commerce to literature and art—have flourished through the development of fragmented and specialized authority. Most centrally here, modern freedom and all of its blessing have thrived through specialized avenues of legal authority, including the specialized powers that the Constitution gives to specialized branches of government. It therefore is not merely unconstitutional but profoundly dangerous that administrative law heads in the opposite direction.

EIGHTEEN

Undivided

Although the Constitution divides the three powers of government among different branches of government, it does not stop there, for it further divides authority within these branches. The consolidating effect of administrative law therefore reaches far. In collapsing tripartite government, the executive's exercise of legislative and judicial powers also collapses the lesser divisions within (or associated with) these powers.

These lesser divisions often are treated as if they were of lesser extent and importance. For example, they typically are viewed simply in terms of legislative bicameralism. But they actually extend much further. Legislative power ordinarily runs through two legislative bodies and one executive body, and judicial power works through three judicial bodies. As a result, administrative lawmaking and adjudication collapse not only the three powers of government but also the divisions among the three bodies that ordinarily control each sort of power.

At stake is not merely structure, but again specialization. Whether the government pursues legislative or judicial power, it ordinarily must act not merely through a single specialized part of government, but through three lesser bodies, each of which has a specialized role. When the government acts administratively, however, it bypasses these specialized bodies and their specialized powers.

The underlying question is one of liberty. Like the main specialization of powers among the branches of government, the subordinate divisions of power within the branches are the foundations of legislative and judicial processes. The consolidation of these divisions therefore deprives Americans of legislative and judicial processes, including much that is guaranteed by the Bill of Rights.

Division and Specialization within Legislative Power

Although legislative power is a specialized power, located in a specialized institution, it has long seemed essential to take the division and specialization further. Accordingly, rather than place legislative power in an undifferentiated legislature, the Constitution divides legislative power and places it in specialized bodies.

The English constitution located legislative power in Parliament, which consisted of the king, the Lords, and the Commons. Somewhat similarly, the U.S. Constitution places legislative power in Congress, subject to a veto in the president. Either way, the legislative process involves three bodies.

Looking back on the English version of this arrangement, DeLolme explained its virtues, observing that whereas the force of executive power requires it to be unified, the danger of legislative power requires it to be divided. Any division in the "executive power" would be a source of conflict, and the executive's power was "confined . . . more easily . . . when undivided." But "the legislative, on the contrary, in order to its being restrained, should absolutely be divided."[1]

This legislative division famously has the advantage of caution—of allowing government to have second and even third thoughts about legislation. Institutions cannot self-consciously be reflective, but the location of legislative power in two legislative houses, followed by a negative in the executive, gives government repeated opportunities to contemplate what it is doing. It thereby can distance itself from popular passions and more generally can minimize its misjudgment.[2]

Especially in America, the division of the legislature channels the diversity of the nation into an institutional form. There are only two houses of Congress, and they therefore cannot really express the nation's diversity, but they at least allow conflicts in the society to find institutional expression. In a unified legislative body, national conflicts would be expressed merely by individual legislators or groups of legislators. In a bicameral legislature, however, the different houses can take up national differences, thus institutionalizing different points of view and the underlying social conflicts.[3]

Indeed, the Constitution establishes not only divided houses but also their specialized powers. Only one house of Congress originates bills for raising revenue, and only the other confirms nominations and ratifies treaties. Underlying these specialized powers are their specialized forms of representation—one type having the potential for a wealthier and longer-term perspective, the other having the potential for a more populist and immediate point of view.

Even the veto power belongs to a specialized body. Although the executive is not representative and is not given the legislative power, this makes it well suited to exercise a negative on legislation. It is, moreover, the body that must exercise the nation's force, and it therefore is apt to see proposed laws from a more practical angle than Congress.

The division of legislative process, however, with all of its institutional advantages, is lost when the executive legislates. At that point, the divided and specialized legislative process gets consolidated in a single institution, which ultimately is controlled by a single person.

The result is a loss of liberty—not the loss of a substantive right, but the loss of the right to be governed only through divided lawmaking. The Constitution's division of the lawmaking process among specialized bodies spares Americans from dangers of unified legislative power. The right to this specialized legislative process, however, gets lost when lawmaking is consolidated in administrative agencies.

The Unconstitutionality of Rump Legislation

Failures to satisfy legislative process have long been a problem in Anglo-American law. The issue was recognized already in England—most notoriously, when the "Rump Parliament" sought to govern by itself. Today, it is a problem in America, where it is even more clearly unconstitutional.

England

The English danger began with the monarch and then shifted to Rump. Either way, however, it was unlawful.

Up through the mid-seventeenth century, it was monarchs who tended to depart from the tripartite process of adopting statutes. As seen in chapter 3, kings often sought to legislate on their own, and at one point their lawmaking proclamations even acquired statutory authorization. Lawmaking proclamations, however, were judged to be unlawful evasions of the legislative process, and the attempt to give them a statutory foundation came to be viewed as an exemplar of absolute power.

Later, the departures from the legislative process shifted toward legislators—the boldest example being the formation of the Rump at the end of the English Civil War. In 1642, when Parliament and Charles I began to raise armies for their approaching conflict, the two houses of Parliament started to legislate without the king. This was bad enough, but it got worse. In December 1648, Colonel Thomas Pride—a parliamentary army officer—purged the House of Commons of insufficiently radical members, and shortly afterward, in January 1649, what was left of the Commons executed the king and abolished the monarchy and the House of Lords. Parliament thus was reduced to a mere part of the Commons—what critics mockingly called the "Rump Parliament."

The Rump, however, could never fully establish its legitimacy, because the English had deep constitutional ideals of divided government. In these ideals, legislation could be made only with the consent of all three elements of the legislative power: the unpurged houses of Parliament and the monarch. The Rump, however, had at least one enduring legacy: an apt name for any attempt to govern with only part of the necessary elements for legislative power.

Tellingly, the enactments that were made by the two houses of Parliament without the king were entitled merely "ordinances." Later, when the House of Commons established itself as the ruling body of the commonwealth, it called its commands "acts."[4] Statutes, however, traditionally required tripartite participation, and after the restoration of the monarchy in 1660, the statute books omitted all of the ordinances and acts adopted during the Interregnum.

Evidently, attempts to collapse the three lawmaking bodies into one or two of these bodies are nothing new. On the contrary, such attempts were widely familiar to eighteenth-century lawyers from recent history, and they were understood to be gross violations of the English constitution.

America

Recognizing the danger, the U.S. Constitution carefully placed the legislative power in the two houses of Congress, with a veto in the president. It thereby barred any rump legislation.

If Congress were to enact that legislative process could be exercised by only one house of Congress, this would be unconstitutional, and the acts of the single house would not be binding—this being what the Supreme Court decided in *INS v. Chada*.[5] Indeed, if Congress were to enact that legislative power could be exercised by the two houses of Congress, without involving the president, this also would be unconstitutional, and the acts of the two houses would not be binding. In other words, even Congress, which is the entire legislative body, would constitute a sort of Rump. Its enactments would be mere ordinances, and the violation of these acts would be of no legal significance.

By the same token, the executive cannot exercise legislative power, even if it has legislative authorization, for when it acts alone, it is a sort of Rump—certainly as much a Rump as the House of Commons once was. Although it would be bad enough for the two houses of Congress to exercise legislative power alone, it is worse for the president or his subordinates to do so, for he constitutionally enjoys only a negative on legislation. Put another way, if Congress cannot delegate legislative power to the two congressional bodies that ordinarily adopt legislation, how can Congress delegate this power to the body that ordinarily has only a veto on legislation? Such, however, is the current reality.

The result is a strange reversal of roles. Administrative lawmaking belongs to the branch of government that constitutionally enjoys only a veto. In contrast, the veto on such lawmaking now requires full, constitutionally authorized legislation adopted by both houses of Congress and the president. Thus, whereas the adoption of legislation once arose from the branch designed to be representative and cautious, it now often comes from the branch designed for effective force. And whereas the veto arose from the forceful part of government, it now in many instances must come from a combination of all branches.

Unsurprisingly, this reverses the quality of legislation and vetoes. The Constitution's arrangement of government combined representative and cautious legislation with decisive vetoes. The administrative arrangement, however, combines unrepresentative rapid-fire lawmaking with indecisive negatives.

The labels for the lawmaking are revealing. Even the defenders of executive legislation do not ordinarily call it "law." Instead, they call it "administrative law," and more specifically they speak of "rules" or "regulations." The Administrative Procedure Act similarly authorizes "rules" and "rule making" rather than law and lawmaking.[6] Thus, like the seventeenth-century advocates of ordinances, the contemporary defenders of administrative law recognize that enactments made outside the tripartite requirement for legislation are not really laws.

Ironically, it would easier to defend the delegation of legislative power to a body altogether outside the government. It often is assumed that the delegation of legislative power to an independent body—whether a private trade association or the United Nations—would be especially problematic, but that the delegation to the executive is permissible because the executive already is part of the government. The delegation to the executive, however, collides with the Constitution's division of the legislative and veto powers, and all the reasons underlying this division. Consequently, even if Congress can delegate legislative power, this cannot overcome the peril of placing legislative power in a mere subset of the bodies that, according to the Constitution, must be part of the legislative process.

Administrative legislation thus collides with the Constitution's legislative process. Put simply, legislative process cannot be exercised by a part of the whole, and administrative legislation thus is the act of a Rump.

Divided and Specialized Judicial Power

Just as the Constitution divides legislative process among three specialized bodies, so too it divides judicial process among three specialized bodies— the judges and two types of juries. Although this specialization is of profound importance for preserving liberty under law, it is abandoned in administrative adjudication.

Already before trial, there is a division of power between judges and grand juries. It will be recalled that warrants come from judges, and that criminal accusations (at least for capital or otherwise infamous crimes) come from grand juries.

At trial, there is a further division, for judges decide questions of law, and petit juries decide questions of fact. To be more precise, a judge decides questions of law and instructs the petit jury on the law, after which the jury gives a verdict and in a civil case determines damages. The judge then enters judgment, and when a criminal defendant is guilty, the judge sentences him.

The judges and the two types of juries not only exercise specialized parts of the judicial process but also are selected through specialized processes. Judges are chosen from among lawyers and, indeed, from a relatively rarified range of lawyers. Jurors, however, are chosen from a broad swath of the public. Thus, although legal questions rest in persons who specialize in law, decisions about accusation and guilt rest in unspecialized members of the community.

This division of judicial power is lost in administrative adjudication. It already has been seen how administrative agencies combine executive, legislative, and judicial power. Additionally, even within their exercise of judicial power, they combine the power of judges and the two types of juries. They investigate and make accusations like grand juries; they hear cases like judges; they decide facts and give verdicts like petit juries. Administrative law thus consolidates the different roles of judges and juries into undifferentiated state power.

This collapse of judicial process is part of the more general triumph of specialized knowledge over specialized authority. Although it is true that many executive officers have valuable specialized knowledge, legislators have the specialized authority of generalists elected by the public, and similarly, jurors have the specialized authority of persons randomly drawn from a swath of the general populace. Their specialized authority, however, is increasinly displaced by the authority of administrators with specialized knowledge—a sort of displacement to which this book will return.

The administrative shift away from the specialization within judicial power has profound consequences for liberty. Most obviously, administrative agencies exercise judicial power without real judges or juries, thus depriving Americans of ordinary judicial process, including jury rights and the due process of law.

Less directly, but more sweepingly, the administrative abandonment of the distinction between judge and jury diminishes liberty by altering the character of the law. When jurors drawn from the public decide the questions of guilt, judges must distinguish between questions of fact and questions of law, thus leading them, on the whole, to speak about the law as a set of generalities distinct from the particulars of cases. In other words, the division between judges and juries encourages judges to enunciate the law in terms that are general and, in this sense, law-like. Additionally, when instructing jurors, judges need to state the law with enough clarity to be understood by members of the public. The distinction between judges and juries thus creates structural incentives for the law to be stated at a level of generality above factual particulars and at a suitable level of clarity—both of which are essential if Americans are to enjoy liberty under law.[7]

It therefore is worrisome that administrative adjudicators consolidate the specialized roles of judges and juries. These officers lack the structural incentives to declare the law in a way that is general and comprehensible, and they therefore tend to interpret statutes and regulations with dizzying complexity, which leaves even phalanxes of corporate lawyers doubtful about what is allowed under law and what is not. The loss of the division between judges and juries thus has profound costs, not only for the individuals who are deprived of judicial process but also, more generally, for a society that hopes to understand and enjoy its freedom.

༻༺ ༻༺ ༻༺

Like the specialized powers of the branches of government, the lesser divisions of power are among the Constitution's most important foundations for liberty. They are the very foundation of legislative and judicial processes. The administrative state, however, obliterates these divisions and thereby crumples legislative and judicial processes into consolidated administrative power.

It is yet another way in which administrative law retreats from specialized authority. Most immediately, it departs from the specialized powers and processes established by the Constitution; more generally, administrative law abandons the tendency toward specialized authority that has been constitutive of modern life and law. Once again, therefore, the administrative consolidation of power conflicts with modernity and returns to the ancient dangers of unspecialized central power.

NINETEEN

Unrepresentative

As part of its specialization of powers, the Constitution places legislative power in Congress—a representative institution. The administrative consolidation of powers, however, establishes unrepresentative lawmaking, and this raises a series of problems.

The most basic difficulty is the lack of consent and obligation. The relationship between obligation, consent, and representation receives little attention from advocates of administrative law. But it surely is significant that administrative agencies are appointed from above rather elected from below. Can an unelected officer really make law? For example, can the secretary of the Department of Agriculture legislate? He is not a representative body, let alone the constitutionally established representative body. So how can he be assumed to legislate with consent of the people? And if without their consent—in particular, their constitutionally authorized mode of consent—how can his commands have any legal obligation?

The problem can be understood in terms of self-government. Whereas the people traditionally ruled themselves through the laws made by their representatives, the government now tends to rule the people through administrative commands. Administrative law thus inverts the relationship between the people and their government, reducing the people to servants and elevating government as their master.

Without Representation, Consent, or Obligation

The need for consent and thus for representation arises from the expectation that law must be not only coercive, in the sense of physical force, but also obligatory. If law were mere force, there would be no need to obey it except under compulsion, and even then, obedience would be merely prudential. It has long been understood, however, that law is not mere force, but a requirement that also comes with obligation, and this points to the need for consent through representation.

Obligation

The difference between law's obligation and its merely coercive effect can be illustrated by traffic statutes. When a statute prohibits driving over seventy miles per hour, drivers have more than one reason to obey. In some instances, they will fear observation by a police officer and on this ground will follow the law. In all instances, however, they also have an obligation to conform to law, even if they do not all feel the obligation.

The sense that law is binding, regardless of enforcement, spares the government and the people the costs of excessive force. If law lacked obligation, or if the public did not feel such obligation, obedience would largely depend on coercive enforcement, the result being both inefficiency and severity. Most persons, however, obey the law even when they do not expect to encounter a police officer, one reason being that they have a sense of the law's obligation. This frees them from coercive enforcement, and it leaves the government free to direct its threats of coercion primarily against outliers who do not sufficiently feel bound by law. A sense of the obligation of law thus can ease the task of government and limit the need for severity against the populace.

Consent and Representation

Although individuals can feel an obligation to obey law for many different reasons, the postmedieval foundation of legal obligation has been the consent of the people. In the prevailing medieval vision, law was binding because it participated in higher verities, including justice, as revealed through reason or natural law. By the fourteenth century, however, European society had become relatively fragmented, and being ever more aware of the diversity of opinions, many European commentators doubted the capacity of human beings to agree about what was reasonable or just.

In these fractured circumstances, the obligation of law increasingly seemed to arise not so much from the justice of a law as from the consent of the community to be bound. Although the community's immemorial customs were obligatory because of the people's tacit consent, its new enactments required their express consent. For example, the people of local communities consented to their local enactments in their local courts, and the people of England consented to their more general statutes in the high court of Parliament.

Underlying the assumption about popular consent were deeper assumptions about the consent of individuals. Nicholas of Cusa already speculated that individuals in nature—in the absence of government—were not yet subject to one another and thus were equally free. And "if by nature men are equally powerful and equally free, the valid and ordained authority of one man naturally equal in power with the others cannot be established except by the choice and consent of the others." In other words, if "by nature all are free," none could hold power over others, except by consent. Thus, "every government," as a matter of nature, "is based on agreement alone and the consent of the subjects." On such foundations, Nicholas and increasingly others concluded that "the binding force of all statutes consists in agreement and consent, tacit or explicit."[1]

Of course, in a large society, such as England, the entire people could not meet in the legislature, and commentators therefore strained to suggest that the people as a whole were present in Parliament. The lords did not need representation, for they could all meet in the upper house, but the commons were too numerous to meet in their house, except by representation. Accordingly, to maintain the consent theory of obligation, some English commentators adopted the fiction that the people as a whole were present in Parliament. For example, in the late fifteenth century, it was argued that an act of Parliament was obligatory even before promulgation because "everyone is party and privy to such an act, and it shall bind everyone."[2]

Yet this vision of the entire community meeting at one time to give their consent was not very plausible. Therefore, rather than pretend that all persons were present in the legislature, commentators increasingly turned to a more layered theory of consent. By remaining in the country, individuals apparently consented to be members of their society or people and subject to its laws. The people, moreover, allegedly had consented in their constitution to be bound by the acts of their representative legislature. Finally, the people in their localities elected representatives to act for them in the legislature. In this way, the consent necessary for the obligation of the law came to rest on the representative character of the lawmaking body.

To be sure, as already noted, the people could accept the legal obligation of custom through their tacit consent, where this was observable from the unchanging character of the custom. The obligation of enacted law, however, could not be discerned in this way, and it therefore needed express consent, if not directly from the people, then at least through their representatives.

Representation thus was the means by which the people obliged themselves. Rather than be coercively ruled by a king's commands, they governed themselves through their own laws.

America

Early Americans embraced this vision of consent and self-government. They assumed that legislation was without obligation unless the people imposed it on themselves in their representative legislature, and they eventually established the nation and its constitution on this ideal.

Taxation was what usually focused attention on such principles. Governments hungry for revenue strained to evade representative legislation and thereby provoked the rejoinder that taxes required consent. John Locke acknowledged that "everyone who enjoys his share of the protection" of civil government should pay his share for it, but added that "still it must be with his own consent, *i.e.* the consent of the majority, giving it either by themselves, or their representatives chosen by them." In contrast, "if any one shall claim a power to lay and levy taxes on the people, by his own authority, and without such consent of the people, he . . . subverts the end of government."[3]

Americans embraced this sort of argument when they were confronted with the Stamp Act and other British taxation. The British already believed that under "our constitution . . . no British subject can be taxed, but . . . of himself, or his own representative," and Americans simply applied this against Parliament.[4] "No taxation without representation" thus became a founding maxim of the nation.

When a congress of the colonies met in 1765, it declared for Americans "that no taxes be imposed on them but with their own consent, given personally or by their representatives." It added that they "are not, and . . . cannot be, represented in the House of Commons," and that therefore "no taxes ever have been, or can be constitutionally imposed on them, but by their respective [colonial] legislatures."[5]

Even many towns declared the principle of representation. The town of Braintree, for example, resolved that it was "a grand and fundamental principle of the British constitution that no freeman should be subjected to any tax to which he has not given his own consent in person or by proxy," and it therefore was "inconsistent with . . . the essential fundamental principles of the British constitution that we should be subjected to any tax imposed by the British Parliament because we are not represented in that assembly in any sense unless it be by a fiction of law."[6] Many other towns repeated these principles.[a]

Although the immediate question was taxation, much more was at stake —namely, all legislation. From the British point of view, Attorney General Richard Hussey worried that there was "no distinction between taxation and any other law," for "[c]onsent seems as necessary to cases where the life and liberty of the subject is concerned as where his property is concerned." Thus, "[i]f the Stamp Act is illegal," then "every other" exercise of parliamentary power in America might be illegal. Indeed, Americans increasingly expected representation in all legislation affecting them. As put by Congress in 1774, "they are entitled to life, liberty, and property, and they have never ceded to any sovereign power whatever, a right to dispose of either without their consent." Indeed, "the foundation . . . of all free government, is a right in the people to participate in their legislative council." As put in 1776 by an American minister, Samuel West, "representation and legislation are inseparably connected."[7]

It thus became a central principle of American constitutional law that binding enactments had to come from the people or their representative legislature. Rather than be ruled with mere force, the people had to govern themselves.

So far did the U.S. Constitution go in recognizing the representative nature of legislative power that it excluded the president from this power. The English constitution located legislative power in Parliament, including not only the Lords and the Commons but also the king. As a practical mat-

---

a. Just how deeply Americans assimilated these ideas about representation is evident from what they said on the streets—for example, in Virginia. In early 1766, a Hobb's Hole merchant, Archibald Ritchie, openly defied the opponents of the Stamp Act by declaring that he would comply with the law. Indeed, he announced "publically at Richmond Court, that he was determined to clear out his vessels on stamped paper; at the same time saying, that he knew where to get such paper." Many Virginians were "enraged." Being "alarmed at the dangerous consequences, that such an iniquitous practice might be productive of to the liberty of their country, if other merchants should pursue so pernicious an example," they met to declare that a British subject "cannot be taxed but by consent of a Parliament in which he is represented by persons of his own choosing." They also vowed to death to prevent the execution of the Stamp Act and warned that "if any abandoned wretch, shall . . . contribute to the introduction or fixture of the Stamp Act in this colony, by using stamped paper, . . . we will with the utmost expedition, convince every such profligate, that immediate danger and disgrace shall attend their prostitute purpose."

Not content with expressing their opinion, these Sons of Liberty—allegedly four hundred of them—went to Hobb's Hole and "drew up in two lines in the main street of the town." Meanwhile, some gentlemen visited Ritchie and invited him to step outside and sign a declaration of remorse, in which he was to swear not to use stamped paper. Under pressure from the crowd, he took off his hat, read the declaration, and then swore to it.[*]

ter, the U.S. Constitution came close to following this model, but when it granted the nation's legislative power to Congress, it carefully specified that this body consisted merely of the Senate and the House of Representatives. Thus, whereas the king's veto was part of the legislative power, the president's veto was not.

Nor should this be a surprise. The United States was founded on the principle that taxes and other binding legislation had to be made by a representative legislature.

The Underlying Realities

The logic of consent and self-government that underlay the need for a representative legislature has become only more powerful since the eighteenth century. It commonly is assumed that traditional principles lose their social context and thus their persuasive force over time. The principle of consent, however, has had the opposite trajectory. It was ahead of social realities in the eighteenth century and came to rest on such realities only in the twentieth.

Social realities have caught up with each level of the theory. Although in the eighteenth century it could not be presumed that slaves had consented to be members of the society, all Americans now are free, and because of globalization, they enjoy much practical freedom to leave and join other societies, thus making almost everyone in the country relatively voluntary members of this society. Moreover, although women, blacks, and even many white men could not vote in the eighteenth century, Americans now generally enjoy this right. Thus, the presumptions of consent—both individual consent to the society and electorial consent to the laws—are no longer so much legal fictions as observable aspects of modern life. Representative government at last lives up to the principle of consent.

Yet now that representation is a realistic foundation for the obligation of laws, administrative lawmaking departs from it. One might expect that, at last, law would come with the consent that could give obligation to its constraints. Administrative rules and interpretations, however, are not made by elected lawmakers, and they thus are without such consent and obligation.

The Unelected Character of Administrators

In defense of administrative law, it may be thought that administrators who make it are representative in their own way. Exactly how they are representative, however, is elusive.

Congress is the only branch of the federal government that consists of elected lawmakers. Indeed, legislators and the president are the only persons in the government of the United States who are elected. All others, including all administrative officers, are merely appointed.

Although the president at least is elected, he is not a representative body. A representative body must to some extent represent the nation's diversity. It therefore cannot consist of a single person, and it must be elected in a way that to some extent reflects diversity, even if only because it is elected by the people in their different states and districts.

Even if the president could be considered a representative body, the reality is that most regulations are not issued by the president. Nor for that matter are they issued by experts in administrative agencies, who at least sometimes have specialized knowledge. Instead, administrative legislation usually is issued by the heads of departments, who typically are not particularly expert and never are elected.

Recognizing the problem, the Administrative Procedure Act seeks to promote "more effective public participation . . . in the rulemaking process." It requires agencies to give "notice" of proposed rulemaking and requires them to "give interested persons an opportunity to participate in the rulemaking through submission of written data, views, or arguments."[8] But that is all. This participation consists merely of being able to write (not to speak) to the rulemakers. It thus is nothing more than the right to petition; it is even less than the ordinary freedom of speech that Americans enjoy with their neighbors; and it leaves administrators almost entirely insulated from the public. The submission of comments therefore is no substitute for elections, and the suggestion of equivalence is laughable. As put by David Baron and Elena Kagan, the notice-and-comment process is "a charade."[9, b]

---

b. Notwithstanding that administrative rulemaking is a sort of rule from above, some academics defend it on democratic grounds, suggesting that notice-and-comment rulemaking amounts to "participatory democracy." Some even claim that an administrative agency is "often a more meaningful site for public participation than Congress." Administrative rules, however, are not made by a representative legislature elected by the people, which is the sort of participation that allows all to participate and that establishes the obligation of law in a republic.

Even when evaluated on their own terms, the claims about "participatory democracy" and "public participation" are puzzling, because the meaningful version of participation in administrative power is neither public nor available to the public. Certainly, some influential corporations and interest groups work closely with administrative agencies to shape policy. But this tends to happen behind closed doors, without access for most Americans.

Francis Lieber long ago commented on the misuse of the terms "law" and "representative":

Whether the name of law be given to personal decrees and arbitrary decisions, is not of the smallest importance. Napoleon, at St. Helena, expressed his surprise at having been called a despot; "I," said he, "who have always acted by law!" This forcibly reminds us of a prominent

Notice-and-comment rulemaking is even more of a charade than it appears to be, because it does not even apply to much administrative lawmaking. Entire categories of lawmaking—such as the interpretation done through guidance, manuals, letter opinions, briefs, etc.—do not require notice, let alone comment. As long as such interpretation appears somewhere, however obscure, it is likely to be carried out by the courts. Thus, even if notice and comment could substitute for representation, this would justify only a small part of administrative lawmaking.

The charade has profound political dangers, for it puts the public in the position of supplicants. Whereas Americans once could think of themselves as participating in representative self-government, they now repeatedly are given notice of an impeding rule and then are left to petition administrators for adjustments. The notice-and-comment process thereby accustoms the public to a subservient role. It reduces them to passive objects of administrative commands who must beg their rulers for relief. Nothing could do more to undermine the capacity of the people to govern themselves under their own laws.

The loss of representation is particularly acute, because the tacit consent of the public is such a poor substitute for the express consent of representatives. Undoubtedly, there can be consent without representation, this being what was traditionally said to give obligation to the common law. Yet the theory of tacit consent made sense for understanding customary law only because it was assumed that the custom would remain unchanged over a very long period, during which there was unbroken acceptance of it. In contrast, legislation is expressly enacted new law, which therefore needs express consent.

Of course, popular submission to administrative legislation could be understood to suggest consent, but not much of it. The populace's general submission to law is too general and passive to reveal much about their consent to particular laws, let alone to obscure administrative regulations or interpretations they have never even heard of. Passive submission may be enough to reveal the consent to remain in a society and be sub-

---

French paper, *The Univers*, which lately stated that it was decidedly in favor of representative government, and that it was only necessary to know what is understood by representative government. *The Univers*—so said the paper itself—understands by this term a legislative corps, which represents the government. I have known, in an official capacity, a patient in a hospital for the insane, who perseveringly maintained that the difference between him and me consisted solely in the name. "Suppose," he used to say, "we patients vote that we are sane and the out-door party is crazy?" "Don't you see?" he would add, with a knowing look.*

ject to its government and laws, but it is not enough to show consent to specific laws.

The theory of popular submission does not seem to be taken seriously even by advocates of administrative law, for they assume that only another regulation or a statute, not mere popular sentiment, can repeal an administrative regulation. Popular opinion matters only if it matters both ways. Accordingly, if active discontent cannot overturn regulations, passive submission cannot justify them.

It may be thought that administrative legislation at least comes with virtual representation. Although the administrative lawmakers themselves are unelected, they are appointed by presidential authority, and they act under congressional authorization or acquiescence. It therefore could be imagined that they are virtually, even if not actually, acting as representatives of the people.

In fact, however, most administrators are not even chosen directly by the president. Although heads of agencies and a few others at the top of each agency are political appointees, selected by the president or his staff, almost all other administrators are hired by existing administrators. Thus, almost all of those who make law through administrative interpretations were never even picked by elected politicians. Far from being elected by the people, let alone elected politicians, they are appointed by other administrators. Their authority thus is not even virtually representative, but is merely that of a self-perpetuating bureaucratic class. Accordingly, the suggestion that their lawmaking comes with virtual representation is illusory.

Virtual representation, moreover, is not a very convincing theory, for it traditionally was an excuse for denying representation to colonists and then to women. For example, although women could not elect representatives and senators, they were said to be virtually represented through their husbands or fathers.[10] Nowadays, the same sort of theory (whether put in terms of "virtual," "delegated," or "derivative" representation) remains an excuse for refusing representation—this time for refusing it to the entire nation. Nor is this a coincidence. As will soon be seen, it was when Americans acquired equal voting rights that much legislation was shifted outside the elected legislature. The virtual representation excuse therefore should be understood in the same way in the past, as a brazen justification for denying representation.

Administrative agencies or officers thus are not representative lawmaking bodies, let alone the Constitution's representative lawmaking body. Perhaps it will be suggested that it is sufficient for administrative power to be mere state coercion. But no one, neither an individual nor a government, has any natural superiority or power over anyone else. Therefore, if a law is not to be mere coercion, it must be made by the people or at least by their representative legislature, and obviously administrative law is not made by either.

Accountability

Among the advantages of a representative lawmaking body is that the lawmakers are accountable to the people. In contrast, administrative law evades this accountability.[11]

Loss of Direct and Specific Accountability

The problem is not simply a loss of accountability, but the loss of direct and specific accountability. Although a series of scholars (including John Hart Ely and David Schoenbrod) point to the accountability issue, others (Eric Posner and Adrian Vermeule) observe that the question is more complicated—that even if the lawmakers in agencies are not specifically accountable, Congress remains "accountable for the performance of agencies generally." Accountability thus is "not lost," but merely "transformed."[12] Indeed, there has been a shift—from direct and specific accountability to indirect and general accountability—but this is not reassuring.

One of the greatest dangers in American society is what economists call "agency costs"—the costs arising from the disparity of interest between those who enjoy power and those whose interests are entrusted to them. In business, such costs notoriously arise from the separation of ownership and control; in government, they arise primarily from the placement of the interests of the people in the hands of public officials.

A concrete response to the agency problem is direct and specific accountability, and this is what is lost in administrative lawmaking. Agency costs are unavoidable in a republic, for it is the nature of republican government to place the interests of the people in the hands of legislators. More generally, such costs are pervasive in a modernized society, which by its nature is specialized. In such a society, no one can do everything—indeed, most people can do only a few things—and many specialized functions therefore must be left to specialists, including legislators, thus creating innumerable opportunities for agency costs. Such a society, moreover, by its nature is highly individuated, and it therefore cannot overcome agency costs merely through communal attachment, but must more substantially rely on mechanisms establishing personal accountability—the direct and specific accountability of those who exercise any function or power for others.

The agency problem that arises when the people place their legislative power in their elected legislators is worrisome enough; the shift of legislative power to unelected lawmakers, however, relocates power to persons who are not directly accountable to the people and thereby adds another layer of agency problems. Indeed, because the heads of agencies are more directly accountable to the president than to Congress, the popular accountability that once reached directly to Congress now must run from Congress to the president, and then down to the heads of agencies. The result is not merely a single set of agency costs, but at least three layers of agency costs.

One might think that administrative lawmakers are directly accountable to the people through their election of the president, but this, too, is indirect accountability. At least when the lawmaking is done by agency heads, the accountability through the president creates only two layers of agency costs, but when it is done through the interpretations of lesser administrative officers, there again are triple-layered agency costs. More fundamentally, this sort of accountability does not involve even a first layer of representation, because the president, although elected, is not a representative body, let alone the Constitution's representative legislative body.[13]

Quite apart from the lack of direct accountability, administrative lawmakers rarely face specific accountability. The beauty of elections is not only that the people can put legislators in Congress, but also that they can remove them. This accountability is specific in the same manner as specific deterrence. And the impending threat of such accountability has the salutary effect (in Samuel Johnson's words) of concentrating the mind.

Of course, Congress sometimes pressures administrative agencies, and occasionally is so insistent that a leading administrator has to leave his office. But most administrative staff are protected in their positions, and even political appointees do not face the predictable and personal accountability of elections. The entire House of Representatives and a third of the Senate confront elections every two years. Yet, among the numerous agency heads who make binding rules, and among the many more administrators who make binding interpretations, few face much risk of being fired for their role in such legislation. In fact, it is difficult to identify more than a handful who have lost their jobs on this account. Nor is this an accident. One of the purposes of administrative power was precisely to insulate lawmaking from politics, including congressional politics.[14]

Recognizing the extent of this insulation, apologists for administrative power sometimes argue that administrators are accountable to other administrators. For example, it is said (by Jerry Mashaw) that "[i]nternal managerial controls can protect private rights and promote fidelity to legislative purposes."[15] But this assumes that limits on administrative power can be entrusted to administrators. It assumes that officials who threaten liberty can safely be left to managerial control rather than elections. It thus adopts the inverted vision of republican government, in which administrators are personally accountable only to higher administrators, not to the people below.[c]

In the end, the accountability of administrators and legislators to the people is very different. Whereas elected legislators are directly and specifically accountable to Americans, administrative lawmakers face only an indirect and general accountability.

Transparency

The accountability of a representative legislature rests not only on the election of legislators but also on the relative transparency of a representative legislature. The identity of legislators and their votes are known; even their debates and committee reports usually are shared with the public. On account of their place in popular politics, moreover, their conduct is covered by journalists and bloggers. It is the sort of openness that is typical of a representative lawmaking body, for a public that chooses its lawmakers will expect to know what they are doing.

In contrast, when legislative power shifts from Congress to administrative agencies, it tends to disappear from public view. What is done by publicly known figures in Congress is done by anonymous bureaucrats in the executive. What is done in open session in one place is done behind closed doors in the other. Whereas the Constitution requires publication of legislative journals and generally allows reporting of legislative debates, nothing requires or even permits publication of internal administrative proceedings.

To be sure, in the exercise of executive power, the executive usually needs

---

c. Georg Wilhelm Friedrich Hegel already argued that administrative officials would not act contrary to public interest—in part because they were accountable to higher officials in the administrative hierarchy. Upon reading this, Karl Marx protested: "[I]f we ask Hegel what is civil society's protection against the bureaucracy, he answers: . . . The hierarchical organization of the bureaucracy. *Control*. This, that the adversary is himself bound hand and foot, and if he is like a hammer *vis-a-vis* those below he is like an anvil in relation to those above. Now, where is the protection against the hierarchy?"*

to deliberate in closed rooms, barred to the public. The application of the nation's lawful force often would be compromised if it became public prematurely, and the advice of executive officers might not be candid if it were apt to be disclosed. But the executive extends this sort of secretiveness to its exercise of legislative power. As a result, when it adopts binding rules and interpretations, little if anything is known of its deliberations.

The problem extends further than the public's inability to visit the executive's little legislative chambers and listen to the debates. Not even the press can keep track of what administrative lawmakers are doing. Administrative lawmaking is so diffuse, complex, and concealed that it is largely beyond outside scrutiny.

Of course, the defenders of administrative law recognize these accountability problems and offer palliatives such as the Administrative Procedure Act and its notice requirement. The mere notice of impending regulations, however, does not even come close to the transparency of public debate conducted by elected representatives. Far from showing transparency, the notice requirement is so meager that it actually reveals the closed character of administrative power.

Continuous Legislators and the Inversion of Public Accountability

One of the distinguishing features of administrative lawmaking bodies is that they can legislate continuously. Although Congress meets regularly, it is not always in session. The executive, however, is continuously in power, so as to be always ready to preserve the interests of the nation. Therefore, when the executive exercises legislative power, it can legislate without interruption.

The result of this institutional continuity is not only more legislation, but an unbroken flow of legislation, thus leaving the people no opportunity to catch up with current administrative regulations before the appearance of yet further decrees. The continuity also affects the caution with which regulations are drafted, for whereas Congress must wait until its next session to adjust its enactments, the executive is confident it can continually tinker, thus often reducing legislation to a series of temporary orders, which it can countermand as it sees fit. At stake therefore is very the nature of legislation, for the executive can reduce its legislation to a stream of commands, thereby making such law not merely a limit on freedom, but a form of uninterrupted control.

Even more seriously, the personal continuity of administrative lawmakers reenforces their sense of themselves as a governing class. As John Locke observed, "where the legislative is in one lasting assembly always in being" there is the danger that "they will think themselves to have a distinct interest, from the rest of the community." Although Locke feared that members of a continuously sitting legislative body would seek "to increase their own riches and power," his larger point was that they would feel themselves to be separate from the rest of the society and to have a different interest.[16]

Milovan Djilas elaborated this sort of point when writing about the "new class" in communist societies. "This new class, the bureaucracy," he wrote, "did not come to power to complete a new economic order but to establish its own and, in so doing, to establish its power over society." Although, like other ruling classes, it "believe[d] that the establishment of its power would result in happiness and freedom for all men," it sought a "monopoly" of power. The emphasis on a monopoly of power obviously did not fit the Western administrative state, and Djilas therefore distinguished between communist and capitalist bureaucrats. The former "have neither masters nor owners over them," and this made them "something different and new: a new class."[17] His label for the extreme bureaucratic class he encountered under communism, however, eventually was recognized as an apt label for the Western bureaucratic class or, more generally, for the intelligentsia who participate in administrative governance or at least in setting its agenda.[18]

None of this is to say that the continuous legislators narrowly seek to preserve merely their own interests. As Djilas recognized at least in passing, they tend to see their exercise of power as an effort to serve the higher ends of society. Daniel Moynihan therefore emphasized that "the self-interest of the new class is merged with a manifestly sincere view of the public interest."[19] But almost all claims for power are sincerely made on behalf of the public, and the sincerity of the concern for the people cannot disguise the assault on their power.

The danger therefore is not merely the self-interest of the continuing lawmaking class, but a regime that pursues the public interest as understood by this class, without direct and specific accountability to the people. Whatever can be said against members of Congress, they are only temporary lawmakers and must submit to the people on election days. Many administrative lawmakers, however, at least those who engage in lawmaking through interpretation, hold power continuously, and therefore exert power over the people for the people's good, without fear of popular removal. Put succinctly, power over the people for the sake of the people, is very different from government of the people, by the people, and for the people.

Administrative power thus inverts public accountability and thereby also the public interest. All lawmakers once were temporary, being accountable to the people and their vision of the public good. Now, however, in many matters, the people are directly accountable to nearly permanent government officials, who act on their vision of the public good, untempered by any sense of personal accountability to the people.

The Question of Class

The loss of popular representation through administrative lawmaking cannot be examined entirely on its own, for (as noted by Thomas West) it curiously followed the expansion of popular representation in legislative elections.[20] Although this could be dismissed as a mere coincidence, it appears to have a more disturbing explanation.

The Puzzle

The conflicting trends are striking. The administrative state first took hold at the federal level in the 1880s after an expansion of suffrage. Indeed, not merely during that early era of administrative law, but repeatedly since then, the expansion of the electorate has been accompanied by the growth of administrative law. This initially may seem odd, for the electoral and administrative developments moved in different directions—the one providing direct accountability to the people in voting, the other diminishing such accountability by removing legislation to administrators.

One of the extraordinary achievements of American life over the past two centuries has been to make the theory of consensual government a reality. Yet when consensual government became a reality, the administrative state undermined that reality by shifting lawmaking away from people and their representatives. Prior to the Civil War, although the theory was one of consent, the reality was that elites often excluded much of the people from being represented. Since then—whether in 1870, 1920, or 1965—the consent theory has become ever more realistic, but each time, after representative government became more open to the people, legislative power increasingly has been sequestered to a part of government that is largely closed to them.

The puzzle becomes all the more acute when one considers some related trends. After Americans began to make their theory of consensual government a reality, many academics, lawyers, and judges began to question the centrality of popular consent through representative legislatures.[21] Although, in their flight from consent, they went in different political directions, and down different methodological paths, many eventually turned to legal realism and its suggestion that law must respond pragmatically to social needs through nonrepresentative mechanisms. Some of those who made this move, such as Benjamin Cardozo, concluded that not only legislatures but also judges could make law; others, such as Frank Goodnow, gave greater emphasis to administrative lawmaking. But whether they placed their faith in judges or administrators, they sought alternatives to legislatures. Evidently, when Americans came close to making a reality of their theory of representation, a growing portion of educated Americans espoused forms of nonrepresentative lawmaking.[d]

Class

An explanation can be found in the role of class. Although administrative power is rarely discussed in terms of class, the two have been closely connected.

Rather than seek popular power, many early advocates of administrative power wanted popular support for a sort of elite power. In the 1880s, Woodrow Wilson believed that "[t]he most despotic of governments under the control of wise statesmen is preferable to the freest ruled by demagogues." Of course, Americans had a free government, and therefore in combating "the error of trying to do too much by vote," Wilson aimed to limit public opinion—to "make public opinion efficient without suffering it to be meddlesome." The key was to confine "public criticism" to "formative" policy and to exclude it from administrative details: "Let administrative study find the best means for giving public criticism this control and for shutting it out from all other interference." Later advocates of administrative law would argue that "[a]dministrative legislation has greater permanence, continuity, and scientific value than legislative administration issuing from fickle popular bodies." One way or another, the point was that administrators, unlike legislators, would not have to bend their principles "to the whim of popular opinion."[22]

This rejection of the popular power exercised through legislatures required a segregation of administrators from political control. Civil service

---

d. Men such as Cardozo, who embraced the judicial route for lawmaking, sometimes candidly admitted that they were responding to their disappointment with legislatures. Cardozo conceded that he might have been "prepared to join" those who rejected the role of "the judicial process" as "a creative agency," but only "if statutes had proved adequate to the bearing of such a burden, or gave promise of being adequate within any future now in sight"—"if only it were true that legislation is a sufficient agency of growth."*

reform ensured that only the right sort of persons would be allowed into government, and it simultaneously secured them against being removed by those who were politically accountable to the people.[23] As a result, the populace now had to trust their administrative rulers. Wilson soothingly explained: "Self-government does not consist in having a hand in everything, any more than housekeeping consists necessarily in cooking dinner with one's own hands. The cook must be trusted with a large discretion as to the management of the fires and the ovens."[24]

Although the advocates of administrative power thought of themselves as pursuing functional advantages for the entire society, the class implications were never far from the surface. Some late-nineteenth-century reformers had responded to popular legislative politics by candidly envisioning a sort of "aristocracy." Proponents of administrative law shared the underlying assumption that the better sort of persons had to exercise power, but they more acceptably referred to them as scientific "experts." Even so, the class prejudice remained visible. Professor John Burgess of Columbia, for example, urged administrative reform while disparaging the "spurious" sort of democratic government in which "the ignorant rule the enlightened" and "the vulgar rule the refined." Documenting such attitudes, William Nelson caustically observes, "Many reformers believed that they themselves constituted precisely the sort of aristocracy needed in government."[25]

Of course, this movement to withdraw legislative power from popular control was allied with politics as well as class. Reformers feared that popular legislation would not be sufficiently progressive, and they therefore sought a better sort of legislation, which would be cordoned off from the inadequately progressive realm of popular politics. Wilson complained "the reformer is bewildered" by the need to persuade "a voting majority of several million heads." Exacerbating this problem was the diversity of the nation, which meant that the reformer needed to influence "the mind, not of Americans of the older stocks only, but also of Irishmen, of Germans, of

Negroes."[26] Rather than attempt to convince such persons, many progressives were eager to shift legislative power to administrative agencies.[e]

Legislators increasingly recognized the political advantages of thereby avoiding accountability for difficult questions. But the underlying intellectual, social, and political demands for the shift of power came from those who viewed legislatures with deep suspicion. Even today, a disdain for popular legislative power remains palpable among many advocates of administrative power—as does a corresponding admiration for expert control—thereby revealing how persistently the ambitions for extralegal power have been allied with anxieties about class and status.[27]

It thus was no accident that the exclusion of people from voting was followed by an exclusion of power from the legislature. Power tends to be seized by anyone who can take it, and ambition therefore is a more substantial explanation of events than conspiracies. Ambition, however, tends to follow opportunities. It therefore was to be expected that the loss of one mode of political exclusion was followed by another. When it no longer was possible to exclude people from representation, the preeminent opportunity to exclude fell to the class that could shift legislative power out of the legislature.

In sociological terms, those who pursued their ambitions and ideals through localized elections and representative legislatures were challenged by those who pursued their ambitions and ideals through the centralized administrative state. With their populism, the latter rebuffed representative legislatures, and with their advocacy of administrative agencies, they opened up opportunities for their own sort of power and interests.

Knowledge

e. Wilson unabashedly elaborated his ethnic and racial fears: "The bulk of mankind is rigidly unphilosophical, and nowadays the bulk of mankind votes." And "where is this unphilosophical bulk of mankind more multifarious in its composition than in the United States?" Thus, "[i]n order to get a footing for new doctrine, one must influence minds cast in every mold of race, minds inheriting every bias of environment, warped by the histories of a score of different nations, warmed or chilled, closed or expanded by almost every climate of the globe."

With these fears of diversity and its implications for progressivism, Wilson embraced a Germanic distaste for democracy. He believed that "[o]ur democracy, plainly, was not a body of doctrine; it was a stage of development"—a stage that had to be left behind. Looking with admiration at Germany and other European nations, he envied their success in "concentrat[ing] legislative leadership,—leadership, that is, in progressive policy." He even praised "monarchy" for "its perfect model of progressive order" and hoped for "concentrating" the United States "by putting leaders forward, vested with abundant authority in the conceptions and execution of policy." He concluded that "we shall remain a nation only by obeying leaders."[*]

When representative legislatures thus gave up ground to administrative agencies, those who prevailed politically because of whom they knew were increasingly displaced by those who prevailed administratively because of what they knew.[28] Although this was partly a difference of class, it was not a matter of class in the narrow conventional sense. Instead, it was a shift in modes of power—a shift from the power exercised through local connectedness to that exercised through the more cosmopolitan authority of knowledge.

The class interest in this unrepresentative lawmaking power was not merely that of an oligarchy—of the administrators who held administrative positions—but of a wide range of Americans who felt discomfort with the hurly-burly realities of electoral politics and who therefore sought a sort of government that better reflected their more elevated and progressive tastes. In many instance, they had left behind the local connectedness of the places where they grew up and had sought the opportunity and prestige of knowledge—especially the specialized academic or scientific knowledge acquired in educational institutions, which flourished by accrediting them, thereby confirming their membership in the new class.

To be sure, most such persons did not acquire an academic degree. And even when they obtained specialized degrees, they tended to be members of the intelligentsia more in spirit than in reality. Vast numbers, however, identified with the prestige of knowledge and thereby enjoyed a sense of participating in a new sort of elite.

Put another way, they found cosmopolitan affinities, a sense of worth, and social status in their supposedly superior intellect, rationality, and knowledge. The formal "scientific" knowledge with which they tended to identify was very different from the more complex communal understanding that traditionally has been essential in politics, but this only accentuated their confidence that they knew better. As a class, therefore, they sympathized with the development of the sort of legislative power that could be exerted on behalf of the intellect, rationality, and knowledge they saw in themselves.

It is in this sense that those who claimed the prerogative to rule without representation were part of a broader "new class." Rather than merely the administrators, or even the intelligentsia, this class included all who were more attached to the authority of knowledge than to the authority of local, political communities. The power of the people to make their own laws through their locally elected representatives thus was challenged by the confidence of an emerging class in the sort of knowledge that was the basis of their social status and their internal sense of merit. Although one might (following Robert Merton) call such persons "cosmopolitans," one might equally (echoing Daniel Bell) understand them as the "knowledge class"— the point being not that they were particularly knowledgeable, but rather that their sense of affinity with cosmopolitan knowledge, rather than local connectedness, was the foundation of their influence and identity.[29]

It cannot be overemphasized that this knowledge class was very broad— that it was not merely administrative and that it cut across the traditional social spectrum. The administrative element of the class included many top administrators and administrative experts. They were joined by legions of lesser lights, who had minimal education, but who found status and upward mobility in their administrative employment, even if only at a clerical level. The knowledge class, however, more expansively included myriads who never set foot inside an administrative agency. Many had acquired specialized knowledge and therefore could imagine that they were participants, or potentially could be participants, in the debates that distantly shaped policy. Yet others merely aspired to such knowledge and therefore, perhaps all the more strongly, identified with the power and advantages associated with it. Such persons recognized the elevating character of specialized knowledge and therefore viewed themselves as part of the knowledge class, although they were not among those who had any chance of exercising influence within it. Quite varied Americans thus affiliated with the new class and its administrative power.

Undoubtedly, there are failings in representative government. Yet the transfer of power from representative legislatures to administrative agencies did not so much cure the failings of representative government as open up opportunities for utterly unrepresentative bodies to make law. The effect was to displace representative government with centralized commands, and to displace the people and their representatives with members of the knowledge class.

Of course, the members of this class tended sincerely to view themselves as selflessly pursuing not their own interest, let alone a class interest, but the public interest. They nonetheless were a class—the cosmopolitan class that has shaped and dominated modernized life. And in light of their identification with their superior knowledge and their corresponding disdain for popular representative politics, it is no wonder that, although they mostly supported expanded suffrage, they also supported the removal of legislative power to administrative agencies staffed by persons who shared their outlook.

The development of administrative power thus cannot be understood merely as a question of law, or even merely as a question of intellectual history. It also must be recognized as a sociological problem—indeed, a profoundly disturbing shift of power. As soon as the people secured the power to vote, a new class cordoned off for themselves a sort of legislative power that they could exercise without representation.

Misalignment of Legislative and Popular Power

The shift of legislative power away from the representative branch of government has implications that go beyond questions of obligation, accountability, and class, for the shift creates a misalignment of legislative and popular power. The stability of government usually depends on a rough alignment of legislative power with the sentiments of the people. In this context, one of the virtues of keeping legislative power in a representative legislature is that this provides a safety mechanism against legislation that drifts too far from the firm foundation of popular opinion.

Of course, Congress often departs from popular opinion and even from most understandings of the public interest, and this is not always to be regretted. And, of course, administrative agencies often are attentive to what the public will accept. A representative legislature, however, is structured to remain in sympathy with the people, and it therefore is less likely than administrative agencies to misjudge what is acceptable.

It therefore is worrisome that legislative power no longer is confined to the representative body of government. Whereas legislators regularly must face up to their constituents, administrators can choose to whom they listen, and when they therefore make regulations without sufficient attention to public sentiment, they tend to stimulate unnecessary and potentially vigorous resentment against government. Indeed, because administrators are so hidden and anonymous, their overreaching is apt to cause resentment not merely against particular persons and enactments, but against government in general.[30]

Thus far, administrative law has avoided much rancor because its burdens have been felt mostly by corporations. Increasingly, however, administrative law has extended its reach to individuals. The entire society therefore now has opportunities to feel its hard edge. As a result, like seventeenth-century English kings who took their prerogative beyond what the public could bear, the administrative state is moving in a direction that is apt to provoke more resentment than obedience.

෪෪෪

In a republic, it is not too much to expect that law will be made by a legislature composed of representatives of the people. It is, in fact, the very nature of a republic to be governed by laws made by this sort of specialized legislative body.

Nonetheless, administrative legislation is unrepresentative. It therefore is without consent, without obligation, and without popular accountability. Indeed, it is form of class power, without a regular means aligning itself to popular sentiment. None of this bodes well, but it is exactly what might be expected when a people no longer merely govern themselves, but are forced to comply with the commands of unelected administrators.

The history of government is largely a story of elite power and popular subservience. Americans, however, turned this old model upside down. By establishing a republican form of government, they eventually made themselves masters and made their lawmakers their servants. More than two centuries later, the shell of this republican experiment remains. Within it, however, another government has arisen, in which new masters once again assert themselves, issuing commands as if they were members of a ruling class, and as if the people were merely their servants. Self-government thus has given way to a system of submission.

TWENTY

Subdelegated

A common defense of administrative law and its consolidation of powers is delegation. A principal can delegate his power to an agent, and on this basis Congress is said to delegate legislative and judicial power to the executive.

A major effect of this delegation argument is to break down the specialization of government powers. Whereas the Constitution preserves the specialization of government powers by placing them in their own specialized parts of government, delegation seems to explain how they nonetheless can be consolidated within the executive.

As it happens, the delegation defense often is more theoretical than realistic, because much executive legislation and adjudication goes beyond congressional authorization.[a] Nonetheless, delegation is an appealing theory for defenders of administrative law, as it seems the best means of justifying the otherwise unlawful consolidation of powers.

The delegation excuse, however, misstates the problem, for the difficulty is not delegation, but subdelegation. By means of the Constitution, the people delegate power to government. In particular, they delegate a specialized power to each branch of government. Accordingly, when Congress purports to give its legislative power to the executive, the question is not whether the principal can delegate the power, but whether the agent can subdelegate it.

Of course, where Congress authorizes the executive to exercise a rule-making power that is not legislative, there is no unlawful subdelegation.

---

a. Agencies often have issued binding regulations without statutory authority. Indeed, the standard statutory phrase for authorizing interpretive and procedural rules (as shown by Thomas Merrill and Kathryn Watts) has been systematically misread since the 1970s to justify agencies in execising a more general rulemaking power.[*]

The subdelegation problem thus arises primarily where Congress authorizes others to make legally binding rules, for this binding rulemaking,
by its nature and by constitutional grant, is legislative. In such matters, a
congressional attempt to authorize administrators amounts to an unlawful
subdelegation of legislative power.[1]

The Debate

Defenders of administrative law tend to slap down objections to it with
the slogan "The nondelegation doctrine is dead."[2] In response, critics of
administrative law often answer, as if in a Monty Python skit, "Not dead
yet!" But there is nothing comic about this sort of exchange, for it is utterly
misleading to frame the debate in terms of "the nondelegation doctrine,"
let alone its death.

The debate is complicated by the equivocations of the Supreme Court.
Although the Court has not, since 1935, invalidated a statute on grounds
of nondelegation, nor has it fully rejected the doctrine. Instead, it simultaneously worries about delegation and permits it. In response to its worries, the Court requires Congress to offer agencies at least an "intelligible
principle"—apparently on the assumption that where Congress provides
such guidance, the agencies are merely filling in details and thus are not
making, but merely executing the law.[3] On this fiction, the Court can pretend that Congress is not delegating legislative power. But even where Congress fails to provide intelligible guidance, the Court hesitates to enforce
its own weak standard. Rather than really require Congress to supply an
"intelligible principle," the Court usually merely interprets the authorizing
statutes to avoid the difficulty.[4]

These judicial equivocations have left the so-called nondelegation doctrine hanging onto life with little more than a thread. The notion of an
"intelligible principle" sets a ludicrously low standard for what Congress
must supply, and therefore, whether or not Congress gives such guidance,
it still is delegating the vast bulk of the lawmaking. Indeed, the Supreme
Court sometimes takes an especially tolerant approach to congressional
delegations on theory that they are "inherent necessities of . . . government
coordination."[5] Recognizing all of this, the debate about the lawfulness of
administrative law largely ignores the "intelligible principle" doctrine and
instead focuses on the death of the nondelegation doctrine.

Yet (as already suggested) the framing of the debate in terms of the nondelegation doctrine is misleading. For one thing, so narrow a focus suggests

that the lawfulness of administrative law turns on the question of delegation. There clearly, however, are many objections to administrative law that do not concern delegation.

Moreover, when the debate is framed in terms of nondelegation, the question gets flipped around. The Constitution places legislative power in Congress and judicial power in the courts, and it therefore is the administrative divergence from the Constitution that needs to be explained, whether by delegation or some other principle. The initial move therefore is the defense of administrative law in terms of delegation, and the nondelegation doctrine is merely the supposed response.

Thus, when defenders of administrative law frame the question in terms of "nondelegation," they shift the burden of persuasion from the claims about delegation that might justify administrative law to the opposing claims about nondelegation. This lawyer's trick nicely throws the question to the other side, but if the larger question about the constitutionality of administrative law is to be taken seriously, it must be understood more seriously—not merely as a lawyer's game about nondelegation, but as the real-world problem of whether Congress can transfer its powers.

Making matters worse, the focus on "the nondelegation doctrine" reduces the controversy to one of mere doctrine, as if no larger principle were at stake. This emphasis on doctrine suggests that the question can be resolved simply by looking to case law, thus allowing the snappy argument that "the nondelegation doctrine is dead." It does not make sense, however, to place profound problems of constitutional law on precedents relating to a narrow doctrine, let alone a doctrine stated so narrowly that it fails to give expression to the underlying principle. Again, if the defense of administrative law is to be taken seriously, it needs to be understood more seriously—not as a technical slap-down, but as a dispute about principle.[b]

---

b. Although this book focuses on the principle of delegation rather than a nondelegation doctrine, some of the arguments about such a doctrine are important. For example, Gary Lawson argues that a non-delegation doctrine can be discerned in the necessary and proper clause. Lawson urges that the clause's grant of power is subject to a reasonableness limitation and that the "proper" requirement incorporates "structural principles." More generally, Lawson and Patricia Granger propose a jurisdictional interpretation of the "proper" requirement. All of this is very valuable as far it goes, but it is important to keep in mind two more basic points.

First, delegation is a principle underlying all grants of power by the people, and thus the barrier to subdelegation is not merely a doctrine or implication derived from the Constitution's text. And because the barrier to subdelegation arises from the initial delegation of power by the people, it precludes much more than the subdelegation of legislative power through the necessary and proper clause. More broadly, it bars any subdelegation of legislative power.

To this end, it is essential to put aside the focus on nondelegation and to concentrate instead on the underlying principle of delegation. It thereby becomes possible to observe—what usually is missed—that administrative law is merely a matter of subdelegation. When a principal delegates power to an agent, the agent ordinarily cannot subdelegate the power to a sub-agent, as this runs counter to the apparent intent of the principal. In individual circumstances, this is a matter of personal freedom; in politics, it is a foundation of constitutional liberty.

Delegation As a Constitutional Principle

Defenders of administrative law (such as Cass Sunstein) demand historical evidence of a nondelegation doctrine and protest that the Constitution does not expressly adopt such a doctrine.[6] But this misses the point, for there clearly was an underlying principle about delegation, which had implications for subdelegation. Delegation was the principle by which the people established their republic and kept their power superior to that of their government, including its legislature.

The best evidence of the pervasiveness of the principle is that it already was applied at a constitutional level to English monarchs. It has been seen that they traditionally had a prerogative power to dispense with the law. Yet if the dispensing power was inherent in the monarch, could she delegate it? Queen Elizabeth had done precisely this. Probably to raise money, she granted one of her courtiers "the penalty and benefit of a penal statute, with power to dispense with the said statute."[7] This was of dubious legality, for it was one thing to sell the right to receive the fines collected under a statute, but quite another to convey the power to dispense with the act.[c]

When, in 1605, under Elizabeth's successor James I, the judges were asked for an advisory opinion about her grant, all of them resolved that it was "utterly against law":

Second, although it is true that the necessary and proper clause does not authorize the subdelegation of legislative power, this is not merely because of the implications of the words "necessary" and "proper." More concretely, as will be seen, the necessary and proper clause authorizes Congress to do what is necessary and proper for carrying out *vested* powers, and it thereby avoids granting Congress any authority to restructure such powers.[*]

c. Even the Crown lawyers who drafted the grant recognized that Elizabeth could not give away the formal power to dispense with the statute, for a dispensation was possible only under her great seal. They therefore stipulated that the recipient of her grant could authorize the lord chancellor or keeper of the great seal to make dispensations "to whom he pleased."[*]

[W]hen a statute is made *pro bono publico*, and the king (as the head of the commonwealth, and the fountain of justice and mercy) is by the whole realm trusted with it, this confidence and trust is so inseparably joined and annexed to the royal person of the king in so high a point of sovereignty, that he cannot transfer it to the disposition or power of any private person, or to any private use: for it was committed to the king by all his subjects for the good of the commonwealth.

Thus, even under James I, the judges recognized that the king's prerogative power came from his subjects—that he was exercising a power delegated by the people. As a result, "the king cannot commit the sword of his justice, or the oil of his mercy, concerning any penal statute to any subject." Having been given to the king, these royal powers "cannot by law be transferred."[8]

It is a conclusion that American judges might well recall. Of course, English judges could not hold legislative acts unlawful, for Parliament was the high court, and its acts were akin to its judgments. Therefore, although the judges could bar the king from delegating his powers, they could not overturn any act of the legislature delegating its powers. Nonetheless, if the English judges could hold a royal act unlawful because it transferred a power that the people placed in their sovereign, American judges should not have much difficulty holding congressional acts unlawful for transferring a power that the people have placed in their legislature.

In fact, parliamentary subdelegations were widely understood to be unlawful. Englishmen of whiggish views tended to argue that legislative power came from the people and that the legislature therefore could not subdelegate its power to others. John Locke, for example, recognized that in England "the legislative" consisted of the king in Parliament and that it enjoyed "but a delegated power from the people." Locke's expression of these ideas was particularly influential and has been noted by a range of scholars (including Larry Alexander, Ernest Gellhorn, and Saikrishna Prakash). Most generally, Locke argued that "the constitution of the legislative" was "the original and supreme act of the society, antecedent to all positive laws in it, and depending wholly on the people," and therefore "no inferior power can alter it."[9] More specifically, he argued that the people's delegation of legislative power to the legislative body precluded it from transferring its power.

As Locke explained, "The legislative cannot transfer the power of making laws to any other hands. For it being but a delegated power from the people, they, who have it, cannot pass it over to others." This followed not simply from their constitution, but from the nature of constitutions:

> The people alone can appoint the form of the commonwealth, which is by constituting the legislative, and appointing in whose hands that shall be. And when the people have said, We will submit to rules, and be governed by laws made by such men, and in such forms, no body else can say other men shall make laws for them; nor can the people be bound by any laws, but such as are enacted by those, whom they have chosen, and authorized to make laws for them. The power of the legislative[,] being derived from the people by a positive voluntary grant and institution, can be no other, than what that positive grant conveyed, which being only to make laws, and not to make legislators, the legislative can have no power to transfer their authority of making laws, and place it in other hands.

On these assumptions, both constitutional law and "the law of God and nature" barred subdelegation. Thus, "[t]he legislative neither must nor can transfer the power of making laws to anybody else, or place it anywhere but where the people have."[10]

The application of these constitutional ideals to Parliament became evident in 1716 in the debates over the Septennial Act. In 1694, Parliament adopted the Triennial Act, which required that Parliament meet and have new elections at least every three years, and although this was merely a statute, it was understood by Whigs to be declaratory of a constitutional principle. In 1716, however, the Whigs sought to preserve their parliamentary majority, and they therefore passed the Septennial Act. This statute abandoned triennial elections and thereby extended the duration of the existing Parliament, thus giving members of Parliament, mostly Whigs, longer terms than those for which they were elected.

Taking up whiggish arguments, Tories complained that Parliament had reconveyed its power. John Snell, for example, quoted John Locke to show that "the purpose of this bill . . . is not within the compass of the trust reposed in us by the people." Reciting Locke's familiar assumption that "[t]he power of the legislative" was "derived from the people by a positive voluntary grant and institution," Snell further quoted that the legislative "can be no other than what that positive grant conveyed" and that "the legislative can have no power of transferring their authority of making laws, and placing it in other hands." Accordingly, the Septennial Act was "an open violation of the peoples liberties, or, to speak most mildly of it, a breach of our trust." Notwithstanding these arguments, the bill passed, but this prompted further protest, most prominently from a group of Lords, that the act was "in subversion of so essential a part of our constitution."[11]

From the time of the Septennial Act until after the American Revolution, it is difficult to find acts of Parliament that subdelegated legislative power. Thereafter, substantial delegations slowly become apparent. In 1783, at the end of the war with America, Parliament authorized the king in council to adjust duties on foreign trade with the United States. Parliament carefully authorized this power only until the end of its next session, thus making the king's power dependent on a renewal of the statutory authorization. Subject only to this caution, however, orders in council thereafter became a conventional form of subdelegated legislation on foreign trade. Eventually, in the 1830s and '40s, Parliament authorized commissions to issue binding regulations on domestic matters, beginning of course with regulations that bound the poor.[12] At least, however, until after the American Revolution, Parliament generally did not delegate legislative power.

The exceptions prove the rule. In one sort of exception, Parliament authorized royal regulations restricting the export of arms and ammunition. In another type of execption, Parliament authorized royal regulations imposing quarantines—usually on vessels arriving in times of plague, but sometimes also domestically to limit cattle distemper.[13] These exceptions had historical explanations in terms of residual elements of the king's prerogative.[d] But the underlying explanation was that Parliament was willing

---

d. The historical explanations were problematic. First, the king's quarantine power was sometimes justified as a remnant of his traditional prerogatives. As observed by Francis Sullivan, the "performance of quarantine" was among "the ancient and undoubted prerogatives of the king alone," and a subject who disobeyed the king's quarantine regulations was punishable "as if these acts were exercised by the whole legislature." Recognizing the constitutional danger in such an argument, Sullivan promptly added that "with respect to making general rules and ordinances, affecting the previous rights of the people, the case is very different."

Second, the royal power to regulate exports of arms and ammunition was at times grounded on the king's property rights. In this view, he had a property interest in all English deposits of saltpeter, thus giving him a personal power over the export of ammunition. Such an argument, however, did not support his control over arms, and it thus was too narrow to do the work attributed to it.

In short, the historical justifications tended to be either constitutionally questionable or too narrow. The absolute power of Parliament was therefore a more solid, if dangerous foundation for the king's power to issue binding regulations on quarantines and the export of arms and ammunition.

The prerogative underpinnings, however, were not irrelevant, for the statutes authorized only the king in council, not his subordinates, to make the regulations. This suggests that Parliament was recognizing an inherent personal royal authority rather than a broader executive power. Incidentally, the cattle distemper required a quarantine within the country rather than merely at the border, and because the quarantine thereby went dangerously beyond traditional quarantines, Parliament gave only temporary authority for the distemper regulations—an auin an emergency to let the king act temporarily outside the law. Parliament was often said to enjoy absolute power, and on this assumption, it violated constitutional principles to authorize irregular measures in emergencies.

One way or another, beyond these narrow exceptions, Parliament (until after the American Revolution) largely lived up to the constitutional principle against any delegation of legislative power. Constitutional debates about delegation therefore continued to focus on the Septennial Act.

From a Tory perspective, as expressed by Blackstone, the Septennial Act proved that Parliament had an absolute power to "change and create afresh even the constitution of the kingdom and of parliaments themselves." In contrast, from a radical Whig viewpoint, the statute was a lone departure from constitutional principle. DeLolme argued that "if we except" the Septennial Act, "we shall not find" that Parliament had changed "any law" enacted since the Restoration that "may really be called constitutional."[14] The statute thus was interpreted in different ways, either to confirm that Parliament had a power above the constitution or to show that it generally was limited by the constitution.

Either way, the Septennial Act was anything but an example of what a legislature could do under law. Americans such as James Madison therefore tended to take up the Tory view, but now as a complaint—the statute being proof that the English considered "the authority of the parliament . . . transcendent and uncontrollable, as well with regard to the constitution, as the ordinary objects of legislative provision."[15]

Whereas in England the legislature enjoyed this absolute power over the constitution, in America legislatures were constitutionally limited, and they therefore could not claim to transfer their power. In particular, because the people's delegation of legislative power was legally binding on the legislature, the legislature could not subdelegate this power. The way in which an ordinary American worked through such ideas can be seen in the notebook of George Gilmer—a military officer from Virginia. Echoing Locke, he wrote: "Government [is] dissolved when the legislative is altered broken or dissolved." More publicly, an essayist observed that legislative power could not be "transferred," as this would "surpass the power of legislation and require the assent of the people at large." Again, "Mr. Locke's reasoning upon this head seems to be decisive. The legislature cannot transfer the power of making laws to any other hands; for it being a delegated power from the people, they who have it cannot pass it over to others."[16]

---

thority that lasted merely eight months and then to the end of the next session of Parliament, at which point there had to be another authorization statute.*

Subdelegation thus turned on the central question of modern government, whether power arises from the people or from government. Some Englishmen defended the delegation of legislative power on the ground that the final power of the society rested in Parliament, which therefore had absolute power, including a power to transfer its lawmaking powers to others. On both sides of the Atlantic, however, advocates of limited government recognized that if the supreme power was in the people, their constitution limited the legislature, not least by confining legislative power where the people had put it. To suggest otherwise was to conclude that power arose from the legislature rather than from the people and that its power could trump theirs.

Considered from a slightly different angle, the people's delegation of legislative power to their elected legislature was the very nature of republican government. As Madison explained in *Federalist* number 10, the first of the "great points of difference between a democracy and a republic" was "the delegation of the government, in the latter, to a small number of citizens elected by the rest."[17] From this perspective, the subdelegation of legislative power to administrative agencies departs not merely from the constitution, but from republican government itself.

Evidently, far from being a mere doctrine or a mere nicety of political theory, the effect of delegation in precluding any subdelegation was a foundation of political freedom. In a republican government, the people delegated legislative power to their representatives and to them alone. And in a constitutional government, after the people transferred such power to their legislature, the legislature could not constitutionally transfer the power to others. On these overlapping assumptions, when the people of the United States delegated legislative power to Congress, they barred Congress from subdelegating it.[e]

---

e. Among the defenses of subdelegation is the suggestion (by Adrian Vermeule and Eric Posner) that the prohibition against subdelegation of legislative power means simply: "Neither Congress nor its members may delegate to anyone else the authority to vote on federal statutes or to exercise other *de jure* powers of federal legislators."

This theory is without historical support. Indeed, it collides with the widespread eighteenth-century assumption (noted in earlier chapters) that legislative power was not merely the power that a constitution happened to place in the legislature, but more fundamentally was a specialized type of power that needed to be kept in the legislature.

The theory also is conceptually awkward, for it reduces the legislative powers of Congress to the voting powers of individual legislators, thus collapsing the power of the legislative body into the power enjoyed by its members. When the theory is understood in a way that avoids this difficulty—for example, when it is understood to mean that only Congress can make acts of Congress—it becomes so minimal and obvious as to be nearly a tautology.*

386 / Chapter Twenty

The Principle Standing Alone

Even when the constitutional analysis is cast aside and delegation is considered as a mundane legal principle, delegation does not do the work attributed to it. Rather than justify administrative legislation, the concept of delegation actually shows that Congress cannot subdelegate its lawmaking power.

Under agency law, even a principal faces limits on what he can delegate. He cannot delegate an act which is illegal. Nor can he delegate the performance of an act that is personal in its nature.[18]

The limits on agents are even greater, for they enjoy only such power as has been delegated to them. The initial delegation thus implies *potestas delegata non potest delegare*—that delegated power cannot be further delegated. The logic is simply that if the principal selects his agent for her knowledge, skill, trustworthiness, or other personal qualities, he presumably gave the power to her, not anyone else. Of course, a principal could expressly authorize subdelegation, but he could not otherwise be understood to have intended this. As put by Justice Story in an early Supreme Court case, "the general rule of law is that a delegated authority cannot be delegated."[19]

On such reasoning, the principle of delegation bars any subdelegation of legislative power. In the Constitution, the people delegate legislative powers to Congress. The people, moreover, specify that they grant the legislative powers to a Congress "consist[ing] of a Senate and House of Representatives," with members chosen in specified ways. The delegation to Congress thus is to a body chosen for its institutional qualities, including members chosen by their constituents for their personal qualities. Congress and its members therefore cannot subdelegate their power.

Express Bar to Subdelegation

Not content to rely merely on the implication from the principle of delegation, the Constitution emphasizes that *all* legislative powers granted to the United States shall be in Congress. It thereby expressly bars the subdelegation of such powers.

Defenders of delegated administrative power protest that the Constitution does not expressly bar the delegation of legislative power—as put by Cass Sunstein, it "does not in terms forbid delegation of that power."[20] But it is strange to complain that a question of underlying principle must rest on the Constitution's terms, and it is stranger still to make such a complaint without even considering the Constitution's words.

When granting executive or judicial power, the Constitution does not speak of *all* such power. It states, "The executive Power of the United States shall be vested in a President of the United States of America" and subsequently provides for the appointment of officers of the United States. Similarly, it states, "The judicial Power of the United States, shall be in one supreme Court, and in such inferior Courts as the Congress may . . . ordain and establish." By omitting the word *all*, the Constitution avoids granting these powers exclusively to the president or the Supreme Court, thus leaving room for some executive power to be allocated to a range of executive officers and some judicial power to be allocated to inferior courts.

In contrast, when granting legislative power, the Constitution speaks of *all* legislative powers. It recites: "All legislative Powers herein granted shall be vested in a Congress of the United States." The Constitution authorizes no inferior legislative bodies, and the Constitution therefore can be explicit that Congress enjoys *all* legislative powers. Thus, for example, although the president can subdelegate some executive power to his subordinates, Congress cannot subdelegate any of its legislative powers, for they all rest in Congress.[f]

Of course, the Constitution could have expressly authorized the subdelegation of some legislative power. It then would have dropped the word *all* and added a phrase permitting Congress to subdelegate one power or another. But this is exactly what the Constitution did not do. As observed

---

f. A hint of this conclusion about *all* legislative powers (even if not the underlying argument from the contrasting words of Articles II and III) can be found in Justice Clarence Thomas's concurrence in *Whitman v. American Trucking Associations.* Thomas Merrill argues against this concurrence by suggesting that, although Article I initially places legislative powers in Congress, it allows Congress to delegate them.

In support of his conclusion, Merrill does not point to any body of eighteenth-century opinion, but this does not mean there is no eighteenth-century evidence. As observed in this chapter, radical whigs through much of the eighteenth century and, more generally, late eighteenth-century Americans typically assumed that when the people in their constitution placed legislative power in the legislature, this body could not then subdelegate its power.

On behalf of his view, Merrill focuses on the words of the U.S. Constitution, noting that Article I conveyed to Congress only the legislative powers "herein granted." He surely is correct that the Constitution thereby aimed to "avoid any inference that Congress was being given plenary legislative authority." But it is unclear how this is relevant to the question of subdelegation. Certainly, the goal of limiting Congress to the enumerated legislative powers does not explain why Article I stated that *all* of the legislative powers shall be vested in Congress. The word is not redundant, however, when one turns to the delegation problem. Whereas Articles II and III omitted this word in order to allow their powers to be given, respectively, to officers subordinate to the president and to inferior courts, Article I carefully assured that *all* of the granted legislative powers were to be in Congress, thereby precluding any shift of such powers to other bodies.*

in chapter 5, some state constitutions generally granted legislative power to their legislatures and then expressly left room for them to subdelegate the suspending power to their executives. The U.S. Constitution, however, did not authorize any subdelegation.

Americans clearly understood how to write constitutions that expressly permitted the subdelegation of legislative power to the executive, and they did not do this in the federal constitution. On the contrary, as apparent from the word *all*, they expressly barred any such subdelegation.

Counterexamples

Notwithstanding the simple pattern observed here in federal lawmaking, there were many local and other rules that arose in more complex circumstances and that therefore require more detailed consideration. It is particularly worth examining these other rules because they sometimes have been taken to be models for the sort of subdelegation that now underlies administrative law. The local and other examples, however, need to be understood on their own terms, and they do not really offer support for the subdelegation of federal legislative power.

State "Delegation" to Municipalities

States are often said to delegate local legislative power to municipalities and other local bodies, and it therefore may be thought that this delegation of legislative power offers a model for such delegation at the federal level. Municipal legislation, however, has long been very different from administrative legislation.

Traditionally, much local lawmaking in England was without central authorization. Just as local custom was understood to arise from the local people, local legislation came from their self-governing bodies. Gradually, however, many local bodies sought the legitimacy of royal charters that authorized them to make local law. Indeed, the efficacy of local law came to depend on its enforceability in royal courts, and therefore an entire body of law developed on the question of which local customs and enactments would be recognized by the courts as part of the law of the land.[21] Along the same lines, in America, it came to be understood that all local legislation in a state was binding only as permitted by state law.

Local lawmaking, however, typically was understood not as a delegated exercise of the state's general legislative power, but rather as a distinctly local sort of representative legislation—authorized and limited by the state but arising from the local populace. The local consent was essential, for only by this means could the local law be binding. Consequently, although a state could establish local governments, including their boundaries, it generally was taken for granted that where a state authorized local legislative power, it had to leave this local legislation in a local represenative body. By the same token, it was understood that the state could not give local representative bodies legislative power over matters outside their locality—the only exception in America being for adjacent areas that were not yet incorporated.

Thus, although nowadays local power is sometimes said to be delegated, it cannot be understood to be delegated in the same sense as administrative power. Rather than a delegated portion of general legislative power, it is a distinctively local sort of legislative power, which must be authorized by the state, but which is located in a representative body, and which thus derives its legitimacy from local elections.

Federal "Delegation" to Territories

Another version of the claim that local legislative power is delegated can be observed in the federal authorization of such power in the territories. Such authorization sometimes is seized upon as a justification for delegated administrative lawmaking, but once again, it is very different.

Like the state authorization of power in municipalities, the federal authorization of power in the territories merely concerns local legislation. As with the state authorization, moreover, the federal authorization recognizes that, if there is to be local legislative power, it must arise from the local population. Again, therefore, it is not so much a top-down delegation of general legislative power as an authorization of a local legislative power that comes from below. If this is delegation, it is delegation of a distinctive sort.

These assumptions about local legislation based in local representation can be observed even in the District of Columbia. Although the Constitution gave Congress the power "[t]o exercise exclusive Legislation in all Cases whatsoever, over such District," this seems to have meant "exclusive" as to the states that ceded land for the district. Accordingly, in deference to the principle of local self-government, Congress in 1802 authorized a local representative government there, with local lawmaking power. Only much later, in 1874, did Congress deviate from this approach by placing the government of the District of Columbia in appointed commissioners. Since 1973, however, Congress has reverted to placing the government of the district in local hands.[22] Although the people of the district do not have the right to vote for federal legislators, it is widely understood that, if there is to be a local legislative power for the district, it should be under local control.

As it happens, the poverty of municipal, territorial, or other local legislation as a model for administrative law is recognized in Supreme Court doctrine. Municipalities, territories, and the District of Columbia all enjoy expansive local legislative power in their localities, without any need to justify what they do in terms of state or federal legislative policies. Put another way, the localities are limited by state or federal law but are not confined to carrying out such law.

In contrast, it has been seen that under Supreme Court doctrine, administrators can legislate only where Congress has set forth an "intelligible principle" to guide them. Thus, at least in theory, administrative lawmakers must limit themselves to carrying out congressional commands. Of course, as a practical matter, this is not much of a limitation, but it shows that, even in the theory of administrative law, the municipal, territorial, and other local legislation is very different from administrative legislation. These two types of legislation arise from divergent assumptions, and the lawfulness of the one does not show the lawfulness of the other.

Municipal Delegation to Administrative Bodies

A further argument from local legislation observes that American municipalities, already in the eighteenth century, sometimes authorized health boards and other subordinate bodies to exercise particular legislative and judicial powers. The suggestion is that the early municipal subdelegation offers a justification for congressional delegation. The analogy, however, is weak.

Unlike the federal constitution, municipal charters often blurred rather than separated legislative, executive, and judicial powers. The charter of the city of New York gave legislative power to the Common Council, consisting of the mayor, recorder, three or more aldermen, and three or more assistants, and it established judicial power in the Mayor's Court, consisting of the mayor, recorder, and three to five aldermen.[23]

These municipal constitutions, moreover, had long been understood to allow some municipal rearrangements of power. Such constitutions came from above rather than below—from the Crown in England and from state legislatures in America—and they therefore were not always considered fundamental in the same way as constitutions from the people. For example, a long line of cases, since at least the sixteenth century, had allowed municipal legislative bodies to restrict suffrage, and although eighteenth-century cases attempted to limit these deviations from municipal constitutions, the common law continued to leave room for such violations.[24] It therefore is not surprising that municipalities did not always confine their legislative and judicial powers to the mechanisms established by their charters.[g]

The subdelegation of legislative or judicial power by municipalities therefore cannot be taken to show the lawfulness of such subdelegation by Congress. Instead, the subdelegation merely reveals the loose drafting and still looser interpretation of many eighteenth-century municipal charters.

Rules of Court

Courts have long made rules to govern their proceedings, and they sometimes have done so with legislative authorization. Such rules therefore have been seized upon as early examples of delegated legislation.[25] Court rules, however, generally were not considered legally binding.

The rules of a court usually affected a range of persons, without quite binding them. Most immediately, they directed court officers. Similarly, they directed lawyers, who were understood to be officers of the court. In limiting what these officers could do, court rules also laid out the conditions for bringing actions or making defenses—for example, that plaintiffs had to file their motions with the file clerk and that defendants had to respond within a specified time.

Because court rules were not understood to impose legally binding constraints, they were the judicial equivalent of executive orders to executive officers—as when the Treasury issued regulations instructing treasury officers about the distribution of pensions. Such regulations incidentally revealed how members of the public could qualify for pensions, but they did this by instructing executive officers rather than binding the public. Of course, one might not find it entirely satisfying to consider rules of court mere orders to officers, and courts could give unusual effect to such rules by holding offenders in contempt of court. Nonetheless, it made more sense

---

g. For example, municipalities increasingly left health regulation—mostly sanitary and quarantine precautions against epidemics—in the hands of administrative officers, usually members of boards of health and sometimes health commissioners. Even so, it is difficult to find eighteenth-century instances in which such boards or commissioners made binding rules for persons on land rather than on vessels, except where the board was elected and thereby (as in Boston) acquired the power ordinarily enjoyed by selectmen, or where the city charter did not separate governmental powers (as in New York).*

to view rules of court as orders to officers than to view them as binding constraints of law, in the manner of a statute against theft. Courts therefore could issue such rules without intruding on legislative power.[h]

The courts, moreover, had for centuries enjoyed their own power to make their rules, and there was reason to think that this power was inherent in the courts or at least implied by their being established to do justice. As a result, when Congress offered statutory authorization for such rules, it was not clearly delegating power. Congress had the power to establish the courts, and it therefore could authorize the courts to make rules, and even could limit their rulemaking authority, but if the power to make rules of courts was inherent in the very existence of a court, it was not obvious that the congressional authorization involved a delegation of power, let alone of legislative power.

The question came before the Supreme Court in 1825 in *Wayman v. Southard*. Congress had authorized federal courts to follow the forms of process of the states in which they sat, subject to alterations and additions made by the federal courts, and in *Wayman* this authorization of the courts was challenged as an unconstitutional delegation of legislative power. Speaking for the Court, Chief Justice Marshall explained that although Congress could regulate the courts, it also could authorize the courts to regulate themselves, for such regulation was not exclusively or strictly legislative. "It will not be contended, that Congress can delegate to the courts, or to any other tribunals, powers which are strictly and exclusively legislative." Nonetheless, "Congress may certainly delegate to others, powers which the legislature may rightfully exercise itself," and these included the power to make rules of court.[26]

Marshall did not elaborate the distinction between the "strictly and exclusively legislative" powers and those that were merely among those that "the legislature may rightfully exercise." Instead, he merely observed, "The line has not been exactly drawn which separates those important subjects, which must be entirely regulated by the legislature itself, from those

---

h. Rules of court thus stood in contrast to the fees owed by litigants to court officers. Because such fees had to be binding, they had to be enacted by statute, and where they had not been enacted, judges had to treat any claim for a fee as a matter of restitution. Echoing Chief Justice Holt, Chief Justice Edmund Pendleton of Virginia opined in 1774 that, in the absence of legislation imposing a fee, the judge in a case "may direct what in his opinion is a reasonable fee, but this is not binding and conclusive on the party[,] who may insist on its being tried by a jury on a quantum meruit—and if the jury find it a reasonable [fee] it then becomes an established fee." In recognition of the distinction between setting fees and making rules of court, Congress later authorized the federal courts to make rules but reserved to itself the power over fees.*

of less interest, in which a general provision may be made, and power given to those who are to act under such general provisions to fill up the details."[27, i]

Marshall shied away from discussing the underlying principle—that Congress could not delegate a power to make legally binding rules—because the process at stake in *Wayland* was an execution and a replevin bond taken on the execution. The rules on such process could well be understood to bind members of the public, not merely direct court officers. As observed by counsel in opposition to the delegation, the rules on execution and replevin were those "by which the citizen shall be deprived of his liberty or property, to enforce a judicial sentence," and "the power to prescribe such rules belongs exclusively to the legislative department."[28] It thus was doubtful whether the court rules at stake in *Wayland* were justifiable under the traditional conception of legislative power. Rather than deal with this problem, Marshall evaded by generalizng that Congress could delegate rulemaking where it was not exclusively legislative.

The power to make binding laws, however, was considered naturally legislative, and to the extent the Constitution granted legislative powers, it carefully stated that they all shall be vested in Congress. It therefore is difficult to distinguish between exclusively legislative matters, which are confined to Congress, and other legislative matters, which can be vested elsewhere. Indeed, this sort of distinction is unnecessary for understanding situtations such that in as *Wayland*, for one need only recognize that, although Congress can make rules of court that are legally binding, a court cannot. A court can issue rules of court directing its officers and can fire officers who fail to comply, but even with congressional authorization, it cannot make its rules binding in the sense of having the obligation of law—this being the problem with the particular rules of court in *Wayland*, a problem that Marshall was unwilling to confront.

The logic of the traditional distinction can be substantiated by applying it to another supposed delegation of legislative power, the congressional authorization of executive regulations directing executive officers in the distribution of government benefits. As already suggested, these regula-

---

i. Some commentators (notably Gary Lawson) rely on Marshall's notion of importance as a measure of what cannot be subdelegated. Marshall's generalization, however, clearly was not intended by him to be the measure of what Congress could not do; nor could so vague a generalization have usefully served as such a measure. In fact, the executive has long made important and lawful rules (including rules on the duties of executive officers, on aliens, and on the distribution of benefits). It thus is mistaken to focus on importance as the measure of what could not be left to the executive.*

tions affect the officers and potential recipients but do not bind them and therefore need not be enacted by the legislature. Of course, Congress could directly adopt such regulations and make them legally binding, whether on executive officers or the broader public. But when the executive makes regulations, it is another matter. Then, although the executive can fire officers who do not comply, the regulations cannot be considered legally binding.

In short, many rules—such as rules of court and rules on how executive officers should distribute benefits—can be subject to the power of different parts of government, but with different effects. Rules that are mere directions to subordinate officers can come from the courts or the executive, but legally binding rules must come from Congress.

Court rules therefore do not support the claims for delegated administrative legislation. Like other regulations directing government officers, they are no precedent for regulations that bind.

Military Orders

Perhaps the most revealing counterexample can be found in military orders. Although some of these orders look very much like delegated legislation, they are an exception that proves the rule.

As already noted, military law has long been distinct from civilian law, and one central difference is that military law allows delegated legislation. Under the authority of the commander in chief, a military officer can issue orders that bind subordinates in the manner of legislation, and these orders are enforceable in the military justice system. Only Congress, however, can make rules that bind in the civilian system, and the Constitution therefore authorizes Congress to make rules for the military.

The Constitution's treatment of the military thus does not show the lawfulness of delegated lawmaking power. On the contrary, it confirms that such delegation is not possible in the civilian system.

Indeed, military orders are exactly what are precluded in civilian life, and they thus are a reminder of why legislative power cannot be delegated. It will be recalled that, as to civilian executive officers, the executive cannot issue legally binding orders. Thus, if an executive officer, even in a most sensitive position, refuses to obey an order, he cannot be prosecuted for the mere refusal. Of course he can be fired, and if his conduct violates statutory prohibitions on mis- or malfeasance in office, he can be sued or prosecuted, but that is all. For example, if Congress were to enact that civilian executive officers have a legal duty to obey rules or orders, this would be of dubious constitutionality, for it would give superior executive officers a binding lawmaking or adjudicatory power. In other words, only in the military can the executive issue binding orders to its officers, and except where disobedience to military orders violates a rule made by Congress, such orders are enforceable only in the military justice system.[29]

How then can the executive issue legally binding orders or rules to the people of the United States? If the president cannot issue such orders even to the executive's civilian officers, and if the people are not military subordinates of the president, neither he nor his officers can issue binding orders to the people.

The relationship of military officers to their subordinates is not the model for the relationship of executive officers to the people of the United States. The people of the United States are subject to the laws made by their legislature, not to mere executive commands.

No Delegation of a Dispensing Power

Among the powers not delegated to Congress was the power to waive or dispense with the obligation of law. This power nonetheless has been revived in administrative law, the underlying assumption being that, if Congress can delegate legislative power, it also can delegate the power to dispense with the delegated legislation. Congress, however, cannot delegate a power it does not have.

Already in England and eighteenth-century America, it was recognized that the dispensing power was not part of the legislative power. The suspending power was an aspect of the legislative power, for the legislature itself could pass a statute to repeal or temporarily abate prior legislation. As seen in chapter 5, however, the dispensing power was not legislative, for it was understood to relieve persons of a law that was left unamended and unmodified. Nor was it an executive or judicial power, because the executive and the courts could not alter the law. Thus, although some American constitutions permitted the suspending power and even its delegation, none of them authorized the dispensing power or its delegation.

It therefore is puzzling how Congress can delegate the executive to waive or dispense with any law, for Congress itself does not have any such power. The argument that Congress can delegate a lawmaking power at least rests on the reality that the Congress has the lawmaking power. But the argument that Congress can delegate a waiver or dispensing power lacks any such foundation, for not even Congress can spare persons from compliance with a statute it does not alter or qualify.

Of course, if the waivers came in the form of regulations, it at least would be coherent to justify them as a subdelegated exercise of legislative power. Congress always can modify the effect of one statute by passing another. Accordingly, if the subdelegation of legislative power were lawful, the executive could easily adopt an administrative rule limiting the reach of an earlier one.

Administrative waivers, however, are not regulations or amendments to regulations. On the contrary, they are exercises of power not only outside the law but also outside administrative rulemaking. As explained by the DC Circuit, a waiver is different from rulemaking, because it is not adopted through an "agency process for formulating, amending, or repealing a rule."[30]

It therefore is of no use to protest, as do some defenders of waivers, that when Congress authorizes them, it merely is delegating its power to pass special legislation. In special acts, Congress at least modifies the effect of one statute by passing another. In contrast, waivers are not adopted as rules or amendments to rules. Rather, they are mere executive dispensations. They simply are letters that the government sends privately to favored persons, purporting to relieve them from compliance with regulations that remain unmodified.

Thus, even if agency rules are a form of delegated legislative power, mere dispensations or waivers are not. Not being legislative, they are not part of the power enjoyed by Congress. They therefore are not something that Congress could subdelegate, even if subdelegation were lawful.

Subdelegation of Judicial Power

Regardless of whether subdelegation were constitutional as to legislative power, it still would run into difficulty with judicial power. Administrative law tends to be justified as a delegation of legislative power, without much being said about any delegation of judicial power. But the administrative adjudication also rests on assumptions about delegation, and this raises particularly serious problems.[31]

It is one thing to claim that Congress can subdelegate its legislative power to the executive, but how can Congress subdelegate judicial power to the executive? The judicial power belongs to the courts rather than Congress, and Congress therefore has no judicial power to delegate. Is it to be assumed that Congress can delegate the power of another branch? Thus far, not even the defenders of administrative law have argued this. The reality is that the Constitution grants "[t]he judicial Power of the United States" to the courts, and therefore even if such power could be subdelegated, Congress is not the branch that could do this.

Adding to the difficulty is that not even the courts or their judges can delegate judicial power. Already in the medieval year books it was said that "judicial power" could "not be assigned." Thus, as put by an early law lecturer, "if the king makes me a justice, and grants me that I may appoint another person at my pleasure, that is void."[32] At common law, in other words, judicial power was inalienable. It was delegated to the judges on account of their learning and integrity, and they therefore could not subdelegate it.

As it happens, there once was considerable scholarship on the subdelegation of judicial office, but it does not offer support for administrative adjudication. In Roman times, the emperor delegated his judicial power in his provinces to his proconsuls, and each proconsul delegated at least part of this power to his deputy. The main dispute was whether a proconsul could delegate his judicial power before he entered his province, and thus before he himself enjoyed any such power, or only upon his arrival. Following the Roman model, the civil and canon laws allowed the delegation of judicial power, and along such lines English kings issued commissions for the civilian Court of Delegates, which had appellate jurisdiction in ecclesiastical and admiralty cases.[33]

The common law, however, took a very different approach, as explained in the seventeenth century by Sir Leoline Jenkins—a leading British civil law judge. He noted that, in the Roman or civil law, "[t]he prince makes a judge and gives him power to make a deputy in the province committed to him." The common law, however, made no such assumption: "Our law is that a judge cannot make a deputy . . . for he is constituted upon presumption of his knowledge and integrity (qualities personal and not communicable)."[34]

Of course, judges appointed clerks to undertake merely ministerial tasks, and they often consulted each other and their clerks. Similarly, the chancellor appointed masters in Chancery for ministerial tasks.[35] But judges could not delegate their office or duty of giving judgment, for they were commissioned as judges to exercise their own, independent judgment. Accordingly, "[n]o judicial power, or power to hold a court and decide causes, can be delegated." As summarized in the twentieth century, "the common law knows of no such institution as a deputy judge."[36, j]

---

j. Already at the time of the prerogative courts, one of the objections to the High Commission and other ecclesiastical courts was "because they judge, or exercise jurisdiction by depu-

From this common law perspective, not even the judges and their courts, let alone Congress, can subdelegate judicial power. In the Constitution, the people of the United States delegate judicial power to courts composed of judges, and as evident from the nomination and confirmation process, judges are appointed for their personal qualities. The judges therefore cannot transfer their office, and the courts cannot transfer their power. Regardless of what they authorize, moreover, the Constitution precludes anyone from becoming a judge of the courts without nomination and confirmation. Thus, even if the courts or judges were inclined to subdelegate judicial power to the executive, it is not apparent how they could do it.

Privatization of Legislative and Judicial Powers

Perhaps the most extraordinary sort of subdelegation is the transfer of legislative and judicial powers not merely to executive agencies, but to private bodies. This sort of delegation is widespread. The resulting privatized power is used to govern investment advisors, securities and commodities exchanges, participants in the exchanges, accountants, clinical laboratories, higher education, nuclear power production, and agricultural marketing. In all of these areas, the federal government authorizes private bodies to engage in binding legislation by enacting rules, standards, or other measures of compliance, and to engage in binding adjudication by means of accrediting, certifying, and licensing.

Of course, if the government merely authorized private bodies to determine and give notice of legal duties or rights, the delegation would not amount to a delegation of legislative or judicial power. But the government typically subdelegates legislative and judicial powers, and in both ways it privatizes powers that the people placed in the government.

The government suggests that the result is private "self-regulation." And, of course, voluntary self-regulation among private parties can be valuable. But the binding legislative power of the government is not the private voluntary power of private parties; it belongs to representatives of the whole people, not to private interests; and there is nothing of self-government in giving dominant economic interests the power to legislate or adjudicate in their own industries, where they can protect themselves and hold down the weak. Far from "self-regulation," this is a gross dereliction of duty.[37]

In fact, this sort of delegation revives the medieval distribution of eco-

---

ties." This delegation was "against the nature of an office of *confidence or trust*," for "as it is *personally inherent*, so it must be personally discharged, and not transported to another."[*]

nomic control to guild-like bodies. Like its medieval predecessor, it allows powerful economic forces, acting with government authority, to bind both themselves and others at the cost of the freedom and constitutional choices of the people. It thus returns to the preconstitutional world in which the government's relinquishment of its powers enables the prevailing forces in each industry to become the real rulers in their fiefdoms.

The danger is not only legislative but also judicial, for even when the private bodies do not legislate, they tend to adjudicate, usually through licensing. The Food and Drug Administration, for example, relies on institutional review boards to license the use of drugs and devices in safety and efficacy tests, and Health and Human Services relies on such boards to license the transfer of medical information (what used to be called "free speech") under HIPAA—the Health Insurance Portability and Accountability Act.

Like government agencies, these private licensing bodies decide who or what is subject to constraint without offering the due process of law. Indeed, because they are private, they can act entirely in private, without hearings or other administrative process. Other administrative adjudication—even much administrative licensing—offers at least its faux process, with ersatz judges, mock courtroom hearings, and imitation rules of evidence. Most of the licensing delegated to private bodies, however, is largely hidden from public view and does not include even the faux process.[38] The delegation of the licensing thus completely evades the due process of law.

Even more than agency licensing, this delegated licensing allows the government to engage in wholesale enforcement and suppression. The Constitution requires the government to act against the public through retail proceedings—through the case-by-case due process of the courts. Licensing, however, permits the government to avoid retail proceedings against offenders, and the delegated licensing enables it even to avoid administrative process. The government thereby can suppress conduct wholesale, without bringing retail proceedings against members of the public, and even without according hearings to those who plead for permission.[k]

Recognizing the dangers of privatizing legislative and judicial powers,

---

k. Most soberingly, the government applies this wholesale suppression to speech. First Amendment scholars often theorize that the licensing of speech or the press is no more dangerous than post-publication constraints. Licensing, however, particularly the delegated licensing, allows the government to suppress speech wholesale, and in fact administrative agencies have reintroduced this sort of suppression on a massive scale.

In the seventeenth century, the Star Chamber delegated much of its licensing of the press to a trade association (the Stationers Company) and to the universities. As a result, rather than have to rely on retail prosecutions in a court with the due process of law, or even on retail prosecutions in the Star Chamber with its inquisitorial process, the government could rely on

the Administrative Conference of the United States acknowledges the risks at the state level but differentiates the federal privatization by emphasizing that it is "audited," which usually means self-auditing or other private auditing. Neither in principle nor as a practical matter does auditing really overcome the difficulties. With or without the auditing, the power delegated to private institutions is even less accountable than that delegated to administrative agencies.[39]

In defense of the privatization of legislative and judicial powers, the federal government offers the telling excuse that it is not competent to regulate some industries. As put by the Administrative Conference of the United States, self-regulation can be preferable to government regulation where the self-governing entities are "directly involved in the regulated activity" and thus may have "more detailed knowledge of the operational or technical aspects of that activity." Obviously, however, as also recognized by the Administrative Conference, self-regulation opens up "significant risks" of "capture of the regulators by the regulated industry" and of "creating barriers to entry or competition."[40]

The whole point of a constitution is to give power to government, so that it can protect individuals and their groups from the predatory tendencies of others. Nonetheless, across much of the American economy, the government now "delegates" its legislative and judicial power to the most powerful interests in society, allowing them to govern the weaker. The risks from economic forces are serious enough on their own, and when combined with privatized government power, they are even worse.

Democratic Control and Administrative Capture

Notwithstanding the weaknesses of the delegation theory, it enjoys considerable support on the assumption that an elected Congress exercises over-

---

the private organizations to control what got printed. The result was to shift control from retail proceedings to wholesale censorship.

Along the same lines, the government nowadays subdelegates control over speech and publication to private organizations and thereby avoids the necessity of particular legal or even administrative prosecutions. For example, just as the Star Chamber once delegated licensing of the press to the universities, Health and Human Services now delegates the licensing of offensive and otherwise disturbing speech and publication in or about human-subjects research—giving the task to universities and, in particular, to their Institutional Review Boards. These boards enforce HHS and other restrictions on speech, partly by threatening scholars with dismissal, but mostly by suggesting that if they are "uncooperative" in submitting to the speech restrictions, the boards will impede their future inquiry and publication. By such means, vast amounts of utterly harmless and profoundly valuable research and its publication have been suppressed.*

sight and control. From this point of view, "democratic" control—actually representative control—can take care of any administrative misconduct.[41] It is no longer always clear, however, who controls whom.

In the traditional version of this danger, a monarch or executive purchased control of the legislature simply by offering personal favors to legislators. The English Crown in the eighteenth century notoriously corrupted Parliament by giving pensions and other benefits to members of Parliament and their relations. Continental rulers also followed this practice, thus shifting control from the purported lawmakers to the executive. Recognizing the effect, Barthold Niebuhr observed in 1822 that, "[w]ith such a power, a chamber can generally be bought; and then the ministerial influence is but the more absolute, while all odium falls upon the nominal law-makers."[42]

The danger under American administrative agencies is slightly different. Agencies sometimes protect themselves from congressional oversight by offering personal favors to congressmen and their families. The administrative influence over Congress, however, more typically plays upon the desire of congressmen to get reelected. Agencies sometimes become politically engaged. Even more seriously, they quietly use their distribution of funds or their binding power in ways that get the attention of legislators. Thus, when a state or an employer within a state needs money, or when they need waivers from overbearing regulations, they and their congressmen become very dependent on the relevant agencies.[43]

The last defense of delegation—that of democratic control—is thus rather dubious. As a formal matter Congress controls executive agencies, but in reality agencies have much power to influence Congress. Congressional control therefore cannot be taken for granted. The nominal lawmakers still enjoy enough power to be blamed for government failings, but the administrative lawmakers have secured considerable independence.

⟨∾⟨∾⟨∾

Far from being merely an abstruse doctrinal matter, the principle of delegation and its implications for subdelegation are the foundation of republican government and constitutional limits. And once this is recognized, delegation is no defense. The people made the original delegation of power, and thus any delegation to the executive is merely a subdelegation, which violates the delegation made by the people.

In barring the subdelegation of legislative power, the Constitution does not rest merely on the general principle of delegation. In addition, with the word *all*, the Constitution expressly bars the subdelegation of legislative powers. As for the supposed delegation of judicial power, the courts and judges cannot subdelegate this power, and Congress cannot give away what belongs to the courts.

To be sure, Congress can authorize the other branches to make non-binding rules, and it can establish and authorize courts to make binding adjudications. But the power to bind, whether by legislation or adjudication, was delegated by the people, respectively, to Congress and the courts, and Congress therefore cannot transfer any such power to anybody.

TWENTY-ONE

Unfederal

Thus far, part IV has focused on how the administrative consolidation of power threatens the horizontal specialization within the federal government, including the divided and representative character of the legislative branch. There also, however, is a vertical specialization between the federal government and the states. Although, on the face of the matter, administrative law does not affect this vertical specialization, it actually goes far toward undermining the federal character of the United States.

Eroding Federalism

The administrative interference with state law is only part of a broader erosion of federalism. This interference, however, stands out as singularly dangerous and unjustified.

The most prominent threat to the vertical specialization of power has been the expansion of congressional power. The Constitution grants Congress only enumerated powers, thus giving the federal government great power over only a specialized range of national matters, such as interstate commerce and the military, and leaving the states with a more general power. The Supreme Court, however, has interpreted some of the enumerated congressional powers very broadly. Thus, whereas traditionally only the states had general legislative power, this now is very nearly shared by the federal government. As a result, federal legislation cuts sharply into the underlying general legislative power of the states.

At least, however, when Congress exercises its expansive power, it relies on enacted federal laws to trump state laws. In contrast, when administrative agencies exercise legislative power, they use mere executive rules and interpretations to brush aside state law.

This matters because administrative law is a much more fertile source of restrictions than the law made by the people or by Congress. The people themselves must agree to constitutional amendments, and the two houses of Congress and the president must agree to statutes, but the executive by itself can adopt federal regulations and thereby render contrary state law and other state action void. Thus, as observed by Bradford Clark, the erosion of the separation of powers also erodes federalism.[1]

The Supremacy of the Law of the Land

The Constitution protects the federal character of American government not only by limiting congressional power and separating federal powers. In addition, it protects federalism through the supremacy of the law of the land.

Supremacy Clause

This protection of federalism is most salient in the Constitution's text. As explained by Clark, when the Constitution specifies what is the supreme law of the land, it addresses whether the executive can make law that binds the states.

After giving Congress legislative power, the Constitution defines "the supreme Law of the Land." In particular, this clause defines the supreme law of the land to include only three things: "This Constitution, and the Laws of the United States which shall be made in Pursuance thereof; and all Treaties made, or which shall be made, under the Authority of the United States, shall be the supreme Law of the Land; and the Judges in every State shall be bound thereby, any Thing in the Constitution or Laws of any State to the Contrary notwithstanding." Other than the Constitution itself and treaties, the laws that amount to the supreme law of the land are "the laws of the United States which shall be made in pursuance" of the Constitution. Much therefore rests on what these laws are.

Clark points out that the laws of the United States made in pursuance of the Constitution appear to be only those made by Congress, not regulations made by the executive. The Constitution carefully places legislative power in Congress, and it specifies the procedures by which Congress can make law. In this context, only the acts of Congress amount to the laws made in pursuance of the Constitution. The supreme law of the land thus does not include administrative rules or interpretation.[2]

On behalf of the claim that administrative law binds the states, it may be thought that when the Constitution speaks of "the laws of the United States which shall be made in pursuance thereof," it means not only the laws made in accord with its lawmaking procedures but also the rules made by procedures authorized by Congress. Yet when the Constitution needed to include laws not made in accord with the Constitution's lawmaking procedures, it defined the supreme law of the land in terms of what was done "under the authority of the United States."

The Constitution had to recognize not only future treaties, made from 1789 onward, but also those adopted earlier by the United States—especially the 1783 Treaty of Paris, which settled the War of Independence against Britain. The Constitution therefore could not specify treaties "made in pursuance" of the Constitution, but instead had to say that "all treaties made, or which shall be made, under the authority of the United States, shall be the supreme Law of the land." Quite apart from what this meant for treaties, it shows that the Constitution distinguished laws made "in pursuance" of the Constitution from those made "under the authority of the United States," thus confirming that the laws made "in pursuance" of the Constitution meant those adopted in accord with its procedures.[3]

The Constitution's text thus reveals how systematically the supreme law of the land includes only the Constitution, acts of Congress, and treaties. Administrative rules, interpretations, and guidance are not part of the supreme law of the land, and they therefore are not supreme over state law.

The Underlying Principle of Supremacy

It is usually assumed that the supremacy mentioned by the Constitution is the supremacy of federal law over state law, and certainly it is at least this. The supremacy of the law of the land, however, has an older history, which reveals an underlying principle of supremacy—one that confirms that administrative acts are not supreme, let alone law.

Already in England, where there were no states, there were questions about the supremacy of the law of the land. The doubts arose because the pope claimed that his canon law was binding in England. In response, Tudor monarchs insisted that their law, the law of the land, was supreme within their realm. This elevation of the law of the land, however, had not only foreign but also domestic implications. After English monarchs relied on the law of the land to resist papal power, English lawyers increasingly stood on the same ground to reject extra- and supralegal royal power.[4]

In other words, the supremacy of the law of the land initially developed against external ecclesiastical law, then against domestic prerogative rule, and only later against the American states. It thus becomes evident that the supremacy of the law of the land mentioned in the U.S. Constitution was not merely an expression of federalism, but was a deep principle about the supremacy of a sovereign's law in its land.

From this perspective, the supreme law of the land stands in contrast not only to state law but also to federal acts that are not the supreme law of the land. Just as in England the supremacy of the law of the land was a response to extralegal prerogative power, so in America it is a rejection of extralegal administrative power. Hence, the supremacy clause's careful inclusion of only treaties, the Constitution, and "the Laws of the United States which shall be made in Pursuance thereof." The text thus follows the underlying principle that the supreme law of the land excludes extralegal power. And this confirms that only the federal law enumerated in the supremacy clause—not rules, interpretations, guidance, or other extralegal acts—can defeat state law.

Federal administrative acts, although they come from the federal government, are not part of the supreme law of the land, and therefore contrary state law is not void. Of course, state law is void when contrary to the supreme law of the United States, but it cannot be displaced by federal actions outside the supreme law of the land.

Administrative law, however, ignores all of this. Although it is not part of the supreme law of the land, it purports to trump state law, and it thereby exaggerates the erosion of federalism. To be sure, it primarily breaks down the horizontal specialization within the federal government, but it also destroys the vertical specialization between the federal government and state governments.

Waivers and Federalism

One of the justifications for administrative waivers is that they allow federal administrators to adjust federal administrative rules to the needs of different states. From this point of view, although federal administrative regulations often cut sharply into state law, federal waivers can accommodate state diversity and thereby become instruments of federalism.

Waivers undoubtedly allow federal agencies to soften the effect of their rules, and states generally are grateful that, when threatened by agency rules, they can plead for agency waivers. This use of waivers, however, does not address the underlying problem that executive commands now enjoy supremacy over state laws. If waivers are the new face of federalism, this is only because administrative waivers offer the most immediate relief from administrative rules—thus making the states dependent on one sort of absolute power to relieve them from another. Put another way, the danger from absolute power in lawmaking is hardly a justification for further absolute power in dispensing.

Waivers thus are not so much a solution as just another part of the larger problem. Although waivers may seem valuable if one is aiming to make absolute power palatable, they are really just another element of administrative or absolute power.

Moreover, because agencies can withhold their waivers from insufficiently compliant states, the waivers are as much a threat to federalism as the rules from which they offer relief. Indeed, agencies often use their waivers to give only temporary relief. The agencies can use waivers to pacify initial opposition to their regulations, until they eventually can get uniform state compliance. Thus, rather than leave room for state variation and federalism, waivers frequently serve merely as a sugar coating on centralized administrative power to make the pill go down more smoothly.

Once again, administrative power is dangerous. In addition to threatening the specialization of power within the federal government, it also undermines the specialization of power between the states and the federal government. At multiple levels, therefore, it consolidates power.

States As Federal Agencies

From the federal administrative perspective, all other organizations—whether states, businesses, or nonprofits—are potential subordinate administrative agencies. A notable effect of administrative power has therefore been gradually to transform states into subordinate federal agencies.

In France, local districts are merely administrative agencies of the central government. In the United States, however, the states are limited but distinct sovereignties, which draw their power from their own peoples through their own constitutions. Thus, although state law is subject to federal law, even federal law cannot commandeer the states.

Nonetheless, the federal government uses the full range of its powers, both statutory and extralegal, to get the states to act as its agents—not least as its administrative agents. Rather than enact and enforce statutes regulating individuals, the federal government increasingly uses its statutes, administrative regulations, interpretations, and guidance to get states to regulate persons under their control. For example, under the Resource Conservation and Recovery Act, although the Environmental Protection Agency can work through its own regulations and enforcement, it can give states permission to carry out equivalent regulatory and enforcement programs of their own. By this means, as with waivers, the federal agency allows state variation, but the broader effect is to recruit states into federal administrative service. Indeed, the threat of overbearing federal administrative action becomes the means of pressing the states into becoming local agents of federal administrative power.

Administrative power thus does more than consolidate powers within the federal government. It also tends to consolidate state power into federal power—even to the point of reducing the states to federal administrative agencies.

❦❦❦

Part IV has shown how administrative law consolidates power. Absolute power was extralegal, supralegal, and consolidated, and administrative law revives all of these aspects of absolutism, including, as seen here, the consolidation of power.

Modern life and freedom consist largely of specialized spheres of authority. Recognizing this tendency, and seeking to turn it into a means of preserving liberty, the Constitution systematically creates specialized divisions.

In particular, as has been seen in this part, the Constitution grants specialized powers; it delegates these powers to specialized branches and does not permit subdelegation; it even places the legislative and judicial powers in institutions divided within themselves. In addition, it locates the legislative power in a specialized representative body, thus ensuring that the laws enjoy consent and obligation. Last but not least, it defines the supreme law of the land to include acts of Congress, but not administrative lawmaking, thereby preserving the specialized role of the federal government in relation to the states.

Administrative law, however, destroys all of this specialization. It amalgamates all that the Constitution kept apart and thereby systematically establishes consolidated government.

PART V

Absolute Power

Administrative power is in various ways a sort of absolute power. Its un-lawfulness therefore is profound. The full depth of the danger, however, remains to be seen.

This part therefore explores the absolute character of administrative power. Chapter 22 reviews the ways in which administrative law is abso-lute. Chapter 23 then examines claims about the necessity of administra-tive power. Necessity was the traditional conceptual foundation for abso-lute power, and it remains central for the modern administrative version of it. Chapter 24 brings the danger down to earth by showing that administra-tive power is not merely a revival of absolute power, but in fact is a direct continuation of it. Indeed, it shows that this continuity ran through Ger-many. Chapter 25 completes the book by discussing some of the remain-ing obstacles or concerns that may seem to stand in the way of finding administrative law unlawful.

TWENTY-TWO

Absolutism

Administrative law is more deeply unlawful than has been understood. This book observes that administrative law runs contrary not only to the Constitution but also to the nature of lawful and especially constitutional government in Anglo-American society. In particular, it argues that administrative law is a form of absolute power. This is, of course, a serious charge, and this chapter therefore steps back from the details to take an overview of the question.

Three Aspects of Administrative Absolutism

The term "absolute power" is apt to be misunderstood, for it has come to be used as a term of abuse, more persuasive as a denunciation than as a description. At the same time, it has at least three concrete meanings that are useful for understanding administrative law.

Administrative law is a sort of absolute power primarily because (as explored in parts I and II) it is extralegal—because it is a binding power exercised outside the law. Absolute power was exercised not through, but outside regular law and adjudication. Thus, when English kings used their prerogative to bind subjects without working through acts of Parliament or the judgments of the courts, these monarchs were said to be exercising their irregular, extraordinary, or absolute prerogative. Similarly, these days, when the executive uses administrative legislation or adjudication to bind subjects, it steps outside constitutionally established law and adjudication to exercise an irregular, extraordinary, or absolute power.

Administrative power thereby threatens the principle of rule through the law and the courts. Many commentators discuss "the rule of law" without much clarity about what they mean, thus provoking skepticism as to whether it is a useful concept. The ideal of rule through law, however, is more tangible, and it has been the foundation of the Anglo-American legal system since at least the time of Bracton, who wrote that "there is no king where will rules rather than law."[1] The U.S. Constitution echoes this old ideal by granting only legislative, executive, and judicial powers to the government, and by placing each in its own branch of government. The Constitution thereby requires the government to rule not through mere executive edicts, but through acts of Congress and the judgments of the courts. By evading these mechanisms, administrative law cuts through the fabric of lawful government—the sort of government conducted through the law and the courts—and it thereby has rapidly reversed what took nearly a thousand years to achieve.

As a secondary matter (as seen in part III), administrative law is irregular or absolute in being above the law. Judges have an office of independent judgment in accord with the law of the land, and they therefore ordinarily cannot defer to anything but the law and their own judgment of it. Nonetheless, they now defer to administrative power, thus treating it as if it were above the law of the land. It thus turns out that the law of the land is not supreme and that administrative law is a power above the law—a power so elevated that the judges do not hold it to account in the same manner as other government acts.

In addition to being extra- and supralegal, administrative law (as shown in part IV) consolidates power, and it thus is absolute in a third sense. Like prerogative power, administrative power has eclipsed the government's essential fragmentation, including its specialized, representative, divided, and federal character.

Of course, there are other possible understandings of absolute power—a fourth being the conception of it as unqualified or unlimited. This is by far the broadest understanding of absolute power, and it is the least relevant to administrative law. It therefore is an important reminder of the need to focus here on the other conceptions.

Thus, in at least in three ways, administrative law is a sort of absolute power. It is an extra- and supralegal consolidated power, and on each account, it not only conflicts with the law but also is more profoundly unlawful.

Soft Absolutism

The danger of absolute power may seem improbable in the relatively civilized circumstances of contemporary life. In a democratic society, however, the threat comes more from soft, paternalistic absolutism than from brutal absolutism. Lurid visions of past absolutism therefore should not distract attention from the sort of absolutism that flourishes today.

Hints of this soothing absolutism became apparent already under Enlightenment monarchs such as Frederick the Great of Prussia and Joseph II of Austria. Their vision was aptly summarized in the motto "Everything for the people, nothing by the people."[2] Yet the European (and eventually Soviet) versions of this caring absolutism remained as hard edged as the hierarchies that exercised power. A more substantial development of soft absolutism was therefore left to the United States.

Tocqueville

The problem of soft absolutism is centrally American because the United States was the first large-scale attempt at popular rule. In these circumstances, rather than fear the tyranny of a single tyrant, Americans had to face what Alexis de Tocqueville called the "tyranny of the majority." This democratic tyranny was outwardly much softer than the traditional versions, but was still a sort of tyranny. As Montesquieu already noted, in a republic, "though there is no external pomp that indicates a despotic sway, yet every moment it is sensibly felt."[3]

Looking at America, Tocqueville added that "the type of oppression which threatens democracies is different from anything there has ever been in the world before," and therefore such "old words as 'despotism' and 'tyranny' do not fit." Instead, the danger to Americans would come from "an immense, protective power which is alone responsible for securing their enjoyment and watching over their fate." This was a "brand of orderly, gentle, peaceful slavery."[4]

This protective, paternalistic slavery strangely combined democratic choice and central control. "Our contemporaries are ever prey to two conflicting passions: they feel the need of guidance, and they long to stay free. Unable to wipe out these two contradictory instincts, they try to satisfy them both together," and so they seek "a government which is unitary, protective, and all-powerful, but elected by the people." It thus was a strange beast, "ultramonarchical" in its body and "republican in its head"—a "monstrosity" that combined "administrative despotism and the sovereignty of the people."[5]

The danger of this soft, democratic, administrative despotism was that it would turn adults into children, gradually depriving them of their power to govern themselves. The soft "[s]ubjection in petty affairs . . . never drives men to despair, but continually thwarts them and leads them to give up using their free will. It slowly stifles their spirits and enervates their souls."

The people thereby would find themselves in a paradox of personal incompetence and popular sovereignty—the one justifying their subjection and the other their power:

> Those democratic peoples which have introduced freedom into the sphere of politics, while allowing despotism to grow in the administrative sphere, have been led into the strangest paradoxes. For the conduct of small affairs, where plain common sense is enough, they hold that citizens are not up to the job. But they give these citizens immense prerogatives where the government of the whole state is concerned. They are turned alternatively into the playthings of the sovereign and into his masters, being either greater than kings or less than men.

Administrative governance thereby would threaten democratic government, not with hard blows to the body, but with gentle fetters on the soul. Yet this was dangerous enough, for a "people who have entirely given up managing their own affairs" would not "make a wise choice of those who are do that for them."[6]

Thus far, although America had "governmental" centralization, it was blessed by the near absence of "administrative" centralization. As a result, the majority in the United States "still lacks the most advanced instruments of tyranny." Nonetheless, Tocqueville feared that "no nations are more liable to fall under the yoke of an administrative centralization than those with a democratic social condition," and he understood that such power "only serves to enervate the peoples that submit to it."[7]

Roscoe Pound

Among those who came to understand the prescience of Tocqueville's fears was Roscoe Pound. He was a legal realist, and he had led the realist demand for discretionary administrative enforcement of "standards." From 1916 through 1936, moreover, he was the dean of Harvard Law School, and he thereby enjoyed a bully pulpit for his views.[8] But although he was deeply learned in German jurisprudence, he was profoundly attached to the common law, and he recognized the danger that administrative law was reviving prerogative power.

In particular, Pound worried about administrative adjudication. He had laid important foundations for administrative rulemaking, and (as shown by Joseph Postell) he was willing to accept administrative adjudication as a temporary expedient, until the regular courts became more flexible. Increasingly, however, he came to realize that such adjudication was becoming permanent.[9]

Although Pound repeatedly expressed his fears about administrative adjudication, his final cri de coeur came in 1946, when the fascist threat to liberty had run its course and the communist threat remained. Like so many of his contemporaries, Pound was not untainted, for he briefly had embraced Nazism as a counterbalance to communism, but he surely was no longer proud of this or of the award he had received in 1934 from the Nazi government.[10]

Now, in early 1946, when Congress was preparing to adopt the Administrative Procedure Act, Roscoe Pound echoed Tocqueville's concerns. Pound was not opposed to administrative law, but he recognized part of the danger and wanted clearer limits. He therefore bluntly repeated what he had been saying for decades with increasing urgency: that administrative power was a sort of "administrative absolutism"—to be precise, that the common law tradition of ruling through the courts of law was losing ground to rule "by government determination."[11]

Pound ultimately cautioned against the substitution of force for law:

> There has come to be a cult of force throughout the world. In place of the political and legal theory on which our government was founded . . . new theories are being advanced. Instead of our fundamental doctrine that government is to be carried on according to law we are told that what the government does is law. Instead of a law which thinks of citizens and officials as equally subject to law, we are told of a public law which subordinates the citizen to the official. . . .

In this context, arguments from inevitability and benevolence were not reassuring:

> A give-it-up philosophy of law and government is being widely taught. We are told that law is to disappear in the society of the future. We are told of a society in which an omnicompetent and benevolent government will provide for the satisfaction of the material wants of everyone and there will be no need of adjusting relations or ordering conduct by law since everyone will be satisfied. Thus there will be no rights. There will only be a general duty of passive obedience. We need to be vigilant that while we are combat-

ing regimes of this sort, as they have developed in dictatorships and totalitar-
ian governments, we do not allow a regime of autocratic bureaus to become
so intrenched at home as to lead us in the same direction.[12]

As Tocqueville foresaw, a democracy might passively accept benevolent absolutism.

A half century later, when Walter Gellhorn recalled his role in drafting the Administrative Procedure Act, he sarcastically observed: "I had not
known, until Dean Pound spoke, that reorganizing and modernizing the
adjudicatory process of federal bodies . . . [was] 'in the spirit of the absolute ideas which have been making headway all over the world.'" Gellhorn
defiantly added that the advocates of administrative law were not discour-
aged by "[b]lustery words of this kind."[13]

In a sense, Pound's words really were bluster. When he spoke about dictatorship and totalitarianism, he failed to heed Tocqueville's caution that
the "old words" such as "despotism" and "tyranny" did not exactly fit the
newer danger. Pound's most vigorous and public complaints, moreover,
came too late—not when administrative law was introduced, at the turn
of the century, but in the 1920s, and then most forcefully in the 1930s
and '40s, when it was being consolidated and refined. Pound himself had
helped to justify administrative law at a time when it might have been more
easily opposed, and his denunciation of it was therefore easily dismissed as
the stridency of an apostate.

Above all, however, what made Pound's rhetoric ring hollow was that he
did not really oppose extralegal power. Instead, he merely aimed to regularize it and to limit its usurpation of the courts. Accordingly, even when he
protested against absolutism, he usually meant only excessive administrative discretion, particularly in adjudication.[a] Once such excrescences were
tempered, the administrative state, he thought, could be rendered moderate and lawful, along the lines of the German *Rechtsstaat*. Thus, although
Pound aptly complained about "absolutism," he did not recognize what
this meant, and he did not really want to slay the beast. Instead, he hoped
to domesticate it—as if safety could be achieved by persuading the creature
to sit down for a civilized dinner.

a. Pound's complaints about absolutism tended to be so diffuse, confused, or inconsistent
that they are difficult to nail down. He often reduced absolutism to discretion, he usually failed
to distinguish discretion in the sense of discernment from discretion in the sense of an exercise
of will, and he condemned much administrative adjudication while largely tolerating administrative lawmaking.

It is difficult to recognize, let alone mobilize against, a sort of lawlessness that does not fit the conventional and dramatic vision of tyranny. But over time it can become easier. The old absolute prerogative began softly and initially provoked ineffectual protests. Only slowly did it reveal its harder edges, and only then did the risk of power outside and above the law come to be widely appreciated. Similarly, administrative power has for a long time seemed innocuous and even benevolent; even to many of its critics it has appeared a necessity that simply has gotten out of hand. Nonetheless, it gradually is revealing itself, and it thereby will come be understood for what it is.

Administrative power is absolute power. It consolidates power outside and above the law, and in each of these ways, it is the very antithesis of law, especially constitutional law.

TWENTY-THREE

Necessity

Necessity has long been understood to rise above the law, and it therefore is no surprise that it has been a central justification for both traditional absolute power and for its contemporary administrative manifestation. This chapter therefore examines the claim of necessity, its constitutional significance, and its empirical foundation.

A Continuing Necessity

Administrative power ultimately rests on claims of necessity. This was true of the Crown's prerogative power, and it again is true of the executive's administrative power, but now with a greater emphasis on the continuing character of the necessity.

The principle of necessity has long been linked to assumptions about a right or even duty of self-preservation, and it therefore, in theory, was a two-edged sword, which could cut in different directions. As put by an eighteenth-century commentator, necessity could arise not "only in the instance of the crown," but also "in instances of private subjects." Most dramatically, although it could justify extralegal governmental power, it also could justify the extralegal power of the people. It thus could equally have authoritarian and revolutionary implications.[1]

When necessity was cited in support of extralegal power, however, its revolutionary implications tended to get cast aside. If necessity was to explain the government's extralegal power, without equally stimulating extralegal power against the government, the open-ended principle of necessity had to be reduced to a one-sided principle of sovereign necessity—or reason of state.

This state necessity was prototypically an emergency, such as an invasion or rebellion. Such an assault, from within or without, could threaten the very survival of the nation. It therefore might seem to justify a ruler, temporarily, to work outside and above the regular legislative and judicial power.

The sovereign necessity, however, that justifies administrative law is simultaneously less dramatic and more profound. Rather than an emergency necessity, which justifies temporary powers outside and above the law, it is a continuing necessity, which is said to require a permanent shift in governmental powers. As James Landis knowingly explained, although war was the conventional foundation for claims of necessity, "peace, too, has its special requirements." It was these quotidian exigencies that now required administrative power: "The insistence upon the compartmentalization of power along triadic lines gave way in the nineteenth century to the exigencies of governance. Without too much political theory but with a keen sense of the practicalities of the situation, agencies were created whose functions embraced the three aspects of government." The government therefore "vests the necessary powers with the administrative authority it creates," and it is "not too greatly concerned" if it thereby "does violence to the traditional tripartite theory of governmental organization." Although most advocates of administrative law are not quite as candid as Landis about the necessary violence to constitutional law, they make clear that constitutional law must bend to governmental necessities. Kenneth Culp Davis, for example, declares that "each of the three major [constitutional] theories—the rule of law, separation of powers, and nondelegation—can and should be modified to bring it into accord with the realities of modern government."[2]

These claims about the realities or necessities of government in modern society place administrative law on enduring shifts in underlying conditions rather than the sharp exigency of passing events. A sense of structural necessity thus supports the structural or permanent adjustment of constitutional law.

On such foundations, the courts throughout the twentieth century have seemed to rely on necessity to justify administrative power. As early as 1918, Professor John Cheadle observed that "there seems to be a growing tendency in the decisions to give prominence to the supposed 'necessity' of the case, even while admitting—unnecessarily, perhaps—that this delegation appears contrary to the letter if not to the spirit of the Constitution." Although the cases did not always admit they were responding to necessity, legal realists were ready to conclude that this was what the courts were really doing—"that acceptance by the courts of the practice of delegating rule-making power is merely a recognition of governmental necessities." In fact, it became utterly commonplace to observe that, notwithstanding the constitutional objections, administrative powers were "sustained" by the courts "because of the recognition of the necessity which prompts them."[3]

The Supreme Court itself has repeatedly justified administrative law on the basis of the alleged continuing necessity. Congress's power in relation to the other branches, the Court writes, "must be fixed according to common sense and the inherent necessities of the government coordination." As a result, "[d]elegation by Congress has long been recognized as necessary in order that the exertion of legislative power does not become a futility." Basing this governmental necessity on a social necessity, the Court adds that, "in our increasingly complex society, replete with ever changing and more technical problems, Congress simply cannot do its job absent an ability to delegate power under broad general directives." These layers of governmental and underlying social necessity have become a standard refrain.[4, a]

As already hinted, the scholarly and judicial arguments from necessity usually remain ambiguous about whether the necessity merely bends the Constitution or actually cuts through it. At the formal surface of constitutional theory, it is said that the Constitution can be adjusted to the changing national landscape; at a level closer to the ground, however, what gives force to the theory is the assumption that governmental and sociological needs are determinative—that these practical exigencies require the constitutional adjustment and that the Constitution would break if it did not bend. Rather than clarify whether the point is entirely constitutional or extraconstitutional, this sort of argument trades on the ambiguity, seeking the legitimacy of constitutional law while resting on harsher implications about necessitous circumstances.

Revealingly, the arguments about continuing necessity do not bother with the possibility of a constitutional amendment to authorize administrative law. An enduring necessity is one that can be addressed through regular law, including regular constitutional law—notably, by going to the people for a constitutional amendment. A persistent necessity therefore

a. At least once, in *Schechter Poultry Corp. v. United States*, the Supreme Court cautioned against the repeated claims of necessity. Speaking about statutes that subdelegated rulemaking power, the Court said that "the constant recognition of the necessity and validity" of such enactments "cannot be allowed to obscure the limitations of the authority to delegate, if our constitutional system is to be maintained." The Court acknowledged that "[e]xtraordinary conditions may call for extraordinary remedies," but "[e]xtraordinary conditions do not create or enlarge constitutional power." Thus the "powers of the national government are limited by the constitutional grants," and "[t]hose who act under these grants are not at liberty to transcend the imposed limits because they believe that more or different power is necessary."*

is a poor excuse for lawless acts. Recognizing this, arguments for absolute power traditionally depended on claims about emergency necessities, in which the king or executive plausibly could argue that he temporarily had to act outside and above the law to save the nation. Nowadays, however, it is suggested that a non-emergency continuing necessity justifies continuing government action outside and above the law.

This is especially odd because American constitutions were designed to avoid giving any justification for any extra- or supralegal power. They carefully gave governments enough power to meet their emergency needs within the law, precisely to avoid any claims for a necessary power outside and above the law. For example, Madison thought guarantees of rights "where emergencies may overrule them, ought to be avoided."[5] Accordingly, the claim about a continuing necessity is puzzling. If violent emergencies cannot justify the government in temporarily exercising power outside regular law and adjudication, how can a continuing and utterly mundane necessity justify a permanent exercise of such power?

This is, however, what has happened. Administrative law relies not on a wartime emergency, but on a continuing peacetime necessity, and it thereby seeks not a temporary, but a permanent power outside and above the law. Rather than a transient lawlessness, this is a lawlessness all the time.

Of course, this permanent state power outside and above the law is nothing new. Jean Bodin learnedly expounded it for sixteenth-century monarchs, and Carl Schmitt less learnedly for twentieth-century fascists. But there is a difference. Whereas Schmitt theorized about the exception from law, which could justify governance outside the constitutional order, Bodin regularized irregular power on the basis of a sovereign authority that, far from being exceptional, was central. And administrative law reveals an even stronger contrast. Along the lines discussed by Schmitt, Hitler repeatedly agitated Germans into a sense of emergency, mobilizing the democratic masses by exciting them into a permanent sense of crisis. In contrast, along the lines suggested by Bodin, American administrative law came to rest more sedately on the everyday necessity of exercising sovereignty over society—thus basing extralegal power on the structural depth of the necessity rather than on any sharp temporal edge.

Worried about genuine emergencies, Adrian Vermeule (most recently in conjunction with Eric Posner) has argued that "ordinary administrative law" offers the appearance of legal regularity, but at the same time leaves spaces for administrative discretion. This discretion, he argues, can be found not simply in crude "black holes," but more typically in "grey holes," which look relatively law-like while permitting a shift toward something

more grim, especially during emergencies. In justifying these legal open-
ings for extralegal power, Vermeule relies on Carl Schmitt, without noting
that he was describing absolute power.[6]

At stake here, however, is the lawfulness of binding administrative
law even where it is entirely clear, and even in entirely mundane, non-
exceptional circumstances. Not merely in its black and grey holes, but in its
very fabric, administrative law is an exercise of absolute power—the power
outside and above the law. Although its little exceptions of varying shades
rest on claims about intermittent necessities, administrative law as a whole
is an exception—a permanent exception based on claims about a continuing structural necessity. The sad reality is that ideas about continuing necessity have been used to justify an entire regime of concentrated extra- and
supralegal power.

Necessary and Proper

The Constitution authorizes Congress to do what is "necessary and proper"
for carrying out the government's other powers, and on this account, the
argument that administrative law is necessary has often seemed to enjoy
a constitutional foundation. It would be odd, however, for the Constitution to have authorized Congress to do simply what is necessary, as this
would have given Congress the absolute power that Americans resented
in Parliament. In fact, although the necessary and proper clause granted
Congress power in terms of necessity, it carefully avoided making this a
power defined by mere necessity. Of particular significance here, the clause
limited Congress to doing what was necessary and proper for carrying out
vested powers.

Necessity

Proverbially, necessity had no law—meaning it had no limit. It thus could
not be satisfied through law, nor could it be confined under law.

Being a claim that seemed naturally above law, necessity was a standard
argument for absolute power. On behalf of an absolute sovereign, it was
said that he had the final judgment about what was necessary, and that the
judges had to defer to his judgment.

The primary change in the eighteenth century was a relocation of this
power: Parliament rather than the monarch now claimed absolute sovereignty. The legislature therefore became the final judge of what was necessary, and its acts were owed judicial deference on this ground. The con-

ventional model of absolute power thus came to consist of a legislative authority to respond to necessity, and a judicial duty to defer to the legislative judgment.

This relocation of absolute power complicated its character. When exercised by the Crown, it was a power exercised outside the law, but now when exercised by the legislature, it usually was exercised through legislation. And although it once had been above the law in the sense that it was owed judicial deference, it now also was thought to be above the law in the sense that it was unlimited—an unlimited legislative power to respond to the nation's needs.

Of course, absolute legislative power, justified by necessity, was what American utterly rejected in 1776. As James Iredell recounted a decade later, Americans "were not ignorant of the theory of the necessity of the legislature being absolute in all cases, because it was the great ground of the British pretensions." Americans in their constitutions therefore repudiated all absolute power, whether in the legislature, the executive, or the courts. In the U.S. Constitution, for example, they located all binding government power in Congress and the courts, and placed all government power, including congressional power, under law. Thus, unlike Parliament, Congress lacked absolute power; it had no authority to exceed or act above the law, not even on grounds of necessity.[7]

The Problem and the Solution

The problem was that the federal government would occasionally need to respond to unanticipated circumstances, and this posed a challenge for constitutional law. Somehow, the Constitution had to acknowledge such a necessity without authorizing a power outside and above the law. In Iredell's words, a constitution had "to impose restrictions on the legislature, that might still leave it free to all useful purposes, but at the same time guard against the abuse of unlimited power."[8] One of the great accomplishments of the U.S. Constitution was to bring some essential points of necessity within the law, thus allowing the government to flourish, without allowing it to exercise any absolute power.

The easy route would have been simply to leave the new government to claim implied powers. At common law, as shown by Robert Natelson, an express grant of power impliedly included such incidental powers as were necessary for carrying out the express power.[9] The Constitution therefore could have left the new federal government to rely on the implication of incidental or necessary powers. This, however, would have invited profound risks. Most seriously, it would have left Congress the opportunity to claim too much by implication. It even might have allowed Congress to assert a nearly general power of necessity and thus absolute power.

The alternative solution was to specify and thereby limit the power to do what was necessary. Among those who had worried about the problem was John Witherspoon. In his lectures at Princeton, he observed how human failings were apt to undermine human law. For example, as a result of the failures of human language and foresight, human laws rarely were accurate enough to accommodate the full range of future needs. Necessity therefore often required individuals and governments to act above the law. There consequently "will remain a great number of cases in which . . . rights of necessity are to be used, even in the best regulated civil society"— indeed, even "after the most mature deliberation and foresight of probable events, and provision for them by specific laws."[10] Perhaps, therefore, like individuals, legislatures inevitably would sometimes need to act above the law.

Fortunately, there was a solution. In Witherspoon's words, "[i]f the law described circumstantially what might be done, it would be no longer a right of necessity, but a legal right."[11]

This cure, however, was not as easy as Witherspoon thought. Although he assumed the law could describe the circumstances in which government might have to act from necessity, his most notable student was doubtful. After drafting the U.S. Constitution, James Madison explained that it would have been "chimerical" to have "attempted a positive enumeration of the powers" that Congress might need. It was possible, however, for the Constitution to grant Congress incidental powers "under the general terms 'necessary and proper.'"[12]

On this theory, the necessary and proper clause authorized Congress "[t]o make all Laws which shall be necessary and proper for carrying into Execution the foregoing Powers, and all other Powers vested by this Constitution in the Government of the United States, or in any Department or Officer thereof." The clause thus gave Congress express authority for doing what was incidental or necessary for carrying out the government's other powers.

Although this clause merely spelled out what otherwise could have been implied, it clarified much. It specified that the power arising from necessity rested in Congress rather than the other parts of government, that the power was limited to what was necessary for carrying out the government's other powers, and that the power was confined to what was both necessary and proper for such ends.[b]

Above all, the necessary and proper clause thereby tamed absolute power. In providing for Congress to pursue necessity through and under law, it acknowledged claims of necessity. But it required these claims to be made through and under the law rather than outside or above it—in particular, it required such claims to be made in accord with the necessary and proper clause—and it thereby avoided authorizing absolutism.

Amnesia about Absolutism

Unfortunately, scholars and judges have largely forgotten the old claim of absolute power and its foundation in necessity, and they therefore have not fully understood the peril that the necessary and proper clause had to avoid. It thus is no surprise that they have read the clause very loosely.

For example, by reading the word "proper" out of the clause, and by taking a broad view of federal powers, the Supreme Court has reduced the clause to a general authorization for Congress to act of necessity. The Court thereby interprets the clause to justify the very claim of legislative necessity that Americans had rejected in Parliament and sought to avoid in Congress.[13]

Making matters worse, the Court defers to Congress's judgment about what is necessary and proper—thus treating Congress as if, like Parliament, its judgments about necessity were above the law. Of course, as noted by Chief Justice Marshall in *Maryland v. McCulloch*, Congress enjoys the power to chose among the necessary and proper means. The necessary and proper clause, however, was designed to avoid parliamentary-style absolutism, and therefore, although the clause leaves Congress complete freedom of choice within the sphere of what is necessary and proper, it bars Congress from going further. In England, Parliament claimed absolute power and therefore expected judicial deference to its legislative judgments about necessity, but in America, the necessary and proper clause precludes this danger by stating its measure of congressional power as a matter of law, thus ensuring that the judges must enforce it.

Nonetheless, the judges defer to Congress about whether a particular

---

b. The history of the clause (as shown by Robert Natelson) confirms that the word "proper" was an additional requirement. In the Committee of Detail, Chancellor John Rutledge of South Carolina suggested that the clause should authorize Congress "to make all laws necessary to carry the foregoing powers into execution." Recognizing the risk of such broad phrasing, the committee later inserted the words "and proper."*

chosen means is necessary and proper for carrying out the Constitution's ends. They thereby return to the deferential posture of the English judges and come close to reviving the absolute legislative power that Americans in their constitutions clearly sought to defeat. The result has been an open path for authorizing administrative law.[c]

Vested Powers

Notwithstanding these judicial departures from the necessary and proper clause, the clause cannot be relied upon as a foundation for administrative law, for it allows Congress to do only what is necessary and proper for carrying out the powers *vested* in the branches of government. This structural aspect of the clause has been largely ignored, but it matters because it ties the means to structurally limited ends.

Already in England, there were hints that because legislative power was vested in Parliament, not even a claim of necessity could justify Parliament in shifting legislative power. It will be recalled (from chapter 3) that when Henry VIII sought to exercise legislative power through his proclamations, he found that he needed parliamentary authorization. The result was the Act of Proclamations, which Parliament justified on grounds of a double necessity: It said that necessity required it to authorize the king to exercise legislative power where he considered it a necessity. Yet Parliament's enactment of this statute, as has been seen, came to be widely viewed as the most extraordinary assault on liberty in English history. Evidently, although Parliament could do much on grounds of necessity, this did not include delegating the legislative power vested in the legislature.

Rather than leave such a conclusion to implications from history, the necessary and proper clause expressly limited Congress to doing what was necessary and proper for carrying out vested powers. If the clause had simply authorized Congress to do what is necessary and proper for carrying out other constitutional powers in the abstract, without regard to where the Constitution placed them, then the clause might have justified Congress in rearranging the powers of government. It then might have justified

---

c. Curiously, Congress often transfers to the executive the very sort of power that Congress enjoys under the necessary and proper clause. In many instances, a federal statute authorizes an agency or its head to make such rules as it considers "necessary and appropriate" or "necessary or appropriate" for carrying out the statute. This sort of statute evidently gives the executive a power to make the laws necessary and proper for carrying into execution part of the government's powers, and it thus gives the executive some of the power that the Constitution in the necessary and proper clause gives to Congress.

the Supreme Court in arguing (as it did in *Sunshine Anthracite Coal Co. v. Adkins*) that Congress's delegation of its legislative power to the executive is "necessary in order that the exertion of legislative power does not become a futility."[14] All of this, however, assumes that Congress can do what is necessary and proper to carry out a legislative power disembodied from the legislature.

Instead, the necessary and proper clause ties what is legislatively necessary and proper not merely to the other powers, but to the other powers as vested in the government and its component bodies. In the words of the clause, Congress can make laws necessary and proper "for carrying into Execution the foregoing Powers, and all other Powers vested by this Constitution in the Government of the United States, or in any Department or Officer thereof." Thus, Congress is authorized to do what is necessary and proper for carrying out not legislative powers in general, but the legislative powers vested in Congress; not simply executive power, but the executive power vested in the president; not simply judicial power, but that vested in the courts.[15]

The clause thereby carefully avoids giving Congress authority to relocate these powers. When Congress authorizes administrative lawmaking, it shifts legislative power to the executive, and it thereby displaces the legislative power vested in Congress. Similarly, when Congress authorizes administrative adjudication, it shifts judicial power to the executive, and it thereby displaces the judicial power vested in the courts. It thus does not carry out these powers as vested in Congress and the courts, but rather subverts them, and it therefore cannot find support in the necessary and proper clause.

This point can be succinctly stated in terms of means and ends. James Madison and, later, John Marshall explained that the necessary and proper clause authorized the particular means necessary and proper to carry out the Constitution's general ends. As by now should be evident, however, the ends are not simply powers, but are vested powers—powers located in particular persons or parts of government. And the vested character of these ends limits the lawful means. For example, when Congress places legislative power in the executive, it is subverting rather than carrying out the legislative power vested in Congress. And when Congress places judicial powers in the executive, it is undermining rather than effectuating the judicial power vested in the courts. These means therefore cannot be justified by the necessary and proper clause.

In sum, although the current understanding of the necessary and proper clause seems to justify administrative law, it actually runs into problems.

Generally, the current interpretation opens up the danger of absolute legislative power—the parliamentary-style power and the judicial deference to it—that the Constitution, including the necessary and proper clause, emphatically sought to avoid. More specifically, the current interpretation fails to recognize that the clause authorizes what is necessary and proper only for carrying out *vested* powers, thus witholding from Congress any power to shift legislative or judicial power to the executive.

Necessity and Modernity

Although necessity is an old justification for absolute power, it is used on behalf of administrative power with a modern sociological twist: that administrative law is necessary in a modernized society. To give a lawful gloss to this claim, it is said that the law itself permits its adaptation to changed circumstances, this being the theory of the living constitution. But the underlying strength of the argument is not so much legal as sociological, and as already hinted, it sometimes comes with suggestions of historical inevitability.

In this vision, in which modernity itself necessitates administrative power, opposition to such power seems antimodern and unrealistic. It is not clear, however, how one should judge whether administrative law is required by modern society. In fact, there are reasons to think that the power exercised through and under law is much better suited to modernity.[16, d]

Complexity

Administrative law often is said to be necessary because of the complex character of modern society. But why this complexity requires administrative law remains unclear.

The simplest version of the complexity argument suggests that socioeconomic complexity requires complex regulation and that this must be administrative. Modern society undoubtedly is more specialized and in this sense complex than traditional society. The next assumption, however, that a complex society needs complex rules, is by no means obvious. As Richard

---

d. The claim that extralegal power is a necessary response to modernity is questioned here mostly on its merits. Nonetheless, it also could be viewed as suspect on account of its history. Extralegal power has been defended as necessary, and the alternative has been condemned as obsolete, since at least the sixteenth century. (See note b in chapter 25.) Accordingly, when considered over time, the claim seems to be not so much about obsolescence as really about the necessity of extralegal power in all circumstances, regardless of changes in society.

Epstein has observed, it also is possible to have simple rules for a complex society.[17] Of course, there are costs to each approach, and the merits of one over the other in any area of law is an empirical question, which cannot be settled here. But that is precisely the point: Just as it cannot be taken for granted that simple rules are necessary, so too it cannot be assumed that complex regulations are necessary.

Even if regulatory complexity is generally needed, statutes can be just as complex and subtle as administrative rules. Both types of enactment can be highly detailed, and both can be drafted by experts—the only difference being that statutes are adopted by Congress rather than by heads of agencies. The need for complex regulation therefore does not show the need for administrative rules.

Another version of the social complexity argument is that a complex society requires continual and in-depth federal control. The distinctive character of modernized society, however, has been its freedom or fragmentation of authority, and it therefore is not evident that social complexity requires so much control. On the contrary, for many purposes the very opposite may be true. If the tendency of modernized society is toward freedom or at least social fragmentation, continual direction by the federal government may actually be inconsistent with modernity. This, too, is an empirical question that cannot be resolved here, but at the very least it cannot be merely assumed that sociological complexity requires the weight of administrative control.[18]

Yet another version of the argument is that, because of changes in society, government must give direction to society in ways that cannot be reduced to rules. From this perspective, statutes or regulations set open-ended standards, and administrative agencies flexibly apply them with licences or waivers. It is not evident, however, why the modernity of society requires the government to impose duties without reducing them to rules. The supposition seems to be that there is something distinctively irregular about modernized relationships or other circumstances, which places them beyond the regularity of rules, but whatever this irregularity is, it has yet to be identified. On this amorphous foundation, however, it is said to be necessary for administrative agencies to subject Americans not only to administrative rules but also to discretionary administrative applications of open-ended standards.

All such administrative complexity burdens Americans with the problem of discerning what the government wants. One once could learn the law without consulting government. Now, however, one must follow rules that are too complex to be understood without consulting the issuing agency for its interpretations, and one must anticipate the enforcement and other discretionary decisions of administrators. One therefore must chase administrators down the corridors of power to glean from them their latest interpretations, policies, and plans. Although this is possible for businesses large enough to enjoy an efficiency of scale in lobbyists and lawyers, it is utterly daunting for individuals and even for many moderately sized businesses. And this is worrisome. The freedom and prosperity of a modernized society is not possible when most individuals and institutions have difficulty figuring out what they lawfully may do.[e]

Thus, even if necessity could justify extra- and supralegal power, it is not apparent that modern society really requires this extra- and supralegal power. On the contrary, there is reason to think that modernity requires rule by and under law.

Rapid Change

Another justification for the sociological necessity of administrative power focuses on the speed of change in modern society—the suggestion being that the rapidly developing character of modern life requires rapidly changing regulation. Life and law, in this view, must move at the same frenetic pace.

Yet even with this vision of fast-paced regulation, there is no need for administrative law, for Congress can act as quickly as agencies when it is motivated to do so.[19] Whereas regulations usually require publication in the *Federal Register* at least thirty days before they become effective, Congress faces no such formal time constraints. To be sure, it does not meet every day of the year, but it usually meets at least some days every month. Congress thus is almost always ready to act, and fears about the pace of legislation do not rest on the legislature's incapacity.

Instead, what is discussed in terms of speed is usually a concern about the political pace of legislation in Congress. The argument that administrative law is necessary to keep up with the tempo of modern society is typi-

---

e. Recognizing the opacity of administrative law, the Department of Labor at one point proposed that it should treat workers and employers "as its customers." On this basis, it concluded that "customer service includes making it easy for employers to find out what the law requires of them, keeping the rules simple and easy to understand, and protecting individuals' rights during the inspection and penalty process, particularly when inadvertent violations can result from misunderstanding of the standards." Of course, if Americans really were customers of government, there would be no problem with obscure regulations, as the unhappy customers could simply walk away.*

cally a claim about the need to circumvent the delays inherent in popular representative politics. The question about the necessity of speed therefore cannot be taken at face value, but must be supplemented with a recognition that there is an underlying question as to whether congressional or bureaucratic judgments are better measures of the need for new legislation.

In fact, the press of administrative legislation is not nearly as urgent as often assumed—a good illustration being the Food and Drug Administration's licensing of new drugs and biologics. The FDA reports that (on average from 2001 through 2010) it annually received thirty applications for new drugs or biologics and approved twenty-three of them.[20] This is not an overwhelming amount of business, and it suggests that the FDA could just as well make recommendations for Congress to adopt by statute.

More generally, there is reason to doubt whether most areas of law regularly need to be altered to accommodate the rapid evolution of society. For example, many of the rules governing securities, television, and radio are older than most of the administrators implementing the rules. Although this does not prove the merit of such rules, it forcibly suggests that there is no necessary connection between the pace of technological and legal change. At least in some key areas, rapid legal change is not needed.[21]

Once again, therefore, the necessity does not live up to its billing. Although necessity has long been said to justify absolute power, it is questionable whether modern society actually requires administrative power.

Discretion

A further explanation of why administrative law is sociologically necessary focuses on the need for binding administrative discretion. From this point of view, as already hinted, the irregularity and rapid change of modern life seem to require discretionary administrative power.

This discretion, however, is very different from the law that laid the foundations for modern society. The common law and then the Constitution established a society in which persons enjoyed a freedom to do as they pleased up to the limits imposed by law, and the Anglo-American legal system thereby contributed much to the development of modern society, its freedom, and its wealth.

In contrast, discretionary administrative power threatens the confidence of individuals and their organizations in their legally protected freedom. Such power imposes binding constraints without the benefit of representation or the political process. It imposes judicial decisions without the due process of law and other basic procedural rights. More generally, it leaves Americans subject to consolidated power—the dangerous combination of legislative, executive, and judicial power.

In such ways, administrative discretion leaves Americans insecure in their freedom. Why invest, if a mere administrator, without much political or legal constraint, can later prohibit your investment? Why even enter a business, if an administrator, without even adopting a regulation, can use an interpretation or waiver to give advantages to your competitors? Why even begin academic research if an administrator can command you to shut it down or can limit what you learn and what you publish? Discretionary administrative power thus deprives Americans of security in their freedom, and it thereby reduces investment, wealth, innovation, experimentation, and personal happiness.

Accordingly, it is difficult to believe that such discretion is a necessary response to modernized society. In fact, what seems necessary in such a society is freedom under law.

Particularized Commands Rather than General Rules

Underlying the claims for complex, rapid, and discretionary administrative power is an assumption that the details of modern life require almost equally detailed legislation. From this perspective, nearly every new technological or industrial development must be addressed point by point, thus reducing law from general rules to a series of particularized commands.[f]

The Food and Drug Administration, for example, licenses new drugs and medical devices one by one, responding to distinct technological developments with distinct legal edicts. Although the authority of the FDA is very general, its use of licensing to authorize each new drug or device is largely particularized.

Undoubtedly, new drugs and devices need regulation, and surely in some instances they need particularized regulation, in which they are forbidden or allowed one by one, but is particularized regulation necessary in all instances? The question matters because overreliance on the particularized sort of regulation comes with consequences. Although the FDA's particularized approach has saved Americans from some dangerous drugs, it also has denied them access to many valuable drugs. Nor should this be

---

f. Put in Lockean terms, much of administrative law displaces "standing laws" with mere "extemporaneous . . . decrees."*

a surprise. The FDA licensing system relies on centralized predictions about safety and efficacy, and it thereby concentrates rather than disperses the risk of errors. This is especially a problem because the FDA does not get much credit for lives saved by drugs, but does get blame for lives lost. It therefore systematically tends to err on the side of denying permission. Indeed, it inhibits the development of entire fields of new medicines—most worrisomely, new antibiotics.[22] There thus is good reason to shift to a less harmful approach—one that would impose particularized prohibitions in some instances, but only more general prohibitions in others. For example, as already suggested, Congress could receive recommendations from the FDA and then could simply ban the sale or interstate transportation of specified types of drugs, leaving the rest to negligence law.

The broader point is that if particularized control is not always necessary, and often is harmful, then administrative law is not so clearly necessary. When one assumes, in accord with a sociological theory, that particularized control is necessary across an entire field, such as drugs and medical devices, then it is difficult to imagine that Congress can be up to the task, and administrative law seems necessary. But when it turns out that particularized control is only sometimes beneficial, then the scale of the problem diminishes, and it no longer is so clear that administrative law is needed.

There is further reason to doubt the necessity of administrative law when one recognizes that general rules of law can sometimes adapt to technological change and complexity much better than particularized controls. It will be seen shortly that agencies have difficulty keeping up to date with science. For now, the other side of the equation must be considered: that general rules can keep pace.

Negligence law nicely illustrates how general rules can be more flexible in adapting to complexity and change than particularized commands. Although the standard of care in negligence is stated generally, what it requires in any field evolves in response to the development of scientific and technical knowledge. In the use of drugs, for example, the standard of care becomes more burdensome when one or another firm discovers drugs that are less risky than others. Negligence thereby leaves room for the evolution of scientific knowledge, and as a result companies must compete to live up to the shifting implications of the standard of care. Even something as basic as negligence law is thus less rigid than particularized administrative rules and licensing.

This is not to say that negligence solves all problems, or that more specific legal restrictions are without value, but rather that the necessity of particularized controls has been exaggerated. When one takes a more balanced understanding of the problem, it is by no means clear that administrative law (or any other form of absolutism) is necessary.

Private Power

In explaining the modern necessity of administrative power, commentators sometimes assert that this power is a necessary response to the danger from corporations in modern society. Certainly, private power can be dangerous. It is not evident, however, why any danger from private power requires not only broad government power but also extralegal power.

Congress has wide substantive powers—powers that have been expanded in the twentieth century to be almost a general governmental power. As a result, the federal government already has more than enough power to legislate regarding corporations. The argument from the danger of private power therefore comes down to how federal power is exercised—the suggestion being that the administrative concentration of federal powers is necessary to defeat concentrated corporate power. But is it really necessary to embrace the one danger in order to counter the other?

In fact, administrative law is especially susceptible to corporate interests, and thus far from being a remedy against the power of large corporations, it tends to become an avenue for their influence. The very concentration of powers in administrative agencies makes agencies valuable partners for concentrated private interests and thus attractive targets for control. These dangers began to be evident already in the formation of the Interstate Commerce Commission—the first major federal administrative body.[g] And by now, when dominant private players draft the regulations affecting them

g. In 1887, in the Interstate Commerce Act, Congress established the Interstate Commerce Commission and gave it administrative power over the railroads. The statute therefore is widely recognized as having created the first major federal administrative agency. What is less widely understood is that the railroads themselves wanted the establishment of this agency. In the words of one congressman, "all the railroad companies and railroad attorneys and railroad experts seek a commission."

Congress considered an alternative bill, which would have directly imposed duties on the railroads, without establishing a commission. But, as put by Representative John H. Reagan of Texas—chair of the Committee on Commerce—the railroads preferred a commission because it allowed them "greater chances for trickery and evasion; with whatever chances there may be for their controlling in their interest the appointment of the commission, or of controlling the commission in their interest after it shall be appointed." They understood, moreover, that it was to their advantage to have a statute that "puts the commission between the complaining citizen and the railroad, instead of allowing the citizen to appeal directly to the courts for redress of his wrongs." A contemporary book even went so far as to declare: "Such a body would sooner or later become a mere bulwark or outpost for the defense of corporate abuses, instead of a fortress of popular rights."*

and negotiate limits on agency enforcement proceedings against them, it is stranger than ever to view administrative power as a check on corporate power.[h]

Indeed, there is reason to fear that the accommodations between administrative agencies and large corporations are much more dangerous to the public than the preexisting danger from either direction. Such accommodations allow the government to co-opt the companies large enough to resist it, and allow such companies to impose costs on their competitors, thereby undercutting competition and innovation. Worst of all, such accommodations leave the rest of the society subject to the coordinated strength of government and private power.

Thus, rather resolve the corporate problems of modern life, administrative power exacerbates them. Modernity, yet again, is no excuse for this extralegal power.

Science

Last but not least, it is widely assumed that administrative law meets the needs of modernity by relying on scientific knowledge. In what sense, however, is it modern or scientific to rely on centralized knowledge about science? In some instances, such knowledge can be sophisticated. But on the whole, the administrative combination of consolidated power and specialized knowledge collides with the empirical skepticism that drives modern science, for it relies on science as a body of more or less knowable truths rather than a diversified mode of skeptical inquiry.

An initial difficulty is the personnel problem. According to administrative theory, administrative rules and licensing will be up to date and well adapted to technological change, because agencies will employ administrators with technical expertise at least as advanced as that which prevails in regulated industries.[23] Science, however, is not just a matter of technical knowledge, which can be predictably applied by skilled technicians. The pace and complexity of science in the private sector leaves most government experts far behind. Private companies often rise and fall on the quality of their scientists, and as technologies evolve, the successful companies can hire yet more top scientists. The companies thus acquire new personnel to match the changing science, and they often transform the science precisely by cultivating the right personnel. Most administrative agencies, in

h. For example, when the Federal Communications Commission proposed net neutrality rules in the summer of 2010, it invited six industry lobbyists to do the drafting.[*]

contrast, cannot continually change and add to their personnel, and they cannot expect to hire experts in new areas of technology who can match the skills of the private scientists who are actually developing these new fields.[24, i]

Even if the personnel difficulty could be solved, there remains the deeper problem of relying on a centralized understanding of science. Administrative regulation rests on the assumption that government agencies are apt to reach the correct conclusions about science. This, however, is unlikely. Scientific advancement depends on experimentation. It arises not from the expert authority of centralized decisionmakers, but from the dispersed authority of diverse scientists, who engage in repeated experiments. In other words, what matters for scientific development is diversified trial and error rather than centralized rationality. Therefore, when agencies attempt to reduce the debated frontiers of science to centrally known expertise, expressed in regulations, there is a substantial danger that they will act on mistaken scientific assumptions. And when they fall back on what can be known with confidence, they will tend to establish yesterday's science as today's regulatory truth.

Thus, in matters ranging from social complexity to scientific knowledge, the necessity of administrative law is questionable. Necessity has long been the justification for absolute power, and this time the necessity is said to arise from the nature of modern society. Modern society, however, especially in America, tends to be fractured and in need of the liberty protected by law. It therefore is worrisome that administrative power consists of consolidated power outside and above the law. Far from clearly advancing the development of modern society, this sort of power appears to impede it.

---

i. Of course, one might think that, however weak the expertise of agencies, it is greater than that of Congress. Yet even where agencies have employees with sufficient expertise, these experts do not actually adopt the new rules. Although subordinate experts in an agency may do the drafting, the person who has the authority to issue the rules is typically the head of the agency, who often will have little technical knowledge.

On this basis, James Landis himself mocked "the legend of agency 'expertise.'" This "was a nice word for the defenders of the administrative process and it had value in demonstrating to the judiciary . . . that the solution" of a "particular problem," if "at all reasonable, should be left to persons who were presumably familiar with it. . . . But on whole does it exist? It obviously exists in the staffs of many of our agencies. But at the top level, where the responsibility of decision rests, one cannot be too sure."

Administrative lawmaking thus does not necessarily rest on greater technical expertise or advice than congressional lawmaking. If agencies were to submit their rules to Congress for it to enact or not, bureaucratic knowledge and drafting would remain available. All that would change is that Congress, rather than the head of an agency, would have the final word on whether to adopt the regulations.*

Necessity As an Empirical Question

Although administrative law is defended as necessary, it is striking that the claim of necessity tends to be abstract rather than empirical. Rather than rest on evidence, it relies on the conceptual strength of the idea of necessity. This lack of an empirical foundation is odd, for if administrative law really is necessary, there should be some substantial evidence of this.[j]

Traditionally, when a king or Parliament exercised absolute power, there was no need for empirical evidence of the necessity, for one of the privileges of sovereignty was the power simply to declare the necessity. In cases of national security, or times of emergency, it often seemed essential for the preservation of the nation that the sovereign not be required to explain the necessity or its empirical foundations. More generally, the discretion to decide whether there was a necessity was a crucial part of absolute power, and therefore, once the sovereign asserted the need, the judges had to defer. It therefore is no surprise that the necessity underlying extra- and supralegal power was merely the abstract concept of necessity.

The necessity for administrative law, however, cannot rest on the abstract declaration of an absolute sovereign. Instead, it is an open academic and legal question, and because it concerns a thesis about the real world, it must rest on empirical data. Accordingly, those who argue for the necessity of administrative law cannot expect to be persuasive unless they offer persuasive evidence of the necessity. Put generally, those who justify departures from the Constitution on empirical grounds have the burden of proving their empirical claims.

The evidentiary problem is particularly acute because the necessity is being used to justify such an extraordinary power. If it really is necessary that the Constitution should be brushed aside or at least bent out of shape, and if it really is necessary to establish a consolidated power outside and above the law, then the necessity should be demonstrably real. The necessity that would justify all of this is presumably a powerful and manifest force. It therefore is not too much to expect empirical evidence showing that the necessity is more than an intellectual construct.

In providing such evidence, the advocates of administrative power have much work ahead them, for it cannot be assumed that the alleged need for administrative law is equally strong across the board. Generic evidence

---

j. Woodrow Wilson already acknowledged that "[t]he object of administrative study is to rescue executive methods from the confusion and costliness of empirical experiment and set them upon foundations laid deep in stable principle."*

therefore will not suffice. For example, even if there were evidence of the need for administrative legislation, this would not necessarily be evidence of the need for administrative adjudication. Similarly, even if there were evidence of the need for executive legislation on health care, this would not necessarily show the need for such legislation on the environment. Indeed, the need for administrative rulemaking on one type of drug would not be dispositive about the need for such rulemaking on another type. And, obviously, the proof of a necessity in the 1880s would not be proof of any such necessity in the 1890s, let alone more than century later.

This particularized approach to evidence is no more than what courts expect every day in their cases. Accordingly, it is not too much to ask from those who insist on the necessity of twisting or even breaking the Constitution so as to establish consolidated power outside and above the law. If the necessity is real, there should be some hard evidence. The proponents of administrative law, however, have not offered any scientifically serious empirical evidence. None at all.

Nor, to top it off, have they offered such evidence to the relevant judges of the necessity. Without much evidence, the advocates of administrative power have persuaded themselves. But the power to decide on the necessity of changing the Constitution lies in the people. Accordingly, if there really is substantial empirical evidence for the necessity of extra- and supralegal power, those who advocate this power should present the evidence to the people.

❧❧❧

Necessity is a powerful argument, and it should be taken seriously. But it comes with a history—an ugly past that suggests it should be viewed with profound caution.

Traditionally, necessity was said to have no law, and it thus was a fundamental excuse for absolute power. On similar grounds, it nowadays has come back to life as a justification for administrative power, and as in the past, the alleged necessity is more conceptual than empirical. Once again, therefore, the danger is that an abstract claim of necessity, unsupported by empirical evidence, has bent or broken through the law, leaving government with absolute power.

TWENTY-FOUR

The German Connection

This book, thus far, has argued that American administrative law revives absolute power. Now, the argument can be taken further. Not merely a natural recurrence of absolute power, American administrative law is a historical continuation of such power.

To understand this, it is necessary to trace the development of what became administrative law. Absolute power, both extra- and supralegal, developed in the hands of mostly Continental civilian scholars, and although it was defeated in England and America, it continued to flourish on the Continent. There it gradually acquired administrative form, and in this shape it then found its way back to the common law nations. Tellingly, both the Continental evolution of absolute power into administrative form, and the shift of such power to America, took largely German paths. Thus, mostly through German connections, there has been much continuity from absolute to administrative power.

Caveats

Some initial words of caution seem advisable. Although this chapter observes the continuity of many absolutist ideas as transmitted through Germany, readers should not leap to conclusions about what such an argument entails.

It would be a mistake, for example, to assume that German ideas were in any strong sense a cause of what happened in the Anglo-American sphere. The late-nineteenth-century Americans who advocated administrative power were responding mainly to their domestic fears and desires, and they drew upon on a range of sources. They ended up assimilating elements of the heritage of Continental civilian absolutism, as transmitted through German scholarship, partly because their own anxieties and hopes led them to see their situation through lenses borrowed from the Continent, and partly because the German ideas seemed to solve American problems. Whether or not the problems really got solved, Americans thereby adopted what became some standard ways of conceptualizing and justifying administrative power.

Another potential misunderstanding concerns political theory. Most American legal commentators ignore both the absolutist civilian heritage and the German pathway, but at least some historians note the German connection, and their insights need to be pursued more systematically.[1] Even the best of this historical scholarship, however, concentrates so much on the transmission of German political and administrative theory to America that it misses the underlying civilian absolutist tradition. In fact, the old foundation of prerogative and administrative power was the civil law, and what got conveyed to Americans through the German theory included many of the underlying civilian-derived assumptions, which persisted long after their civilian origins and German transmission were forgotten.[2]

Once this is recognized, it becomes apparent that American administrative power is not simply a revival of the old consolidated extra- and supralegal power. Rather, it is in some ways a direct continuation of that absolutist tradition. And both this derivation and its road through Germany confirm how profoundly administrative power conflicts with Anglo-American ideals of law.

A final word of caution concerns the role of the Germans. It would miss the point to suppose that this chapter focuses on Germany gratuitously or that it is suggesting anything invidious about Germans. On the contrary, the focus is on Germany because Germany had a distinctive place in the history of administrative power, and the implications reach far beyond Germany because human failings are not confined to any one nation. Germans once formed a nation of free peoples and free institutions, and the role of administrative power in changing that offers lessons for all peoples, including Americans.

In short, the argument here does not make strong assumptions about causation, theory, or Germans. Instead, it focuses on something more concrete: the continuity of civilian-derived absolutist assumptions and their transmission through Germany.

From Civilian Absolutism to Administrative Law

Much of contemporary administrative law—at least in its conceptual and constitutional framework—derives from the extra- and supralegal rule by European monarchs that was justified by civilian scholars as absolute power. Over the centuries, this power was systematized as administrative power, and thus what once was recognized as absolute power acquired modern expression in another form.

Ideas about the absolute power of temporal rulers developed mostly within the learned law—the academic study of Roman-derived canon and civil law. As today, academic inquiry offered an opportunity to explore a vision of law that rose above national legal systems, and this sort of jurisprudential study flourished with the rediscovery of Roman legal texts. On these foundations, scholars pursued ideas outside the limitations of particular lands, theorizing in a manner that seemed cosmopolitan and intellectually exciting. As Francis Bacon explained about one of his civilian-style endeavors, it "leave[s] the wit of man more free to turn and toss."[3]

Of course, the academic shift to these elevated levels of inquiry threatened English law. As early as the twelfth century, an English chronicler praised the virtues of the civil law but worried that its proponents would use it to displace "communis status arbitria"—the judgment of the established community. By the mid-twelfth century the danger was such that King Stephen declared Roman law should have no place or at least no authority in England.[4]

The academic fascination with the civil law, and the political discomfort, became all the greater when medieval and early modern civilian commentators expounded ideas of absolute power. Their founding text (as suggested in chapter 3) was the Roman maxim "What pleases the prince has the force of law."[5] Being eager for patronage, and intrigued with ideas of necessity that rose above the forms of law, many of the academics who studied the civil law drew upon this maxim to justify extra- and supralegal power—not the will of a community acting through its regular, communally adopted law, but the will of a ruler exercised outside and above such law.[6] Civilian commentators thus adopted a dual conception of governmental power, and they were pleased to think that this revealed their combination of idealism about law and realism about state necessity. They thereby, however, tore apart the fabric of regular lawmaking authority, leaving Continental Europeans with a more ominous understanding of state authority than the English.

Recognizing the injury from their candid acknowledgment of absolutism,

most civilian commentators sought to bind it up with at least theoretical re-
straints. They said that the ruler could not exercise absolute power to take
property without *causa*, or cause. They added that he could not be presumed
to have intended to act contrary to law unless he did so expressly—that is,
unless he adopted a non obstante clause, in which he expressly recited that
he was carving out a dispensation from a specific enactment. Most broadly,
they reassuringly presented absolute power as exceptional.[7]

Nonetheless, the breach in expectations of lawfulness had been sanctified by scholarship, and learned men would soon take it further. English
lawyers traditionally had hesitated to generalize that the king had absolute
power, and when in the sixteenth century they acknowledged that such a
power existed in the monarch, they not only treated it as exceptional but
also typically confined it within the safety of particular prerogatives that
were acknowledged by law. In contrast, learned civilians tended to consider the ruler's absolute authority a transcendent general power, and as
already suggested, most of their limitations on it were more academic than
effectual.[8]

Jean Bodin was the most systematic of those who seized upon this opening. Candidly theorizing—what had long been apparent—that the exception was in fact central, he declared that absolute power was the defining
feature of sovereignty.[9] Civilian absolutism thus entered political theory,
and it soon licensed rulers to choose as they pleased between lawful governance and simple state power.

This absolute power most clearly began to take an administrative form
when civilian-influenced lawyers, clerics, and other bureaucrats increasingly exercised absolute power on their ruler's behalf. In the fifteenth and
sixteenth centuries—whether in kingdoms, little principalities, or city-
states—rulers came to depend on their bureaucratic minions to make and
enforce their extralegal commands. This tendency was pursued perhaps
most systematically in German states, and it was transformative, for it gave
civilian scholars an opportunity not only to enjoy patronage and power
but also to systematize autocratic rule.[10] That this was turning into a different sort of absolutism was recognized only later. Already, however, the
pursuit of absolute authority though the acts of bureaucrats was initiating
the transmutation of absolute power into administrative power.

The administrative version of absolutism acquired prominence when
Prussian kings systematized their absolute power in the spirit of Enlightenment rationality. Justinian had long before declared his *Institutes* to be
based on legal science, and civilian academics often insisted upon the scientific character of their inquiries.[11] Building on this tradition, but with

an Enlightenment twist, Prussian monarchs rationalized their exercise of power through administrative codification. This process reached its classic expression in the Prussian Civil Code—initiated by Frederick the Great and promulgated by his successor in 1794. Although other Enlightenment monarchs, including Catherine the Great of Russia and Joseph II of Austria, also pursued administrative codes, the Prussian version was the preeminent example. Thus, long before Max Weber extolled rational bureaucracy under hierarchical control, the Prussian code had become the model of scientific or at least systematic rationality in the exercise of absolute power.

Probably inspired by the Continental codes and the underlying German legal literature, Jeremy Bentham espoused his own vision of codification. Unlike the enlightened monarchs of his era, Bentham favored representative government, but in other ways he echoed their absolutism. Already on the Continent, civilian-derived theory rejected the natural law theory of sovereignty and legal obligation; it reduced law to the sovereign's command; it suggested that he should codify his laws; it celebrated the role of the state in maximizing happiness. Adaptations of these elements appeared in Bentham's philosophy, and especially as transmitted by his student John Austin, this "positivism" would prepare the way for administrative power in common law countries.[12]

The systematized absolutism that developed in Prussia and German-influenced lands first became recognized as "administrative" in France. Although under the Bourbons it was a matter of the royal pleasure, in the Republic and under Napoleon it was regularized and renamed *droit administratif*. Napoleon thereby (as noted by Dicey) "gave full expression" to the ancien régime's "royal prerogative." No longer confined by the customary constraints on the king's personal authority, absolute power now flourished as an enlightened manifestation of uninhibited state power. Thus, what the earlier regime had done in legislative *ordonnances*, interpretative *déclarations*, and particularized *édits*, the new one did even more vigorously through administrative equivalents.[13]

Underlying administrative power was often the police power. This was the Continental term for the general power of the state to secure *Ordnung*, or order, and it had its most profound appeal in Germany. As put by the Prussian code, "To make the necessary provisions for preserving public peace, security, and order, and for averting dangers threatening the public or individuals, is the police function." Anxieties about order thus justified the police power. And because this sweeping power did not differentiate legislative, judicial, and executive roles, it seemed to vindicate an undifferentiated administrative authority, including executive legislation and adjudication. Catherine the Great explained the legislative implications in her *Nakaz*, or Instruction: "The order in general in a state is frequently understood by the term *police*," and "[i]t needs regulations, rather than laws." Recognizing this sort of justification, Francis Lieber condemned administrative power as "police government."[14, a]

a. The police power has long provided legitimacy for administrative power. *Policey* or *polizei* was a word used since the fifteenth century by French and German lawyers to refer to the domestic interests of civil government. The *droit de police*, or police power, was thus the power "to make particular orders for the government of all of the inhabitants of a town, or territory." Like the word "administrative," *police* initially was often used in relation to local governance, and it therefore was applied "chiefly unto three things," namely "small commodities" such as victuals, "trades" or "occupations," and "streets, or highways." Being derived from the Greek word "polis," however, it could reach the full range of domestic concerns, and like the word "administrative," it increasingly was used as a name not merely for the local power of local governments, but for the full domestic sovereign power of the state. Accordingly, when Continental jurisdictions transformed the monarch's absolute authority into the state's administrative authority, they often spoke in terms of the police power.

The term "police" entered the common law through men such as Blackstone, who were steeped in the civil law, and through cosmopolitan reformers such as Patrick Colquhoun. As late as 1815, a British commentator could still consider it a French term, but it gradually became widely familiar, not least in American constitutional law.

This Continental term was not inconsequential. Most narrowly, the word was appropriated in England and America as an elevated name for the sort of officers previously known as "constables." More broadly, it gave Americans a legalistic name for a general domestic government power, and in this role it eventually undermined the specialized and enumerated powers established by American constitutions.

Americans traditionally had established the power of their governments in terms of specialized legislative, executive, and judicial powers, not an unspecialized police power. Therefore, when Americans initially established their state constitutions, they did not mention the police power without making clear that this general domestic power belonged to the people rather than any one part of government. The 1776 Pennsylvania Constitution recited that "the people of this state have the sole, exclusive and inherent right of governing and regulating the internal police of the same"—a provision also adopted in North Carolina, Delaware, Maryland, and Vermont. Similarly, in 1777, the New York Constitution stated that the power to establish "a new form of government and internal police" belonged to "the people."

Such caution would not last long. The word "police" offered a technical-sounding name for a general governmental power in domestic matters, and this increasingly attracted American lawyers. Unsurprisingly, the police power and the constitutional limitations on it were most systematically expounded in the United States by a lawyer who studied in Germany, the Göttingen-trained Christopher Tiedeman. He, however, was only one of many nineteenth-century Americans who attributed the police power to the states and even, partly, to the federal government. Although he and some other lawyers tried to limit the damage, this consolidated vision of government power sliced through the separated powers (not to mention the enumerated powers), and it thereby went far toward justifying the administrative state.

Although the police power no longer is prominent as a justification for administrative governance, its early heritage and its implications can still be observed in the notion of policy. Whereas the U.S. Constitution authorizes the federal government to rule through law, the government nowadays carries out "policy," whether through statutes, administrative rules, interpretations, guidance, or other administrative demands. Law has thus largely given way to policy.[*]

On one justification or another, the absolute power that so many civilian academics and their successors had been peddling since the Middle
Ages eventually became not only prerogative power but also its successor,
administrative power. The English had finally defeated the power outside
the law in the seventeenth century, and Americans had more thoroughly
vanquished it in their constitutions. On the Continent, however, and with
particular academic zeal in Germany, the old absolute power went largely
unchecked, except to be modernized and made more efficient in administrative form.

Absolute power thus never really went away. After being expounded in
the study of the civil law, it eventually found expression in personal monarchical prerogative and then, even more systematically, in the state's administrative power. Much changed when monarchs accustomed themselves
to the rigors of bureaucracy, but absolute power persisted in administrative
form.

German Anti-Constitutional Scholarship

For the constitutionality of administrative power in America, what would
matter was not the practical detail of Continental administrative law, but
the German scholarship on administrative and more generally state power.
Americans drew many of their particular administrative plans from the
English, but it was mostly from the Germans that they imbibed an academic idealization of administrative power and a corresponding contempt
for power exercised through and under law, including a contempt for many
of the formalities of constitutional law.

Germans

Ideas of administrative power flourished among German academics. These
scholars differed on the role of civilian ideas, for whereas some looked
back to the Roman Empire and its civilian heritage, others preferred more
Germanic traditions. Few, however, were unaffected by civilian ideas, and
although some hoped to find limitations on power, almost all were deeply
imbued with at least the underlying civilian assumptions about the legitimacy of consolidated extra- and supralegal state power.[15]

In the sixteenth century, many German scholars had hoped to use civil
law to limit the absolute power of princes. Such hopes, however, soon
faded, and academics trained in the civilian tradition increasingly aligned
themselves and their learning with an enlightened absolutism.[16] In the sev-

enteenth and eighteenth centuries, civilian absolutist assumptions not only persisted in law but also became integrated into other studies, including a wide range of cameralist and political inquiries. Civilian-derived ideas thereby remained the academic foundation for absolute power, whether exercised personally or administratively.

No German did more to raise the civilian-derived administrative tradition to a philosophical level than Georg Wilhelm Friedrich Hegel. Original as he was in his philosophy, Hegel built upon familiar ideas, including those about the administrative state. Civilian-influenced German scholars already had elevated the state rather than the people as the judge of the public interest and had upheld the state's administrative commands rather than a popularly-enacted constitution as the measure of liberty. Hegel inevitably was familiar with such ideas, and he incorporated aspects of them into his own. He distinguished the state from the mere government and theorized that it evolved organically over history with its society, thus revealing that it was not limited by the people through an act of their will. Envisioning the state as the central moral person in society, he assumed that the state was engaged in a continual struggle against the private pursuit of self-interest, and from this perspective he asserted the power of the state over selfish private claims, including private claims of legal rights. Indeed, he assumed that private rights were "subjective" and that "objective" freedom could be found only in the state. He therefore complained that in England "objective freedom or rational right is . . . sacrificed to formal right and particular private interest." To combat this sort of danger, Hegel held that the state could not be accountable to the people through representative government, but instead would have to govern through an administrative class—a "universal class"—so called because he thought it would identify with the state and its elevated moral aims in opposition to the narrow private interests of society.[17]

Other Germans went even further. Whereas Anglo-American academics traditionally found the obligation of law in consent, many Germans reduced the state to a brutal reality. Heinrich von Treitschke (whose students would range from W. E. B. DeBois to Georg Simmel) boldly declared, "The state is force." In the more measured liberal tone of Rudolph von Jhering, "Coercion put in execution by the State forms the absolute criterion of law," and "[w]hether this coercion is put into execution by the court . . . or by the administrative authorities is indifferent. All rules which are realized in this way are law." Realpolitik thus came with a stark realism about law. No longer based on divine authority, absolute power now seemed to rest more securely on an empirical foundation, and the will of the ruler, once celebrated by civilians, now flourished as the power or will of the state.[18]

It will seen below that many Germans at the same time sought a legalistic account of state power and therefore demanded what they called a *Rechtsstaat*. In other words, they hoped for a state that would exercise its administrative power in a law-like manner. They had inherited, however, an administrative state, and therefore, even in their vision of a *Rechtsstaat*, they had to take for granted the primacy of the state and its administrative power.

The leading German scholars of administrative law, ranging from Lorenz von Stein to Rudolph von Gneist, tended to be liberal Hegelians—meaning that they were liberal as to society but authoritarian in their understanding of the state. Like other German liberals, they were inclined (as put by Robert Miewald) to view "a relatively progressive bureaucracy as the surest defense against an unrestrained monarchy." But in thereby accepting a systematized version of prerogative rule, they also legitimized it.[19] Indeed, they took satisfaction in the orderly and rational exercise of the state's administrative power, and they justified the bureaucratized version of the old absolutism by repeating the old civilian disparagement of constitutional governance and forms.

Far from ignoring popular sentiment, the advocates of administrative power assumed that the state's unified will could be understood as an expression of the unified will of the people. In the nineteenth century, it no longer was plausible to espouse an absolute royal prerogative in opposition to popular feelings. But an absolute administrative power, carried out by the state on behalf of the people, could be reconciled with populist tendencies. The key was to assume that the people had a unified interest or will and that this undergird the unified state in carrying out its will through administrative power.

The German proponents of administrative power especially disdained any constitutional separation of powers. Civilians had long rejected popular constitutional limitations, including any division of sovereignty, and when Montesquieu in the eighteenth century popularized the separation of powers, civilian-trained German scholars of administrative power (such as Johann von Justi) emphatically demurred.[20] Nineteenth-century German scholars continued in the same vein. For example, Hegel dismissed the conventional separation of powers as incompatible with state unity, and Treitschke fervently taught that the "whole doctrine of the three authorities in the State and their division is the toy of theory and playful fancy." Instead, "[t]he essence of the State is its unity, and that State is best organized in which these three powers are united in one supreme and independent hand."[21]

These sorts of absolutist ideals found fertile ground in German anxieties about national divisions. As summarized by M. J. C. Vile, "The impulse of the German attack upon the doctrine of the separation of powers was . . . that same horror of the destruction of the essential unity of state power which had characterized absolutist theories for centuries."[22] The Germans, however, took it further than most, for perhaps in response to their divisions, they often associated the unity of the state with the unity of society. Unlike the English and Americans, who found freedom in specialization and division, large numbers of Germans distrusted the specialized authority that was central in constitutional governance.

Of course, many Germans refused to join the anti-constitutionalist chorus. Many choristers, moreover, came from other nations. Nonetheless, it was the Germans who sang most passionately.

The dark possibilities for America were evident already in the nineteenth century. When Tocqueville came to the United States, he found little evidence of binding administrative constraints, and he was puzzled as to why they prevailed on one continent and not another. In contrast, Hegel, saw an incomplete state. Suspicious of democracy, he thought society achieved its highest expression in a state that arose organically from its history and that exercised power through a bureaucracy. He therefore denied that the new nation on the other side of the Atlantic was yet a "Real State," saying that it was only an unknown "land of the future."[23]

Americans

The largely untempered German learning found its way to America partly through academia. Since the Middle Ages, the study of the common law had been confined mostly to the Inns of Court and private apprenticeships—not merely from tradition, but from a self-conscious attempt to exclude the danger of academic law. In contrast, the study of the civil law had thrived in Continental and especially German universities—spawning derivative approaches in law, sociology, and political science. These approaches tended to repudiate the study of civilian doctrine but largely perpetuated civilian assumptions favoring consolidated state power outside and above the law, and many Americans imported these civilian-style ideas. As put by Roscoe Pound, administrative ideas "come to us chiefly from the modern

Roman administrative regime of continental Europe," especially from the "continental writers" on the subject.[24]

By the nineteenth century, German universities were particularly rigorous in their academic methods, and in Germany, therefore, the most extreme views of state power found sophisticated expression in the most up-to-date of learned institutions. The scientific model of academic inquiry developed in Germany was widely admired in the United States, and German ideas thereby found an open path into American universities. Thousands of late-nineteenth-century American scholars, eager to overcome their parochialism, flocked to Germany and returned with ideas about scientific study, which they then introduced into American academic life. By the 1880s, it could be observed that the "science of administration" was "finding its way into college courses in this country." The German scholarship on administrative power thus became the avenue for a sort of learning incompatible with American law.[25]

This was particularly apparent in the study of political science. Not merely at Columbia, Johns Hopkins, and Michigan, but soon in dozens of schools, Germanic ideas reached thousands of graduate students and then undergraduates. Charles Merriam in 1903 observed the results: "In the movement toward the study of politics during the last few decades, the leaders, almost without exception, have been men trained in German schools, familiar with German methods, and profoundly influenced by German ideas." Unsurprisingly, he added that "the influence of the German school is most obvious" in the displacement of "the contract theory of the origin of the state" by "the idea of the function of the state." The "German thinkers" had "assailed" the theory that "the state originates in an agreement between men" and had substituted, in a strange marriage of Hegel and Darwin, "the historical, organic, evolutionary idea." With this ominous historicism, reaching from primitive origins to brave new possibilities, German academics and their American followers idealized the state as having an organic or at least evolutionary relation to the society, with equally broad functions. These academics thereby "expanded" their understanding of "[t]he purpose of the state" from the protection of individuals and their individual interests to a "general care for the interests of the community."[26]

Like the Germans, many of the Americans sought social unity through the state. They were well aware, for example, of the views of Rudolf von Gneist. This nationalist liberal jurist at least sought to limit the arbitrary dictates of autocratic administrative power by establishing a *Rechtsstaat* of administrative law, but at the same time he worked (sometimes with Bismarck) to establish consolidated administrative power as the means of achieving a consolidated society. In the words of a progressive American admirer, Gneist held that "the political state exists in order to combat, and . . . to neutralize, the selfish forces working in society." From this German and even Hegelian perspective, administrative law could have deep moral appeal for progressive American academics in their struggle against trusts, monopolies, and other forms of selfishness.[27, b]

Indeed, many Americans, not just progressives or academics, drew upon the German ideas, without worrying too much about their implications for liberty. Of course, like some of the academics, the non-academics tended to get their Germanic assumptions second- or thirdhand, and by the turn of the century Americans increasingly left aside German ideas about the organic character of the state. Vast numbers, however—certainly many progressives, but also many socialists and conservatives—accepted civilian-derived ideas about extralegal power and more general Germanic notions about a unified and moral state enjoying a developmental or evolution-

b. Many scholars emphasize the distinctively Hegelian aspects of these developments. Perry Miller writes that the post–Civil War embrace of Hegelian idealism was "one of the most radical revolutions in the history of the American mind." Commenting on the administrative implications, John Marini observes that the "theory upon which the administrative state is based . . . developed as a practical outgrowth of German idealist philosophy," and "stands in sharp contrast to the government created by a limited constitution."

The emphasis on Hegel, however, although sometimes justified, can also obscure the complexity of the German ideas and how they were employed in America. Undoubtedly, German ideas about state or administrative power were often framed in Hegelian terms—for example, by Stein and Gneist—and this also was evident in America. Many of the American adaptations of German administrative thought, however, soon went in non-Hegelian directions or at least included a host of non-Hegelian elements.

Even more basically, one must distinguish between a philosophical and a historical approach to the question. Notwithstanding the philosophical appeal of attributing legal developments, such as American administrative law, to a philosopher such as Hegel, a more historical approach can recognize the degree to which Hegel himself was giving expression to aspects of a long tradition of civilian-derived German thought. For purposes of this inquiry, what mattered about Hegelian concepts is that they became an avenue for Germanic ideas about the state, including civilian-derived ideas about extralegal power. Of course, this is not to agree with Karl Marx's caustic words: "What Hegel says about 'the Executive' does not merit the name of a philosophical development. Most of the paragraphs [in his *Philosophy of Right*] could be found verbatim in the Prussian code." Instead, the point is more balanced—that part of Hegel's philosophy echoed Germany's civilian and administrative heritage.

There consequently is a risk in overemphasizing the philosophical approach. It usually runs back merely to Hegel, and it thus tends to obscure the underlying historical continuity, which runs back all the way to civil and ultimately Roman law. At least until the late nineteenth century, this historical heritage was still widely understood, and just because much of it has been forgotten does not mean that its legacy is past.*

ary relation to society.[c] With these ideals, increasingly put in "pragmatic" American terms, many Americans expected the state to pursue moral ends by employing administrative power in opposition to selfish private claims, including claims of rights. Unfortunately, in thus assimilating administrative power, these Americans typically did not pause to consider how profoundly alien it was to American life.[28]

In particular, such Americans tended to embrace the anti-constitutional implications. For example, when American scholars of politics adopted Germanic ideas about the state's administrative power, many also echoed the Germanic assault on separation of powers and constitutional limits.

Even before World War I, most Americans who studied political theory had abandoned their fascination with German scholarship. Many still held Germanic views about the state, but they now typically put aside the German authorities to tackle more practical questions about the implementation of administrative power. Yet far from a rejection of Germanic approaches to government power, this was a sign of how much the *Staatstheorie* had been assimilated. Overtly Germanic scholarship was becoming old fashioned, but by 1914 administrative law was well on its way to becoming an accepted part of American government, and (as will be seen) the Germanic ideas would remain significant.[29]

Development of Administrative Law in America

To understand how the German ideas came to be relevant in the United States, it is necessary to step back to the mid-nineteenth century, to trace the American development of administrative law. Administrative power is often assumed to have been a creation of the New Deal, but it actually became a significant part of American government during earlier efforts at reform—first in municipalities, and then increasingly in the states and the federal government. It was in this context, during the last decades of the nineteenth century, that Americans began systematically to rely on German ideas.

---

c. Administrative law was sought or at least accepted by large numbers of Americans who were not narrowly progressive. On the one hand, for example, some socialists in 1895 declared that, on account of "social necessity," "all branches of production" should come "under the control of the people through the people's central administrative authorities." On the other hand, even a conservative such as Elihu Root conceded that administrative law was among "the necessities of our situation"—although he also worried that administrative agencies "carry with them great and dangerous opportunities for oppression." Thus, |i]f we are to continue a government of limited powers these agencies of regulation must themselves be regulated"—in particular, the "limits of their power over the citizen must be fixed and determined."*

Municipalities

Practical experience with administrative governance initially became a part of American life in municipalities. After the English began to exercise administrative power through commissions—notably the Poor Law Commission in 1834 and especially boards of health in 1848—some American states followed suit. On both sides of the Atlantic, local governments had never been fully brought in line with the constitutional ideals about the separation of powers, and they therefore were particularly open to administrative developments.

At the local level, the Continental models for administrative power appear to have been of little interest. The English who established the preeminent administrative commissions, the boards of health, were well aware of the underlying German model, but most Americans who sought these bodies probably assumed that they were simply adopting English mechanisms.

In New York and other states, state legislatures established municipal commissions in order to sidestep the political power of city bosses and the danger of corruption, and in New York in 1870 the city bosses and their allies fought back in a public controversy over the constitutionality of government by commission. Although the dispute was at least as much about legislative interference with city governance as about the larger questions of administrative power, there was much debate about these larger constitutional questions. Mayor Martin Kalbfleisch of Brooklyn, for example, protested that each commission was a "monstrous un-American compound of legislative and executive functions in one body." This "double character" of a commission "saves it from checks both ways," for it "has the powers of both branches of the city government and the limitations of neither."[30, d]

This and other municipal controversies increasingly attracted broader attention. When the New York newspapers condemned commissions as

---

d. The debate was spurred largely by Governor John Thompson Hoffman's complaints that the legislature had created independent boards and commissions (on police, fire, and heath), which are "not elected by the people of the localities or appointed by the authorities thereof." This was, according to Hoffman, "an evasion of the spirit of the [New York] Constitution." As a remedy, he proposed that there be new charters for the affected cities, "in order to insure an early return to the system of local self-government as guaranteed by the Constitution."

Of course, the underlying story was not so elevated. Hoffman had previously been mayor of New York City, and he was elected governor with the assistance of William Tweed. Once in the governor's office, Hoffman proposed the new city charters, including one for New York City, and although he argued for this on grounds of constitutional law and municipal freedom from legislative interference, it obviously suited the desires of Tammany Hall.*

threats to "democracy," the *Nation* in 1870 felt obliged to respond that "those administrative bodies" had done "beneficial political work" during the past two decades. In the *Nation's* view, commissions filled a political gap, and thus it was valuable to have "commissioners with absolute power of administration."[31]

During the closing decades of the century, many academics, journalists, progressives, and others persistently explored municipal reform, and it was at this point that German ideas became prominent. At one level, Germany seemed to offer a model of good municipal governance—as when a popular magazine published articles entitled "The Government of German Cities: The Municipal Framework" and "What German Cities Do for Their Citizens: A Study of Municipal House-Keeping."[32]

At a broader level, Continental and especially German anti-constitutional ideas could justify municipal administrative power, and no one personified this realization more than Frank Goodnow. After studying in Paris and Berlin, he became a professor of law and political science at Columbia University, where he published treatises on administrative law and municipal government and even wrote a chapter on municipal corruption in Bryce's *American Commonwealth*. When Goodnow delivered his German ideas directly to the public—as in his 1897 books *Municipal Problems* and *Comparative Administrative Law*—the foreign anti-constitutional ideas provoked as much anxiety as assent.[e] By the beginning of the next century, however, he had learned to present his views with less overt reliance on German sources—for example, in his 1904 *City Government in the United States* and the next year, more generally, in his *Principles of Administrative Law of the United States*. The former began by self-consciously confining itself "almost exclusively to a study of American conditions"; the latter began by repudiating Alfred Dicey's complaint about the foreign character of administrative law by observing that this sort of power "includes many matters which are and must be the subject of legal regulation in English-speaking countries."[33]

---

e. In reviewing Goodnow's *Municipal Problems*, a Kentucky newspaper was generally favorable, but it cautioned:

> Much will have to be done towards changing public sentiment before we shall be able to adopt any of Mr. Goodnow's theories. He has drawn . . . on the experience in German and French municipalities, where these problems have been so much more successfully met than with us, owing largely no doubt to the genius for administration manifested by these peoples who have been subject to the civil law; and we have an idea that we are dishonoring our traditions if we draw from other sources than our Anglo-Saxon ancestors. We have a secret feeling, too, that inefficiency is often a badge of individual freedom.[*]

There always is reason to doubt the persuasiveness of academic and especially foreign academic ideas, but by the turn of the century German ideas of state power dominated not only the Anglo-American study of political theory but also many practical studies of municipal reform. American scholars and their students set out with German thoroughness to study the German approach to municipal problems, and the resulting books and dissertations included a wide array of case studies and overviews.[f]

Revealingly, municipal reform organizations quoted the academics and even published their own volumes. The American Civic Association in 1911 issued *A German City Worthy of Emulation: A Study of Frankfort-on-the-Main as An Example in Municipal Administration*. In 1913, the Newport Improvement Association invited Professor John Burgess of Columbia to speak on municipal reform, and his candidly Prussian ideas seem to have impressed the association, for it shortly aftward invited him to prepare a report on changing Newport's charter. More expansively, the City Commissioners of Houston engaged Frank Putnam to go to Germany and study the "leading municipalities in that country" because Houston could learn "important lessons" by studying "the methods which have been so successful in many of the most progressive cities of Germany." The commissioners published his results in 1913 as *City Government in Europe: Houston's Inquiry into Municipal Organization and Administration in the Principal Cities of Great Britain and Germany; with a Report of Findings and Recommendations for Houston's Guidance in Developing a Great Seaport City on the Gulf of Mexico*. At least prior to World War I, German ideas flourished in both academic and municipal inquiries about municipal power.[34]

Federal Government

German ideas became more broadly significant when the federal government began to establish administrative power. At that point, progressive Americans needed to explain this power and its constitutionality, and for such purposes German academic ideas seemed invaluable.

Already before the overt federal development of administrative law in 1887, there were hints. For example, in 1869, after the commissioner of internal revenue adopted a regulation that established how much taxpayers

---

f. The case studies included *Berlin: A Study of Municipal Government in Germany* (1889), *Municipal Improvements in Boston and Germany* (1899), and *Municipal Administration in Germany as Seen in the Government of a Typical Prussian City, Halle* (1901). Among the overviews were *European Cities at Work* (1913) and *Municipal Life and Government in Germany* (1914).

owed, the Supreme Court upheld the regulation as binding without really focusing on what was at stake. Perhaps this was merely an unselfconscious departure from the traditional prohibition on executive rules that bound the public. Perhaps, however, it also was a harbinger of the future.[g]

A clearer step toward federal administrative power was the Civil Service Reform Act of 1883. Prussia was the model of a merit-based bureaucracy, and the 1883 statute brought this system to Washington. Its sponsor, Senator George Pendleton, had studied at Heidelberg, and its main advocate in the House, Representative John Kasson of Iowa, had repeatedly served in Europe as a diplomat. Both therefore must have understood what they were proposing for the United States.[35]

Already in the campaign for the Civil Service Act, merit selection was recognized as a step toward the sort of administrative power that prevailed on the Continent. E. L. Godkin—founder of the *Nation*—argued in the *Century Illustrated Magazine* in 1882 that much of the "social transformation" that had occurred "since 1815, in France, or England, or Germany," consisted of "improvements in administration," and that "the best legislative changes" would have been "fruitless . . . without improved administrative machinery for their execution." The implications seemed clear: "We cannot very much longer postpone the work which other nations have accomplished. . . . Our turn will come next, and, in spite of 'politics,' will probably come soon."[36]

The initial substantive step was the Interstate Commerce Act. After some states experimented with state railroad commissions, Congress in 1887 established the Interstate Commerce Commission with powers to compel

g. Initially, when courts said that executive rules had the force of law, they meant only that the rules bound executive officers. For example, in *Harvey v. United States*, a judge of the Court of Claims said in 1867 that "rules and regulations relating to the subjects on which a department acts . . . are made by its head under an act of Congress conferring that power, and thereby giving to such regulations the force of law." Notwithstanding the breadth of these words, the judge was speaking about regulations by which the Treasury Department merely governed the conduct of its officers, and even in this regard, his conclusion traditionally would have been considered an overstatement.

Two years later, however, in *United States v. Barrows et al.*—the 1869 case mentioned in the text—the Supreme Court attributed the force of law to internal revenue regulations that bound members of the public. The authorizing statute imposed a tax on oil, with an "allowance for leakage as may be established by the regulations of the commissioner of internal revenue." The leakage in the case exceeded the standardized measure of leakage recognized by the commissioner's regulations, but the Court repudiated a claim for the actual leakage on the ground that "the per centum of deduction being fixed by a regulation of the department, in conformity to an act of congress, becomes a part of the law, and of as binding force as if incorporated in the body of the act itself." The regulation thereby set the tax.*

testimony and impose rates on the railroads, thus giving the commission a judicial power. Although its supporters tended to brush aside constitutional complaints, its opponents protested that the act transferred judicial power to a mere commission, thus taking it away from the courts. Albert Fink— the eminent German-American railroad engineer—protested that in a "free country" men could not simultaneously serve as "lawmakers, judges, and sheriffs." In the House of Representative, John Reagan of Texas observed that the American people were "not accustomed to the administration of the civil law through bureau orders," and that "[t]his system belongs in fact to despotic governments, not to free republics."[37, h]

A different and more lasting recognition of the constitutional question came from a young academic, Woodrow Wilson. He understood that the "creation of national commissioners of railroads, in addition to the older state commissions, involves a very important and delicate extension of administrative functions." It therefore was when Congress created the federal commissioners, in 1887, that Wilson declared the importance of German ideals for American administrative power.[38]

Wilson had been teaching himself German, so he could read German political and administrative theory in the original. Like many American scholars, he sometimes (as shown by Robert Miewald) "mistranslated" it. On the whole, however, in his publications and lectures, Wilson applied "warmed-over German theory" to American government.[39]

He acknowledged that administration "is a foreign science, speaking very little of the language of English or American principle" and that it "has been developed by French and German professors." In fact, Prus-

h. Senator John Morgan proposed to amend the bill with the proviso that "[t]he commissioners appointed under this act shall not exercise either legislative or judicial powers." When this was opposed, he wondered whether perhaps the commissions "are even more than that; they are autocrats." Indeed, Senator Joseph Brown complained that the commission would be a "little Star Chamber."

Recognizing how much was at stake, Professor William Graham Sumner of Yale observed in 1887 in the *North American Review*: "Now that the royal power is limited, and that the old military and police states are in the way of transition to jural states, we are promised a new advance to democracy. What is the disposition of the new state as regards the scope of its power? It unquestionably manifests a disposition to keep and use the whole arsenal of its predecessors." Sumner even took aim at the Hegelianism: "We are told that the state is an ethical person. This is the latest form of political mysticism. Now, it is true that the state is a mystical person in just the same sense as a business firm, a joint stock corporation, or a debating society." But this was "far from the meaning and utility of the dogma that the state is an ethical person." That was a "modern form of dogmatism designed to sacrifice the man to the institution which is not good for anything except so far as it can serve the man." Summarizing "the coming power," Sumner called it "omnicracy."*

sia was "where administration has been most studied and most nearly perfected."[40]

Going further, Wilson candidly admitted the mixed blessing of this "absolute" Prussian heritage. "We should not like to have had Prussia's history for the sake of having Prussia's administrative skill; and Prussia's particular system of administration would quite suffocate us. It is better to be untrained and free than to be servile and systematic." He hoped, however, for the best of both worlds: "Still there is no denying that it would be better yet to be both free in spirit and proficient in practice. It is this even more reasonable preference which impels us to discover what there may be to hinder or delay us in naturalizing this much-to-be-desired science of administration."[41] He thereby brushed aside the conflict between administrative power and American liberty. Indeed, as will be seen shortly, he already was anticipating how there might be German-style solutions to the American constitutional objections.

Wilson, of course, was not alone in such views. Instead, what stood out about him was that when Congress in 1887 established the Interstate Commerce Commission, Wilson announced the American significance of Continental ideas of administrative power. Systematic thought about administrative power and its constitutionality now seemed to many Americans inescapably necessary, and German ideas therefore would matter.

Conduits for German Ideas

German ideas could make a difference only because they already were beginning to enter American public life. Some of the pathways were general, some academic, and some governmental, but the Germanic administrative ideas had a broad appeal that cut across these distinctions.

It was an era in which educated men could not help but be aware of Prussian administrative achievements. Prussia and then Germany were notorious for their administrative prowess, and Americans therefore could read about it in their newspapers. They could gain further insight by reading biographies of Frederick the Great or of Baron Stein—the great Prussian administrative reformer.

More centrally, after late-nineteenth-century American scholars of political science and sociology became fascinated with German scholarship, they taught generations of students the Germanic skepticism about constitutional limitations, consent, and the separation of powers, and the Germanic love of the state and administrative authority. Having echoed these ideas in countless essays and dissertations, the students then repeated such notions at yet other schools and ultimately took them to Washington. Like their German progenitors, American teachers of political science had good reason to believe that they were training administrators for the state.[42]

Already in the late nineteenth century, as shown by Michael Lacey, the District of Columbia had a thriving intellectual community of scientifically minded bureaucrats who were "work[ing] out the premises for the modern regulatory state." They were deeply read in academic literature, and they were very open to what one of them, Lester Ward, called the "legislation . . . done by the executive branch."[43]

The bureaucrats, including academics and their students, tended to press for greater administrative power. For example, Professor Henry Carter Adams of the University of Michigan—the economist who served as statistician for the Interstate Commerce Commission—gave a speech in 1907 urging that "judicial supervision" of the commission should be displaced by "administrative supervision." In justification of this, Adams explained that the government was "woefully deficient" in "administrative agencies" dealing with "industrial affairs" and suggested that this reflected a constitutional difference: "The marked difference between the German constitution and the American Constitution is that we overestimate the exercise of judicial functions, and underestimate the exercise of administrative or supervisory functions; whereas in Germany the reverse is true." He had "no intent to disparage the importance of judicial administration," but "the other method of making effective government control over industrial affairs contains the greater hope."[44]

The academic ideas found their way directly into the 1912 presidential election. Theodore Roosevelt had imbibed German ideas of administrative power from John Burgess at Columbia Law School, and Roosevelt and his Progressive Party repeatedly appealed to voters with such notions. Tellingly, even Republicans in the election felt obliged to endorse administrative power.

When Woodrow Wilson prevailed, the highest executive officer in the nation went to a man who, for more than a quarter century, had favored German theories of administrative power. In the political realm, when Wilson established the Federal Trade Commission and strengthened the Interstate Commerce Commission, he knew he could not openly appeal to German ideas. Even in the academic sphere, the remaining enthusiasm for overtly German arguments were losing steam, and they became especially awkward after the commencement of World War I. By then, however, the underlying German-style assumptions had already become well established in American universities and government.

The transmission of academic ideas on administrative power was formalized in 1916 by the establishment of Washington's first think tank, the Institute for Government Research—soon to be renamed the Brookings Institution. Publicly, this early think tank issued volumes promoting "scientific" approaches to administrative "efficiency." Privately, it pursued the same mission by cultivating working relationships with administrators. Indeed, it self-consciously recognized that, although forceful demands were effective against legislators in a representative body, a more accommodating tone was best when working with administrative legislators. Therefore, rather than engage in any "public indictment of present conditions" and "public propaganda" for reforms, it took a "sympathetic attitude" and aimed at "cooperating" with officials.[45] This would become the twentieth-century style of "policymaking," in which sympathetic cooperation with extralegal power often displaced open political debates about law.

The institute's board of trustees was headed by Frank Goodnow, who had recently become president of Johns Hopkins. Although he had reached international fame by drafting the 1914 Chinese constitution, he would have greater effect in disseminating his Germanic vision of administrative power through the institute.[i] Its director was Princeton professor William Willoughby—twin brother of Johns Hopkins professor Westel Willoughby—and although William was the lesser academic, he more systematically brought administrative ideas to the government. In German fashion, he predictably distinguished the state from the government and rejected the separation of powers—arguing, instead, for a functional distribution of powers, including "administration as a distinct branch of government." His real skill was in translating administrative power into simplistic American terms. For example, he described "Congress as a board of directors," and administrative agencies as the "means by which it may ensure that its orders are in fact carried out."[46, j]

German ideas thus found a wide range of conduits into American life.

i. He based the Chinese constitution on the Japanese model and thus gave the powers of the Japanese emperor to the Chinese president. In practical terms, this meant the president had broad "administrative" power, including "large powers of legislation."[*]

j. Both Goodnow and Willoughby had earlier, in 1910, served on President Taft's Commission on Economy and Efficiency. After it failed to make much of an impression, the two academics realized that they could exert greater influence by standing just outside the government. Under Willoughby's leadership, scholars at the institute tended to seek American versions of the *Rechtsstaat*, in which administrative power was effective and efficient, but was structured to limit its abuses.

Of course, Americans pursued administrative power in response to their domestic anxieties, and even in academic institutions Americans soon lost patience with academics who persisted in citing German sources. Nonetheless, when Americans in the late nineteenth century and the beginning of the twentieth explored administrative power, they had many opportunities to learn from ideas drawn from Germany—so much so that such ideas soon seemed American.

Anti-Constitutional Justifications

As Wilson anticipated, German thought would be profoundly important for American administrative law. It is not always possible to sort out exactly what was taken from Germany, let alone whether it would have developed in America without the German inspiration. Clearly, however, much was derived from Germany and ultimately from earlier civilian assumptions, as can now be traced in the anti-constitutional justifications.

Of course, Americans also adopted some specific administrative programs from Germany—most notably, Bismarck's workers' compensation. Americans even appear to have adopted many civilian-derived administrative procedures from Germany or the Continent.[k]

More generally, though, Americans adopted German ideas to overcome the constitutional obstacles to administrative power. Once these Germanic justifications were popularized, there was no need to cite Germans, and after 1914 Americans had particularly strong reasons to repackage the Continental ideas to suit domestic sensibilities. But it is no coincidence that when Americans defended the constitutionality of administrative law, they relied on ideas familiar from German academics. Indeed, throughout the twentieth century, Germanic anti-constitutional ideas were among the leading constitutional justifications for administrative power.

---

k. It thus is no accident that there are astonishing similarities between the practices of the English High Commission and some American administrative commissions. For example, the High Commission had its own lawyers draft accusations and had its own commissioners determine the sufficiency of the charges. Then, after the commission issued letters or orders requiring defendants to appear and respond, it would try and punish them. Although American agencies were not designed to imitate these High Commission practices, it should be no surprise that the similarities sometimes reached down into such astonishing detail.

More generally, the German desire for a *Rechtsstaat* appears have found expression in the arbitrary and capricious standard. Jhering observed that when an "enactment of the administrative authorities" in Prussia was not "lawful," it was deemed "arbitrary." Similarly, in America, when courts hold administrative acts unlawful under the Administrative Procedure Act, they usually do so on the ground that it is arbitrary and capricious.[*]

Escaping Constitutional Limits

One of the most basic German responses to constitutional law was to deny or at least temper its application to administrative power. Whereas Anglo-American constitutions limited both the legislative and the executive branches, Continental and especially German scholars tended to assume that administration lay beyond reach of constitutional law.[47]

The notion that absolute or administrative power lay beyond constitutional limits began already with civilian conceptions of royal or prerogative authority. Echoing civilian arguments about the place of sovereign power above the law, James I in England had evaded constitutional limits by insisting that matters of state were within "the absolute prerogative of the Crown" and so were not "to be disputed" in the courts. Similarly, in seventeenth-century Prussia, it was said that "Regierungssachen sind keine Justizsachen."[48] Taking up this old civilian absolutism, many nineteenth-century German and other Continental scholars denied that administrative power was subject to constitutional law, let alone judicial enforcement of it.

The narrow reach of constitutional law on the Continent was regretted by some Germans. The great historian Barthold Niebuhr had once been a Prussian administrator, and when in 1822 he looked back at the recent Continental attempts to establish popular power, he feared that the effort was incomplete: "In most of the late attempts at establishing free institutions, nations have committed the great mistake of seeking liberty in the legislative branch only, or mainly." This was a mistake because "liberty depends at least as much upon the administrative branch (*Verwaltung*) as upon any other." A better approach was evident across the water: "The English are the only modern European nation who have acted differently; and the freedom of North America rests upon this great gift from Old England even more than on the representative form of her government, or anything else."[49] In other words, constitutional assurances of a representative legislature lost much of their value if there were not constitutional limits on administrative power.

Many other German scholars, however, were perfectly comfortable in distinguishing between constitutional and administrative matters. For example, when Treitschke rejected the separation of powers, he instead divided power into "the constitutional and administrative categories"—the one being the state's "unified will," and other being the detailed expression and application of this will.[50]

Following this German division, even if not specifically Treitschke, Woodrow Wilson repeatedly distinguished "between constitutional and administrative questions." John Austin, a half-century earlier, already had taught how, in the civilian tradition, "public law . . . is frequently divided into *constitutional* and *administrative*," but Wilson in the 1880s vigorously espoused this view. He recognized that previously, in America, administrative law was "not separated from constitutional law." But he thought the distinction important because it "may deliver us from the too great detail of legislative enactment," and thereby "give us administrative elasticity and discretion."[51]

Wilson therefore emphasized the difference "between the province of constitutional law and the province of administrative function." He reasoned: "The broad plans of governmental action are not administrative; the detailed execution of such plans is administrative. Constitutions, therefore, properly concern themselves only with those instrumentalities of government which are to control general law."[52] Whatever the quality of Wilson's reasoning, he was committed to the civilian-derived German vision that administrative power lay beyond constitutional limits.[1]

Soon, even Americans who betrayed no attachment to German ideas were urging that the courts should refrain from interfering with administrative power. Charles Evans Hughes had no love for German administrative ideas, but he probably was at least vaguely familiar with them from his years at Columbia Law School, and when in 1907 he was serving as governor of New York, he defended administrative power from the New York courts. He did so by arguing that when the courts applied the state's constitution, they should not interfere with "questions of administration"— with what Hughes dismissed as "all these matters of detail." Recognizing

1. Recognizing with whom he was disagreeing, Wilson purported to quote Niebuhr that liberty, at least on the Continent, "depends incomparably more upon administration than upon constitution." Wilson admitted that "[a]t first sight this appears to be largely true"—that, "[a]pparently, facility in the actual exercise of liberty does depend more upon administrative arrangements than upon constitutional guarantees; although constitutional guarantees alone secure the existence of liberty." But then (revealing his Germanic anti-constitutionalism) Wilson asked, "upon second thought—is even so much as this true?"

The distinction between constitutional and administrative questions was often aligned with a further German distinction between political and administrative matters. Arguing in 1887 that "[a]dministrative questions are not political questions," Wilson wrote: "This is a distinction of high authority; eminent German writers insist upon it as of course. Bluntschli, for instance, bids us separate administration alike from politics and from law. Politics, he says, is state activity 'in things great and universal,' while 'administration, on the other hand,' is 'the activity of the state in individual and small things. Politics is thus the special province of the statesman, administration of the technical official.'" Of course, he hastened to add, "But we do not require German authority for this position; this discrimination between administration and politics is now, happily, too obvious to need further discussion."*

that the judges felt constitutional scruples, he suggested that they rather than the constitution were the obstacle, for "[w]e are under a constitution, but the constitution is what the judges say it is." And he motivated them by adding a thinly veiled threat: If courts pursued the constitution into "these administrative matters," there would be "a propaganda advocating a short-term judiciary," and the courts would be subjected to "that hostile and perhaps violent criticism from which they should be shielded." If not by logic, then by threats, he would persuade judges to refrain from applying the constitution to administrative power.[53]

Although a candid distinction between constitutional and administrative questions could not easily be maintained at the surface of American law, many Americans had been exposed to the German distinction and concluded that administrative questions should not be subjected to judicial severity.[54] In placing absolute power beyond constitutional law, civilian scholars had been hostile to any judicial reconsideration of it, and even into the twentieth century the Germans barred regular courts from reviewing administrative power.[55] Of course, so sweeping a prohibition was not plausible in common law countries, and the Anglo-American version was therefore to allow jurisdiction but to expect deference. James I, for instance, understood that he could not always prevent the common law courts from taking jurisdiction, but he at least expected these courts to defer to his absolute prerogative, including the judgments and interpretations adopted by his prerogative tribunals. Similarly, in the twentieth century, Americans did not simply copy the German rejection of jurisdiction over administrative acts, but instead adopted a softer version, in which courts could take jurisdiction but had to defer.

The effect was to preserve the ideals of constitutional law and judicial review, but not much of the substance. Publicly the ideals remained; in reality, however, administrative power was mostly protected from constitutional law. And far from being cynical, this made sense from the administrative point of view.[m]

---

m. The Germanic distinction between administrative and constitutional law had implications not only for judges but also administrative agencies—for example, in suggesting that they could transcend their statutory authority. When teaching that "the functions of government are in a very real sense independent of legislation, and even of constitutions," Wilson already concluded that "[a]dministration cannot wait upon legislation, but must be given leave, or take it, to proceed without specific warrant in giving effect to the characteristic life of the state." This sort of attitude has become commonplace, as evident in the many administrative actions that stretch beyond their congressional authorization.*

State Power and Individual Rights

Another anti-constitutional justification drawn from Germany was the elevation of the state above personal rights. Americans traditionally had assumed that government derived from an act of the people and ultimately even from the consent of individuals, and on this foundation, they understood their constitutional rights to trump government power. They increasingly learned from the Germans, however, that the state was the source of all law and rights and that it thus had priority over rights. Many Americans thereby came to assume that administrative power trumped individual rights and could reshape them to satisfy government interests.

The absolutist assumptions that the Germans inherited from civilians elevated the state above all other interests in society and established state power, not least administrative power, as the measure of individual freedom. From this perspective, even when German administrative scholars allowed that the state could establish administratively enforceable rights against the state, they upheld the state as the source of such rights and insisted that the state could alter them. Even a scholar as liberal as Georg Jellinek could go so far as to say: "The individual personality is not the basis but the result of the legal community."[56]

Although Americans typically held back from such extremes, and insisted that they valued individual liberty, many adopted a Germanic view of the state's power over rights. They argued that the state rather than the people was the source of liberty and that individuals therefore were subject to the state's judgment about how far individual rights had to give way to state interests. At Columbia, for example, Burgess concluded that the state "formed for itself a constitution" and that it itself was "the source of individual liberty." Indeed, he defined sovereignty as "original, absolute, unlimited, universal power over the individual subject and over all associations of subjects." Such views were commonplace. Professor James Garner declared that sovereignty "can be bound only by its own will, that is, it can only be self-limited," and according to Westel Willoughby, the state is "not a creature of law."[57]

Following this Germanic vision of the state, leading advocates of administrative power taught that individual rights restrained administrative action only as the state determined expedient. Wilson thought that the "inviolability of persons," as protected by a bill of rights, did "not prevent the use of force by administrative agents for the accomplishment of the legitimate objects of government." Instead, a bill of rights "simply prevents malicious, unreasonable, arbitrary, unregulated direction of force against individuals."[58] Goodnow argued that an individual's rights were "conferred upon him . . . by the society to which he belongs" and that what they were could therefore be "determined by the legislative authority in view of the needs of that society. Social expedience, rather than natural right, is thus to determine the sphere of individual freedom of action." He even feared that an "insistence on individual rights" could "become a menace when social rather than individual efficiency is the necessary prerequisite of progress," and he therefore took satisfaction that "the sphere of governmental action is continually widening and the actual content of individual rights is being increasingly narrowed."[59, n]

The implication was that judges had to accept administrative intrusions on rights. After progressive legislatures authorized administrative power, Goodnow urged that judges should recognize the "wide discretion" of legislative bodies in constitutional interpretation, as this was essential for "[a]ttempts to change the structure of our political system and so to modify the content of private rights as to bring them in conformity with modern conditions." Such attitudes obviously remain influential. As put by a contemporary commentator (Peter Strauss), "social changes brought about by industrial and post-industrial economies" could not have been anticipated by the Constitution, and "American judges have responded to this challenge, on the whole, by interpreting the Constitution in ways that confirm the structural changes that have been made, and by reinterpreting citizens' rights in light of the changed arrangements."[60]

German ideas thus paved the way for the administrative reduction of rights. Although the twentieth century usually is depicted as an era of expanded liberty, the very opposite was true where constitutional rights conflicted with administrative power. Ken Kersch notes this in Fourth and Fifth Amendment rights, and the point can be made more broadly. Following the influx of German ideas, administrative power has almost systematically overridden constitutional rights—nearly all of the procedural rights and even some substantive rights.

---

n. Of course, societal efficiency was understood to include mere administrative efficiency. Westel Willoughby—a professor of political science at Johns Hopkins and the managing editor of the *American Political Science Review*—generalized in 1910 about "Administrative Necessity as a Source of Federal Power." Under this heading, he explained that "the principle of administrative efficiency has been employed to permit the field of individual rights to be entered." In other words, the Supreme Court "has frankly argued that where, for the efficient performance of the administrative duties laid upon the general government, it is necessary that an administrative order should take the place of a judicial process, the private rights of person and property are not to be allowed to stand in the way."*

Consolidation Rather than Separation

Even more significant was the civilian and Germanic disdain for the separation of powers and the corresponding celebration of consolidated state
power. Whether drunk at full strength or watered down to make it more
palatable, this hostility to the separation of powers became a staple of
twentieth-century constitutional justifications for administrative power.

The most pedantically German examinations of separation of powers
were too abstruse to be very persuasive in America—as can be illustrated
by George H. Smith's essay "The Theory of the State." Smith was a devotee of Wilhelm Roscher—the German scholar who popularized the notion
of "enlightened absolutism"—and like other Americans who imbibed the
German spirit, Smith had little patience for the tripartite division of powers, complaining that it lacked "scientific accuracy." Instead, after elaborate
functional analysis, he concluded that the state had "rights," including "the
administrative rights"—namely, "the right of legislation, and that of government (*Imperium*)." A Romano-Germanic vision of the state's unity, functions, and rights thus displaced the American vision of federalism, separation of powers, and rights reserved by the people.[61]

Arcane as Smith's essay may seem, it won a munificent prize from the
American Philosophical Society in 1895, and this is suggestive. Smith's
overtly German vision would not get far, but the Germanic rejection of
separation of powers and the substitution of functionalist analysis was by
now moving beyond academic departments into general academic conversation, and it would soon become a standard constitutional defense of administrative law.

A more progressive sociological version of the Germanic approach
was taken by Goodnow, who urged the consolidation of government as a
means of achieving the consolidation of society. He followed Gneist in emphasizing the "historical development" of society in opposition to the contractual vision underlying the Constitution, arguing that "all attempts to
place society on a contractual basis" were "worse than useless in that they
retard development." Like Gneist, he aimed to overcome social fragmentation through the consolidation of the state, arguing that a contractual vision of law, and the resulting elevation of constitutionally fixed principles,
seemed to stand in the way of "modern progressive" social reform. Against
the danger from such principles, Goodnow adopted what Merriam called
"a new line of division" against the separation of powers—arguing that the
functions of the state consisted simply of the "expression of the will of
the state" and the "execution of that will," in both of which administra-

tive power was essential. By means of this "centralized and consolidated" power, the will of the people in establishing separate governmental powers could be reduced to "the will of the state."[62]

Probably the simplest versions of the German ideas were the most persuasive, and the way that a mundane devotee of administrative power could reject the separation of powers can be observed in the work of John Mabry Mathews. After teaching political science at Princeton and then Illinois, and working for the Efficiency and Economy Commission of Illinois, he summarized his teaching in his 1917 book *Principles of American State Administration*. Like Wilson and others, he argued that "efficient administration, formerly considered more appropriate to monarchical governments, is no less essential to a democratic government and is, indeed, intimately connected with the furtherance of true democracy." To this end, he concluded that "it is necessary for the people to rid themselves of some venerable ideas and traditional notions, such as allegiance to the principles of separation of powers and checks and balances."[63]

The point is not that these particular expositions were influential, or that the German sources for the rejection of separation of powers were regularly acknowledged, but rather that simplified Americanized versions of such ideas had gradually become commonplace. Looking back in 1920 over the past half century, Merriam observed the separation of powers had been "slowly translated . . . from a principle of liberty to a rule of political convenience."[64]

Comparative, Sociological, and Functional Reasoning

At a jurisprudential level, Americans often drew (directly or indirectly) on German comparative, sociological, and functional reasoning. By this means, Americans were able to explain the constitutionality of administrative law within a broader intellectual framework.

To transcend the chasm between Continental administrative power and American constitutions, Americans turned to comparative study. Civilian scholarship and, more recently, Jhering's realism had already inspired Germans to do much comparative study of administrative law, especially along functionalist lines, and Americans, such as Wilson and Goodnow, soon followed. Although the immediate goal was to trace differences, the larger effect was to suggest the functional interchangeability of different mechanisms. According to Wilson, comparative study revealed "a unity in structure and procedure" that would lead to "the upsetting of many pet theories as to the special excellence of some one system of government." As put by Goodnow, "The forms and methods of administrative action" were "everywhere essentially the same."[65, o]

The sociology and political science drawn from Germany became particularly valuable resources for academic proponents of administrative law, for these "sciences" invited scholars to adopt supposedly scientific sociological terms, which could cut through the legal doctrines of different societies. This had been Goodnow's move when he drew a supposedly "new line of division"—between the expression and the execution of the will of the state—in place of the separation of powers. By focusing in this way on what they considered the functional realities across legal systems, scholars delegitimized American constitutional principles that stood in the way of administrative law.[66]

The functionalist path around constitutional obstacles did not deny the administrative concentration of powers, but recast it in reassuring functionalist terms. As observed by Robert Miewald, German academics pursued "endless classifications" of governmental "functions," and Americans soon also adopted this end run around constitutional forms. For example, instead of accepting the "artificial" separation of powers, Wilson favored an "organic differentiation" and "division of functions," explaining that this was "simply an argument from convenience, in the highest sense of that term." In other words, government "is modified by its environment, necessitated by its tasks, shaped to its functions by the sheer pressure of life."[67]

Most broadly, the sociological functionalism had the advantage of giving a scientific veneer to the old absolutist claims about necessity above law. At one level, this could be framed in pragmatic terms, as when it was said that "[n]o administrative tribunal would be able to function if it were guided solely by rules of law." At an underlying level of historical sociology, it could be added that "[r]egulation by law . . . no longer works" because of the "congested conditions of modern life." Combining these approaches, advocates of administrative power often argued in terms of both functional necessity and historical inevitability. A law professor who joined the bench, Cuthbert W. Pound, bluntly explained about administrative agencies: "They are here to stay. They are an organic growth. Our complex industrial and commercial problems cannot be handled otherwise." Ger-

o. In 1928, Freund also published a comparative study of administrative power, and like Wilson and Goodnow, he found that any "difference . . . diminishes as we scrutinize our own laws more carefully." But the level of Germanic detail that Goodnow explored in 1897 was no longer of much interest when Freund pursued it three decades later.*

man ideas about the sociological inevitability of administrative law thus found American expression.[68]

In such ways, American advocates of administrative law responded to constitutional obstacles with civilian-derived German ideas. They embraced a Germanic limit on the application of constitutional law to administrative agencies, a Germanic conception of how administrative power could reduce rights, a Germanic contempt for the separation of powers and other constitutional formalities, and a Germanic vision of the functional and historical necessity of administrative power. These were constitutional justifications in anti-constitutional terms. The students trained in such attitudes soon became bureaucrats, lawyers, and judges, and in these positions they eventually swept away the constitutional impediments.

The *Rechtsstaat*

Accentuating the absolute character of American administrative law was the partial American adoption of the German *Rechtsstaat*. The incompleteness of the American adoption of this German vision has been observed by Daniel Ernst, and the implications are sobering.[69] Whereas some German academics systematically attempted to regularize administrative power by reducing it to administrative law, Americans systematically left room for the very administrative discretion that the Germans rejected.

Germany

Germany was so far immersed in absolutism that the German version of the rule of law was merely the regularization of absolute power. The first step came when enlightened Germans, in the eighteenth century, sought to limit the opportunity for a ruler's arbitrary whim by reducing the absolute power of the prince to the administrative power of his bureaucrats. Recognizing the advantages of systematizing state power, Prussian monarchs encouraged this bureaucratization, striving to make Prussia the model of administrative efficiency.

The second step came when liberal Germans in the nineteenth century hoped to regularize the administrative power of bureaucrats into administrative rules. Rather than submit to discretionary administrative power, Robert von Mohl in the 1830s and other reformers aimed to establish a bureaucracy that would govern through a formalized administrative law, with appeals to the courts, and within the framework of constitutional law—this being the strongest ideal of the *Rechtsstaat*.[70]

This strong version, however, could not get far in Germany, and it failed most publicly with the stillbirth of the imperial constitution proclaimed in 1849 in Frankfurt. Advocates of the *Rechtsstaat* had secured a provision that "[t]he administrative legal system is abolished; the courts will decide about all cases of infringements on the law." This, however, was too radical for much of Germany, and when support for the constitution was not forthcoming, it was not only the constitution and a united Germany that seemed doomed. Thereafter, only a diminished *Rechtsstaat*, without recourse to the regular courts, was possible. Although Prussia eventually established appeals from administrative decisions to administrative courts, it preserved the state and its administrative power from accountability in the ordinary courts.[71]

Even in this weak version of the *Rechtsstaat*, with appeals only to administrative courts, these tribunals did their best to assimilate the administrative system to a legal system. Although the Prussian code authorized any administrative actions necessary for preserving order, the administrative courts understood this as a limitation and on this basis rejected administrative actions they deemed unnecessary for such ends. Through the efforts of Georg Jellinek and other scholars, moreover, Germans came to recognize that the state could subject itself to administrative rights, which individuals could enforce in the administrative courts.[72] The *Rechtsstaat* thus was profoundly valuable in its German context, for it allowed Germans to enjoy a law-like version of absolute power and thereby to come as close to law as was possible under extralegal rule.

Although this was as much as the Germans could hope for, it was a regularization of absolute power, and it thus was much less than Americans took for granted. Scholars on both sides of the Atlantic (including R. C. van Caenegem, Daniel Ernst, and Kenneth Ledford) have tended to understand the *Rechtsstaat* as the "rule of law," and on this basis have assumed that there is little significant difference between administrative rule and the traditional Anglo-American rule through and under law.[73] In fact, the *Rechtsstaat* was merely an elevated version of administrative power, one designed to mimic law but still based on state power outside regular law. Even in enforcement, the *Rechtsstaat* offered trial and review only by administrative judges in the administrative system, not trial and review by real judges standing on their own authority. Thus, although stated in legal terms, it was very different from the Anglo-American ideal of government through and under law.

None of this should be a surprise. The sad reality was that the Germans were stuck with the administrative version of prerogative power. The German understanding of the rule of law was therefore primarily to have the government constrain itself in the manner of law, but this meant simply that the government had to work through administrative law rather than mere administrative power, and that it had to offer some sort of review in administrative courts. This *Rechtsstaat*, or rule of law, was a far cry from rule through and under law.[74]

America

Nonetheless, Americans took up the notion of the rule of law. And they did not even live up to this.

In America, the administrative enterprise could be acceptable only under the rubric of "law," and it therefore is unsurprising that American academics tended to speak in terms of "administrative law" rather than mere "administrative power." They were familiar, moreover, with the significance of the names used in Europe, whether the French *droit administratif* or the German *Rechtsstaat*.

As noted by Daniel Ernst, however, the reality of the *Rechtsstaat* made little headway in America. Whereas German liberals struggled to move from discretionary administrative power to nondiscretionary administrative rules, many American progressives fled headlong from nondiscretionary legal rules to discretionary administrative power. Put in terms of theory, although the Germans included liberals such as Otto Mayer, Americans sometimes went more in the direction of Carl Schmitt.[p]

p. The American rejection of the *Rechtsstaat* was painfully evident in discussions of how administrative standards should displace legal rules. Roscoe Pound and Felix Frankfurter welcomed administrative discretion in applying standards as necessary for the flexibility required in a modern society. Pound acknowledged that there were "dangers" in "committing the application of legal standards to administrative bodies" but justified administrative power as the means of applying standards in place of rules where the latter would be insufficiently flexible to accommodate "special circumstances." Similarly, although Frankfurter recognized the danger of "abuses of caprice and oppression," he desired an administrative power "flexible enough to meet the flexibilities of life." Such a viewpoint was apt to appeal to these men who were so comfortable in the exercise of power.

Less powerful and more candid, Ernst Freund supported administrative law but with greater caution. He acknowledged, on the one hand, that there was "no room for administrative power in combating plain illegality" and, on the other, that "a professed regime of liberty is likewise intolerant of administrative power." Nonetheless, he thought there was a middle ground for administrative power between "plain illegality" and "liberty." He concluded that the "proper province of administrative power" lies in matters in which "it would be very difficult to separate what is lawful from what is unlawful without administrative arrangements." This had some common ground with Pound's argument for administrative administration of standards, but with a blunt recognition of the cost for liberty. Ultimately, as explained by Daniel Ernst,

Even in providing for administrative review, the Americans did not follow the best of the German example. The Germans at least elevated administrative courts as genuinely independent bodies and had them provide de novo review. Americans, however, generally established the worst of both worlds. On the one hand, they usually left administrative review within the relevant agency, often conducted by its politically appointed head or by a board appointed by him. On the other hand, they reduced the courts' review to a deferential look at administrative acts on the basis of a factual record created by the agency itself.

The resulting American venture was thus not even a *Rechtsstaat*. Although Americans had borrowed from the Germans, they were heading in a different direction. Americans had drawn upon a line of ideas that ran from the civilians to the Germans, but rather than simply borrow wholesale from this tradition, Americans tended to rely on the Germanic notions to conceptualize and justify their own extralegal project, which tilted toward administrative discretion more than an administrative version of law.

Those who regretted this direction of administrative power included some of its most notable advocates. Woodrow Wilson worried about the administrative shift "from law to personal power." He complained in 1908 that "[p]ublic officers were "administering not rules of law but their own discretionary opinions." To be sure "[w]e are all advocates of a firm and comprehensive regulation," but "[i]f there must be commissions, let them be, not executive instrumentalities having indefinite powers capable of domineering as well as regulating, but tribunals of easy and uniform process acting under precise terms of power in the enforcement of precise terms of regulation." Having done so much to encourage German-style administrative power, Wilson now protested the failure to exercise this power in a law-like manner.[75]

Such protests, however, were not in the long term very persuasive. Administrative power remained extralegal power—a power different from that exercised through law—and thus even a relatively law-like version of this power was difficult to defend as a matter of law. As in the past, moreover, there was no obvious stopping point outside the law. Thus, even a rela-

---

Freund thought "administrative discretion" was "tolerable only until experience under open-ended *standards* suggested the content of a certain *rule*."

The embrace of standards stood in contrast to the traditional assumption that government could exercise power only through law and thus only as to perfect rights or duties. These were rights or duties that were considered enforceable (whether in the state of nature or in civil society), and one essential characteristic of a perfect right or duty was that it was capable of being stated as a rule. From this traditional perspective, which protected liberty through and under law, a right or duty that could not be stated as a rule was merely imperfect and thus unenforceable.[*]

tively rule-bound version of extralegal power opened up the temptation to pursue more discretionary versions, thus leading to cascading expansions of this power.

One of the most poignant commentaries on the American departure from the *Rechtsstaat* came in the work of Ernst Freund. Daniel Ernst shows that Freund desperately sought to advance this ideal, hoping that Americans could adopt administrative power without embracing extremes of administrative discretion. But his efforts were of little avail. Shortly before his death (as Ernst notes) Freund recalled his borrowings from the Continent and lamented how much had been left behind. He wrote that his "ideas about administrative law were undoubtedly influenced by Goodnow, who in his turn was influenced by continental jurists and treatises, but the process of transmission brought eliminations and substitutions; and now the presentation of an entirely new plan appears to break the old traditions completely."[76] The result was mere administrative power, and although couched in terms of "administrative law," it did not meet even the German ideal of how it should imitate law.[q]

Much evidently was lost in the transatlantic crossing. Whether in administrative lawmaking or adjudication, the liberal German vision of administrative law, the *Rechtsstaat*, was reduced to the progressive American vision of administrative power. The *Rechtsstaat* was, in the words of Daniel Ernst, "A Transatlantic Shipwreck."

q. Even in attempting to tame the danger of absolute power, American administrative law followed the Continental civilian-style model. As noted earlier in this chapter, the late medieval civilian commentators who embraced absolute power also hoped to moderate its perils. Yet having espoused absolute power—a power above law—they could not subdue it with law, and they therefore could only caution that a ruler had to limit himself by following rational mental processes. The ruler, they said, had to state a cause (*causa*) when he departed from the law; he had to be explicit about any intent to dispense with the law (as in non obstante clauses); more generally, he had to act reasonably.

Not coincidentally, Americans incorporated such limits into their administrative law—as if these academic palliatives could really substitute for constitutional limits. When issuing rules, agencies must meet notice-and-comment requirements, but can escape this requirement where they offer the feeble reassurance that they have "good cause." Although agencies typically must act through rules, they can dispense with them where (as in the old non obstante clauses) they explicitly waive compliance with a specified rule. Administrative law even harks back to civilian ideas in relying on vapid reasonableness tests to define limits on executive power—for example, in providing for deference to rational, reasonable, or non-arbitrary decisionmaking under the Administrative Procedure Act and *Chevron*.

In all of these ways, administrative law substitutes soft civilian-style academic rationality for the hard edges of Anglo-American law. The common law protected liberty with clear-cut divisions of authority. In contrast, administrative law emulates the civilian pattern, in which consolidated power is subject to largely academic limits of good cause, specificity, and reasonableness.

Blindness

None of this is to say that American exponents of administrative power were knowing advocates of absolutism. Nor is it to say that they were pro-tofascists. Rather, the point is more mundane. Almost all persons are at-tracted to power, and Americans drank—indeed, drank deeply—from a poisonous well.[77]

Obviously, the ways in which administrative authority could go wrong became most vivid not in America, but on the Continent. Extralegal power had long flourished in France, Germany, and Russia, and in the nineteenth century it had acquired scientific legitimacy in the form of administrative power, but it was in the twentieth century that the costs of this heritage became most painfully apparent. Although nineteenth-century Germans had moved from administrative power to the *Rechtsstaat* ideal of admin-istrative law, they thereby established liberal legitimacy for a system of ex-traordinary executive authority, and when the Nazis came to power they took advantage of this authority. Moreover, where the Nazis found even administrative law too cumbersome, they reintroduced mere administra-tive power alongside it, thus establishing what Ernst Fränkel in 1941 called a "dual state," in which "normative" general and administrative law was combined with "prerogative" administrative power. Further east, the Rus-sians had done their best to follow the German shift toward the *Rechtsstaat*, but without even a thin layer of law controlling the emperor. After their revolution they reverted from administrative law back to mere administra-tive power—this time in party rather than imperial hands. The ideas that had justified monarchical abuse in past centuries thus lent themselves to systems that were much worse.[78]

This might have been a source of embarrassment for advocates of a type of "law" that had such deep foundations in German legal scholar-ship. But it was not. Roscoe Pound expressed concern about "administra-tive absolutism" and about its connection to "the rise and vogue of dicta-tors elsewhere."[79] As already noted, however, he remained committed to an administrative *Rechtsstaat*, and he therefore rejected only some aspects of administrative power. In any case, he was too inconsistent and blustery to have even a chance of being persuasive.

Most advocates of administrative law expressed no self-doubt. It was easy to ignore the German and more generally Continental foundations of administrative power. Already before World War I, the casebook method of teaching had the effect of stripping Continental sources from the teaching of administrative law, thus allowing professors to avoid any unpleasant reactions in class.[80] Moreover, treatises increasingly offered Americanized versions of the German arguments on deference, administrative power over rights, separation of powers, functionalism, and the sociological inevitability of administrative law, and it therefore was possible to assimilate these German views without any discomforting reminders about their origins. By 1914, moreover, the courts had upheld significant aspects of administrative power, and by the 1940s their legitimization of it was nearly complete. Americans advocates of administrative law therefore never felt obliged to reconcile their endeavor with its Continental sources and uses.

Nonetheless, it was difficult to avoid recognizing what lay not far in the background, including the old civilian absolutism, its continuity in French and German administrative law, and its celebration in German political theory. The problem with those who drew upon the German and other Continental ideas was not that these men were evil, but that they were so committed to their project that they were indifferent to the danger. As Thomas Merrill observes about one of them, they became cheerleaders for administrative power. Having taken this stance, most of them disdainfully brushed aside contrary considerations.[81]

Indeed, they embraced a tradition that was notorious for its incompatibility with American law and liberty. The connection between absolute and administrative power was not a secret. In the most prominent book on constitutional law of the late nineteenth century, Dicey began by observing that "the views of the prerogative maintained by Crown lawyers under the Tudors and the Stuarts bear a marked resemblance to the legal and administrative ideas which at the present day under the Third Republic still support the *droit administratif* of France."[82]

The Americans who espoused administrative power, however, had little patience for history and even less for law. As has been seen, they preferred to speak in German-derived sociological terms about functional realities and about the historical inevitability of administrative power in modern society. Like their German intellectual forebears, moreover, they dismissed constitutional obstacles as mere formalities, usually with a tone of contempt. It is a style that has not altogether passed.[83]

That governments seek power, including absolute power, should be no surprise. What is disappointing is that so many Americans drew upon absolutist ideas without pausing to consider the significance of their civilian and German heritage or why such ideas had been rejected by Anglo-American constitutional law.

ᏻᏻᏻ

The history of how absolute power was systematized into administrative law, and how it came to be adopted in America, has been largely forgotten by American lawyers. But it bears remembrance.

Painful as it must be for administrative scholars to acknowledge, administrative power has a long and ugly history. It began as absolute power at least in the Middle Ages, it persisted into modern times on the Continent, and from there it spread to America. Thus, rather than simply a restoration of absolute power, administrative law is actually a continuation of such power. And what this implies for America becomes concrete when one recognizes the central role of Germany in the early development of administrative power on the Continent and in the later migration of such power to the United States.

TWENTY-FIVE

Obstacles

Notwithstanding that administrative power is profoundly unlawful, there remain a series of conventional objections that are apt to be raised in opposition to this conclusion. These obstacles can be serious for some constitutional questions, but they turn out to be rather less serious for administrative law. Indeed, when one considers the depth of the objections to administrative law, the obstacles to concluding that it is unlawful appear very thin, even brittle.

Reliance

Even when administrative law is recognized as theoretically unconstitutional, it is defended on grounds of reliance. From this perspective, Americans have come to rely on it, and it is unjust to disappoint their expectations. This sort of argument, however, is not very persuasive as to administrative law.

Undoubtedly, many Americans rely on the substantive duties imposed through administrative law—for example, the duties that protect against dangerous drugs. Any such substantive duties, however, can just as well be imposed by statute and enforced in the courts. For example, Congress could adopt regulations proposed by the Food and Drug Administration, and then the FDA and private parties could pursue violations of the law in the courts.

Accordingly, even though there is reliance on the valuable substantive policies adopted in administrative law, it cannot be assumed that there is reliance on administrative law. The policy is different from the mode of enacting and enforcing it, and if there really is much reliance on the administrative mode of enactment and enforcement, there should be some serious empirical evidence of this. Not for the first time, the defense of administrative law depends on an empirical question for which no empirical evidence has been offered.

The empirical question only gets worse when one realizes that the claim about reliance is rarely accompanied by much detail about who exactly relies on administrative law or in what ways. This is disturbing because, to the extent that the reliance on administrative law is really reliance on the mode of enacting and enforcing it, rather than on the substance, it appears to play into the hands of powerful interests.

Many large corporations and other complex organizations have come to rely on administrative lawmaking and adjudication as a form of government power that is peculiarly susceptible to behind-the-scenes negotiations. Small businesses, in contrast, cannot similarly expect to reach private accommodations with administrators. Nor can individual Americans. On the whole, the larger the private organization, the more it relies on administrative power as a means of arranging special deals for itself, thereby allowing it to reach accommodations that would never survive the accountability of popular politics or judicial process.

The corporate reliance on administrative law is based on corporate access. To an overwhelming degree, it is corporations, their lawyers, and their lobbyists, not ordinary individuals, who have a role in the formation of administrative rules and interpretations and in decisions about the initiation or settlement of administrative prosecutions. This makes some sense, because administrative power most directly imposes duties on corporations. Overall, however, the corporate access to administrators reenforces the power of the powerful and excludes ordinary citizens. The result is reliance for the well placed, not for others.[1]

This reliance by only part of the society is especially troubling because it is reliance on unlawful power and on the judges' deference to it. Is this reasonable reliance? And what about the reliance of the rest of the society on the laws, especially the Constitution? Is that not reasonable reliance?

Whatever the merits of a reliance argument, it must recognize the reliance on both sides of the question. And when both sides are recognized, the argument that reliance justifies otherwise unlawful administrative power becomes a strange proposition: that the reliance by the powerful on unlawful power defeats the reliance by the rest of the society on the law.

The usual reliance argument thus is one sided and unpersuasive. Rather than legitimize administrative law, it suggests the importance of recognizing its unconstitutionality.

Living Constitution

The living constitution is a conventional theory for justifying constitutional change. As applied to administrative law, however, it does not so much justify constitutional change as stand in its way.

Open Ended

One problem is that the living constitution is too open ended to justify any particular constitutional change. Although it offers a critique of fixity in constitutional law, it does not make clear why one sort of development is better than another.

Thus, even if one accepts the premises of the living constitution, there remains an open question as to whether administrative law is justified. The living constitution opens up the possibility of change outside constitutional amendments, but it is too general a theory to reveal whether administrative law was the right sort of change.

Entrenchment

Another difficulty is that when the living constitution is applied to existing constitutional developments, such as administrative law, it shifts from a theory of change to a theory of entrenchment. To be sure, the theory is well known for justifying relatively recent expansions of constitutional liberties. But it also offers a defense for long-past accretions of government power and concomitant losses of rights. Indeed, as soon as a change has occurred, the theory shifts from challenging the law to preserving it, and whatever one thinks of the expanded rights, the expanded powers and diminished rights are worrisome.

The danger of blind support for any prior change is particularly apparent in administrative law. Although administrative law seemed a bold new form of governance in 1887 and even in 1906, it now, after a century of bureaucratic expansion, often looks more like a surviving dinosaur.

It therefore is disconcerting to hear the constitutionality of administrative law defended on a theory that preserves the past on the ground that it once was new. If the living constitution is to be a mode of change, it cannot be understood as preventing constitutional challenges to fossilized constitutional arrangements.

Consent

Among the foundations of the living constitution is the notion of popular consent. The judges, in this view, introduce constitutional change, and it acquires consent when the people accept what the judges have done. This sort of popular acquiescence may, perhaps, reveal consent to some constitutional changes, but at least as applied to administrative law, it offers a particularly weak sort of consent.

The poverty of the consent is evident already from the lack of notice. To amend the Constitution, a constitutional convention, or two-thirds of both houses of Congress, must propose an amendment, and three-quarters of the states must ratify it. Somewhat similarly, to amend a statute, a senator or representative must propose a bill, and the two houses of Congress must vote on it. Even to amend a regulation, an administrative agency ordinarily must comply with the Administrative Procedure Act's notice-and-comment requirements.

Under the living constitution, however, the notice tends to be minimal, and this certainly was true in the development of administrative law. When Americans advocated administrative power, they rarely were explicit about the constitutional change. When the courts, moreover, upheld the constitutionality of administrative power, they tended to offer reassurances that it was not very different or new. For example, when the Supreme Court upheld the delegated taxing power in the 1890 tariff, it told Americans that this power was "not an entirely new feature," but had "the sanction of many precedents in legislation."[2] This sort of equivocation was hardly notice of constitutional change, and it therefore is difficult to conclude that popular acquiescence in the court's decision really amounted to consent.[a]

Further impoverishing the consent under the living constitution is the lack of concentrated deliberation, let alone self-conscious national decisionmaking. When authorizing constitutional change, the Constitution provides for layers of deliberation in Congress or a constitutional convention and then in state legislatures or conventions. The debates about con-

---

a. Not surprisingly, some of the most candid accounts of administrative law came from its most ambivalent supporters. The 1912 Republican platform cautiously declared that "much . . . may be committed to a federal trade commission, thus placing in the hands of an administrative board many of the functions now necessarily exercised by the courts." Even the Republicans, however, did not point out the constitutional costs. For example, they urged that a trade commission would "avoid delays and technicalities incident to court procedure," but they said nothing about the loss of trials before independent judges and juries or, more generally, about the loss of due process of law in the courts.*

stitutional change thus get concentrated into the very bodies that clearly have authority to amend the Constitution, and the result is a highly deliberative and self-conscious national decision for or against amendment. The living constitution, however, allows judges to introduce the change and then leaves individuals to acquiesce or protest—as if after-the-fact deliberation and decisionmaking by scattered persons, who lack authority on their own to change the Constitution, were likely to be even remotely as concentrated and self-conscious as the decisionmaking established by the Constitution. Certainly, the public response that occurred after the courts sanctioned administrative law did not have the concentrated deliberative decisionmaking one could expect of a body that is confident of its power to act for people in changing the Constitution.

The inadequacy of the consent becomes especially acute when one considers how the elite of the knowledge class shifted power to themselves and then claimed the acquiescence of the people. As administrators they asserted extralegal power; as judges they upheld the constitutionality of this power; as academics they justified the administrators and judges in terms of the living constitution. The result has been to turn consent upside down. Whereas the Constitution once could be changed only through an express act of the people, now an express act of the people is necessary to counteract the judges who change the Constitution. Otherwise, the people are said to acquiesce in what the judges do.

Considered in the cold light of legal realism, both the living constitution and its application to administrative law have shifted power from the people to the knowledge class and particularly its elite. Through the use of their theory-making power, this elite transferred the constitution-making power to the judicial members of their class, and they then used that power to justify the transfer of lawmaking and adjudicatory powers to the administrative members of their class. And this is called "consent."

Evolution

Even more than consent, what underlies the living constitution is a sociological assumption about the evolution of law—an assumption that law adapts to its circumstances. Yet rather than justify administrative law, this assumption calls it into question.

Although the living constitution argument about administrative power squarely claims that such power is modern and is necessary for modernized society, it repeatedly has been seen here that this argument deserves skepticism. Administrative power is a revival of prerogative power. Indeed, it is the most recent manifestation of an ancient tendency to exercise con-solidated power outside and above the law, and it therefore seems anything but modern. Even in its alleged necessity, its modernism must be doubted, for as so often in the history of absolute power, the arguments for its neces-sity tend to be more stylized than empirical.

In fact, the sociological character of the United States suggests that the Constitution's arrangements are better adapted to the nation's society than administrative law. The United States enjoys a prototypically modernized society, which is specialized, diverse, and free. In the academic traditions of the civil law, it seemed essential to deploy absolute power precisely to suppress the social, political, and legal fragmentation associated with mo-dernity. In the common law tradition, however, the fractured qualities of modernity have flourished under the protection of the law. They even have found expression in the law, whether in its specialization of government powers or in its protection of individual rights.

In this context, it becomes apparent that administrative law tends to be a dead weight on the modernized nature of American society. This is not the place for detailed empirical studies of the enervating effects of ad-ministrative law, but it clearly consolidates power outside and above the law, it evades many constitutional processes and rights, and it displaces self-government with a system of government directives. In such ways, it burdens Americans with commands that come from persons elevated with centralized power in place of laws arising from the diverse and disorderly complexity of American society. It thereby cuts against the sociological ten-dencies that underlie the freedom of modern American life and against the legal protection for such freedom. Thus, rather than the wave of the future, it is an undertow dragging the nation into the stagnation of an antiquated Continental vision of society.

Of course, administrative law developed in America during the century that witnessed the most extravagant experiments in consolidated extra- and supralegal power, and it therefore should be no surprise that, even in America, there was a drift in this direction. Fortunately, the drift did not go nearly as far as in many other nations, but the general tendency is re-vealing. It is a reminder that administrative law was a product of its times and that times change. As admirable and modern as extralegal and consoli-dated powers seemed in one century, they can be recognized in another to be outdated and unsophisticated, even dangerous and unfree.

The question therefore is not whether the living constitution justifies administrative law, but rather whether this theory has become an excuse for entrenching an antiquated constitutional arrangement. On the theory that government must evolve to meet the needs of a modernized society, the living constitution strangely entrenches an innovation that dates back over a century—indeed, many centuries—thus maintaining a petrified vision of extralegal, supralegal, and consolidated power in a diverse and free society.[b]

Precedent

Precedent may seem to favor administrative law. Certainly, after a century of precedents upholding administrative law, it may be doubted whether the judges are free to correct their errors. The precedents, however, are not conclusive.

---

b. Tellingly, the living constitution's arguments about consent and evolution are themselves an echo of absolutism, for they pick up on a long line of civilian-style arguments about acquiescence and obsolescence. Although the history deserves more detailed treatment than it can receive here, a brief summary may be illuminating. Put simply, the arguments from acquiescence and obsolescence were of civilian origin; they were successfully employed on the Continent on behalf of absolute power; but in England the use of such arguments to justify absolutism was repudiated, initially as an affront to common law and statutory liberties, and then more emphatically as a matter of constitutional law.

Acquiescence, for example, was alleged to justify the dispensing power. It was said "that albeit kings and princes cannot make laws, but with the consent of the people, yet may they dispense with any positive law, by reason that of long time they have used so to do . . . for long custom maketh a law." In response, John Ponet—the bishop of Winchester—observed that "evil customs (be they never so old) are not to be suffered, but utterly to be abolished," and "none may prescribe [that is, claim prescription] to do evil, be he king or subject." More generally, it was argued, in *Vindiciæ Contra Tyrannos*, that "no such prescription nor prevarication can justly prejudice the right of the people."

Along similar lines, when prerogative tribunals drew upon civilian ideas to suggest that the due process of law was obsolete, common lawyers insisted on their ancient rights. The High Commission justified its violations of Magna Charta and the medieval due process statutes by arguing that these old enactments were "antiquate[d] . . . and worn out of use." Outraged, James Morice asked: "Where is now . . . the Great Charter of England" and "Where is now the statute . . . that no man be put to answer without . . . due process"?

There thus is nothing new about justifying absolute power, prerogative or administrative, on grounds of acquiescence and obsolescence. These were standard civilian excuses for absolute power, and the contemporary versions of these claims should be recognized as the same old apologies for the same old lawlessness.

Precisely to cut short such arguments, many common lawyers in the seventeenth century insisted that the English constitution had originally been enacted, the implication being that it could not be adjusted except by a new enactment by the people. The lawyers thereby ended up embracing the fiction that the enactment was lost in the mists of time, but their goal was anything but fanciful or antiquarian, for they aimed to forestall the civilian arguments that eroded legal limits on power. Americans pursued this end more concretely by actually enacting their constitutions, and even adopting them as acts of record, which could not be defeated with claims of acquiescence or obsolescence. Nonetheless, such claims have been revived, and as in the past they are employed to justify extra- and supralegal power.*

Precedent and Principle

The obligation of precedent tends to conflict with the pursuit of legal principles, and the greater the attachment to precedent, the greater the conflict. Eventually, therefore, precedents have to give way.

Judges traditionally viewed precedent merely as evidence of the law. On this assumption, they felt obliged to follow precedent only where they could not discern an answer from the law itself—indeed, according to Matthew Hale, only where it was *in equilibrio*.[3] Now, however, judges claim that precedents are binding not merely as evidence, but in the manner of the law itself.

So strong a view of precedent is apt to pile error upon error, with little chance of judicial correction, thus creating a cascade of deviations away from the Constitution. As a result, precedent increasingly does not reveal the law but threatens it, putting at risk all that the Constitution once established. Of course, this tension can superficially be excused by assuming that judges can develop constitutional law in accord with changing principles, but this does not really address the danger of an approach to precedent that systematically pulls the judges away from the Constitution.

One way or another, precedents cannot spare judges from considering principles. It is widely said that judges cannot mechanically follow the law, and if so, they also cannot mechanically follow precedent. Certainly, on a question as important as administrative law, judges cannot simply cite their prior cases, but must pause to consider what they are doing. And if they are free to play with the Constitution in legitimizing administrative power, they surely are at liberty to play with their own precedents in overturning it. They therefore cannot hide behind their precedents and must address the merits of the question. Indeed, they must ask themselves whether they really want the responsibility for sustaining consolidated power outside and above the law.

Threats and Precedents

An additional reason for hesitating to accept the precedents arises from their history. The history of administrative precedents almost never gets mentioned in contemporary scholarship. It is clear, however, that early advocates for administrative power used threats to persuade the courts, and this has implications for the ensuing precedents.

Repeatedly, when the constitutionality of administrative law was challenged in the early twentieth century, the proponents of this power responded with threats. Whereas James I threatened the judges, American advocates of extralegal power threatened the courts, but their desire to shift judicial votes was similar.

Already when Congress and the president, in the Hepburn Act in 1906, expanded the power of the Interstate Commerce Act, they made "the implied threat" (according to Thomas Merrill) that if the Supreme Court "did not back off" from its standards of judicial review, "more drastic action, such as stripping the Court of jurisdiction over ICC matters or creating a specialized court, would be in the offing." Such threats, in fact, were numerous, systematic, and public. In 1907 (as seen in chapter 24), Governor Charles Evans Hughes threatened the courts in New York. In 1909, a member of the Interstate Commerce Commission, Charles Prouty, warned that if the judges opposed the Commission's power over the railroads, the resulting popular protest "would not stop until the Constitution itself had been so altered as to enable the people to deal properly with these public servants." In 1911, when Frank Goodnow pressed for administrative law and other changes in his *Social Reform and the Constitution*, he concluded by theorizing about the different threats that might be used to "induce the courts" to move in a more "progressive" direction; indeed, these threats dominated the final chapter of his book.[4] The next year, progressives widely endorsed the recall of judges, or at least their decisions; most prominently, the Progressive Party candidate, Theodore Roosevelt, urged such measures on behalf of administrative power.[5] A quarter century later, his cousin Franklin Delano Roosevelt actually sought legislation against the Supreme Court. Ironically, Chief Justice Hughes was then on the receiving end.[c]

The threats often came with commendations of legal realism. The point was that if the judges understood their role in realist terms, they could bow to pressures without thinking that they were departing from their office as judges—indeed, they might feel bound to give way. Hughes (it will be recalled) urged the judges to consider that "[w]e are under a Constitution, but the Constitution is what the judges say it is." Similarly, Goodnow wanted the courts to recognize that they had "a really political function." In such ways, judges were to bend with the times. Thurman Arnold later captured part of the underlying ethos. He exhorted his readers to "accept

---

c. The threats came with a host of accompanying arguments. For example, progressives often legitimized their assault on the courts by raising questions about the authority of the judges to hold statutes unconstitutional. Taking this approach, Teddy Roosevelt supported popular recall of judicial decisions by observing that in "England, Germany, France—every civilized country of Europe— . . . the judge has no power of reviewing the constitutionality of any legislative act."[*]

the world as it is," on the ground that "[p]rinciples, once formulated into a logical system, and accepted, seem to paralyze action in the actual arena of human affairs." As a result, "great constructive achievements in human organization have been accomplished by unscrupulous men who violated most of the principles which we cherish."[6]

The threats against the courts need to be recognized as part of the history of American administrative law. Of course, the judges convinced themselves that they remained independent, and surely in some instances they did. Since then, moreover, judicial acquiescence has been normalized with soothing generalities about pragmatism, institutional prudence, and what Alexander Bickel calls the "passive virtues."[7] The threats themselves, however, cannot be swept under the rug, for they raise questions about the independent judgment of the judges. They thereby call into doubt the early precedents for administrative law, and because the early cases laid the foundation for later cases, the threats are relevant to the full line of precedents on administrative power.

Precedents that depart from principle are not persuasive. Nor are those that follow in the wake of systematic threats against the courts.

Time No Cure

Ultimately, time is no cure. Although time can put many legal problems to rest, some problems are so serious that they remain alive, generation after generation.

Of course, as noted already in the introduction, the constitutional question about administrative law is no longer the same as in the past. The issue then was whether there could be administrative exceptions to the constitutionally established avenues of legislative and judicial power. What once seemed a mere variation, however, has since become a central mode of governance—a full-scale alternative to the constitutionally established forms of government. The question thus has altered, and it therefore is irrelevant whether prior generations acquiesced on the question that was evident to them.

Yet even if the question remains the same, it is too serious to be cured by time—let alone by the accompanying reliance, acquiescence, evolution, and precedents. Administrative power is merely the most recent manifestation of a recurring danger, one that has always come back, if not in one century, then another. In each iteration, prerogative and administrative, it has claimed to have acquiescence and to have displaced obsolete legal formalities, but each time it thereby has threatened rule through and under law. It therefore stimulated the development of constitutional law, and it remains incompatible with the nature of Anglo-American constitutions.

Indeed, administrative governance is a sort of power that has long been understood to lack legal obligation. It is difficult to understand how laws made without representation, and adjudications made without independent judges and juries, have the obligation of law; instead, they apparently rest merely on government coercion. They therefore cannot be perpetuated on a theory of consent or acquiescence, and they traditionally would have had the potential to justify revolution. Certainly, when the English Crown justified its absolute power as constitutional, the English and eventually the Americans engaged in revolutions against it.

The recurrence of this sort of danger is already apparent in the alienation of so many Americans from the government. It often is said that Americans increasingly are suspicious and resentful of government, but this should not be a surprise when the executive takes power out of the hands of the people and their constitutionally authorized bodies and places it in the hands of elusive administrators.

Administrative power thus inflicts a much deeper wound than time can heal. More than a century has passed since the executive began regularly to constrain Americans with administrative rules and adjudications. All the time in the world, however, cannot give these mere commands the obligation of law, and the longer this coercion persists, the more one must fear that the remedy also will be forceful.[d]

Judicial Principles

The need to recognize earlier errors becomes especially powerful when the judges run up against principles directly applicable to themselves. Even if they ignore the constitutional principles that apply to other parts of government and to the people, they cannot afford to ignore the principles that define their own office.

One such principle is that of rule through the law and the courts. In departing from this principle, administrative power evades the judicial power given to the courts and makes a mockery of the due process of law, jury

---

d. Nearly a century before the English Civil War, John Ponet observed that although "absolute authority" could be "colored and dissembled for a season, yet doth it at length burst out, and worketh the revenge with extremity."*

trial, and other procedural rights. Once the judges realize this, they will have difficulty adhering to their precedents without knowingly compromising their own power and office.

Even more central to their office is their duty to follow the law of the land. The judges are bound by their office and thus their oaths to follow the law as best they can. Of course, some judges assume that this includes a power to reshape the law where it is uncertain. Even so, the judges cannot follow an extra- and supralegal power—a power exercised not through and under the law, but outside and above it. When judges enforce this irregular power, even if with the feeble excuse of precedent, they threaten their own role and identity, for it is apt to turn them from judges of law into instruments of mere power.

Another principle that is central to judicial office is the duty of judges to exercise independent judgment. Judges have an office or duty that requires them to exercise their own, independent judgment. Therefore, when deferring to administrative lawmaking, interpretation, and factfinding, judges must consider whether, instead of exercising independent judgment about the law, they are bowing to a power above the law. This was the theory on which absolute monarchs expected judges to defer to prerogative power, and when judges now defer to such power in administrative form, they evidently are again submitting to a power above the law. The judges therefore must weigh their precedents against the degrading prospect of continuing to defer to supralegal power and thus continuing to relinquish their own, independent judgment.

The candid deference of the judges to administrative interpretation even has implications for the authority of judicial interpretations. Judicial holdings in cases have long enjoyed authority as evidence of the law. The authority of the judges in expounding the law, however, rests on their office of judgment—on the assumption that they hold an office in which they strive merely to exercise judgment, understanding, or discernment about the law.[8] Otherwise, their opinions cannot be understood as evidence of the law. On this basis, however, if they candidly abandon their own judgment in favor of the judgment of the executive, in what sense are their holdings authoritative? Evidently not as exercises of judgment. Therefore, when judges defer to administrative interpretations, it becomes difficult to take seriously the idea that the judges are authoritative expositors of the law.

Administrative law thus threatens all that judges venerate, including rule through and under law, due process of law, jury trial, the supreme law of the land, the judicial power of the courts, the office and independence of judges, and the authority of judicial interpretation. Therefore, if only to preserve their office or sense of identity, judges cannot afford to cling to their precedents. They have not been true to the law, but they still perhaps can be true to themselves.

Practical Judicial Fears

Of course, judges will worry about a host of practical complications that may arise in addressing administrative power. But most such complications are manageable.

For example, judges may reasonably wonder whether they really should hold all administrative power unconstitutional in a single all-or-nothing decision. So sweeping a conclusion could cause serious dislocations. Such a decision, however, is unlikely to be necessary. Step-by-step corrections usually are sufficient to bring judicial opinions back into line with the law, and in any case the judges usually will have reason to focus on the narrowest grounds for finding unconstitutionality. An incremental approach to administrative law is thus likely to prevail.

The judges may also worry that, if they hold statutes void for delegating legislative power, they will have difficulty determining which statutes are too open ended and which are not. This fear, however, is misplaced, for the judges need not approach the problem by asking whether Congress unlawfully delegates power. The more immediate problem is that administrative agencies unlawfully constrain Americans. Therefore, rather than have to evaluate the underlying statutes, judges would merely have to examine administrative edicts and hold them void where they purport to bind. This obviously is a much narrower and more concrete legal problem, which would not strain the competence of the judges.

Lower court judges are apt to have special concerns. In particular, they may be reluctant to hold administrative power unlawful before the Supreme Court reaches this conclusion. The Supreme Court's reasoning, however, is not always predictable, and lower court judges have a profoundly important role in exploring analytical paths and thus opening up possibilities for the Supreme Court to consider. Accordingly, when lower courts try out new lines of reasoning, and especially when they thereby bring judicial doctrine back in line with the Constitution, it should not be assumed that they are challenging the high court. On the contrary, they usually are trying to ascertain the law as best they can, and they thereby give the Supreme Court a chance to get it right.

Last but not least, even where lower court judges feel constrained in their decisions by Supreme Court precedents, they are not bound to justify these precedents in their opinions. Adherence to precedent does not entail silence about the law. On the contrary, judges have a duty to be truthful and accurate in their exposition of the law. Therefore, even when following the precedents on administrative power, lower court judges remain free—indeed, they are bound by duty—to expound the unlawfulness of such power.

❧❧❧

Whereas administrative law is deeply unlawful, the obstacles to accepting this conclusion are disturbingly thin. Undoubtedly, in some areas of law, concerns about reliance, the living constitution, precedent, and judicial practicalities can be very serious. It is far from clear, however, that they are substantial enough to justify absolute power—the consolidated power that is not only against law but also beyond and above the law. When raised in defense of this dangerous power, the supposed obstacles look like lame excuses for not facing up to the ugly reality.

The past may be a different county, but parts of it look disturbingly like the present. Certainly, when studying the absolute prerogative, it is difficult to avoid the impression that one is seeing an earlier manifestation of administrative power.

Although binding administrative power is widely said to be a novelty, which developed in response to the necessities of modern life, it is as ancient as the desire for consolidated power outside and above the law. It returns to the absolute prerogative, replete with similar legislative and judicial evasions, and similar justifications in necessity. Administrative power thus is dangerous and unlawful in ways not conventionally recognized.

Absolute Power and the Constitutional Response

The danger of prerogative or administrative power—in contrast to mere executive power—arises not simply from its unconstitutionality, but more generally from its revival of absolute power. Rather than a specialized governmental power exercised through and under law, it is a consolidated governmental power outside and above the law. It therefore traditionally was recognized as absolute, but whereas it once provoked the development of constitutional law, it now threatens to overwhelm the Constitution.

Like the English Crown before the development of English constitutional law, the American executive seeks to exercise power outside the law and the adjudications of the courts. Like the Crown, moreover, it demands judicial deference to this power, thus claiming a power not only outside the law but also above it. Like the Crown, it thereby consolidates the specialized powers of government. Administrative power thus returns to prerogative power, and as in the past, this absolute power threatens to evade a wide range of regular law, adjudication, institutions, processes, and rights.

Constitutional law, however, developed precisely to bar this sort of consolidated extra- and supralegal power. Although the English had long been familiar with the notion of a constitutional enactment establishing government, they gave it prominence in the seventeenth century as an answer to the prerogative. The constitution was understood to be the source of all government power, and it therefore left the government no power above the law. Moreover, by placing legislative power in the legislature, and judicial power in the courts, it clarified that the government had to rule through regular law and adjudication. Indeed, it was understood to place the lawmaking and judicial powers in specialized institutions and to subject these powers to specific processes and rights.

Americans echoed all of this in their constitutions. They made clear that their governments enjoyed power only under the constitutional law made by the people and that the law of the land was supreme. They specified that their governments were to exercise legislative power through the acts of their legislatures, and judicial power through the adjudications of their courts, and they subjected these powers to constitutional processes and rights. Going further than the English, Americans in their constitutions made clear that not only their executives but even their legislatures were without absolute power.

As a result, the governments established by Americans could bind them only through regular legislation and adjudication, not through executive acts. Of course, there were some state and especially local deviations from this ideal. And even at the federal level, there were exceptions at the margins—for example, legislatively in military rules and in territorial and other local lawmaking, and judicially in military orders, congressional subpoenas, and warrants under a suspension of habeas. Yet far from being arbitrary, these exceptions largely defined the basic ideal that the government could not bind its subjects through executive edicts. Instead, overall, it could bind them only through its law and the acts of its courts.

Nonetheless, prerogative power has crawled back out of its constitutional grave and come back to life in administrative form. Put another way, administrative power has resuscitated the consolidated power outside and even above the law that once was recognized as absolute. It thereby has imposed on America the very power that constitutional law had defeated in England—a power contrary to the nature of Anglo-American societies and their constitutional law.

A Recurring Threat

Far from being a past solution to a past problem, the constitutional response to absolute power was a farsighted attempt to address persistent tendencies in human nature. Throughout the history of the common law, rulers and dominant classes have been discontent with constraints and ambitious for power, and they therefore have restlessly pursued power not only through the law but also outside and above it. In response, there have been repeated attempts to place legal limits on both avenues of power—to restrain the power pursued within constitutional avenues and, even more basically, to bar any pursuit of binding power down irregular paths.

The English struggled for more than half a millennium to protect their liberty from extra- and supralegal power. They did this in 1215 in Magna Charta's provision on the law of the land, in 1354 and 1368 in the statutes on due process, in 1610 in the Commons' petition to James I, in 1628 in the Petition of Rights, in 1641 in the abolition of the prerogative courts, in 1689 in the Declaration of Rights, and finally in 1763 in the rejection of general warrants. On these foundations, Americans repudiated extra- and supralegal power even more decisively in their constitutions—in their state constitutions, the federal constitution, and two years later in the federal bill of rights.[a]

The danger came back with a vengeance, however, after Americans learned from their German cousins to disdain constitutional formalities and to welcome administrative law. This bureaucratized version of the old absolute power held out the promise of addressing social problems with rational Germanic efficiency. At the same time, it shifted power from representative government to administrative experts and, more generally, the knowledge class, who thought they knew what was best for the people. On such grounds, large numbers of Americans welcomed administrative law, without pausing to consider that it was the very antithesis of law.

Evidently, the lust for power outside the law is a recurring danger, and it is confined neither to monarchies nor to the past. Understanding this,

a. Incidentally, although this book examines English prerogative power to understand American administrative power, there also is much to be learned about England from the later, American experience. Any such use of history in reverse may initially seem odd. In showing the recurring nature of extra- and supralegal power, however, American history suggests that it is a mistake to consider absolutism a merely historical, let alone a merely old, local, or otherwise parochial problem.

Americans in their constitutions carefully repudiated power outside or above the law. Their constitutions, however, could no longer hold off the danger when an increasingly dominant knowledge class abandoned its attachment to the straight and narrow paths of law in pursuit of broader avenues of extra- and supralegal power.

The result, as in the past, is an alternate, parallel system of law, which is not law, but mere command, and which increasingly crowds out real law. Americans thus must live under a dual system of government, one part established by the Constitution, and another circumventing it.

Liberty under Law

At stake is nothing less than liberty under law. Ideally in common law systems, and even more emphatically under the U.S. Constitution, all persons enjoy liberty under law—meaning the freedom to do as they please up to the constraints of law. This liberty thus is all that law does not forbid.

Already in England, those who protested extralegal power demanded their full liberty under the limits of law. Although they were disparaged for urging disobedience, they answered that they owed obedience to law, not subservience to mere power. As put by James Morice in 1593, "We . . . the subjects of this kingdom are born and brought up in due obedience, but far from servitude and bondage," they were "subject to lawful authority and commandment," not "licentious will and tyranny." They therefore insisted on "enjoying by limits of law and justice our lives, lands, goods, and liberties in great peace and security."[1]

Four centuries later, extralegal power again threatens the liberty demarcated by law. Of course, administrative law is said to have statutory authority. This, however, does not alter the fact that administrative law confines Americans, not through law, but outside it, thus displacing the liberty under law with a subjugation to administrative command.

The liberty established by the Constitution is a liberty under law, not a liberty under administrative fiat. It is a complete freedom to do whatever is not forbidden by law, and any attempt to impose extralegal constraints is unconstitutional.

Sociology and Freedom

Also at stake is the modernized character of American society and how the law responds by protecting freedom through and under the law. Although it is said that administrative power is a necessary response to the complexities of modern society, this argument is remarkably close to the old suggestion about the necessity of the prerogative, and once again such an argument justifies a consolidated power profoundly at odds with the nature of modern life and liberty.

The claims for a consolidated extra- and supralegal power have long conflicted with the changing nature of human society—especially with the specialization that lies at the heart of modernity. From the Middle Ages onward, the English and then Americans found freedom amid the specialization and related divisions of modernized life. They persistently, moreover, sought to protect their liberty and way of life by confining their governments to specialized institutions that bound them only in specialized ways through and under the law.

It therefore was no coincidence that the danger of absolute power developed and flourished on the Continent or that it was resisted most successfully in England and America. On the Continent, governments have long relied on civilian traditions of absolute power to impose order on their societies, and when confronted by the fractures of modernity, they have responded with their old combination of anxiety and absolutism.

In England and America, however, the fracturing of authority came earlier, and it entered the traditions of these societies, including their law. The English and then Americans found their freedom in their divisions of authority and in the law that preserved these divisions, and they struggled to preserve the law that thus preserved their rights. In this way, since the Middle Ages, the common law has come to frame the modernity and freedom of Anglo-American life. When prerogative power systematically threatened this freedom with consolidated power outside and above the law, the English turned to constitutional law to protect their legal system, its divisions of authority, and its protections for freedom. Unsurprisingly, in their especially fractured society, Americans pursued these constitutional goals with even greater vigor. They barred any consolidated power, any power outside the law, and any power above the law.

Of course, these various forms of absolute power collide not only with the law that has flourished in Anglo-American society but also, more fundamentally, with the society itself. Whereas the society has thrived on diverse, specialized, and dispersed authority, administrative agencies impose homogenous, unified, and centralized power.

This conflict is not recognized by advocates of administrative power, but it increasingly is felt by those who are subject to administrative coercion. In modernized and especially American society, each individual feels his own authority, and therefore resents the attempts of others, including government, to impose constraints against his wishes. Anglo-American law over the past centuries has therefore increasingly allowed individuals to elect their lawmakers and more generally to enjoy expanded freedom. For a little more than a century, however, administrative power has cut back on this participation and freedom, and it thus is no surprise that Americans increasingly feel alienated from their government. Absolute power is dangerous in all societies, but in a free society, it is dangerous not only because of what it imposes but also because of what it is apt to provoke.

Constitutional Violations

Once it is clear how administrative power revives absolute power, and how this power conflicts with the nature of American law, liberty, and society, one can dig into the details of how it violates the Constitution. Because it returns to the very power that constitutional law developed in order to defeat, it does more than simply depart from one or two constitutional provisions. It systematically steps outside the Constitution's structures, thereby creating an entire anti-constitutional regime.

The U.S. Constitution bars any power above the law by establishing all of the government under law. It then bars any consolidated power outside the law by distinguishing the three specialized powers and placing them in specialized institutions, thus requiring legislative power to be exercised only through the law, and judicial power only through the decisions of the courts. The Constitution then subjects legislative and judicial powers to various processes and rights. All of these constitutional limits, however, are brushed aside by administrative power.

In returning to prerogative lawmaking, administrative lawmaking violates both the grant of legislative power and the division of legislative power. To the extent administrative lawmaking renders contrary state law void, it also goes beyond the supremacy clause. Indeed, not being made by a representative body, let alone the constitutionally established representative body, it has no legal obligation.

As for its return to prerogative adjudication, administrative adjudication violates the grant of judicial power to the courts and the division of this power between the judges and the two sorts of juries. It even denies Americans their right to judges ratified by the Senate, who are protected in tenure and salary, and who have an office of exercising independent judgment in accord with the law of the land.

The administrative adjudication also denies judicial process—what is protected as the due process of law. Administrative adjudication is justified on the ground that it offers such process as is due and that due process centrally confines only the courts. The principle of due process of law, however, concerned any exercise of judicial power, and it developed precisely to defeat the prerogative or administrative adjudication that kings conducted outside the regular courts. This was why it was not the due process of prerogative or administrative rules, but the due process of law, meaning judicial decisions in accord with the law, in the courts of law, according to their traditional procedures. Administrative adjudication therefore cannot escape the guarantee of due process of law.

Indeed, administrative adjudication violates most of the rights concerning judicial power. These include not only the due process of law but also, among other things, the rights relating to grand juries, petit juries, warrants, and self-incrimination. Like due process, these procedural rights developed most basically in response to prerogative proceedings, and they therefore were understood not merely as limits on the courts, but more generally as limits on the judicial power, whoever exercises it. It thus is profoundly mistaken to assume that these rights centrally limit only the courts, let alone merely criminal proceedings in courts. On the contrary, although they confine the courts in their exercise of judicial power, they also completely bar the executive from exercising such power.

In support of its extralegal legislative and judicial power, the administrative regime demands judicial deference. As in the era of the prerogative, the judges have an office or duty to exercise independent judgment in accord with the law of the land. Nonetheless, they defer to administrative lawmaking as if it were above the law, thus denying the supremacy of the law of the land. They also defer to administrative interpretation and fact-finding. In such ways, the judges deny parties their right to the independent judgment of regular judges and juries. The shocking character of this deference becomes apparent when one realizes that, even under James I, English judges refused to defer to most prerogative or administrative lawmaking, interpretation, and fact-finding. American judges, however, do not hesitate to defer.

Apologists for administrative power thus must overcome many constitutional objections. They must put aside the separation or specialization of powers, the grants of legislative and judicial powers, the internal divisions of these powers, the unrepresentative character of administrative lawmaking, the nonjudicial character of administrative adjudication, the obstacles to subdelegation, the problems of federalism, the due process of law, and almost all of the other rights limiting the judicial power. Last but not least, the defenders of administrative power must brush aside the danger of absolute power—the danger of consolidated power exercised outside the law and its courts, and often even above the law. Altogether, it is a tall order.

Administrative Excuses

The usual administrative excuses will not suffice. In fact, they are feeble. Administrative power is said to be justified by the necessary and proper clause. This, however, fails to recognize that the clause was carefully drafted to bar any claim for judicial deference to a legislative judgment about necessity. Parliament's absolute power rested on the finality of its judgment about the necessity of its enactments—a judgment to which the judges had to defer. To avoid this absolute legislative power and the corresponding judicial deference, the necessary and proper clause grants a power limited by law, which the judges therefore have a duty to enforce.

More specifically, the clause carefully bars any redistribution of constitutional powers. It authorizes Congress to enact what is necessary and proper only for carrying out the "vested" powers, including the powers vested by the Constitution in Congress and the courts. By confining Congress to carrying out the legislative power vested in Congress, and the judicial power vested in the courts, the clause makes clear that Congress cannot use the clause to shift these powers to other institutions.

Another excuse for administrative power is that the U.S. Constitution could not have anticipated this sort of governance and that the Constitution therefore should not be understood to bar it. Anglo-American lawyers, however, were accustomed to claims of extralegal power. The historic struggles of the common law had been largely about the threat from consolidated power exercised outside and above the law, and from the Middle Ages through the eighteenth century, the common law repeatedly responded to these claims, most prominently through the development of constitutional law.

The continuity of the old prerogative threat and the new administrative threat is not only conceptual but also historical, for administrative power was derived (mostly by way of German scholarship) from the old civilian traditions of absolute power. Administrative power thus was a later expression of the same absolutism that was evident in prerogative power. Both conceptually and historically, therefore, the suggestion of constitutional innocence is mistaken. The extralegal exercise of power, whether called "prerogative" or "administrative," was something the U.S. Constitution systematically forbade.

For example, in defense of administrative power it is suggested that, because this power operates outside Congress and the courts, it is not subject to the structures, processes, and rights imposed by the Constitution. Constitutional law, however, developed to bar extralegal exercises of legislative and judicial power. Accordingly, the grant of legislative powers to Congress clearly prohibits any executive exercise of such power, and the grant of judicial power to the courts clearly forbids any executive adjudication. Similarly, the due process of law, the right to a jury, and the privilege against self-incrimination all developed as constitutional rights in response to the prerogative or administrative exercise of judicial power. Accordingly, the conclusion that these rights do not really or fully apply to administrative proceedings simply ignores one of the basic reasons for having these rights.

In addition, administrative power cannot be justified on grounds of congressional subdelegation. Some of the most salient examples of early English prerogative legislation and adjudication had legislative authorization, or at least acquiescence, and nonetheless were condemned as violations of law and barred by constitutional law. Americans were familiar with this history, and when they delegated powers to their legislatures and courts, they left no room for any subdelegation, except where they expressly allowed it. For example, in their state constitutional provisions on the suspending power, they expressly allowed a subdelegation of this legislative power. But in the U.S. Constitution, they did not authorize any subdelegation of legislative power. On the contrary, they granted *all* legislative power to Congress, and they thereby expressly precluded the subdelegation of legislative power to any other body. Thus, like the other constitutional excuses, the delegation argument is not reassuring.

A further apology for administrative power comes in the mantra that it is subject to judicial review. But this is no excuse for constitutional violations prior to judicial review. Nor is it an excuse for the deference that passes as judicial review.

Far from offering reassurance, congressional delegation and judicial review have become fig leaves that cannot cover up the reality of nearly independent administrative power. Perhaps they once lent some credibility to administrative power by suggesting that it was subject to legislative and judicial oversight. Nowadays, however, agencies often exercise administrative power with little regard to whether or not Congress delegated it, and with little fear of the deferential judicial review. Administrative power thus has become largely independent of its supposed legal constraints, and is well on its way to becoming the primary mode by which the government controls the people. As a result, the congressional delegation and judicial oversight have come to be fictions—reassuring fables more than real sources of legitimacy.

The most telling excuses are those from mere necessity. The advocates of administrative power repeatedly fall back on the necessity of such power—not simply the constitutional necessity allowed by the necessary and proper clause, but a more radical underlying necessity. Sometimes it is a practical necessity; sometimes, a sociological necessity. Either way, this argument revives the standard defense of absolute power, as refined by German academics. Advocates of such power often emphasize that the necessity does not so much break the law as merely bend it. As in the past, however, the force of the argument comes to rest on the force of the underlying necessity, buttressed with Germanic contempt for constitutional forms. Altogether it is a strange way to understand American constitutional law.

The Role of Class in a Republic

Not far below the surface of the constitutional questions is the nagging problem of class. The growth of administrative power in America has followed the expansion of suffrage—an expansion that increasingly has opened up voting to all the people. It therefore is necessary to consider whether there is a connection.

It would appear that the new, cosmopolitan, or knowledge class embraced popular suffrage with a profound caveat. They tended to favor popular participation in voting, but they also tended to support the removal of much legislative power from legislatures. The almost paradoxical result has been to agonize over voting rights while blithely shifting legislative power to unelected administrators.

The underlying discontent was with representative government. Throughout the nineteenth and twentieth centuries, reformers struggled for the people to have equal representation and thus to enjoy the power to govern themselves. The reformers told themselves that, if only the people had power, reasonable and righteous government would prevail. When the people gradually acquired this power, however, the results were disappointing for the knowledge class. The members of this class had established their status, influence, and sense of self-worth through their assiduous pursuit of rationality and specialized knowledge, and they were troubled that popularly elected legislatures did not operate in line with the qualities they so admired in themselves.

Some members of the new class worked to shift legislative power to the judiciary; others urged that much of it be removed to the executive. What seemed lacking in popularly controlled legislatures was thus to be supplied by learned judges or, more broadly, by rational administrative experts. Administrative power, in other words, was one of the avenues for power by and on behalf of a class that understood authority not merely in terms of the equal rights of all the people, but more deeply in terms of their own rationality and specialized knowledge.

It therefore is necessary to understand administrative power not only as a matter of law but also as an avenue of class power. Of course, this is not to say that the knowledge class was a sharply defined class in the conventional sense; nor is it to say that the advocates of administrative power were insincere or narrowly self-interested; nor even is it to say that, in repeatedly speaking about authorizing persons with "scientific knowledge" or "expertise," they were speaking in code about a power grab. Nonetheless, administrative power has been a mode of class power.

Of course, the elite of the knowledge class enjoyed much more real power than the rest of it. Only its elite really had the opportunity to shape administrative rules and adjudication or otherwise to mold policy. Nonetheless, they did all of this with the sympathies typical of their class, and much of the class therefore could identify with them and what they did.

There is much to be said for knowledge, including the specialized knowledge that has arisen within the broader specialization that has shaped modernity. Knowledge, however, is not understanding. Certainly, the specialized knowledge, scientific or pseudoscientific, that has flourished within the knowledge class is not self-knowledge. Moreover, even if the knowledge of those in this class ran deeper, it would not justify them in claiming for themselves the power of the people and their representatives. The superior knowledge of individuals or classes may justify them in the fruits of their labor, but it does not warrant them to exercise a power belonging to others. Particularly when the strength of the society as a whole rests on the distribution of authority among all the people and among the different parts of government, this arrogation of power, even if accomplished by persuasion, is unjustified. And when the shift of power is to a class that trains itself to be persuasive and powerful, the shift should be viewed with the deepest suspicion.

The removal of legislative power from popular to administrative control must be viewed with particular distrust because the knowledge class not only enlarged its own power but also sanctified the arrangement from the bench. Members of this class taught that the judiciary inevitably had to exercise lawmaking power, including constitution-making power, and of course when they put on robes, they used their judicial exercise of legislative power to justify the administrative exercise of such power. Coming from the judges, such decisions reassured the populace. In retrospect, however, it is profoundly disturbing that a class shifted the power of the people and their representatives to the courts and the executive, and that it then relied on judicial lawmaking to legitimize the executive's administrative lawmaking. Whatever one might conclude from this, it is not legitimacy.

Exacerbating the class problem are perceptions of interest. The rulemaking class understands itself to be acting for the public interest, and with this elevated sense of itself, it often reveals aristocratic scorn for the classes that candidly pursue self-interest. Of course, as in the past, the dominant class is not really singing:

> Bow, bow, ye lower middle classes!
> Bow, bow, ye tradesmen, bow, ye masses.[2]

Nonetheless, much of the knowledge class shares the sense of contempt felt by a traditional aristocracy, and they therefore often sing a disdainful and dangerous tune.

In charity, it must be recognized that the administrative sequestration of popular and representative power was an expression of predictable sociological tensions. For thousands of years, but most rapidly in recent centuries, the growing development of mobility and communication spurred the specialization of labor, knowledge, and ultimately of life that characterizes what is called "modernity." On the one hand, these fractured circumstances opened up opportunities for the development of personal and political freedom, including ideals about equal liberty, consent, and the power of the people as exercised through their representatives. On the other hand, the same fragmented circumstances gave rise to the growing authority of specialized knowledge and the class that enjoys this knowledge. These two developments obviously are apt to collide, and when specialized knowledge prevailed over specialized governmental powers, the result was administrative power.

None of this, however, was inevitable. It is not surprising that those with growing power wanted more. But the knowledge class had many avenues for power, and there was no need for it to secure a place in government through the old device of extra- and supralegal power. It therefore is disappointing that a class so empowered by its specialized knowledge has been so eager to displace specialized government through and under law.

The U.S. Constitution could carefully erect its barriers to absolutism, but it could not prevent an increasingly dominant class from abandoning the Constitution and securing popular acquiescence in its exercise of precisely the power that Constitution most systematically prohibits.

Prussification

Whereas Americans once enjoyed liberty and had duties only under their own laws, enforced in independent courts, Prussians traditionally lived under their regime's administrative commands, enforced by administrative courts. Thus, although Americans were bound by law because it came from below, Prussians were bound by administrative power because it came from above. In this sense, for Prussians, civilian commands were fundamentally akin to military commands.

The danger from administrative law thus can be understood as the risk of introducing Prussian-style rule. Of course, Prussia was a militarized society, and America is the opposite. But administrative law increasingly subjects Americans to mere executive commands, and therefore, no longer only in the military, but throughout the society, Americans must obey orders. As in Prussia, moreover, the administrative officers who impose these orders are generally not accountable in the courts for their unlawful acts, for as in Prussia the courts protect administrative officers and defer to administrative power.

Of course, one may take comfort in the democratic authority of Congress, but even a democratized and largely decent version of Prussian governance has no place in the United States. The danger is that even while the legislature acts with the power of the people, the administration acts against them with the power of the state, thus forcing them to submit to the commands of officials and accustoming them to obedience—not obedience to laws of their own representatives, but obedience to the commands of those in authority. As observed by the Prussian scholar Barthold Niebuhr, "We are swallowed up by bureaucracy; all public spirit is smothered. And then, of what use is a representative and debating council, as in France, if all the rest is founded on the principle of this concentrated bureaucracy—if the minister has to carry out the general law into all its details?"[3]

Lest this point about the Prussification of American governance seem an exaggeration, it should be noted that something similar was recognized by one of the earliest American scholars of administrative law. Frank Goodnow divided administrative power into "five great administrative branches"— "*viz.*, foreign, military, judicial, financial, and internal affairs"—and he explained that, in all of them, "the relations of the individual with the administration resulting from the action of the administration will . . . be essentially the same." In other words, the executive command over the civilian population was "essentially the same" as the executive command over the military. The underlying point was that "we find the administration acting everywhere as the delegate of the sovereign and exercising powers of compulsion over those persons who are in obedience to the state."[4]

The obligation of law is very different from obedience to the state. Traditionally, the law was to be obeyed because it enjoyed obligation—because it rested on the power of the people to govern themselves through law made by themselves or their representatives. Under the administrative regime, however, executive commands must be obeyed because they are the will of the state, backed by its compulsion. This is Prussification.

Ordnung

Underlying Prussian administrative rule in Germany was the earlier introduction of the ideal, if not always the reality, of *Ordnung*. An attachment to order is often assumed to be an inherant national trait of Germans, but there is reason to believe it is a historical artifact, a cultural development that was established in part through administrative power. From this perspective, the establishment of *Ordnung* in German life is disturbing, for it is uncannily suggestive of later, American developments.

The notion of *Ordnung* became pervasive in the sixteenth century, and as has been explained by Gerald Strauss—a distinguished scholar of Reformation-era Germany—it had administrative foundations. It was espoused by "organization-minded bureaucrats"—by "theologians, lawyers, academics, professional administrators sitting on joint executive bodies and closely tied, both organizationally and personally, to ruling princes and magistrates." They were a "socially homogenous band of functionaries who had, by the middle of the sixteenth century, come to occupy most of the positions of administrative authority and intellectual influence in the intertwined offices of state, bench, church, and academy," and they were "imbued with the result-oriented ethos of the reforming activist."

> They did not see eye to eye on every issue. But they were linked by a common over-all objective, which was to drag society, no matter how unwillingly, into the sixteenth century. They were linked in other ways, too: by . . . class consolidation, by the privileges attendant upon social ascent, and by

daily working contact with one another in the political, financial, and ecclesiastical bodies whose collective deliberations guided the business of early modern government.

"Some were intellectuals, but their arena was not the study or the lecture hall; it was the political stage." There, they hoped to turn law and administrative regulations "into the chief agent of social cohesion," and of course they "consolidate[d] their political, and thereby their social, position by exalting the virtues of bureaucratic centralism."[5]

According to Strauss, "order" was the "code word" for their agenda, and like American administrative ordering, German order meant eradicating independent authority and self-government:

> It meant the curtailment of local autonomies and their integration in a spreading system of state offices. . . . "Order," in practice, meant a single body of civil and criminal law; it meant appellate jurisdiction transferred from local, domainial, village, or town courts to supervening territorial—that is to say, state—benches. It meant the replacement of amateur law finding by professional jurisprudence. It meant that village elders, town councils, seigneurial deputies were being subordinated in their authority to princely bureaucrats. It meant "orderly" administrative channels—which is to say hierarchy, always favoring the upper echelons. . . . It meant the threat of eradication held over the entire farrago of notions and practices that made up traditional piety, and their replacement by an academically defined and politically sanctioned orthodoxy. It meant common standards for Christian living, improving rules for putting one's house in order, officially declared and enforced canons of civic decency and good citizenship. It meant schools organized to educate, on one level, a culturally homogenous cadre of lay and clerical office holders and, on the other, an essentially docile mass of subjects. It meant weakening many of the attachments linking people to their native places and bonding them instead to designated administrative units, the parish and the district.[6]

Of course, the bureaucratic ordering of contemporary America is very different from the bureaucratic ordering of sixteenth-century Germany. But German history is suggestive of the dangers of allowing an administrative class to rule a traditionally free people.

The underlying tendency then, as now, was toward control—almost as though "[s]ociety could function only if every instant of public and private conduct was covered by its directive." The result now, as then, is "a petty world of trivial derelictions, requiring constant admonition, censure, punishment, above all unremitting vigilance."[7]

The danger was not merely the stifling effect of submitting to the hectoring demands of an upwardly mobile class with an elevated sense of its knowledge; even more seriously, the risk was that of systematically depriving a people of the expectation and experience of governing themselves, whether politically or even personally. Germans would live for centuries under the *Ordnung* imposed by administrative power, until eventually they were fully accustomed to being ruled. Americans only more recently have been subjected to administrative governance, and it would be a mistake to assume that they will follow the German path. Nonetheless, the order imposed by an administrative class is a familiar problem with familiar dangers.[b]

Soft Despotism

Although it would be an exaggeration to denounce administrative power as mere tyranny or despotism, this power is profoundly worrisome. Even soft absolutism or despotism is dangerous.

In democratic circumstances, administrative power can be a particularly benevolent version of absolute power, and it therefore often seems more enervating than immediately threatening. What begins softly, however, is apt to become harsh. The Star Chamber itself long seemed an apparently valuable institution, but absolute power invites arrogance and then abuse, and the Star Chamber soon became sufficiently oppressive that its abolition was an opening step in what became the English Revolution. As Acton warned, "Power tends to corrupt, and absolute power corrupts absolutely."

The danger in the United States is apparent in many ways. Most dramatically, when presidents and their officers become accustomed to issuing binding administrative edicts, they can easily drift into utterly arbitrary and

---

b. The Germans even developed a name for the persons who came to need administrative order. They were *Ordnungsmenschen*. Max Weber wrote:

> This passion for bureaucratization . . . makes one despair. It is . . . as if we should become, with knowledge and will, men who need "order" and nothing but order, who become nervous and cowardly if this order wavers for a moment, and helpless if they are wrenched out of their exclusive adaptation to this order. That the world may know nothing further than such *Ordungsmenschen*—we are engaged in this development all the same, and the central question is not how we can promote and hasten it still further but rather what we have to set against this machinery to keep a remnant of humankind free from the parceling out of the soul, from this exclusive mastery of the bureaucratic ideal of life.*

despotic acts, such as seizing private property and detaining entire ethnic groups, even citizens, without habeas corpus. In this sense, cases such as *Youngstown Sheet & Tube Co. v. Sawyer* and *Korematsu v. United States* should be understood as intimations of where administrative power can lead—as recently confirmed by *Hamdi v. Rumsfeld*.

More seriously, administrative power corrupts not only rulers but also the ruled. It accustoms an otherwise self-governing people to a regime of potentially pervasive control, and it thereby (as already suggested) gradually deprives them of their capacity for self-rule.

Administrative law therefore should be recognized for what it is. It is a version of absolute power, and although it is mild compared to other versions, it is more than bad enough.

Candor

An essential step toward recognizing the threat is candor. Speaking truth to power does not always work, but plainspoken debate can open up closed questions, including those about administrative power.

There is a jarring disconnect between what is taught and celebrated in constitutional law and what is accepted in administrative law. The one offers a vision of divided power exercised through and under law; the other presents the reality of consolidated power exercised outside and above the law. This contrast between law and mere state power invites forthright treatment, and the first step in this direction is simply a matter of words.

Legal Vocabulary

Although administrative power presents itself in the legitimizing vocabulary of law, scholars and judges should not dignify extralegal power in this way. Instead, when discussing administrative power, they should eschew words suggestive of law.

The very phrase *administrative law*, for example, should be understood as a fig leaf which gives legal cover to extralegal lawmaking. Similarly, the terms *administrative court* and *administrative law judge* disguise extralegal exercises of judicial power. As put by Justice William Howard Taft, an administrative tribunal is "miscalled a court."[8]

It also is inaccurate to talk about administrative lawmaking in terms of the *delegation* of legislative power; what really is at stake is its unlawful subdelegation. As for the *delegation* of waivers or of judicial power, this is a misnomer, because Congress cannot delegate any power it does not have.

To speak of *due process* in administrative hearings is to depict administrative proceedings as if they were lawful proceedings with the due process of law in district courts. Along similar lines, it is mistaken to talk about *appeals* from administrative decisions, to refer to administrative adjudicators as *judges*, or to call their binding directives *orders*, *subpoenas*, or *warrants*. Moreover, because an administrative tribunal is not a court, its administrative documentation cannot be considered *the record*, although it could be considered a private record and thus evidence offered by one of the parties. Whatever one wishes to call administrative power, it is not law or judicial authority, and it should not be given any name that suggests as much.

Absolutist Vocabulary

Just as administrative power should not be graced with the vocabulary of law, so too the vocabulary of absolute power should not intrude into law. This has become commonplace and dangerous.

For example, American lawyers often speak of *necessity*. The Constitution leaves room for necessity, but only as a basis for Congress to act through and under the law. The arguments for administrative power, however, often play on an ambiguity, offering a theory about necessity within the law but supporting it with suggestions about a societal necessity that rises above the law. It therefore is essential to remember the old role of necessity as a foundation for power outside and above the law. On this basis, one can begin to appreciate the limits in the necessary and proper clause and the dangers of a more open-ended reliance on necessity.

Another absolutist term is *deference*. James I demanded that the judges defer to his power outside the law on the theory that it also was above the law. Common law judges, however, have an office of independent judgment, in which they must follow the law of the land. Therefore, as in the time of James I, they cannot defer. Although they must recognize the power established by law in the other branches of government, they cannot show *deference* to the other branches without giving up their own, independent judgment and recognizing a power above the law.[9]

Perhaps the most deeply embedded absolutist term is *administrative*. It was the French label for the systematized absolute power that, by the nineteenth century, had largely displaced the more personal or prerogative absolute power. Over time, administrative power has become familiar, but it remains profoundly dangerous.

Although the encroachment of these absolutist terms needs to be resisted, the underlying problem is absolute power itself. On account of its administrative revival, this danger now threatens the constitutional law that was designed to defeat it. Absolute power, however, remains unlawful. Whether extralegal, supralegal, or consolidated, it is unconstitutional and contrary to the very nature of Anglo-American constitutional law and society.

NOTES

INTRODUCTION

a. Philip Hamburger, "Beyond Protection," Columbia Law Review, 1: 1823, 1834–51 (2009).

b. *Goldberg v. Kelly*, 397 U.S. 254, 262 (1970) and *Mathews v. Eldridge*, 424 U.S. 319 (1976); Charles Reich, "The New Property," Yale Law Journal, 73: 733 (1964); William W. VanAlstyne, "The Demise of the Right-Privilege Distinction in Constitutional Law," Harvard Law Review, 81:1439 (1968).

d. Richard A. Epstein, "Why the Modern Administrative State Is Inconsistent with the Rule of Law," NYU Journal of Law & Liberty, 3: 491 (2008); David Dyzenhaus, *The Constitution of Law: Legality in a Time of Emergency*, 42 (Cambridge: Cambridge University Press, 2006). Closer to the approach taken here is some of the scholarship on emergency powers. In focusing on emergency exercises of administrative power, however, such scholarship does not recognize how quotidian administrative power threatens rule through and under the law. More generally, it does not systematically and concretely distinguish rule through and under law from the rule of law. Clinton L. Rossiter, *Constitutional Dictatorship: Crisis Government in the Modern Democracies*, 3 (Westport: Greenwood Press, 1979); Clement Fatovic, *Outside the Law: Emergency and Executive Power*, 8 (Baltimore: Johns Hopkins University Press, 2009); Benjamin A. Kleinerman, *The Discretionary President: The Promise and Peril of Executive Power*, x–xi (Lawrence: University Press of Kansas, 2009); Nomi Claire Lazar, *States of Emergency in Liberal Democracies*, 5 (Cambridge: Cambridge University Press, 2009).

1. The author is indebted to many scholars for their advice, particularly those who wrestled with substantial parts of the manuscript or gave detailed comments. These scholars include Corey Brettschneider, Steven Calabresi, John Duffy, Harold Edgar, Daniel Ernst, Charles Fried, Victor Gourevitch, Michael Greve, Lotte Hamburger, John Harrison, Gary Lawson, Ronald Levin, Clarisa Long, John Manning, Jerry Mashaw, Jud Matthews, Thomas Merrill, Gillian Metzger, Henry Monaghan, Nicholas Parrillo, Glen Robinson, Susan Rose-Ackerman, Guenther Roth, Edward Rubin, Peter Strauss, Adrian Vermeule, and (not least) the two anonymous readers for the press. The author also is grateful to Columbia Law School, George Mason Law School, and the Liberty Fund for holding workshops on portions of the manuscript, and to Dean David Schizer of Columbia Law School for funding a conference on

it. By such means, the manuscript was subjected to vigorous critiques from diverse points of view.

For permission to quote manuscripts in their possession, the author gratefully acknowledges the British Library, the Earl Gregg Swem Library at the College of William and Mary, Harvard Law School Special Collections, the Library of Congress, the Library of Virginia, the London Municipal Archives, the Massachusetts Historical Society, the New Hampshire State Archives, the Pennsylvania Historical Society, the U.S. National Archives, and the Virginia Historical Society.

Whether in relying on printed or manuscript sources, this book silently modernizes most quotations. In particular, it does this by using contemporary spelling; by abandoning archaic second-person pronouns (so that *thou, thee,* and sometimes *ye* become *you*); by extending contractions and abbreviations; by contracting separate words into one where this has become conventional; by correcting misplaced or absent apostrophes; by reducing unnecessary capitalization and italicization, except where it matters for emphasis or clarity, and except where the capitalization signals the beginning of a sentence.

2. As put by an early commentator, "administrative law implies that branch of modern law under which the executive department of government, acting in a quasi legislative or quasi judicial capacity, interferes with the conduct of the individual for the purpose of promoting the well-being of the community." Cuthbert W. Pound, "Constitutional Aspects of Administrative Law," in *The Growth of Administrative Law,* 111 (St. Louis: Thomas Law Book Co., 1923). This was what Ernst Freund called "control," or the "power over persons and property." "Ernst Freund—Pioneer of Administrative Law," University of Chicago Law Review, 29: 755, 760, 778 (1962). The resulting line of division between constraint and benefit remains evident even in the Administrative Procedure Act. When this statute imposes procedural requirements on administrative rulemaking, it carefully excludes rules relating to "public property, loans, grants, benefits, or contracts," and it thereby focuses on rules that constrain. 5 U.S.C. §553(a)(2).

3. This contradiction has been noted by Thomas G. West, "Progressivism and the Transformation of American Government," in *The Progressive Revolution in Politics and Political Science: Transforming the American Regime,* 19, ed. John Marini & Ken Masugi (Lanham: Rowman & Littlefield Publishers, 2005).

CHAPTER ONE

a. Mashaw's scholarship notes that assumptions about the absence of administrative power "in the first century of the Republic" give rise to "deep concerns about the legitimacy of the modern administrative state. If these images of our constitutional practices and commitments are true, then our current arrangements represent a radical departure from original understandings." In this context, Mashaw's work on administration during the nation's first century aims to provide "a more balanced view of the constitutional status of administration in our system of governance" by showing that there have been "basic continuities." Jerry L. Mashaw, *Creating the Administrative Constitution: The Lost One Hundred Years of American Administrative Law,* 4, 6, 286 (New Haven: Yale University Press, 2012). See also Eric A. Posner & Adrian Vermeule, "Interring the Nondelegation Doctrine," University of Chicago Law Review, 69: 1721, 1736 (2002); Cass R. Sunstein, "Nondelegation Canons," University of Chicago Law Review, 67: 315, 322–23 (2000).

1. Larry Alexander & Saikrishna Prakash, "Reports of the Nondelegation Doctrine's Death Are Greatly Exaggerated," University of Chicago Law Review, 70: 1297 (2003); Larry Alexander & Saikrishna Prakash, "Delegation Really Running Riot," Virginia Law Review, 93: 1035 (2007); Bradford Clark, "Separation of Powers As a Safeguard of Federalism," Texas Law Review, 79: 1321, 1430 (2001); Ken I. Kersch, *Constructing Civil Liberties: Discontinuities in the Development of American Constitutional Law*, 112 (Cambridge: Cambridge University Press, 2004); Gary Lawson, "The Rise and Rise of the Administrative State," Harvard Law Review, 107: 1231 (1994); Gary Lawson, "Delegation and Original Meaning," Virginia Law Review, 88: 327 (2002); Theodore J. Lowi, "Two Roads to Serfdom: Liberalism, Conservatism, and Administrative Power," American University Law Review, 36: 295, 296 (1987); Theodore J. Lowi, *The End of Liberalism: Ideology, Policy, and the Crisis of Public Authority*, 143–44 (New York: W. W. Norton & Co., 1969); Ronald J. Pestritto, "The Progressive Origins of the Administrative State: Wilson, Goodnow, and Landis," Social Philosophy & Policy, 24: 16 (2007); Michael B. Rappaport, "The Selective Nondelegation Doctrine and the Line Item Veto: A New Approach to the Nondelegation Doctrine and Its Implications for *Clinton v. City of New York*," Tulane Law Review, 76: 265 (2001); Martin H. Redish, *The Constitution As Political Structure*, 142–43, 157–58 (New York: Oxford Univerity Press,1995); David Schoenbrod, *Power without Responsibility: How Congress Abuses the People through Delegation*, 13 (New Haven: Yale University Press, 1993).

2. Charles Reich, "The New Property," Yale Law Journal, 73: 733, 770 (1964); Gary Lawson, "Burying the Constitution under a TARP," Harvard Journal of Law & Public Policy, 33: 55 (2010). Similarly, Edward Rubin notes an administrative return to medieval tendencies. Edward Rubin, *Beyond Camelot: Rethinking Politics and Law for the Modern State*, 155, 173 (Princeton: Princeton University Press, 2005).

3. *Goldberg v. Kelly*, 397 U.S. 254, 262 (1970), quoting *Cafeteria & Restaurant Workers Union v. McElroy*, 367 U.S. 886, 895 (1961).

4. For a clear analysis of the four powers, including the fourth, "administrative power," see Thomas Christie, review of *Oeuvres de Jerome Petion, Membre de l'Assemblée Constituante, de las Convention Nationale, & Maire de Paris* (1793), Analytical Review, 15: 98 (1793). The fourth concerned "the newly created provincial assemblies, erected on purpose to superintend the collection of the imposts, the preservation and repair of roads and canals, and, in short, everything that concerned the interior government of the provinces." Ibid.

   One of the earliest Americans to allude to four powers was the New York lawyer and judge, Elisha P. Hurlbut. In 1840, he observed: "The civil officers of the State are divided into four classes, viz. legislative, executive, judicial, and administrative." The last was "a very numerous class of officers," and it was doubtful whether many of them really exercised what is here considered administrative power—a binding executive power. The clearest example consisted of the bank commissioners, who "visit the monied incorporations of the state which are made subject to their power, and examine their books and papers, thoroughly inspect their affairs, and make such inquiries as are necessary to ascertain their actual condition, and their ability to fulfil their engagements." E. P. Hurlbut, *Civil Office and Political Ethics*, 49, 73 (New York: 1840). For the commissioners and their power of examination, see the New York safety fund acts, particularly An Act to Create a Fund for the Benefit of the Creditors of Certain Monied Corporations, and for Other Purposes, §§15–18 (Apr. 2, 1829), *The Revised Statutes of New York*, 1: 606 (Albany: 1836).

5. Peter Strauss writes: "The civil service, largely insulated from politics, may appropriately be regarded as the fourth effective branch of government wholly without regard to the arguably special position of the independent commissions." Peter L. Straus, "The Place of Agencies in Government: Separation of Powers and the Fourth Branch," Columbia Law Review, 84: 573, 582 (1984).
6. James M. Landis, *The Administrative Process*, 2, 12, 88 (New Haven: Yale University Press, 1938).
7. Adrian Vermeule, "Our Schmittian Administrative Law," Harvard Law Review 122: 1095, 1102–03, 1132 (2009); Eric A. Posner & Adrian Vermeule, *The Executive Unbound: After the Madisonian Republic*, 104–07 (New York: Oxford University Press, 2010).

CHAPTER TWO

a. For unconstitutional conditions, consent decrees, and the notion of government by contract, see Philip Hamburger, "Unconstitutional Conditions: The Irrelevance of Consent," Virginia Law Review, 98: 479, 548–49, 565–67, (2012).
c. *A Speech Against the Suspending and Dispensing Prerogative*, 21–22, 6th ed. (London: 1767).

1. Francis Oakley, *Omnipotence, Covenant, & Order: An Excursion in the History of Ideas from Abelard to Leibniz*, 109–10 (Ithaca: Cornell University Press, 1984).
2. For example, the fifteenth-century civilian Jason de Mayno quoted Baldus about the power of the pope and the prince to do what is "supra ius et contra ius, et extra ius." R. W. Carlyle & A. J. Carlyle, *A History of Mediæval Political Theory in the West*, 6: 83, 149, 460 (New York: Barnes & Noble, n.d.).
3. Much learned work has been done on the medieval development of ideas of absolute power. For ideas about God's potential to have ordained his law to be different from the law he ordained, and for the characterization of this as a sort of "absolute" power, see William J. Courtenay, *Capacity and Volition: A History of the Distinction of Absolute and Ordained Power*, 87 (Bergamo: Pierluigi Lubrina Editore, 1990). For the power to exercise will irregularly, outside ordained law, which came to be called "absolute" power in the context of political and legal debate, see Francis Oakley, *Omnipotence, Covenant, & Order: An Excursion in the History of Ideas from Abelard to Leibniz*, 43, 63 (Ithaca: Cornell University Press, 1984).
4. For the place of absolute prerogatives in the context of English law, see David S. Berkowitz, "Reason of State in England and the Petition of Right, 1603–1629," in *Staatsräson: Studien zur Geschichte eines politischen Begriffs*, 165, ed. Roman Schnur (Berlin: Duncker & Humbolt, 1975). The English (as will be observed in chapter 24) attempted to confine absolute power within particular prerogatives and attempted to define its boundaries by law. On this basis Glenn Burgess questions whether absolutism is a useful concept for understanding English history. Glenn Burgess, *Absolute Monarchy and the Stuart Constitution*, 34–36, 210–11 (New Haven: Yale University Press, 1996). There were, however, many versions of absolutism, and it is unclear why one should discount absolutism in England because it usually was not taken as far or generally as in some other places. In fact, the English understanding of absolute power in the context of ordinary law had deep Continental roots.
5. In the thirteenth century, it often was said that "[t]he king is prerogative," meaning that he is exceptional, and "the term *prerogative* is hardly used except in this adjectival manner." Frederick Pollock & Frederic William Maitland, *The History of English*

Law, 1: 512, ed. S. F. C. Milsom (Cambridge: [Cambridge] University Press, 1968). Only later did the word become a label for an exceptional royal power, as when Thomas Starkey complained that the "prerogative in power granted to princes is the destruction of all laws and policy." Thomas Starkey, *A Dialogue between Pole and Lupset*, 69, ed. T. F. Mayer, Camden Fourth Series, vol. 37 (London: Camden Society, 1989). See also ibid., 83.

6. Francis Oakley, *Omnipotence, Covenant, & Order: An Excursion in the History of Ideas from Abelard to Leibniz*, 105 (Ithaca: Cornell University Press, 1984).

7. Letter from John Adams to William Hooper (ante Mar. 27, 1776), in *Legal Papers of John Adams*, 4: 76 (Cambridge: Belknap Press, 1979). So far did Americans go in this direction that when Madison worried about the threat from legislative tyranny, he complained that the "founders of our republics" seem "never for a moment to have turned their eyes from the danger to liberty from the overgrown and all-grasping prerogative of an hereditary magistrate." James Madison, Federalist Number 48, in *The Federalist*, 333, ed. Jacob E. Cooke (Middletown: Wesleyan University Press, 1961).

INTRODUCTION TO PART I

1. Gary Lawson, "The Rise and Rise of the Administrative State," Harvard Law Review, 107: 1231, 1248 (1994); Bradford Clark, "Separation of Powers As a Safeguard of Federalism," Texas Law Review, 79: 1321 (2001); Bradford Clark, "Putting the Safeguards Back into the Political Safeguards of Federalism," Texas Law Review, 80: 327 (2001); Bradford Clark, "The Supremacy Clause As a Constraint on Federal Power," George Washington Law Review, 71: 91 (2003); Bradford Clark, "Constitutional Compromise and the Supremacy Clause," Notre Dame Law Review, 83: 1421 (2008); Bradford Clark, "The Procedural Safeguards of Federalism," Notre Dame Law Review, 83: 1681 (2008); David Schoenbrod, *Power without Responsibility: How Congress Abuses the People through Delegation*, 99 (New Haven: Yale University Press, 1993).

CHAPTER THREE

b. Letter from Stephen Gardiner to Protector Somerset (Oct. 14, 1547), in *The Letters of Stephen Gardiner*, 399, ed. James Arthur Miller (Cambridge: [Cambridge] University Press, 1933) (interior quotation marks omitted).

d. *Solicitor General v. Louche & Holland* (Oct. 16, 1608), in *Les Reportes del Cases in Camera Stellata 1593 to 1609*, at 79, by John Hawarde, ed. William Paley Baildon (Privately Printed: 1894).

e. *Solicitor General v. Louche & Holland* (Oct. 16, 1608), in *Les Reportes del Cases in Camera Stellata 1593 to 1609*, at 328, by John Hawarde, ed. William Paley Baildon (Privately Printed: 1894).

f. Coke, *Reports*, 12: 75.

1. A king enjoyed the power to issue proclamations with the advice of his council, and this occasionally may have restrained him. Nonetheless, proclamations were understood to be issued by the king, not by his council, and when Englishmen discussed the power of the king to make law through his proclamations, they repeatedly echoed the old Roman assumption that the ruler's will or pleasure had the effect of law.

2. The maxim was from Ulpian's version of the *Lex Regia*, as recited by Justinian's *Digest* (I.iv.1.pr) and his *Institutes* (I.ii.6) (*quod principi placuit legis habet vigorem*).

3. Bracton, *On the Laws and Customs of England*, 2: 33, ed. Samuel E. Thorne (Cambridge: Belknap Press, 1968) ("there is no rex where will rules rather than lex"); John Fortescue, *De Laudibus Legum Angliæ*, 26 (chap. IX), 130–31, 134 (chap. XXXIV), ed. Francis Gregor & Andrew Amos (Cincinnati: 1874). Another English rejection of the civilian justification for proclamations came from John Ponet, who warned against the danger where "princes' wills may stand for laws." [John Ponet], *A Short Treatise of Politike Pouuer, and of the True Obedience which Subjects Owe to Kynges and Other Ciuile Gouernours*, sig. [E7v] (n.p.: 1556).

    Even the civilians had qualms. When commenting on the text "What has pleased the prince has the force of law," Accursius quoted the *Codex* that "[n]ot every statement of the judge is a sentence," and then added: "So too not every statement of the prince is a law." Brien Tierney, "'The Prince Is Not Bound by the Laws': Accursius and the Origins of the Modern State," Comparative Studies in Society and History, 5: 378, 397 (1963). It was the English, however, who more systematically contained the danger.

4. *Tudor Royal Proclamations*, 1: xxx–xxxi, ed. Paul L. Hughes & James F. Larkin (New Haven: Yale University Press, 1964). The king had the prerogative to establish weights and measures by proclamation, and to mint coins and to declare their value by proclamation. It came to be understood, however, that these prerogatives probably could not amount to a power to alter the legally binding duties of subjects. Thus, notwithstanding the claims of the Crown, it was doubted whether, after the monarch had established a weight, measure, or alloy, he could "legally change the established weight or alloy of money, without an act of Parliament." Joseph Chitty, *A Treatise on the Law of the Prerogatives of the Crown*, 197 (London: 1820), quoting seventeenth-century sources. See also John Baker, "Human Rights and the Rule of Law in Renaissance England," Northwestern University Journal of International Human Rights, 2: 5 (2004). Avoiding any such uncertainty, the U.S. Constitution give Congress the power to regulate the value of money and to fix the standard of weights and measures. U.S. Const., Art. I, §8.

    As for binding subjects to accept coins, it became clear that this could not be done by proclamation. Thus, in attacking Wood's copper halfpennies and farthings, Jonathan Swift argued in 1724: "The king never issues out a proclamation but to enjoin what the law permits him. He will not issue out a proclamation against law, of if such a thing should happen by mistake, we are no more obliged to obey it than to run our heads into the fire." M. B. Drapier [Jonathan Swift], *A Letter to Mr. Harding the Printer* (i.e., Drapier's Letter No. II), in *The Prose Works of Jonathan Swift*, 6: 41, ed. Temple Scott (London: George Bell & Sons, 1903).

5. Put another way, "the limitations imposed by law upon the prerogative powers of the Crown operate only in the relations between the king and his subjects, or foreigners within his protection," and thus "[a]n act done by the Crown outside the range of English (or British) law is said to be an Act of State." Maurice Amos, *The English Constitution*, 125 (New York: Longmans, Green & Co., 1930). More accurately, there traditionally was a distinction between subjects (including foreigners within protection) and non-subjects. The former owed allegiance and thus both had obligation to and enjoyed the protection of the law; the others had neither the obligation nor the protection. Philip Hamburger, "Beyond Protection," Columbia Law Review, 109: 1826 (2009).

    It sometimes is said that the king had a prerogative to use his proclamations to license his subjects' foreign travel. The barrier to such travel without license, however, arose from a medieval statute. See ibid., 1872, n. 166, quoting Matthew Hale, *Prerogatives of the King*, 296–97, ed. D. E. C. Yale (London: Selden Society, 1976). Moreover, it will be seen in chapter 6 that there was an exception for the licensing of some cross-border or offshore matters.

6. *Tudor Royal Proclamations*, 1: xxvii, ed. Paul L. Hughes & James F. Larkin (New Haven: Yale University Press, 1964). According to another scholar, who conducted a statistical analysis of royal proclamations, "[t]he striking revelation" is that "early Tudor proclamations seldom made new law." R. W. Heinze, *The Proclamations of the Tudor Kings*, 59 (Cambridge: Cambridge University Press, 1976).

7. An Act That the Appeals in Such Cases as Have Been Used to be Pursued to the See of Rome Shall Not be from Henceforth Had Nor Used but Within this Realm, 24 Henry VIII, c. 12 (1534); Proclamations (Nov. 16, 1538) (Feb. 26, 1539) (Apr. 1539), in *Tudor Royal Proclamations*, 1: 270, 278, 285, ed. Paul L. Hughes & James F. Larkin (New Haven: Yale University Press, 1964); Letter from Stephen Gardiner to Protector Somerset (Oct. 14, 1547), in *The Letters of Stephen Gardiner*, 391, ed. James Arthur Miller (Cambridge: [Cambridge] University Press, 1933). It is no coincidence that the Act of Proclamations remained silent about the proclamations on corn, as Henry would not have wanted to draw attention to the views of the judges.

8. An Act that Proclamations Made by the King Shall Be Obeyed, 31 Henry VIII, c. 8 (1539).

9. Ibid. There has been much skepticism as to whether the Act of Proclamations should be understood in terms of absolutism, but the terms of the act itself show that the tension between ordinary and extraordinary power was central.

10. Ibid.

11. Ibid. (Commas have been added silently for ease of reading.) In providing that proclamations could be issued under pains and penalties, and in providing that they were to be obeyed as though they were made by act of Parliament, the statute apparently was referring only to such proclamations as were made under the authority of the statute. M. L. Bush, "The Act of Proclamations: A Reinterpretation," *American Journal of Legal History*, 27: 33, 39, 40, 41 (1983).

12. An Act that Proclamations Made by the King Shall be Obeyed, 31 Henry VIII, c. 4 (1539). In an attempt to mitigate the lawlessness of prosecutions for violations of proclamations, and in a prerogative court, the statute authorized the prosecutions only against those who wilfully or obstinately offended against proclamations, thus confining these proceedings to instances of contemptuous violations.

13. 31 Henry VIII, c. 8. (Commas have been added silently for ease of reading.)

14. Even the statute's partial limits on lawmaking proclamations were viewed by contemporaries as valuable barriers to absolutism. Stephen Gardiner observed that, during the contentious parliamentary debates on the statute, Parliament secured "a plain promise that, by authority of the act for proclamations, nothing should be made contrary to an act of parliament or common law"—this being the third element of the proviso. Letter from Stephen Gardiner to Protector Somerset (Oct. 14, 1547), in *The Letters of Stephen Gardiner*, 391, ed. James Arthur Miller (Cambridge: [Cambridge] University Press, 1933). Later, in 1559, John Aylmer said that those who "in King Henry VIII's days would not grant him that his proclamations should have the force of statute were good fathers of the country." M. L. Bush, "The Act of Proclamations: A Reinterpretation," *American Journal of Legal History*, 27: 33, 45 (1983). If he meant that the statute did not have this effect, he was among those who interpreted the proviso to mean more than it did. Ibid.

15. Although another statute authorized Henry VIII to make ordinances for Wales, this did not receive the same attention in constitutional debates as the Act of Proclamations. 34–35 Henry VIII, c. 26 (1542–43).

16. Proceeding in the Bill of Apparel (10–13 March, 1575), *Proceeding in the Parliaments of Elizabeth I*, at 1: 454, ed. T. E. Hartley (London: Leicester University Press, 1981). Other members, by contrast, did not think "the matter to be so dangerous," for "the proclamation is circumscribed within certain limits, and the penalty set down expressly in the act." Ibid., 455. Even they, however, objected to the bill as it was drafted, and although another version was passed by the Commons, it died in the Lords.

17. David Hume, *The History of England from the Invasion of Julius Caesar to the Revolution of 1688*, at 5: 266–67 (Indianapolis: Liberty Classics, 1983).
    William Blackstone came as close to such views as his politics allowed. He was a politic Tory, who assumed that in every society there had to be a body with absolute power, and that in England this body was Parliament. He therefore rejected the possibility of legal limits on Parliament. Far from justifying lawmaking proclamations, however, he condemned the Act of Proclamations. Writing about Henry VIII's later years, Blackstone explained: "[T]he royal prerogative was then strained to a very tyrannical and oppressive height; and, what was the worst circumstance, its encroachments were established by law, under the sanction of those pusillanimous parliaments, one of which to its eternal disgrace passed a statute, whereby it was enacted that the king's proclamations shall have the force of acts of parliament." Blackstone assumed that there was an "absolute despotic power, which must in all governments reside somewhere," but he differed from early-seventeenth-century advocates of the prerogative, for he thought the English constitution placed the absolute sovereign power not in the king, but in Parliament. William Blackstone, *Commentaries on the Law of England*, 1: 156, 4: 424 (Oxford: 1765).

18. David Hume, *The History of England from the Invasion of Julius Caesar to the Revolution of 1688*, at 5: 267 (Indianapolis: Liberty Classics, 1983).

19. F. W. Maitland, *The Constitutional History of England*, 253 (Cambridge: [Cambridge] University Press, 1909).

20. An Act for the Repeal of Certain Statutes, 1 Edward VI, c. 12, §IV (1547).

21. *Proclamation, Prerogative* (1555–56), Dalison, *Reports*, 20. The text here prints (with minor adjustment) the slightly abbreviated translation adopted by Hallam, Anson, and Maitland. According to another report, the judges said that "no proclamation by itself may make a law which was not a law before, but may only confirm and ratify an old law, and not change it." And although "various precedents were shown out of the Exchequer to the contrary . . . the justices had no regard to them." Additional Ms. 24845, fol. 31, British Library, as translated by John Baker, "Human Rights and the Rule of Law in Renaissance England," Northwestern University Journal of International Human Rights, 2: 3 (2004).

22. *Proceedings in the Parliaments of Elizabeth I*, at 1: 239, ed. T. E. Hartley (Apr. 20, 1571) (London: Leicester University Press, 1981); ibid., 2: 321. Similarly, William Fleetwood—the recorder of London—wrote about kings that, "for anything that is in alteration or abridgment of the common law they have no power to ordain." Liber Fleetwood, Guildhall Ms. 86, fol. 1[v], London Municipal Archives.

23. *Att. Gen. v. Parker et al.* (1597), in *Les Reportes del Cases in Camera Stellata 1593 to 1609*, at 78–79, by John Hawarde, ed. William Paley Baildon (Privately Printed: 1894). The court also punished some justices of the peace who had failed to enforce

some proclamations and other orders of the Privy Council. The council had sent out letters instructing justices of the peace to enforce its orders against engrossing corn, but it sent these letters only to the judges at the assizes, and through them to the leading justices of the peace in each county. As a result, the other, lesser justices of the peace "never knew the substance of them, nor of the council's orders concerning grain. But *ignorantia legis non excusat.*" Ibid. Egerton viewed proclamations, orders, and other prerogative decrees as laws—even as commands above the law—and therefore ignorance was no excuse.

24. Lord Keeper's Speech (May 18, 1603), in *Les Reportes del Cases in Camera Stellata 1593 to 1609*, at 161–62, by John Hawarde, ed. William Paley Baildon (Privately Printed: 1894). In a related dispute, the council claimed that it "could alter or order the placing of persons of honor or office" to allow a member of the council, Burleigh, to sit next to Justice Christopher Yelverton when he sat on nisi prius. This was an affront both to the judge and to the law, and Yelverton therefore protested that "the Council of State could not alter the course of the common law," and if so, "he would be sorry it could." Ibid., 151.

25. Ibid., 329. Similarly, when Attorney General Henry Yelverton brought an information for building without brick, though on old foundations, contrary to a proclamation, "it was said, that proclamations were so far just, as they were made *pro bono publico.*" *Armested's Case*, Hobart 251 (Star Chamber, 1619). For another such prosecution, see *Case of Savage* et al. (1607), in *Les Reportes del Cases in Camera Stellata 1593 to 1609*, at 318, by John Hawarde, ed. William Paley Baildon (Privately Printed: 1894).

26. John Cowell, *The Interpreter*, sig. Ddd3[r]–[Ddd4r] ("prerogative of the king") (Cambridge: 1607).

27. *A Booke of Proclamations* (London: 1609); Speech of Sir Edwin Sandys (Feb. 17, 1610), in *Proceedings in Parliament 1610*, at 2: 357, ed. Elizabeth Read Foster (New Haven: Yale University Press, 1966) (complaining that this was "a wrong bruit"). For other accounts of the rumor, see ibid., 2: 22, n. 49. The Commons later noted "the care taken to reduce all the proclamations made since your Majesty's reign into one volume, and to print them in such form as acts of parliament have been." This "seemeth to imply a purpose to give them more reputation and more establishment than heretofore they have had." Ibid., 2: 259.

28. House of Commons, Petition of Temporal Grievances (July 7, 1610), in *Proceedings in Parliament 1610*, at 2: 258–59, ed. Elizabeth Read Foster (New Haven: Yale University Press, 1966).

29. Ibid., 2: 259. Indeed, "some [proclamation were] made shortly after a session of parliament for matter[s] directly rejected in the same session, other appointing punishments to be inflicted before lawful trial and conviction; some containing penalties in form of penal statutes; some referring the punishment of offenders to courts of arbitrary discretion, which have laid heavy and grievous censures upon the delinquents; some, as the proclamation for starch, accompanied with letters commanding inquiry to be made against the transgressors at the quarter sessions; and some vouching former proclamations, to countenance and warrant the latter." Ibid.

30. Ibid., 2: 259–60. In support of this sort of conclusion by the House, its members had earlier argued that proclamations were "not binding" because they "can neither make, nor declare laws" and that "[t]he king by his charter cannot change or alter the laws of the land in anything but by Parliament." [Ellesmere], The Speech of the Lord Chancellor of England, in the Exchequer Chamber, Touching the Post-Nati

(1608), in *Law and Politics in Jacobean England: The Tracts of Lord Chancellor Ellesmere*, 208, ed. Louis A. Knafla (Cambridge: Cambridge University Press, 1977); Speech by Fuller (June 23, 1610), in *Proceedings in Parliament 1610*, at 2: 154, ed. Elizabeth Read Foster (New Haven: Yale University Press, 1966).

31. Ibid., 2: 259–60.

32. Bracton, *On the Laws and Customs of England*, 2: 305, ed. Samuel E. Thorne (Cambridge: Belknap Press, 1968); *De Natura Legis Naturæ: The Works of Sir John Fortescue*, I: 200 (I.x), ed. Thomas Fortescue (London: 1869), who argued against the label. For more on these points and the rest of the history of the idea, see Philip Hamburger, *Law and Judicial Duty*, 81–90 (Cambridge: Harvard University Press, 2008). For the positions of Bailyn and Wood, see Philip Hamburger, *Law and Judicial Duty*, 70–71 (Cambridge: Harvard University Press, 2008).

33. Speech of Hoskyns (June 23–28, 1610), in *Parliamentary Debates in 1610*, at 76, ed. Samuel Rawson Gardiner (London: Camden Society, 1862); Speeches of Martyn and Hobart (June 29, 1610), ibid., 89–90.

34. The linkage was obvious and sometimes was emphasized. Edward Alford declared in November that "we stand upon impositions and proclamations." Esther S. Cope, "Sir Edward Coke and Proclamations, 1610," American Journal of Legal History, 15: 216–17 (1971).

35. [James Whitelocke], *A Learned and Necessary Argument To Prove that Each Subject Hath a Propriety in His Goods*, 11 (London: 1641); House of Commons, Petition of Temporal Grievances (July 7, 1610), in *Proceedings in Parliament 1610*, at 2: 266, ed. Elizabeth Read Foster (New Haven: Yale University Press, 1966). Whitelocke also contrasted the common law position to a contrary civilian maxim, saying it was a "[m]axim of ours" that "the King cannot alter the Law." [James Whitelocke], *A Learned and Necessary Argument To Prove that Each Subject Hath a Propriety in His Goods*, 11 (London: 1641).

36. *Chevron U.S.A. Inc. v. National Resources Defense Council, Inc.*, 467 U.S. 837, 844, 865 (1984).

37. *Case of Proclamations* (Sept. 20, 1610), Coke, *Reports*, 12: 74–75.

38. A Proclamation Signifying his Majesties Pleasure Touching Some Former Proclamations (Sept. 24, 1610), in *A Booke of Proclamations*, 235–36 (London: 1609). This proclamation came four days after the initial consultation with Coke.

39. Coke, *Reports*, 12: 75.

40. Certain Resolutions Concerning Proclamations (Oct. 26, 1610), in Esther S. Cope, "Sir Edward Coke and Proclamations, 1610," American Journal of Legal History, 15: 221 (1971); *Case of Proclamations* (1610), Coke, *Reports* 12: 75–76. Elaborating his point, he explained, "that which cannot be punished without proclamation, cannot be punished with it." Ibid., 75.

41. Ibid., 75.

42. Roger Twysden, *Certaine Considerations upon the Government of England*, 89–90 (London: Camden Society, 1849); Matthew Hale, *The Prerogatives of the King*, 141, ed. D. E. C. Yale (London: Selden Society, 1976). See also ibid., 171, 172. When the House of Commons in 1641 investigated the prerogative legislation of Charles I, it condemned "his majesty's proclamations . . . as illegal and against the liberty of the subject." Resolution (Oct. 30, 1641), in *The Journal of Sir Simonds D'Ewes, From the First Recess of the Long Parliament to the Withdrawl of King Charles from London*, 56, ed. Willson Havelock Coates (New Haven: Yale University Press, 1942).

43. Matthew Bacon, *A New Abridgment of the Law*, 4: 188–89 (London: 1778). See also William Blackstone, *Commentaries on the Laws of England*, 1: 270 (Oxford: 1765).

44. David Hume, *The History of England from the Invasion of Julius Caesar to the Revolution of 1688*, 5: 266–67 (Indianapolis: Liberty Classics, 1983).

45. A Devonshire-Freeholder, "Proclamations have not the Force of Law," in *The Political Register and Impartial Review*, 218–20 (1771). Even the laws that consisted of "immemorial customs" had "their beginning and continuance from the laws of nature, and the universal consent of the nation." Ibid.

46. Francis Stoughton Sullivan, *Lectures on the Constitution and Laws of England: With a Commentary on Magna Charta*, 184–85, ed. Gilbert Stuart (London: 1776). Sullivan recognized that the key point was the reality of legislative power rather than any labels, for it was "to little purpose whether we call them laws or not, since they are such in effect." Ibid.

47. Jean Louis DeLolme, *The Constitution of England; or, An Account of the English Government*, 55 (I.iv) (Indianapolis: Liberty Classics, 2007).

CHAPTER FOUR

a. George Buchanan, *De Jure Regni Apud Scotos*, 44 (n.p.: 1680).

b. [James Whitelocke], *A Learned and Necessary Argument To Prove that Each Subject Hath a Proprietary in His Goods*, 6, 11, 15 (London: 1641).

1. Philip Hamburger, *Law and Judicial Duty*, 225–32 (Cambridge: Harvard University Press, 2008).

2. *The Digest of Justinian*, lix–lx (The Confirmation of the Digest), ed. Alan Watson (Philadelphia: University of Pennsylvania Press, 1998).

3. *Codex* (I.xiv.1), in *The Civil Law*, 12: 85, trans. Samuel Parsons Scott (Cincinnati: Central Trust Co., 1932). See also *Codex* (I.xiv.11).

4. When explaining that the power to expound the law rested in the judges, Chancellor Christopher Hatton (in the late 1580s) also discussed the Roman-style power of lawmaking interpretation and why it did not rest even in Parliament. His argument rested on Parliament's elective character. Although Parliament was the lawmaker in England, and although it therefore could alter the law with a new statute, the periodic need for re-election of its lower house deprived it of the continuing power to interpret that once had been claimed by Roman emperors. Thus, in England, it was "an absurd thing to make an exposition go further than either the words, or the intention" by asking the legislators for their subsequent interpretation, for when "the assembly of Parliament" was "ended," then "their authority is returned to the electors." So clearly was their authority returned, "that if they were altogether assembled again for interpretation by a voluntary meeting, *Eorum non esset interpretari*"—not one of the statutes should be interpreted by them.

   Accordingly, the only authoritative interpretation that remained possible in England was the more modest sort done by judges when discerning "the intent of the maker." This was "the interpretation" that the common law judges had "in their hands, and their authority no man taketh in hand to control." Christopher Hatton, *A Treatise Concerning Statutes, or Acts of Parliament: And the Exposition Thereof*, 28–30 (London: 1677). For another example of such reasoning, see William Fleetwood, *The Office of a Justice of the Peace, Together with Instructions, How and In What Manner Statutes Shall Be Expounded*, 98 (London: 1658). Somewhat similar arguments were later made by St. George Tucker in the 1782 Virginia case *Commonwealth v. Caton et al.*, otherwise known as the *Prisoners' Case*. See Philip Hamburger, *Law and Judicial Duty*, 549 (Cambridge: Harvard University Press, 2008).

5. Thomas Ridley, *A View of the Civile and Ecclesiastical Law*, 211, 212 (London: 1607).

6. *Prohibition del Roy* (1608), Coke, *Reports*, 12: 63.

7. Julius Caesar's Notes, Lansdowne Ms. 160, as printed in Roland G. Usher, "James I and Sir Edward Coke," English Historical Review, 18: 669, 673 (1903).

8. *Prohibition del Roy* (1608), Coke, *Reports*, 12: 63–65. Usher observes that Coke's account probably conflates a series of discussions at the council table. Roland G. Usher, "James I and Sir Edward Coke," English Historical Review, 18: 669 (1903).

9. *Case of Proclamations*, Coke, *Reports*, 2: 74–75 (1610).

10. Roger Twysden, *Certaine Considerations upon the Government of England*, 87 (London: Camden Society, 1849); Matthew Bacon, *A New Abridgment of the Law*, 4: 190 (London: 1778); ibid., 1: 555. The second passage quoted from Bacon actually was an adaptation of a passage in Justice Fortescue Aland, *Reports of Select Cases*, iii (preface) (London: 1748). For the conception of judicial precedents as evidence of the law, but not more than evidence, see Philip Hamburger, *Law and Judicial Duty*, 228–29 (Cambridge: Harvard University Press, 2008).

11. For the development of the Star Chamber into a distinct, although not entirely separate court, see chap. 8, endnote 4.

12. According to one study, "The period under consideration is remarkable for the fact that during its course the country was virtually governed by proclamations and orders in council. Nor is it possible to challenge the competence of the court in the matter. An order is made by the king in council, very often by the council after its judicial session in the Star Chamber. It is not surprising that the council *qua* judicial body should devise and apply sanctions for its own legislative measures." Henry E. I. Phillips, "The Last Years of the Court of Star Chamber 1630–41," Transactions of the Royal Historical Society, 4th ser., 21: at 117 (1939).

13. See, for example, *A Decree of Starre-Chamber, Concerning Printing*, sig. [A3v] (London: 1637).

14. Decree in Star Chamber Concerning Books (1566), in *Sources of English Constitutional History*, 388, ed. C. Stephenson & F. G. Marcham (New York: Harper & Brothers, 1937); Decree in Star Chamber Concerning Printers (1586), ibid., 389; *A Decree of Starre-Chamber, Concerning Printing* (London: 1637).

For a decree on apparel, see the command cited in Proclamation (Feb. 12, 1580), in *Tudor Royal Proclamations*, 2: 461, ed. Paul L. Hughes & James F. Larkin (New Haven: Yale University Press, 1969). See also *A Decree of Starre-Chamber: Concerning Inmates, and Divided Tenements, in London or Three Miles About*, sig. [C4v] (London: 1636). For an account of the 1633 Star Chamber decree on the price of victuals and horsemeat, see John Southerden Burn, *The Star Chamber: Notices of the Court and Its Proceedings*, 132 (London: 1870). For the 1633 decree baring vintners from dressing meat, see *The Journal of Sir Simonds D'Ewes, From the Beginning of the Long Parliament to the Opening of the Trial of the Earl of Strafford*, 546, ed. Wallace Notenstein (New Haven: Yale University Press, 1923). Also note a Star Chamber decree regulating the soap trade (Aug. 23, 1633), in *The Journal of Sir Simonds D'Ewes, From the First Recess of the Long Parliament to the Withdrawl of King Charles from London*, 55, n. 4 (entry of Oct. 30, 1641), ed. Willson Havelock Coates (New Haven: Yale University Press, 1942).

Regarding the regulation of tenements, a commission appointed by the Star Chamber informed the court that these cases were "infinite" in number—indeed, that it "found three hundred faulty in this, and in four large houses they found now 8,000 inhabitants, and the last great plague 800 out of them died of the pest." John Hawarde, *Les Reportes del Cases in Camera Stellata 1593 to 1609*, at 329, ed. William Paley Baildon (Privately Printed: 1894). The court also required building in brick. Ibid., 319.

15. *A Decree of Starre-Chamber: Concerning Inmates, and Divided Tenements, in London or Three Miles About*, sig. [C4v] (London: 1636).

16. An Act for the Regulating of the Privy Council and for Taking Away the Court Commonly called the Star Chamber, 16 Charles I, c. 10 (1641).

17. Maitland notes that there had been a "cessation of any attempts to tax merchandise without parliamentary authority from the reign of Richard II to the reign of Mary." F. W. Maitland, *The Constitutional History of England*, 259 (Cambridge: [Cambridge] University Press, 1909).

18. Samuel R. Gardiner, *History of England from the Accession of James I. to the Outbreak of the Civil War, 1603–1642*, at 2: 12 (New York: AMS Press, 1965).

19. [James Whitelocke], *A Learned and Necessary Argument To Prove that Each Subject Hath a Proprietary in His Goods*, 6 (London: 1641). For statistical comparisons of the rates, see Michael J. Braddick, *The Nerves of State: Taxation and the Financing of the English State, 1558–1714*, at 53–54 (Manchester: Manchester University Press, 1996).

20. [James Whitelocke], *A Learned and Necessary Argument To Prove that Each Subject Hath a Propriety in His Goods*, 8 (London: 1641). For the sixteenth- and seventeenth-century use of "natural" to refer to what was innate or native to a country, see OED, s.v. "natural."

21. [James Whitelocke], *A Learned and Necessary Argument To Prove that Each Subject Hath a Proprietary in His Goods*, 14 (London: 1641); House of Commons, Petition of Temporal Grievances (July 7, 1610), in *Proceedings in Parliament 1610*, at 2: 266, ed. Elizabeth Read Foster (New Haven: Yale University Press, 1966); Speech of Thomas Hedley (June 28, 1610), ibid., 2: 190.

22. Speech of Edmund Waller on Shipmoney (1640), in *Historical Collections*, 3: 1339, ed. John Rushworth (London: 1721).

23. For the way in which questions of administrative detention came to be understood in terms of the king's right to avoid specifying the cause of detention on a return of a writ of habeas, see Philip Hamburger, "Beyond Protection," Columbia Law Review, 109: 1906–07 (2009).

24. Petition of Right, 3 Charles I, c. 1 (1628).

25. An Act Declaring the Rights and Liberties of the Subject and Settling the Succession of the Crown, 1 William & Mary, sess. 2, c. 2 (1689). This followed the wording of a proposed statute that had been introduced as early as 1685. See manuscript copy of bill in possession of author.

26. *Brewster v. Kidgell* (K.B. 1698), Holt's Opinions, Add. Ms. 35979, fol. 109[v]–110[r], British Library, discussed in Philip Hamburger, *Law and Judicial Duty*, 94 (Cambridge: Harvard University Press, 2008). See also Comberbach, *Reports*, 466.

27. This is why it restricted its 1689 Declaration of Rights to declaring existing rights and largely dropped its assertion of new rights.

28. A Subsidy Granted to the King of Tonnage and Poundage, And Other Sums of Money Payable upon Merchandise Exported and Imported, 12 Charles II, c. 4 (1660).

29. *Brewster v. Kidgell* (K.B. 1698), Holt's Opinions, Add. Ms. 35979, fol. 109[v]–110[r], British Library, quoted and discussed in Philip Hamburger, *Law and Judicial Duty*, 94 (Cambridge: Harvard University Press, 2008). See also Comberbach, *Reports*, 466.

CHAPTER FIVE

a.   *Journals of the House of Commons*, 31: 15 (Nov. 18, 1766); *The Parliamentary History of England*, 16: 245 (London: 1813); John Lord Campbell, *The Lives of the Lord Chancellors and Keepers of the Great Seal of England*, 5: 265–66 (London: John Murray, 1849); Philip Ward Jackson, *Public Sculpture of the City of London*, 163–64 (Liverpool: Liverpool University Press, 2003); Engraving of William Beckford's Statue (c. 1771) (without caption).

b.   That the 1852 steamboat statute did not formally authorize waivers is clear from its words. After laying out rules for inspectors to follow in inspecting boilers, it provided that "the same rules shall be observed in regard to boilers heretofore made, unless the proportion between such boilers and the cylinders or some other cause renders it manifest that its application would be unjust, in which cases the inspectors may depart from these rules, if it can be done with safety." An Act to Amend an Act Entitled "An Act to Provide for the Better Security of the Lives of Passengers on Board of Vessels Propelled in Whole or in Part by Steam," and For Other Purposes, §9 (Aug. 30, 1852), *Public Statutes at Large of the United States*, 10: 65. It is on this basis that Mashaw concludes that "the inspectors were allowed to waive any of the rules in the statute concerning boiler requirements if their application would be unjust and the inspectors determined that variance from the rules could be accomplished with safety." Jerry L. Mashaw, *Creating the Administrative Constitution: The Lost One Hundred Years of American Administrative Law*, 193 (New Haven: Yale University Press, 2012).

Incidentally, so loose a statement of an officer's alternative duties as appeared in the 1852 act was rather unusual. More typically, Congress spelled out the alternative duty with greater specificity—as can be illustrated by the 1853 amendments to the 1852 statute. After authorizing inspectors to grant licenses on one set of standards, Congress added that they "may approve of boilers and steam-pipes made prior to the first day of July next, and subsequent to the passage of the act approved the thirtieth of August, eighteen hundred and fifty-two . . . if the same be not made with stamped iron: *Provided* it shall appear that stamped iron could not be seasonably procured." Similarly, after instructing inspectors to require metallic lifeboats, it authorized the inspectors "upon satisfactory proof that the owner or owners of a steamer are unable to obtain seasonably or upon reasonable terms, a metallic life-boat, as required by said act, or that such a boat is unsuited to the navigation in which a steamer is employed, to accept in any such case a substitute or substitutes for such metallic lifeboat: *Provided*, such substitute shall in their judgment afford safe and suitable means of preserving life in case of accident." Although the difference between waivers and alternative instructions can be difficult to parse, these provisions provided alternative instructions rather than a simple authority to waive or dispense with the standard instructions. A Resolution in Amendment of a Joint Resolution Relating to the Duties of Inspectors of Steamers . . . , §§2–3 (Mar. 3, 1853), *Public Statutes at Large of the United States*, 10: 262.

1.   For the necessity justification underlying dispensations, see Gaines Post, *Studies in Medieval Legal Thought: Public Law and the State, 1100–1322*, at 264–67 (Princeton: Princeton University Press, 1964).

2.   Matthew Paris, *English History*, 2: 422, trans. J. A. Giles (London: Bohn, 1853); [John Ponet], *A Short Treatise of Politike Pouuer, and of the True Obedience which Subjects Owe to Kynges and Other Ciuile Gouernours*, sig. [B6v] (n.p.: 1556). According to Paris,

the non obstante clause became familiar in England in approximately 1251. Nearly three centuries later, Thomas Starkey wrote that "there be few laws and statutes in parliament ordained, but by placards and license obtained of the prince, they are broken and abrogate[d] and so to the commonweal do little profit, even like as dispensations have do[ne] in the pope's law, which hath been the destruction of the law of the church." Thomas Starkey, *A Dialogue between Pole and Lupset*, 69, ed. T. F. Mayer, Camden Fourth Series, vol. 37) (London: Camden Society, 1989).

For scholarship on the introduction and development of non obstante clauses in England, see William Prynne, *Brief animadversions on, Amendments of, & Additional Explanatory Records to, The Fourth Part of the Institutes of the Lawes of England*, 129–33 (London: 1669); Alexander Luders, "The Birth and Parentage, Rise and Fall of Nonobstante," in *Tracts on Various Subjects in the Law and History of England*, 327 (London: 1810); Paul Birdsall, "'Non Obstante': A Study in the Dispensing Power of English Kings," in *Essays in History and Political Theory in Honor of Charles Howard McIlwain*, 37 (Cambridge: 1937). For the canon law, see William J. Courtenay, *Capacity and Volition: A History of the Distinction of Absolute and Ordained Power*, 92–98, (Bergamo: Pierluigi Lubrina Editore, 1990).

3.   Thomas Smith, *De Republica Anglorum*, 60, ed. L. Alston (1583; Cambridge: 1906). For the *mala in se* distinction, see Vaughan, *Reports*, 330–59; Matthew Bacon, *A New Abridgment of the Law*, 4: 178 (London: 1778). For early hints of some of the doctrine against privileges that intruded on the rights of others, see Gaines Post, *Studies in Medieval Legal Thought: Public Law and the State, 1100–1322*, at 279 (Princeton: Princeton University Press, 1964).

4.   For what look like early dispensations and some early hints of a power to suspend or modify statutes, see "The Early Statutes," in *The English Parliament in the Middle Ages*, essay xxv, 25–26, 39, ed. H. G. Richardson & G. O. Sayles (London: Hambledon Press, 1981); S. B. Chrimes, *English Constitutional Ideas in the Fifteenth Century*, 279–83 (Cambridge: Cambridge University Press, 1936).

5.   An Act Concerning Monopolies and Dispensations with Penal Laws and the Forfeiture Thereof, 21 James I, c. 3 (1624). See also Coke, *Institutes*, 3: 186. (Commas have been added silently for ease of reading.)

6.   George R. Abernathy, "Clarendon and the Declaration of Indulgence," Journal of Ecclesiastical History, 11: 59–60, 62 (1960); His Majesty's Declaration to All His Loving Subjects (Mar. 15, 1672), in *The Stuart Constitution, 1603–1688: Documents and Commentary*, 407, ed. J. P. Kenyon (Cambridge: Cambridge University Press, 1966); *Journals of the House of Commons*, 251 (Feb. 10, 1672).

7.   Trial of Sir Edward Hales (1686), in *State Trials*, 11: 1196; King James the Second His Gracious Declaration to All His Loving Subjects for Liberty of Conscience (Apr. 4, 1687), in *The Stuart Constitution, 1603–1688: Documents and Commentary*, 411, ed. J. P. Kenyon (Cambridge: Cambridge University Press, 1966).

8.   Petition of Seven Bishops (May 18, 1688), in *The Stuart Constitution, 1603–1688: Documents and Commentary*, 441, ed. J. P. Kenyon (Cambridge: Cambridge University Press, 1966).

9.   *The Declaration of His Highness, William Henry, by the Grace of God, Prince of Orange, &c. of the Reasons Inducing Him to Appear in Arms in the Kingdom of England . . .* ([1688]), in *The History of the Desertion*, 52–53, by [Edmund Bohun] (London: 1689).

10.   Speeches of Henry Capel and William Williams (May 16, 1689), in *The Debates of the House of Commons, From the Year 1667 to the Year 1694*, at 9: 257–58, by Anchi-

tell Gray (London: 1763). Echoing such views, Hume later wrote that "the legislative power of the Parliament was a mere fallacy; while the sovereign was universally acknowledged to possess a dispensing power, by which all the laws could be invalidated, and rendered of no effect." David Hume, *The History of England from the Invasion of Julius Caesar to the Revolution of 1688*, at 4: 363 (app. III) (Indianapolis: Liberty Classics, 1983).

11. Declaration of Rights, 1 William & Mary, sess. 2, c. 2 (1689). As put by one member of Parliament, his colleagues had been "tender in not taking away all dispensing power." Speech of Sir John Lowther (May 16, 1689), in *The Debates of the House of Commons, From the Year 1667 to the Year 1694*, at 9: 255, by Anchitell Gray (London: 1763). This relatively cautious rejection of the dispensing power had a long history, as evident from Ponet's view that rulers could not dispense with positive laws, "unless the makers of the laws give them express authority so to do." [John Ponet], *A Short Treatise of Politike Pouuer, and of the True Obedience which Subjects Owe to Kynges and Other Ciuile Gouernours*, sig. [C7v] (n.p.: 1556).

For the politics underlying the Declaration of Rights (but with little recognition of the early history of dispensations or their later potential), see Carolyn A. Edie, "Tactics and Strategies: Parliament's Attack upon the Royal Dispensing Power, 1597-1689," American Journal of Legal History, 29: 197 (1985); Carolyn A. Edie, "Revolution and the Rule of Law: The End of the Dispensing Power," Eighteenth-Century Studies, 10: 34 (1977).

12. Richard Brown, *Church and State in Modern Britain, 1700-1850*, at 304-05 (London: Routledge, 1991).

13. *Journals of the House of Commons*, 31: [3] (Nov. 11, 1766); *Parliamentary History*, 16: 246, n. (1803). The statute was An Act for Improvement of Tillage and the Breed of Cattle, 22 Charles II, c. 13 (1670). As explained by a later law dictionary, an embargo in time of war on shipping and thereby on subjects leaving the realm "will be equally binding as an act of parliament, because founded upon a prior law. . . . But a proclamation to lay an embargo in time of peace upon all vessels laden with wheat (though in time of a public scarcity,) being contrary to law, and particularly to a statute then in force (22 C. 2. c. 13) the advisors of such a proclamation, and all persons acting under it, always found it necessary to be indemnified by special acts of parliament." Thomas Edlyne Tomlins, *Law-Dictionary*, vol. 2 ("king" V.3) (London: 1835).

14. *Journals of the House of Commons*, 31: 23 (Nov. 24, 1766); John Lord Campbell, *The Lives of the Lord Chancellors and Keepers of the Great Seal of England*, 5: 216-17 & 265-67 (London: John Murray, 1849).

15. *A Speech Against the Suspending and Dispensing Prerogative*, 14, 6th ed. (London: 1767). This pamphlet was compiled from arguments made in a range of speeches in November and December 1766. Hargrave later commented that "the doctrine of dispensing with and suspending laws was as foreign to the real general question, which was then to be decided upon, as it ever is alarming." Francis Hargrave, *Jurisconsult Exercitations*, 2: 298 (London: 1811).

16. *Annual Register for 1767*, at 48; *State Necessity Considered as a Question of Law*, 30 (London: 1766). The emergency was such that, although the House would take a month to resolve the constitutional question, it promptly, on the first day it met, unanimously resolved that the king should continue the embargo and that it should be extended to include barley and malt. *Journals of the House of Commons*, 31: 6 (Nov. 11, 1766).

17. Ibid., 47.
18. *A Speech Against the Suspending and Dispensing Prerogative*, 9, 12, 6th ed. (London: 1767).
19. *State Necessity Considered as a Question of Law*, 3, 7–10, 12 (London: 1766).
20. Ibid., 48–49.
21. In particular, the indemnification statute recited that all lawsuits and prosecutions brought on account of the order should be discharged and held void. An Act for Indemnifying Such Persons as Have Acted for the Service of the Public, in Advising or Carrying into Execution the Order of Council of the Twenty-Sixth Day of September Last, for Laying an Embargo on All Ships Laden with Wheat or Wheat Flour; and for Preventing Suits in Consequence of the Said Embargo, 7 George III, c. 7 (1767). For the history of the bill, see "The History of the Last Session of Parliament," London Magazine, 37: 11–12 (1768).
22. *State Necessity Considered as a Question of Law*, 8 (London: 1766).
23. *Annual Register, or a View of the History, Politicks, and Literature for the Year 1766*, at 38 (London: 1767).
24. Debates in both Houses on the Bill of Indemnity for those Concerned in the Late Embargo (Nov. 24, 1766), in *Parliamentary History*, 16: 249 (London: Hansard, 1813).
25. *A Speech Against the Suspending and Dispensing Prerogative*, 13, 24, 6th ed. (London: 1767).
26. William Blackstone, *Commentaries on the Laws of England*, 1: 160 (Oxford: 1765).
27. "Debates in the House of Representatives, on the Subject of the Tender-Act (so called) (March 24, 1788)," Independent Chronicle (Boston) (Apr. 3, 1788). The bill was an attempt to revive a statute that had expired, and although it was passed after debate, it apparently did not have the governor's support and did not become law.
28. Ibid.
29. Ibid. Incidentally, a hint of attitudes toward administrative dispensations can be discerned in a short squib, complaining about how someone was "excused from militia fines and duty." The piece began: "Is it true, that the Lieutenant assumed any dispensing power over the militia law?" "For the Chronicle of Freedom," Independent Gazetteer (Philadelphia) (Aug. 24, 1782).
30. Mass. Const. of 1780, Pt. II, Chap. VI, Art. I.
31. The South Carolina and New Hampshire constitutions did not specify a pardon power.
32. Mass. Const. of 1780, Pt. I, Chap. II, Sec. I, Art. VIII; N.Y. Const. of 1777, Art. XVIII; Va. Const. of 1776. The Virginia provision was the subject of dispute in 1780, after a statute allocated the pardoning power to both houses of the legislature.
33. Maryland Declaration of Rights of 1776, §7; Mass. Const. of 1780, Pt. I, Declaration of Rights, Art. 20. The six constitutions were those of Maryland, Massachusetts, Virginia, and New Hampshire in 1784, and North Carolina and Vermont in 1786.
34. The 1679 Habeas Corpus Act protected the writ of habeas corpus, and the Declaration of Rights in 1689 recognized that the law could not be suspended, except by Parliament or under its authority. Thereafter, the power to suspend the writ of habeas lay in Parliament.
35. Mass. Const. of 1780, Pt. II, Chap. VI, Art. VII. In other respects, however, such provisions barred executive suspensions.
36. See the constitutions of Delaware, Georgia, New York, Pennsylvania, South Carolina, and New Hampshire in 1776, and Vermont in 1777.

37. Pa. Const. of 1790, Art. IX, Sec. 12.
38. *Little v. Barreme*, 6 U.S. 170 (1804).
39. Ibid., 179.
40. An Act respecting Quarantines and Health Laws, §1 (Feb. 25, 1799), *Public Statutes at Large of the United States*, 1: 619. For the lobbying for this bill, see "Correspondence between the Citizens of New-York and Philadelphia, Respecting Arrangements to Guard against Pestilential Diseases," Medical Repository, 2: 358 (Dec. 2, 1798).
41. Treasury communications, both printed and manuscript, have been examined for evidence that the secretary of the treasury dispensed with the relevant reporting periods.
42. Some statutory provisions authorized the president to waive the statutory duties of other executive officers in promoting or otherwise dealing with subordinates, especially military officers. For example, in 1866, the president was "authorized to waive the examination of such officers in the pay department of the navy as are on duty abroad, and cannot at present be examined, as required by law." This sort of statute merely restored to the president some of the discretionary authority over subordinates that had been taken from him by the statute requiring the examination of the relevant naval officers. An Act to Regulate the Appointment of Paymasters in the Navy, and Explanatory of an Act for the Better Organization of the Pay Department of the Navy (June 21, 1866), *Public Statutes at Large of the United States*, 14: 70. See also An Act to Provide for the Examination of Certain Officers of the Army and to Regulate Promotions Therein (Oct. 1, 1890), ibid., 26: 562.

    Along somewhat similar lines, when Congress authorized the secretary of the navy to accept up to six Japanese students designated by the Empire of Japan for instruction at Annapolis, it provided that he "may, in the case of the said persons, modify or dispense with any provisions of the rules and regulations of the said academy which circumstances may, in his opinion, render necessary or desirable." A Resolution to Admit Certain Persons to the Naval Academy (July 27, 1868), *Public Statutes at Large of the United States*, 15: 261.
43. For example, an 1861 statute authorized the commissioner of patents "to dispense in future with models of designs when the design can be sufficiently represented by a drawing." Tellingly, however, this allowed him to dispense with his statutory duties in granting a privilege, and by specifying when he was to depart from his instructions, the statute really laid out an alternate rule. An Act in Addition to "An Act to Promote the Progress of the Useful Arts," §5 (Mar. 2, 1861), *Public Statutes at Large of the United States*, 12: 247.

CHAPTER SIX

b. Cornelius M. Kerwin and Scott R. Furlong, *Rulemaking: How Government Agencies Write Law and Make Policy*, 8 (Washington, DC: CQ Press, 2011) (misdating the statutes as 1796 and as "[t]wenty years later"); An Act to Regulate the Collection of Duties on Imports and Tonnage, §61 (Mar. 2, 1799), *Public Statutes at Large of the United States*, 1: 673; An Act for the Assessment and Collection of Direct Taxes and Internal Duties, §4 (July 22, 1813), ibid., 3: 26.
d. *Documents Accompanying a Bill Authorizing the Accounting Officers of the Treasury Department to Give Credit to Certain Collectors of the Customs for Allowances Paid by Them to the Owners and Crews of Fishing Vessels, Presented February 10, 1809* (Washington, DC: 1809). Congress responded with An Act Authorizing the Accounting Officers of the Treasury Department to Give Credit to Certain Collectors of the Customs

for Allowances Paid by Them to the Owners and Crews of Fishing Vessels (June 28, 1809), *Public Statutes at Large of the United States*, 2: 552.

e. Letter from Felix Grundy to Levi Woodbury (Sept. 8, 1838), Record Group 56, Correspondence of the Office of the Secretary of the Treasury, Letters Received from the Attorney General, 1831–1910, Box 1, at National Archives II, College Park, MD; Letter from Felix Grundy to Levi Woodbury (Dec. 19, 1838), ibid.

In December 1838, the Treasury relied on administrative necessity to justify its interpretation of the duties of customs collectors, and it thereby provoked Grundy to explain to Woodbury that only Congress, not the Treasury, could alter the customs laws. Customs collectors had developed convenient practices for dealing with unascertained and protested duties, but although the practices seemed administratively convenient, they had allowed the New York collector, Samuel Swartwout, to embezzle over a million dollars in duties. When Woodbury began to face the consequences, he wrote to the attorney general to inquire about the lawfulness of the practices, and he hinted at their justification in administrative necessity:

> On an importation of goods liable to cash duties, some time must unavoidably elapse before the duties thereon can be calculated and the exact amount payable ascertained. It appears to be the practice in such cases, to receive from the importer a sum of money deemed sufficient to cover the amount, when ascertained, and any deficiency is afterwards made up, or the surplus refunded by the collector, as the case may be. These funds the collector designates as money taken and held for unascertained duties.

Grundy responded:

> It seems to me that the intention of those, who originally framed our revenue laws was, that the duties should be ascertained, and paid, where cash duties are imposed, before the goods are delivered to the owner. But it is understood that in some ports this is wholly impracticable, and therefore, a departure in practice . . . is indispensable. This state of things, could not have been foreseen, by those, who originally passed the acts of Congress, under which the revenue is still collected. The vast increase of the commerce of the United States, and its concentration, at particular ports, renders that impracticable, which at an early period could easily be effected. If the law cannot be executed according to its letter and probable intention on account of the altered circumstances of the affairs of the country, Congress alone can supply the proper remedy. In the meantime[,] however, until Congress shall act, such Treasury regulations should be adopted and enforced as will best secure the objects of the law. It could never have been the intention of Congress, that a Collector should receive money for duties, under a private arrangement with the importer and keep the money in his hands until it was convenient for him to cause the amount of duties to be ascertained. If such practice were to be tolerated, it might be the interest of the collector to postpone the ascertainment of the duties, as the in the meantime, he would have uncontrolled use of the money. It would also increase the danger of faithlessness in the collector, by permitting large amounts of money to remain with him and under his individual control, instead of being the Treasury of the United States.
>
> The tenor and spirit of the all our revenue laws, seem to inculcate the idea, that the intention of Congress has at all times been, that money collected for revenue, should be promptly placed in the Treasury and not be permitted to remain in the hands of the collectors. Therefore in any regulations you may make upon this subject, that object should be constantly kept in view.

That the laws were "wholly impracticable," and that "a departure in practice" was "indispensable," was no excuse.

In the same letter, incidentally, Woodbury also inquired about the lawfulness of the prevailing treatment of protested duties. Especially in the larger ports, it was common for an importer to dispute the duty determined by the customs collector. Therefore, "with the view of getting possession of his goods," the importer would pay the collector under protest "and at one the same time give that officer notice not to pay over the money to the government." Of course, the importer would immediately institute a suit against the collector "to recover back the amount so paid." After reciting all of this, Woodbury asked Grundy: "Can a collector legally retain in his hands, beyond the control of the Department, and distinct from his other funds, arising from duties, money so received?" The attorney general answered:

> [U]nder the laws of Congress in relation to duties on imported articles, it is the duty of the collector to carry into execution, the instructions of the Treasury Department, and to conform his acts to them. If in doing this, he shall collect more money, than the Judiciary shall afterwards in an action against the collector by the importer, adjudge to have been due to the government, there can be no doubt, that it is the duty of the government to save the collector from injury. But the question you present, is of a very different character. It is whether the collector has the legal right to retain the money so received in his own hands, beyond the control of the department &c. My opinion is, that no such right exists, and that the collector should, notwithstanding such protest, and suit by the importer, pay over to the Treasury, all moneys by him received, under such circumstances, as though no protest had been made or suit commenced.

The attorney general then reiterated that if the importer prevailed in court, "it would be the duty of the government, promptly to discharge such judgment, and release the collector from its consequences." Ibid.

f.   Circular to Collectors, Appraisers, and other officers of the Customs from R. J. Walker (July 6, 1847), Circular Letters of the Secretary of the Treasury (T Series) 1789–1878, National Archives Microfilm No. 735, Reel 3, Vol. 3, p. 310. See also Robert Mayo, *A Synopsis of the Commercial and Revenue System of the United States, As Developed by Instructions and Decisions of the Treasury Department for the Administration of the Revenue Laws*, 436 (Washington, DC: 1847).

g.   Alexander Bickel, *The Least Dangerous Branch: The Supreme Court at the Bar of Politics*, 236 (1962, New Haven: Yale University Press, 1986); Philip Hamburger, *Law and Judicial Duty*, 132–41, 159–78 (Cambridge: Harvard University Press, 2008).

h.   Edith G. Henderson, *Foundations of English Administrative Law: Certiorari and Mandamus in the Seventeenth Century*, 32–33 (Cambridge: Harvard University Press, 1963); Matthew Bacon, *A New Abridgment of the Law*, 1: 655 (London: 1778).

i.   For the setting of wages, see W. A. S. Hewins, "Regulation of Wages by the Justices of the Peace," Economic Journal, 8: 345 (1898); Richard B. Morris & Jonathan Grossman, "The Regulation of Wages in Early Massachusetts," New England Quarterly, 11: 471, 499 (1938). For the declining role of justices of the peace in setting of wages and bread prices in America, see William E. Nelson, *The Common Law in Colonial America: Volume II: The Middle Colonies and the Carolinas, 1660–1730*, at 55 (Oxford: Oxford University Press, 2012). In colonial South Carolina, the legislature in 1749 limited the dangers of having justices of the peace exercising legislative power by having the commissary general publish "the current price of fine flour at Charlestown." William Simpson, *The Practical Justice of the Peace and Parish-Officer, of His Majesty's Province of South-Carolina*, 49 (Charlestown: 1761). For legislative price setting during wartime, see Kenneth Scott, "Price Control in New England during the Revolution," New England Quarterly, 19: 453 (1946).

m.   Civis, *Remarks on the Embargo Law: In Which Its Constitutionality, as Well as Its Effects on the Foreign and Domestic Relations of the United States, Are Considered*, 7–8 (New York: 1808).

n.   *Locke's Appeal*, 72 Pa. St. 491, 498 (1873). For other cases, see citations in *Bouvier's Law Dictionary*, 285 (New York: Banks Law Publishing Co., 1928).

1.   Kenneth Culp Davis, "A New Approach to Delegation," University of Chicago Law Review, 36: 713, 719–20 (1969); Jerry L. Mashaw, *Creating the Administrative Constitution: The Lost One Hundred Years of American Administrative Law*, 7, 46, 56, 77, 126, 166 (New Haven: Yale University Press, 2012); Eric A. Posner & Adrian Vermeule, "Interring the Nondelegation Doctrine," University of Chicago Law Review, 69: 1721, 1736 (2002); Cass R. Sunstein, "Nondelegation Canons," University of Chicago Law Review, 67: 315, 322–23 (2000). For responses, though on different terms than here, see Gary Lawson, "Delegation and Original Meaning," Virginia Law Review, 88: 327, 398–403 (2002); Michael B. Rappaport, "The Selective Nondelegation Doctrine and the Line Item Veto: A New Approach to the Nondelegation Doctrine and Its Implications for *Clinton v. City of New York*," Tulane Law Review, 76: 265, 310 (2001).

Some commentators suggest that Hamilton wanted the executive to enjoy administrative power, and in support of this conclusion they quote Hamilton's definition of administration in *The Federalist*:

> The administration of government, in its largest sense, comprehends all the operations of the body politic, whether legislative, executive or judiciary, but in its most usual, and perhaps in its most precise signification, it is limited to executive details, and falls peculiarly within the province of the executive department. The actual conduct of foreign negotiations, the preparatory plans of finance, the application and disbursement of the public moneys, in conformity to the general appropriations of the legislature, the arrangement of the army and navy, the direction of the operations of war; these and other matters of a like nature constitute what seems to be most properly understood by the administration of government.

Alexander Hamilton, Federalist Number 72, in *The Federalist*, 486–87, ed. Jacob E. Cooke (Middletown: Wesleyan University Press, 1961), quoted by Daniel P. Carpenter, *The Forging of Bureaucratic Autonomy: Reputations, Networks, and Policy Innovation in Executive Agencies, 1862–1928*, at 37 (Princeton: Princeton University Press, 2001). None of these executive actions, however, bound subjects of the United States. Although Hamilton pressed for broad legislative power in Congress, he did not argue for what here is understood as administrative power.

2.   They write that legislative power was the power "to make laws/rules for the governance of society." Larry Alexander & Saikrishna Prakash, "Reports of the Nondelegation Doctrine's Death Are Greatly Exaggerated," University of Chicago Law Review, 70: 1297, 1326 (2003).

3.   For example, immigrants and other aliens who could be presumed to have accepted allegiance were considered to have become at least temporary subjects. Philip Hamburger, "Beyond Protection," Columbia Law Review, 109: 1823, 1850–54 (2009).

4. John Locke, *Two Treatises of Government*, 273 (II.ii.9), ed. Peter Laslett (Cambridge: Cambridge University Press, 1988); William Blackstone, *Commentaries on the Law of England*, 1: 57 (Oxford: 1765). Of course, there was a difference of opinion as to whether the will of the legislature was enough, by itself, to give obligation to law. Blackstone, for example, took the arch-Tory line that, "in relation to those laws which enjoin only *positive duties*, and forbid only such things as are not *mala in se* but *mala prohibita* merely, annexing a penalty to noncompliance, here I apprehend conscience is no farther concerned, than by directing a submission to the penalty, in case of a breach of those laws." Ibid., 1: 57–58.

5. An Act for establishing an Executive Department, to be denominated the Department of Foreign Affairs, §1 (July 27, 1789), *Public Statutes at Large of the United States*, 1: 29; An Act for regulating the Military Establishment of the United States, §11 (Apr. 30, 1790), ibid., 1: 121. Earlier, it was enacted that pensions to disabled Revolutionary soldiers were to be paid by the United States "under such regulations as the President . . . may direct." An Act Providing for the Payment of the Invalid Pensioners of the United States (Sept. 29, 1789), ibid., 1: 95.

6. An Act Making Provision for the [payment of the] Debt of the United States, 1st Congress, §6 (Aug. 4, 1790), ibid., 1: 140.

7. It later was said about the distinction between regulations and instructions: "This distinction is inherent in the nature of the two things. An instruction is a direction to government the conduct of the particular officer to whom it is addressed. A regulation affects a class or classes of officers." *Landram v. United States* (1880), 16 Ct. Cl., 74; 27 Int. Rev. Rec., 80.

8. The first printed comptroller's circular, with instructions and an explanation of forms, appears to have come in December 1789. Circular from Nicholas Eveleigh (Dec. 1, 1789), Record Group 56, Treasury Department Circulars 1789–1798, Vol. 1, p. 35.5, at National Archives II, College Park, MD. The printing of circulars from the secretary and the comptroller seems to have become standard by May 1791. See Record Group 56, Treasury Department Circulars 1789–1798, Vol. 1, pp. 71ff., at National Archives II, College Park, MD.

    For an English example, see *Instructions by the Commissioners of His Majesty's Customs in America, to ____ who is appointed ____ of the Customs at the Port of ____ in America* (n.p.: [1767?]).

9. *Rules and Regulations Respecting the Recruiting Service*, [3] ([Philadelphia: 1798]); Regulations to be Observed by the Deputy Postmaster in the United States, *The Post-Office Law with Instructions, Forms and Tables of Distances, Published for the Regulation of the Post Offices*, 36 (Philadelphia: 1798). For another example of printed regulations from 1798, see *Regulations Respecting Extra-Allowances to Officers* ([1798]), issued by Secretary of War James McHenry.

10. As a result, directives to officers about the distribution of benefits were increasingly accompanied by publications explaining to the public how they could apply for the benefits. See, for example, *Circular to Registrars and Receivers of the United States Land Offices in Re[gard? to] Military Land Warrants [rest of title missing]* (May 3, 1855) ([Washington, DC: 1855]); *Instructions and Forms to Be Observed by Persons Applying to the Pension Office for Bounty Land under the Act of March 3, 1855* (Washington, DC: 1855). For earlier regulations directing officers in handling claims to bounty lands, see *Rules and Regulations to Be Observed in Substantiating Claims to Bounty Land, under the Act of Congress of the 5th of March, 1816, Entitled "An Act Granting Bounties in Land and Extra Pay to Certain Canadian Volunteers"* ([1816?]).

11. *Lockington's Case* (Pa. 1813), American Law Journal, 5: 92–94 (1814). For a discussion of this case and the place of enemy aliens in American law, see Philip Hamburger, "Beyond Protection," Columbia Law Review, 109: 1896–97 (2009). For a more general account of the different treatment of American and aliens, and how Congress left "to courts the enforcement of penalties against the person of citizens," see Leonard D. White, *The Federalists: A Study in Administrative History*, 441 (New York: Macmillan Co., 1961). Note that the power to license and control non-subjects had been a lawful part of the royal prerogative, and in America was part of the force of the nation belonging to the executive, although at least partly subject to congressional statutes authorizing and thereby limiting it.

12. Letter from Alexander Hamilton to Otho H. Williams (July 19, 1792), in *The Papers of Alexander Hamilton*, 12: 50, ed. Harold C. Syrett & Jacob E. Cooke (New York: Columbia University Press, 1967).

13. Circular to the Collectors of the Customs (July 20, 1792), in *The Papers of Alexander Hamilton*, 12: 57–62, ed. Harold C. Syrett & Jacob E. Cooke (New York: Columbia University Press, 1967). See also original in Record Group 56, Treasury Department Circulars 1789–1798, Vol. 1, p. 114, at National Archives II, College Park, MD.

    As early as October 1789, Hamilton told collectors in a circular that some of the discounts they granted on duties were "not in my opinion the true construction" of the relevant statute. Circular from Alexander Hamilton (Oct. 6, 1789), Circular Letters of the Secretary of the Treasury (T Series) 1789–1878, National Archives Microfilm No. 735, Reel 2, Vol. 1, p. 6. Two months later, he wrote: "My opinion having been several times asked on the following points, I think it proper, in order to produce uniformity of practice to convey it in a circular instruction." Circular from Alexander Hamilton (Dec. 18, 1789), and Circular from Alexander Hamilton (Dec. 23, 1789), Record Group 56, Treasury Department Circulars 1789–1798, Vol. 1, p. 38, at National Archives II, College Park, MD. See also Circular Letters of the Secretary of the Treasury (T Series) 1789–1878, National Archives Microfilm No. 735, Reel 2, Vol. 1, p. 27.

    Comptrollers soon were also sharing their interpretations, as when Oliver Wolcott wrote a circular giving his opinion and noting that it was one "in which the Attorney General, who has been consulted concurs." Circular from Oliver Wolcott (June 25, 1792), Record Group 56, Treasury Department Circulars 1789–1798, Vol. 1, p. 113, at National Archives II, College Park, MD.

14. Circular to the Collectors of the Customs (July 20, 1792), in *The Papers of Alexander Hamilton*, 12: 57–62, ed. Harold C. Syrett & Jacob E. Cooke (New York: Columbia University Press, 1967).

15. Letter from Alexander Hamilton to Otho H. Williams (July 19, 1792), ibid., 55. He might have added that, by the same token, inferior executive officers could resign if they considered an interpretation unlawful. Two years later, on the eve of the Whiskey Rebellion, when Congress added duties on the sale of foreign wines and distilled spirits, it took the precaution of confirming that the duties were to be collected "subject to the superintendence, control and direction of the department of the treasury." An Act Laying Duties on Licensing for Selling Wines and Foreign Distilled Spirituous Liquors by Retail, §4 (June 5, 1794), *Public Statutes at Large of the United States*, 1: 378.

    A half century later, when another treasury secretary enjoined receivers of public money and the registers of land offices to comply with "existing instructions" for the security of public money, he closed his circular with a warning: "Any omission on the part of the officers before referred to comply strictly with the above instructions, and not satisfactorily explained, will be made the ground of a report to the President for the removal of the delinquent." Circular to Registers and Receivers of the Public Money from R. J. Walker (June 17, 1847), Circular Letters of the Secretary of the Treasury (T Series) 1789–1878, National Archives Microfilm No. 735, Reel 3, Vol. 3, pp. 306–07.

16. For example, in October 1789, Hamilton wrote to customs collectors: "A doubt has been expressed by some collectors, whether vessels are liable to pay tonnage at each entry. On this point the opinions of counsel have been taken: in conformity to which it is my duty to inform you that the tonnage duty must be paid in all cases where it is necessary for a vessel to make an entry unless such cases are otherwise especially provided for by law." Circular from Alexander Hamilton (Oct. 20, 1789), Circular Letters of the Secretary of the Treasury (T Series) 1789–1878, National Archives Microfilm No. 735, Reel 2, Vol. 1, p. 12. The next month, he wrote that, "thinking it expedient in a case of mere construction to assist my own judgment by the advice of professional men, I stated the questions which had been submitted to me to two gentlemen of the law in this city, eminent for their ability; and I herewith transmit a copy of the opinions they have given." He added that "my own judgment, upon full reflection, corresponds in every particular with the opinion given to me." Circular from Alexander Hamilton (Nov. 30, 1789), Record Group 56, Treasury Department Circulars 1789–1798, Vol. 1, pp. 27–28, at National Archives II, College Park, MD. See also Circular Letters of the Secretary of the Treasury (T Series) 1789–1878, National Archives Microfilm No. 735, Reel 2, Vol. 1, p. 16.

   For the Treasury's later reliance on opinions of the attorney general, see, for example: Circular from Alexander Hamilton (Aug. 6, 1792), Record Group 56, Treasury Department Circulars 1789–1798, Vol. 1, p. 123, at National Archives II, College Park, MD; Circular from Oliver Wolcott (Aug. 24, 1794), Record Group 56, Treasury Department Circulars 1789–1798, Vol. 1, p. 156a, at National Archives II, College Park, MD.

17. Circular from Alexander Hamilton (July 23, 1792), Record Group 56, Treasury Department Circulars 1789–1798, Vol. 1, p. 122, at National Archives II, College Park, MD. Moreover, where construction was difficult—as on the duties on brass in plates and sheets—Hamilton admitted as much: "The thing is not free from doubt; but . . . [in light of various reasons] I adopt the construction which exempts from duty brass in the former as well as the latter shape." Circular from Alexander Hamilton (Aug. 6, 1792), Record Group 56, Treasury Department Circulars 1789–1798, Vol. 1, p. 123, at National Archives II, College Park, MD.

18. Circular from Alexander Hamilton (July 22, 1792), Record Group 56, Treasury Department Circulars 1789–1798, Vol. 1, p. 116, at National Archives II, College Park, MD. For the attorney general's opinion enclosed by Hamilton, see Letter from Edmund Randolph to Alexander Hamilton (June 21, 1792), Record Group 56, Treasury Department Circulars 1789–1798, Vol. 1, p. 120, at National Archives II, College Park, MD. (The opinion is not among the published opinions of attorneys general.)

19. For an early exception, see Circular to Collectors, Naval Officers, and Surveys (Dec. 28, 1793), in A Synopsis of the Commercial and Revenue System of the United States, As Developed by Instructions and Decisions of the Treasury Department for the Administration of the Revenue Laws, 235, by Robert Mayo (Washington, DC: 1847).

20. Report of the Attorney General, of Fees and Regulations Proper to be Established in the

Courts of the United States, Published by Order of the House of Representatives, 4 (Philadelphia: Francis Child, 1795).

21. Jerry L. Mashaw, *Creating the Administrative Constitution: The Lost One Hundred Years of American Administrative Law*, 102, 104 (New Haven: Yale University Press, 2012).

22. Circular (Jan. 23, 1818), in *A Synopsis of the Commercial and Revenue System of the United States, As Developed by Instructions and Decisions of the Treasury Department for the Administration of the Revenue Laws*, 98, by Robert Mayo (Washington, DC: 1847).

    For example, later that year, after Congress passed new customs statutes, the Comptroller's Office distributed copies of the new acts to collectors together with a circular noting an open "question" about the export "drawback or bounty" on some types of spirits (those distilled from molasses and those on refined sugar made out of sugar imported into the United States). Would such goods be entitled to the drawback during an interim period between two statutes regulating the subject? To avoid confusion, Comptroller Anderson notified the collectors that he and the secretary of the treasury were of the opinion that there could be no drawback for such goods. He also instructed the customs officers on the evidence they were to rely upon and the forms they were to use. *Duties Payable on Goods, Wares and Merchandise . . .* , 13–14, 2nd ed. (New York: Day & Turner, 1819). All of this interpretation merely instructed collectors; it did not bind or constrain the public.

    Andrews was not the first comptroller to issue circulars reviewing interpretation problems. For example, when circulating the sixth volume of the laws of the United States, Gabriell Duvall wrote, "I embrace this opportunity to communicate my instructions on several subjects which appear to require attention." Circular from G. Duvall (Dec. 22, 1804), Record Group 56, Treasury Department Circulars 1799–1816, Vol. 2, p. 232a, at National Archives II, College Park, MD. Andrews, however, appears to have been more systematic.

23. Robert Mayo, *A Synopsis of the Commercial and Revenue System of the United States, As Developed by Instructions and Decisions of the Treasury Department for the Administration of the Revenue Laws*, ix (Washington, DC: 1847); Treasury Department, *General Regulations, No. 63: Abstract of Decisions on Questions Submitted to the Treasury Department Arising under the Laws Affecting Revenue and Commerce, in Force since December 1, 1846, and under Treaty Stipulations with Foreign Powers* (Washington, DC: 1856).

24. *Elliott v. Swartwout*, 35 U.S. 10 Pet. 137 153 (1836).

25. An Act to Provide Revenue from Imports, and to Change and Modify Existing Laws Imposing Duties on Imports, and for Other Purposes, §24 (Aug. 30, 1842), *Public Statutes at Large of the United States*, 566.

26. *U.S. v. Irving*, 42 U.S. 250, 261 (1843).

27. Internal Revenue Law, §22, in *A Compendium of Internal Revenue Laws, with Decisions, Rulings, Instructions, Regulations, and Forms*, 13, by J. B. F. Davidge & I. G. Kimball (Washington, DC: W. H. & O. H. Morrison, 1871). For the binding effect of such regulations on officers, see *In re Huttman*, 70 Fed. Rep., 699, 701 (D.Ct. D.Kan. 1895). The earliest federal statutes on the subject were not even this broad. For example, under a 1789 act of Congress, officers were subject to penalty upon being convicted for willfully neglecting or refusing to perform their duties under the statute. An Act for Registering and Clearing Vessels, Regulating the Coasting Trade, and for Other Purposes, §34 (Sept. 1, 1789), *Public Statutes at Large of the United States*, 1: 65. For other examples, see Leonard D. White, *The Federalists: A Study in Administrative History*, 425–26 (New York: Macmillan Co., 1961).

The English rule on resignation was that an officer remained in office until he secured acceptance of his resignation, but American jurisdictions divided on this question. Officers of the United States could leave their offices, and avoid liability for non-performance, without getting an acceptance. For the cases, see Floyd R. Mechem, *A Treatise on the Law of Public Offices and Officers*, 263–64 (Chicago: Callaghan & Co., 1890).

28. Although military orders generally were directed only at soldiers and sailors, this was not true under martial law, but that obviously was not a precedent for civilian administrative law.

29. 6 Henry VI, c. 5 (1427); *Rookes Case* (C.P. 1598), Coke, *Reports*, 5: 100a.

30. Ibid.; Matthew Bacon, *A New Abridgment of the Law*, 1: 655 (London: 1778), citing Hard., 146.

Alan Cromartie suggests that Robert Callis in his 1622 reading at Gray's Inn took a view opposite to Coke's. Alan Cromartie, "The Constitutionalist Revolution: The Transformation of Political Culture in Early Stuart England," *Past & Present*, 163: 91 (1999). There is a risk, however, of overstating their differences. Whereas Coke strained to assimilate all discretion to a legal discretion, Callis acknowledged the legal discretion that was done according to law and then openly propounded another discretion, which "is the absolute judge of the cause, and gives the rule." Yet even in thus departing from Coke's analysis in *Rooke's Case*, Callis relied upon Coke to suggest how such discretion was to be exercised in a law-like manner, and he even added, "I had rather trust to the worst certain law, than to give too much way to the uncertain discretion of the commissioners." *The Reading of That Famous and Learned Gentleman, Robert Callis Esq; Sergeant at Law, Upon the Statute of 23 H. 8. Cap. 5. of Sewers: As it was Delivered by Him at Grays-Inn, in August, 1622*, at 86 (London: 1647). Baker observes that Coke's attitude toward discretion persisted in the eighteenth century. J. H. Baker, *An Introduction to English Legal History*, 151 (London: Butterworths, 2002).

31. 23 Henry VIII, c. 5 (1531–32); Matthew Bacon, *A New Abridgment of the Law*, 1: 654 (London: 1778). Such ordinances expired with the commissions, although by statute, the commissioners could extend the life of these directives for one year after their commission came to an end. *Court Minutes of the Surrey & Kent Sewer Commission*, 1: vi, 112 ([London]: London County Council, 1909).

32. *The Reading of That Famous and Learned Gentleman, Robert Callis Esq; Sergeant at Law, Upon the Statute of 23 H. 8. Cap. 5. of Sewers: As it was Delivered by Him at Grays-Inn, in August, 1622*, at 227 (London: 1647).

33. For parish road surveyors, see Edith G. Henderson, *Foundations of English Administrative Law: Certiorari and Mandamus in the Seventeenth Century*, 18 (Cambridge: Harvard University Press, 1963). Although the assessments were a matter of discernment, the appointment of days for roadwork involved more discretion. Along the same lines, justices of the peace, with the assent of local constables, determined the assessments necessary for the repair of local bridges and appointed collectors, who could distrain for nonpayment. Ibid., 20. The assumptions about discernment also applied to parish assessments for the poor. Ibid., 22.

34. Saunders Welch, *Observations on the Office of Constable*, 6 (London: 1754); William Nelson, *The Office and Authority of a Justice of the Peace*, 189 (London: 1739). The constable also traditionally could command others to assist him, but this also was not more than a determination and notice of a duty imposed by law.

35. Michael Dalton, *The Country Justice*, 17, 20 (London: 1622).

36. Ibid.

37. Copy of resolution sent to Clerk of the Council (Jan. 28, 1789), in Library of Virginia, Governor Beverley Randolph Papers, Box 58; Va. Const. of 1776, Declaration of Rights, §5.

38. Local knowledge was directly significant in the rule: "No person shall be licensed unless the selectmen shall approve of him, and shall recommend him as a person of sober life and conversation, and suitably qualified and provided for that employment, and attached to the constitution and laws." *Abstract of the Laws for the Regulation of Licensed Houses: Published by Order of the Court of Sessions of the County of Essex*, 4 (Salem: June 12, 1821).

39. Michael Dalton, *The Country Justice*, 346 (London: 1622).

40. "A Catholic Christian," Letter to Mrs. Rind, Virginia Gazette (Rind) (May 12, 1774). Religious dissenters at various times turned to Virginia's county courts, to its council, and to its legislature for licenses. Even when the legislature decided upon the licenses, it was acting under the English Toleration Act and thus was expected by the dissenters to act as a licenser—that is, without exercising legislative will.

41. An Act to Regulate Trade and Intercourse with the Indian Tribes, §1 (July 22, 1790), *Public Statutes at Large of the United States*, 1: 137.

42. An Act for the More Effectual Preservation of Peace in the Ports and Harbors of the United States, and in the Waters under Their Jurisdiction, §4 (Mar. 3, 1805), *Public Statutes at Large of the United States*, 2: 341.

43. Circular from Robert Gallatin (May 25, 1805), Record Group 56, Treasury Department Circulars 1799–1816, Vol. 2, at p. 237, at National Archives II, College Park, MD.

44. An Act for Registering and Clearing Vessels, Regulating the Coasting Trade, and for Other Purposes (Sept. 1, 1789), *Public Statutes at Large of the United States*, 1: 55; An Act to Amend an Act Entitled "An Act to Provide for the Better Security of the Lives of Passengers on Board of Vessels Propelled in Whole or in Part by Steam," and for Other Purposes (Aug. 30, 1852), *Public Statutes at Large of the United States*, 10: 61; Jerry L. Mashaw, *Creating the Administrative Constitution: The Lost One Hundred Years of American Administrative Law*, 187 (New Haven: Yale University Press, 2012).

45. The act of Congress immediately preceding the 1852 steamboat statute was An Act Making Appropriations for the Transportation of the United States Mail by Ocean Steamers and Otherwise . . . (Aug. 30, 1852), *Public Statutes at Large of the United States*, 10: 61.

46. William W. Adams, "Constitutional History: Development of Admiralty Jurisdiction in the United States, 1789–1857," Western New England Law Review, at 8: 157, 163, 165, 180 (1986); An Act to Establish the Judicial Courts of the United States, §9 (Sept. 24, 1789), *Public Statutes at Large of the United States*, 1: 77; An Act Extending the Jurisdiction of the District Courts to Certain Cases, Upon the Lakes and Navigable Waters Connecting Them (Feb. 26, 1845), ibid., 5: 726.

47. For an early example of congressionally imposed licensing as means of general domestic regulation, see An Act to Regulate the Sale of Viruses, Serums, Toxins, and Analogous Products in the District of Columbia, to Regulate Interstate Traffic in Said Articles, and for Other Purposes (July 1, 1902), *Public Statutes at Large of the United States*, 32: 728.

48. An Act to Authorize the President of the United States, under Certain Conditions, to Suspend the Operation of the Act Laying an Embargo . . . (Apr. 22, 1808), *Public Statutes at Large of the United States*, 2: 490

Earlier statutes that authorized the president to do more than merely determine facts included the 1794, 1799, and 1800 statutes for suspension of embargoes. For example, the 1794 suspension statute authorized the president, while Congress was not in session, to embargo vessels, including American vessels, "whenever, in his opinion, the public safety shall so require . . . under such regulations as the circumstances of the case may require." An act to Authorize the President of the United States to Lay, Regulate and Revoke Embargoes, §1 (June 4, 1794), *Public Statutes at Large of the United States*, 1: 372. The 1799 statute, adopted during the so-called quasi war with France, erected statutory barriers to trade with France but authorized the president "to remit and discontinue" them "if he shall deem it expedient and consistent with the interest of the United States." An Act further to Suspend the Commercial Intercourse between the United States and France . . . §4 (Feb. 9, 1799), ibid., 1: 614.

49. Speech of Philip Key (Apr. 13 & 19, 1808), *Annals of Congress*, 18: 2118, 2125, 2212, 2213–14; discussed by David P. Currie, *The Constitution in Congress: The Jeffersonians, 1801–1829*, at 148–50 (Chicago: University of Chicago Press, 2002).

50. Speech of Philip Key (Apr. 19, 1808), *Annals of Congress*, 18: 2212, 2213, 2215; discussed by David P. Currie, *The Constitution in Congress: The Jeffersonians, 1801–1829*, at 148–50. See also Speech of John Rowan (Apr. 19, 1808), *Annals of Congress*, 18: 2232–37. For attempts to cure the constitutional defect, see the amendments proposed by Key and Randolph (Apr. 19, 1808), *Annals of Congress*, 18: 2240–42.

Outside Congress, a commentator protested that "this delegation of power from congress to the president" was "objectionable, on constitutional grounds" and thus was a "nullity." He added: "We here behold congress transferring their powers to the president. And this . . . is the first time I have ever heard of a constitutional delegation of power from one branch of the government to another. Nay, I had always thought that it was the true spirit of our constitution, to keep the great departments of our state distinct." Civis, *Remarks on the Embargo Law; in Which Its Constitutionality, as Well as Its Effects on the Foreign and Domestic Relations of the United States, Are Considered*, 7–8 (New York: 1808).

51. An Act to Interdict the Commercial Intercourse between the United States and Great Britain and France . . . , §11 (Mar. 1, 1809), *Public Statutes at Large of the United States*, 2: 530–31. See similarly An Act concerning the Commercial Intercourse between the United States and Great Britain and France . . . , §4 (May 1, 1810), ibid., 2: 606. For the act of state doctrine, see Anthony J. Bellia, Jr., & Bradford Clark, "The Federal Common Law of Nations," Columbia Law Review, 109: 1 (2009). Other such statutes included are discussed, even if not well understood, in *Marshall Field & Co. v. Clark*, 143 U.S. 649 (1892).

According to Jerry Mashaw, "[t]he nondelegation issue [in the 1809 statute] reached the Supreme Court in 1813" in *Cargo of the Brig Aurora v. United States*, 11 U.S. 382 (1813). He writes that "[t]he Supreme Court dismissed the delegation concern with the almost offhand declaration that Congress could limit the duration of a statute's operation by the occurrence of a fact and have that fact established by presidential proclamation." Jerry L. Mashaw, *Creating the Administrative Constitution: The Lost One Hundred Years of American Administrative Law*, 99 (New Haven: Yale University Press, 2012). The printed opinion of Justice William Johnson, however, does not appear to have directly addressed the issue, and Mashaw appears to be relying on the argument by counsel that "[t]he legislature did not transfer any power of legislation to the President. They only prescribed the evidence which should be admitted of a fact, upon which the law should go into effect." 11 U.S. 387.

52. An 1822 statute provided that

> in the event of the signature of any treaty or convention concerning the navigation or commerce between the United States and France, the president . . . is . . . authorized, should he deem the same expedient, by proclamation, to suspend, until the end of the next session of Congress, the operation of the act, entitled "An act to impose a new tonnage duty on French ships and vessels," and for other purposes; and also to suspend, as aforesaid, all other duties on French vessels . . . which may exceed the duties on American vessels . . .

An Act in Addition to the Act Concerning Navigation, and Also to Authorize the Appointment of Deputy Collectors, §2 (May 6, 1822), *Public Statutes at Large of the United States*, 3: 681.

CHAPTER SEVEN

a. 5 U.S.C. §553(b)(B); 5 U.S.C. §553(d)(3); Jeffrey S. Lubbers, *A Guide to Federal Agency Rulemaking*, 116 (Chicago: American Bar Association, 2006).

b. Walter Gellhorn, *Federal Administrative Proceedings*, 122 (Baltimore: Johns Hopkins Press, 1941).

c. Office of Management and Budget, Final Bulletin for Good Guidance Practices, *Federal Register*, 72: 3439–40 (Jan. 25, 2007).

d. Department of Labor, *Accompanying Report of the National Performance Review Office of the Vice President*, 51–52 (Washington, DC: Sept. 1993).

e. *Copcutt v. Board of Health*, 35 N.E. Reporter at 322.

h. Ernst Freund, *Administrative Powers over Persons and Property*, 17, 28, 129, 132–34 (Chicago: University of Chicago Press, 1928); James M. Landis, *The Administrative Process*, 52 (New Haven: Yale University Press, 1938); Communications Act, 47 U.S.C. §203(a)(2).

i. Ernst Freund, *Administrative Powers over Persons and Property*, 17, 28, 129, 132–34 (Chicago: University of Chicago Press, 1928).

1. 5 U.S.C. §§553 & 555–57.

2. 5 U.S.C. §§554–57; Joan Flynn, "The Costs and Benefits of 'Hiding the Ball': NLRB Policymaking and the Failure of Judicial Review," Boston University Law Review, 75: 387, 390, 413, 421, 422 (1995).

3. 5 U.S.C. §§553. For the case law requiring supporting data, see Jeffrey S. Lubbers, *A Guide to Federal Agency Rulemaking*, 283 (Chicago: American Bar Association, 2006). Some statutes also require advance notice of proposed rulemaking. Ibid., 210.

4. Negotiated Rulemaking Act (2000), 5 U.S.C. §§561–70. According to proposals in 1993 by the Department of Labor, negotiation would allow the department to "reach consensus with those affected by the rule" and thereby to "face less litigation, if not eliminate it entirely, for rules developed through this process." On this basis, the department concluded that, to avoid litigation over its rules, it "should seek opportunities to foster consensus through rulemaking." Department of Labor, *Accompanying Report of the National Performance Review Office of the Vice President*, 13, 15 (Washington, DC: Sept. 1993).

Commentators have observed that negotiated rulemaking can lead to unlawful rules that otherwise would have been challenged by one of the participants in the negotiating process. William Funk, "When Smoke Gets in Your Eyes: Regulatory Negotiation and the Public Interest: EPA's Woodstove Standards," *Environmental Law* 18: 55, 57 (1987); Peter L. Strauss, *Administrative Justice in the United States*, 254 (Durham: Carolina Academic Press, 2002).

5. *Skidmore v. Swift & Co.*, 323 U.S. 134 (1944); *Christensen v. Harris County*, 529 U.S. 576 (2000); *United States v. Mead Corp.*, 533 U.S. 218 (2000); Jeffrey S. Lubbers, *A Guide to Federal Agency Rulemaking*, 507–12 (Chicago: American Bar Association, 2006). Sometimes agencies, such as the Environmental Protection Agency, are subject to their own informal rulemaking requirements, which cannot so easily be evaded. Clean Air Act §307(d); 42 U.S.C. §7607(d).

6. John F. Manning, "Nonlegislative Rules," George Washington Law Review, 72: 893 (2004). For varying degrees of skepticism about guidance, see Robert A. Anthony, "Three Settings in Which Nonlegislative Rules Should Not Bind," Administrative Law Review, 53: 1313 (2001); Robert A. Anthony, "Interpretive Rules, Policy Statements, Guidances, Manuals, and the Like: Should Federal Agencies Use Them to Bind the Public?," Duke Law Journal, 41: 1311, 1326 (1992); John Manning, "Constitutional Structure and Judicial Deference to Agency Interpretations of Agency Rules," Columbia Law Review, 96: 612, 617 (1996); Thomas O. McGarity, "Some Thoughts on 'Deossifying' the Rulemaking Process," Duke Law Journal, 41: 1385 (1992); David Zaring, "Best Practices," New York University Law Review, 81: 294 (2006). For a summary of so-called *Skidmore* deference and "respect," see *Christensen v. Harris County*, 529 U.S. 576, 587 (2000); Jeffrey S. Lubbers, *A Guide to Federal Agency Rulemaking*, 507–20 (Chicago: American Bar Association, 2006).

7. For the arm-twisting, see Lars Noah, "Administrative Arm-Twisting in the Shadow of Congressional Delegations of Authority," Wisconsin Law Review, 873, 874 (1997).

8. For example, it has been observed that, rather than rely on waivers to achieve "situational justice" or "equity," the Occupational Safety and Health Administration employs them as a "central element" of its "policymaking apparatus." Peter H. Schuck, *The Limits of Law: Essays on Democratic Governance*, 163 (Boulder: Westview Press, 2000).

9. To be precise, the statute states:

    For the purpose of establishing national primary and secondary ambient air quality standards, the Administrator shall within 30 days after December 31, 1970, publish, and shall from time to time thereafter revise, a list which includes each air pollutant—(A) emissions of which, in his judgment, cause or contribute to air pollution which may reasonably be anticipated to endanger public health or welfare; (B) the presence of which in the ambient air results from numerous or diverse mobile or stationary sources; and (C) for which air quality criteria had not been issued before December 31, 1970 but for which he plans to issue air quality criteria under this section.

    42 U.S.C. §7408(a). See also *American Trucking Associations, Inc. v. Environmental Protection Agency*, 175 F.3rd 1027 (1999).

10. *Indus. Union Dept. v. Amer. Petroleum Inst.*, 448 U.S. 607, 706 (1980). See also Roscoe Pound, "The Administrative Application of Legal Standards," Annual Report of American Bar Association, 42: 12–13 (1919).

11. House of Commons, Petition of Temporal Grievances (July 7, 1610), in *Proceedings in Parliament 1610*, at 2: 261, ed. Elizabeth Read Foster (New Haven: Yale University Press, 1966).

12. An Act to Reduce the Revenue and Equalize Duties on Imports, and for Other Purposes, §3 (Oct. 1, 1890), *Public Statutes at Large of the United States*, 26: 567; *Marshall Field & Co. v. Clark*, 143 U.S. 649, 680 (1892); Tariff Act of 1922, H.R. 7456,
§§316–17, at 95–98 (Washington, DC: Government Printing Office, 1922). Along
similar lines, see *Buttfield v. Stranahan*, 192 U.S. 470 (1904). Generally, see *Tariff Acts
Passed by the Congress of the United States from 1789–1909* (Washington, DC: Government Printing Office, 1909).

13. Another possible limit on the summary abatement of public nuisances was the occasional suggestion that the abatement was limited to property of trifling value. The
Supreme Court, for example, in 1894 upheld the abatement of fishing nets on the
ground that the nets were of little value and the owners had a subsequent remedy
for the goods themselves or their value. *Lawton v. Steele*, 152 U.S. 133 (1894).

14. An Act for Promoting Public Health (Aug. 31, 1848), 11 & 12 Victoria, c. 63. The
Germans were well known for their police regulation of health, leading Robert von
Mohl to boast that "[m]edical police is both in theory and practice essentially German." Even in France, "where anything is done, German principles and arrangements are closely imitated." Robert von Mohl, *Polizei-Wissenschaft*, 135, as quoted
by Edwin Chadwick, *Report on the Sanitary Condition of the Labouring Poor* (1842), as
quoted by Noga Morag-Levine, *Chasing the Wind: Regulating Air Pollution in the Common Law State*, 71 (Princeton: Princeton University Press, 2003).

15. An Act to Create a Metropolitan Sanitary District and Board of Health . . . , Chap. 74,
§§12 & 14, *Laws of the State of New York Passed at the Eighty-Ninth Session of the Leg-
islature*, 1: 122, 125 (Albany: 1866). Section 12 authorized the power to issue ordinances by incorporating, inter alia, Internal Regulations for the Preservation of the
Public Health of the City of New York, Title III, Art. I, §2, in *Laws and Ordinances
Relative to the Preservation of the Public Health*, 31, ed. George W. Morton (New York:
Mayor & Commissioners of Health, 1860). See also Susan Wade Peabody, *Historical
Study of Legislation Regarding Public Health in the States of New York and Massachusetts*,
95 (Chicago: University of Chicago Press, 1909). For earlier grants of such powers, see ibid., 93. See also Frank J. Goodnow, "Summary Abatement of Nuisances
by Boards of Health," Columbia Law Review, 2: 203 (1902). For the 1848 English
statute and the American imitation, see Noga Morag-Levine, *Chasing the Wind:
Regulating Air Pollution in the Common Law State*, 72–73 (Princeton: Princeton University Press, 2003). For earlier German boards, see Marc Raeff, *The Well-Ordered
Police State: Social and Institutional Change through Law in the Germanies and Russia,
1600–1800*, at 131–32 (New Haven: Yale University Press, 1983); Diethelm Klippel, "Reasonable Aims of Civil Society: Concerns of the State in German Political
Theory in the Eighteenth and Early Nineteenth Centuries," in *Rethinking Leviathan:
The Eighteenth-Century State in Britain and Germany*, 81, 94, ed. John Brewer & Eckhart Hellmuth (Oxford: Oxford University Press, 1999).

16. *Metropolitan Board of Health v. Heister*, 37 N.Y. 661 (1868). A Pennsylvania case already had held that the Philadelphia Board of Health had final jurisdiction to determine the fact of a nuisance. *Kennedy v. The Board of Health*, 2 Pa. St. 366 (Pa.
Supreme Court, 1845).

17. 37 N.Y. 671–72; *People ex rel. John Copcutt v. Board of Health of City of Yonkers*, 140
N.Y. 1, 35 N.E. Reporter 320, 321 & 323 (1893).

18. Henry Bixby Hemenway, *Legal Principles of Public Health Administration*, 202 (Chicago: T. H. Flood & Co., 1914); Frank J. Goodnow, *The Principles of the Administrative*

Law of the United States, 337–38 (New York: G. P. Putnam's Sons, 1905). For the development of the notice and hearing justification in lower New York courts in the nineteenth century, and its rejection by the court of appeals, see Susan Wade Peabody, *Historical Study of Legislation Regarding Public Health in the States of New York and Massachusetts,* 95–96 (Chicago: University of Chicago Press, 1909).

19. 47 U.S.C. §301 (2001).

20. For this point, see Francis Staughton Sullivan, *Lectures on the Constitution and Laws of England,* 186 (London: 1776).

21. For a defense of the candid waiver of statutory requirements, see David J. Baron & Todd D. Rakoff, "In Defense of Big Waiver," Columbia Law Review, 113: 265 (2013).

22. For an example of how a waiver of a regulation can be a waiver of the underlying statute, see Philip Hamburger, "Health-Care Waivers and the Courts," National Review Online (Mar. 14, 2010), at http://www.nationalreview.com/articles/261982/health-care-waivers-and-courts-philip-hamburger.

23. For the *numerus clausus* principle, see Thomas W. Merrill & Henry E. Smith, "Optimal Standardization in the Law of Property: The *Numerus Clausus* Principle," Yale Law Journal, 110: 1 (2000); Henry Hansmann & Reinier Kraakman, "Property, Contract, and Verification: The *Numerus Clausus* Problem and the Divisibility of Rights," Journal of Legal Studies, 31: 373 (2002).

24. For the use of waivers to buy off opposition, see Peter H. Schuck, *The Limits of Law: Essays on Democratic Governance,* 150 (Boulder: Westview Press, 2000).

25. John Dickinson, *Administrative Justice and the Supremacy of the Law in the United States,* 89–90 (Cambridge: Harvard University Press, 1927). On the other side of the Atlantic, see also Cecil T. Carr, *Delegated Legislation,* 22–23 (Cambridge: Cambridge University Press, 1921).

INTRODUCTION TO PART 2

a. St. George Tucker, Law Lectures, 6: 220, Tucker-Coleman Papers, Mss. 39.1 T79, Box 62, Special Collections Research Center, Earl Gregg Swem Library, College of William and Mary.

1. Gary Lawson, "The Rise and Rise of the Administrative State," Harvard Law Review, 107: 1231, 1248 (1994); Caleb Nelson, "Adjudication in the Political Branches," Columbia Law Review, 107: 559, 625 (2007). See also Theodore J. Lowi, "Two Roads to Serfdom: Liberalism, Conservatism, and Administrative Power," American University Law Review, 36: 295, 303 (1987); and John Manning, "Separation of Powers As Ordinary Interpretation," Harvard Law Review, 124: 1939, 2020 (2011), although Manning takes a broad view of the "public rights" that can be adjudicated by the executive.

Richard Fallon takes seriously the risks of the administrative adjudication but assumes that judicial review, even with some deference, is a sufficient remedy. Richard H. Fallon, "Of Legislative Courts, Administrative Agencies, and Article III," Harvard Law Review, 10: 915, 984, 989 (1998). James Pfander similarly recognizes the dangers but offers another, more textual justification of administrative adjudication, suggesting that Congress's power "[t]o constitute tribunals inferior to the supreme Court" reveals an authority for administrative tribunals outside the courts. James E. Pfander, "Article I Tribunals, Article III Courts, and the Judicial Power of the United States," Harvard Law Review, 118: 643, 650 (2004). The tribunals inferior to the president cannot easily be understood as tribunals inferior to the Supreme Court, except in the very different sense that all governmental bodies are subject to the adjudications of the courts.

2. Roscoe Pound, "The Judicial Office in the United States," *Proceedings of the 20th Annual Session of the Iowa State Bar Association*, 104–05 (1914).

CHAPTER EIGHT

1. [Richard Cosin], *An Apologie for Sundrie Proceedings by Jurisdiction Ecclesiasticall*, 2: 1–2 (London: [1593]). In the original, there are parentheses around the words "by law."

    Academic lawyers justified this jurisdiction over extralegal offenses by claiming that they "may be Englished by the general term of *misdemeanors*." Ibid., 2. Such offenses, however, obviously were more than merely misdemeanors. Richard Crompton—a common law expert on jurisdiction—more candidly observed that, although some of the misdemeanors punished in Star Chamber were among those punishable by the law of the land, the rest were "such as receive no special punishment, by either the common or statute law." Laying out the civilian justification, he explained that these crimes were those that "in the civil law are called *crimina extraordinaria*— crimes requiring extraordinary punishment, for which no certain punishment exists, but for which there is arbitrary judicial commitment. [Richard Crompton], *Star-Chamber Cases, Shewing What Causes Properly Belong to the Cognizance of That Court*, 11 (preamble) (London: 1630) ("in the civil law [they] are called *crimina extraordinaria quia extra ordine puniuntur, unde certæ nullæ pænæ existunt; sed arbitrio iudicis committuntur*"), citing Justinian, *Digest*, XXXXVII.11.

    The offense of seditious libel illustrates how this extralegal jurisdiction was apt to be abused. The common law recognized "libels," or written defamations, to be criminal, on the ground that they were apt to provoke quarrels. But it did not distinctively punish those written against government officials. Not content with this, the Star Chamber around 1600 began to prosecute such defamation as "seditious libels," thus developing a new, more serious criminal charge on the theory that the offenders were "not sufficiently provided for by the laws otherwise." [Richard Crompton], *Star-Chamber Cases, Shewing What Causes Properly Belong to the Cognizance of That Court*, 10 (preamble) (London: 1630). Precisely because the law did not punish seditious libels, the Star Chamber claimed jurisdiction to do so.

2. William Hudson, "A Treatise of the Court of Star Chamber," in *Collectanea Juridica*, 2: 107, ed. Francis Hargrave (London: 1792). The treatise was written no later than 1621. Thomas Barnes, "Mr. Hudson's Star Chamber," in *Tudor Rule and Revolution: Essays for G. R. Elton from His American Friends*, 286, ed. DeLloyd J. Guth & John W. McKenna (Cambridge: Cambridge University Press, 2008).

3. An Act Giving the Court of Starchamber Authority to Punish Divers Misdemeanors, 3 Henry VII, c. 1 (1487); *Select Cases before the King's Council in the Star Chamber Commonly Called the Court of Star Chamber, A.D. 1477–1509*, at lix–lxi, ed. I. S. Leadam (London: Selden Society, 1902).

4. Certainly, the statute confirmed the court's controverted power to examine defendants on oath. Ibid., lxiv.

    J. H. Baker seems to hint that in 1487 the Court of Star Chamber was not yet a distinct court that could be distinguished from a regular meeting of the king's council. He also suggests that the 1487 statute concerned a "special tribunal" of the council, the jurisdiction of which was later "absorbed into that of the Star Chamber." In support of these conclusions, he notes that "it was not until 1540 that the Court of Star Chamber and the Privy Council became so separate that they had their own officials and records," and that the marginal note, "pro Camera Stellata," which appears in the Parliament Rolls at the head of the 1487 statute, "seems to have been an interpolation." J. H. Baker, *An Introduction to English Legal History*, 102 (London: Butterworths, 1979). The blurred line between the council and its meetings as a court in Star Chamber, however, does not mean that there was not yet a Court of Star Chamber. Indeed, the title of the 1487 statute, as recorded in the Parliament Rolls, is "An act giving the court of Starchamber authority to punish various misdemeanours." It therefore seems mistaken to suggest, on the one hand, that the Star Chamber was not yet really distinct from the council and, on the other, that the 1487 statute established a distinct special tribunal. Although the evidence is spare, it indicates that there already was a Court of Star Chamber, which was developing as an extension of the council, and that Parliament gave it expanded jurisdiction. For the judicial role of the council and the Star Chamber's early history, see *Select Cases before the King's Council in the Star Chamber Commonly Called the Court of Star Chamber, A.D. 1477–1509*, at lix–lxxi, ed. I. S. Leadam (London: Selden Society, 1902).

5. This was notably the case with Archbishop John Whitgift's 1583 *Articles Touching Preachers*. See *Select Statutes and Other Constitutional Documents Illustrative of the Reigns of Elizabeth and James I*, at xxxix, ed. G. W. Prothero (Oxford: Clarendon Press, 1913).

6. Ibid., xliv.

7. Commission, 42 Ass. pl. 5 (1368). The words of the judges were recited in *The Argument of Master Nicholas Fuller, in the Case of Thomas Ladd, and Richard Maunsell*, 16 (n.p.: 1607). Whitelocke relied on this as a case "where the judges took away a commission from one, that had the power given by it to him under the great seal, to take ones person, and to seize his goods before he was indicted." [James Whitelocke], *A Learned and Necessary Argument To Prove that Each Subject Hath a Proprietary in His Goods*, 16 (London: 1641). See also Coke, *Institutes*, 2: 54; Matthew Bacon, *A New Abridgment of the Law*, 4: 174 (London: 1778), citing, inter alia, Brooke, *Abridgment*, Commissions 3, 15, 16.

8. *Reports from the Lost Notebooks of Sir James Dyer*, 1: 24, ed. J. H. Baker (London: Selden Society, 1994); *The Reports of Sir John Spelman*, 2: 380, ed. J. H. Baker (London: Selden Society, 1977).

9. *Scroggs v. Coleshill* (1559), Dyer, *Reports*, 2: 175b; *Reports from the Lost Notebooks of Sir James Dyer*, 1: 24, ed. J. H. Baker (London: Selden Society, 1994); *The Reports of Sir John Spelman*, 2: 380, ed. J. H. Baker (London: Selden Society, 1977); J. H. Baker, "Personal Liberty under the Common Law, 1200–1600," in *The Common Law Tradition: Lawyers, Books and the Law*, 343–44 (London: Hambledon Press, 2000). The final quote comes from [James Whitelocke], *A Learned and Necessary Argument To Prove that Each Subject Hath a Proprietary in His Goods*, 16 (London: 1641). See also *The Argument of Master Nicholas Fuller, in the Case of Thomas Ladd, and Richard Maunsell*, 17 (n.p.: 1607).

10. House of Commons, Petition of Temporal Grievances (July 7, 1610), in *Proceedings in Parliament 1610*, at 2: 260, ed. Elizabeth Read Foster (New Haven: Yale University Press, 1966).

11. [James Morice], *A Briefe Treatise of Oathes, Exacted by Ordinaries and Ecclesiastical Judges, To Aunswere Generalie to All Such Articles or Interrogatories as Pleaseth them to*

Propound: And of Their Forced and Constrained Oathes Ex Officio, Wherein is Proved that the Same are Unlawful, 50 ([Middleburg: c. 1590]); Order (Oct. 15, 1602), in *Les Reportes del Cases in Camera Stellata 1593 to 1609*, at 157, by John Hawarde, ed. William Paley Baildon (Privately Printed: 1894); *Anon.* (1627), in *The Star Chamber: Notices of the Court and Its Proceedings*, 98, by John Southerden Burn (London: 1870). For more on resistance to the commission's process and sentences, see Roland G. Usher, *The Rise and Fall of the High Commission*, 124 (Oxford: Clarendon Press, 1968).

12. Ethan H. Shagan, "The English Inquisition: Constitutional Conflict and Ecclesiastical Law in the 1590s," Historical Journal, 47: 541–43 (2004).

13. *The Argument of Master Nicholas Fuller, in the Case of Thomas Ladd, and Richard Maunsell*, 3 (n.p.: 1607).

14. William Hudson, "A Treatise of the Court of Star Chamber," in *Collectanea Juridica*, 2: 4–5, ed. Francis Hargrave (London: 1792). See also, for example, ibid., 16.

15. An Act for the Regulating of the Privy Council and for Taking Away the Court Commonly called the Star Chamber, 16 Charles I, c. 10 (1641). (Commas have been added silently for ease of reading.)

16. An Act for the Repeal of a Branch of a Statute Primo Elizabeth Concerning Commissioners for Causes Ecclesiastical, 16 Charles I, c. 11 (1641). (Commas have been added silently for ease of reading.) Later in the century, after the Interregnum, the High Commission was revived, but not for long.

17. An Act for the Regulating of the Privy Council and for Taking Away the Court Commonly called the Star Chamber, 16 Charles I, c. 10 (1641); Roger Twysden, *Certaine Considerations upon the Government of England*, 87 (London: Camden Society, 1849). Note that when Parliament made its declaration about the ordinary course of the law, it did not mention persons, for the king and his council (as will be seen in chap. 11) were understood to have a narrow emergency power of arrest.

18. Philip Hamburger, *Law and Judicial Duty*, 125–26 (Cambridge: Harvard University Press, 2008).

19. Letter from Thomas Jefferson to Philip Mazzei (Nov. 1785), in *Papers of Thomas Jefferson*, 9: 69, ed. Julian P. Boyd (Princeton: Princeton University Press, 1954); Extracts from Law-Writers, 99 (entry dated Dec. 12, 1787), William Plumer Papers, Reel 19, Library of Congress. According the printed report, which Plumer was merely summarizing, Mansfield said: "A court of equity is as much bound by positive rules and general maxims concerning property (though the reason of them may now have ceased,) as a court of law is." *Doe, ex dismiss. Long v. Laming* (K.B. 1760), Burrow, *Reports*, 2: 1108. This was also echoed in *The Works of James Wilson*, 2: 479, ed. Robert Green McCloskey (Cambridge: Belknap Press, 1967).

20. Jean Louis DeLolme, *The Constitution of England; or, An Account of the English Government*, 294 (II.xvii) (Indianapolis: Liberty Classics, 2007).

21. Ibid., 294–95 (II.xvii).

22. Ibid., 241 (II.xvi).

CHAPTER NINE

1. See Philip Hamburger, *Law and Judicial Duty*, chap. 5 (Cambridge: Harvard University Press, 2008).

2. Ibid., 159–60.

3. *Year Books of Edward II*, 12: 17 (the volume for 5 Edward II., 1312), ed. William Craddock Bolland (London: Selden Society, 1916). As observed by Holdsworth,

there were other instances in which the judges do not seem to have been so independent, but at least some of them are easily distinguishable. William Holdsworth, *A History of English Law*, 2: 561–64 (London: Sweet & Maxwell: 2003).

4. J. C. Holt, *Magna Charta*, 461 (Cambridge: Cambridge University Press, 1992); *The Book of Oaths and the Several Forms Thereof, both Ancient and Modern*, 121–22 (London: 1689) (translating oath enrolled and printed with 20 Edward III, c. 1 (1346)). Although this oath was often in later centuries associated with 18 Edward III, this point is corrected in *Statutes of the Realm*, 1: 306.

5. *De Natura Legis Naturæ* (I.xvi), in *The Works of Sir John Fortesque*, 1: 205, ed. Thomas Fortescue (London: 1869).

6. See Philip Hamburger, *Law and Judicial Duty*, 514–15 (Cambridge: Harvard University Press, 2008).

7. Coke, *Institutes*, 2: 51; Giles Jacob, *Law Dictionary*, sig. Fff2[v] ("judge") (London: 1732). For further details, see Philip Hamburger, *Law and Judicial Duty*, chap. 4 (Cambridge: Harvard University Press, 2008).

8. *The Book of Oaths*, 3 (London: 1689); *The Book of Oaths*, 144–45 (London: 1649). For the personnel of the Star Chamber, see *A Brief Collection of the Queenes Majesties Most High and Most Honorable Courtes of Recordes*, Camden Miscellany, 20: 22–23, Camden Third Series, vol. 83 (London: Royal Historical Society, 1953).

9. Philip Hamburger, *Law and Judicial Duty*, chaps. 18 & 19 (Cambridge: Harvard University Press, 2008).

10. Theodore F. T. Plucknett, *A Concise History of the Common Law*, 459 (Boston: Little, Brown & Co., 1956).

11. Jean Louis DeLolme, *The Constitution of England; or, An Account of the English Government*, 201 (II.xii) (Indianapolis: Liberty Classics, 2007).

12. [John Hawles], *The Englishmans Right: A Dialogue between a Barrister at Law, and a Jury-Man*, 5 (London: 1680).

13. An Act for Granting and Applying Certain Stamp Duties . . . , 5 George III, c. 12 (1765).

14. *Hale and Fleetwood on Admiralty Jurisdiction*, liii, ed. M. J. Prichard & D. E. C. Yale (London: Selden Society, 1993). Notwithstanding the allegation about the high seas, some overlapping of jurisdictions was allowed, such as for goods spoiled at sea and then sold on land and for some actions for wages. Ibid., lvi, xci.

15. Instructions Adopted by the Braintree Town Meeting (Sept. 24, 1765), in *Papers of John Adams*, 1: 138–39 (Cambridge: Belknap Press, 1977); Resolutions of the Stamp Act Congress (Oct. 19, 1765), in *Documents of American History*, 58, ed. Henry Steele Commager (New York: Appleton, Century, Crofts, 1948).

16. An Act for the Better Securing the Dependency of this Majesty's Dominions in America upon the Crown and Parliament of Great Britain, 6 George III, c. 12 (1766).

17. "To the Printers," Boston Gazette and Country Journal (July 15, 1765); "Continued from our last," New-London Gazette [aka Connecticut Gazette] (Oct. 11, 1765).

18. N.J. Const. of 1776, Art. XXII.

19. In England, civil cases for more than forty shillings were within the jurisdiction of the common law and its courts—thus making forty shillings the point at which the right to a jury traditionally began in non-criminal cases. In some American states, this starting point for common law jurisdiction had been allowed to rise—in New Jersey, for example, it had risen to six pounds. Below such a threshold, the legislature could give justices of the peace a summary jurisdiction over civil claims without violating the right to a jury, but above the jurisdictional threshold, there was a right

to a jury in a regular court of law. This was the floor not merely for the jurisdiction of the courts, but more generally for the law itself. State legislatures therefore could not give much judicial power to justices of the peace without colliding with their constitutions. Philip Hamburger, *Law and Judicial Duty*, 410–11 (Cambridge: Harvard University Press, 2008).

20. Letter from Nathaniel Scudder to Henry Laurens (June 17, 1780), Dreer Collection, Members of Old Congress, Vol. 8:2, p. 111, Pennsylvania Historical Society, Philadelphia, discussed by Michael S. Adelberg, "A Combination to Trample All Law Underfoot," *New Jersey History*, 115: 3, 11 (1997).

21. N.J. Const. of 1776, Art. XXII.

22. For details of the case and why it is clear that the court held the act unconstitutional, see Philip Hamburger, *Law and Judicial Duty*, 407–22 (Cambridge: Harvard University Press, 2008).

23. *Macgregore v. Furber*, Rockingham County Inferior Court, Minute Book, New Entries, May term 1786, Case No. 113, New Hampshire State Archives. For other cases, see Philip Hamburger, *Law and Judicial Duty*, 422–35 (Cambridge: Harvard University Press, 2008).

24. An Act for the Recovery of Small Debts in an Expeditious Way and Manner, Original Acts (Nov. 9, 1785), New Hampshire State Archives; "A Citizen" (Dec. 8, 1785), *New Hampshire Gazette* (Dec. 16, 1785).

25. *Macgregore v. Furber*, Certified Record of Judgment, Rockingham County Superior Court Record No. 9320, New Hampshire State Archives; *Macgregore v. Furber*, Rockingham County Inferior Court, Minute Book, New Entries, May term 1786, Case No. 113, New Hampshire State Archives.

CHAPTER TEN

b. *A True Copy of the Lord Andevers Two Speeches To the Lords in Parliament; The One Concerning the Star-Chamber; The Other Concerning the Pacification: Both of Which Were Formerly Corrupted and Abused by a False Copy Printed*, 2 (London: 1641).

c. Edward Coke, *Institutes*, 2: 50.

1. Richard H. Helmholz, "The Privilege and the *Ius Commune*: The Middle Ages to the Seventeenth Century," in *The Privilege against Self-Incrimination: Its Origins and Development*, 36–38, by Charles M. Grey, John H. Langbein, et al. (Chicago: University of Chicago, 1997).

2. [James Morice], *A Briefe Treatise of Oathes, Exacted by Ordinaries and Ecclesiastical Judges, To Aunswere Generalie to All Such Articles or Interrogatories as Pleaseth them to Propound: And of Their Forced and Constrained Oathes Ex Officio, Wherein is Proved that the Same are Unlawful*, 30 ([Middleburg: c. 1590]). Thus, "in causes capital or otherwise criminal, these our laws neither urge by oath nor force by torment any man to accuse or excuse himself, but reject the oath as unbeseeming a well governed state or commonwealth." Ibid., 31. Similarly, in Parliament, he carefully said "wrested oaths" were "contrary to all legal proceedings" as "we are constrained to be . . . accusers . . . of ourselves." Speech of James Morice (Feb. 27, 1593), in *Proceedings in the Parliaments of Elizabeth I*, 3: 31–32, ed. T. E. Hartley (London: Leicester University Press, 1995).

Even a civilian such as Cosin acknowledged that "it is not holden by any law in England, nor by practice of any court here used; that a man should be examined upon his oath, touching a crime, whereby his life or any of his limbs may be endangered." [Richard Cosin], *An Apologie for Sundrie Proceedings by Jurisdiction Ecclesias-ticall*, 2: 38 (London: [1593]). He similarly conceded that "the defendant's oath in cause capital, neither is used nor allowed by the laws of this realm." Ibid., 2: 68.

3. [James Morice], *A Briefe Treatise of Oathes, Exacted by Ordinaries and Ecclesiastical Judges, To Aunswere Generalie to All Such Articles or Interrogatories as Pleaseth them to Propound: And of Their Forced and Constrained Oathes Ex Officio, Wherein is Proved that the Same are Unlawful*, 9 ([Middleburg: c. 1590]). The oath as used in the High Commission was "You shall swear to answer all such interrogatories as shall be offered unto you and declare your whole knowledge therein, so God help you." Mary Ballantine Hume, *The History of the Oath Ex Officio in England*, 6 (Ph.D. thesis, Harvard University, 1923).

4. *Earl of Kent's Case* (May 1, 1605), in *Les Reportes del Cases in Camera Stellata 1593 to 1609*, at 203–04, by John Hawarde, ed. William Paley Baildon (Privately Printed: 1894). For the exclusion of interrogatories taken in the ecclesiastical courts, see ibid., and for the exclusion of examinations in Chancery, see ibid., 270. Levy argues that there were different standards for different courts, not yet a rule against self-incrimination, but recognizes that the problem was not confined to the High Commission. Leonard W. Levy, *Origins of the Fifth Amendment: The Right against Self-Incrimination*, 257 (New York: Oxford University Press, 1968).

5. In 1587, the Star Chamber ordered that when defendants, after admonition, failed to "make direct answers" to interrogatories, they were to be committed to the Fleet prison and ordered to pay costs to the plaintiff. Case 288, Order of Star Chamber (Oct. 27, 1587), Star Chamber Reports, f. 89[r–v], Harvard Law School Ms. 1128, in English Legal Manuscripts, R-54 (Fiche H-1776–329 to 335). Similarly, see order (May 25, 1596), John Hawarde, *Les Reportes del Cases in Camera Stellata 1593 to 1609*, at 46, ed., William Paley Baildon (Privately Printed: 1894).

    In 1597, the Star Chamber added that the failure to answer interrogatories amounted to a confession. In a prosecution brought by a private party in Star Chamber, Attorney General Coke secured an order of the court that "if the defendant will not answer [interrogatories], *tenetur pro confesso*"—held to be confession. "[T]hus, if a man prefers a bill and [the defendant] will not answer, it is not held as a confession; but on this answer the plaintiff shall serve interrogatories, and if the defendant will not answer these, *tenetur pro confesso*." *Rede v. Boothes* (Nov. 4, 1597), ibid., 90. Similarly, see ibid., 74. Although Mary Hume discusses such issues, she confuses the evidence on refusal to answer the charges and refusal to answer interrogatories. Mary Ballantine Hume, *The History of the Oath Ex Officio in England*, 121–22 (Harvard Ph.D. Thesis 1923).

    Incidentally, Coke and his colleagues opined in 1606 that the High Commission could not use force to impose questions before charges were brought. At least by 1631, however, the commissioners got around this by relying on the *pro confesso* presumption. Roland G. Usher, *The Rise and Fall of the High Commission*, 247–48 (Oxford: Clarendon Press, 1968). For examples, see ibid.; the case of Nathaniel Wickens (c. 1636), in *The High Commission: Notices of the Court, and Its Proceedings*, 28, by John Southerden Burn (London: 1865); Henry E. I. Phillips, "The Last Years of the Court of Star Chamber 1630–41," Transactions of the Royal Historical Society, 4th ser., 21: 103, 113–14 (1939).

6. William Hudson, "A Treatise of the Court of Star Chamber," in *Collectanea Juridica*, 2: 127, ed. Francis Hargrave (London: 1792); John Southerden Burn, *The Star Chamber: Notices of the Court and Its Proceedings*, 49–50 (London: 1870); *Select Cases before*

the King's Council in the Star Chamber Commonly Called the Court of Star Chamber, A.D. 1477–1509, at xvii, ed. I. S. Leadam (London: Selden Society, 1902). For the prevalence of *ore tenus* proceedings, see *Reports from the Lost Notebooks of Sir James Dyer*, 1: lxxxviii, ed. J. H. Baker (London: Selden Society, 1994).

7. *Att. Gen. v. Johnes* (1600), in *Les Reportes del Cases in Camera Stellata 1593 to 1609*, at 116, by John Hawarde, ed. William Paley Baildon (Privately Printed: 1894). In theory, the defendant had to confess before being thus hauled into court and summarily convicted, but in reality mere obstinacy sufficed. Henry E. I. Phillips, "The Last Years of the Court of Star Chamber 1630–41," Transactions of the Royal Historical Society, 4th ser., 21: at 113 (1939). In 1607, when Coke was chief justice of common pleas, he protested that "on *ore tenus* they ought only to proceed on confession, and not otherwise, notwithstanding it appear plainly to be true." John Hawarde, *Les Reportes del Cases in Camera Stellata 1593 to 1609*, at 330, ed. William Paley Baildon (Privately Printed: 1894).

8. Leonard W. Levy, *Origins of the Fifth Amendment: The Right against Self-Incrimination*, 301, 304, 307, 313 (New York: Oxford University Press, 1968); M. R. T. MacNair, "The Early Development of the Privilege against Self-Incrimination," Oxford Journal of Legal Studies, 10: 66 (1990); J. H. Langbein, "The Criminal Trial before the Lawyers," University of Chicago Law Review, 45: 263 (1978); John Langbein, "The Historical Origins of the Privilege against Self-Incrimination at Common Law," Michigan Law Review, 92: 1047, 1048 (1994); John Lanbein, "The Privilege and Common Law Criminal Procedure: The Sixteenth to the Eighteenth Centuries," in *The Privilege against Self-Incrimination: Its Origins and Development*, 82, by Charles M. Grey, John H. Langbein, et al. (Chicago: University of Chicago, 1997); John H. Wigmore, "The Privilege against Self-Crimination: Its History," Harvard Law Review, 15: 633 (1902).

9. *A Short Discourse; Being the Judgment of Several of the Most Learned Doctors of the Civil Law; Concerning the Practise of their Courts, and of the Oath Ex Officio*, in *The Life and Acts of the Most Reverend Father in God, John Whitgift*, appendix to bk. III, at 137, by John Strype (London: 1718); [Richard Cosin], *An Apologie for Sundrie Proceedings by Jurisdiction Ecclesiasticall*, 3: 51, 53 (London: [1593]). For the history of arguments that such proceedings were medicinal rather than punitive, see Richard H. Helmholz, "The Privilege and the *Ius Commune*: The Middle Ages to the Seventeenth Century," in *The Privilege against Self-Incrimination: Its Origins and Development*, 30, by Charles M. Grey, John H. Langbein, et al. (Chicago: University of Chicago, 1997).

10. [Richard Cosin], *An Apologie for Sundrie Proceedings by Jurisdiction Ecclesiasticall*, 3: 113 (London: [1593]); York Commission Act Book, as quoted by Roland G. Usher, *The Rise and Fall of the High Commission*, vi, xxx–xxxi, xxxiii (Oxford: Clarendon Press, 1968); Coke, *Institutes*, 4: 238; *Th'Appelation of Iohn Penrie, Unto the Highe Courte of Parliament*, 43 (n.p.: 1589). In Star Chamber, private complainants could recover relief, such as damages or "restitution of that which is unjustly taken away by force or fraud," but such cases gave rise to both punishment and recompense, and they therefore were understood to be criminal in nature, even if also partly civil. William Hudson, "A Treatise of the Court of Star Chamber," in *Collectanea Juridica*, 2: 225–27, ed. Francis Hargrave (London: 1792). For speculation about the fate of early civil complaints in Star Chamber, see *Select Cases before the King's Council in the Star Chamber Commonly Called the Court of Star Chamber, A.D. 1477–1509*, at lxviii, ed. I. S. Leadam (London: Selden Society, 1902).

11. A Short Discourse; Being the Judgment of Several of the Most Learned Doctors of the Civil Law, in *The Life and Acts of the Most Reverend Father in God, John Whitgift*, appendix to bk. III, at 136–37, by John Strype (London: 1718). (The *Short Discourse* probably was drafted in large part by Richard Cosin.) More generally, see Richard H. Helmholz, "The Privilege and the *Ius Commune*: The Middle Ages to the Seventeenth Century," in *The Privilege against Self-Incrimination: Its Origins and Development*, 28, by Charles M. Grey, John H. Langbein, et al. (Chicago: University of Chicago, 1997). Defending directly incriminating questioning, Cosin wrote: "I hear . . . that *in the Star-Chamber a man is not driven to answer directly to the fact itself, but only to the circumstances of the fact, as was in Trussers Case, as is said.*" To this he responded, "But I am certainly informed . . . that the practice of that court is clean otherwise." [Richard Cosin], *An Apologie for Sundrie Proceedings by Jurisdiction Ecclesiasticall*, 3: 55 (London: [1593]).

 Technically, in the canon law, *fama* was a matter of "common report" or rumor, but the term seems often to have been used rather loosely in connection with High Commission proceedings to include most sorts of suspicion, however poorly verified. For a brief summary of the more traditional technical distinctions, see Leonard W. Levy, *Origins of the Fifth Amendment: The Right against Self-Incrimination*, 23 (New York: Oxford University Press, 1968). For the decline of "preliminary inquests to establish existence of *fama publica* before subjecting defendants to the oath," see Richard H. Helmholz, "The Privilege and the *Ius Commune*: The Middle Ages to the Seventeenth Century," in *The Privilege Against Self-Incrimination: Its Origins and Development*, 41, by Charles M. Grey, John H. Langbein, et al., (Chicago: University of Chicago, 1997). When English civilians in the 1590s were put on the defensive, they spoke of how "when by circumstance once known abroad," persons come to be "vehemently suspected," they were subject to the "suspicion and fame of crimes." A Short Discourse, in *The Life and Acts of . . . Whitgift*, appendix to bk. III, at 136, by John Strype (London: 1718).

12. Ibid., 137; [Richard Cosin], *An Apologie for Sundrie Proceedings by Jurisdiction Ecclesiasticall*, 2: 45 (London: [1593]); [James Morice], *A Briefe Treatise of Oathes, Exacted by Ordinaries and Ecclesiastical Judges, To Aunswere Generalie to All Such Articles or Interrogatories as Pleaseth them to Propound: And of Their Forced and Constrained Oathes Ex Officio, Wherein is Proved that the Same are Unlawful*, 21 ([Middleburg: c. 1590]). Morice's care in critiquing the civilians is revealed by how exactly he quoted the *Short Discourse*.

13. [James Morice], *A Briefe Treatise of Oathes, Exacted by Ordinaries and Ecclesiastical Judges, To Aunswere Generalie to All Such Articles or Interrogatories as Pleaseth them to Propound: And of Their Forced and Constrained Oathes Ex Officio, Wherein is Proved that the Same are Unlawful*, 8 ([Middleburg: c. 1590]); William Hudson, "A Treatise of the Court of Star Chamber," in *Collectanea Juridica*, 2: 169, ed. Francis Hargrave (London: 1792). Penry complained of "tyrannous inquisition" like that of Spain in the High Commission. *Th'Appelation of Iohn Penrie, Unto the Highe Courte of Parliament*, 43 (n.p.: 1589). Indeed, Lord Burghley told Archbishop Whitgift that "the inquisitions of Spain use not so many questions to comprehend and trap their preys," and that "this kind of proceeding is too much favoring the Romish inquisition." Letter from William, Lord Burghley to Archbishop Whitgift (July 1, 1584), in *The High Commission: Notices of the Court, and Its Proceedings*, 13, by John Southerden Burn (London: 1865). For the date, see *Calendar of State Papers, Domestic Series, of the Reign of Elizabeth, 1581–1590*, at 2: 188, ed. Robert Lemon (London: 1865). For

other allusions to the Spanish inquisition, see Mary Ballantine Hume, *The History of the Oath Ex Officio in England*, 75, 79, 80, 94, 116 (Ph.D. thesis, Harvard University, 1923)

14. Speech of James Morice (Feb. 27, 1593), in *Proceedings in the Parliaments of Elizabeth I*, 3: 32, ed. T. E. Hartley (London: Leicester University Press, 1995). The narrow concern about the commission's statutory jurisdiction led the common law judges in 1606 to conclude that "though where parties are proceeded withal *ex officio*, there needeth no libel, yet ought they to have the cause made known unto them for which they are called *ex officio*, before they be examined, to the end it may be appear unto them before their examination, whether the cause be of ecclesiastical cognizance, otherwise they ought not to examine them upon oath." Coke, *Institutes*, 2: 616. For another version of the opinion, see *An Oath before an Ecclesiastical Judge Ex Officio*, Coke, *Reports*, 12: 26.

15. *The Argument of Master Nicholas Fuller, in the Case of Thomas Ladd, and Richard Maunsell*, 3 (n.p.: 1607).

16. [Richard Cosin], *An Apologie for Sundrie Proceedings by Jurisdiction Ecclesiasticall*, 3: 53 (London: [1593]).

17. An Act for the Repeal of a Branch of a Statute Primo Elizabeth Concerning Commissioners for Causes Ecclesiastical, 16 Charles I, c. 11 (1641). (Commas have been added silently for ease of reading.)

18. Leonard W. Levy, *Origins of the Fifth Amendment: The Right against Self-Incrimination*, 301, 304, 307, 313 (New York: Oxford University Press, 1968); M. R. T. MacNair, "The Early Development of the Privilege against Self-Incrimination," Oxford Journal of Legal Studies, 10: 66 (1990); J. H. Langbein, "The Criminal Trial before the Lawyers," University of Chicago Law Review, 45: 263 (1978). See also John H. Wigmore, "The Privilege against Self-Crimination: Its History," Harvard Law Review, 15: 633 (1902).

    The scholarship on the subject has suffered from a whiggish search for the origins of the common law "rule" against self-incrimination, with the resulting tendency to omit what is not a rule adopted in a holding by a court—as when a recent article sharply distinguishes between "oppositional use" and "legal use" of the rule, a distinction that tends to downplay the elements that contributed to constitutional ideas. See, for example, M. R. T. MacNair, "The Early Development of the Privilege against Self-Incrimination," Oxford Journal of Legal Studies, 10: 70 (1990). Indeed, the search for *the rule* and its origins is even more broadly misleading because the legal arguments against self-incrimination were diverse and not all of them ended up producing the later rule.

19. Virginia Bill of Rights of 1776; Leonard W. Levy, *Origins of the Fifth Amendment: The Right against Self-Incrimination*, 409 (New York: Oxford University Press, 1968).

20. Speech of James Morice (Feb. 27, 1593), in *Proceedings in the Parliaments of Elizabeth I*, 3: 34, ed. T. E. Hartley (London: Leicester University Press, 1995); Treatise on the Oath *Ex Officio*, in *Cartwrightiana*, 43, ed. Albert Peel & Leland H. Carlson (London: George Allen & Unwin, 1951), quoting Fox's account of a letter to Thomas Phillips from his congregation.

    Another critic wrote: "Let the party accused stand on the one side and the accuser on the other side and let the judge sit, and judge the cause"; otherwise the king would be "a murderer before God." Treatise on the Oath *Ex Officio*, in *Cartwrightiana*, 44, ed. Albert Peel & Leland H. Carlson (London: George Allen & Unwin, 1951).

21. William Hudson, "A Treatise of the Court of Star Chamber," in *Collectanea Juridica*, 2: 126, ed. Francis Hargrave (London: 1792); Speech of James Morice (Feb. 27, 1593), in *Proceedings in the Parliaments of Elizabeth I*, 3: 31, ed. T. E. Hartley (London: Leicester University Press, 1995). See also Morice's account of proceedings "upon secret, malicious, and sinister information, and sometimes again upon bare and naked suspicion." Ibid., 36.

    According to a noted civilian, a judge could act "either upon relation made unto him by some other, or upon his own mere motion, without any relation from others." [Richard Cosin], *An Apologie for Sundrie Proceedings by Jurisdiction Ecclesiasticall*, 2: 6 (London: [1593]). Thus, "an ordinary or delegate . . . that proceedeth of office, is not bound to make proofs of the same (saving before his superior judge, if an appellation be brought and do lie) because it sufficeth, that the same is apparent and known upon himself." Ibid., 2: 36–37. As in the Continental inquisition, informal "[d]enunciation" was valued as "a special means of stirring up the office" of the judge. This was "[a] relating of some man's crime unto a judge, to the end to have the offender reformed or punished; yet without that solemn inscription by the denouncer, which the law requires in an accusation." Ibid., 2: 38. Being a "general inquiry," rather than a "special inquiry," it allowed the judge to "secretly receive the witnesses depositions in writing (for the information of the court) before the supposed offender be cited." Ibid., 2: 53, 56.

22. [Richard Cosin], *An Apologie for Sundrie Proceedings by Jurisdiction Ecclesiasticall*, 1: 54 (London: [1593]) (quoting one of his opponents); *Certain Considerations Touching the Better Pacification and Edification of the Church of England* (1604), in *Works of Francis Bacon*, 2: 519 (London: 1826); *The Argument of Master Nicholas Fuller, in the Case of Thomas Ladd, and Richard Maunsell*, 26 (n.p.: 1607).

23. *The Christian Mans Triall: or, A True Relation of the First Apprehension and Several Examinations of John Lilburne*, 7–8, 2nd ed. (London: 1641).

24. [James Morice], *A Briefe Treatise of Oathes, Exacted by Ordinaries and Ecclesiastical Judges, To Aunswere Generalie to All Such Articles or Interrogatories as Pleaseth them to Propound: And of Their Forced and Constrained Oathes Ex Officio, Wherein is Proved that the Same are Unlawful*, 9 ([Middleburg: c. 1590]); *The Argument of Master Nicholas Fuller, in the Case of Thomas Ladd, and Richard Maunsell*, 4 (n.p.: 1607). One defendant protested, "I desire . . . that I may not have them both for mine accusers and judges." *Th'Appelation of Iohn Penrie, Unto the Highe Courte of Parliament*, 49 (n.p.: 1589).

25. The commission instructed the commissioners that "if you find any who either shall deny to lend [to] us, or shall make delays or excuses, let them know they do thereby incur our high displeasure; and if they persist in their obstinacy notwithstanding that, then you shall examine such persons upon oath, whether he hath been dealt withal . . . to refuse to lend, or to make excuse for his not lending: who hath so dealt with him, and what speeches or persuasions he or they have used, tending to that purpose." Instructions Which Our Commissioners for the Loan of Money are Exactly and Effectually to Observe and Follow, in *The Constitutional Documents of the Puritan Revolution, 1625–1660*, at 55, ed. Samuel Rawson Gardiner (Oxford: Clarendon Press, 1958). See also Leonard W. Levy, *Origins of the Fifth Amendment: The Right against Self-Incrimination*, 262 (New York: Oxford University Press, 1968).

26. Petition of Right, 3 Charles I, c. 1 (1628).

27. An Act for the Repeal of a Branch of a Statute Primo Elizabeth Concerning Commissioners for Causes Ecclesiastical, 16 Charles I, c. 11 (1641).

28. [James Morice], *A Briefe Treatise of Oathes, Exacted by Ordinaries and Ecclesiastical Judges, To Aunswere Generalie to All Such Articles or Interrogatories as Pleaseth them to Propound: And of Their Forced and Constrained Oathes Ex Officio, Wherein is Proved that the Same are Unlawful*, 19, 54–55 ([Middleburg: c. 1590]).

29. Coke, *Institutes*, 2: 103–04. The hidden character of the proceedings has been excused on the ground that it arose simply from the written character of the evidence. Roland G. Usher, *The Rise and Fall of the High Commission*, 113 (Oxford: Clarendon Press, 1968). The reliance on written evidence outside the courtroom, however, was part of the more general civilian reliance on judges rather than open accusations before a court and community. Usher also excuses the High Commission by suggesting that its meetings were "private" rather than "secret"—meaning that the accused and his friends usually "could find out what was going on"—as if this made it a public trial. Ibid.

30. William Sharp McKechnie, *Magna Charta: A Commentary on the Great Charter of King John*, 375 (New York: Burt Franklin, n.d.). Note that the word "and" in the final phrase is a translation of *vel*, which literally meant *or*, although here, according to McKechnie, it "almost beyond doubt" was understood to mean *and*. Ibid., 381–82.

31. 28 Edward III, c. 3 (1354); None Shall be Put to Answer Without Due Process of Law, 42 Edward III, c. 3 (1368). See also Mary Ballantine Hume, *The History of the Oath Ex Officio in England*, 17–18 (Ph.D. thesis, Harvard University, 1923).

32. Speech of James Morice (Feb. 27, 1593), in *Proceedings in the Parliaments of Elizabeth I*, 3: 32, 36, ed. T. E. Hartley (London: Leicester University Press, 1995).

33. [James Morice], *A Briefe Treatise of Oathes, Exacted by Ordinaries and Ecclesiastical Judges, To Aunswere Generalie to All Such Articles or Interrogatories as Pleaseth them to Propound: And of Their Forced and Constrained Oathes Ex Officio, Wherein is Proved that the Same are Unlawful*, 37 ([Middleburg: c. 1590]). More generally, he argued that "the king by his commission or grant, otherwise than by Parliament, may not change or alter the laws of this realm, nor the order, manner or form of the administration of justice." Ibid.

34. *The Argument of Master Nicholas Fuller, in the Case of Thomas Ladd, and Richard Maunsell*, 10 (n.p.: 1607), more or less quoting 42 Edward III, c. 3 (1368).

35. Ibid., 29.

36. House of Commons, Petition of Temporal Grievances (July 7, 1610), in *Proceedings in Parliament 1610*, at 2: 261, ed. Elizabeth Read Foster (New Haven: Yale University Press, 1966). The Commons made the second point in connection with the local versions of the Star Chamber.

37. Proceedings against Sara Jones, etc. (Lambeth, late April, 1632, & Consistory in St. Paul's, May 8, 1632), *Reports of Cases in the Courts of Star Chamber and High Commission*, 285 292, 294–95, ed. Samuel Rawson Gardiner (London: Camden Society, 1886). More than four decades earlier, Penry similarly complained that he had not been "tried by any lawful authority." *Th'Appelation of Iohn Penrie, Unto the Highe Courte of Parliament*, 50 (n.p.: 1589).

38. Edward, Earl of Clarendon, *The History of the Rebellion and Civil Wars in England Begun in the Year 1641*, at 1: 374 (Apr. 1, 1641), ed. W. Dunn MaCray (Oxford: Clarendon Press, 1888).

39. An Act for the Regulating of the Privy Council and for Taking Away the Court Commonly called the Star Chamber, 16 Charles I, c. 10 (1641). Hale shortly afterward echoed this point in various ways. Sir Matthew Hale, *The Prerogatives of the King*, 183, ed. D. E. C. Yale (London: Selden Society, 1976).

CHAPTER ELEVEN

c. Y.B., Mich. 12 Edward 3, pl. 23 (1338), in *Year Books of the Reign of King Edward the Third: Years XII and XIII*, at 54, Rolls Series no. 31, part B, vol. 2, ed. Luke Owen Pike (London 1885). Two centuries after Shareshull, Justice Anthony Fitzherbert complained about "general citations" from bishops, who "cite men to appear before them . . . without expressing any cause, are against the law." Anthony Fitzherbert, *The New Natura Brevium*, 1: 41 (London: 1794). The High Commission sometimes used general warrants, but not without protest. Shortly before Parliament abolished the commission, the House of Commons heard about the commission's conduct in *Burton's Case* and resolved that the "searching and seizing" of his books and papers were "by color of a general warrant dormant from the high commissioners; and that the said warrant is against law, and the liberty of the subject." Resolution on Burton's Case (Mar. 12, 1641), in *Historical Collections*, 4: 207, ed. John Rushworth (London: 1721).

d. *Canadian Freeholder* (1776), in *State Trials*, 19: 1169–70. Similar comments are quoted in Eric Schnapper, "Unreasonable Searches and Seizures of Papers," Virginia Law Review, 71: 869, 878, 896, 901 (1985).

1. For an illustration of a warrant issued by the court, see John Hawarde, *Les Reportes del Cases in Camera Stellata 1593 to 1609*, at 111–12, ed. William Paley Baildon (Privately Printed: 1894).

   The Crown went out of its way to ensure that the personnel of the law courts and the prerogative courts overlapped. In particular, some prerogative judges also were law judges or at least justices of the peace. As a result, some of the judges of the prerogative tribunals had independent power to issue warrants on probable cause. Most prerogative judges, however, had no such foundation for their warrants, and the prerogative courts systematically insisted on their own authority to issue orders and warrants.

2. Henry Barrow, *A Plain Refutation of Mr. George Giffarde's Reproachful Booke* (Dort: 1591), in *The Writings of Henry Barrow, 1590–1591*, at 197, 318, ed. Leland H. Carlson (London: George Allen & Unwin, 1966). A member of the commission had "absolute power in his own name . . . to cite, summon, judge, and punish." Ibid., 209.

3. Order (Oct. 15, 1602), in *Les Reportes del Cases in Camera Stellata 1593 to 1609*, at 157, by John Hawarde, ed. William Paley Baildon (Privately Printed: 1894).

4. For the role of multiple writers in creating Martin, see *The Just Censure and Reproof of Martin Junior*, 186 (n.p.: [1589]), in *The Martin Marprelate Tracts: A Modernized and Annotated Edition*, xxxiv–xlvi, ed. Joseph L. Black (Cambridge: Cambridge University Press, 2008).

5. Resolution in Prynne's Case (Apr. 20, 1641), in *Historical Collections*, 4: 228, ed. John Rushworth (London: 1721); Resolution in Leighton's Case (Apr. 21, 1641), ibid.; Resolution in Bastwick's Case (Feb. 22, 1641), 4: 193. These and related materials are collected in [William Bollan], *The Freedom of Speech and Writing upon Public Affairs Considered*, 92–98 (London: 1766). Even the Irish House of Lords complained that the proceedings of the High Commission were "in many causes without legal warrants." A Schedule of Some Part of the Grievances . . . of this Kingdom voted in the Lord's House in Ireland, the 18th February 1640, in *Proceedings in the Opening Session of the Long Parliament*, 3: 82, ed. Maija Jansson (Rochester: University of Rochester Press, 2001).

6. As summarized by Amar, "If an executive . . . magistrate issued the warrant, the verdict of *Wilkes v. Wood* and of Blackstone seems clear." In Blackstone's words, it "was 'no warrant at all.'" Akhil Reed Amar, "Fourth Amendment Principles," Harvard Law Review 107: 757, 780 (1994).

7. Matthew Hale, *Historia Placitorum Coronæ*, 2: 105–06 (London: 1736). This was written around the middle of the seventeenth century.

8. Ibid., 109, 150.

9. *A Letter Concerning Libels, Warrants, the Seisure of Papers, and Sureties for the Peace of Behavior*, 58, 6th ed. (London: J. Almon, 1766). He elaborated, "It must either be sworn that I have certain stolen goods, or such a particular thing that is criminal in itself, in my custody, before any magistrate is authorized to grant a warrant to any man to enter my house and seize it." Ibid.

10. Opinion of the Judges on Unlawful Imprisonments (June 9, 1591), in *A History of English Law*, 5: 495–97, by William Holdsworth (London: Sweet & Maxwell: 2003). The opinion survived in two versions, and the differences eventually, in the 1630s, provoked controversy. *State Trials*, 3: 76–77; J. A. Guy, "Origins of the Petition of Right Reconsidered," in *Law, Liberty, and Parliament: Selected Essays on the Writings of Sir Edward Coke*, 328, ed. Allen D. Boyer (Indianapolis: Liberty Fund, 2004). For part of the context, but not clearly the central details, see John P. Dawson, "The Privy Council and Private Law in the Tudor and Stuart Periods: II," Michigan Law Review, 48: 627, 648–52 (1950).

11. *Darnel's Case* (1626), in *State Trials*, 3: 10, quoted by J. R. Tanner, *English Constitutional Conflicts of the Seventeenth Century 1603–1689*, at 270 (Cambridge: University Press, 1966).

12. Petition of Right, 3 Charles I, c. 1 (1628).

13. [Henry Parker], *Observations Upon Some of His Majesties Late Answers and Expresses*, 45 ([London: 1642]).

14. Paul Halliday, *Habeas Corpus: From England to Empire*, 242 (Cambridge: Belknap Press, 2010). By focusing on the mechanical details, including the continued use of common law writs of habeas, Halliday misses both the broader questions of politics and the deeper questions of lawfulness, and he thereby misses the most interesting consequences of the Habeas Corpus Act. The most sensitive account of the political context, ignored by Halliday, remains Andrew Amos, *The English Constitution in the Reign of King Charles the Second*, 170–205 (Cambridge: C. J. Clay, 1857).

15. It has been suggested that detentions under suspension acts were not clearly lawful, but were merely without remedy. Trevor W. Morrison, "Hamdi's Habeas Puzzle: Suspension As Authorization?," Cornell Law Review, 91: 411, 432 (2006); Trevor W. Morrison, "Suspension and the Extrajudicial Constitution," Columbia Law Review, 107: 1533, 1543–51 (2007). In fact, the seventeenth-century evidence relied upon by Morrison's article consists of only one quotation, which, when recited in full, does not support the position for which it is quoted. Instead, it indicates that the remedy lay in Parliament: "This [bill] cannot secure them from answering in Parliament; if they commit a person without cause, they must answer it to the law, and the kingdom." Anchitell Grey, *Debates of the House of Commons, From the Year 1667 to the Year 1694*, at 9: 276 (May 25, 1689) (London: 1763). Indeed, Williams prefaced this by arguing: "I take the privy councillor[s], to act in execution of this bill as trustees for the kingdom. . . . Privy councillors are not all lawyers, and I would have that clause for their safety. . . . [I]f they have no reason for what they do, I tell them to their faces, they must answer for it in Parliament." Ibid., 275–76.

In the eighteenth century, moreover, a suspension of habeas clearly was under-stood to render administrative detentions lawful. Amanda L. Tyler, "Is Suspension a Political Question?," Stanford Law Review, 59: 333, 386 (2006); Amanda L. Tyler, "Suspension As an Emergency Power," Yale Law Journal, 118: 600, 613 (2009). See also David L. Shapiro, "Habeas Corpus, Suspension, and Detention: Another View," Notre Dame Law Review, 82: 59, 86–87 (2006).

16. U.S. Const., Art. I, §9. Habeas corpus had been protected by acts of Parliament, and therefore, after the end of the king's suspending power with the Declaration of Rights in 1689, the writ could only be suspended by Parliament through legis-lation—as when in 1777 Parliament adopted the first of a series of suspension acts aimed at Americans. Not surprisingly, therefore, when the U.S. Constitution permit-ted suspension of habeas, it enumerated this in the guarantee of habeas together with the other limits on the power of Congress.

17. Drawde Kekatihw [Edward Whitaker], The Ignoramus Justices 18 (London: 1681). Whitaker was arguing against a general warrant issued at the Middlesex sessions at Hick's Hall against dissenters, and he added, "that officer that acts by such general warrant, if he shall apprehend any person thereon, and it prove that the person so apprehended be innocent of the crimes charged upon, the constables, or other of-ficer, are accountable for the same as false imprisonment, for that general warrant will not bear the officer harmless." Ibid.

18. Matthew Hale, Historia Placitorum Coronæ, 2: 150 (London: 1736).

19. Articles of Impeachment of High-Treason and Other Great Crimes and Misdemean-ors against Sir William Scroggs, Chief Justice of the Court of King's Bench (Jan. 5, 1681), in Cobbett's Parliamentary History of England, 4: 1276 (London: 1808).

20. William Hawkins, A Treatise of the Pleas of the Crown, 2: 81–82 (II.xiii.10) (London: 1726).

21. [Philip Carteret Webb], Copies Taken from the Records . . . Of Warrants Issued by Secre-taries of State for Seizing Persons Suspected of Being Guilty of Various Crimes, Particularly, of Being the Authors, Printers, and Publishers of Libels, from the Restoration to the Present Time (London: 1763); State Trials, 19: 1415.

22. William Blackstone, Commentaries on the Laws of England, 4: 287 (Oxford: 1769). The problem was that, although the Privy Council, as a judicial body, could issue warrants, "no single privy councilor, nor any number of privy councilors not met in council as a board, can pretend to such a power." In other words, "the being a privy councilor or secretary of state, does not make a man a justice of peace, and more authority or jurisdiction no secretary ever claimed." Accordingly, in the 1760s, a commentator could observe that, to allow secretaries of state and other privy coun-cillors to issue warrants, "it has of late been always the practice to insert by name every privy councilor into the commissions of the peace." A Letter Concerning Libels, Warrants, the Seizure of Papers, and Sureties for the Peace of Behavior, 48–49, 6th ed. (London: J. Almon, 1766). For some of the earlier history of this practice, see the arguments of Sir Bartholomew Shower in Proceedings between the King, Thomas Kendal, and Richard Roe (K.B. 1695), in A Selection Collection of Remarkable Trials, 78–79 (London: 1744).

For example, when Parliament in 1710 barred post office employees from open-ing mail, it took care to authorize the principal secretaries of state to issue warrants authorizing the opening of letters. But they did this in their judicial capacity as jus-tices of the peace, and on this understanding, the statute specified that they had to sign "an express warrant . . . for every such opening[,] detaining[,] or delaying"—the point being that "[a] general warrant is not sufficient." An Act for Establishing a General Post-Office for all Her Majesties Dominions . . . , 9 Anne, c. 10, §41–42 (1710); *The Right of British Subjects to Petition and Apply to their Representatives Asserted and Vindicated*, lix ([London: 1734]).

23. In the earlier habeas proceeding, in which Wilkes sought his release from prison, Chief Justice Pratt simply assumed that secretaries of state enjoyed the power of justices of the peace. George Rudé, *Wilkes and Liberty: A Social Study of 1763–1774*, at 27 (Oxford: Clarendon Press, 1962). By contrast, in later trials, it would become apparent that Secretary of State Halifax could not be considered a justice of the peace. In the action for damages against Wood, however, Chief Justice Pratt seems to have been somewhere between such opinions, and he did not clearly resolve the question.

24. *The Annual Register, or a View of the History, Politicks, and Literature 1763*, at 145 (London: 1764). Hawkins also said: "There is no authority in our law books that mention these kinds of warrants, but in express terms condemn them." Ibid. For similar opinions, see *Money v. Leach* (K.B. 1765), William Blackstone, *Reports*, 1: 555, 562; *Huckle v. Money* (C.B. 1763), Wilson, *Reports* (K.B.), 2: 206; *Entick v. Carrington* et al (K.B. 1765), Wilson, *Reports* (K.B.), 2: 275.

25. *Wilkes v. Wood* (C.P. 1763), in *State Trials*, 19: 1167. Blackstone wrote that a general warrant was "illegal and void for it's uncertainty; for it is the duty of the magistrate, and ought not to be left to the officer, to judge of the ground of suspicion." William Blackstone, *Commentaries on the Laws of England*, 4: 288 (Oxford: 1769). For the limited value of administrative usage, see *Money v. Leach* (K.B. 1765), William Blackstone, *Reports*, 1: 555, 562 (1781).

26. See, for example, Petition of Charles Paxton (1752), in *Legal Papers of John Adams*, 2: 133, ed. L. Kinvin Wroth & Hiller B. Zobel (Cambridge: Belknap Press, 1965).

27. Ibid., 2: 110. The editors of the *Legal Papers of John Adams* write that "even with probable cause, the officer who searched and found nothing was liable in damages for the trespass." Ibid., 110–11. This proposition, however, is not supported by the cited cases, which clearly concern other issues. See ibid., 125, n. 62, and cases cited there. For the internal guidelines, within the customs office, for searches under writs of assistance, see Elizabeth Evelynola Hoon, *The Organization of the English Customs System 1696–1786*, at 272 (1938; reprint, Newton Abbot: David & Charles, 1968).

28. *Legal Papers of John Adams*, 2: 111, ed. L. Kinvin Wroth & Hiller B. Zobel (Cambridge: Belknap Press, 1965).

29. Thomas Hutchinson, *The History of the Province of Massachusetts Bay*, 3: 67, ed. Lawrence Shaw Mayo (Cambridge: Harvard University Press, 1936).

30. Ibid.

31. Petition of Lechmere, in *Legal Papers of John Adams*, 2: 112–13, ed. L. Kinvin Wroth & Hiller B. Zobel (Cambridge: Belknap Press, 1965).

32. Ibid., 138 & 144. Although the text here relies on the John Adams's second, more polished account, it clearly reflects the character of Gridley's argument as set out in Adams's initial notes. See, ibid., 123.

33. Ibid., 117.

34. When applications were made for writs of assistance again in 1773, a Boston newspaper in 1773 observed that such a writ "is of the nature of general warrants so justly clamored against by the people of England a few years ago." Boston Gazette (Apr. 12, 1773), as quoted by Maurice Henry Smith, *The Writs of Assistance Case*, 476 (Berkeley: University of California Press, 1978). For the response in 1773 in Vir-

ginia, see Proceedings of the Virginia Committee of Correspondence (Aug. 10, 1773 & Jan. 6, 1774), in *Revolutionary Virginia: The Road to Independence*, 2: 41–42, 59–63, ed. William J. Van Schreeven & Robert L. Scribner (Charlottesville: University Press of Virginia, 1975). More generally, for an illustration of how American lawyers assimilated English law against general warrants, see the notes of Francis Dana on the subject. Francis Dana's Legal Notes, Slip endorsed "General Warrants" (second item in folder), Dana Family Papers, N-1088, Box 34, Massachusetts Historical Society, Boston. The latest citation is Burrow, *Reports*, 3: 1767, thus showing the notes to have been written in 1771 or subsequently.

35. The Townshend Revenue Act (June 29, 1767), in *Documents of American History*, 64, ed. Henry Steele Commager (New York: Appleton, Century, Crofts, 1948).

36. Maurice Henry Smith, *The Writs of Assistance Case*, 2–5 (Berkeley: University of California Press, 1978). For further details about each state, see Horace Gray, "Writs of Assistance," in *Reports of Cases Argued and Adjudged in the Superior Court of the Province of Massachusetts Bay, between 1761 and 1772 by Josiah Quincy, Junior*, 500–11, ed. Samuel M. Quincy (Boston: 1865).

37. Maryland Declaration of Rights of 1776, Art. 23.

CHAPTER TWELVE

a. See Philip Hamburger, "Beyond Protection," Columbia Law Review, 109: 1823, 1894–98 (2009).

b. *Magruder v. United States*, Second Opinion, in *Court of Claims: Reports and Digest of Opinions*, 80–81 (New York: 1856); *Todd v. United States*, ibid., 148; *Accardi v. United States*, ibid., 80; *Beatty's Executor v. United States*, ibid., 86, *Sturges, Bennett & Co. v. United States*, ibid., 230.

c. Robert Mayo, *A Synopsis of the Commercial and Revenue System of the United States, As Developed by Instructions and Decisions of the Treasury Department for the Administration of the Revenue Laws*, 431 (Washington, DC: 1847); An Act for the Establishment of a General Land Office in the Department of the Treasury (April 25, 1812), *Public Statutes at Large of the United States*, 2: 716; An Act Supplementary to the Several Acts Providing for the Settlement and Confirmation of Private Land Claims in Florida, §4 (May 23, 1849), ibid., 4: 284–85.

d. Letter from John J. Crittenden to President Millard Fillmore (Sept. 12, 1850), Record Group 56, Correspondence of the Office of the Secretary of the Treasury, Letters Received from the Attorney General, 1831–1910, Box 1, at National Archives II, College Park, MD. See also Opinion of William Wirt (July 27, 1824), *Official Opinions of the Attorneys General of the United States*, 1: 678.

e. *Rex v. Savage* (K.B. 1519), in *Reports of Cases by John Caryll*, 2: 704, ed. J. H. Baker (London: Selden Society, 2000); *Bowman & Others, Devisees of Cattel, v. Middleton* (May term, 1792), Bay (S.C.), *Reports*, 1: 254–55. See also William Shepheard, *Of Corporations, Fraternities, and Guilds*, 68, 79 (London: 1659); Giles Jacob, *Law Dictionary*, s.v. "Corporation," sig. Aa2,4[v] (London: 1732).

f. *Attorney General. v. Donatt* (Ex. Ch. 1561), in *Reports from the Lost Notebooks of Sir James Dyer*, 1: 49–50, ed. J. H. Baker (London: Selden Society, 1994). For other cases, see Hamburger, *Law and Judicial Duty*, 195, n. 43 (Cambridge: Harvard University Press, 2008).

g. Matthew Bacon, *New Abridgment of the Law*, 4: 207 (London: 1778), citing Lucas 131.

h.   Debates (Mar. 14, 1621), in *Commons Debates 1621*, at 2: 219, ed. Wallace Notestein, Frances Helen Relf & Harley Simpson (New Haven: Yale University Press, 1935).

i.   An Act to Establish the Post-Office and Post-Roads within the United States, §21 (May 8, 1794), *Public Statutes at Large of the United States*, 1: 362; *The Post-Office Law with Instructions, Forms and Tables of Distances, Published for the Regulation of the Post Offices*, 21 §21 (Philadelphia: 1798).

k.   An Act for Taking Away the Revenue Arising by Hearth-Money, 1 William & Mary, c. 10 (1688).

l.   An Act for the Speedy and Effectual Recruiting of his Majesty's Land Forces and Marines, 30 George III, c. VIII, §9 (1757). The king could "suspend or enforce the execution of this act" as he judged "expedient," but rather than a suspension of the act, this was merely a suspension of its execution. Ibid., §33.

o.   *Murray's Lessee v. Hoboken Land & Improvement Co.*, 59 U.S. 272, 280–81, 282, 283 (1856).

q.   An Act for the Due Regulation of Public Houses, §15, *The Laws of the Commonwealth of Massachusetts*, 1: 381 (Boston: 1801); *Abstract of the Laws for the Regulation of Licensed Houses: Published by Order of the Court of Sessions of the County of Essex*, 7 (Salem: June 12, 1821).

1.   Gary Lawson, "The Rise and Rise of the Administrative State," Harvard Law Review, 107: 1231, 1248 (1994); Caleb Nelson, "Adjudication in the Political Branches," Columbia Law Review, 107: 559, 625 (2007). The conflation of binding adjudications and others is commonplace. See, for example, Paul M. Bator, "The Constitution As Architecture: Legislative and Administrative Courts under Article III," Indiana Law Journal, 65: 233, 239 (1990).

2.   Jerry L. Mashaw, *Creating the Administrative Constitution: The Lost One Hundred Years of American Administrative Law*, 73, 75 (New Haven: Yale University Press, 2012).

3.   Philip Hamburger, "Beyond Protection," Columbia Law Review, 109: 1873–98, 1921–40 (2009).

4.   For the Virginia statute and Madison's role, see Philip Hamburger, "Beyond Protection," Columbia Law Review, 109: 1932, 1939 (2009). Madison explained to Jefferson that "[t]his act empowers the executive to confine or send away suspicious aliens, on notice from Congress that their sovereigns have declared or commenced hostilities against U.S. or that the latter have declared war against such sovereign." Letter from James Madison to Thomas Jefferson (Jan. 22, 1786), in *The Papers of Thomas Jefferson*, 9: 197, ed. Julian P. Boyd (Princeton: Princeton University Press, 1950). For the federal act, see An Act Respecting Alien Enemies, Chap. 66 (July 6, 1798), *Public Statutes at Large of the United States*, 1: 577. For interpretation of its provisions for the license of enemy aliens, see Philip Hamburger, "Beyond Protection," Columbia Law Review, 109: 1894–98.

5.   An Ordinance for Regulating the Treasury, and Adjusting the Public Accounts, Journals of Congress, and of the United States in Congress Assembled: For the year 1781, at 7: 185 (Sept. 11, 1781); Willard Eugene Hotchkiss, *The Judicial Work of the Comptroller of the Treasury*, 13 (Ithaca: Cornell University Press, 1911); An Act to Establish the Treasury Department, §3 (Sept. 2, 1789), *Public Statutes at Large of the United States*, 1: 66.

6.   Speech of James Madison (June 29, 1789), in *Documentary History of the First Federal Congress of the United States of America*, 11: 1080, ed. Charlene Bangs Bickford,

Kenneth R. Bowling & Helen E. Veit (Baltimore: Johns Hopkins University Press, 1992).

7.   In the 1780s, in Virginia, some judges briefly and not very successfully explored the possibility of appealing from a Treasury decision to the courts. A 1788 statute created new district courts and appointed four new judges. Philip Hamburger, *Law and Judicial Duty*, 570 (Cambridge: Harvard University Press, 2008). One of these new judges, St. George Tucker, pressed the state's auditor, John Pendleton, for his salary to be paid beginning from the date that his commission was signed, rather than from the date that he took his oath under the commission. When the auditor consulted the state's attorney general, James Innes opined that "the four additional Judges appointed under the district court law ought to receive their salaries from the date of their respective commissions, provided they have signified their acceptance thereof to the executive in due time." John Pendelton, Case for the Attorney General's opinion (July 2, 1788) together with the opinion by James Innes, Edmund Randolph Executive Papers, Box 54, Library of Virginia. Two of the judges, Tucker and John Tyler, brought suits in the Court of Chancery, and from there, by adjournment, to the Court of Appeals. Tucker persisted and had his appeal dismissed. *St. George Tucker v. The Auditor* (June 23–24, 1789), Supreme Court of Appeals, Order Book No. 1, 1779–1789, at 146, Library of Virginia.

      Tyler, however, was more astute. Prior to the judgment against Tucker, Tyler's counsel "requested the court not to proceed to give an opinion in this case it being his intention to dismiss his appeal in the said Court of Chancery." *John Tyler v. The Auditor* (June 22, 1789), ibid., 144. Although Tyler thus retreated, he recognized that, being a district court judge, he was apt to get further in a district court. He thereby obtained "ten pounds for payment of so much adjudged by the District Court to be due to John Tyler esquire as a judge; being the difference between the time of his appointment and qualifications." *Journals of the Council of the State of Virginia*, 5: 209 (Sept. 21, 1790), ed. Sandra Gioia Treadway (Richmond: Virginia State Library, 1982).

8.   "Office of the Attorney General," National Register, 3: 241 (Apr. 19, 1817).

9.   Willard Eugene Hotchkiss, *The Judicial Work of the Comptroller of the Treasury*, 30–31 (Ithaca: Cornell University Press, 1911). For early experiments along these lines and proposals for what became the Court of Claims, see Robert Mayo, *A Synopsis of the Commercial and Revenue System of the United States, As Developed by Instructions and Decisions of the Treasury Department for the Administration of the Revenue Laws*, 427, 431 (Washington, DC: 1847). For the subpoena power of the Court of Claims, see An Act to Establish a Court for the Investigation of Claims against the United States, §3 (Feb. 24, 1855), *Public Statutes at Large of the United States*, 10: 612. More generally, for the rules of the court, broken down by date and source, see *The Law of Claims against Government, Including the Mode of Adjusting Them and the Procedure Adopted in Their Investigation*, 313, Report No. 134, House of Representatives, 43rd Congress, 2nd Session (Washington, DC: Government Printing Office, 1875).

10. *De Groot v. United States*, 72 U.S. 419 (1866); *United States v. Union Pacific Co.*, 98 U.S. 569, 603 (1878); *Miles v. Graham*, 268 U.S. 501 (1925); but reconsidered in *Williams v. United States*, 289 U.S. 553 (1933).

11. As put by the Supreme Court, "Nothing passes a perfect title to public lands, with the exception of a few cases, but a patent"—the exceptions being "where Congress grants lands in words of present grant." *Wilcox v. Jackson*, 38 U.S. 498, 499 (1939).

12. Letter from James Buchanan to unknown recipients (Dec. 12, 1859), in *Decisions of*

the Interior Department in Public Land Cases and Land Laws Passed by the Congress of the United States: Together with the Regulations of the General Land Office, 681, ed. W. W. Lester (Philadelphia: 1860).

For the evolution of appeals, see No. 417 (Aug. 11, 1858), in *Decisions of the Interior Department in Public Land Cases and Land Laws Passed by the Congress of the United States: Together with the Regulations of the General Land Office*, 379, ed. W. W. Lester (Philadelphia: 1860). For the quotation, see Henry N. Copp, *The American Settler's Guide: A Brief Exposition of the Public Land System of the United States of America*, 13–14 (Washington, DC: Published by the Editor, 1880).

13. Letter from Secretary J. Thompson to S. G. Stevens (Mar. 16, 1858), in *Decisions of the Interior Department in Public Land Cases and Land Laws Passed by the Congress of the United States: Together with the Regulations of the General Land Office*, 679, ed. W. W. Lester (Philadelphia: 1860). For the availability of judicial remedies, see also Letter from Attorney General J. S. Black to Interior Secretary Jacob Thompson (Sept. 29, 1859) (regarding the Jimeno ranch), in *Decisions of the Interior Department in Public Land Cases and Land Laws Passed by the Congress of the United States: Together with the Regulations of the General Land Office*, 642, ed. W. W. Lester (Philadelphia: 1860). See also Caleb Nelson, "Adjudication in the Political Branches," Columbia Law Review, 107: 559, 578 (2007).

14. It was conventional to distinguish between "particular privileges" and the more "general liberties of the people"—even if the particular rights ultimately rested upon the general liberties. *Norris v. Staps* (C.P. 1616), Hobart, *Reports*, 211.

15. E. Wyndham Hulme, "The History of the Patent System under the Prerogative and at Common Law," Law Quarterly Review, 46: 141, 152 (1896). Crown lawyers in the reigns of Elizabeth and James deliberately went beyond these traditional ideas about lawful patents. See, for example, Francis Bacon's speech of Nov. 20, 1601, reproduced in William Hyde Price, *The English Patents of Monopoly*, 154 (Cambridge: Harvard University Press, 1913).

16. An Act concerning Monopolies and Dispensations with Penal Laws, and the Forfeitures thereof, 21 James I, c. 3, §§1–2 (1624). (Commas have been added silently for ease of reading.)

17. Ibid., §6. The statute also required that the letters patent "be not contrary to the law nor mischievous to the state by raising prices of commodities at home, or hurt of trade, or generally inconvenient." Ibid.

18. Coke, *Institutes*, 3: 181.

19. An Act to Promote the Progress of Useful Arts, §1 (Apr. 10, 1790), *Public Statutes at Large of the United States*, 1: 110. The 1793 statute clarified that it allowed patents for things "not previously known or used before the application." An Act to Promote the Progress of Useful Arts; and to Repeal the Act Heretofore Made for That Purpose, §1 (Feb. 21, 1793), ibid., 1: 320–21.

20. An Act to Promote the Progress of Useful Arts, §1 (Apr. 10, 1790), *Public Statutes at Large of the United States*, 1: 110; An Act to Promote the Progress of Useful Arts; and to Repeal the Act Heretofore Made for That Purpose, §1 (Feb. 21, 1793), ibid., 1: 320–21. For the early history of the patent system, see Edward C. Walterscheid, *To Promote the Progress of Useful Arts: American Patent Law and Administration, 1798–1836* (Littleton: Fred B. Rothman & Co. 1998).

The abandonment of the patent committee in 1793 largely removed the government's discretion in granting patents and thereby created a registration system. And because the registration system failed adequately to protect patent rights, it has been argued that "the courts are not always more efficient than an administrative agency in defining property rights." John F. Duffy, "The FCC and the Patent System: Progressive Ideals, Jacksonian Realism, and the Technology of Regulation," University of Colorado Law Review, 71: 1071, 1126 (2000). The initial grant of a patent, however, was a grant of a privilege, and it therefore cannot be assumed that the poor experience with the registration of patents shows the advantages of administrative adjudication for protecting property rights.

21. An Act to Promote the Progress of Useful Arts; and to Repeal the Act Heretofore Made for That Purpose, §9 (Feb. 21, 1793), *Public Statutes at Large of the United States*, 1: 322–23.

22. An Act to Promote the Progress of Useful Arts, and to Repeal All Acts and Parts of Acts Heretofore Made for That Purpose, §2–7 (July 4, 1836), *Public Statutes at Large of the United States*, 5: 118–19.

23. Paul M. Bator, "The Constitution As Architecture: Legislative and Administrative Courts under Article III," Indiana Law Journal, 65: 233 (1990). Similarly, David Currie has found lawmaking power in the postmaster general's statutory power to hire persons to build roads and to decide where to establish post offices, even though this was merely a power to provide services. David P. Currie, *The Constitution in Congress: The Federalist Period*, 149 (Chicago: University of Chicago Press, 1997).

Incidentally, for a rare surviving copy of published regulations edited for republication, see *Regulations for a System of Letter Carriers in the Cities of the United States, under the 41st Section of the "Act to Change the Organization of the Post Office Department," &c. Approved 2d July, 1836* ([c. 1836]), issued by Post Master J. Page, Printed Ephemera Collection; Portfolio 231, Folder 11, Library of Congress. Of course, it consists entirely of directions to postmasters and carriers.

24. Letter from George Washington to John Jay (July 18, 1788), in *Documentary History of the Ratification of the Constitution*, 16: 596, ed. John P. Kaminski & Gaspare J. Saladino (Madison: Wisconsin Historical Society, 1986). For the background, see ibid., 16: 540–41. For the threat to liberty, see ibid., 16: 561, 562, 579, 581 & 586. For analysis of the problem as a matter of custom, usage, practice, or an institution, see ibid., 16: 558, 562, 579 & 588.

25. Caleb Nelson, "Adjudication in the Political Branches," Columbia Law Review, 107: 559, 562, 578 (2007).

26. Note that early police regulations did not direct or authorize officers to constrain the public beyond what was permissible for constables. For example, New York City police officers possessed "all the common law and statutory powers of constables, except for the service of civil process." *Rules and Regulations for the Government and Guidance of the Metropolitan Police Force of the State of New York*, 19 (New York: Geo. F. Nesbitt & Co., 1857). The way that police officers gradually acquired a power to give binding orders is suggested by an 1871 law, adopted by the District of Columbia, requiring police officers to "regulate" the conduct of hackney coaches, and imposing a fine on drivers who refused to obey. *Compiled Statutes in Force in the District of Columbia*, 1: 350 (Washington: Government Printing Office, 1894).

27. Their assessments were owed by those who were understood to benefit from the work and who had a pre-existing duty to carry it out. Ida Darlington, "The London Commissioners of Sewers and Their Records," Journal of the Society of Archivists, 2: 196, 200 (1962). Although these duties and benefits ordinarily were attributed to the adjacent landowners, commissions sometimes took a broader view of who was benefited and owed the duties, and therefore charged all of the inhabitants. See, for

example, *The Records of the Commissioners of Sewers in the Parts of Holland, 1547–1603*, at 1: 66, 67, 94, ed. A. Mary Kirkus (Lincoln: Lincoln Record Society, 1959).

28. Edith G. Henderson, *Foundations of English Administrative Law: Certiorari and Mandamus in the Seventeenth Century*, 28–29 (Cambridge: Harvard University Press, 1963).

29. *The Reading of That Famous and Learned Gentleman, Robert Callis Esq; Sergeant at Law, Upon the Statute of 23 H. 8. Cap. 5. of Sewers: As it was Delivered by Him at Grays-Inn, in August, 1622*, at 80 (London: 1647); Ida Darlington, "The London Commissioners of Sewers and Their Records," Journal of the Society of Archivists, 2: 196, 207 (1962).

30. *The Reading of That Famous and Learned Gentleman, Robert Callis Esq; Sergeant at Law, Upon the Statute of 23 H. 8. Cap. 5. of Sewers: As it was Delivered by Him at Grays-Inn, in August, 1622*, at 82, 139 (London: 1647); Edith G. Henderson, *Foundations of English Administrative Law: Certiorari and Mandamus in the Seventeenth Century*, 28–29 (Cambridge: Harvard University Press, 1963). As might be expected of administrative officers, the commissioners sometimes let their surveyors make presentments of matters that by statute belonged to the juries, and one commentator attempted to reconcile this practice with the law by suggesting that the surveyor in such instances was merely making a "supplemental presentment." *The Reading of That Famous and Learned Gentleman, Robert Callis Esq; Sergeant at Law, Upon the Statute of 23 H. 8. Cap. 5. of Sewers: As it was Delivered by Him at Grays-Inn, in August, 1622*, at 84 (London: 1647). For the varied number of jurors nominated (although always more than twelve and not more than twenty-four) see *Court Minutes of the Surrey & Kent Sewer Commission*, passim ([London]: London County Council, 1909); *The Records of the Commissioners of Sewers in the Parts of Holland, 1547–1603*, at 1: xxvii, ed. A. Mary Kirkus (Lincoln: Lincoln Record Society vol. 54, 1959). For the multiple functions of the juries, see Sidney Webb & Beatrice Webb, *English Local Government: Statutory Authorities for Special Purposes*, 26 (London: Longmans, Green & Co., 1922).

31. *The Reading of That Famous and Learned Gentleman, Robert Callis Esq; Sergeant at Law, Upon the Statute of 23 H. 8. Cap. 5. of Sewers: As it was Delivered by Him at Grays-Inn, in August, 1622*, at 138, 140–41 (London: 1647). An apologist for the commissions, Robert Callis, strained to uphold their dignity by arguing that they were courts of record—his point being not unlike that of the contemporary scholars who insist that bankruptcy adjudicators need to be called "judges." Callis was candid enough, however, that he made his arguments in a guarded manner, as when he said that the commissioners had the power "to make orders and decrees, which are judgments in effect." Ibid., 129.

The power to imprison was the measure of a court of record, and Callis therefore tried to show that commissions of sewers had this power. But he had to acknowledge that any such imprisonment might seem "to sway somewhat against the grand charter of England, and against the liberty of a free-born subject." In the end, therefore, he could make only the strained argument that the commissioners had a power to imprison for contempt and that a failure to obey their orders should be understood as a contempt. Ibid., 133. The reality remained, however, that the commissioners were not a court of record, and therefore although they could commit persons for "a contempt in the face of their court," they could not, even on a theory of contempt, imprison a person merely "for disobeying their orders." Matthew Bacon, *A New Abridgment of the Law*, 1: 655 (London: 1778).

Incidentally, the traditional difference between a fine and an amercement is revealing. A fine could be imposed only by a court of record for a violation of law. In contrast, an amercement could be imposed for a contempt either by a court of record or by a court that was not of record. But whereas the court of record could levy the amercement itself, the court that was not of record ultimately had to rely on a court of record to enforce its amercement.

32. See, for example, John Dickinson, *Administrative Justice and the Supremacy of the Law in the United States*, 5, n. 5 (Cambridge: Harvard University Press, 1927).

33. John Paul, *A Clear and Compendious System of the Excise Laws, Methodically Arranged, and Alphabetically Digested*, 93–94 (London: 1779).

34. See, for example, *Cases Relating to the Duties of Excise, And to the Jurisdiction of Justices of the Peace, Upon Informations Laid Before Them for Offense against the Laws of Excise* (London: 1715); *Abstract of Cases and Decisions on Appeals Relating to the Tax on Servants* (London: 1781); *Cases Which Have Been Determined by the Judges Relative to the Duties on Houses and Windows, and on Inhabited Houses* (n.p.: 1782).

35. John Paul, *A Clear and Compendious System of the Excise Laws, Methodically Arranged, and Alphabetically Digested*, 93–94 (London: 1779).

36. [Timothy Cunningham], *The History of Our Customs, Aids, Subsidies, National Debts, and Taxes*, pt. III, p. 21 (London: 1761); William Blackstone, *Commentaries on the Laws of England*, 1: 308 (Oxford: 1765).

37. Ibid.; Samuel Johnson, *A Dictionary of the English Language*, sig. 8L[v] ("excise") (London: 1755). For American complaints, see those collected in James Thomson Callender, *A Short History of the Nature and Consequences of Excise Laws; Including Some Account of the Recent Interruption to the Manufactories of Snuff and Refined Sugar* (Philadelphia: 1795). In addition, English debates about the excise were published in American newspapers, including a complaint in 1789 about "Pitt's Excise Inquisition," Correspondence (London, June 29), Norwich Packet and the Country Journal (Sept. 18, 1789).

38. An Act Repealing . . . the Duties Heretofore Laid upon Distilled Spirits Imported from Abroad, and Laying Others in Their Stead; and Also Upon Spirits Distilled within the United States, for Appropriating the Same, §44 (Mar. 3, 1791), *Public Statutes at Large of the United States*, 1: 209; An Act Making Further Provision for Securing and Collecting the Duties on Foreign and Domestic Spirits, Stills, Wines and Teas, §9 (June 5, 1794), ibid., 380.

39. Stephen Dowell, *A History of Taxation and Taxes in England*, 3: 77 (London: Longmans, Green & Co., 1888); Thomas M. Cooley, *A Treatise on the Law of Taxation*, 158 (Chicago: Callaghan & Co., 1876); Anne Woolhandler, "Delegation and Due Process: The Historical Connection," Supreme Court Review, 223, 237, 243 (2008); An Act to Provide for the Valuation of Lands and Dwelling-Houses and the Enumeration of Slaves within the United States, §19 (July 9, 1798), *Public Statutes at Large of the United States*, 1: 588.

40. Leonard D. White, *The Federalists: A Study in Administrative History*, 451–52 (New York: Macmillan Co., 1961).

41. *The Documentary History of the Supreme Court of the United States, 1789–1800*, at 4: 723–29, ed. Maeva Marcus (New York: Columbia University Press, 1992).

42. Jerry L. Mashaw, *Creating the Administrative Constitution: The Lost One Hundred Years of American Administrative Law*, 75 (New Haven: Yale University Press, 2012).

43. *The Documentary History of the Supreme Court of the United States, 1789–1800*, at 4: 723, ed. Maeva Marcus (New York: Columbia University Press, 1992).

44. An Act to Provide for the Settlement of the Claims of Widows and Orphans Barred by the Limitations Heretofore Established, and to Regulate the Claims to Invalid Pensions (Mar. 23, 1792), *Public Statutes at Large of the United States*, 1: 243–44.

45. *The Documentary History of the Supreme Court of the United States, 1789–1800*, at 6: 53–54, 370–71, ed. Maeva Marcus (New York: Columbia University Press, 1998); *Hayburn's Case*, 2 U.S. 409 (1792).

46. *Gordon v. United States*, 69 U.S. 561 (1864).

47. Jerry L. Mashaw, *Creating the Administrative Constitution: The Lost One Hundred Years of American Administrative Law*, 76 (New Haven: Yale University Press, 2012). As for the significance for "the modern administrative state," see ibid., 85.

48. Opinion of Ryder & Murray (July 12, 1750), in Elizabeth Evelynola Hoon, *The Organization of the English Customs System 1696–1786*, at 276 (1938; reprint, Newton Abbot: David & Charles, 1968); An Act Repealing . . . the Duties Heretofore Laid upon Distilled Spirits Imported from Abroad, and Laying Others in Their Stead; and Also Upon Spirits Distilled within the United States, for Appropriating the Same, §44 (Mar. 3, 1791), *Public Statutes at Large of the United States*, 1: 209. See also An Act to Provide for Mitigating or Remitting the Forfeitures, Penalties and Disabilities Accruing in Certain Cases Therein Mentioned, §3 (Mar. 3, 1797), ibid., 1: 506; An Act Providing Compensation . . . §8 (Feb. 28, 1799), ibid., 1: 626. For the probable cause requirement, see An Act Repealing . . . the Duties Heretofore Laid upon Distilled Spirits Imported from Abroad, and Laying Others in Their Stead; and Also Upon Spirits Distilled within the United States, for Appropriating the Same, §§32, 38 (Mar. 3, 1791), ibid., 1: 207–08.

    As put by Leonard White, "[t]he collector (with the district attorney) appeared in the role of prosecutor; the importer, shipmaster, or owner, in the role of defendant; the penalties and forfeitures were imposed by the judge." Leonard D. White, *The Federalists: A Study in Administrative History*, 446 (New York: Macmillan Co., 1961). For the assumption in early federal law that forfeitures were penalties, see ibid., 445.

49. James Bradby, *A Treatise on the Law of Distress*, 1 (New York: 1808). For the view that distress was a sort of administrative adjudications, see Paul M. Bator, "The Constitution As Architecture: Legislative and Administrative Courts under Article III," Indiana Law Journal, 65: 233, 246 (1990); Jerry L. Mashaw, *Creating the Administrative Constitution: The Lost One Hundred Years of American Administrative Law*, 115, 218, 352, n. 130 (New Haven: Yale University Press, 2012).

50. James Bradby, *A Treatise on the Law of Distress*, 38 &, more generally, chap. III (New York: 1808). Caleb Nelson suggests that distraint in the nineteenth century could be viewed as making "inroads" on the general assumption that the government could bind or constrain subjects only through judicial proceedings. Caleb Nelson, "Adjudication in the Political Branches," Columbia Law Review, 107: 559, 586 (2007). Distress, however, was an ancient common law remedy for parties owed fixed debts. It thus put the government in no better position than, for example, a landlord seeking to collect rent owed by a delinquent tenant.

51. *Murray's Lessee v. Hoboken Land & Improvement Co.*, 59 U.S. 272, 284 (1856).

52. Goodnow relied on a series of such instances—the distress warrant in *Murray's Lessee*, the notices given by tax assessors, and the orders issued to aliens—to suggest that administrative officers generally had the power to bind. Even Goodnow, however, acknowledged that these cases were "decided largely in view either of historical considerations or of the plenary power of the government." Frank J. Goodnow, *The Principles of Administrative Law of the United States*, 335–37 (New York: G. P. Putnam, 1905).

53. See, for example, *Warrant for Regulating the Necessary Stoppages from the Dragoons and*

Foot, For Answering the Expense Born by the Regiment (Apr. 29, 1732). This was issued, by his majesty's command, under the signature of Secretary of War William Strickland. It restated and slightly amended an earlier "Regulation of Weekly Pay and Stoppages . . . for answering the Expenses customarily born by the Regiment" that was "Commonly called Grass-Money."

54. *Murray's Lessee v. Hoboken Land & Improvement Co.*, 59 U.S. 272, 279 (1856); Paul M. Bator, "The Constitution As Architecture: Legislative and Administrative Courts under Article III," Indiana Law Journal, 65: 233, 246 (1990).

55. 59 U.S. 272, 279. In fact, the traditional practice established by state statutes was for town selectmen or assessors to determine the delinquent amount and then to issue warrants to a tax collector or constable to distrain the taxpayer's goods to that amount. The Court upheld the use of distress warrants by tax collectors against delinquent taxpayers in *Springer v. United States*, 102 U.S. 586 (1880), although with a rather excessive interpretation of Marshall's statement in *McCulloch v. Maryland* that "[t]he power to tax involves the power to destroy." Ibid., 593.

56. Much research remains to be done on nonjudicial orders and warrants, whether those issued by the Crown and its officers or by American executives and their subordinates.

57. Sir Matthew Hale, *The Prerogatives of the King*, 183, ed. D. E. C. Yale (London: Selden Society, 1976); Wyndham Beawes, *Lex Mercatoria Redivida*, 2: 507, 513 (Dublin: 1795); Emily Kadens, "The Last Bankrupt Hanged: Balancing Incentives in the Development of Bankruptcy Law," Duke Law Review, 59: 1229 (2010).

58. See An Act to Establish a Court for the Investigation of Claims against the United States, §3 (Feb. 24, 1855), *Public Statutes at Large of the United States*, 10: 612. For example, see *Decisions of the Interior Department in Public Land Cases and Land Laws Passed by the Congress of the United States: Together with the Regulations of the General Land Office*, 339, 391, 396–97, 399, 401, ed. W. W. Lester (Philadelphia: 1860).

59. An Act to Establish an Uniform System of Bankruptcy throughout the United States, §§4–5, 14–15 (Apr. 4, 1800), *Public Statutes at Large of the United States*, 2: 22–23, 25 (1800).

60. The surviving debates are sketchy, but the concerns about taking judicial power out of the courts was mentioned by Representative Dana of Connecticut, who argued against abolishing the 1800 statute: "As to the particular objections made to the law, amendments may remove them. If the district judge shall be empowered to revise and disallow, in case he sees fit, the proceedings of the commissioners; that is, possess the ultimate right of deciding on the whole business, many of the existing objections will be removed." Speech of Samuel W. Dana (Feb. 18, 1803), *Annals of Congress*, 562. See also ibid., 563.

61. An Act to Establish a Uniform System of Bankruptcy throughout the United States, §§1, 4–7 (Aug. 19, 1841), *Public Statutes at Large of the United States*, 5: 441, 443–446 (1841). For court orders to testify, see also, for example, *Rules and Forms in Bankruptcy, in the District Court, of the Eastern District of Pennsylvania*, 21 (§17) (Philadelphia: 1841); *Rules and Forms in Bankruptcy, in the District Court of the United States, for the District of Massachusetts*, 5 (§X), 8 (§XV) ([Boston]: 1842).

62. An Act to Establish a Uniform System of Bankruptcy throughout the United States, §§5–7 (Mar. 2, 1867), *Public Statutes at Large of the United States*, 14: 514, 519–20.

63. In addition, parish officers in some states still retained a power to indenture or apprentice indigent children whose parents were dependent on parish aid, but increas-

ingly only with the consent of the justices of the peace or other judicial officers. For New York, see David M. Schneider, *The History of Public Welfare in New York State*, 117 (Chicago: University of Chicago Press, 1938).

64. See, for example, Peter L. Strauss, *Administrative Justice in the United States*, 42 (Durham: Carolina Academic Press, 2002).

65. For the inspection, see An Act Repealing . . . the Duties Heretofore Laid upon Distilled Spirits Imported from Abroad, and Laying Others in Their Stead; and Also Upon Spirits Distilled within the United States, for Appropriating the Same, §§19, 25, 26 & 29 (Mar. 3, 1791), *Public Statutes at Large of the United States*, 1: 203–06. For the regulations, see An Act Concerning the Duties on Spirits Distilled within the United States, §5 (May 8, 1792), ibid., 1: 269.

66. An Act Repealing . . . the Duties Heretofore Laid upon Distilled Spirits Imported from Abroad, and Laying Others in Their Stead; and Also Upon Spirits Distilled within the United States, for Appropriating the Same, §§32, 38 (Mar. 3, 1791), ibid., 1: 207–08. This last point, about the officer's burden of showing probable cause, was balanced by another presumption: that the lack of the requisite mark or certificate on imported containers of spirits was presumptive evidence that the containers were liable to forfeiture, thus allowing excise officers to seize them and making it necessary at trial for the owner to prove that the spirits were imported in accord with law. Ibid., §27, at 206.

   Of course, even with probable cause, an officer was responsible for taking care of seized property. As summarized in the early nineteenth century, "If any officer of the revenue seize goods without probable cause, he is responsible for all the losses and injuries, however occasioned. If with probable cause, he is responsible only for injuries occasioned by ordinary neglect." Richard Peters, *A Full and Arranged Digest of Cases, Decided in the . . . Courts of the United States*, 3: 129 (Philadelphia: 1839). For a more elaborate statement in an underlying case held before Chief Justice Story, see *Burke v. Trevitt*, 1 Mason's C.C.R. 96,101–02 (1816).

67. An Act Repealing . . . the Duties Heretofore Laid upon Distilled Spirits Imported from Abroad, and Laying Others in Their Stead; and Also Upon Spirits Distilled within the United States, for Appropriating the Same, §35 (Mar. 3, 1791), *Public Statutes at Large of the United States*, 1: 207.

68. Somewhat similarly, when Congress incorporated the Bank of the United States, it allowed the Treasury to inspect general accounts relating to statements owed to the Treasury, but not private accounts: "The officer at the head of the treasury department . . . shall be furnished . . . with statements of the amount of the capital stock of the said corporation, and of the debts due to the same; of the monies deposited therein; of the notes in circulation, and of the cash in hand; and shall have a right to inspect such general accounts in the books of the bank, as shall relate to the said statements. *Provided*, That this shall not be construed to imply a right of inspecting the account of any private individual or individuals with the bank." An Act to Incorporate the Subscribers to the Bank of the United States, §7, paragraph XVI (Feb. 25, 1791), ibid., 1: 195.

69. For the limits on search and seizure limits of privately owned papers, see Eric Schnapper, "Unreasonable Searches and Seizures of Papers," Virginia Law Review, 71: 869 (1985); Donald A. Dripps, "'Dearest Property': Digital Evidence and the History of Private 'Papers' As Special Objects of Search and Seizure," Journal of Law and Criminology, 103: 49 (2013).

CHAPTER THIRTEEN

a.   William Hudson, "A Treatise of the Court of Star Chamber," in *Collectanea Juridica*, 2: 225–27, ed. Francis Hargrave (London: 1792).

b.   On the need for prosecutions to secure forfeitures of goods seized by customs officers, see Elizabeth Evelynola Hoon, *The Organization of the English Customs System 1696–1786*, at 275 (1938). There is nothing new about the attempt to recast criminal penalties as administrative forfeitures. When James I adopted proclamations that imposed penalties on his subjects, he occasionally sought to minimize legal objections by speaking of the penalties as forfeitures. No one, however, was deceived. The House of Commons petitioned that "no fine or forfeiture of goods or other pecuniary or corporal punishment may be inflicted upon your subjects . . . unless they shall offend against some law or statute of this realm in force at the time of their offense committed." House of Commons, Petition of Temporal Grievances (July 7, 1610), in *Proceedings in Parliament 1610*, at 2: 259–60, ed. Elizabeth Read Foster (New Haven: Yale University Press, 1966).

c.   For the authority of the judges in expounding the law, see Philip Hamburger, *Law and Judicial Duty*, chaps. 7 & 17 (Cambridge: Harvard University Press, 2008).

d.   5 U.S.C. §706(2).

e.   *The Reformation of the Ecclesiastical Laws of England, 1552*, at 193, ed. James C. Spaulding (Kirksville: Sixteenth Century Essays & Studies, 1992).

f.   U.S. Court of Appeals for Veterans Claims, Order in No. 11-2408, *Constance Copeland v. Eric K. Shinseki* (July 27, 2012). Both side argued for such a power. Appellant's Response to Order for Supplemental Briefing; Appellee's Memorandum of Law, in Response to the Court's Order of July 27, 2012.

h.   *United States v. Morton Salt*, 338 U.S. 636, 642 (1950).

i.   Ibid., 652.

k.   Pa. Const. of 1776, Chap. 2, §25; N.Y. Const. of 1777, Art. XLI; Mass. Const. of 1780, Pt. I, Art. XII; New Hampshire Bill of Rights of 1784, Art. XVI; Virginia Bill of Right of 1776, Sec. 8; North Carolina Declaration of Rights of 1776, Art. IX; Maryland Declaration of Rights of 1776, Arts. 19 & 21; New Jersey Constitution of 1776, Art. XXII; Georgia Constitution of 1777, Art. LXI.

m.   William Blackstone, *Commentaries on the Laws of England*, 1: 118 (Oxford: 1765); *Trial of Alexander Addison*, 17 (Lancaster: 1803); *The Constitutionalist: Addressed to Men of All Parties in the United States by an American*, 38 (Philadelphia: 1804); *Atlas Roofing Company, Inc. v. Occupational Safety and Health Review Commission*, 430 U.S. 442, 450 (1977); Marcus Dirk Dubber, *The Police Power: Patriarchy and the Foundations of the American Republic*, 106–07, 111 (New York: Columbia University Press, 2005). On the multiple meanings of the word *ius*, see *Lexicon Iuridicum: Hoc est, Iuris Civilis Et Canonici in Schola Atque Foro usitatarum vocum Penus*, 520 (n.p.: 1607), which observed, "Ius pluribus modis dicitur, hoc est, multa significat." For an example of the German debate over *ius publicum*, see Justus Henning Böhmer, *Introductio in Jus Publicum Universale*, 64–65 (Frankfort: 1771).

Incidentally, the contemporary public rights doctrine should not be confused with ideas of sovereign immunity. The latter doctrine protects the government from being sued in court. The public rights doctrine, on the other hand, allows the federal government to bring claims against members of the public outside of court and without a jury.

n.   *State v. Clerk of Patasquank County Court* (N.C. Superior Court 1778), discussed in

Philip Hamburger, *Law and Judicial Duty*, 383–91 (Cambridge: Harvard University Press, 2008).

o. See, for example, *Stone v. Farmers' Loan & Trust Co.*, 116 U.S. 307 (1886).

p. For the application of the hearing requirement in the last half of the nineteenth century, see Anne Woolhandler, "Delegation and Due Process: The Historical Connection," Supreme Court Review, 223, 236–43 (2008).

q. *Goldberg v. Kelly*, 397 U.S. 254, 262 (1970). See also *Mathews v. Eldridge*, 424 U.S. 319 (1976). For the belief about the expansion of liberty, see, for example, Peter L. Strauss, *Administrative Justice in the United States*, 14 (Durham: Carolina Academic Press, 2002). The loss of liberty is part of the *more is less* problem. For these sorts of trade-offs, see Philip Hamburger, "More Is Less," Virginia Law Review, 90: 835 (2004), and Philip Hamburger, "Getting Permission," Northwestern Law Review, 101: 405, 413–15 (2007).

s. *In re Mark Strouse* (U.S. D.Ct. Nev., 1870), Internal Revenue Record and Customs Journal, 11: 182, 183 (June 4, 1870). For other such revenue cases, see J. B. F. Davidge & I. G. Kimball, *A Compendium of Internal Revenue Laws, with Decisions, Rulings, Instructions, Regulations, and Forms*, 306–14 (Washington, DC: W. H. & O. H. Morrison, 1871).

v. 42 U.S.C. §9606(b).

w. *Interstate Commerce Commission v. Brimson*, 154 U.S. 447, 462 (1894). For the traditionally narrow concept of contempt of court, and for the expansion of contempt in ways that deny the due process of law, see John C. Fox, *The History of Contempt of Court: The Form of Trial and the Mode of Punishment*, 6, 8, 202, 207 (Oxford: Clarendon Press, 1927). As for bankruptcy commissions, note that, already in England, a refusal to obey a warrant from commissioners of bankruptcy was held by the chancellor not to be a contempt of his court. Wyndham Beawes, *Lex Mercatoria Redivida*, 1: 127–28 (Dublin: 1795), citing a case of 1710.

1. Gary Lawson, "The Rise and Rise of the Administrative State," Harvard Law Review, 107: 1231 (1994); Caleb Nelson, "Adjudication in the Political Branches," Columbia Law Review, 107: 559 (2007).

    See also Richard H. Fallon, "Of Legislative Courts, Administrative Agencies, and Article III," Harvard Law Review, 10: 915, 919 (1998); James E. Pfander, "Article I Tribunals, Article III Courts, and the Judicial Power of the United States," Harvard Law Review, 118: 643, 646 (2004).

2. Ernst Freund, *Administrative Powers over Persons and Property*, 17, 35 (Chicago: University of Chicago Press, 1928). Freund contrasted Germany and America on this point. "In Germany the general power of the police authorities to issue particular orders extends to the correction of all conditions threatening harm to public peace, safety, or order." In other words, administrative officers could direct binding orders to persons in particular instances; and this distinguished them from their Anglo-American counterparts: "In contrast to the law prevailing in the greater part of Germany. . . . Anglo-American law knows no general administrative power to issue orders to individuals. Such a power belongs in our system only to courts of equity, and, as a power to subpoena witnesses and to compel them to give evidence, to the courts of common law." Whereas in Germany this power was administrative, in America it was judicial. Ibid., 140.

3. The Supreme Court had a glimpse of the problem in *Northern Pipeline Co. v. Mara-*

thon Pipeline Co., 458 U.S. 50 (1982), in which it held a bankruptcy statute unconstitutional for allowing executive officers to adjudicate private rights.

4. For a federal illustration of the division between civil actions and criminal proceedings on indictments and informations, see An Act Supplementary to the Act Intituled "An Act Concerning the District of Columbia," §2 (Mar. 3, 1801), *Public Statutes at Large of the United States*, 2: 115. For discussions, see Zephaniah Swift, *A System of the Laws of the State of Connecticut*, 2: 180–83 (Wyndham: 1796); Nathan Dane, *A General Abridgment and Digest of American Law*, 5: 254–57 (Boston: 1824); "History and Development of Qui Tam," Washington University Law Quarterly, 81, 90 (1972); Harold J. Krent, "Executive Control over Criminal Law Enforcement: Some Lessons from History," American University Law Review, 38: 275, 297–303 (1989).

5. 5 U.S.C. §554(d). For one of myriad discussions of the prosecutorial role of agencies, see *Final Report of the Attorney General's Committee on Administrative Procedure*, 208–09 (Washington, DC: U.S. Government Printing Office, 1941). Similarly, a recent commentator mentions "the agency's staff—its prosecutors, one could say," see Peter L. Strauss, *Administrative Justice in the United States*, 205, n. 76 (Durham: Carolina Academic Press, 2002).

6. Ernst Freund, *Administrative Powers over Persons and Property*, 32 (Chicago: University of Chicago Press, 1928). For a detailed survey of review structures within agencies, including question of finality, see Russell L. Weaver, "Appellate Review in Executive Departments and Agencies," Administrative Law Review, 48: 251 (1996).

7. Peter L. Strauss, *Administrative Justice in the United States*, 207, n. 78, 210 (Durham: Carolina Academic Press, 2002).

8. *A Blackletter Statement of Federal Administrative Law*, 9 (Chicago: American Bar Association, 2004). One commentator writes about the FAA: "Most administrators expect their staff to review the hearing record, and may not personally review the record. The administrators may or may not read the briefs. As a result, the review process tends to vary." More generally, he observes that, at some agencies, "[t]he agency head meets with subordinates for only a brief period, focusing on a few major issues, and may not read the record or any of the briefs." Russell L. Weaver, "Appellate Review in Executive Departments and Agencies," Administrative Law Review, 48: 251, 265, 288 (1996).

9. For the 1992 survey, see Charles H. Koch, Jr., "Administrative Presiding Officials Today," Administrative Law Review, 46: 271, 278 (1994). The numbers were more than twice as high for administrative law judges in the Social Security Administration, but as they decide benefits, the argument here rests on the figures from administrative law judges outside that agency. In this connection, note that the case load of administrative law judges increasingly has shifted from regulation to benefits. Daniel J. Gifford, "Federal Administrative Law Judges: The Relevance of Past Choices to Future Directions," Administrative Law Review, 49: 1, 59–60 (1997).

The sanctions on administrative law judges are imposed by the Federal Merit Systems Protection Board, thus conveniently allowing agencies to say that they cannot punish their administrative law judges for nonconformity. For example, the Environmental Protection Agency declares:

> [N]or can the Agency decrease an ALJ's salary or otherwise negatively effect the other terms and conditions of their employment. Further, all ALJs are appointed essentially "for life," in that there is no mandatory retirement age for ALJs and ALJs can only be removed from their positions for "good cause" es-

tablished and determined by the Federal Merit Systems Protection Board on the record after a hearing, and thus cannot be removed arbitrarily or for political reasons.

EPA, Office of Administrative Law Judges, *Practice Manual*, 3 (July 2011). Nonetheless, the Federal Merit Systems Protection Board can "decrease an ALJ's salary or otherwise negatively effect the other terms and conditions of their employment" for failing to comply with the EPA's regulations.

10. 5 U.S.C. §554(d); *A Blackletter Statement of Federal Administrative Law*, 11–12 (Chicago: American Bar Association, 2004).

11. As put by one commentator, "the APA created a paradox of independent trial-level adjudicators whose decisions could be reviewed and overturned by officials who lacked comparable protection." Although "[s]ome reviewing officials have protections designed to ensure their independence; most do not." Indeed, most "do not have job security, and can be removed at will." Russell L. Weaver, "Appellate Review in Executive Departments and Agencies," Administrative Law Review, 48: 251, 252, 271 (1996).

12. F. W. Maitland, *Constitutional History of England*, 263 (Cambridge: [Cambridge] University Press, 1909).

13. In fact, Fourth and Fifth Amendment rights appear to have been deliberately reduced to make way for the administrative state. Ken I. Kersch, *Constructing Civil Liberties: Discontinuities in the Development of American Constitutional Law*, 112–17 (Cambridge: Cambridge University Press, 2004).

14. Josh Chafetz, "Executive Branch Contempt of Congress," University of Chicago Law Review, 1083, 1127 (2009).

15. *United States v. Morton Salt*, 338 U.S. 632, 636, 642 (1950).

16. Ibid., 641. The Federal Trade Commission concluded its proceedings against the corporation with an order to file a "report of compliance"—an order affirmed with modifications by a decree of the court of appeals. Morton Salt filed the reports, and "there the matter appears to have rested for a little upwards of four years," when the commission, acting on its own, "ordered additional and highly particularized reports to show continuing compliance" with the order and the decree. In other words, this was a case in which the demand for a compliance report was not even tucked behind the fig leaf of a judicial decree from a court or even an agency. The administrative demand for a compliance report in *Morton Salt* thus looks startlingly like an inquisitorial inquiry—an administrative version of a grand jury investigation, which requires disclosure of information about the occurrence of crimes. The Supreme Court, however, upheld the administrative demand for compliance reports, saying that administrative agencies could employ a process that "at times is inquisitorial." Ibid., 636, 640.

17. Ibid., 642.

18. Ibid., 642–43.

19. Ibid., 652–53 (internal quotation marks omitted). The second passage quoted was from *Oklahoma Press Publishing Co. v. Walling*, 327 U.S. 186, 208 (1946).

20. 5 U.S.C. §554(b)(3).

21. In both the New Jersey case and the New Hampshire case, the courts not only held the administrative proceedings unconstitutional but also the statutes. See Philip Hamburger, *Law and Judicial Duty*, 407–35 (Cambridge: Harvard University Press, 2008).

22. As candidly explained by one agency, its administrative judges act "as both the judge

and jury." EEOC, Frequently Asked Questions about the Federal Sector Hearing Process, http://www.eeoc.gov/federal/fed_employees/faq_hearing.cfm.

23. As summarized in the mid-eighteenth century, "[t]he power of a justice of the peace is in restraint of the common law, and in abundance of instances is a tacit repeal of that famous clause in the great charter, that a man shall be tried by his equals; which also was the common law of the land long before the great charter." Richard Burn, *Justice of the Peace, and Parish Officer*, 159 (London: 1756).

24. *District of Columbia v. Clawans*, 300 U.S. 617 (1937), citing Felix Frankfurter & Thomas G. Corcoran, "Petty Federal Offenses and the Constitutional Guaranty of Trial by Jury," Harvard Law Review, 39: 917 (1926). For *Clawans*, and how Frankfurter regretted its extension in later cases, see Ken I. Kersch, *Constructing Civil Liberties: Discontinuities in the Development of American Constitutional Law*, 114–15 (Cambridge: Cambridge University Press, 2004).

25. *Atlas Roofing Company Inc. v. Occupational Safety and Health Review Commission*, 430 U.S. 442, 450 (1977). Although the Supreme Court has backed away from the "public rights" justification, it still concludes that "the public rights doctrine reflects simply a pragmatic understanding that, when Congress selects a quasi-judicial method of resolving matters that 'could be conclusively determined by the Executive and Legislative Branches,' the danger of encroaching on the judicial powers is reduced." *Thomas v. Union Carbide*, 473 U.S. 568, 570 (1985). Of course, this case concerned a binding adjudication, and thus one that was not really within the authority of the executive and legislative branches. For skepticism about the contemporary public rights doctrine, see Kenneth S. Klein, "The Validity of the Public Rights Doctrine in Light of the Historical Rationale of the Seventh Amendment," Hastings Constitutional Law Quarterly, 21: 1013 (1994).

26. An agency can close hearings only to the extent it can show a compelling interest. *Detroit Free Press v. Ashcroft*, 2002 U.S. App. Lexis 17646, 2002 Fed App. 0291P (6th Cir. 2002).

27. Coke, *Institutes*, 2: 103–04.

28. *Hi-Tech Furnace Systems, Inc. v. FCC*, 224 F.3d 781, 787–90 (D.C. Cir. 2000).

29. For this point, and the example, see Michael Asimow, *A Guide to Federal Agency Adjudication*, 70 (Chicago: American Bar Association, 2003).

30. 5 U.S.C. §706(2)(A). Although the statute recites "arbitrary" and "capricious" as alternative measures, the courts usually unite them in a conjoined standard. Indeed, they often do not clearly distinguish these standards from the "substantial evidence" standard.

31. Roland G. Usher, *The Rise and Fall of the High Commission*, 151 (Oxford: Clarendon Press, 1968).

32. Michael Asimow, *A Guide to Federal Agency Adjudication*, 76 (Chicago: American Bar Association, 2003).

33 5 U.S.C. §§551(6) & 556(d).

34. CERCLA, 42 U.S.C. §9607(b). Although the emphasis here is on the violation of due process, note Gary Lawson's argument that the specification of standards of proof "is an essential part of the judicial decision-making process," and that therefore statutory specifications of such standards "represent a direct challenge to the principle of decisional independence." Gary Lawson, "Controlling Precedent: Congressional Regulation of Judicial Decision-Making," Constitutional Commentary, 18: 191, 219 (2001).

35. Ernst Freund, *Administrative Powers over Persons and Property*, 154 (Chicago: Univer-

sity of Chicago Press, 1928). He was writing about both the burden of proof and the bar to admission of new evidence.

36. Peter L. Strauss, *Administrative Justice in the United States*, 47 (Durham: Carolina Academic Press, 2002).

37. *Emspak v. United States*, 349 U.S. 190 (1955).

38. *United States v. Morton Salt*, 338 U.S. 636, 642–43 (1950).

39. This locution turns up already in an early case on the power of a railroad commissioner, *State ex rel. Caldwell v. Wilson*, North Carolina Reports, 121: 425, 464 (N.C. 1897). One of the headnotes in the case bluntly explained: "'Due process' is such process as is due to the particular circumstances of a case according to the law of the land. It does not necessarily imply a regular proceeding in a Court of justice or after the manner of such Courts, and a party cannot be said to have been deprived of his property 'without due process' when he has had a fair hearing according to the modes of proceeding applicable to such case." Ibid., 426.

40. Peter L. Strauss, *Administrative Justice in the United States*, 13 (Durham: Carolina Academic Press, 2002).

41. The scholarship of Nicholas Rosenkranz notes the passive voice in most of the first eight amendments, and how this stands in contrast to the active voice of the First Amendment. But rather than accept the implication that the procedural amendments thereby limit all parts of government, his work suggests that each of the passive guarantees mainly limits a single part of government other than Congress—for example that the due process clause "is essentially a restriction on what the *executive* branch may do *in the absence of a law.*" Nicholas Rosenkranz, "The Objects of the Constitution," Stanford Law Review, 63: 1005, 1042 (2011). Although this is valuable in recognizing the passive voice, it takes too narrow a view of the significance. For example, a court surely can violate due process by condemning a defendant without trial, and Congress can violate it by authorizing such proceedings.

42. St. George Tucker, Law Lectures, p. 4 of four loose pages inserted in volume 2, Tucker-Coleman Papers, Mss. 39.1 T79, Box 62, Special Collections Research Center, Earl Gregg Swem Library, College of William and Mary. Of course, he quoted Coke.

43. Charles Reich notes how licensing puts affected persons in the position of supplicants. Charles Reich, "The New Property," Yale Law Journal, 73: 733, 751 (1964). For the way in which licensing "reverses the ordinary presumption of liberty" and thereby alters the relationship of individuals to government, see Philip Hamburger, "Getting Permission," Northwestern Law Review, 101: 405, 418–19 (2007).

44. Writing about the 1794 federal licensing of auctioneers, Leonard White observes that "[t]he federal purpose was to tax, not to regulate." Leonard D. White, *The Federalists: A Study in Administrative History*, 401 (New York: Macmillan Co., 1961). For the collection of reports, note that ships had to deposit their ship's registers with the collector, and that by retaining the registers, he could ensure compliance with reports owed by law to him. Ibid., 446.

45. John F. Manning, "Nonlegislative Rules," George Washington Law Review, 72: 893 (2004). For the arm-twisting, see Lars Noah, "Administrative Arm-Twisting in the Shadow of Congressional Delegations of Authority," Wisconsin Law Review, 873, 874 (1997). For varying degrees of skepticism about guidance, see Robert A. Anthony, "Three Settings in Which Nonlegislative Rules Should Not Bind," Administrative Law Review, 53: 1313 (2001); Robert A. Anthony, "Interpretive Rules, Policy Statements, Guidances, Manuals, and the Like—Should Federal Agencies Use Them to Bind the Public?," Duke Law Journal, 41: 1311, 1326 (1992); John Man-

ning, "Constitutional Structure and Judicial Deference to Agency Interpretations of Agency Rules," Columbia Law Review, 96: 612, 617 (1996); Thomas O. McGarity, "Some Thoughts on 'Deossifying' the Rulemaking Process," Duke Law Journal, 41: 1385 (1992); David Zaring, "Best Practices," New York University Law Review, 81: 294 (2006). For a summary of so-called *Skidmore* deference and "respect," see *Christensen v. Harris County*, 529 U.S. 576, 587 (2000); Jeffrey S. Lubbers, *A Guide to Federal Agency Rulemaking*, 507–20 (Chicago: American Bar Association, 2006).

46. Peter L. Strauss, Todd D. Rakoff & Cynthia R. Farina, *Gellhorn and Byse's Administrative Law Cases and Comments*, 289 (New York: Foundation Press, 2003). For some of the dangers of this sort of bargaining in place of rule through law, see Theodore J. Lowi, *The End of Liberalism: Ideology, Policy, and the Crisis of Public Authority*, 147–49 (New York: W. W. Norton & Co., 1969).

47. Lars Noah, "Administrative Arm-Twisting in the Shadow of Congressional Delegations of Authority," Wisconsin Law Review, 873, 876–82 (1997).

48. As put by one commentator, agencies "frequently include regulatory provisions in the[ir] administrative consent decrees that they could not impose directly on a regulated entity." Lars Noah, "Administrative Arm-Twisting in the Shadow of Congressional Delegations of Authority," Wisconsin Law Review, 873, 892 (1997).

49. Mark Rothstein, "OSHA after Ten Years: A Review and Some Proposed Reforms," Vanderbilt Law Review, 34: 71, 110, n. 234 (1981). The case was *Marshall v. Barlow's, Inc.*, 436 U.S. 307, 320–21 (1978). More generally, for the extortionate use of power to investigate, see Charles Reich, "The New Property," Yale Law Journal, 73: 733, 750 (1964).

50. Along somewhat similar lines, Charles Reich observes: "The penumbral government power is, indeed, likely to be greater than the sum of the granted powers. Seeking to stay on the safe side of an uncertain, often unknowable limit, people dependent on largess are likely to eschew any activities that might incur official displeasure." Charles Reich, "The New Property," Yale Law Journal, 73: 733, 751 (1964).

51. James Lindgren, "Unraveling the Paradox of Blackmail," Columbia Law Review, 84: 670 (1984); James Lindgren, "The Elusive Distinction between Bribery and Extortion: From the Common Law to the Hobbs Act," UCLA Law Review, 35: 815 (1988).

52. *Endicott Johnson Corp. v. Perkins*, 317 U.S. 501, 509 (1943). As summarized by one commentator, "the standards for issuance and enforcement of subpoenas are in fact highly permissive." In adjudication, agencies can issue subpoenas and to a degree enforce subpoenas; in investigations, agencies need courts to enforce subpoenas, but the review "is not itself likely to be demanding." Peter L. Strauss, *Administrative Justice in the United States*, 44, 266–67 (Durham: Carolina Academic Press, 2002).

53. *Colonnade Catering Corp. v. United States*, 397 U.S. 72 (1970); *United States v. Biswell*, 406 U.S. 311 (1972); Statement of Alito, J., in *Huber v. N.J. Department of Environmental Protection*, 562 U.S. __ (2011).

54. Some recognition of this can be found in *Marshall v. Barlow's, Inc.*, 436 U.S. 307, 321, 323 (1978).

55. *Marshall v. Barlow's, Inc.*, 436 U.S. 307, 320–21 (1978).

56. 49 U.S.C. §32707. Similarly, for a municipal example, see *Engineering & Manufacturing Services, LLC v. Ashton*, 2007 U.S. Dist. Lexis 67784 (N.D. Ohio, Sept. 13, 2007), in which the Cleveland fire department obtained a warrant "to get to know the property."

57. See, for example, Peter L. Strauss, *Administrative Justice in the United States*, 42 (Durham: Carolina Academic Press, 2002).

58. *In re Meador & Bros.*, Law Times, 2: 140 (U.S. Dist. Ct. Ga. 1869).

59. *Donovan v. Dewey*, 452 U.S. 594 (1981); *New York v. Burger*, 482 U.S. 691 (1987).

60. The connected buildings, used for mixed agricultural and industrial purposes, were typical of New England farms. Thomas C. Hubka, *Big House, Little House, Back House, Barn: The Connected Farmhouse of New England*, viii, xii, 9, 10, 13, 50, 62, 65–66, 77, 98, 119–20, 122, 125, 146–48, 180–81, 189–90, 192–93, 195, 203–04, 222–23 (Lebanon: University Press of New England, 1984). Connected buildings also were frequent in many towns. The legislature of colonial South Carolina authorized justices of the peace to enter any "bakehouse, warehouse, or outhouse" to inspect bread without a warrant, but rather than an example of a search authorized by an administrative warrant, this was simply an inspection authorized by a statute.

61. "Draft Writ of Assistance in Hand of Governor Thomas Hutchinson, George G. Wolkins, 'Writs of Assistance in England,'" Proceedings of the Massachusetts Historical Society, 3rd ser., 66: 357, 362 (1936–41). (Commas have been added silently for ease of reading.) Virginians complained about the government's entry into "houses[,] shops[,] and cellars." Proceedings of the Virginia Committee of Correspondence (Jan. 6, 1774), in *Revolutionary Virginia: The Road to Independence*, 2: 62, William J. Van Schreeven & Robert L. Scribner (Charlottesville: University Press of Virginia, 1975).

62. Petition of Lechmere, *Legal Papers of John Adams*, 2: 141–42, ed. L. Kinvin Wroth & Hiller B. Zobel (Cambridge: Belknap Press, 1965).

63. A later case supplies an illustration. Where the Philadelphia board of health abated a public nuisance on a vacant lot, the state supreme court held that although a judicial warrant was necessary for entry into a "house, store, cellar, or other enclosure," this was not required for entry into a "vacant lot." *Kennedy v. Board of Health*, 2 Pa. 366 (Pa. Supr. Ct. 1845), WL 5260 (Pa.).

64. "*In re Meador & Bros.*," Law Times, 2: 140, 144, 147 (U.S. Dist. Ct. Ga. 1869).

65. The statute in *Meador* provided that, "to aid in the prevention, detection, and punishment of any frauds" in relation to internal taxes, and "to examine into the efficiency and conduct of all officers of internal revenue within his district," a supervisor of internal revenue shall have power "to examine all persons, books, papers, accounts, and premises, and to administer oaths, and to summon any person to produce books and papers, or to appear and testify under oath before him." Ibid., 141.

66. "[F]ailure to respond may be taken as an admission, or as a basis for refusing permission to cross-examine a relevant witness." Peter L. Strauss, *Administrative Justice in the United States*, 266, n. 286 (Durham: Carolina Academic Press, 2002) (citing cases).

67. *Endicott Johnson Corp. v. Perkins*, 317 U.S. 501, 509 (1943).

68. In re *Office of Inspector General, Railroad Retirement Board*, 933 F.2d 276, 277 (5th Cir. 1991). For an only slightly different position, note the view that a court "must do more than 'rubber-stamp' the issuance of an administrative subpoena," but "the court's review of an administrative subpoena is extremely limited." *United States v. Witmer*, 835 F. Supp. 208, 220 (M.D. Pa. 1993). As put by an academic, "A summary procedure is employed in district court to test these issues, and one's impression of the cases is that enforcement is not often refused." Peter L. Strauss, *Administrative Justice in the United States*, 267 (Durham: Carolina Academic Press, 2002).

69. *Federal Maritime Commission v. South Carolina State Ports Authority et al.*, 535 U.S. 743, 756, 763–64 (2002)—the penultimate quotation being from *Butz v. Economou*, 438 U.S. 478, 513 (1978).

70. Act to Regulate the Collection of Duties on Imports and Tonnage, §68 (Mar. 2, 1799), *Public Statutes at Large of the United States*, 1: 677. For other authority to enter or board vessels, see §54, ibid., 1: 668. For earlier statutory provisions regarding entry on to vessels, to collect documents, to inspect, and to search, see ibid., 40, 156–57 & 164.

CHAPTER FOURTEEN

a. Francis Lieber, *On Civil Liberty and Self-Government*, 106–07, n. 4 (Philadelphia: 1877).

1. Coke, *Institutes*, 2: 186–87.
2. Speech of Edward Coke (Mar. 25, 1628), in *Commons Debates 1628*, at 2: 101, ed. Robert C. Johnson & Maija Jansson Cole (New Haven: Yale University Press, 1977).
3. Matthew Hale, *The Prerogatives of the King*, 7, 269, ed. D. E. C. Yale (London: Selden Society, 1976).
4. Ibid., 141. Intriguingly, this was the penultimate paragraph of one of Hale's manuscripts of his book. Although one can only speculate, it is suggestive about why he put the manuscript aside, presumably during the Interregnum.

    In a case on taxes, Chief Justice Holt assumed that, "by the original frame and constitution of the government," legislation "must be by an act made by the whole legislative authority." *Brewster v. Kidgell* (K.B. 1698), Holt's Opinions, Add. Ms. 35979, fol. 109[v]–110[r], British Library.
5. Roger Twysden, *Certaine Considerations upon the Government of England*, 87 (London: Camden Society, 1849).
6. *State Necessity Considered as a Question of Law*, 6 (London: 1766).
7. Caleb Nelson, "Adjudication in the Political Branches," Columbia Law Review, 107: 559, 590 (2007). St. George Tucker explained that "all the courts of the U.S. must be composed of judges holding their offices during good behavior." St. George Tucker, Law Lectures, p. 4 of four loose pages inserted in volume 2, Tucker-Coleman Papers, Mss. 39.1 T79, Box 62, Special Collections Research Center, Earl Gregg Swem Library, College of William and Mary.
8. Francis Lieber, *On Civil Liberty and Self-Government*, 89, 178–79 (London: 1853). By the same token, he added, neither were they to be subject "to the dictation of mobs, nor any people who claim to be *the* people." Ibid., 89.
9. A. V. Dicey, *Introduction to the Law of the Constitution*, 179, 183, 189 (London: MacMillan & Co., 1924).
10. John Dickinson, *Administrative Justice and the Supremacy of the Law in the United States*, 35 (Cambridge: Harvard University Press, 1927).
11. Ibid., 37. For Dickinson's reliance on judicial review, see Thomas Merrill, "Article III, Agency Adjudication, and the Origins of the Appellate Review Model of Administrative Law," Columbia Law Review, 111: 939, 976 (2011). Similarly, see Paul M. Bator, "The Constitution As Architecture: Legislative and Administrative Courts under Article III," Indiana Law Journal, 65: 233, 268 (1990).

CHAPTER FIFTEEN

a. *United States v. Vowell & McLean*, 9 U.S. 368 (1809).

1. A Speech in the Star Chamber (June 20, 1616), in *The Political Works of James I*, at 333, ed. Charles Howard McIlwain (Cambridge: Harvard University Press, 1918).
2. *The Letters and the Life of Francis Bacon*, 5: 363, ed. James Spedding (London: 1869).

3.   Speech of Henry Yelverton (June 29, 1610), in *Parliamentary Debates in 1610*, at 87–88, ed. Samuel Rawson Gardiner (London: Camden Society, 1862).

4.   Speech of Richard Martyn (June 29, 1610), ibid., 89; Speech of Edward Coke (Mar. 24, 1628), in *State Trials*, 3: 68. Coke also said, "The king hath no prerogative, but that which the law of the land allows him." *Case of Proclamations* (1610), Coke, *Reports*, 12: 76. By mid-century, even distinguished royalists agreed: "We hold only what the law holds: the king's prerogative and the subject's liberty are determined, and bounded, and admeasured by a written law what they are; we do not hold the king to have any more power . . . but what the law gives him." *The Cordial of Judge Jenkins, For the Good People of London* (1648), in *The Works of the Grave and Learned Lawyer Judge Jenkins*, 131 (London: 1648).

     Coke is reported at one point to have to have said, "There is prerogative indisputable, and prerogative disputable. Prerogative indisputable, is that the king hath to make war: disputable prerogative is tied to the laws of England." Speech of Edward Coke (1620), in *Cobbett's Parliamentary History of England*, 1: 1193 (London: 1806). The truncated report of the debate leaves his meaning unclear, but he probably meant that the law was the measure of where the king had absolute discretion and where he did not.

5.   Henry Barrow, *A Plain Refutation of Mr. George Giffarde's Reproachful Booke* (Dort: 1591), in *The Writings of Henry Barrow 1590–1591*, at 316, ed. Leland H. Carlson (London: George Allen & Unwin, 1966).

6.   *The Argument of Master Nicholas Fuller, in the Case of Thomas Ladd, and Richard Maunsell*, 30–31 (n.p.: 1607). Although different from his argument in court, this pamphlet at least suggests the character of Fuller's argument.

7.   *Prohibitions del Roy*, Coke, *Reports*, 12: 64.

8.   Sir Matthew Hale, *The Prerogatives of the King*, 180, ed. D. E. C. Yale (London: Selden Society, 1976).

9.   See chap. 4, endnote 4.

10. That this was Coke's point in *Bonham's Case* has not been understood, but it is clear from a range of evidence, as shown in Philip Hamburger, *Law and Judicial Duty*, 622–30 (Cambridge: Harvard University Press, 2008).

11. Philip Hamburger, *Law and Judicial Duty*, 225–30 (Cambridge: Harvard University Press, 2008).

12. *Earl of Shaftesbury's Case* (K.B. 1677), in *Modern Reports*, 1: 148. After this was argued by Wallop on behalf of Shaftesbury, the attorney general conceded, "that which is said of the judges' power to expound statutes cannot be denied." Ibid., 154.

13. A Speech in the Star Chamber (June 20, 1616), in *The Political Works of James I*, at 333, ed. Charles Howard McIlwain (Cambridge: Harvard University Press, 1918).

14. Roscoe Pound, *The Spirit of the Common Law*, 73–74 (Boston: Marshall Jones Co., 1921).

15. "An Elector" [James Iredell], "To the Public," *North Carolina Gazette* (Newbern) (Aug. 17, 1786). For the office or duty of judges, see Philip Hamburger, *Law and Judicial Duty*, 103, 283 (Cambridge: Harvard University Press, 2008).

16. *Osborne v. Bank of the United States*, 22 U.S. 738, 866 (1824).

17. Some state courts already assumed that they had a duty to follow federal law, as can be observed from the opinions in which Massachusetts and North Carolina judges held state statutes unconstitutional under the Articles of Confederation. See Philip Hamburger, *Law and Judicial Duty*, 597–601 (Cambridge: Harvard University Press, 2008). Of course, when judges, not unreasonably, concluded that the Articles of

Confederation were not really law, they might doubt whether they had any duty to follow them.

18. *Murray's Lessee v. Hoboken Land & Improvement Co.*, 59 U.S. 272, 284 (1856).
19. Ibid.; Caleb Nelson, "Adjudication in the Political Branches," Columbia Law Review, 107: 559, 562, 586 (2007).
20. *Decatur v. Paulding*, 39 U.S. 497, 515 (1840).
21. Reviewing the history, Ann Woolhandler calls such actions "de novo" review. Ann Woolhandler, "Judicial Deference to Administrative Action: A Revisionist History," Administrative Law Review, 43: 197 (1997). Caleb Nelson observes that such review was available only where the executive acts were understood to have gone beyond the discretion of the government—either in binding subjects or in distributing benefits in a way that infringed on their legal rights. Caleb Nelson, "Adjudication in the Political Branches," Columbia Law Review, 107: 559, 563–64 (2007). Most recently, Thomas Merrill analyzes the actions available to members of the public, showing that "[t]he form of action dictated the nature of the 'review.'" Thomas Merrill, "Article III, Agency Adjudication, and the Origins of the Appellate Review Model of Administrative Law," Columbia Law Review, 111: 939, 947 (2011). See also Ernst Freund, *Administrative Powers over Persons and Property*, 234–69 (Chicago: University of Chicago Press, 1928).

    Although Woolhandler's work is valuable for its account of de novo review, it suggests that courts traditionally deferred to administrative exercises of judicial power. Much of her evidence of deference to administrative actions, however, consists of citations to John Dickinson, who in turn cited cases against officers, in which the form of action often determined the outcome. The reliance on Dickinson is unfortunate, for he emphasized the importance of not drawing strong conclusions from cases that denied recovery on account of the requirements for the cause of action. As he explained about mandamus, "[t]he fact that the courts will not issue a writ of mandamus in a given situation" did not mean they "would not review the executive action . . . in some other way." Woolhandler, "Judicial Deference to Administrative Action: A Revisionist History," Administrative Law Review, 43: 210, notes 67& 68, 213; John Dickinson, *Administrative Justice and the Supremacy of the Law in the United States*, 40 (Cambridge: Harvard University Press, 1927). Indeed, the fact that courts increasingly established legal barriers protecting officers in actions against them does not show that there traditionally was any judicial deference, let alone to the executive.
22. For some illustrative Massachusetts tax cases from the 1780s, see Philip Hamburger, *Law and Judicial Duty*, app. I (Cambridge: Harvard University Press, 2008).
23. Thomas Merrill, "Article III, Agency Adjudication, and the Origins of the Appellate Review Model of Administrative Law," Columbia Law Review, 111: 951, 953 (2011).
24. *Elliott v. Swartwout*, 35 U.S. 137, 153 (1836).
25. *Lee v. Lincoln*, 15 F.Cas. 210, No. 8195 (1841).
26. Ibid.
27. *Floyd v. Barker* (1607), Coke, Reports, 12: 24; Thomas Wood, *An Institute of the Laws of England*, 443 (London: 1772).
28. See, for example, the discussion of the carriage tax in chap. 16, endnote 9.
29. *U.S. v. Irving*, 42 U.S. 250, 260, 262–63 (1843).

CHAPTER SIXTEEN

a. *Cary v. Curtis*, 44 U.S. 236, 250 (1845).

b. Ernst Freund, "Historical Survey," in *The Growth of Administrative Law*, 12–15 (St. Louis: Thomas Law Book Co., 1923); Ernst Freund, *Administrative Powers over Persons and Property*, 243 (Chicago: University of Chicago Press, 1928); David E. Engdahl, "Immunity and Accountability for Positive Government Wrongs," Colorado Law Review, 44: 1, 22–23, 41 (1972). See also John Mabry Mathews, *Principles of American State Administration*, 161–62 (New York: D. Appleton & Co., 1917).

e. Anthony Fitzherbert, *La Graunde Abridgement*, 2: fol. 83r, "Monstrance de Fait," No. 182 ([London]: 1577) (citing case of 16 Henry VI); Y.B., Michaelmas 1 Henry VII, 4, pl.5.

f. A. V. Dicey, *Introduction to the Study of the Law of the Constitution*, 225 (Indianapolis: Liberty Classics, 1982); James G. Randall, "The Indemnity Act of 1863: A Study in the War-Time Immunity of Governmental Officers," Michigan Law Review, 20: 590–91 (1922).

h. *Final Report of the Attorney General's Committee on Administrative Procedure*, 209–11 (Washington, DC: U.S. Government Printing Office, 1941). For the adoption of the "substantial evidence" standard in appeals from administrative proceedings, see *ICC v. Union Pacific Railroad Co.*, 222 U.S. 541 (1912), as noted by Thomas W. Merrill, "The Origins of American-Style Judicial Review," in *Comparative Administrative Law*, 389, 397, ed. Susan Rose-Ackerman & Peter L. Lindseth (Cheltenham: Edward Elgar, 2010).

i. Samuel Rutherford, *Lex Rex: The Law and the Prince*, 252–53 (xxvii.1 & 3) (London: 1644). As evident from his allusion to "inferior judges," Rutherford took a Presbyterian view of government.

j. For Madison's understanding of departmentalism and the more conventional view, see Philip Hamburger, *Law and Judicial Duty*, 225–34, 550–54 (Cambridge: Harvard University Press, 2008).

1. Among the scholarship that is skeptical of judicial deference is Martin Shapiro, *Who Guards the Guardians: Judicial Control of Administration*, 173 (Athens: University of Georgia Press, 1988); Martin Shapiro, *The Supreme Court and Administrative Agencies*, 265 (New York: Free Press, 1968).

2. Jack Lively, *The Social and Political Thought of Alexis de Tocqueville*, 171 (Oxford: Clarendon Press, 1965). See also David E. Engdahl, "Immunity and Accountability for Positive Government Wrongs," Colorado Law Review, 44: 17, 19 (1972). Long before, Twysden explained: "None of [the king's prerogatives] can be a warrant for any employed by him to do wrong or injury to any man, but he must answer the party grieved in an ordinary court of justice, and be punished according to law." Roger Twysden, *Certaine Considerations upon the Government of England*, 87 (London: Camden Society, 1849).

3. Robert Mayo, who in the 1840s edited existing Treasury circulars—vigorously criticized the old lines between administrative and judicial proceedings. He was sympathetic to customs collectors and other such officers, and he complained bitterly about the unequal treatment of different types of government officers, arguing that there should be a uniform method of determining disputes under a centralized at least semi-judicial tribunal. Robert Mayo, *A Synopsis of the Commercial and Revenue System of the United States, As Developed by Instructions and Decisions of the Treasury*

Department for the Administration of the Revenue Laws, 427, 432 (Washington, DC: 1847).

4. An Act Making Appropriations for the Civil and Diplomatic Expenses of the Government for the Year Eighteen Hundred and Thirty-Nine, §2, *Public Statutes at Large of the United States*, 5: 348–49.

5. *Cary v. Curtis*, 44 U.S. 236, 242 (1845).

6. Ibid., 253.

7. An Act Explanatory of an Act Entitled, "An Act Making Appropriations . . ." (Feb. 26, 1845), *Public Statutes at Large of the United States*, 5: 727.

8. These problems were discussed in *People ex rel. John Copcutt v. Board of Health of City of Yonkers*, 140 N.Y. 1, 35 N.E. Reporter 320, 322 (1893).

9. The late-eighteenth-century mechanism that was similar to an appeal came in the form of a separate cause of action, but functioned as an appeal. When imposing an excise on carriages, Congress in 1796 provided for two levels of appeal within the Treasury—initially from the inspection officers to their district supervisors, and then to the secretary of the Treasury. After that, Congress allowed an aggrieved taxpayer to bring a suit against the district supervisor to recover the duties paid. According to the statute, the parties maintaining such suits were "confined to the assignment and proof of such facts and matters" as they had "previously stated" to the supervisors in the administrative appeal. This presumably required plaintiffs to wait until there was a final decision by the secretary and to bring claims only against the supervisors. Of particular interest here, because of the statutory delay and the limit on the matters that could be proved, the independent actions by taxpayers functioned like appeals. An Act Laying Duties on Carriages for the Conveyance of Persons; and Repealing the Former Act for that Purpose, §9 (May 28, 1796), *Public Statutes at Large of the United States*, 1: 481, discussed by Leonard D. White, *The Federalists: A Study in Administrative History*, 455 (New York: Macmillan Co., 1961); Jerry L. Mashaw, "Recovering American Administrative Law: Federalist Foundations, 1787–1801," Yale Law Journal, 115: 1256, 1309 (2006). For the politics of the carriage tax and its fate in *Hylton v. United States*, see Charlotte Crane, "Reclaiming the Meaning of 'Direct Tax,'" http://ssrn.com/abstract=1553230.

10. Peter L. Strauss, *Administrative Justice in the United States*, 336 (Durham: Carolina Academic Press, 2002); *United States v. Morgan*, 313 U.S. 409, 422 (1941). Similarly, Justice Jackson justified *Skidmore* deference in terms of "good judicial administration." *Skidmore v. Swift & Co.*, 323 U.S. 134, 140 (1944).

11. *Cary v. Curtis*, 44 U.S. 236, 253 (1845).

12. Frank J. Goodnow, *The Principles of Administrative Law of the United States*, 396–97 (New York: G. P. Putnam, 1905).

13. Edmund M. Parker, "Administrative Courts for the United States," in *Proceedings of the American Political Science Association at Its Sixth Annual Meeting*, 46, 49 (Baltimore: Waverly Press, 1910); Frank J. Goodnow, *Selected Cases on the Law of Officers, Including Extraordinary Legal Remedies*, 438 (Chicago: Callaghan & Co., 1906). Goodnow had a point, although a rather disturbing one, when he vehemently protested: "We can do no better than endeavor to beat it into the heads of the legal profession that notwithstanding our boasted protection of private rights in this country, those rights are as a matter of fact much less protected against administrative action than they are under the system of administrative courts in vogue upon the continent of Europe." Daniel R. Ernst, "Ernst Freund, Felix Frankfurter, and the American *Rechtsstaat*: A Transatlantic Shipwreck, 1894–1932," Studies in American Political

Development, 23: 171, 178, n. 51 (2009), quoting *Proceedings of the American Political Science Association*, 64 (1909).

14. John Dickinson, *Administrative Justice and the Supremacy of the Law in the United States*, 42 (Cambridge: Harvard University Press, 1927).

15. W.N.M., "The Power of an Executive to Construe Statutes Pertaining to His Department As a Reason for Denying Mandamus," University of Pennsylvania Law Review, 78: 407 (1930).

16. Alexander Hamilton, Federalist Number 78, in *The Federalist*, 525, ed. Jacob E. Cooke (Middletown: Wesleyan University Press, 1961).

17. 5 U.S.C. §706.

18. 5 U.S.C. §706.

19. Philip Hamburger, *Law and Judicial Duty*, chap. 10 (Cambridge: Harvard University Press, 2008).

20. "An Elector" [James Iredell], "To the Public," *North Carolina Gazette* (Newbern) (Aug. 17, 1786); *Marbury v. Madison* (1803), 5 U.S. 137, 177–78.

21. *Citizens to Preserve Overton Park, Inc. v. Volpe*, 401 U.S. 402, 416 (1971); *Motor Vehicle Manufacturers Association v. State Farm Mutual Automobile Insurance Co.*, 463 U.S. 29 (1983); *U.S. Airwaves, Inc. v. FCC*, 232 F.3d 227, 233 (D.C. Cir. 2000).

22. *Sierra Club v. Costle*, 657 F.2d 298, 410 (D.C. Cir. 1981).

23. *Chevron U.S.A. Inc. v. National Resources Defense Council, Inc.*, 467 U.S. 837, 844, 865 (1984). The case ostensibly addresses the provision of the Administrative Procedure Act stating that judges shall hold unlawful and set aside agency action, findings, and conclusions found to be "in excess of statutory jurisdiction, authority, or limitations, or short of statutory right." 5 U.S.C. §706. It also has been understood to address questions about the arbitrary and capricious measure. John F. Duffy & Michael Hertz, *A Guide to Judicial and Political Review of Federal Agencies*, 96–102 (Chicago: American Bar Association, 2005). Revealingly, one commentator speaks of "*Chevron* obedience" in order to suggest "the obligation of courts to accept reasonable agency determinations." Peter L. Strauss, *Administrative Justice in the United States*, 371 & n. 104 (Durham: Carolina Academic Press, 2002). The breadth of *Chevron* deference was recently emphasized in *City of Arlington v. Federal Communications Commission*, 509 U.S. __ (2013).

24. *Skidmore v. Swift & Co.*, 323 U.S. 134 (1944); *Christensen v. Harris County*, 529 U.S. 576 (2000); *United States v. Mead Corp.*, 533 U.S. 218 (2000).

In justifying *Skidmore*, Peter Strauss writes: "Cases reaching back well into the nineteenth century had reasoned that settled administrative interpretations, or administrative interpretations contemporaneous with enactment, are 'entitled to very great respect,' and ought not be disturbed if they are possibly within the meaning of statutory language, or 'overruled without cogent reasons.'" Peter L. Strauss, "'Deference' Is Too Confusing—Let's Call Them 'Chevron Space' and '*Skidmore* Weight,'" Columbia Law Review, 112: 1143, 1154 (2012). None of the pre–Civil War cases cited by Strauss, however, support his conclusions. An 1827 case explained that it concerned a "contemporaneous construction" by commissioners that also "seems to have received, very shortly after, the sanction of the legislature." *Edwards' Lessee v. Darby*, 25 U.S. 206, 210 (1827). An 1832 case was really about recognizing reliance on long-standing constructions. *United States v. State Bank of North Carolina*, 31 U.S. 29, 39 (1832). Only the 1877 case cited by Strauss suggested something closer to deference. *United States v. Moore*, 95 U.S. 760, 763 (1877).

25. *Thomas Jefferson University v. Shalala*, 512 U.S. 504, 510–11 (1994); *Auer v. Robbins*,

519 U.S. 452 (1997) (quotation marks omitted); John Manning, "Constitutional Structure and Judicial Deference to Agency Interpretations of Agency Rules," Columbia Law Review, 96: 612 (1996); *Bowles v. Seminole Rock & Sand Co.*, 325 U.S. 410 (1945).

26. For the *Case of Proclamations*, see chap. 3. For *Bonham's Case*, see Philip Hamburger, *Law and Judicial Duty*, app. I (Cambridge: Harvard University Press, 2008).

27. Henry Monaghan defends judicial deference to administrative interpretation of statutes by suggesting that the deference merely recognizes the underlying power of Congress to delegate lawmaking power to executive agencies. Henry P. Monaghan, "'Marbury' and the Administrative State," Columbia Law Review, 83: 1, 6 (1983). This explanation, however, runs into difficulty. The immediate problem is what the courts say about what they are doing. Rather than say that they are recognizing the authority of agencies to make law, the courts candidly say that they are putting aside their interpretation in deference to administrative interpretation. A larger problem is the confusion of legislative and judicial powers. Even if Congress could subdelegate binding lawmaking power to the executive, the power to make authoritative interpretations is distinctively judicial. Judges therefore cannot defer to executive interpretations without giving up a central element of their office, and as will be seen later, Congress cannot delegate a power it does not have.

28. 5 U.S.C. §706. The rare exception is when a court of appeals sends an appeal to a district court to create a record.

29. Thomas Merrill, "Article III, Agency Adjudication, and the Origins of the Appellate Review Model of Administrative Law," Columbia Law Review, 111: 939, 974–75, n. 71 (2011).

30. Thurman Arnold, *The Symbols of Government*, 189–90 (New Haven: Yale University Press, 1935).

31. Thomas Merrill, "Article III, Agency Adjudication, and the Origins of the Appellate Review Model of Administrative Law," Columbia Law Review, 111: 951, 959, 963 (2011).

32. Roscoe Pound, "Executive Justice," American Law Register, 55: 137, 139 (Mar. 1907). He added:

> In general, the cases prior to 1880 tend to hold all matters involving a hearing and determination, where the liberty, property or fortune of the citizen may be affected, to be judicial and not capable of exercise by executive functionaries. Since 1880, the cases, at first requiring an appeal or a possibility of judicial review, but later beginning to cast off even that remnant of judicial control, tend strongly to hold every sort of power that does not involve directly an adjudication of a controversy between citizen and citizen—and in the cases of disputes over water-rights and election-contests some which do—to be administrative in character and a legitimate matter for executive boards and commissions.

Ibid., 140.

CHAPTER SEVENTEEN

a. St. George Tucker, Law Lectures, 6: 220, Tucker-Coleman Papers, Mss. 39.1 T79, Box 62, Special Collections Research Center, Earl Gregg Swem Library, College of William and Mary; Alexander Hamilton, Federalist Number 78, in *The Federalist*, 523, ed. Jacob E. Cooke (Middletown: Wesleyan University Press, 1961).

b. For Wood and other skeptics about the separation of powers, see Edward S. Corwin, "The Progress of Constitutional Theory between the Declaration of Independence and the Meeting of the Philadelphia Convention," in *American Constitutional History: Essays by Edward S. Corwin*, 4, ed. Alpheus T. Mason & Gerald Garvey (New York: Harper Torchbooks, 1964); Gordon S. Wood, "Judicial Review in the Era of the Founding," in *Is the Supreme Court the Guardian of the Constitution*, 155, ed. Robert A. Licht (Washington, DC: AEI Press, 1993). For responses, see Saikrishna B. Prakash & John C. Yoo, "The Origins of Judicial Review," University of Chicago Law Review, 70: 931 (2003); Philip Hamburger, *Law and Judicial Duty*, 400–05 (Cambridge: Harvard University Press, 2008). For an account that attributes separation of powers to early Americans but only relatively late, around the time of the Revolution, see Stephen G. Calabresi, Mark E. Berghausen & Skylar Albertson, "The Rise and Fall of Separation of Powers," Northwestern Law Review, 106: 527 (2012). It does not recognize the intellectual origins of separation in specialized faculties or the recognition of separation as early as the fourteenth century.

c.   William Blackstone, *Commentaries on the Laws of England*, 1: 51–52 (Oxford: 1765).

1.   For the Madisonian view, which focused on keeping apart the branches of government, see James Madison, Federalist Number 47, in *The Federalist*, 324–25, ed. Jacob E. Cooke (Middletown: Wesleyan University Press, 1961). For the alternative view, that the three branches were "assigned different powers," see, for example, Arnold I. Burns & Stephen J. Markman, "Understanding Separation of Powers," Pace Law Review, 7: 575, 582 (1987). Incidentally, Madison's understanding of entire or complete separation entailed by the separation of powers was very similar to his understanding of the purity of church and state required by his vision of the "separation of church and state."

      Of course, the success of political parties undermines the effect of the separation of powers. Daryl Levinson & Richard Pildes, "Separation of Parties, Not Powers," Harvard Law Review, 119: 2312 (2006). Yet this is not to say there is no point in adhering to separation, as evident from the implications of separation for administrative power.

2.   E.g., Hervaeus Natalis c. 1315, discussed by Brian Tierney, *Religion, Law, and the Growth of Constitutional Thought, 1150–1650*, at 45 (Cambridge: Cambridge University Press, 1982); Brian Tierney, "Hierarchy, Consent, and the 'Western Tradition,'" Political Theory, 15: 649 (1987).

3.   Modus Tenendi Parliamentum, sec. XVIII, in M. V. Clarke, *Medieval Representation and Consent*, 381 (London: Longmans, Green & Co., 1936), as translated by Francis D. Wormuth, *The Origins of Modern Constitutionalism*, 60 (New York: Harper & Brothers, 1949). The original is "contra defectus legum originalium, iudicialium, et executorarium"—the second comma being present in one variant but not another. *Parliamentary Texts of the Later Middle Ages*, 75 & 108, ed. Nicholas Pronay & John Taylor (Oxford: Clarendon Press, 1980). This is translated in the 1980 edition as "against the defects of customary law, the law of the courts and the executive"— apparently on the assumption that "legum" is used here in contrast to "lex." Ibid., 88. In the entire *Modus*, however, the word "lex" is not used at all, and "legum" is used only in this instance.

4.   Philip Hamburger, *Law and Judicial Duty*, 149–50 (Cambridge: Harvard University Press, 2008).

5.   Francis D. Wormuth, *The Origins of Modern Constitutionalism*, 60 (New York: Harper & Brothers, 1949); W. B. Gwyn, *The Meaning of the Separation of Powers Doctrine*, 54, 64 (New Orleans: Tulane University Press, 1965); M. J. C. Vile, *Constitutionalism*

and the Separation of Powers, 57 (Indianapolis: Liberty Fund 1998). For example, John Sadler attributed three personal qualities to parts of government: "I cannot deny original power to the Commons, judicial to the Lords, executive to the King." Francis D. Wormuth, *The Origins of Modern Constitutionalism,* 61 (New York: Harper & Brothers, 1949) In a more up-to-date manner, Samuel Rutherford differentiated the executive power of the king, the legislative power of Parliament, and the judicial power of the judges, who were to judge independently of the king. [Samuel Rutherford], *Lex, Rex: The Law and the Prince,* 160, 178–79 (xx) (London: 1644).

6. *Case of Paty et al.* (Q.B. 1705), *The Judgements Delivered by the Lord Chief Justice Holt in the Case of Ashby v. White and Others, and in the Case of John Paty and Others,* 60 (London: 1837).

7. Francis Osborne [William Pitt], in London Journal (July 4, 1730), as quoted by W. B. Gwyn, *The Meaning of the Separation of Powers Doctrine,* 97 (New Orleans: Tulane University Press, 1965).

8. Montesquieu, *The Spirit of the Laws,* 185–86 (XI.vi) (Dublin: 1751). As to Locke's views, see John Locke, *Two Treatises of Government,* 275 (II.ii.13), ed. Peter Laslett (Cambridge: Cambridge University Press, 1988); Philip Hamburger, "Revolution and Judicial Review: Chief Justice Holt's Opinion in *City of London v. Wood,*" Columbia Law Review 94: 2127 (1994). Locke's analysis of the state of nature obviously was of particular significance for the separation of judicial from legislative power. At a more concrete level, although Locke did not separate a judicial power from the executive, he held it was "necessary there should be a power always in being, which should see to the execution of the laws that are made, and remain in force. And thus the legislative and executive power come often to be separated." Locke, *Two Treatises of Government,* 365 (II.xii.144). See also ibid., 324–25 (II.viii.88). In other respects, however, Locke's conceptions of government powers went in a very different direction.

9. Montesquieu, *The Spirit of the Laws,* 186 (XI.vi) (Dublin: 1751).

10. Ibid., 186 (XI.vi). Although Venice had "different tribunals" exercise legislative, executive, and judicial powers, there remained "the mischief" that "these different tribunals are composed of magistrates all belonging to the same body; which constitutes almost one and the same power." Ibid., 187 (XI.vi).

11. Thomas Jefferson, *Notes on the State of Virginia,* 195 (London: 1787); James Madison, Federalist Number 47, in *The Federalist,* 324, ed. Jacob E. Cooke (Middletown: Wesleyan University Press, 1961) (commas have been added).

12. John Locke, *Two Treatises of Government,* 272 (II.ii.8), 275 (II.ii.13), ed. Peter Laslett (Cambridge: Cambridge University Press, 1988).

13. Ibid., 132 (II.x.132). An American newspaper summarized: "All citizens are equal, and originally possess of legislative, executive, judiciary and military powers." "A Few Plain Maxims of Common Sense," Virginia Independent Chronicle (Mar. 19, 1788).

14. Edmund Randolph, Ms. Notes of Argument in *Commonwealth v. Lamb &c.,* James Madison Papers, 91: 104, at pp. 9 & 11, Library of Congress; *Report of the Committee of the Council of Censors, Appointed to Enquire, "Whether the Constitution has been preserved inviolate in every part, and whether the legislative and executive branches of government have performed their duty as guardians of the people, or assumed to themselves or exercised other or greater powers, than they are entituled to by the Constitution,"* 4 (Philadelphia: Francis Bailey, 1784). (Note that this is the twenty-seven-page pamphlet published under this title.)

Arguing that some such powers were retained by individuals even after the adoption of a constitution, the Rev. Moses Mather preached in a prominent revolutionary sermon that "[b]y nature, every man . . . is his own legislator, judge, and avenger, and absolute lord of his property," and similarly, "[i]n civil government, rightly constituted, every one retains a share in the legislative, taxative, judicial, and vindictive powers." [Moses Mather], *America's Appeal to the Impartial World*, 7 (Hartford: 1775).

15. James Madison, Federalist Number 37, in *The Federalist*, 235, ed. Jacob E. Cooke (Middletown: Wesleyan University Press, 1961).

16. James Madison, Federalist Number 47, in *The Federalist*, 324–325, ed. Jacob E. Cooke (Middletown: Wesleyan University Press, 1961).

17. N.H. Const. of 1784, Art. XXXVII. The convention that framed this constitution had observed that "although there is a considerable majority for keeping the executive power separate from the legislative; yet there is . . . a diversity of sentiment concerning the manner, and hands, in which the same should be deposited." *An Address of the Convention for Framing a Constitution of Government for the People of New Hampshire*, 2 (Portsmouth: 1783). Similarly, a New Hampshire minister noted, "I might show how the several powers of government are nicely adjusted, so as to have a mutual check on each other, and despotic power guarded against by keeping the legislative, judicial and executive powers, distinct and separate, an essential arrangement in a free government." Samuel M'Clintock, *A Sermon Preached Before the Honorable The Council, and the Honorable the Senate and House of Representatives, of the State of New Hampsire, June 3, 1784: On Occasion of the Commencement of the New Constitution and Form of Government*, 24 (Portsmouth: 1784).

18. *Report of the Committee of the Council of Censors*, 18 (Philadelphia: 1784); St. George Tucker, Law Lectures, p. 4 of four loose pages inserted in volume 2, Tucker-Coleman Papers, Mss. 39.1 T79, Box 62, Special Collections Research Center, Earl Gregg Swem Library, College of William and Mary. That such views were widely discussed in Philadelphia is suggested by the observation of a newspaper essay that "each of these branches, of right, exercises all authority, devolved by the community, which property belongs to it, unless the contrary be clearly expressed." A.B., Pennsylvania Gazette (Apr. 28, 1784), as quoted by M. J. C. Vile, *Constitutionalism and the Separation of Powers*, 153 (Indianapolis: Liberty Fund, 1998).

Gary Lawson views "the Constitution's three 'vesting' clauses as effecting a complete division of otherwise unallocated federal governmental authority among the constitutionally specified legislative, executive, and judicial institutions." Thus, "[a]ny exercise of governmental power, and any governmental institution exercising that power, must either fit within one of the three formal categories thus established or find explicit constitutional authorization for such a deviation." Gary Lawson, "Territorial Governments and the Limits of Formalism," California Law Review, 78: 853, 857 (1990). John Manning protests that the Constitution's allocation of powers must be somewhat open ended because the document contains no separation-of-powers clause. John Manning, "Separation of Powers As Ordinary Interpretation," Harvard Law Review, 124: 1939, 1944 (2011). But this fails to recognize the degree to which the Constitution establishes its separation of powers as the default when it grants specialized powers to specialized branches of government. The Constitution establishes its separation of powers, and then qualifies it in various ways, and it therefore is a mistake to qualify the separation of powers in other ways.

19. Montesquieu, *The Spirit of the Laws*, 186 (XI.vi) (Dublin: 1751).

20. Christopher Hitchens, *Hitch-22: A Memoir*, 51 (Crows Nest: Allen & Unwin, 2010).

21. Focusing on administrative legislation, David Schoenbrod observes that delegation endangers liberty. David Schoenbrod, *Power without Responsibility: How Congress Abuses the People through Delegation*, 107 (New Haven: Yale University Press, 1993).

22. For the functionalist approach, see Peter L. Strauss, "The Place of Agencies in Government: Separation of Powers and the Fourth Branch," Columbia Law Review, 84: 573, 597 (1984). For the formalist view, see Gary Lawson, "Territorial Governments and the Limits of Formalism," California Law Review, 78: 853, 859–60 (1990). For an attempt to split the difference, see John Manning, "Separation of Powers As Ordinary Interpretation," Harvard Law Review, 124: 1939, 1940–44 (2011).

23. A. V. Dicey, *Lectures on the Relation between Law and Public Opinion in England during the Nineteenth Century*, xliii–iv, preface to the 2nd, 1914, ed. (London: Macmillan & Co., 1940).

24. Montesquieu, *The Spirit of the Laws*, 187 (XI.vi) (Dublin: 1751). According to Ernst Freund, the "feeling" that the law "is inadequate to check undesirable practices and that additional grounds of restraint should be established" constitutes "in itself . . . a bias which inevitably communicates itself to a policy-enforcing authority." Writing about the Trade Commission of 1914, Freund also explained, "The dispute usually does not turn upon the truth or falsity of the facts established by the commission, but upon the truth or falsity of its conclusions," which "must in the nature of things be largely matter of opinion, and the difference between law and fact becomes obscure. A bias, even an unconscious bias, may determine which way the decision will fall." Ernst Freund, "Historical Survey," in *The Growth of Administrative Law*, 31–32 (St. Louis: Thomas Law Book Co., 1923).

25. John Dickinson, *Administrative Justice and the Supremacy of the Law in the United States*, 23 (Cambridge: Harvard University Press, 1927). Charles Reich observes that "commonly the initial tribunal is a hearing office, but the final decisions is by the dispensing agency itself." Charles Reich, "The New Property," Yale Law Journal, 73: 733, 752 (1964).

26. Bruce Wyman, *Principles of Administrative Law*, 321 (St. Paul: 1903). According to Charles Reich, "Nor should the same persons sit as legislator, prosecutor, judge and jury, combining all the functions of government in such a way as to make fairness virtually impossible." Charles Reich, "The New Property," Yale Law Journal, 73: 733, 784 (1964).

27. Peter L. Strauss, Todd D. Rakoff, Cynthia R. Farina & Gillian E. Metzger, *Gellhorn and Byse's Administrative Law Cases and Comments*, 16 (New York: Foundation Press, 2011).

28. John Locke, *Two Treatises of Government*, 351 (II.ix.124–26), ed. Peter Laslett (Cambridge: Cambridge University Press, 1988), discussed in Philip Hamburger, "Revolution and Judicial Review: Chief Justice Holt's Opinion in *City of London v. Wood*," Columbia Law Review, 94: 2134 (1994).

29. Philip Hamburger, "Revolution and Judicial Review: Chief Justice Holt's Opinion in *City of London v. Wood*," Columbia Law Review, 94: 2127 (1994).

30. Ibid., 2152.

31. The principle that one should not be judge in one own case has recently been critiqued by Adrian Vermeule on the ground that the maxim is applied inconsistently. After surveying a wide range of instances in which the principle has been invoked or has been left aside, Vermeule concludes that the maxim cannot even be relied upon

as a presumption against impartiality because "central structural features of the constitutional system" are inconsistent with it. Adrian Vermeule, "Contra *Nemo Iudex in Sua Causa*: The Limits of Impartiality," Yale Law Journal, 122: 100, 110 (2012).

In the common law, however, the principle against being judge in one's own case traditionally was not stated in absolute terms, for it developed merely as a presumption of interpretation—namely, that a grant of judicial power should not be interpreted to permit the recipient to be judge in his own case, unless the grant specifically authorized this. D. E. C. Yale, "*Judex in Propria Causa*: An Historical Excursus," Cambridge Law Journal, 33: 87, 96 (1974). The principle thus was not rigid, but simply a basis for something like equitable interpretation. Common lawyers tended to understand the danger of flatly applying abstract moral principles to the rough texture of human institutions, and it therefore should be no surprise that when they explored the principle about not being judge in one's own case, they left ample room for variation.

Put more broadly, there is a danger that Vermeule's approach elevates principles beyond what they can bear. Certainly, if the principle against being judge in one's own case is expected to explain the exceptions to it, it cannot be viewed as very accurate or predictive. No human ideal is so unequivocal that it is beyond qualification by other considerations, and it therefore is no objection to an ideal that it sometimes must give way to other ideals or even merely other concerns. In this instance, the fact that the makers of constitutions and other laws have (for good or bad reasons) often judged it necessary to carve out exceptions to the principle, does not show that the principle fails to summarize a profound moral presumption against biased adjudication.

In addition, there is a question of context or domain. Although Vermeule evaluates the principle in the context of the full range of governmental decisions, it traditionally had a much narrower application in Anglo-American law and philosophy. It conventionally was employed mainly to understand the relationship of government to its subjects, and in this context, the Constitution goes far in following the principle. On the whole, as seen in part II, the U.S. Constitution allows the government to bind subjects judicially only through the courts and their judges—in particular, judges who have an office of independent judgment in accord with the law, and who are constitutionally protected in this office. When considered in this context, the Constitution's departures from the principle are not nearly as serious as Vermeule's analysis suggests.

32. A paper prepared for the Administrative Conference of the United States recognizes that "trial-type adjudications are held before scores of federal agencies, each having its own set of practice and procedure rules." On this basis, it urges that the agencies employ "similar practice and procedure," so as to reduce adjudication costs, expedite and simplify proceedings, and simplify the role of all persons. Michael Cox, "The Model Adjudication Rules (MARs)," T. M. Cooley Law Review, 11: 75, 76 (1984).

33. Ernst Freund, *Administrative Powers over Persons and Property*, 33 (Chicago: University of Chicago Press, 1928).

34. *Encyclopedia of Public Administration and Public Policy: K–Z*, at 2: 1087, ed. Jack Rabin (CRC Press, 2003); Max Weber, "Legal Authority with a Bureaucratic Administrative Staff," in *Economy and Society*, 2: 225, ed. Guenther Roth & Claus Wittich (Berkeley: University of California Press, 1978).

35. Karl R. Popper, *Conjectures and Refutations: The Growth of Scientific Knowledge* (London: Routledge, 2003); Imre Lakatos, *Proofs and Refutations* (Cambridge: Cambridge University Press, 1976).

36. Robert King Merton, *The Sociology of Science: Theoretical and Empirical Investigations,* 277 (Chicago: University of Chicago Press, 1973).

37. Note the Supreme Court's allusion in *Chevron* to "the incumbent administration's views of wise policy." *Chevron U.S.A. Inc. v. National Resources Defense Council, Inc.,* 467 U.S. 837, 865 (1984). Distinguishing between empiricism and rationalism, one commentator observes: "Here was an intellectual orientation, finally, that often failed to express the humility and skepticism one expects with empiricism, and instead revealed a sweep and severity of which the stoutest rationalists would have been proud." R. Jeffrey Lustig, *Corporate Liberalism: The Origins of Modern American Political Theory, 1890–1920,* at 155 (Berkeley: University of California Press, 1982).

CHAPTER EIGHTEEN

1. Jean Louis DeLolme, *The Constitution of England; or, An Account of the English Government,* 153 (II.iii) (Indianapolis: Liberty Classics, 2007).

2. For the benefits of divided legislative power, whether in terms of caution, restraint of transient popular passions, or avoiding the risks of bad laws, see John F. Manning, "The Nondelegation Doctrine As a Canon of Avoidance," Supreme Court Review, 233, 239–40 (2000); David Schoenbrod, *Power without Responsibility: How Congress Abuses the People through Delegation,* 119 (New Haven: Yale University Press, 1993).

3. Along these lines, recent scholarship notes the value of bicameralism both for the sake of caution and for getting different perspectives. Adrian Vermeule, "Second Opinions and Institutional Design," Virginia Law Review, 97: 1435, 1467 (2011)

4. *Acts and Ordinances of the Interregnum, 1642–1660,* ed. C. H. Firth & R. S. Rait (London: His Majesty's Stationary Office, 1911). To be precise, the shift from ordinances to acts occurred on Jan. 16, 1649. Ibid., 1257.

5. *INS v. Chada,* 462 U.S. 919 (1983).

6. 5 U.S.C. subchapter II, §551 (4) & (5).

7. Aspects of these dangers are evident in England, where civil juries have been largely abolished. J. H. Baker, *An Introduction to English Legal History,* 81 (London: Butterworths, 1979).

CHAPTER NINETEEN

a. "Proceedings of the Sons of Liberty (March 1, 1766)," Maryland Gazette (Mar. 27, 1766), in Tyler's Quarterly Historical and Genealogical Magazine, 16: 111–14 (1935).

b. Peter H. Schuck, *The Limits of Law: Essays on Democratic Governance,* 256 (Boulder: Westview Press, 2000); Francis Lieber, *On Civil Liberty and Self-Government,* 108 (Philadelphia: 1859). See also John A. Rohr, *To Run a Constitution: The Legitimacy of the Administrative State,* 100 (Lawrence: University Press of Kansas, 1986). For a relatively early American argument that industries should be represented in the government with specialized cabinet offices, see LL.B. [Almont Barnes], *Administrative Organization: A Consideration of the Principle Executive Departments of the United States Government, in Relation to Administration,* 42, 81–82 (Washington, DC: William H. Morrison, 1884).

c. Karl Marx, *Critique of Hegel's "Philosophy of Right,"* 53, ed. Joseph O'Malley (Cambridge: Cambridge University Press, 1970).

d. Benjamin N. Cardozo, *The Growth of the Law*, 132–33 (New Haven: Yale University Press, 1924).

e. Woodrow Wilson, "The Study of Administration," Political Science Quarterly, 2: 197, 208–09 (1887); Woodrow Wilson, "Character of Democracy in the United States," Atlantic Monthly, 64: 577, 582, 588 (1889).

1. Nicholas of Cusa, *De Condordantia Catholica* (II.xiv–xv), in *Medieval Political Ideas*, 1: 192, 2: 418, ed. Ewart Lewis (London: Routledge & Kegan Paul, 1954). Such ideas became familiar among common lawyers long before Locke adopted them. Chief Justice Henry Hobart noted that "by law of nature . . . all men are free, and cannot be brought under the dominion of any." *Moore v. Hussey et al.* (C.P. 1609), Hobart, *Reports*, 99. Hale even introduced his work on the prerogative with this sort of analysis. Matthew Hale, *The Prerogatives of the King*, 1, ed. D. E. C. Yale (London: Selden Society, 1976).

2. Arguments of Cases in the Inner Temple in the Time of Edward IV and Henry VII, in *Readings and Moots at the Inns of Court in the Fifteenth Century*, 2: 139, case no. 25, ed. Samuel E. Thorne & J. H. Baker (London: Selden Society, 1990). As put by Sir Thomas Smith, "every Englishman is intended to be there present, either in person or by procuration and attorneys, of what preeminence, state, dignity, or quality soever be he, from the Prince . . . to the lowest person of England," and therefore "the consent of the Parliament is taken to be every mans consent." Thomas Smith, *De Republica Anglorum*, 35 (London: 1583).

3. John Locke, *Two Treatises of Government*, 362 (II.xi.140), ed. Peter Laslett (Cambridge: Cambridge University Press, 1988).

4. *Annual Register for 1766*, at 38 (London: 1767).

5. Resolutions of the Stamp Act Congress (Oct. 19, 1765), in *Documents of American History*, 58, ed. Henry Steele Commager (New York: Appleton, Century, Crofts, 1948).

6. Instructions Adopted by the Braintree Town Meeting (Sept. 24, 1765), in *Papers of John Adams*, 1: 138 (Cambridge: Belknap Press, 1977). With greater emphasis on the practical considerations, the Virginia resolves of 1765 stated: "That the taxation of the people by themselves, or by persons chosen by themselves to represent them, who can only know what taxes the people are able to bear, or the easiest method of raising them, and must themselves be affected by every tax laid on the people, is the only security against a burdensome taxation, and the distinguishing characteristic of British freedom, without which the ancient Constitution cannot exist." Virginia Stamp Act Resolves (May 30, 1765), in *Documents of American History*, 56, ed. Henry Steele Commager (New York: Appleton, Century, Crofts, 1948).

7. Lawrence Henry Gipson, "The Great Debate in the Committee of the Whole House of Commons on the Stamp Act, 1766, As Reported by Nathaniel Ryder," Pennsylvania Magazine of History and Biography, 86: 18 (1962); Declaration and Resolves of the First Continental Congress (Oct. 14, 1774), *Journals of the Continental Congress*, 1: 63ff., in *Documents of American History*, 83, ed. Henry Steele Commager (New York: Appleton, Century, Crofts, 1948); Samuel West, *On the Right to Rebel against Governors* (Boston: 1776), in *American Political Writing during the Founding Era, 1760–1805*, at 419, ed. Charles S. Hyneman & Donald S. Lutz (Indianapolis: Liberty Press, 1983).

8. Administrative Procedure Act, 5 U.S.C. §553 & §591(2). At the same time, §553 exempts interpretative rules and "general statements of policy."

9. David Baron & Elena Kagan, "*Chevron's* Nondelegation Doctrine," Supreme Court Review, 201, 231–32 (2001). See also Jody Freeman, "Collaborative Governance in the Administrative State," U.C.L.A. Law Review, 45: 1, 12 (1997).

10. See, for example, Letter from R. H. Dana, in *Woman Suffrage Unnatural and Inexpedient*, 17 (Boston: 1886). For an answer to this sort of argument, see *Equal Rights for Women: A Speech by George William Curtis in the Constitutional Convention of New York*, 10 (Lansing: Michigan Woman Suffrage Association, 1872). For the development of the phrase as a British defense against colonial complaints, see review of *The Crisis; or, a Full Defence of the Colonies*, Gentleman's Magazine, 36: 6 (Jan. 1766); *The Cambridge Modern History*, 7: 194 (New York: Macmillan Co., 1906).

11. John Hart Ely, *Democracy and Distrust: A Theory of Judicial Review*, 131–34 (Cambridge: Harvard University Press, 1980); David Schoenbrod, *Power without Responsibility: How Congress Abuses the People through Delegation*, 99, 105 (New Haven: Yale University Press, 1993); Martin Shapiro, "Administrative Law Unbounded: Reflections on Government and Governance," Indiana Journal of Global Legal Studies, 8: 369, 372 (2001).

12. Eric A. Posner & Adrian Vermeule, "Interring the Nondelegation Doctrine," University of Chicago Law Review, 69: 1721, 1749 (2002).

13. For the view that administrative lawmaking is accountable through presidential elections, see Jerry L. Mashaw, *Greed, Chaos, and Governance: Using Public Choice to Improve Public Law*, 152 (New Haven: Yale University Press, 1997).

14. See, for example, Frank J. Goodnow, *The Principles of Administrative Law of the United States*, 13 (New York: G. P. Putnam, 1905).

15. Jerry L. Mashaw, *Creating the Administrative Constitution: The Lost One Hundred Years of American Administrative Law*, 9 (New Haven: Yale University Press, 2012).

16. John Locke, *Two Treatises of Government*, 361 (II.xi.138), ed. Peter Laslett (Cambridge: Cambridge University Press, 1988).

17. Milovan Djilas, *The New Class: An Analysis of the Communist System*, 38, 32, 44 (New York: Frederick A. Praeger, 1957).

18. B. Bruce-Briggs, "An Introduction to the Idea of the New Class," in *The New Class?*, 2, ed. B. Bruce-Briggs (New York: McGraw-Hill Book Co., 1979). Historians such as Anthony Smith have noted the "rise of the bureaucratic state" from the late Middle Ages onward, which "encouraged the growth of a wealthy bourgeois class and an allied intelligentsia," and "it was this new stratum that inherited the traditions and concepts of statecraft built up during the preceding centuries, as well as the machinery of state with which to implement their interests and policies." Anthony D. Smith, *The Ethnic Origins of Nations*, 132 (Oxford: Blackwell, 1995). On the interests pursued by early modern German administrators, see Marc Raeff, *The Well-Ordered Police State: Social and Institutional Change through Law in the Germanies and Russia, 1600–1800*, at 22 (New Haven: Yale University Press, 1983).

19. Daniel P. Moynihan, "Equalizing Education: In Whose Benefit?," Public Interest, 83 (Fall 1972), discussed in B. Bruce-Briggs, "An Introduction to the Idea of the New Class," in *The New Class?*, at 2, ed. B. Bruce-Briggs (New York: McGraw-Hill Book Co., 1979). Samuel Gompers more sardonically observed, "There is a very close connection between employment as experts and the enthusiasm for human welfare." Daniel P. Moynihan, "Equalizing Education: In Whose Benefit?," Public Interest, 83 (Fall 1972).

20. For this contradiction, see Thomas G. West, "Progressivism and the Transformation of American Government," in *The Progressive Revolution in Politics and Political Sci-*

ence: Transforming the American Regime, 19, ed. John Marini & Ken Masugi (Lanham: Rowman & Littlefield Publishers 2005).

21. Surveying the shift that has occurred in educated opinion, Edwin Godkin—editor of the *Nation*—asked, "What is really the attitude of educated men toward universal suffrage today? As a general rule I think they really mistrust or regret it, but accept it as inevitable." Of course, there were many possible responses. Godkin himself concluded: "I do not look for the improvement of democratic legislatures in quality in any moderate period. What I believe democratic societies will do, in order to improve their government . . . is to restrict the power of these assemblies and shorten their sittings, and to use the referendum more freely." Edwin Lawrence Godkin, *Problems of Modern Democracy*, 201–02, 297 (New York: Charles Scribner's Sons, 1896). For his anxieties about class and leadership in America, see Stow Persons, *The Decline of American Gentility*, 149–50 (New York: Columbia University Press, 1973).

22. Woodrow Wilson, *Cabinet Government in the United States*, 20, ed. Thomas K. Finletter (1879; Stamford: Overbrook Press, 1947); Woodrow Wilson, "The Study of Administration," Political Science Quarterly, 2: 214–15 (1887); John Preston Comer, *Legislative Functions of National Administrative Authorities*, 16–17 (New York: Columbia University Press, 1927).

23. Incidentally, civil service reform already was a path to tenure in eighteenth-century Germany. Rudolf Vierhaus, "The Prussian Bureaucracy Reconsidered," *Rethinking Leviathan: The Eighteenth-Century State in Britain and Germany*, 134, ed. John Brewer & Eckhart Hellmuth (Oxford: Oxford University Press, 1999).

24. Woodrow Wilson, "The Study of Administration," Political Science Quarterly, 2: 197, 214 (1887).

25. *Address of Professor John W. Burgess Made on the Invitation and at the Request of the Newport Improvement Association, September 5th, 1913*, at 28 [i.e., 23] (1913) (Bulletin of the Newport Improvement Association, no. 2); William E. Nelson, *The Roots of American Bureaucracy*, 90 (Cambridge: Harvard University Press, 1982). See also Nancy Cohen, *The Reconstruction of American Liberalism, 1865–1914*, at 111 (Chapel Hill: University of North Carolina Press, 2002); R. Jeffrey Lustig, *Corporate Liberalism: The Origins of Modern American Political Theory, 1890–1920*, at 152 (Berkeley: University of California Press, 1982). Lustig writes of how "Benthamite elites informed by Baconian facts could easily substitute 'scientific lawmaking' for the older activities of juries, legislatures, and political parties." Ibid., 171. Lustig notes how Croly eventually "lamented that prewar liberals like himself never saw how much their ideas actually served to keep "'economic and social power predominantly in the hands of one class.'"

26. Woodrow Wilson, "The Study of Administration," Political Science Quarterly, 2: 197, 208–09 (1887). As put by one scholar, "Administration can remove the necessity of building a public consensus in favor of reform." Dennis J. Mahoney, *Politics and Progress: The Emergence of American Political Science*, 136 (Lanham: Lexington Books, 2004).

27. A recent article reports:

> Former White House Budget Director[,] Peter Orszag, penned a piece this week in the New Republic arguing, as the title says, "Why we need less democracy." Orszag wrote that "the country's political polarization was growing worse— harming Washington's ability to do the basic, necessary work of governing." His solution? "[W]e need to minimize the harm from legislative inertia by

relying more on automatic policies and depoliticized commissions for certain policy decisions. In other words, radical as it sounds, we need to counter the gridlock of our political institutions by making them a bit less democratic."

. . . Last year, former auto czar Steve Rattner wrote in his book, "Overhaul," "Either Congress needs to get its act together or we should explore alternatives. . . . If our country wants to do a better job of solving its problems, it needs to find a way to let talented government officials operate more like they do in the private sector."

"Obama-Style Democracy: Bureaucrats Know Best," Washington Examiner (Sept. 28, 2001).

28. For this distinction, see Robert K. Merton, *Social Theory and Social Structure*, 454 (New York: Free Press, 1968). Merton similarly distinguishes between what is known and what, at a local level, is understood. Ibid., 547.

29. Robert K. Merton, *Social Theory and Social Structure*, 447 (New York: Free Press, 1968); Daniel Bell, *The Coming of Post-industrial Society: A Venture in Social Forecasting*, 343–45 (New York: Basic Books, 1973). Although Bell sometimes suggests that the knowledge class forms an elite of "knowledge workers," his writing is more relevant here when he speaks more broadly about affiliation with the "prestige and status" of intellectual communities. Ibid.

   Also relevant are Michael Lacey's observations about the development of Washington bureaucrats who "advocated a new style of knowledge governance and were among the first Americans to try to work out the premises for the modern regulatory state." Michael J. Lacey, "The World of the Bureaus: Government and the Positivist Project in the Late Nineteenth Century," in *The State and Social Investigation in Britain and the United States*, 127 & passim, ed. Michael J. Lacey & Mary O. Furner (Washington, DC: Woodrow Wilson Center Press, 1993). According to R. Jeffrey Lustig, "here was an empiricism which claimed to vindicate common sense and the common man, employed by an elitist middle class bent on making the submerged masses more like itself." R. Jeffrey Lustig, *Corporate Liberalism: The Origins of Modern American Political Theory, 1890–1920*, at 155 (Berkeley: University of California Press, 1982). On cosmopolitian sensibilities in America, see John Fabian Witt, *Patriots and Cosmopolitans: Hidden Histories of American Law* (Cambridge: Harvard University Press, 2007).

   Writing about administrators in sixteenth- and seventeenth-century Germany, Marc Raeff writes: "Membership in the new elites was not defined primarily by social origins but rather by professional competence, so that members of both new old and new strata could join them. The old elites, as defined by birth and outdated functions, were displaced by professional technicians." Marc Raeff, *The Well-Ordered Police State: Social and Institutional Change through Law in the Germanies and Russia, 1600–1800*, at 174 (New Haven: Yale University Press, 1983).

30. Writing about German governance in the early modern era, one scholar observes: "The physical separation between administrators and administered reinforced the feeling of separation between the sovereign authority and the population." Marc Raeff, *The Well-Ordered Police State: Social and Institutional Change through Law in the Germanies and Russia, 1600–1800*, at 161 (New Haven: Yale University Press, 1983).

CHAPTER TWENTY

a. Thomas W. Merrill & Kathryn Tongue Watts, "Agency Rules with the Force of Law: The Original Convention," Harvard Law Review, 116: 467, 591 (2002).

b. Gary Lawson, "Discretion as Delegation: The "Proper Understanding of the Non-delegation Doctrine," 73 George Washington Law Review 235, 237, 254, 258 (2005); Gary L. Lawson and Patricia B. Granger, "The Proper Scope of Federal Power: A Jurisdictional Interpretation of the Sweeping Clause," Duke Law Journal, 43: 267, 274 (1994); Gary Lawson, "Delegation and Original Meaning," Virginia Law Review, 88: 327, 347 (2002).

c. *Penal Statutes* (1605), Coke, *Reports*, 7: 36b–37a.

d. Francis Staughton Sullivan, *Lectures on the Constitution and Laws of England*, 183 (London: 1776). The king had a prerogative in saltpeter, which was understood to belong to him, even if under the land of his subjects, and saltpeter thus was part of his prerogative in the sense of his lawful property. *The Case of the King's Prerogative in Saltpeter* (1607), 12 Coke, Reports, 12.

e. Eric A. Posner & Adrian Vermeule, "Interring the Nondelegation Doctrine," University of Chicago Law Review, 69: 1721, 1723 (2002). For another critique, see Larry Alexander & Saikrishna Prakash, "Reports of the Nondelegation Doctrine's Death Are Greatly Exaggerated," University of Chicago Law Review, 70: 1297 (2003).

f. *Whitman v. American Trucking Associations*, 531 U.S. 457, 487 (2001) (concurrence); Thomas W. Merrill, "Rethinking Article I, Section I: From Nondelegation to Exclusive Delegation," Columbia Law Review, 104: 2097, 2101, 2118, 2121, 2129 (2004).

g. *The Board of Health. Commonwealth of Massachusetts: . . . An Act to Empower the Town of Boston to Choose a Board of Health, and for Removing and Preventing Nuisances* ([Boston:] Russell & Cutler [1798]); *Health Laws of New-York*, 22–23, 39 (New York: 1805); *In Board of Health, May 7, 1810: Order, That the Following Rules and Regulations for Establishing the Police of the Burying Grounds and Cemetaries, and for Regulating the Burial of the Dead, within the Town of Boston, Have the Force of Law, on and after the First Day of July Next* ([Boston: 1810]).

  Of course, some cities, during emergencies, took measures not obviously authorized by law—as when the mayor of Baltimore issued a proclamation "forbidding the entrance in the city of Baltimore, or within three miles thereof, of all persons whomsoever, as well as all baggage or other goods, which have come from the city of Philadelphia, until they shall at least have been fifteen days absent therefrom." James Calhoun, Mayor of Baltimore, Proclamation (Aug. 18, 1798), in *Memoirs of the Yellow Fever*, 25–26, by William Currie (Philadelphia: 1798). See also Proclamation (Sept. 15, 1798), ibid., 80–81.

h. Opinion on the Power of the General Court to Establish Fees (May 4, 1774), in *The Letters and Papers of Edmund Pendleton 1734–1803*, at 1: 83, ed. David John Mays (Charlottesville: Virginia Historical Society, 1967).

i. Gary Lawson, "Delegation and Original Meaning," Virginia Law Review, 88: 327, 356 (2002); Gary Lawson, "Discretion as Delegation: The "Proper Understanding of the Nondelegation Doctrine," George Washington Law Review, 73: 235, 236, 265 (2005).

j. *An Appeal to the Parliament; or Sions Plea against the Prelacie*, 40 (n.p.: [1628?]).

k. Philip Hamburger, "IRB Licensing," in *Who's Afraid of Academic Freedom* (New York: Columbia University Press, 2014). See also Philip Hamburger, "Unconstitutional Conditions: The Irrelevance of Consent," Virginia Law Review, 98: 479 (2012); Philip Hamburger, "Getting Permission," Northwestern Law Review, 101: 405 (2007).

1. There are a range of scholarly arguments against delegation, but they tend to distinguish in a rather open-ended manner between permissible and nonpermissible

delegations of legislative power, and they thus typically do not recognize the sharp barrier to any delegation of the power that the Constitution locates in the legislature. See Gary Lawson, "Delegation and Original Meaning," Virginia Law Review, 88: 327 (2002); Michael B. Rappaport, "The Selective Nondelegation Doctrine and the Line Item Veto: A New Approach to the Nondelegation Doctrine and Its Implications for *Clinton v. City of New York*," Tulane Law Review, 76: 265 (2001); Martin H. Redish, *The Constitution As Political Structure*, 5–16 (New York: Oxford University Press, 1995); David Schoenbrod, *Power without Responsibility: How Congress Abuses the People through Delegation* (New Haven: Yale University Press, 1993).

2. The tone of supporters of administrative law is captured by this statement: "The only certainties about the nondelegation doctrine are that it lacks a precise constitutional foundation, it is incapable of precise formulation and application, and it is doubtful whether it even exists at all." Douglas C. Michael, "Federal Agency Use of Audited Self-Regulation As a Regulatory Technique," Administrative Law Review, 47: 171, 195–96 (1995).

3. For a version of the mere execution theory, see Eric A. Posner & Adrian Vermeule, "Interring the Nondelegation Doctrine," University of Chicago Law Review, 69: 1721, 1725 (2002).

   In arguing that executive rules merely execute the law, the article by Posner and Vermeule claims that this "simple conception has deep roots in American public law"—by which the article appears to mean it was rooted by c. 1900. Even this, however, is not evident from the two cases cited to support the proposition. Although the Supreme Court in *United States v. Grimaud* stated that "the authority to make administrative rules is not a delegation of legislative power," the Court was speaking about the rules governing the use of public property, and whether it meant more than this far from clear. *United States v. Grimaud*, 220 U.S. 506, 521 (1911). As for the other case cited for support, *Railroad & Warehouse Commission v. Chicago, Milwaukee & St. Paul Railroad Co.*, 38 Minn. 281, 37 N.W. 782, 788 (1888), it was reversed by the Supreme Court in *Chicago, M. & St. P. Ry. Co. v. Minnesota*, 134 U.S. 418 (1890).

4. *Panama Refining v. Ryan*, 293 U.S. 388 (1935); *Schechter Poultry Co. v. United States*, 295 U.S. 495 (1935); *Mistretta v. United States*, 488 U.S. 361 (1989), quoting *J. W. Hampton, Jr., & Co. v. United States*, 276 U.S. 394, 409 (1928) (quotation mark omitted); John F. Manning, "The Nondelegation Doctrine As a Canon of Avoidance," Supreme Court Review, 240, n. 90 (2000); Cass R. Sunstein, "Nondelegation Canons," University of Chicago Law Review, 67: 315 (2000). Manning observes that the interpretation to avoid excessively broad delegation adds an additional problem of judicial interference with congressional choices. Manning, Supreme Court Review, 223 (2000). Generally, though, as Justice Scalia has noted, "We have almost never felt qualified to second-guess Congress regarding the permissible degree of policy judgment that can be left to those executing or applying the law." *Whitman v. American Trucking Ass'ns*, 531 U.S. 474–75 (2001) (quotation marks omitted).

5. *Mistretta v. United States*, 488 U.S. 361, 372 (1989) (internal quotation marks omitted).

6. Cass R. Sunstein, "Nondelegation Canons," University of Chicago Law Review, 67: 315, 322 (2000).

7. *Penal Statutes* (1605), Coke, *Reports*, 7: 36b–37a.

8. Ibid. For the sake of readability, the quotation printed as an indented block has been adjusted: A comma has been omitted after the word "mercy," and a semicolon

after the phrase "trusted with it" has been printed as a comma. The unlucky recipient of the grant may have been Edward Dyer, who was authorized to dispense with the 1563 Leather Act. Carolyn A. Edie, "Tactics and Strategies: Parliament's Attack upon the Royal Dispensing Power, 1597–1689," at 208, American Journal of Legal History, 29: 197 (1985). For a list of grants that gave statutory penalties and a dispensing power to private persons, see William Hyde Price, *The English Patents of Monopoly*, 146–47 (Cambridge: Harvard University Press, 1913).

The Statute of Monopolies also rejected the delegation of the dispensing power. As Coke summarized, "It appeareth by the preamble of this act that all grants of the benefit of any penal law, or of power to dispense with the law, or to compound for the forfeiture, are contrary to the ancient fundamental laws of this realm." Coke, *Institutes*, 3: 186.

More generally, on the inalienability of sovereignty, see Ernst H. Kantorowicz, *The King's Two Bodies: A Study in Mediaeval Political Theology*, 347–58 (Princeton: Princeton University Press, 1957); Peter Riesenberg, *Inalienability of Sovereignty in Medieval Political Thought*, 22 (New York: Columbia University Press, 1956); Gaines Post, *Studies in Medieval Legal Thought: Public Law and the State, 1100–1322*, at 281 & 415–33 (Princeton: Princeton University Press, 1964). Not surprisingly, "the canonistic doctrine of 'Inalienability' was articulated and became the norm in England much earlier than in other European countries." Ernst H. Kantorowicz, "Inalienability," Speculum, 39: 488, 502 (1954).

9. John Locke, *Two Treatises of Government*, 362 (II.xi.141); 373 (II.xiii.157), ed. Peter Laslett (Cambridge: Cambridge University Press, 1988); Ernest Gellhorn, "Returning to First Principles," 36 American University Law Review, 36: 345, 347–48 (1987); Larry Alexander & Saikrishna Prakash, "Reports of the Nondelegation Doctrine's Death Are Greatly Exaggerated," University of Chicago Law Review, 70: 1297 (2003).

10. John Locke, *Two Treatises of Government*, 362–63 (II.xi.141–42), ed. Peter Laslett (Cambridge: Cambridge University Press, 1988). One sentence in Locke has led to different conclusions about his views. He wrote:

> This legislative is not only the supreme power of the common-wealth, but sacred and unalterable in the hands where the community have once placed it; *nor can any edict of any body else, in what form soever conceived, or by what power soever backed, have the force and obligation of a law, which has not its sanction from that legislative, which the public has chosen and appointed.* For without this the law could not have that, which is absolutely necessary to its being a law, the consent of the society, over whom no body can have a power to make laws, but by their own consent, and by authority received from them. (Italics added)

Ibid., 356 (II.xi.134). On account of the passage in italics, it is said that Locke was open to subdelegation of legislative power. Eric A. Posner & Adrian Vermeule, "Nondelegation: A Post-mortem" University of Chicago Law Review, 70: 1331, 1339 (2003).

This, however, is at best an inference from ambiguity, without considering the context. Rather than leave room for a subdelegation of legislative power, Locke appears to have been assuming that the legislative would sanction the edict of another body by reciting the words of the edict or at least incorporating it by reference—the latter being what Parliament did with the *Book of Rates*. In fact, immediately after the quotation in the preceding paragraph, Locke revealed what he was talking about, for he denied that "any oaths to any foreign power whatsoever, or any domestic subordinate power" could "discharge any member of the society from his obedience to the legislative"—this being a clear allusion to the claims sometimes made by popes for their bulls, indulgences, and other instruments. What Locke evidently had in mind was that papal acts could have the force of law only if adopted by Parliament.

In other words, rather than arguing in favor of delegated legislation, Locke was arguing against the obligation of papal legislation. This conclusion makes sense of both the relevant passage and the surrounding text, and it is consistent with Locke's other passages in which he repeatedly and clearly rejects the subdelegation of legislative power.

11. *The Historical Register*, 368–70, sig. [Ddd3][v]–[Ddd4][v] (London: 1717) (the page numbers are misprinted); Protest (Apr. 14, 1716), *A Complete Collection of All the Protests Made in the House of Lords*, 178 ([London]: 1748). See also the speech of Sir Robert Raymond—a lawyer of moderately Tory sympathies who would become chief justice of King's Bench within a decade. Ibid., 396. For the passages quoted by Snell, see John Locke, *Two Treatises of Government*, 362–63 (II.xi.141), 428 (II. xix.243), ed. Peter Laslett (Cambridge: Cambridge University Press, 1988).

Such arguments ordinarily had belonged to radical Whigs, such as Benjamin Hoadly: "[T]here can be no right, or authority, in those who are concerned in the government of these kingdoms, by any solemn act to alter the essentials of our present constitution. . . . And whatever may be said of some governors, these continue to this day to receive all their right to act as legislators from the free choice of the people; and therefore can have no powers but what are designed and intended, in that free choice, and contract of the people." It thus was "impossible to say whence they should receive authority to decree anything destructive of the public happiness, or to make any such change in the essential parts of our constitution; or whence any necessity should arise, that can oblige the people to acquiesce in any such decree, or in any such change, which they never authorized any persons to make in their names." Benjamin Hoadly, *The Measures of Submission*, 103 (London: 1706).

12. Beginning in 1783, Parliament authorized the king in council "to make such regulations, with respect to duties, drawbacks, or otherwise, for carrying on the trade and commerce between the people and territories belonging to the Crown of Great Britain and the people and territories of the . . . United States, as to his majesty in council shall appear most expedient and salutary." An Act for Preventing Certain Instruments from Being Required from Ships Belonging to the United States of America; and to Give his Majesty, for a Limited Time, Certain Powers . . . , §III, 23 George III, c. 39 (1783). A decade later, a commentator explained: "The orders of his majesty in council regulate the importations of merchandise from the United States of America, to authorize which an act passes every session of Parliament; and the trade with the United States of America will probably continue under that regulation until there shall be a commercial treaty between Great Britain and those states." Accordingly, "it will be always necessary to refer to the last order of council in the London Gazette respecting the importation or exportation of the articles therein mentioned from and to the United States of America." John Nodin, *The British Duties of Customs, Excise, &c.*, 7–8 (London: [1792]). For the Apr. 1, 1791 order in council, see ibid., 9–16. See also *The Papers of Alexander Hamilton*, 13: 397, ed. Harold C. Syrett & Jacob E. Cooke (New York: Columbia University Press, 1967). For similar statutory authorization, allowing orders in council to permit the export of corn, see 31 George III, c. 30 §14 (1791).

The first major domestic delegation of power came in the Poor Laws. An Act for the Amendment and Better Administration of the Laws Relating the Poor in England and Wales, 4 & 5 William IV, c. 76 (1834). For details of the resulting regulations, see John Frederick Archbold, *The Act for the Amendment of the Poor Laws*, 155, 175 (London: 1835).

13. For royal control of exports of arms, ammunition, and gunpowder, including saltpeter, see A Subsidy Granted to the King of Tonnage and Poundage . . . , 12 Charles II, cap. 4, §11 (1660); An Act to Impower his Majesty to Prohibit the Exportation of Salt Petre . . . , 29 George II, cap. 16, §1 (1756).

    For quarantine restrictions at the border, see An Act to Oblige Ships Coming From Places Infected More Effectually to Perform Their Quarantine, 9 Anne, cap. 2 (1710). For examples of quarantine regulations, see Proclamations (Nov. 9, 1710), (Sept. 6, 1711), (Aug. 31, 1712), and Order in Council (May 4, 1728), London Gazette, 1 (6671) (May 4–7, 1728); Order in Council (June 18, 1747), ibid., 5 (8650) (June 16–20, 1747).

    For the distemper statutes, see An Act to Enable his Majesty to Make Rules, Orders and Regulations, More Effectually to Prevent the Spreading of the Distemper which Now Rages amongst the Horned Cattle in this Kingdom, 19 George II, cap. 5 (1746), and the later statutes cited with the statute in Ruffhead's Statutes at Large.

    Incidentally, John Archibold Fairlie cites a series of seventeenth- and eighteenth-century instances of delegated legislation in the form of orders in council (dating from 1680 through 1796), but he does not mention that they all were Scottish or Irish, not English, and therefore cannot be taken as evidence of what was possible under English law. John Archibold Fairlie, *Administrative Procedure in Connection with Statutory Rules and Orders in Great Britain*, 14 (Urbana: University of Illinois, 1927).

14. William Blackstone, *Commentaries on the Laws of England*, 1: 156 (Oxford: 1765); Jean Louis DeLolme, *The Constitution of England; or, An Account of the English Government*, 155 (II.iii) (Indianapolis: Liberty Classics, 2007).

15. James Madison, Federalist Number 53, in *The Federalist*, 361, ed. Jacob E. Cooke (Middletown: Wesleyan University Press, 1961).

16. George Gilmer, Commonplace Book, 134 (before May 1778), Virginia Historical Society, Mss 5:5, G4213:1; "Observations upon the Seven Articles, Reported by the Grand Committee . . . and Now Lying on the Table of Congress" (from the New York Gazetteer of Jan. 29), Virginia Independent Chronicle (Feb. 21, 1787). The last passage, beginning "Mr. Locke's reasoning," was a quotation from the English scholar Thomas Rutherforth, and the internal quotation marks have been omitted. This obviously is suggestive about how Locke's ideas were assimilated through other writings. For more on this, particularly the role of Defoe earlier in the century, see Philip Hamburger, "Revolution and Judicial Review: Chief Justice Holt's Opinion in *City of London v. Wood*," Columbia Law Review, 94: 2148–50 (1994).

17. James Madison, Federalist Number 10, in *The Federalist*, 63, ed. Jacob E. Cooke (Middletown: Wesleyan University Press, 1961). Similarly, Hamilton recognized that the constitutional authority of Congress was its "delegated authority." Alexander Hamilton, Federalist Number 78, ibid., 524. In more general terms, it has been observed: "The entire point of a constitution that governs structure is to enable government to function while restraining the ability of government to restructure itself." Stephen L. Carter, "Constitutional Improprieties: Reflections on Mistretta, Morrison, and Administrative Government," University of Chicago Law Review, 57: 357, 366 (1990).

18. Floyd R. Mechem, *A Treatise of the Law of Agency*, 12 (Chicago: Callaghan & Co., 1889).
19. *Shankland v. Washington*, 30 U.S. 390, 395 (1831). See also *Warner v. Martin*, 52 U.S. 209 (1850).
20. Cass R. Sunstein, "Nondelegation Canons," University of Chicago Law Review, 67: 315, 322 (2000).
21. Philip Hamburger, *Law and Judicial Duty*, 180–85 (Cambridge: Harvard University Press, 2008).
22. An Act to Incorporate the Inhabitants of the City of Washington, in the District of Columbia, §§2 & 6 (May 3, 1802), *Public Statutes at Large of the United States*, 2: 195–96; District of Columbia Home Rule Act (Dec. 24, 1973), Public Law 93–198; 87 Stat. 777.
23. Charter of the City of New York (1730), *Laws and Ordinances, Ordained and Established by the Mayor, Aldermen and Commonalty of the City of New-York*, 7–9 (New York: 1786). Nor was this pattern confined to incorporated municipalities, for New England towns usually were governed by selectmen, who enjoyed a range of different powers, and who sometimes delegated powers to subordinate bodies.
24. For English cases treating corporate charters as constitutions, see Philip Hamburger, *Law and Judicial Duty*, 185–88 (Cambridge: Harvard University Press, 2008).
25. See, for example, Peter L. Strauss, *Administrative Justice in the United States*, 28 (Durham: Carolina Academic Press, 2002).
26. *Wayman v. Southard*, 23 U.S. 1, 42–43 (1825).
27. Ibid., 43.
28. Ibid., 14.
29. In England and some of the states there persisted old ideas about the obligatory character of some local public offices, the underlying assumption being that these were the communal duties of members of the local community—in very traditional English terms, they were the duties of members of the local manor or town court. In such circumstances, acceptance of office was a legal duty, and an officer could not resign without violating his duty. There is no reason, however, to think that such assumptions ever applied to federal officers.
30. *Goodman v. FCC*, 182 F.3rd 987, 993–94 (D.C. Cir. 1999).
31. For the improbability of the delegation of judicial power, see Larry Alexander & Saikrishna Prakash, "Reports of the Nondelegation Doctrine's Death Are Greatly Exaggerated," University of Chicago Law Review, 70: 1297, 1302 (2003). They point out that all sorts of delegations deserve attention. Noting that the necessary and proper clause does not distinguish between the delegation of legislative power and the delegation of other powers, they observe that "if Congress may delegate its legislative powers, there is no sound reason why Congress cannot delegate other powers," including non-legislative powers, thus giving Congress "carte blanche to refashion many of the structural Constitution's most famous features." Larry Alexander & Saikrishna Prakash, "Delegation Really Running Riot," Virginia Law Review, 93: 1035, 1038–39, 1079 (2007).
32. Brooke, *Abridgment*, "Office & Off.," pl. 39 (citing 9 Edward IV, 31); Viner, *Abridgment*, 14: 581; William Marshall's First Lecture (Lincoln's Inn 1516), in *John Spelman's Reading on Quo Warranto*, 61, ed. J. H. Baker (London: Selden Society, 1997).
33. Although the Delegates had broader jurisdiction, most of it consisted of ecclesiastical and admiralty cases. G. I. O. Duncan, *The High Court of Delegates*, 34–35 (Cambridge: [Cambridge] University Press, 1971).

As early as 1552, the Crown considered proposals to temper subdelegation in ecclesiastical courts. The proposals included principles such as that "[t]he person to whom a case is delegated cannot subdelegate it to someone else, unless the case was committed to him by our royal majesty." Even then, such a person "cannot give to his subdelegate the power of [further] subdelegation." *The Reformation of the Ecclesiastical Laws of England, 1552*, at 259, ed. James C. Spaulding (Kirksville: Sixteenth Century Essays & Studies, 1992).

34. Sir Leoline Jenkins, manuscript notes in interleaved copy of Richard Zouche, *Cases and Questions of Right and Judicature, Resolved in the Civil-Law*, 12ff. (Oxford: 1652), copy at University of Lausanne, as published on Google Books. For the relevant passages in Roman law, see Justinian, *Digest* (I.xiv).

35. At least by the last half of the sixteenth century, it was evident that the masters had a ministerial role. John G. Henderson, *Chancery Practice: With Especial Reference to the Office and Duties of Masters in Chancery . . .* , 47–49 (Chicago: T. H. Flood & Co., 1904). Predictably, when Egerton was lord keeper, masters "served in an open judicial capacity." Conventionally, however, the tasks of a master in Chancery were ministerial, including taking affidavits, taxing costs, and administering oaths. W. J. Jones, *The Elizabethan Court of Chancery*, 104–05 (Oxford: Clarendon Press, 1967). The limited power of masters is evident from the meager character of their role even when they came closest to judicial power—for example, when the court asked them to verify matters "alleged to be confessed, or set forth in the defendant's answer." The masters then were to "take consideration of the whole answer or answers of the defendants, and certify not only whether the matter be so confessed or set forth, but also any other matter avoiding that confession, or balancing the same, [so] that the court may receive a clear and true information." *Ordines Cancellariæ: Being Orders of the High Court of Chancery*, 145–46 (London: 1698).

36. Nathan Dane, *A General Abridgment and Digest of American Law*, 6: 423 (Boston: 1823); Roscoe Pound, "The Law School and the Common Law," in *Two Addresses Delivered before the Alumni of the Harvard Law School*, 19 (1920).

37. Administrative Conference of the United States, Recommendation 94–1, *The Use of Audited Self-Regulation As a Regulatory Technique*, 1 (1995).

38. For the treatment of applications for licenses under the Administrative Procedure Act, §558(c), see Michael Asimow, *A Guide to Federal Agency Adjudication*, 155–56 (Chicago: American Bar Association, 2003). Although §558(c) requires agencies to act on applications "with due regard for the rights and privileges of all the interested parties or adversely affected persons," this provision "appears to have little practical effect." Ibid., 156. When suspending or withdrawing a license, the agency must give notice and an opportunity to show or achieve compliance with the licensing requirements, but this "second chance" requirement does not necessarily mean a hearing. Ibid., 158.

39. Ibid., 1. See also Douglas C. Michael, "Federal Agency Use of Audited Self-Regulation As a Regulatory Technique," Administrative Law Review, 47: 171, 178 (1995).

40. Administrative Conference of the United States, Recommendation 94–1, *The Use of Audited Self-Regulation As a Regulatory Technique*, 1 (1995).

41. As sardonically put by Walter Gellhorn, "so long as the representative legislature remains supreme—so long as it can modify or repeal rules the executive has made . . . the danger of tyranny is not overwhelming." Walter Gellhorn, *Federal Administrative Proceedings*, 15 (Baltimore: Johns Hopkins Press, 1941).

42. Francis Lieber, *Reminiscences of an Intercourse with Mr. Niebuhr the Historian during*

a Residence with Him in Rome, in the Years 1822 and 1823, at 59–61 (Philadelphia: 1835).

43. For a description of a particularly overt example of political engagement see Paul A. Gigot, "The Fannie Mae Gang," Wall Street Journal (July 23, 2008). Although threats to withhold funds usually occur below the radar, they sometimes are entirely candid. See Maggie M. Thornton, "Darrell Issa Rahm Emanuel: No Chicago Political Machine," *Maggie's Notebook* (Aug. 4, 2009), http://www.maggiesnotebook .com/2009/08/darrell-issa-rahm-emanuel-no-chicago-political-machine-full-text/.

CHAPTER TWENTY-ONE

1. Bradford Clark, "Separation of Powers As a Safeguard of Federalism," Texas Law Review, 79: 1321 (2001); Bradford Clark, "Putting the Safeguards Back into the Political Safeguards of Federalism," Texas Law Review, 80: 327 (2001); Bradford Clark, "The Supremacy Clause As a Constraint on Federal Power," George Washington Law Review, 71: 91 (2003); Bradford Clark, "Constitutional and the Supremacy Clause," Notre Dame Law Review, 83: 1421 (2008); Bradford Clark, "The Procedural Safeguards of Federalism," Notre Dame Law Review, 83: 1681 (2008).

2. See articles cited in this chapter, endnote 1. Defenders of administrative law have responded that the word "Laws" appears twice in the supremacy clause. On this basis, they suggest that Clark interprets the word inconsistently—that he first reads the word at the beginning of the clause to refer only to enacted laws and then reads the word at the end of the clause to refer to both enacted laws and the common law. Peter L. Strauss, "The Perils of Theory," Notre Dame Law Review, 83: 1567 (2008); Henry Paul Monaghan, "Supremacy Clause Textualism," Columbia Law Review, 110: 731, 769 (2010).

    This complaint about different meanings, however, ignores the text of the supremacy clause, which carefully modifies its uses of the word "Laws" in different ways. The clause begins by speaking of "the Laws of the United States which shall be made in Pursuance thereof," thereby focusing on statutes, and then speaks of "the Law of any State," thereby encompassing all state law, whether statutory or common law. It thus becomes evident that Clark's reading of the supremacy clause does not rest on an inconsistent interpretation of the word "Laws," but rather merely recognizes that, in different places, it modifies the word in different ways. Bradford Clark, "The Procedural Safeguards of Federalism," Notre Dame Law Review, 83: 1681, 1685–87 (2008).

3. Bradford Clark, "Separation of Powers As a Safeguard of Federalism," Texas Law Review, 79: 1321, 1337 (2001).

4. The supremacy of English law was most notably enacted under Henry VIII in An Acte that the Appeles in suche Cases as have ben used to be pursued to the See of Rome shall not be from henseforth had ne used but wythin this Realme, 24 Henry VIII, c. 12 (1534). As William Tyndale explained, the king "ought not . . . to suffer" clerics "to have a several law by themselves," for "one king, one law, is Gods ordinance in every realm." [William Tyndale], *The obedie[n]ce of a Christen man and how Christe[n] rulers ought to governe*, fol. lxxiii[v] ([Antwerp: 1528]). For details of the historical developments, see Philip Hamburger, *Law and Judicial Duty*, 59–64, 202–08 (Cambridge: Harvard University Press, 2008).

CHAPTER TWENTY-TWO

1. Bracton, *On the Laws and Customs of England*, 2: 33, ed. Samuel E. Thorne (Cambridge: Belknap Press, 1968) ("there is no rex where will rules rather than lex").

2. R. C. van Caenegem, *An Historical Introduction to Western Constitutional Law*, 109, 127 (Cambridge: Cambridge University Press, 1995), who also notes that "enlightened absolutism was no less absolutist than the older species." Indeed, "[t]his form of government was merely the last phase of the classic European absolutism, whose origins went back to the Middle Ages." Ibid., 126. Alas, van Caenegem appears to be overly optimistic. Another scholar observes that the Enlightenment idea of *Glückseligkeit*, or happiness, did not distinguish between the good of the society and the good of the state. Diethelm Klippel, "Reasonable Aims of Civil Society: Concerns of the State in German Political Theory in the Eighteenth and Early Nineteenth Centuries," in *Rethinking Leviathan: The Eighteenth-Century State in Britain and Germany*, 76, ed. John Brewer & Eckhart Hellmuth (Oxford: Oxford University Press, 1999).

3. Montesquieu, *The Spirit of the Laws*, 186 (XI.vi) (Dublin: 1751).

4. Alexis de Tocqueville, *Democracy in America*, 691–93 (II.iv.6), ed. J. P. Mayer, trans. George Lawrence (Garden City: Anchor Books, 1969).

5. Ibid., 693–94 (II.iv.6).

6. Ibid., 694 (II.iv.6).

7. Ibid., 88 & 96 (I.i.6), 262–63 (I.ii.8).

8. Indeed, he viewed the separation of powers as an analytic formality. Roscoe Pound, "The Theory of the Judicial Decision," Harvard Law Review, pt. II, 36: 802, 814 (1923). For his drawing on the civilian tradition, see John Fabian Witt, *Patriots and Cosmopolitans: Hidden Histories of American Law*, 226 (Cambridge: Harvard University Press, 2007). For his acceptance of administrative law, even as he criticized its excesses, see N. E. H. Hull, *Roscoe Pound and Karl Llewellyn: Searching for an American Jurisprudence*, 258–60 (Chicago: University of Chicago Press, 1997).

9. Joseph Postell, "The Anti–New Deal Progressive: Roscoe Pound's Alternative Administrative State," Review of Politics, 74: 53, 58, 72, 82–83 (2012).

10. Stephen H. Norwood, *The Third Reich in the Ivory Tower: Complicity and Conflict on American Campuses*, 56–57 (Cambridge: Cambridge University Press, 2009); see John Fabian Witt, *Patriots and Cosmopolitans: Hidden Histories of American Law*, 231 (Cambridge: Harvard University Press, 2007).

11. Roscoe Pound, *Administrative Agencies and the Law*, 7, 26 (New York: American Affairs, 1946).

12. Ibid., 26.

13. Walter Gellhorn, "Birth Pangs of the Administrative Procedure Act," Administrative Law Journal, 10: 51, 52 (1996). Gellhorn was quoting Roscoe Pound, "The Place of the Judiciary in a Democratic Polity," A.B.A. Journal, 27: 133 (1941).

CHAPTER TWENTY-THREE

a. *A. L. A. Schechter Poultry Corp. v. United States*, 295 U.S. 495, 528–30 (1935).

b. Gary Lawson, Geoffrey P. Miller, Robert G. Natalson & Guy I. Seidman, *The Origins of the Necessary and Proper Clause*, 88–89 (Cambridge: Cambridge University Press, 2010).

e. Department of Labor, *Accompanying Report of the National Performance Review Office of the Vice President*, 56 (Washington, DC: Sept. 1993).

f. John Locke, *Two Treatises of Government*, 358 (II.xi.136), ed. Peter Laslett (Cambridge: Cambridge University Press, 1988).

g. Rep. John H. Reagan of Texas, *Congressional Record*, 31 (Dec. 3, 1884); Rep. John H. Reagan of Texas, ibid., 7283–84 (July 21, 1886). See also Rep. Ben Caldwell of Illinois, ibid., 7292 (July 21, 1886). Representative George F. Edmunds protested: "If we can lay down a rule . . . we ought to lay it down as positively as we may, so as to relieve the commission of the responsibility and the danger . . . of their soon being the charms on the watch-chain of the railroad president." Williamjames Hull Hoffer, *To Enlarge the Machinery of Government: Congressional Debates and the Growth of the American State, 1858–1891*, at 161 (Baltimore: Johns Hopkins University Press, 2007). In contrast to Reagan, Shelby Collum wanted to avoid "all hard-and-fast rules," and instead sought a statute that "could not possibly harm the railroads or other business interests of the nation." Stephen Skowronek, *Building a New American State: The Expansion of Administrative Capacities, 1877–1920*, at 145 (Cambridge: Cambridge University Press: 1982).

Note that there were open accusations that legislators received passes from the railroads so they could visit their constituents free of charge. *Debate in Forty-Ninth Congress on the Bill to Establish a Board of Commissioners on Interstate Commerce, and to Regulate Such Commerce, Etc.*, 318–21 (Washington, DC: 1887) (debate on May 11, 1886).

h. Tim Wu, *The Master Switch: The Rise and Fall of Information Empires*, 287 (New York: Vintage Books: 2011). Wu adds: "[T]he FCC decided to let industry draft the rule. If that sounds like a dereliction of the agency's duty to make the law itself, all that can be said is that the process is hardly unprecedented." Ibid., 288.

i. James M. Landis, "The Administrative Process—the Third Decade," *Administrative Law Review*, 13: 17, 21 (1960).

j. Woodrow Wilson, "The Study of Administration," *Political Science Quarterly*, 2: 197, 210 (1887).

1. *State Necessity Considered as a Question of Law*, 10 (London: 1766).

2. James M. Landis, *The Administrative Process*, 2, 12, 88 (New Haven: Yale University Press, 1938); Kenneth Culp Davis, *Administrative Law: Cases, Text, Problems*, 20 (St. Paul: West Publishing, 1977). Landis also wrote that "the administrative process springs from the inadequacy of a simple tripartite form of government to deal with modern problems." James M. Landis, *The Administrative Process*, 1 (New Haven: Yale University Press, 1938).

Ideas about *perpetua necessitas*, or a mundane but permanent necessity, have also been used for other purposes—as evident in the late medieval development of justifications for annual taxation. So regular an exercise of power was not always necessary for any pressing external reasons, and the necessity thus was in a sense fictional. It therefore came to be justified as "an habitual necessity, though not an actual necessity." In this way, "the meaning of *necessitas* . . . shifted from an outer emergency to an inner administrative need." Ernst H. Kantorowicz, *The King's Two Bodies: A Study in Mediaeval Political Theology*, 287, 289 (Princeton: Princeton University Press, 1957).

3. John B. Cheadle, "The Delegation of Legislative Functions," *Yale Law Journal*, 27: 892, 893 (1918); John B. Andrews, *Administrative Labor Legislation: A Study of American Experience in the Delegation of Legislative Power*, 170 (New York: Harper & Brothers Publishers, 1936); Thomas I. Parkinson, "Functions of Administration in Labor Legislation," *American Labor Legislation Review*, 20: 149 (1930).

4. *J. W. Hampton, Jr. & Co. v. United States*, 276 U.S. 394, 406 (1928); *Sunshine Anthra-*

cite Coal Co. v. Adkins, 310 U.S. 381, 398 (1940); *Mistretta v. United States*, 488 U.S. 361, 372 (1989).

5. Letter from James Madison to Thomas Jefferson (Oct. 17, 1788), in *The Papers of James Madison*, 11: 299, ed. Robert A. Rutland & Charles F. Hobson (Charlottesville: University Press of Virginia, 1977). On national security questions, see Philip Hamburger, "Beyond Protection," Columbia Law Review, 109: 1826 (2009); more generally, see Philip Hamburger, "The Constitution's Accommodation of Social Change," Michigan Law Review, 88: 239 (1989).

6. Adrian Vermeule, "Our Schmittian Administrative Law," Harvard Law Review 122: 1095, 1101, 1132 (2009); Eric A. Posner & Adrian Vermeule, *The Executive Unbound: After the Madisonian Republic*, 104–07 (New York: Oxford University Press, 2010). Other scholars who focus on genuine emergencies, but in a manner less accepting of Schmittian "exceptions," include Harvey Mansfield, "Is the Imperial Presidency Inevitable?" New York Times, Sunday Book Review, BR12 (Mar. 13, 2011); Clement Fatovic, *Outside the Law: Emergency and Executive Power*, 8 (Baltimore: Johns Hopkins University Press, 2009); Nomi Claire Lazar, *States of Emergency in Liberal Democracies*, 5 (Cambridge: Cambridge University Press, 2009); Benjamin A. Kleinerman, *The Discretionary President: The Promise and Peril of Executive Power*, x–xi (Lawrence: University Press of Kansas, 2009).

7. "An Elector" [James Iredell], "To the Public," *North Carolina Gazette* (Newbern) (Aug. 17, 1786).

8. Ibid.

9. Gary Lawson, Geoffrey P. Miller, Robert G. Natalson & Guy I. Seidman, *The Origins of the Necessary and Proper Clause*, chaps. 4 & 5 (Cambridge: Cambridge University Press, 2010).

10. John Witherspoon, Lectures on Moral Philosophy, in *The Works of the Rev. John Witherspoon*, 3: 466–67 (Philadelphia; 1802).

11. Ibid., 3: 468.

12. James Madison, Federalist Number 44, in *The Federalist*, 303–04, ed. Jacob E. Cooke (Middletown: Wesleyan University Press, 1961).

13. For arguments that "proper" limitation bars violations of the separation of powers, see Gary L. Lawson & Patricia B. Granger, "The Proper Scope of Federal Power: A Jurisdictional Interpretation of the Sweeping Clause," Duke Law Journal, 43: 267, 274 (1994).

14. *Sunshine Anthracite Coal Co. v. Adkins*, 310 U.S. 381, 398 (1940).

15. Peter Strauss assumes that the word "Department" in the necessary and proper clause should be understood as a vestigal allusion to particular executive departments, which did not end up being mentioned in the Constitution, thus making it a mere "solipsism," not an allusion to the parts of the government. This is improbable in light of the careful drafting of the Constitution, and untenable in light of conventional approaches to interpretation. But Strauss certainly is correct in saying that the vesting language is "not noticed, and the clause is understood to empower Congress to create the government." Peter L. Strauss, *Administrative Justice in the United States*, 21, n. 42 (Durham: Carolina Academic Press, 2002).

16. One challenge to the claim that federal administrative power was "the natural and adaptive reaction of government to changing conditions" comes in the scholarship of Stephen Skowronek, who observes that this claim "distorts the history of reform" by attributing to social forces what was product of contested politics. Stephen Skowronek, *Building a New American State: The Expansion of Administrative Capacities*,

1877–1920, at viii–ix (Cambridge: Cambridge University Press: 1982). Somewhat similarly, see Thomas K. McGraw, *Prophets of Regulation* (Cambridge: Belknap Press, 1984).

17. Richard A. Epstein, *Simple Rules for a Complex World*, 21 (Cambridge: Harvard University Press, 1995). For a critique, that not all simple rules expand liberty, see Frederick Schauer, "Does Simplicity Bring Liberty," Critical Review, 11: 393 (1997). For a response, observing that Epstein's goal was merely "to attack the conventional rule that substantive legal rules must become ever more complex as society does," see Richard A. Epstein, "The Right Set of Simple Rules: A Short Reply to Frederick Shauer and Comment on G. A. Cohen," Critical Review, 12: 305 (1998).

18. It has long been recognized that the "division of labor" and the other "complexity" in Anglo-American society developed long before the flourishing of administrative law. Roscoe Pound, "Executive Justice," American Law Register, 55: 137, 144 (Mar. 1907).

19. David Schoenbrod, *Power without Responsibility: How Congress Abuses the People through Delegation*, 121 (New Haven: Yale University Press, 1993).

20. NMEs approved by CDER (2010), http://www.fda.gov/downloads/Drugs/Develop mentApprovalProcess/HowDrugsareDevelopedandApproved/DrugandBiologicAp provalReports/UCM242695.pdf.

21. Ernst Freund already questioned "whether as a matter of fact many regulations are not as permanent as statutes, intrenched in the inertia of bureaucratic tradition." Ernst Freund, *Administrative Powers over Persons and Property*, 222 (Chicago: University of Chicago Press, 1928). For a brief study of delays in state regulation, see John B. Andrews, *Administrative Labor Legislation: A Study of American Experience in the Delegation of Legislative Power*, 115–21 (New York: Harper & Brothers Publishers, 1936). Along such lines, the Department of Labor has described its rulemaking process as "cumbersome, slow, and adversarial." Department of Labor, *Accompanying Report of the National Performance Review Office of the Vice President*, 13 (Washington, DC: Sept. 1993).

22. Daniel Carpenter, *Reputation and Power: Organizational Image and Pharmaceutical Regulation at the FDA*, 1, 465–66, 467, 511, 529 (Princeton: Princeton University Press, 2010). According to a recent article in the Washington Post,

> Experts point to three reasons pharmaceutical companies have pulled back from antibiotics despite two decades of screaming alarms from the public health community: There is not much money in it; inventing new antibiotics is technically challenging; and, in light of drug safety concerns, the FDA has made it difficult for companies to get new antibiotics approved.
>
> As a result, only four of the world's 12 largest pharmaceutical companies are researching new antibiotics, said David Shlaes, a drug development veteran and consultant. . . .
>
> Shlaes said that concerns about antibiotic safety—driven by deaths linked to the drug Ketek that came to light in 2006—have made the FDA reluctant to approve new antibiotics. "They've basically made it impossible for companies to develop and market antibiotics in the U.S.," he said.

Brian Vastag, "NIH Superbug Outbreak Highlights Lack of New Antibiotics," Washington Post, Health & Science (Aug. 24, 2012).

23. As put by Walter Gelhorn, there is a "need for continuous expert supervision, capable of ad hoc development to parallel the development of the subject matter

involved." Walter Gellhorn, *Federal Administrative Proceedings*, 9 (Baltimore: Johns Hopkins Press, 1941).

24. For example, the Department of Labor has said of its Mine Safety and Health Administration that its expertise in some "areas of new technology has lagged" and, "[a]s a result, the agency has been unable to maintain its position at the forefront of mining technology." Moreover, "[t]he approval regulations currently administered by MSHA are often inadequate to address modern technology and the demands of the industry. Recently, many industry and foreign government standards have been updated and are more appropriate to present needs." Department of Labor, *Accompanying Report of the National Performance Review Office of the Vice President*, 29 (Washington, DC: Sept. 1993). According to the Administrative Conference, "audited self-regulation" is valuable because regulated entities often have "more detailed knowledge of the operational or technical aspects" of their activities. Administrative Conference of the United States, Recommendation 94–1, *The Use of Audited Self-Regulation As a Regulatory Technique*, 1 (1995).

CHAPTER TWENTY-FOUR

a. Randle Cotgrave, *A Dictionarie of the French and English Tongues*, sig. [Qqq vi] ("police") (London: 1611); The First Supplement to the Grand Instructions (Tatischeff text), chap. XXI, §528, in *The Nakaz of Catherine the Great*, 431, ed. William E. Butler & Vladimir A Tomsinov (Clark: Lawbook Exchange, 2010); Supplement to the Grand Instructions (Macartney-Dukes text), chap. XXI, §538, ibid., 509; *Miscellaneous and Posthumous Works of Henry Thomas Buckle*, 2: 221, ed. Helen Taylor (London: Longmans, Greene & Co., 1872); Pa. Const. of 1776, Art. III; N.Y. Const. of 1777, preamble.

See also Marc Raeff, *The Well-Ordered Police State: Social and Institutional Change through Law in the Germanies and Russia, 1600–1800*, at 5 (New Haven: Yale University Press, 1983); Diethelm Klippel, "Reasonable Aims of Civil Society: Concerns of the State in German Political Theory in the Eighteenth and Early Nineteenth Centuries," in *Rethinking Leviathan: The Eighteenth-Century State in Britain and Germany*, 79, ed. John Brewer & Eckhart Hellmuth (Oxford: Oxford University Press, 1999); Hans Boldt, "Geschichte der Polizei in Deutschland," in *Handbuch des Polizeirechts*, 1, 3 (Munich: C. H. Beck'sche Verlagsbuchhandlung, 1992); David N. Mayer, "The Jurisprudence of Christopher G. Tiedeman: A Study of Laissez-Faire Constitutionalism," Missouri Law Review, 93, 102–03 (1990). Even in emphasizing constitutional limitations "to protect private rights against . . . social reformers," Tiedeman accepted the breadth of the police power. Christopher G. Tiedeman, *A Treatise on the Limitations of Police Power in the United States*, viii (St. Louis: 1886). Although the importance of the "police" in eighteenth- and nineteenth-century America is recognized by Christopher Tomlins, his work emphasizes communal implications without adequately acknowledging the authoritarian element or how late-eighteenth-century Americans avoided this by separating and enumerating powers. Christopher L Tomlins, *Law, Labor, and Ideology in the Early American Republic*, 45–46, 58 (Cambridge: Cambridge University Press, 1993). Similarly, the work of Santiago Legarre understands the police power as the legislative power of the states without recognizing that, in early American constitutions, it was understood as the more general power of the people. Santiago Legarre, "The Historical Background of the Police Power," Journal of Constitutional Law, 9: 745, 748 (2007).

b. *American Thought: Civil War to World War I*, at ix, ed. Perry Miller (New York Rine-
    hart & Co., 1954); John Marini, *Politics of Budget Control: Congress, the Presidency,
    and the Growth of the Administrative State*, 2 (Washington, DC: Crane Russak, 1992);
    Karl Marx, *Critique of Hegel's "Philosophy of Right,"* 44, ed. Joseph O'Malley (Cam-
    bridge: Cambridge University Press, 1970), discussed by Robert D. Miewald, "The
    Origins of Wilson's Thought: The German Tradition and the Organic State," in *Poli-
    tics and Administration: Woodrow Wilson and American Public Administration*, 18, ed.
    Jack Rabin & James S. Bowman (New York: Marcel Dekker, 1984).

c. "Our Goal," People (Feb. 24, 1895) (from Edward Monnell, editor of the Sunday
    edition of the New York Press); Elihu Root, "Address As President of the American
    Bar Association" (Aug. 30, 1916), in *Addresses on Government and Citizenship*, 535
    (Cambridge: Harvard University Press, 1916).

d. "The Governor's Message," Evening Post (Jan. 4, 1870). For the confused politics,
    which defied party distinctions, see "Legislature of New York," Troy Weekly Times
    (Mar. 26, 1870).

e. "Municipal Problems: Local Self-Government Ably Discussed by Prof. Goodnow: A
    Work of General Interest," Morning Herald (Lexington) (May 2, 1897).

g. *Harvey v. United States*, 3 Ct. Cl. 38, 1800 WL 509 (U.S. Ct. Cl. 1867); *United States
    v. Barrows et al.*, 1 Abb.U.S. 351, 24 F. Cas. 1018, 1019 (1869). For cases somewhat
    similar to *Barrows*, see *United States v. Eaton*, 144 U.S. 677 (1892); *Wilkins v. United
    States*, 96 Fed. Rep., 837; Vol. 2, Treas. Dec. No. 21623 (U.S. Cir. Ct. of App. 1899).

h. Williamjames Hull Hoffer, *To Enlarge the Machinery of Government: Congressional De-
    bates and the Growth of the American State, 1858–1891*, at 161–62, 164 (Baltimore:
    Johns Hopkins University Press, 2007); W. G. Sumner, "State Interference," North
    American Review, 145: 109, 115 (1887).

i. "Goodnow Likes Constitution," Columbus Ledger (June 22, 1914).

k. Rudolf von Ihering, *Law As a Means to an End*, 275 (New York: Macmillan Co.,
    1921).

l. Woodrow Wilson, "The Study of Administration," Political Science Quarterly, 2:
    197, 210–11 (1887).

m. Notes for Lectures at Johns Hopkins (1891–94), in *Papers of Woodrow Wilson*, 7: 114,
    ed. Arthur S. Link (Princeton: Princeton University Press, 1969), discussed by Ron-
    ald J. Pestritto, "The Progressive Origins of the Administrative State: Wilson, Good-
    now, and Landis," Social Philosophy & Policy, 24: 16, 41 (2007). For the tendency
    of administrative legislation to trespass beyond its statutory warrant, see Thomas W.
    Merrill & Kathryn Tongue Watts, "Agency Rules with the Force of Law: The Original
    Convention," Harvard Law Review, 116: 467, 591 (2002).

n. Westel Woodbury Willoughby, *The Constitutional Law of the United States*, 1: 62 (New
    York: Baker, Boorhis & Co., 1910).

o. Ernst Freund, "Historical Survey," in *The Growth of Administrative Law*, 15 (St. Louis:
    Thomas Law Book Co., 1923).

p. Roscoe Pound, "The Administrative Application of Legal Standards," Annual Report
    of the American Bar Association, 42: 1, 19 (1919); Ernst Freund, *Administrative Pow-
    ers over Persons and Property*, 27–28 (Chicago: University of Chicago Press, 1928);
    Daniel R. Ernst, "Ernst Freund, Felix Frankfurter, and the American *Rechtsstaat*: A
    Transatlantic Shipwreck, 1894–1932," Studies in American Political Development,
    23: 176, 177, 187 (2009), quoting Felix Frankfurter, review of *The Growth of Ameri-
    can Administrative Law*, Harvard Law Review, 37, 640–41 (1924), and notes from his
    classes.

1. Ken I. Kersch, *Constructing Civil Liberties: Discontinuities in the Development of American Constitutional Law*, 339 (Cambridge: Cambridge University Press, 2004); Ronald J. Pestritto, "The Progressive Origins of the Administrative State: Wilson, Goodnow, and Landis," Social Philosophy & Policy, 24: 16, 40, 42, 51 (2007); Christian Rosser, "Examining Frank J. Goodnow's Hegelian Heritage: A Contribution to Understanding Progressive Administrative Theory," Administration & Society, 20: 1, 25–26 (2012); M. J. C. Vile, *Constitutionalism and the Separation of Powers*, 295 (Indianapolis: Liberty Fund, 1998); Frank Tariello, Jr., *The Reconstruction of American Political Ideology, 1865–1917*, at 53 (Charlottesville: University Press of Virginia, 1982). See also William C. Chase, *The American Law School and the Rise of Administrative Government*, 50 (Madison: University of Wisconsin Press, 1982); Martin Shapiro, *Who Guards the Guardians: Judicial Control of Administration*, 36 (Athens: University of Georgia Press, 1988); Noga Morag-Levine, *Chasing the Wind: Regulating Air Pollution in the Common Law State*, 79 (Princeton: Princeton University Press, 2003). For the contemporary significance of German and American administrative regimes for each other, see Susan Rose-Ackerman, *Controlling Environmental Policy: The Limits of Public Law in Germany and the United States* (New Haven: Yale University Press, 1995).

2. On the continuing role of German ideas in America, Robert Miewald aptly observes the error of assuming that German ideas were no longer significant after the turn of the century: "By the turn of the century, so the argument goes, political science has become domesticated and nothing more is heard of this once-powerful foreign element. I suggest that not all these traces of the early approach were eliminated and that, through such writers as Wilson, a massive dose of the German school found its way into the study of administration in the United States." Robert D. Miewald, "The Origins of Wilson's Thought: The German Tradition and the Organic State," in *Politics and Administration: Woodrow Wilson and American Public Administration*, 17–18, ed. Jack Rabin & James S. Bowman (New York: Marcel Dekker, 1984). Miewald adds that the current obscurity of Lorenz von Stein in the United States "is a sad note on the ahistorical orientation of the discipline." Ibid., 19.

3. Francis Bacon, *The Elements of the Common Lawes of England*, sig. B3[r] (preface) (London: 1630). Bacon wrote this in justification of "delivering of knowledge in distinct and disjoined aphorisms" rather than in "a certain method or order"; ibid., as discussed by Daniel R. Coquillette, *Francis Bacon*, 38 (Stanford: Stanford University Press, 1992).

4. "An English Theologian's View of Roman Law: Pepo, Irnerius, Ralph Niger," in *Rechtshistorische Schriften*, by Hermann Kantorowicz, 240–41, 243 (Karlsruhe: C. F. Müller, 1970); *The Teaching of Roman Law in England*, xxvi, ed. Francis de Zulueta & Peter Stein (London: Selden Society, 1990).

5. The maxim was from Ulpian's version of the *Lex Regia*, as recited by Justinian's *Digest* (1.4.1pr.) and *Institutes* (I.ii.6) ("quod principi placuit legis habet vigorem").

6. Joseph Canning, *The Political Thought of Baldus de Ubaldis*, 74–75 (Cambridge: Cambridge University Press, 1987); Kenneth Pennington, *The Prince and the Law, 1200–1600*, chaps. 2 & 3 (Berkeley: University of California Press, 1993).

7. For the requirement of a non obstante clause, see R. W. Carlyle & A. J. Carlyle, *A History of Mediæval Political Theory in the West*, 6: 149 (New York: Barnes & Noble, n.d.); Walter Ullmann, *The Medieval Idea of Law As Represented by Lucas de Penna: A Study in Fourteenth-Century Legal Scholarship*, 104, n. 3 (New York: Barnes & Noble, 1969). More generally, for the efforts of Continental lawyers to tame the dangers of

absolutism, see Kenneth Pennington, *The Prince and the Law, 1200–1600*, chaps. 3 & 4 (Berkeley: University of California Press, 1993), who also observes, however, that their limitations "did not offer robust protection from the prince's arbitrary authority." Ibid., 120. For the near irrelevance of just cause requirements, see also R. W. Carlyle & A. J. Carlyle, *A History of Medæval Political Theory*, 6: 543 (New York: Barnes & Noble, n.d.), paraphrasing Gentili. For the exceptional character of absolute power, see, for example, Joseph Canning, *The Political Thought of Baldus de Ubaldis*, 74–75 (Cambridge: Cambridge University Press, 1987).

In the wake of World War II, much scholarship has emphasized the civilian theories that limited absolutism. It is understandable that scholars working in Continental law have sought to find in its traditions at least some foundation for limits on state power. It would be a sad mistake, however, to ignore the profound differences between the common law and civil law approaches to power.

8. Twysden wrote that the king's "prerogatives are not numberless, but contain in themselves matter of prescription." Roger Twysden, *Certaine Considerations upon the Government of England*, 87 (London: Camden Society, 1849). For the traditional English focus on particular prerogatives and the way in which this was threatened in the sixteenth century, see W. S. Holdsworth, "The Prerogative in the Sixteenth Century," Columbia Law Review, 21: 561 (1921).

9. Kenneth Pennington, *The Prince and the Law, 1200–1600*, at 276–83 (Berkeley: University of California Press, 1993); Philip Hamburger, *Law and Judicial Duty*, 67 (Cambridge: Harvard University Press, 2008). For the role of such ideas in England already under Henry VIII, see chap. 3, footnote b.

10. For the early development of administrative power in Protestant German states of the last half of the sixteenth century, including the sixteenth-century German *Landesordnungen*, or codes, see Marc Raeff, "The Well-Ordered Police State and the Development of Modernity in Seventeenth- and Eighteenth-Century Europe: An Attempt at a Comparative Approach," American Historical Review, 80: 1221, 1223 (1975); Marc Raeff, *The Well-Ordered Police State: Social and Institutional Change through Law in the Germanies and Russia, 1600–1800*, at 21–23, 49, 55 (New Haven: Yale University Press, 1983). For the role of German Protestantism, see Philip S. Gorski, *The Disciplinary Revolution: Calvinism and the Rise of the State in Early Modern Europe*, 138 (Chicago: University of Chicago Press, 2003). For a caution against attributing too much to Protestantism, see Hajo Holborn, *A History of Modern Germany: The Reformation*, 193 (New York: Alfred A. Knopf, 1959).

11. Justinian, *Institutes, Proemium*, §3–4; Michael H. Hoeflich, "Law and Geometry: Legal Science from Leibniz to Landell," American Journal of Legal History, 30: 95 (1980); Philip Hamburger, "The Development of the Nineteenth-Century Consensus Theory of Contract," Law & History Review, 7: 241,308 (1989).

12. As suggested in the text, Bentham considerably modified some of the Continental ideas. For example, the Enlightenment idea of *Glückseligkeit* or happiness did not distinguish between the good of the society and the good of the state. Diethelm Klippel, "Reasonable Aims of Civil Society: Concerns of the State in German Political Theory in the Eighteenth and Early Nineteenth Centuries," in *Rethinking Leviathan: The Eighteenth-Century State in Britain and Germany*, 76, ed. John Brewer & Eckhart Hellmuth (Oxford: Oxford University Press, 1999).

The connection between Bentham's ideas and the Continental codification was not lost on contemporaries. When Étienne Dumont in 1791 prepared a letter for Bentham to send to the French National Assembly, in which the philosopher offered his services to the legislature in preparing a French code, the letter began by recalling the research done in preparation for the Prussian code. *The Works of Jeremy Bentham*, 10: 268, ed. John Bowring (Edinburgh: William Tait, 1843).

For Bentham's brief account of at least one aspect of administrative power, administrative tribunals, see H. W. Arndt, "Bentham on Administrative Jurisdiction," Journal of Comparative Legislation and International Law, 3rd ser., 21: 198 (1939). More generally, Austin divided "political powers" into "such as are *legislative*, and such as are *executive* or *administrative*," and he noted the civilian tradition of dividing "public law . . . into *constitutional* and *administrative*." John Austin, *The Province of Jurisprudence Determined*, 244, lxxi (London: John Murray, 1832).

13. A. V. Dicey, *Introduction to the Law of the Constitution*, 332 (London: MacMillan & Co., 1924). For royal *ordonnances*, etc., see J. B. Denisart, *Collection de Décisions Nouvelles et de Notions Relatives a La Jurisprudence Actuelle*, 2: 69 (édit) (Paris: 1768). More generally, see Herman Finer, *Theory and Practice of Modern Government*, 741–54 (New York: Henry Holt & Co., 1949); R. C. van Caenegem, *An Historical Introduction to Western Constitutional Law*, 99 (Cambridge: Cambridge University Press, 1995). Even in 1929, the English chief justice could use the phrase "administrative law" and then note that "happily there is no English name for it." Lord Hewart of Bury, *The New Despotism*, 37 (London: Ernest Benn Limited, 1929).

14. Ernst Freund, *Administrative Powers over Persons and Property*, 140, n. 2 (Chicago: University of Chicago Press, 1928), translating *Allgemeine Landrecht für die Preußischen Staaten*, title XVII, §10 (1794), which referred to "das Amt der Polizey"; The First Supplement to the Grand Instructions (Tatischeff Text), chap. XXI, §528, in *The Nakaz of Catherine the Great*, 431, ed. William E. Butler & Vladimir A. Tomsinov (Clark: Lawbook Exchange, 2010); Supplement to the Grand Instructions (Macartney-Dukes text), chap. XXI, §538, ibid., 509; Francis Lieber, *On Civil Liberty and Self-Government*, 1: 46–47, 73, 89 (Philadelphia: 1853). For the German developments, see Conrad Bornhak, *Preussische Staats- und Rechtsgeschichte* (Berlin: Carl Henmanns Verlag, 1903); Herman Finer, *Theory and Practice of Modern Government*, 724–40 (New York: Henry Holt & Co., 1949). For the formative role of civilian academics (the *gemietete Doktoren*, or hired doctors of law), see ibid., 725.

15. For the conflict between Romanists and Germans, see David M. Rabban, *Law's History: American Legal Thought and the Transatlantic Turn to History*, 103 (Cambridge: Cambridge University Press, 2013). For the profound role of Roman and civilian ideas until the end of the nineteenth century, although with greater emphasis on their constitutional potential, see James Q. Whitman, *The Legacy of Roman Law in the German Romantic Era: Historical Vision and Legal Change*, x–xv (Princeton: Princeton University Press, 1990).

16. Ibid., 39.

17. Georg W. F. Hegel, *Philosophy of Mind: Translated from the Encyclopedia of the Philosophical Sciences*, 143, ed. William Wallace (New York: Cosimo, 2008); discussed by Gerhard Casper, "Changing Concepts of Constitutionalism: 18th to 20th Century," Supreme Court Review, 311, 324 (1989), quoting Hegel, *Philosophy of Mind*. For the eighteenth-century German views, see Fania Oz-Salzberger, "Scots, Germans, Republic and Commerce," in *Republicanism: A Shared European Heritage: The Values of Republicanism in Early Modern Europe*, 2: 216, ed. Martin van Gelderen & Quentin Skinner (Cambridge: Cambridge University Press, 2002).

18. W. G. Hastings, "The Development of Law As Illustrated by the Decisions Relating to the Police Power of the State," Proceedings of the American Philosophical

Society, 39: 359, 549 (1900), citing Vorlesungen, 1: 33–323; 2: 11–27; Rudolf von Ihering, *Law As a Means to an End*, 241–42 (New York: Macmillan Co., 1921). For the point about Realpolitik, see Jud Matthews, "Administrative Law in Comparative Perspective: Translating the German Doctrine of Subjective Public Rights," 28–29, 43 (unpublished paper, 2006).

19. Robert D. Miewald, "The Origins of Wilson's Thought: The German Tradition and the Organic State," in *Politics and Administration: Woodrow Wilson and American Public Administration*, 22, ed. Jack Rabin & James S. Bowman (New York: Marcel Dekker, 1984). Miewald concludes: "Any review of the essence of German administrative theory must take account of the ideal state described in [Hegel's] major treatise on political theory, *The Philosophy of Right*." Ibid., 18. For the liberal Hegelians, see Giles Pope, "The Political Ideas of Lorenz Stein and Their Influence on Rudolf Gneist and Gustav Schmoller," German History, 4: 60–61 (1987). See also Erich Hahn, "Rudolf Gneist and the Prussian Rechtsstaat: 1862–78," Journal of Modern History, 49: 1361, 1362 (1977); Mark R. Rutgers, "Can the Study of Public Administration Do without a Concept of the State? Reflections on the Work of Lorenz Von Stein," Administration & Society, 26: 395, 398 (1994); Robert D. Miewald, "The Origins of Wilson's Thought: The German Tradition and the Organic State," in *Politics and Administration: Woodrow Wilson and American Public Administration*, 19–20, ed. Jack Rabin & James S. Bowman (New York: Marcel Dekker, 1984).

20. For Justi's legal training, at Wittenberg, see Ulrich Adam, *The Political Economy of J. H. G. Justi*, 25 (Oxford: Peter Land, 2006). For the eighteenth-century rejection of separation—notably by Justi—see Christian Rosser, "Examining Frank J. Goodnow's Hegelian Heritage: A Contribution to Understanding Progressive Administrative Theory," Administration & Society, 20: 1, 6–7 (2012); Fania Oz-Salzberger, "Scots, Germans, Republic and Commerce," in *Republicanism: A Shared European Heritage: The Values of Republicanism in Early Modern Europe*, 2: 215, ed. Martin van Gelderen & Quentin Skinner (Cambridge: Cambridge University Press, 2002).

21. G. W. F. Hegel, *Philosophy of Right*, 315, 339, §§278 & 300 (Cambridge: Cambridge University Press, 1991); Heinrich von Treitschke, *Politics*, 2: 5, trans. Arthur James Balfour (New York: MacMillan Co., 1916). Of course, Treitschke was not alone in this. For Johann Kaspar Bluntschli's views, see Christian Rosser, "Examining Frank J. Goodnow's Hegelian Heritage: A Contribution to Understanding Progressive Administrative Theory," Administration & Society, 20: 1, 14 (2012). For Mohl and Bluntschli, see M. J. C. Vile, *Constitutionalism and the Separation of Powers*, 270–71 (Indianapolis: Liberty Fund, 1998).

22. M. J. C. Vile, *Constitutionalism and the Separation of Powers*, 270 (Indianapolis: Liberty Fund, 1998).

23. Jack Lively, *The Social and Political Thought of Alexis de Tocqueville*, 169 (Oxford: Clarendon Press, 1965); A. V. Dicey, *Introduction to the Law of the Constitution*, 327 (London: MacMillan & Co., 1924). For the Hegel quotes, see George Wilhelm Friedrich Hegel, *The Philosophy of History*, 85–86, trans. J. Sibree (New York: Dover Publications, 1956); Stephen Skowronek, *Building a New American Sate: The Expansion of Administrative Capacities, 1877–1920*, 6–7 (Cambridge: Cambridge University Press: 1982); G. A. Kelly, "Hegel's America," Philosophy & Public Affairs, 2: 3, 7 (1972).

24. Roscoe Pound, *Administrative Agencies and the Law*, 5 (New York: American Affairs, 1946); Roscoe Pound, "The Recrudescence of Absolutism," Sewanee Review, 47: 18, 24 (1939).

25. Woodrow Wilson, "The Study of Administration," Political Science Quarterly, 2: 197 (1887). Sylvian Fries writes that "thousands of young American scholars" matriculated in German universities in the century after 1820, especially in the late nineteenth century. Sylvia D. Fries, "Staatstheorie and the New American Science of Politics," Journal of the History of Ideas, 34: 391, 392 (1973). It was observed in 1890 that "professors in Germany agree pretty generally that they have had in the last fifteen years no more eager, industrious and able students than those who go from this side the water." "Introductory Note, Proceedings of the American Academic of Political and Social Science," Annals of the American Academy of Political & Social Science, 1: 132 (1890). More generally, see David M. Rabban, Law's History: American Legal Thought and the Transatlantic Turn to History, 66–67, 86–87 (Cambridge: Cambridge University Press, 2013). For the German scientific study of law, see Mathias Reimann, "Nineteenth Century German Legal Science," Boston College Law Review, 318–37 (1990). The German model continued to fascinate Americans into the twentieth century. Ken I. Kersch, Constructing Civil Liberties: Discontinuities in the Development of American Constitutional Law, 246, 262 (Cambridge: Cambridge University Press, 2004). For an amusing instance, see Merlo J. Pusey, Charles Evans Hughes, 1: 70 (New York: Columbia University Press, 1963). Ultimately, as Ronald Pestritto writes about Wilson and Goodnow, they "import[ed] a foreign administrative science into the American system of government." Ronald J. Pestritto, "The Progressive Origins of the Administrative State: Wilson, Goodnow, and Landis," Social Philosophy & Policy, 24: 16, 51 (2007)

26. Charles Edward Merriam, A History of American Political Theories, 338–39 (New York: Macmillan Co., 1903). He noted: "The work of such publicists as Gneist, Stein, Ihering, Bluntschli, Jellinek, and Holtzendorff is clearly evident in the method and thought of present day political scientists." Ibid. More generally, see Sylvia D. Fries, "Staatstheorie and the New American Science of Politics," Journal of the History of Ideas, 34: 391, 403 (1973); Dennis J. Mahoney, Politics and Progress: The Emergence of American Political Science, 3, 8–9, 11 (Lanham: Lexington Books, 2004); Ronald J. Pestritto, "The Progressive Origins of the Administrative State: Wilson, Goodnow, and Landis," Social Philosophy & Policy, 24: 16, 40 (2007).

Dennis Mahoney notes that "the whole of the original faculty of political science at Columbia University spent at least a year studying German universities." Dennis J. Mahoney, Politics and Progress: The Emergence of American Political Science, 22 (Lanham: Lexington Books, 2004). Sylvia Fries observes that at Michigan there were a whole series of courses "in topics which resembled closely the substance of Staatswissenschaft," including, of course, comparative administrative law. As promised by Charles Kendall Adams—the first dean of the University of Michigan's School of Political Science—"[t]he character of the courses and the method of the instruction will be essentially the same as those offered and given in the schools of political science at Paris, Leipzig, Tübingen, and Vienna." In the 1890–91 academic year, one Harvard professor complained, "there was hardly a course in the catalogue" that "did not smack of Verfassungsgeschichte"—German-style constitutional history. Indeed, much of their scholarship often did little more than "translate" the German Staatstheorie into Anglo-American terms. Sylvia D. Fries, "Staatstheorie and the New American Science of Politics," Journal of the History of Ideas, 34: 391, 394, 396 (1973), quoting 1881 address by Charles K. Adams.

27. Ernst Freund, "Historical Survey," in The Growth of Administrative Law, 40 (St. Louis:

Thomas Law Book Co., 1923). For more on Gneist and Freund, see Daniel R. Ernst, "Ernst Freund, Felix Frankfurter, and the American *Rechtsstaat*: A Transatlantic Shipwreck, 1894–1932," Studies in American Political Development, 23: 171, 176–77 (2009); "Ernst Freund—Pioneer of Administrative Law," University of Chicago Law Review, 29: 755 (1962). On Gneist and Bismark, see Frank J. Goodnow, "Local Government in Prussia, I," Political Science Quarterly, 4: 648, 661 (1889).

28. Sylvia D. Fries, "Staatstheorie and the New American Science of Politics," Journal of the History of Ideas, 34: 391 (1973); Ronald J. Pestritto, "The Progressive Origins of the Administrative State: Wilson, Goodnow, and Landis," Social Philosophy & Policy, 24: 16, 40 (2007); Christian Rosser, "Examining Frank J. Goodnow's Hegelian Heritage: A Contribution to Understanding Progressive Administrative Theory," Administration & Society, 20: 1, 10, 16, 18 (2012). In Goodnow's words, the government had to be responsive to a society that was "dynamic or progressive in character." Frank J. Goodnow, *Social Reform and the Constitution*, 1 (1911; reprint, New York: Burt Franklin, 1970). For the complexity of the reception of German ideas—often filtered through American lectures and other secondary American sources—see Christian Rosser, "Examining Frank J. Goodnow's Hegelian Heritage: A Contribution to Understanding Progressive Administrative Theory," Administration & Society, 20: 1, 2, 26.

29. Sylvia D. Fries, "Staatstheorie and the New American Science of Politics," Journal of the History of Ideas, 34: 391, 404 (1973). On the Americanization, see Dennis J. Mahoney, *Politics and Progress: The Emergence of American Political Science*, 30 (Lanham: Lexington Books, 2004). Wilson asked his students: "Have we not in this country an opportunity to recast the whole science of administration for ourselves?" Notes for Lectures at Johns Hopkins (1891–94), in *Papers of Woodrow Wilson*, 7: 122, ed. Arthur S. Link (Princeton: Princeton University Press, 1969).

30. "Brooklyn City . . . Message of Mayor Kalbfleisch," New York Herald (Jan. 4, 1870).

31. "Commissioners," Nation, 203 (Mar. 31, 1870).

32. Albert Shaw, "The Government of German Cities: The Municipal Framework," Century Illustrated Magazine, 48 (2): 296 (1894). Albert Shaw, "What German Cities Do for Their Citizens: A Study of Municipal House-Keeping," Century Illustrated Magazine, 48 (3): 380 (1894). Shaw was a journalist who studied at Hopkins and briefly taught at Cornell.

33. Frank J. Goodnow, *City Government in the United States*, ix (New York: Century Co., 1904); Frank J. Goodnow, *The Principles of Administrative Law of the United States*, 2 (New York: G. P. Putnam, 1905).

34. *Address of Professor John W. Burgess Made on the Invitation and at the Request of the Newport Improvement Association, September 5th, 1913* (1913) (Bulletin of the Newport Improvement Assocation, no. 2). See also *Report of Committee on Charter Revision to the Newport Improvement Association* (Bulletin no. 3) and *Report by Professor John W. Burgess to the Newport Improvement Association Concerning the Petition for the Charter* (Bulletin no. 4). For an example of how municipal reformers relied on academic and popular writers, see Allen Ripley Foote, *Powers of Municipalities: A Discussion of the Report on Municipal Program of the Special Committee of the National Municipal League*, 8, 26 ([Washington, DC: 1898]), quoting Goodnow and Shaw.

35. Williamjames Hull Hoffer, *To Enlarge the Machinery of Government: Congressional Debates and the Growth of the American State, 1858–1891*, at 130–31, 137–38 (Baltimore: Johns Hopkins University Press, 2007).

36. E. L. Godkin, "The Danger of an Office-Holding Aristocracy," *Century Illustrated Magazine*, 24 (2): 28, 33 (1882).

37. Testimony of Albert Fink, *Report of the Senate Select Committee on Interstate Commerce (Testimony)*, 124 (49th Congress, 1st Session, submitted to Senate Jan. 18, 1886) (Washington, DC: Government Printing Office, 1886), discussed by John A. Rohr, *To Run a Constitution: The Legitimacy of the Administrative State*, 98 (Lawrence: University Press of Kansas, 1986); Rep. John H. Reagan of Texas, *Congressional Record*, 7283 (July 21, 1886). For the transfer of legislative and judicial powers, see Rep. Augustus Hill Garland of Arkansas, *Congressional Record*, 568–69 (Jan. 9, 1885). Similarly, see *Political and Commercial Objections to Conferring Judicial Powers upon the Interstate Commerce Commission: An Argument by Joseph Nimmo, Jr., before the Senate Committee on Interstate Commerce, in Relation to the Bill S. 892, Feb. 23, 1892* (Washington, DC: Gibson Bros, 1892). Nimmo said that he could recall only one instance of a federal statute that invested commissioners with judicial power: the 1872 act authorizing circuit courts to appoint shipping commissioners. Ibid., 21.

38. Woodrow Wilson, "The Study of Administration," *Political Science Quarterly*, 2: 197, 201 (1887). It has been observed that "Wilson's contribution was not to fashion new ideas, but to give current Continental European preferences and notions a form that allowed them to be taught and transmitted." Niels Thorsen, "The Origins of Woodrow Wilson's 'The Study of Administration,'" *American Studies in Scandinavia*, 21: 16, 27 (1989). See also M. J. C. Vile, *Constitutionalism and the Separation of Powers*, 293, 304 (Indianapolis: Liberty Fund, 1998); Ronald J. Pestritto, "The Progressive Origins of the Administrative State: Wilson, Goodnow, and Landis," *Social Philosophy & Policy*, 24: 16, 40 (2007); Ernst Freund, *Administrative Powers over Persons and Property*, 146 (Chicago: University of Chicago Press, 1928); Frank J. Goodnow, *Comparative Administrative Law*, 1: v (New York: G. P. Putnam's Sons, 1897); James Q. Whitman, *The Legacy of Roman Law in the German Romantic Era: Historical Vision and Legal Change*, xiii–iv (Princeton: Princeton University Press, 1990).

39. Robert D. Miewald, "The Origins of Wilson's Thought: The German Tradition and the Organic State," in *Politics and Administration: Woodrow Wilson and American Public Administration*, 8, 27, ed. Jack Rabin & James S. Bowman (New York: Marcel Dekker, 1984). His work was "far from a pure expression of the native genius but merely a rephrasing of ideas then current in German administrative thought." Ibid., 8. For his misunderstanding, see ibid., 18, 22.

40. Woodrow Wilson, "The Study of Administration," *Political Science Quarterly*, 2: 202, 204 (1887).

41. Ibid., 2: 207.

42. The establishment of a graduate school in political science, so as to train students to serve the nation in administrative position, was proposed in 1885 by Edmund J. James, in his *Instruction in Political and Social Science*, 18, 20, 23 (Philadelphia: Philadelphia Social Science Association, 1885). See also Robert Adcock, "The Emergence of Political Science As a Discipline: History and the Study of Politics in America, 1875-1910," *History of Political Thought*, 24: 481, 501 (2003); Dennis J. Mahoney, *Politics and Progress: The Emergence of American Political Science*, 20, 55, 148 (Lanham: Lexington Books, 2004). As in Germany, many scholars taught from the perspective of "reforming civil servants." Michael Stolleis, *Public Law in Germany 1800–1914*, at 219 (New York: Berghahn Books, 2001).

43. Michael J. Lacey, "The World of the Bureaus: Government and the Positivist Project

in the Late Nineteenth Century," in *The State and Social Investigation in Britain and the United States*, 127 & passim, ed. Michael J. Lacey & Mary O. Furner (Washington, DC: Woodrow Wilson Center Press, 1993); Lester F. Ward, *The Psychic Factors of Civilization*, 310 (New York: Johnson Reprint Corporation, 1970).

44. Henry C. Adams, "Governmental Supervision of Railway Accounts," Railway Age, 44: 884 (Dec. 20, 1907). The commission aimed "to exercise a controlling influence" on the "administration of railway properties" by the clever expedient of taking a broad interpretation of its authority to dictate methods of accounting to the railways. Ibid.

    For more on the commission's position, see *Twenty-First Annual Report of the Interstate Commerce Commission*, 139–42 (Washington, DC: Government Printing Office, 1907).

45. W. F. Willoughby, "The Institute for Government Research," American Political Science Review, 12: 49, 51, 58–62 (1918). For the founding of the institute, see "Federal Bureau to Probe Many Government Forms," Colorado Springs Gazette (Mar. 14, 1916). Another institution that disseminated administrative ideas was the Public Administration Clearing House in Chicago.

46. W. F. Willoughby, *An Introduction to the Government of Modern States*, 6, 241, 388–89 (1919; New York: Century Co., 1921); W. F. Willoughby, *Principles of Legislative Organization and Administration*, 8 (Washington, DC: Brookings Institution, 1934).

47. Ronald J. Pestritto, "The Progressive Origins of the Administrative State: Wilson, Goodnow, and Landis," Social Philosophy & Policy, 24: 16, 47 (2007).

48. A Speech in the Star Chamber (June 20, 1616), in *The Political Works of James I*, at 333, ed. Charles Howard McIlwain (Cambridge: Harvard University Press, 1918); R. C. van Caenegem, *An Historical Introduction to Western Constitutional Law*, 3, 135–37 (Cambridge: Cambridge University Press, 1995).

49. Francis Lieber, *Reminiscences of an Intercourse with Mr. Niebuhr the Historian during a Residence with Him in Rome, in the Years 1822 and 1823*, at 59–61 (Philadelphia: 1835). Lieber gave this quotation pride of place as the first in his collection. Niebuhr added: "But here (in Rome), in Spain, and in Portugal, there are neither the British principle, nor bureaucratic order, and system, and precision." Ibid.

50. Heinrich von Treitschke, *Politics*, 2: 5, trans. Arthur James Balfour (New York: MacMillan Co., 1916).

51. Outline of Course of Lectures (1831), in John Austin, *The Province of Jurisprudence Determined*, lxxi (London: John Murray, 1832); Woodrow Wilson, "The Study of Administration," Political Science Quarterly, 2: 197, 211 (1887); Notes for Lectures at Johns Hopkins (1891–94), in *Papers of Woodrow Wilson*, 7: 121–22, ed. Arthur S. Link (Princeton: Princeton University Press, 1969). He thus differentiated "between those governmental adjustments which are essential to constitutional principle and those which are merely instrumental to the possibly changing purposes of a wisely adapting convenience." Woodrow Wilson, "The Study of Administration," Political Science Quarterly, 2: 211 (1887). For hints of such views in the writing of William Dean Howells, see Nancy Cohen, *The Reconstruction of American Liberalism, 1865–1914*, at 111 (Chapel Hill: University of North Carolina Press, 2002).

52. Woodrow Wilson, "The Study of Administration," Political Science Quarterly, 2: 197, 212 (1887).

53. Speech before the Elmira Chamber of Commerce (May 3, 1907), in *Addresses of Charles Evans Hughes*, 185–87, ed. Jacob Gould Schurman (New York: G. P. Putnam's Sons, 1916). Astonishingly, Hughes added that the real assault on judicial

independence was to "burden it with these questions of administration." Ibid., 185. See also Merlo J. Pusey, *Charles Evans Hughes*, 1: 203 (New York: Columbia University Press, 1963).

54. The Germanic vision that administrative power stood apart from the constitutional system became sufficiently widespread in America that, in 1934, two scholars at Brookings felt obliged to protest that "a sound system of administrative legislation and adjudication can be attained only by a proper integration of government functions with the constitutional and legal system." Frederick Blachly & Miriam Oatman, *Administrative Legislation and Adjudication*, 17 (Washington, DC: Brookings Institution, 1934).

55. In addition, Prussian courts had "no such power of passing upon the constitutionality of laws," but could simply inquire "whether a law has been passed, or, in administrative cases, an official order issued, in due legal form." Woodrow Wilson, *The State: Elements of Historical and Practical Politics*, 298, §630 (Boston: D. C. Heath & Co., 1911).

56. Georg Jellinek, *System der Subjektiven Öffentlichen Rechte*, 28 (1905), as quoted by Jud Matthews, "Administrative Law in Comparative Perspective: Translating the German Doctrine of Subjective Public Rights," 30 (unpublished paper, 2006). For the vulnerability of rights in the German system, see ibid., 36.

57. John W. Burgess, *Political Science and Comparative Constitutional Law*, 1: 49, 52, 175 (Boston: 1890); James W. Garner, *Introduction to Political Science*, 251 (New York: 1919); Westel W. Willoughby, *An Examination of the Nature of the State*, 224 (New York: 1896). For discussion of Burgess, see Jean M. Yarbrough, *Theodore Roosevelt and the American Political Tradition*, 38–46 (Lawrence: University Press of Kansas, 2012). For discussion of Garner, see Sylvia D. Fries, "Staatstheorie and the New American Science of Politics," Journal of the History of Ideas, 34: 391, 398, 400, 402 (1973); Dennis J. Mahoney, *Politics and Progress: The Emergence of American Political Science*, 28 (Lanham: Lexington Books, 2004). On Burgess's politics, see ibid., 4. As for Burgess's intellectual assumptions, he wrote that "[h]istory in the making" was "the progressive realization of the ideals of the human spirit in all of the objective forms of their manifestation," including law and institutions." Put another ways, these were "progressive revelations of the human reason" in its advance of the human race toward "its ultimate perfection." J. W. Burgess, "Political Science and History," American Historical Review, 2: 401, 403 (1897).

58. Notes for Lectures at Johns Hopkins (1891–94), in *Papers of Woodrow Wilson*, 7: 121–22, ed. Arthur S. Link (Princeton: Princeton University Press, 1969).

59. Ibid., 7: 121–22; Frank Johnson Goodnow, *The American Conception of Liberty and Government*, 11, 12–13, 21 (Providence: Standard Printing Co., 1916). Indeed, he regretted that "the private individual rights of American citizens have come to be formulated and defined, not by representative bodies, as is now the rule in Europe, but by courts." Ibid.

Herbert Croly observed, "Individual freedom is important, but more important still is the freedom of a whole people to dispose of its own destiny." Herbert Croly, *The Promise of American Life*, 178 (New York: Macmillan Co., 1914). Ernst Freund later wrote about the "progressive adjustment of legal checks to official powers . . . in which many observers will be inclined to find the essential contribution of administrative law to our jurisprudence." Ernst Freund, review of Felix Frankfurter & J. Forrester Davison, *Cases and Other Materials on Administrative Law*, Harvard Law Review, 46: 167, 169 (1932).

60. Frank J. Goodnow, *Social Reform and the Constitution*, 5 (1911; reprint, New York: Burt Franklin, 1970); discussed by Ken I. Kersch, *Constructing Civil Liberties: Discontinuities in the Development of American Constitutional Law*, 112–17 (Cambridge: Cambridge University Press, 2004); Peter L. Strauss, *Administrative Justice in the United States*, 13 (Durham: Carolina Academic Press, 2002).

61. George H. Smith, "The Theory of the State," Proceedings of the American Philosophical Society, 34: 181, 183, 263, 266–67, 309–10 (1895). For American interest in Roscher, see W. Cunningham, "Why Had Roscher So Little Influence in England?," Annals of the American Academy of Political & Social Science, 5: 1 (1894).

62. Charles Edward Merriam, *A History of American Political Theories*, 323–24 (New York: Macmillan Co., 1903). See also Frank J. Goodnow, *Social Reform and the Constitution* (1911; reprint, New York: Burt Franklin, 1970); Frank J. Goodnow, *Comparative Administrative Law* (New York: G. P. Putnam's Sons, 1897). At a less theoretical level, Goodnow simply summarized: "Modern political science has . . . generally discarded this theory [of separaton of powers] both because it is incapable of accurate statement, and because it seems to be impossible to apply it with beneficial results." Frank J. Goodnow, *Social Reform and the Constitution*, 218 (1911; reprint, New York: Burt Franklin, 1970).

In light of Goodnow's views and sources, it is revealing that some scholarship relies upon his ideas for understanding early America. For example, recent work (by Jerry Mashaw) concludes that "recovering something like Goodnow's broad vision of administrative law is critically important to understanding what administrative government, and government according to law, was about in the Federalist period" and, indeed, for the next century. Jerry L. Mashaw, "Recovering American Administrative Law: Federalist Foundations, 1787–1801," Yale Law Journal, 115: 1256, 1266 (2006); Jerry L. Mashaw, *Creating the Administrative Constitution: The Lost One Hundred Years of American Administrative Law*, 10 (New Haven: Yale University Press, 2012).

63. John Mabry Mathews, *Principles of American State Administration*, vii, 502 (New York: D. Appleton & Co., 1917).

64. Charles Edward Merriam, *American Political Ideas: Studies in the Development of American Political Thought 1865–1917*, at 143 (New York: Macmillan Co., 1929). Indeed, by the 1930s it was nearly a matter of humor. Roscoe Pound asked: "Now, how about that separation of powers? There is something that is anathema to many of the teachers of government and politics in many of our institutions of learning." Roscoe Pound, "Modern Administrative Law," in *A Legal Institute on Modern Federal Administrative Law, Held at Richmond, Virginia, April 28 and 29, 1939*, at 11 (Richmond: Richmond Press, [1939]).

65. Woodrow Wilson, *The State: Elements of Historical and Practical Politics*, xxxiv–v (Boston: D. C. Heath & Co., 1911); Frank J. Goodnow, *Comparative Administrative Law*, 2: 103 (New York: G. P. Putnam's Sons, 1897). For Jhering, see Michael Stolleis, *Public Law in Germany 1800–1914*, at 430 (New York: Berghahn Books, 2001). On German comparative law scholarship, see Ralf Michels, "The Functional Method of Comparative Law," in *The Oxford Handbook of Comparative Law*, 348, ed. Mathias Reimann & Reinhard Zimmermann (Oxford: University Press, 2008). For antecedents in civilian-derived scholarship, see Julian H. Franklin, *Jean Bodin and the Sixteenth-Century Revolution in the Methodology of Law and History*, 2–3 (New York: Columbia University Press, 1966); Martina Künnecke, *Tradition and Change in Ad-*

ministrative Law: An Anglo-German Comparison, 4 (Berlin: Springer, 2008). Wilson took a comparative approach to studying and teaching, with particular emphasis on Germany. See his Lectures on Administration at Johns Hopkins (1891–93), in *Papers of Woodrow Wilson*, 7: 113, ed. Arthur S. Link (Princeton: Princeton University, 1969); Notes for Lectures at Johns Hopkins (1891–94), in *Papers of Woodrow Wilson*, 7: 117, ed. Arthur S. Link (Princeton: Princeton University, 1969). When listing the literature on the science of administration, Wilson enumerated a wide range of Germans, some Frenchmen, and only one American, Goodnow's 1893 *Comparative Administrative Law*. Ibid., 7: 118–20.

66. For the constitutional implications, see Ronald J. Pestritto, "The Progressive Origins of the Administrative State: Wilson, Goodnow, and Landis," Social Philosophy & Policy, 24: 16, 47 (2007).

67. Robert D. Miewald, "The Origins of Wilson's Thought: The German Tradition and the Organic State," in *Politics and Administration: Woodrow Wilson and American Public Administration*, 24, ed. Jack Rabin & James S. Bowman (New York: Marcel Dekker, 1984); Lectures on Administration (1891), in *Papers of Woodrow Wilson*, 7: 142, ed. Arthur S. Link (Princeton: Princeton University Press, 1969); Woodrow Wilson, *The New Freedom*, 47 (New York: Doubleday, Page & Co., 1913); discussed by Ronald J. Pestritto, "The Progressive Origins of the Administrative State: Wilson, Goodnow, and Landis," Social Philosophy & Policy, 24: 16, 39 (2007).

68. Eugen Ehrlich, *Fundamental Principles of the Sociology of Law*, 56 (1936; reprint, New Brunswick: Transaction Publishers, 2009); John Dickinson, *Administrative Justice and the Supremacy of the Law in the United States*, 10 (Cambridge: Harvard University Press, 1927); Cuthbert W. Pound, "Constitutional Aspects of Administrative Law," in *The Growth of Administrative Law*, 122 (St. Louis: Thomas Law Book Co., 1923). Pound taught at Cornell for nine years and then sat on the New York Court of Appeals. For Ehrlich, see James E. Herget & Stephen Wallace, "The German Free Law Movement As the Source of American Legal Realism," Virginia Law Review, 73: 399, 411–12 (1987).

69. Daniel R. Ernst, "Ernst Freund, Felix Frankfurter, and the American *Rechtsstaat*: A Transatlantic Shipwreck, 1894–1932," Studies in American Political Development, 23: 171, 173, 175, 188 (2009). Although Ernst's article does not recognize how a *Rechtsstaat* differs from a polity that rules through law, it elegantly captures the tension among leading exponents of different visions of administrative law.

70. Michael Stolleis, *Public Law in Germany 1800–1914*, at 229–31 (New York: Berghahn Books, 2001). See also Hiroshi Oda, "The Emergence of *Pravovoe Gosudarstvo* (*Rechtsstaat*) in Russia," Review of Central and East European Law, 25: 373, 379–80 (1999); Kenneth F. Ledford, "Formalizing the Rule of Law in Prussia: The Supreme Administrative Law Court, 1876–194," Central European History, 37 (2004); Martina Künneke, *Tradition and Change in Administrative Law: An Anglo-German Comparison*, 23–24 (Berlin: Springer, 2007); Daniel R. Ernst, "Ernst Freund, Felix Frankfurter, and the American *Rechtsstaat*: A Transatlantic Shipwreck, 1894–1932," Studies in American Political Development, 23: 171, 172, 177 (2009).

71. Michael Stolleis, *Public Law in Germany, 1800–1914*, at 217 (New York: Berghahn Books, 2001); Erich Hahn, "Rudolf Gneist and the Prussian Rechtsstaat: 1862–78," Journal of Modern History, 49: 1361 (1977).

72. Martina Künnecke, *Tradition and Change in Administrative Law: An Anglo-German Comparison*, 110 (Berlin: Springer, 2008); Jud Matthews, "Administrative Law in

Comparative Perspective: Translating the German Doctrine of Subjective Public Rights," 28–29, 31, 44 (unpublished paper, 2006).

73. R. C. van Caenegem, *An Historical Introduction to Western Constitutional Law*, 15 (Cambridge: Cambridge University Press, 1995); Kenneth F. Ledford, "Formalizing the Rule of Law in Prussia: The Supreme Administrative Law Court, 1876–194," *Central European History*, 37: 203, 206 (2004); Daniel R. Ernst, "Ernst Freund, Felix Frankfurter, and the American *Rechtsstaat*: A Transatlantic Shipwreck, 1894–1932," Studies in American Political Development, 23: 171, 177 (2009).

74. Martina Künnecke, *Tradition and Change in Administrative Law: An Anglo-German Comparison*, 23 (Berlin: Springer, 2008).

75. "Law or Personal Power" (April 13, 1908), *The Public Papers of Woodrow Wilson: College and State: Educational, Literary and Political Papers (1875–1913)*, 2: 25, 27–28, ed., Ray Stannard Baker & William E. Dodd (New York: Harper & Brothers, 1925). Wilson sometimes spoke in a way that could be understood to mean that he rejected all administrative power. To businessmen, he said: "Government regulation? Yes, but through the ancient, the stable, the incorruptible instrumentality of law, not through the choice of executive officials." "Address to the Commercial Club of Chicago: The Government and Business" (Mar. 14, 1908), in *Papers of Woodrow Wilson*, 18: 50, ed., Arthur S. Link (Princeton: Princeton University Press, 1974). To select fellow Democrats, he added: "The government of the United States was established to get rid of arbitrary, that is, discretionary executive power. If we return to it, we abandon the very principles of our foundation, give up the English and American experiment and turn back to discredited models of government." "Law or Personal Power" (April 13, 1908), *The Public Papers of Woodrow Wilson: College and State: Educational, Literary and Political Papers (1875–1913)*, 2: 25, ed., Ray Stannard Baker & William E. Dodd (New York: Harper & Brothers, 1925). Wilson, however, clearly understood such statements to repudiate only discretionary administrative power, not a more restrained administrative law.

76. Daniel R. Ernst, "Ernst Freund, Felix Frankfurter, and the American *Rechtsstaat*: A Transatlantic Shipwreck, 1894–1932," Studies in American Political Development, 23: 171, 173, 175–76, 184, 188 (2009); "Ernst Freund—Pioneer of Administrative Law," University of Chicago Law Review, 29: 755, 776 (1962); Ernst Freund, *The Growth of American Administrative Law*, 22–23 (St. Louis, Thomas Law Book Co., 1923). Freund translated *Rechtsstaat* as "rule of law."

77. At least some American academics embraced fascist or at least authoritarian attitudes in administrative law. For the way in which fascism could have "appeal to liberals," see John P. Diggins, "Flirtation with Facism: American Pragmatic Liberals and Mussolini's Facism," American Historical Review, 71: 487, 498 (1966). For the "unsavory" characters involved with the National Recovery Administration, see James Q. Whitman, "Of Corporatism, Fascism and the First New Deal," American Journal of Comparative Law, 39: 747, 755, 768 (1991). Indeed, a thoughtful writer on administrative law was Fritz Morstein Marx, who began his career writing enthusiastically about the Nazis in tracts such as *The German National Revolution*, published in 1933 by the Friends of the New Germany.

78. Ernst Fraenkel, *The Dual State: A Contribution to the Theory of Dictatorship*, xiii, 28, 46 (New York: Oxford University Press, 1941).

   Although the German civil service was sufficiently attached to its tradition of apolitical service to resist full Nazification, the very existence of the civil service was "a heaven-sent boon to Hitler's government," being "an ideal foundation" for his exercise of consolidated power. Herman Finer, *Theory and Practice of Modern Government*, 808 (New York: Henry Holt & Co., 1949). The Nazis, however, revised the character of German administrative authority. In the late nineteenth century, administrative studies were largely supplanted by the study of administrative law. But beginning in 1933, Nazi scholars denounced the notion of administrative law as dogmatic and sought a return to ideas of administrative power, "with an administrative science" focusing on "administrative reality" and justifying "an active, creative, and political administration." To this end, some called for a "'new administrative law'" centered on "'the Führer-idea, community, and national subordination.'" Michael Stolleis, *The Law under the Swastika*, 113, 115, 117–18, trans. Thomas Dunlap (Chicago: University of Chicago Press, 1998). See also ibid., 119–20.

The degree of German influence in Russia is suggested by the fact that "[t]he bureaucratic state of Peter I was denounced as 'foreign' or 'German,'" and that, by the mid-nineteenth century, in some Russian departments, "the percentage of Germans was very high in the upper ranks, reaching 40 percent." Walter M. Pintner, "The Evolution of Civil Officialdom," in *Russian Officialdom: The Bureaucratization of Russian Society from the Seventeenth to the Twentieth Century*, 190, 206, 209, ed. Walter McKenzie Pintner & Don Karl Rowney (Chapel Hill: University of North Carolina Press, 1980). For the Russian reception and rejection of an administrative *Rechtsstaat*, see Hiroshi Oda, "The Emergence of *Pravovoe Gosudarstvo* (*Rechtsstaat*) in Russia," Review of Central and East European Law, 25: 373, 380, 406 (1999).

79. Roscoe Pound, "The Recrudescence of Absolutism," Sewanee Review, 47: 18, 26 (1939).

80. Thus, although Ernst Freund wrote extensively about French and German administrative law in his academic treatises, his 1911 casebook alluded to France and Europe only briefly in the introduction and omitted any mention of Germany, other than in a few footnotes. Ernst Freund, *Cases on Administrative Law: Selected from Decisions of English and American Courts*, 1–2 (St. Paul: West Publishing Co., 1911). A Columbia student recorded that "Goodnow had learned that he must concentrate on American administrative law, and his epoch-making volumes on comparative administrative law were never referred to except as an item in the bibliography announced at the first lecture." William C. Chase, *The American Law School and the Rise of Administrative Government*, 49 (Madison: University of Wisconsin Press, 1982). Cf. James E. Herget & Stephen Wallace, "The German Free Law Movement As the Source of American Legal Realism," Virginia Law Review, 73: 399, 433 (1987).

After World War II, to the limited extent Americans focused on the Continental precedents for administrative law, they naturally focused on the *droit administratif*, not the *Verwaltungsrecht*. See, for example, Bernard Schwartz, *French Administrative Law and the Common-Law World* (New York: New York University Press, 1954). For an English study, see Marguerite A. Sieghart, *Government by Decree: A Comparative Study of the History of the Ordinance in English and French Law* (London: Stevens & Sons, 1950).

81. Thomas Merrill, "Article III, Agency Adjudication, and the Origins of the Appellate Review Model of Administrative Law," Columbia Law Review, 111: 939, 972 (2011). So far did the American advocates go in separating administrative power from its past that they presented it as an American and empirical response to modern life, devoid of prior history or theory. According to men such as James Landis, administrative agencies were "the product, not of dogma or of abstract theory, but of the gradual development of control by a democratic government." They were an "indig-

enous" and "empirical growth," which "always sprung from a concern over things rather than over doctrine." This was too systematic a rejection of *Staatstheorie* and the Continental experience to have been entirely unknowing. Landis, Gellhorn, and many others, however, systematically presented administrative power in such terms, thus unburdening it of its historical and theoretical baggage. James Landis, "The Development of the Administrative Commission: An Address before the Swarthmore Club of Philadelphia, February 27, 1937" (1937), reprinted in Walter Gellhorn, *Administrative Law: Cases and Comments*, 2–3 (Brooklyn: Foundation Press, 1947).

82. A. V. Dicey, "Preface to the First Edition," in *Introduction to the Law of the Constitution*, vii (1885; reprint, London: MacMillan & Co., 1924).

83. Gary Lawson observes that the work of James Landis "fairly drips with contempt for the idea of a limited national government subject to a formal, tripartite separation of powers." Gary Lawson, "The Rise and Rise of the Administrative State," Harvard Law Review, 107: 1231 (1994). For the "anti-legal temper" of scholars of public administration and their contempt for "technical legal rules," see Laurence E. Lynn, "Restoring the Rule of Law to Public Administration: What Frank Goodnow Got Right and Leonard White Didn't," Public Administration Review, 803, 807 (Sept. & Oct. 2009).

CHAPTER TWENTY-FIVE

a. Republican Platform (1912), Walter W. Spooner, *National Party Platforms*, 383, in *History of the State of New York Political and Governmental*, vol. 6, ed. Ray B. Smith (Syracuse: Syracuse Press, 1922).

b. [John Ponet], *A Short Treatise of Politike Pouuer, and of the True Obedience which Subjects Owe to Kynges and Other Ciuile Gouernours*, sig. [B6v] (n.p.: 1556); *Vindiciæ Contra Tyrannos*, 63 (sig. I[1r]) (London: 1648); Speech of James Morice (Feb. 27, 1593), in *Proceedings in the Parliaments of Elizabeth I*, 3: 32, ed. T. E. Hartley (London: Leicester University Press, 1995). For an example of the civilian acquiescence argument about "allowance" and about "consent of the whole realm" given in fact rather than by representatives in Parliament, see [Richard Cosin], *An Apologie for Sundrie Proceedings by Jurisdiction Ecclesiasticall*, 2: 93 ([London: 1593]). For American constitutions as acts of record and the implications for acquiescence, see Philip Hamburger, *Law and Judicial Duty*, 295–98 (Cambridge: Harvard University Press, 2008).

c. Theodore Roosevelt, *Progressive Principles*, 266 (New York: Effingham Wilson, 1913). A report prepared in 1919 for the American Federation of Labor urged a recall of judicial decisions and relied on Bluntschili for the observation that "[i]n most modern states," notably Germany, "there is . . . no legal remedy against the validity and applicability of the law allowed upon the ground that the contents thereof stand in contradistinction to the constitution." Jackson H. Ralston, *Study and Report for American Federation of Labor upon Judicial Control over Legislatures as to Constitutional Questions*, 57 (Washington, DC: Law Reporter Printing Co., 1919).

d. [John Ponet], *A Short Treatise of Politike Pouuer, and of the True Obedience which Subjects Owe to Kynges and Other Ciuile Gouernours*, sig. [B7r] (n.p.: 1556).

1. As put by Charles Reich, many elements of administrative process "favor larger, richer, more experienced companies or individuals over small ones." Charles Reich, "The New Property," Yale Law Journal, 73: 733, 765 (1964).

2. *Marshall Field & Co. v. Clark*, 143 U.S. 649, 690 (1892).

3. Philip Hamburger, *Law and Judicial Duty*, 230–31 (Cambridge: Harvard University Press, 2008).

4. Thomas W. Merrill, "The Origins of American-Style Judicial Review," *Comparative Administrative Law*, 389, 397, ed. Susan Rose-Ackerman & Peter L. Lindseth (Cheltenham: Edward Elgar, 2010) (noting also that "the tenor of Supreme Court decisions in ICC decisions changed dramatically"); Charles A. Prouty, "Court Review of the Orders of the Interstate Commerce Commission," Yale Law Journal, 18: 297, 310 (1909), discussed by Stephen Skowronek, *Building a New American Sate: The Expansion of Administrative Capacities, 1877–1920*, at 260 (Cambridge: Cambridge University Press: 1982); Frank J. Goodnow, *Social Reform and the Constitution*, 343 (1911; reprint, New York: Burt Franklin, 1970). Although Goodnow was particularly loquacious in theorizing about possible measures that could be taken against the judges, another survey of such "remedies" appeared in Jackson H. Ralston, *Study and Report for American Federation of Labor upon Judicial Control over Legislatures as to Constitutional Questions*, 58–63 (Washington, DC: Law Reporter Printing Co., 1919).

5. So deep was the impression made by the progressives that by 1914 judicial recall had become "the subject of college and high-school debate extending throughout the year in various parts of the country, and particularly in the northwest." Theodore Roosevelt, *Progressive Principles*, 72, 255, 273, 325 (New York: Effingham Wilson, 1913); American Bar Association, Report of the Committee to Oppose the Judicial Recall (1914), Washington Law Reporter, 42: 646. The recall was the subject of enough academic debates that the Debaters' Handbook Series even issued a volume on the subject. *Selected Articles on The Recall Including the Recall of Judges and Judicial Decisions*, ed. Edith M. Phelps, 2nd ed. (White Plains: H. W. Wilson Co., 1915).

6. Goodnow, *Social Reform and the Constitution*, 357; Thurman Arnold, *The Symbols of Government*, 5–6 (New Haven: Yale University Press, 1935).

7. Alexander Bickel, *The Least Dangerous Branch: The Supreme Court at the Bar of Politics*, 111 (1962; reprint, New Haven: Yale University Press, 1986).

8. Philip Hamburger, *Law and Judicial Duty*, 228–29 (Cambridge: Harvard University Press, 2008).

CONCLUSION

b. Harvey Goldman, *Politics, Death, and the Devil: Self and Power in Max Weber and Thomas Mann*, 172 (Berkeley: University of California Press, 1992).

1. Speech of James Morice (Feb. 27, 1593), in *Proceedings in the Parliaments of Elizabeth I*, 3: 35, ed. T. E. Hartley (London: Leicester University Press, 1995).

2. W. W. Gilbert & Arthur Sullivan, *Iolanthe or the Peer and the Peri*, 35–36, act 1 (n.p.: J. M. Stoddart, 1882).

3. Francis Lieber, *Reminiscences of an Intercourse with Mr. Niebuhr the Historian During a Residence with Him in Rome, in the Years 1822 and 1823*, at 59–60 (Philadelphia: 1835).

4. Frank J. Goodnow, *Comparative Administrative Law*, 2: 104 (New York: G. P. Putnam's Sons, 1897). Somewhat similarly, other commentators observed: "The Army and Navy regulations resemble codes of law, and extensive systems of regulations are in effect in other departments constituting a vast body of administrative law. Rules and regulations prescribed pursuant to law for the transaction of public business become a part of that body of laws of which the courts take judicial notice." John H.

Finley & John F. Sanderson, *The American Executive and Executive Methods*, 323 (New York: Century Co., 1908).

5. Gerald Strauss, "The Idea of Order in the German Reformation," in *Enacting the Reformation in Germany: Essays on Institution and Reception*, essay XIV, pp. 2, 5–6, 10–13 (Aldershot: Variorum, 1993). Similarly, for the development of an administrative class in Germany, see Marc Raeff, *The Well-Ordered Police State: Social and Institutional Change through Law in the Germanies and Russia, 1600–1800*, at 21–22 (New Haven: Yale University Press, 1983). For an interpretation of these developments in terms of Protestantism, see Philip S. Gorski, *The Disciplinary Revolution: Calvinism and the Rise of the State in Early Modern Europe*, 138 (Chicago: University of Chicago Press, 2003). More generally, for the ordering of German society through administrative ordinances, see ibid., 44, 105, and generally ibid., pt. 2.

6. Gerald Strauss, "The Idea of Order in the German Reformation," in *Enacting the Reformation: Essays on Institution and Reception*, essay XIV, p. 12 (Aldershot: Variorum, 1993).

7. Gerald Strauss, "Protestant Dogma and City Government: The Case of Nuremburg," in *Enacting the Reformation in Germany: Essays on Institution and Reception*, essay IV, pp. 53–54 (Aldershot: Variorum, 1993).

8. *Howat v. State of Kansas*, 258 U.S. 181, 183 (1922).

9. The absolutist terms that deserve caution also include *police power*. As might be expected from its origins (discussed in chapter 24), this phrase has long suggested a general domestic power that transcends the separate powers of government. Along similar lines, the word *policy* is often is used to refer to an executive agenda that is binding in the manner of law, as when the Supreme Court urges respect for policy statements.

INDEX OF CASES

Made in the USA
Las Vegas, NV
13 July 2021